BUSINESS MATHEMATICS

BUSINESS MATHEMATICS

Dr. J.K. SINGH
(M.F.C., F.C.S., Ph.D.)
Associate Professor
Ram Lal Anand College (Evening)
University of Delhi
DELHI

Himalaya Publishing House
ISO 9001:2015 CERTIFIED

Third Edition : 2013
Edition : 2014, 2015, 2017, 2018, 2019, 2022
Edition : 2023

Published by : Mrs. Meena Pandey
for **HIMALAYA PUBLISHING HOUSE PVT. LTD.,**
"Ramdoot", Dr. Bhalerao Marg, Girgaon, Mumbai - 400 004.
Phone: 022-23860170, 23863863; **Fax:** 022-23877178
E-mail: himpub@bharatmail.co.in; **Website:** www.himpub.com

Branch Offices :

New Delhi : "Pooja Apartments", 4-B, Murari Lal Street, Ansari Road, Darya Ganj, New Delhi - 110 002. Phone: 011-23270392, 23278631; Fax: 011-23256286

Nagpur : Kundanlal Chandak Industrial Estate, Ghat Road, Nagpur - 440 018. Phone: 0712-2721215, 2721216

Bengaluru : Plot No. 91-33, 2nd Main Road, Seshadripuram, Behind Nataraja Theatre, Bengaluru - 560 020. Phone: 080-41138821; Mobile: 09379847017, 09379847005

Hyderabad : No. 3-4-184, Lingampally, Besides Raghavendra Swamy Matham, Kachiguda, Hyderabad - 500 027. Phone: 040-27560041, 27550139

Chennai : No. 34/44, Motilal Street, T. Nagar, Chennai - 600 017. Mobile: 09380460419

Pune : "Laksha" Apartment, First Floor, No. 527, Mehunpura, Shaniwarpeth (Near Prabhat Theatre), Pune - 411 030. Phone: 020-24496323, 24496333; Mobile: 09370579333

Cuttack : Plot No. 5F-755/4, Sector-9, CDA Markat Nagar, Cuttack - 753 014, Odisha. Mobile: 09338746007

Kolkata : 3, S.M. Bose Road, Near Gate No. 5, Agarpara Railway Station, North 24 Parganas, West Bengal - 700 109. Mobile: 09674536325

Printed at : Geetanjali Press Pvt. Ltd., Nagpur. On behalf of HPH.

Dedicated to the

Holy Feet

of

Shri Sai Baba of Shirdi

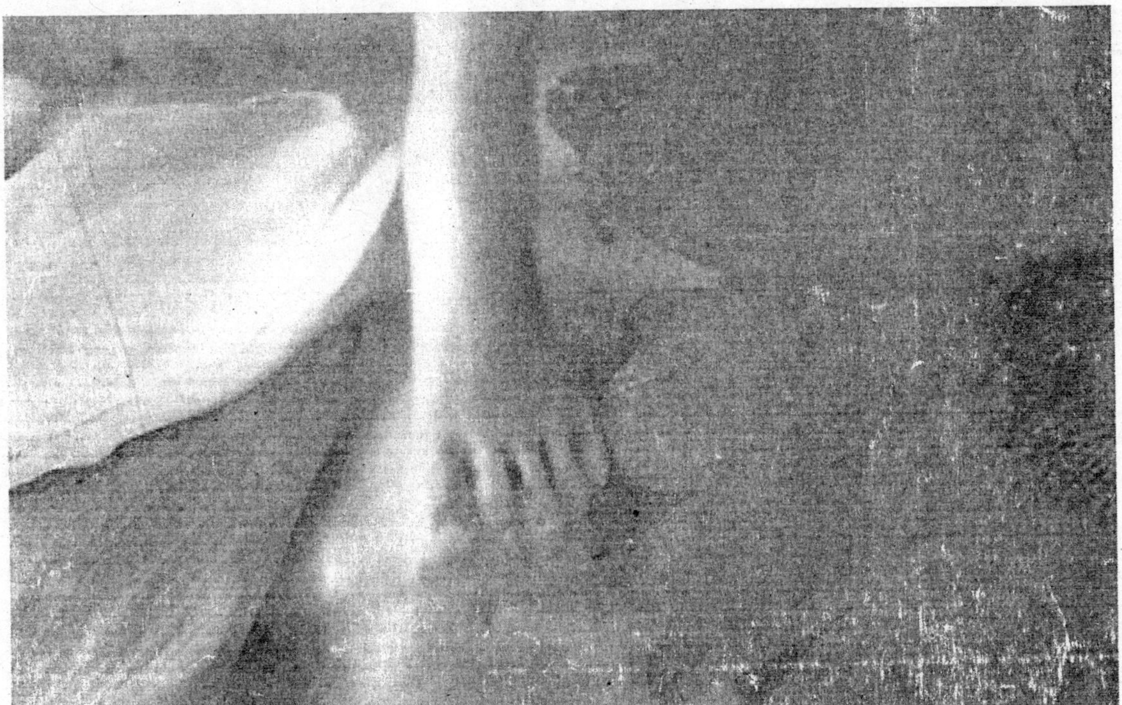

Preface to the Third Edition

I am delighted with the unexpected and overwhelming response of the second edition (alongwith reprint) of this book and the feedback from the users of the book. This has encouraged me to bring enlarged and thoroughly revised third edition of this book. The earlier editions of this book were mainly focusing on syllabus of Delhi University as it was part of suggested reading of the paper Business Mathematics of B.Com. (Honours) course. ***At present, this book find it place in the syllabus of many other Central Universities and management institutions for various academic and management courses including MBA, BBA, etc. Keeping in view the usage of the book by various students in different Universities/Management institutes all over the country, some new chapters, dealing with the following concepts, have been included in the book***

- ❑ Mathematical Induction
- ❑ Arithmetic and Geometric Progression
- ❑ Set theory
- ❑ Permutation and Combination
- ❑ Algebra of Vectors
- ❑ Logarithm

New illustrations have been included in the following chapters

- ❑ Application of Matrices and Determinants
- ❑ Application of Differentiation
- ❑ Application of Integration
- ❑ Linear programming problems

The other features of the book such as – Simple, lucid and plain language, all concepts followed by solved practical illustrations and unsolved exercises, etc. have been kept intact. I hope the users of the book would appreciate the book for its simple style of explaining complex issues relating to commerce and economics.

I express my sincere gratitude to all my colleagues of Delhi University and friends of other Universities/Management institution. My thanks are also due to my family members for their support and encouragement in accomplishment of this task.

Last but not the least, I would also like to thank Shri Neeraj Pandayji and Shri S.K. Joshiji of Himalaya Publishing House for constant supervision in publication of this book and elevating its status to the present level .

(Dr. J.K. Singh)
Associate Professor
Department of Commerce,
Ram Lal Anand College (Eve)
University of Delhi.

Contents

1

Matrices and Determinants – Basic Concepts

HIGHLIGHTS OF THE CHAPTER

- **Introduction**
- **Types of Matrices**
- **Multiplication of Matrix by a Scalar**
- **Transpose of Matrix**
- **Symmetric and Skew Symmetric Matrices**
- **Minors and Cofactors**

INTRODUCTION

Matrix may be defined as a rectangular arrangement of mn numbers into m horizontal rows and n vertical columns. An $m \times n$ matrix is usually written as

$$A = \begin{bmatrix} a_{11} & a_{12} & \cdots & a_{1n} \\ a_{21} & a_{22} & \cdots & a_{2n} \\ \vdots & & & \vdots \\ a_{m1} & a_{m2} & \cdots & a_{mn} \end{bmatrix}$$

The number a_{11}, a_{12}......etc are known as the elements of the matrix A. The chapter deals with the basic concepts of matrix such as addition, subtraction, multiplication and different systems of solving linear simultaneous equations.

TYPES OF MATRICES

(*a*) ***Row Matrix*** : A matrix having only one row is called now matrix. For example, $A = [1, 2, 2, 4]$ is a 1×4 row matrix.

(*b*) ***Column Matrix*** : *A* matrix having only one column is called column matrix. For example,

$$A = \begin{bmatrix} 1 \\ 2 \\ 3 \\ 4 \end{bmatrix} \text{ is a column matrix of the order } 4 \times 1.$$

(*c*) ***Null or Zero Matrix*** : *A* matrix whose all elements are zero is called *a* null matrix or a zero matrix.

(*d*) ***Identity or Unit Matrix :*** A square matrix $A = \left[a_{ij}\right]_{mxn}$ is called an identity or unit matrix if

(*i*) $a_{ij} = 0$ for all $i \neq j$ and

(*ii*) $a_{ii} = 1$ for all $i = j$

Thus, in case of a square matrix, diagonal element is unity and non diagonal element is equal to zero. For example

$$A = \begin{bmatrix} 1 & 0 & 0 \\ 0 & 1 & 0 \\ 0 & 0 & 1 \end{bmatrix}$$

(*e*) ***Square Matrix :*** A matrix of order *nxm* for which $m = n$ *i.e.* number of rows is equal to number of column.

(*f*) ***Upper and Lower Triangular Matrix :*** A square matrix $A = [a_{ij}]$ is called an upper triangular matrix it $a_{ij} = 0$ for all $i > j$

Example $$A = \begin{bmatrix} 1 & 4 & 5 \\ 0 & 2 & 6 \\ 0 & 0 & 9 \end{bmatrix}$$

In case of lower triangular matrix $a_{ij} = 0$ for $i < j$.

Example $$A = \begin{bmatrix} 1 & 0 & 0 \\ 4 & 2 & 0 \\ 5 & 6 & 9 \end{bmatrix}$$

Equality of Matrices

Two matrices are equal if all elements of one matrix is equal to the element of the other matrix in terms of location as well as value. Further, number of rows and column of the two matrix shall also be equal.

Algebra of Matrices

Let *A* and *B* be two matrices each of order *mxn.* The sum of the two matrix is obtained by adding corresponding elements of *A* and *B*. Matrix addition is possible only when they are of the same order *i.e.* number of rows and column of two matrices being added shall be same.

Properties of Matrix Addition

(*a*) Matrix addition is commutative.

i.e. $A + B = B + A$

(*b*) Matrix addition is associative.

i.e. $(A + B) + C = A + (B + C)$

(*c*) ***Existence of Identity :*** The null matrix is the identity element for matrix addition *i.e.* $A + 0 = A = 0 + A$.

(*d*) ***Existence of Inverse :*** For every matrix $A = [a_{ij}]_{mxn}$, there exist a matrix $[-a_{ij}]_{mxn}$ denoted by $-A$, such that

$$A + (-A) = 0 = (-A) + A.$$

Subtraction of Matrices

For two matrices A and B of the same order, we define $A-B = A + (-B)$.

MULTIPLICATION OF MATRIX BY A SCALAR

The matrix obtained by multiplying every element of any matrix by a scalar k is called the scalar multiple of A.

For example, it $A = \begin{bmatrix} 1 & 5 \\ 2 & 3 \end{bmatrix}$

then $4A = \begin{bmatrix} 4 & 20 \\ 8 & 12 \end{bmatrix}$

i.e. each element of matrix A is multiplied with 4.

Properties of Scalar Multiplication

(*i*) $k(A + B) = kA + kB.$

(*ii*) $(k + l)A = kA + lA$

(*iii*) $(kl)A = l(kA)$

(*iv*) $(-k)A = -(kA) = k(-A)$

(*v*) $(-1)A = -A$

TRANSPOSE OF MATRIX

The transpose of any matrix is obtained by changing its rows into column and its column into rows.

i.e. $\left(A^T\right)_{ij} = a_{ji}$ for all $i = 1, 2, ...m, j = 1, 2.....n.$

For example if $A = \begin{bmatrix} 1 & 4 & 2 \\ 3 & 7 & 6 \\ 1 & 3 & 4 \end{bmatrix}$

then $A^T = \begin{bmatrix} 1 & 3 & 1 \\ 4 & 7 & 3 \\ 2 & 6 & 4 \end{bmatrix}$

Properties of Transpose

If A and B are two matrices, then

(*i*) $(A^T)^T = A$

(ii) $(A + B)^T = A^T + B^T$

(iii) $(KA)^T = KA^T$, k is any scalar.

(iv) $(AB)^T = B^T A^T$.

SYMMETRIC AND SKEW SYMMETRIC MATRICES

Symmetric Matrix

A square matrix A is Symmetric Matrix it for all elements

$$a_{ij} = a_{ji}$$

i.e.
$$A = \begin{bmatrix} 1 & 4 & 6 \\ 4 & 8 & 5 \\ 6 & 5 & 2 \end{bmatrix}$$

Thus, a square matrix A is a Symmetric matrix if

$$A^T = A$$

Skew Symmetric Matrix

A square matrix A is a Skew Symmetric matrix if

$$a_{ij} = -a_{ji}$$

i.e.
$$A = \begin{bmatrix} 1 & -2 & -7 \\ 2 & 4 & -6 \\ 7 & 6 & 3 \end{bmatrix}$$

Thus, a square matrix is a skew symmetric matrix if $A^T = -A$.

Properties of Symmetric and Skew Symmetric Matrix

If A is any square matrix, then

(a) $A + A^T$ is a Symmetric matrix.

(b) $A - A^T$ is a Skew-Symmetric matrix.

(c) AA^T and A^TA are Symmetric matrix.

Example 1. **If** $A = \begin{bmatrix} 1 & -2 & -7 \\ 2 & 4 & -6 \\ 7 & 6 & 3 \end{bmatrix}$, $B = \begin{bmatrix} 4 & 0 & 2 \\ 7 & 1 & 4 \\ 2 & 2 & 6 \end{bmatrix}$

Verify that 3 (A + B) = 3A + 3B.

Solution.
$$A = \begin{bmatrix} 3 & 9 & 0 \\ 0 & 8 & -2 \\ 7 & 5 & 4 \end{bmatrix}, \; B = \begin{bmatrix} 4 & 0 & 2 \\ 7 & 1 & 4 \\ 2 & 2 & 6 \end{bmatrix}$$

$$= \begin{bmatrix} 3+4 & 9+0 & 0+2 \\ 0+7 & 8+1 & -2+4 \\ 7+2 & 5+2 & 4+6 \end{bmatrix} = \begin{bmatrix} 7 & 9 & 2 \\ 7 & 9 & 2 \\ 9 & 7 & 10 \end{bmatrix}$$

$$\therefore \quad 3(A+B) = \begin{bmatrix} 3\times 7 & 3\times 9 & 3\times 2 \\ 3\times 7 & 3\times 9 & 3\times 2 \\ 3\times 9 & 3\times 7 & 3\times 10 \end{bmatrix} = \begin{bmatrix} 21 & 27 & 6 \\ 21 & 27 & 6 \\ 27 & 21 & 30 \end{bmatrix}$$

Again $$3A = 3\begin{bmatrix} 3 & 9 & 0 \\ 0 & 8 & -2 \\ 7 & 5 & 4 \end{bmatrix}$$

$$= \begin{bmatrix} 3\times 3 & 3\times 9 & 3\times 0 \\ 3\times 0 & 3\times 8 & 3\times -2 \\ 3\times 7 & 3\times 5 & 3\times 4 \end{bmatrix} = \begin{bmatrix} 9 & 27 & 0 \\ 0 & 24 & -6 \\ 21 & 15 & 12 \end{bmatrix}$$

and $$3B = 3\begin{bmatrix} 4 & 0 & 2 \\ 7 & 1 & 4 \\ 2 & 2 & 6 \end{bmatrix} = \begin{bmatrix} 3\times 4 & 3\times 0 & 3\times 2 \\ 3\times 7 & 3\times 1 & 3\times 4 \\ 3\times 2 & 3\times 2 & 3\times 6 \end{bmatrix}$$

$$= \begin{bmatrix} 12 & 0 & 6 \\ 21 & 3 & 12 \\ 6 & 6 & 18 \end{bmatrix}$$

$$\therefore \quad 3A + 3B = \begin{bmatrix} 9 & 27 & 6 \\ 0 & 24 & -6 \\ 21 & 15 & 12 \end{bmatrix} + \begin{bmatrix} 12 & 0 & 7 \\ 21 & 3 & 12 \\ 6 & 6 & 18 \end{bmatrix}$$

$$= \begin{bmatrix} 9+12 & 27+0 & 6+6 \\ 0+21 & 24+3 & -6+12 \\ 21+6 & 15+6 & 12+18 \end{bmatrix} + \begin{bmatrix} 21 & 27 & 6 \\ 21 & 27 & 6 \\ 27 & 21 & 30 \end{bmatrix}_{3\times 3}$$

$$\therefore \quad 3(A+B) = 3A + 3B$$

Multiplication of Two Matrices

Definition

Let $A = [a_{ij}]_{m\times n}$ and $B = [b_{ji}]_{n\times p}$ be two matrices such that the number of columns in A is equal to the number or rows in B. Then $m \times p$ matrix $[C_{ik}]_{m\times p}$ such that

$$C_{ik} = \sum_{j=1}^{n} a_{ij}\, a_{ik}$$

give the product of the matrices A and B in that order and we write $C = AB$.

The product AB of two matrices A and B exists if and only if the number of columns in A is equal to the number of rows in B.

In the product AB, the matrix A is called the prefactor and the matrix B is called the post factor.

Important Points

1. If the number of columns of A is different from the number of rows of B, the product AB is not defined.
2. If A be of order $m \times n$ and B be of order $n \times p$, then AB is defined and will be of the order $m \times p$.
3. If the product AB exists, then it is not necessary that the product BA will also exist.

Example 2. **If** $A = \begin{bmatrix} 0 & 1 & 0 \\ 3 & 2 & 1 \\ 1 & 0 & 1 \end{bmatrix}$ **and** $B = \begin{bmatrix} 1 & 2 & 3 & 4 \\ 2 & 0 & 1 & 2 \\ 3 & 1 & 0 & 5 \end{bmatrix}$ **then find AB. Does BA exits?**

Solution.

Here the matrix A is of the order 3×3 and the matrix B of the order 3×4. The number of columns of A is equal to the number of rows of B, therefore AB is defined *i.e.*, the product AB exists and it will be a matrix of the order 3×4.

$$AB = \begin{bmatrix} 0 & 1 & 0 \\ 3 & 2 & 1 \\ 1 & 0 & 1 \end{bmatrix} \begin{bmatrix} 1 & 2 & 3 & 4 \\ 2 & 0 & 1 & 2 \\ 3 & 1 & 0 & 5 \end{bmatrix}$$

$$= \begin{bmatrix} 0 \times 1 + 1 \times 2 + 0 \times 3 & 0 \times 2 + 1 \times 0 + 0 \times 1 \\ 3 \times 1 + 2 \times 2 + 1 \times 3 & 3 \times 2 + 2 \times 0 + 1 \times 1 \\ 1 \times 1 + 0 \times 2 + 1 \times 3 & 1 \times 2 + 0 \times 0 + 1 \times 1 \end{bmatrix}$$

$$\begin{matrix} 0 \times 3 + 1 \times 1 + 0 \times 0 & 0 \times 4 + 0 \times 2 + 0 \times 5 \\ 3 \times 3 + 2 \times 1 + 1 \times 0 & 3 \times 4 + 2 \times 2 + 1 \times 5 \\ 1 \times 3 + 0 \times 1 + 1 \times 0 & 1 \times 4 + 0 \times 2 + 1 \times 5 \end{matrix}\Bigg]$$

$$= \begin{bmatrix} 2 & 0 & 1 & 0 \\ 10 & 7 & 11 & 21 \\ 4 & 3 & 3 & 9 \end{bmatrix}_{3\times4}$$

Since the number of the columns of B is not equal to the number of rows of A, therefore the product AB does not exist.

Example 3. **(*a*) If** $\begin{bmatrix} x+y & y-z \\ z-2x & y-x \end{bmatrix} = \begin{bmatrix} 3 & -1 \\ 1 & -1 \end{bmatrix}$, **find x, y, z**

(*b*) If $\begin{bmatrix} x-y & 2x+z \\ 2x-y & 3z+w \end{bmatrix} = \begin{bmatrix} -1 & 5 \\ 0 & 13 \end{bmatrix}$, **find x, y, z, w.**

Solution.

(*a*) Using equality of matrices

$x + y = 3$ ....(*i*) $\qquad y - z = -1$ ....(*ii*)

$z - 2x = 1$ ....(*iii*) $y - x = 1$ ....(*iv*)

Adding (*i*) and (*iv*), we get $2y = 4$

$\therefore y = 4 \div 2 = 2$

$\therefore$ From (*i*) $x + 2 = 3 \Rightarrow x = 3 - 2 = 1$

From (*ii*) $2 - z = -1 \Rightarrow z = 2 + 1 = 3$

$\therefore x = 1, y = 2, z = 3$

(*b*) Using equality of matrices

$x + y = -1$ ....(*i*) $2x + z = 5$ ....(*ii*)

$2x - y = 0$ ....(*ii*) $3z + w = 13$ ....(*iv*)

Subtracting (*i*) from (*iii*), we get $x = 1$

$\therefore$ From (*iii*) $2(1) - y = 0 \quad \Rightarrow \quad y = 2$

From (*ii*) $2(1) + z = 5 \quad \Rightarrow \quad z = 5 - 2 = 3$

From (*iv*) $3(3) + w = 13 \quad \Rightarrow \quad w = 13 - 9 = 4$

$\therefore x = 1, y = 2, z = 3, w = 4$

Example 4. Let $A = \begin{bmatrix} 3 & 4 \\ 3 & 2 \end{bmatrix}$, $B = \begin{bmatrix} 1 & 3 \\ -2 & 5 \end{bmatrix}$

$C = \begin{bmatrix} -2 & 5 \\ 3 & 4 \end{bmatrix}$

Find each of the following :

(*i*) *A* + *B*, (*ii*) *A* – *B*, (*iii*) 3*A* – *C*, (*iv*) *AB*, (*v*) *AB*

Solution.

(*i*) $A + B = \begin{bmatrix} 3 & 4 \\ 3 & 2 \end{bmatrix} + \begin{bmatrix} 1 & 3 \\ -2 & 5 \end{bmatrix}$

$= \begin{bmatrix} 3+1 & 4+3 \\ 3-2 & 2+5 \end{bmatrix} = \begin{bmatrix} 4 & 7 \\ 1 & 7 \end{bmatrix}$

(*ii*) $A - B = \begin{bmatrix} 3 & 4 \\ 3 & 2 \end{bmatrix} - \begin{bmatrix} 1 & 3 \\ -2 & 5 \end{bmatrix} = \begin{bmatrix} 3-1 & 4-3 \\ 3+2 & 2-5 \end{bmatrix}$

$= \begin{bmatrix} 2 & 1 \\ 5 & -3 \end{bmatrix}$

(*iii*) $3A - C = 3\begin{bmatrix} 3 & 4 \\ 3 & 2 \end{bmatrix} - \begin{bmatrix} -2 & 5 \\ 2 & 4 \end{bmatrix}$

$= \begin{bmatrix} 9 & 12 \\ 9 & 6 \end{bmatrix} - \begin{bmatrix} -2 & 5 \\ 3 & 4 \end{bmatrix} = \begin{bmatrix} 9+2 & 12-5 \\ 9-3 & 6-4 \end{bmatrix} = \begin{bmatrix} 11 & 7 \\ 6 & 2 \end{bmatrix}$

(iv) $AB = \begin{bmatrix} 3 & 4 \\ 3 & 2 \end{bmatrix}\begin{bmatrix} 1 & 3 \\ -2 & 5 \end{bmatrix} = \begin{bmatrix} 3(1)+4(-2) & 2(3)+4(5) \\ 3(1)+2(-2) & 3(3)+2(5) \end{bmatrix}$

$$= \begin{bmatrix} 3-8 & 6+20 \\ 3-4 & 9+10 \end{bmatrix} = \begin{bmatrix} -5 & 26 \\ -1 & 19 \end{bmatrix}$$

(v) $BA = \begin{bmatrix} 1 & 3 \\ -2 & 5 \end{bmatrix}\begin{bmatrix} 3 & 4 \\ 3 & 2 \end{bmatrix} = \begin{bmatrix} 1(3)+3(3) & 1(4)+3(2) \\ -2(2)+5(3) & -2(4)+5(2) \end{bmatrix}$

$$= \begin{bmatrix} 2+9 & 4+6 \\ -4+15 & 8+10 \end{bmatrix} = \begin{bmatrix} 12 & 10 \\ 11 & 2 \end{bmatrix}$$

***Example 5.* (*a*) Find *X* if**

$$Y = \begin{bmatrix} 3 & 2 \\ 0 & 4 \end{bmatrix} \text{ and } 2X + Y = \begin{bmatrix} 1 & 0 \\ -3 & 2 \end{bmatrix}$$

(*b*) Find *X* and *Y* if

$$X + Y = \begin{bmatrix} 7 & 10 \\ 2 & 5 \end{bmatrix} \text{ and } X - Y = \begin{bmatrix} 3 & 0 \\ 0 & 3 \end{bmatrix}$$

Solution.

(*a*) $2X + Y = \begin{bmatrix} 1 & 0 \\ -3 & 2 \end{bmatrix} \Rightarrow 2X = \begin{bmatrix} 1 & 0 \\ -3 & 2 \end{bmatrix} - Y$

$$\therefore \quad 2X = \begin{bmatrix} 1 & 0 \\ -3 & 2 \end{bmatrix} - \begin{bmatrix} 3 & 2 \\ 0 & 4 \end{bmatrix} = \begin{bmatrix} 1-3 & 0-2 \\ -3-0 & 2-4 \end{bmatrix} = \begin{bmatrix} -2 & -2 \\ -3 & -2 \end{bmatrix}$$

$$\therefore \quad X = \frac{1}{2}\begin{bmatrix} -2 & -2 \\ -4 & -2 \end{bmatrix} = \begin{bmatrix} -1 & -1 \\ -3/2 & -1 \end{bmatrix}$$

(*b*) $X + Y = \begin{bmatrix} 7 & 10 \\ 2 & 5 \end{bmatrix}$

$$X - Y = \begin{bmatrix} 3 & 0 \\ 0 & 3 \end{bmatrix}$$

Addition these matrics, we get

$$(X+Y)+(X-Y) = \begin{bmatrix} 7 & 10 \\ 2 & 5 \end{bmatrix} + \begin{bmatrix} 3 & 0 \\ 0 & 3 \end{bmatrix} = \begin{bmatrix} 7+3 & 10+0 \\ 2+0 & 5+3 \end{bmatrix}$$

$$2X = \begin{bmatrix} 10 & 10 \\ 2 & 8 \end{bmatrix},$$

$$X = \frac{1}{2}\begin{bmatrix} 10 & 10 \\ 2 & 8 \end{bmatrix} = \begin{bmatrix} 5 & 5 \\ 1 & 4 \end{bmatrix}$$

Now $$X + Y = \begin{bmatrix} 7 & 0 \\ 2 & 5 \end{bmatrix}$$

$$\Rightarrow \quad Y = \begin{bmatrix} 7 & 0 \\ 2 & 5 \end{bmatrix} - X = \begin{bmatrix} 7 & 0 \\ 2 & 5 \end{bmatrix} - \begin{bmatrix} 5 & 5 \\ 1 & 4 \end{bmatrix}$$

$$= \begin{bmatrix} 7-5 & 0-5 \\ 2-1 & 5-4 \end{bmatrix} = \begin{bmatrix} 2 & -5 \\ 1 & 1 \end{bmatrix}$$

$$\therefore \quad X = \begin{bmatrix} 5 & 5 \\ 1 & 4 \end{bmatrix}; \; Y = \begin{bmatrix} 2 & -5 \\ 1 & 1 \end{bmatrix}$$

Example 6. **If** $A = \begin{bmatrix} 3 & 2 \\ 4 & 1 \end{bmatrix}$ **and** $B = \begin{bmatrix} a & b \\ 3 & 5 \end{bmatrix}$ **find** a **and** b **such that** $AB = BA$. **Compute** $3A + 5B$.

Solution : We have

$$AB = \begin{bmatrix} 3 & 2 \\ 4 & 1 \end{bmatrix}\begin{bmatrix} a & b \\ 3 & 5 \end{bmatrix} = \begin{bmatrix} 3a+6 & 3b+10 \\ 4a+3 & 4b+5 \end{bmatrix}$$

$$BA = \begin{bmatrix} a & b \\ 3 & 5 \end{bmatrix}\begin{bmatrix} 3 & 2 \\ 4 & 1 \end{bmatrix} = \begin{bmatrix} 3a+4b & 2a+b \\ 29 & 11 \end{bmatrix}$$

If $AB = BA$, we must have

$$4a + 3 = 29$$

$$4b + 5 = 11$$

Solving for a and b, we get $a = \frac{13}{2}$, $b = \frac{3}{2}$

Now $$3A + 5B = \begin{bmatrix} 9 & 6 \\ 12 & 3 \end{bmatrix} + \begin{bmatrix} \frac{65}{2} & \frac{15}{2} \\ 15 & 25 \end{bmatrix} = \begin{bmatrix} \frac{83}{2} & \frac{27}{2} \\ 28 & 28 \end{bmatrix}$$

Example 7. **Find the matrix** A **such that**

$$A\begin{bmatrix} 3 & 4 \\ 6 & 2 \end{bmatrix} = \begin{bmatrix} 2 & 8 \\ 9 & 4 \end{bmatrix}$$

Solution. The resultant matrix is a 2×2 matrix and the post factor of A is also a 2×2 matrix, therefore A must be a 2×2 matrix. Let

$$A = \begin{bmatrix} a & b \\ c & d \end{bmatrix}$$

Therefore, the given equation can be written as

$$\begin{bmatrix} a & b \\ c & d \end{bmatrix}\begin{bmatrix} 3 & 4 \\ 6 & 2 \end{bmatrix} = \begin{bmatrix} 2 & 8 \\ 9 & 4 \end{bmatrix}$$

$$\Rightarrow \quad \begin{bmatrix} 3a + 6b & 4a + 2b \\ 3c + 6d & 4c + 2d \end{bmatrix} = \begin{bmatrix} 2 & 8 \\ 9 & 4 \end{bmatrix}$$

$$\Rightarrow \quad 3a + 6b = 2,\ 4a + 2b = 8,\ 3c + 6d = 9,\ 4c + 2d = 4.$$

Solving these equations simultaneously for a, b, c and d, we obtain

$$a = \frac{22}{9},\ b = \frac{8}{9},\ c = \frac{1}{3},\ \text{and } d = \frac{4}{3}.$$

Hence the matrix A is

$$A = \begin{bmatrix} \frac{22}{9} & -\frac{8}{9} \\ \frac{1}{3} & \frac{4}{3} \end{bmatrix}$$

***Example 8.* If** $A = \begin{bmatrix} 1 & 2 \\ 3 & 4 \end{bmatrix}$, $B = \begin{bmatrix} 1 & 0 \\ 2 & -3 \end{bmatrix}$ **and** $C = \begin{bmatrix} 1 & -1 \\ 0 & 1 \end{bmatrix}$, **show that** $A(B + C) = AB + AC$.

Solution. We have

$$B + C = \begin{bmatrix} 1 & 0 \\ 2 & -3 \end{bmatrix} + \begin{bmatrix} 1 & -1 \\ 0 & 1 \end{bmatrix} = \begin{bmatrix} 2 & -1 \\ 2 & -2 \end{bmatrix}$$

$$\therefore \quad A(B + C) = \begin{bmatrix} 1 & 2 \\ 3 & 4 \end{bmatrix}\begin{bmatrix} 2 & -1 \\ 2 & -2 \end{bmatrix} = \begin{bmatrix} 6 & -5 \\ 14 & -11 \end{bmatrix}$$

Also

$$AB = \begin{bmatrix} 1 & 2 \\ 3 & 4 \end{bmatrix}\begin{bmatrix} 1 & 0 \\ 2 & -3 \end{bmatrix} = \begin{bmatrix} 5 & -6 \\ 11 & -12 \end{bmatrix}$$

and

$$AC = \begin{bmatrix} 1 & 2 \\ 3 & 4 \end{bmatrix}\begin{bmatrix} 1 & -1 \\ 0 & -1 \end{bmatrix} = \begin{bmatrix} 1 & 1 \\ 3 & 1 \end{bmatrix}$$

$$\therefore \quad AB + AC = \begin{bmatrix} 5 & -6 \\ 11 & -12 \end{bmatrix} + \begin{bmatrix} 1 & 1 \\ 3 & 1 \end{bmatrix} = \begin{bmatrix} 6 & -5 \\ 14 & -11 \end{bmatrix}$$

Thus $A\ (B + C)\ AB + AC$.

***Example 9.* If** $A = \begin{bmatrix} 0 & 1 \\ 1 & 0 \end{bmatrix}$ **and** $B = \begin{bmatrix} 0 & -i \\ i & 0 \end{bmatrix}$, **where** $i^2 = -1$. **Verify that** $(A + B)^2 = A^2 + B^2$.

Solution. Using the data given above, we have

$$A + B = \begin{bmatrix} 0 & 1 \\ 1 & 0 \end{bmatrix} + \begin{bmatrix} 0 & -i \\ i & 0 \end{bmatrix} = \begin{bmatrix} 0 & 1 - i \\ 1 + i & 0 \end{bmatrix}$$

$$(A + B)^2 = (A + B)\ (A + B)$$

$$= \begin{bmatrix} 0 & 1 - i \\ 1 + i & 0 \end{bmatrix}\begin{bmatrix} 0 & 1 - i \\ 1 + i & 0 \end{bmatrix} = \begin{bmatrix} 2 & 0 \\ 0 & 2 \end{bmatrix}$$

Also $$A^2 = \begin{bmatrix} 0 & 1 \\ 1 & 0 \end{bmatrix}\begin{bmatrix} 0 & 1 \\ 1 & 0 \end{bmatrix} = \begin{bmatrix} 1 & 0 \\ 0 & 1 \end{bmatrix}$$

and $$B^2 = \begin{bmatrix} 0 & -i \\ i & 0 \end{bmatrix}\begin{bmatrix} 0 & -i \\ i & 0 \end{bmatrix} = \begin{bmatrix} 1 & 0 \\ 0 & 1 \end{bmatrix}$$

$$\therefore \quad A^2 + B^2 = \begin{bmatrix} 1 & 0 \\ 0 & 1 \end{bmatrix} + \begin{bmatrix} 1 & 0 \\ 0 & 1 \end{bmatrix} = \begin{bmatrix} 2 & 0 \\ 0 & 2 \end{bmatrix}$$

Hence $(A + B)^2 = A^2 + B^2$.

Exercise 1.1

1. If $A = \begin{bmatrix} 1 & 0 \\ -1 & 7 \end{bmatrix}$ and $I = \begin{bmatrix} 1 & 0 \\ 0 & 1 \end{bmatrix}$, find k so that $A^2 = 8A + kI$. [$k = -7$]

2. If $A = \begin{bmatrix} 3 & 1 \\ -1 & 2 \end{bmatrix}$, show that $A^2 - 5A + 7I_2 = 0$

3. If $A = \begin{bmatrix} 2 & -1 \\ 3 & 2 \end{bmatrix}$ and $B = \begin{bmatrix} 0 & 4 \\ -1 & 7 \end{bmatrix}$, find $3A^2 - 2B$ $\left[\textit{Answer}: \begin{bmatrix} 3 & -20 \\ 38 & -11 \end{bmatrix}\right]$

4. If $\begin{bmatrix} 1 & 1 & x \end{bmatrix}\begin{bmatrix} 1 & 0 & 2 \\ 0 & 2 & 1 \\ 2 & 1 & 0 \end{bmatrix} = 0$, find x. [$x = -2$]

5. If $A = \begin{bmatrix} -2 \\ 4 \\ 5 \end{bmatrix}$, $B = \begin{bmatrix} 1 & 3 & -6 \end{bmatrix}$, verify $(AB)^T = B^T A^T$

6. If $A = \begin{bmatrix} 2 & 4 & -1 \\ -1 & 0 & 2 \end{bmatrix}$, $B = \begin{bmatrix} 3 & 4 \\ -1 & 2 \\ 2 & 1 \end{bmatrix}$, find $(AB)^T$

7. If $A = \begin{bmatrix} 3 & 2 \\ 4 & 1 \end{bmatrix}$, and $B = \begin{bmatrix} a & b \\ 3 & 5 \end{bmatrix}$, find a and b such that $AB = BA$. Compute $3A + 5B$.

8. Find the matrix A such that

$$A\begin{bmatrix} 3 & 4 \\ 6 & 2 \end{bmatrix} = \begin{bmatrix} 2 & 8 \\ 9 & 4 \end{bmatrix}$$

Q.9. If where $A = \begin{bmatrix} 0 & 1 \\ 1 & 0 \end{bmatrix}$ and $B = \begin{bmatrix} 0 & -i \\ i & 0 \end{bmatrix}$, $i^2 = -1$, verify that $(A + B)^2 = A^2 + B^2$.

Q.10. If $A = \begin{bmatrix} 1 & 2 \\ 3 & 4 \end{bmatrix}$, $B = \begin{bmatrix} 1 & 0 \\ 2 & -3 \end{bmatrix}$ and $C = \begin{bmatrix} 1 & -1 \\ 0 & 1 \end{bmatrix}$ show that $A(BC) = (AB)C$.

Example 10. **Evaluation Determinant of**

$$A = \begin{bmatrix} -1 & 5 & -2 \\ 2 & 1 & 0 \\ 2 & 7 & 3 \end{bmatrix}$$

Solution.

$$|A| = -1(1 \times 3 - 0 \times 7) - 5(2 \times 3 - 0 \times 2) - 2(2 \times 7 - 2 \times 1)$$
$$= -1(3) - 5(6) - 2(12)$$
$$= -3 - 30 - 24 = -57.$$

Example 11. **Evaluate**

$$\begin{vmatrix} a + ib & c + id \\ -c + id & a - ib \end{vmatrix}$$

Solution.

$$\Delta = \begin{vmatrix} a + ib & c + id \\ -c + id & a - ib \end{vmatrix}$$
$$= (a + ib)(a - ib) - (-c + id)(c + id)$$
$$= (a + ib)(a - ib) + (c - id)(c + id)$$
$$= (a^2 + b^2) + (c^2 + d^2) \qquad [\because i^2 = -1]$$
$$= a^2 + b^2 + c^2 + d^2$$

Example 12. **Prove that**

$$= \begin{vmatrix} 1 + a^2 - b^2 & 2ab & -2b \\ 2ab & 1 - a^2 + b^2 & 2a \\ 2b & -2a & 1 - a^2 - b^2 \end{vmatrix} = \left(1 + a^2 + b^2\right)^3$$

Solution. Let

$$\Delta = \begin{vmatrix} 1 + a^2 - b^2 & 2ab & -2b \\ 2ab & 1 - a^2 + b^2 & 2a \\ 2b & -2a & 1 - a^2 - b^2 \end{vmatrix}$$

$$= \begin{vmatrix} 1 + a^2 + b^2 & 0 & -b\left(1 + a^2 _ b^2\right) \\ 0 & 1 + a^2 + b^2 & a\left(1 = a^2 + b^2\right) \\ 2b & -2a & 1 - a^2 - b^2 \end{vmatrix} \begin{pmatrix} R_1 \to R_1 + bR_3 \\ R_2 \to R_2 - aR_3 \end{pmatrix}$$

$$= \left(1 + a^2 + b^2\right)^2 \begin{vmatrix} 1 & 0 & -b \\ 0 & 1 & a \\ 2b & -2a & 1 - a^2 - b^2 \end{vmatrix}$$

$$= \left(1 + a^2 + b^2\right)^2 \left\{ \begin{vmatrix} 1 & a \\ -2a & 1 - a^2 - b^2 \end{vmatrix} - b \begin{vmatrix} 0 & 1 \\ 2b & -2a \end{vmatrix} \right\}$$

(Expanding along first row)

$$= (1 + a^2 + b^2)^2 \, [(1 - a^2 - b^2 + 2a^2) - b\,(-2b)]$$

$$= (1 + a^2 + b^2)\,(1 + a^2 + b^2) = (1 + a^2 + b^2)^3.$$

Example 13. **Show that**

$$\begin{vmatrix} y + z & x & y \\ z + x & z & x \\ x + y & y & z \end{vmatrix} = (x + y + z)(x - y)^2$$

Solution. Let

$$\Delta = \begin{vmatrix} y + z & x & y \\ z + x & z & x \\ x + y & y & z \end{vmatrix}$$

Performing $R_1 \to R_1 + R_2 \to R_3$, we get

$$\Delta = \begin{vmatrix} 2(x + y + z) & x + y + z & x + y + z \\ z + x & z & x \\ x + y & y & z \end{vmatrix} \qquad \textit{(Property 5)}$$

$$= (x + y + z) \begin{vmatrix} 2 & 1 & 1 \\ z + x & z & x \\ x + y & y & z \end{vmatrix}$$

Performing $C_1 \to C_1 - 2C_2$ and $C_2 \to C_2 - C_3$, we get

$$\Delta = (x + y + z) \begin{vmatrix} 0 & 0 & 1 \\ x - z & z - x & x \\ x - y & y - z & z \end{vmatrix} \qquad \textit{(Property 5)}$$

$$= (x + y + z)\,[(x - z)\,(y - z) - (z - x)\,(x - y)]$$

(Expanding along first row)

$$= (x + y + z)\,(x - z)\,[(y - z) + (x - y)]$$

$$= (x + y + z)\,(x - z)^2.$$

Example 14. **Show that** $\begin{vmatrix} 1 & 1 & 1 \\ a & b & c \\ a^2 & b^2 & c^2 \end{vmatrix}$

$$= (a - b)(b - c)(c - a)(a + b + c).$$

Solution. Applying $C_2 \to C_2 - C_1$ and $C_3 \to C_3 - C_1$, we get

$$\Delta = \begin{vmatrix} 1 & 0 & 0 \\ a & b - a & c - a \\ a^3 & b^3 - c^3 & c^3 - a^3 \end{vmatrix} = \begin{vmatrix} b - a & c - a \\ b^3 - a^3 & c^3 - a^3 \end{vmatrix}$$

(*Expanding along* R_1)

$$= (b - a)(c - a)\begin{vmatrix} 1 & 1 \\ b^2 + ab + a^2 & c^2 + ca + a^2 \end{vmatrix}$$

$$= (b - a)(c - a)[(c^2 + ca + a^2) - (b^2 + ab + a^2)]$$

$$= (b - a)(c - a)[(c^2 - b^2) + a(c - b)]$$

$$= (b - a)(c - a)(c - b)(c + b + a)$$

$$= (a - b)(b - c)(c - a)(a + b + c).$$

Example 15. **Prove that**

$$\begin{vmatrix} a^2 & a^2 - (b - c)^2 & bc \\ b^2 & b^2 - (c - a)^2 & ca \\ c^2 & c^2 - (a - b)^2 & ab \end{vmatrix} = (a - b)(b - c)(c - a)(a + b + c)(a^2 + b^2 + c^2)$$

Solution. Applying $C_2 \to C_2 - 2C_1 - 2C_3$, we get

$$\Delta = \begin{vmatrix} a^2 & -\left(a^2 + b^2 + c^2\right) & bc \\ b^2 & \left(a^2 + b^2 + c^2\right) & ca \\ c^2 & (a^2 + b^2 + c^2) & ab \end{vmatrix}$$

$$= \left(a^2 + b^2 + c^2\right)\begin{vmatrix} a^2 & 1 & bc \\ b^2 & 1 & ca \\ c^2 & 1 & ab \end{vmatrix}$$

Interchanging C_1 and C_2

$$= \left(a^2 + b^2 + c^2\right)\begin{vmatrix} 1 & a^2 & bc \\ 1 & b^2 & ca \\ 1 & c^2 & ab \end{vmatrix}$$

Multiplying R_1, R_2 and R_3 by a, b and c respectively.

$$= \left(a^2 + b^2 + c^2\right) \times \frac{1}{abc}\begin{vmatrix} a & a^2 & abc \\ b & b^2 & abc \\ c & c^2 & abc \end{vmatrix}$$

$$= \left(a^2 + b^2 + c^2\right) \times \frac{abc}{abc}\begin{vmatrix} a & a^2 & 1 \\ b & b^2 & 1 \\ c & c^2 & 1 \end{vmatrix}$$

$$= \left(a^2 + b^2 + c^2\right) \times \begin{vmatrix} 1 & a & a^3 \\ 1 & b & b^3 \\ 1 & c & c^3 \end{vmatrix}$$

$$\Delta = (a^2 + b^2 + c^2) \times (a - b)(b - c)(c - a)(a + b + c)$$

or $$\Delta = (a - b)(b - c)(c - a)(a + b + c)(a^2 + b^2 + c^2)$$

***Example 16.* Solve the linear equations**

$$2x + 3y = 5$$

$$3x - 2y = 1$$

with the help of determinants.

Solution.
$$D = \begin{vmatrix} 2 & 3 \\ 3 & -2 \end{vmatrix} = 2(-2) - 3(3) = -4 - 9 = -13$$

$$D_1 = \begin{vmatrix} 5 & 3 \\ 1 & -2 \end{vmatrix} = 5(-2) - 1(3) = -10 - 3 = -13.$$

$$D_2 = \begin{vmatrix} 2 & 5 \\ 3 & 1 \end{vmatrix} 2(1) - 3(5) = 2 - 15 = -13.$$

$$x = \frac{D_1}{D} = \frac{-13}{-13} = 1$$

$$y = \frac{D_2}{D} = \frac{-13}{-13} = 1.$$

Cramer's Rule : (in case of three variables)

The same rule can be applied to solve the equations in three unknows.

If
$$a_1x + b_1y + c_1z = d_1$$
$$a_2x + b_2y + c_2z = d_2$$
$$a_3x + b_3y + c_3z = d_3$$

Then $x = \frac{D_1}{D}, \; y = \frac{D_2}{D}, \; z = \frac{D_3}{D}$ where

(i) $$\Delta = \begin{vmatrix} a_1 & b_1 & c_1 \\ a_2 & b_2 & c_2 \\ a_3 & b_3 & c_3 \end{vmatrix}$$

i.e. the determinant of the coefficients of x, y, z.

(ii) $$D_1 = \begin{vmatrix} d_1 & b_1 & c_1 \\ d_2 & b_2 & c_2 \\ d_3 & b_3 & c_3 \end{vmatrix}$$

i.e. the determinant obtained from D by replacing a's, the coefficient of x by d's.

(iii) $$D_2 = \begin{vmatrix} a_1 & d_1 & c_1 \\ a_2 & d_2 & c_2 \\ a_3 & d_3 & c_3 \end{vmatrix}$$

i.e. the determinant obtained from D by replacing b's, the coefficients of y by d's.

(iv) $$D_3 = \begin{vmatrix} a_1 & b_1 & d_1 \\ a_2 & b_2 & d_2 \\ a_3 & b_3 & d_3 \end{vmatrix}$$

i.e. the determinant obtained from D by replacing c's. The coefficients of z by d's.

Example 17. **Solve the following system of equations by means of determinants**

$$x + y + z - 7 = 0$$
$$x + 2y = 3z - 16 = 0$$
$$x + 3y + 4z - 22 = 0$$

Solution : The given system of equations is

$$x + y + z = 7$$
$$x + 2y = 3z = 16$$
$$x + 2y + 4z = 22$$

$$D = \begin{vmatrix} 1 & 1 & 1 \\ 1 & 2 & 3 \\ 1 & 3 & 4 \end{vmatrix} = 1(8 - 9) - 1(4 - 3) + 1(3 - 2) = -1 - 1 + 1 = -1$$

$$D_1 = \begin{vmatrix} 7 & 1 & 1 \\ 16 & 2 & 3 \\ 22 & 3 & 4 \end{vmatrix} = 7(8-9) - 1(64-66) + 1(48-44) = -7 + 2 + 4 = -1.$$

$$D_2 = \begin{vmatrix} 1 & 7 & 1 \\ 1 & 16 & 3 \\ 1 & 22 & 4 \end{vmatrix} = 1(64-66) - 7(4-3) + 1(22-16) = -2 - 7 + 6 = -3.$$

$$D_3 = \begin{vmatrix} 1 & 1 & 7 \\ 1 & 2 & 16 \\ 1 & 3 & 22 \end{vmatrix} = 1(44-48) - 1(22-16) + 7(3-2) = -4 - 6 + 7 = -3.$$

Now $x = \dfrac{D_1}{D} = \dfrac{-1}{-1} = 1$

$$y = \frac{D_2}{D} = \frac{-3}{-1} = 3$$

$$z = \frac{D_3}{D} = \frac{-3}{-1} = 3$$

Hence $x = 1,\ y = 3,\ z = 3.$

Exercise 1.2

1. Solve the following system of equation using various rules.

(*i*) $2x - y = 17$

$3x + 5y = 6$ $(x = 7,\ y = -3)$

(*ii*) $5x - 7y + z = 11$

$6x - 8y - z = 15$

$3x + 2y - 6z = 7$ $(x = 1,\ y = -1,\ z = -1)$

(*iii*) $x + y + z = 1$

$ax + by + cz = k$

$a^2x + b^2y + c^2z = k^2$

$$\left[x = \frac{(c-k)(k-b)}{(c-a)(a-b)},\ y = \frac{(k-c)(a-k)}{(b-c)(a-b)},\ z = \frac{(b-k)(k-a)}{(b-c)(c-a)}\right.$$

(*iv*) $\dfrac{2}{x} + \dfrac{3}{y} + \dfrac{10}{z} = 4$

$\dfrac{4}{x} - \dfrac{6}{y} + \dfrac{5}{z} = 1$

$\dfrac{6}{x} - \dfrac{9}{y} + \dfrac{20}{z} = 2$ $(x = 2,\ y = 3, \text{ and } z = 5)$

Q.2. Solve the following using Cramer's rule

(*a*) $x - 2y = 4,\quad -3x + 5x = -7$

(*b*) $2x - y = 1,\quad 7x - 2y = -7$

(*c*) $2x - y = 17,\quad 3x + 5y = 6$

(*d*) $3x + y = 19,\quad 3x - y = 23$

(*e*) $2x - y = -2,\quad 3x + 4y = 3$

(*f*) $2x + 3y = 10,\quad x + 6y = 4$

[**Ans. :** (*a*) $x = -6, y = -5$, (*b*) $x = -3, y = -7$, (*c*) $x = 7, y = -3$

(*d*) $x = 7, y = -2$, (*e*) $x = -\frac{5}{11}, y = \frac{12}{11}$, (*f*) $x = \frac{16}{3}, y = -\frac{2}{9}$]

MINORS AND COFACTORS

Minor : If A is any square matrix of the order n, then minor m_{ij} of a_{ij} is the determinant of the square sub-matrix of order $(n-1)$ obtained by leaving i^{th} row and j^{th} column of A.

For example

(*a*) Minor of a square matrix $A = \begin{vmatrix} 1 & -5 \\ 3 & 2 \end{vmatrix}$

will be $M_{11} = 2, M_{12} = 3, M_{21} = -5$ and $M_{22} = 1$.

Likewise

Minor of $A = \begin{vmatrix} 2 & 3 & 1 \\ -4 & 1 & 2 \\ 2 & 1 & 3 \end{vmatrix}$

will be $M_{11} = \begin{vmatrix} 1 & 2 \\ -1 & 3 \end{vmatrix} = (1 \times 3 - (-1) \times 2) = 5$

$$M_{12} = \begin{vmatrix} -4 & 2 \\ 2 & 3 \end{vmatrix} = (4 \times 3 - 2 \times 2) = -16$$

$$M_{13} = \begin{vmatrix} -4 & 1 \\ 2 & 1 \end{vmatrix} = [-4 \times -1 - (1 \times 2)] = 4 - 2 = 2.$$

Similarly minors of other elements can be calculated.

Cofactors : If $A = [a_{ij}]$ be any square matrix. Then the cofactor. C_{ij} of a_{ij} in A is equal $(-1)^{i+j}$ times the determinant of the sub matrix of order $(n - 1)$ obtained by leaving i^{th} row and j^{th} column of A.

$$C_{ij} = (-1)^{i+j} (a_{ij})$$

Example if $A = \begin{bmatrix} 4 & -5 \\ 2 & 1 \end{bmatrix}$ then

$C_{11} = 1,$ $\quad C_{12} = (-1)^{1+2}\ (2) = -2$

$C_{21} = (-1)^{2+1}\ (-5) = 5$ $\quad C_{22} = (-1)^{2+2}\ (4) = 4$

Adjoint and Inverse of a Matrix

Adjoint of any square matrix may be defined as transpose of its cofactors matrix.

$$\therefore \text{ If } \quad A = \begin{bmatrix} a_{11} & a_{12} & a_{13} \\ a_{21} & a_{22} & a_{23} \\ a_{31} & a_{32} & a_{33} \end{bmatrix}$$

then its cofactor matrix

$$C = \begin{bmatrix} c_{11} & c_{12} & c_{13} \\ c_{21} & c_{22} & c_{23} \\ c_{31} & c_{32} & c_{33} \end{bmatrix}$$

and the transpose of the cofactor matrix will be given as.

$$\text{Adj } (A) = C' = \begin{bmatrix} c_{11} & c_{21} & c_{31} \\ c_{12} & c_{22} & c_{32} \\ c_{13} & c_{23} & c_{33} \end{bmatrix}$$

Inverse of any Matrix A

Following steps are followed to calculate inverse of any matrix A.

(*a*) Find determinant of A, $|A|$.

(*b*) If $|A| = 0$, it implies A is a singular matrix and therefore inverse is not feasible.

If $|A| \neq 0$, then proceed further.

(*c*) Calculate the cofactors of elements of given matrix A.

(*d*) Find transpose of the cofactor matrix. If will be adjoint matrix.

(*e*) Divide adjoint of the given matrix A by the determinant $|A|$. The resultant will be inverse of the matrix A.

$$\therefore \quad A^{-1} = \frac{1}{|A|} \, adj \ A.$$

Properties of Inverse of Matrix

(*a*) $(A^{-1})^{-1}$ A *i.e.* inverse of the inverse of original matrix is the original matrix itself.

(*b*) $AA^{-1} = A^{-1}A = I_n$ where I is the identity matrix.

Example 18. **If** $A = \begin{bmatrix} 1 & 2 & -3 \\ 2 & 3 & 2 \\ 3 & -3 & -4 \end{bmatrix}$

Find inverse of A.

Solution. $$|A| = \begin{vmatrix} 1 & 2 & -3 \\ 2 & 3 & 2 \\ 3 & -3 & -4 \end{vmatrix}$$

$$= 1(-12+6) - 2(-8-6) - 3(-6-9) = 67.$$

Cofactors

$C_{11} = -6,$ $C_{21} = 17$ $C_{31} = 13$

$C_{12} = 14$ $C_{22} = 5$ $C_{32} = -8$

$C_{13} = -15$ $C_{23} = 9$ $C_{33} = -1$

$$adj\ A = \begin{bmatrix} -6 & 14 & -15 \\ 17 & 5 & 9 \\ 13 & -8 & 1 \end{bmatrix}^T = \begin{bmatrix} -6 & 17 & 13 \\ 14 & 5 & -8 \\ -15 & 9 & -1 \end{bmatrix}$$

$$A^{-1} = \frac{1}{|A|}\ adj\ A = \frac{1}{67}\begin{bmatrix} -6 & 17 & 13 \\ 14 & 5 & -8 \\ -15 & 9 & -1 \end{bmatrix}.$$

Example 19. **Find the inverse of the matrix.**

$$\begin{bmatrix} 4 & -2 & 1 \\ 7 & 3 & 3 \\ 2 & 0 & 1 \end{bmatrix}$$

Solution. Let

$$A = \begin{bmatrix} 4 & -2 & 1 \\ 7 & 3 & 3 \\ 2 & 0 & 1 \end{bmatrix}$$

Then $|A| = (4)(3) - (-2)(1) + (1)(-6) = 8 \neq 0.$

Thus A^{-1} exists and is given by $A^{-1} = \frac{1}{|A|}\ adj\ A.$

To find adj A, let C_{ij} denote the cofactor of a_{ij}, the element in the ith row and jth column of $|A|$. Thus

$C_{11} = 3$ $C_{12} = -1$ $C_{13} = -6$

$C_{21} = 2$ $C_{22} = 2$ $C_{23} = -4$

$C_{31} = -9$ $C_{32} = -5$ $C_{33} = 26$

$$adj\ A = \begin{bmatrix} 3 & 2 & -9 \\ -1 & 2 & -5 \\ -6 & -4 & 26 \end{bmatrix}$$

Hence $$A^{-1} = \frac{1}{|A|} adj\ A = \frac{1}{8}\begin{bmatrix} 3 & 2 & -9 \\ -1 & 2 & -5 \\ -6 & -4 & 26 \end{bmatrix}.$$

Example 20. **Given** $A^{-1} = \begin{bmatrix} 5/7 & 1/7 \\ 3/7 & 2/7 \end{bmatrix}$, **evaluate** $A^2 + 2A$.

Solution. The determinant of A^{-1} will be

$$|A^{-1}| = \frac{10}{49} - \frac{3}{49} = \frac{7}{49} = \frac{1}{7} \neq 0$$

Therefore $$A = \left(A^{-1}\right)^{-1} = \frac{1}{|A^{-1}|} adj \left(A^{-1}\right)$$

$$= 7\begin{bmatrix} 2/7 & -1/7 \\ -3/7 & 5/7 \end{bmatrix} = \begin{bmatrix} 2 & -1 \\ -3 & 5 \end{bmatrix}$$

Now $$A^2 = A \cdot A = \begin{bmatrix} 2 & -1 \\ -3 & 5 \end{bmatrix}\begin{bmatrix} 2 & -1 \\ -3 & 5 \end{bmatrix} = \begin{bmatrix} 7 & -7 \\ -21 & 28 \end{bmatrix}$$

all hence $$A^2 + 2A = \begin{bmatrix} 7 & -7 \\ -21 & 28 \end{bmatrix} + \begin{bmatrix} 4 & -2 \\ -6 & 10 \end{bmatrix} = \begin{bmatrix} 11 & -9 \\ -27 & 38 \end{bmatrix}$$

Example 21. **Find matrix** A **such that** $A\begin{bmatrix} 3 & 4 \\ 6 & 2 \end{bmatrix} = \begin{bmatrix} 2 & 8 \\ 9 & 4 \end{bmatrix}$

Solution. Let $B = \begin{bmatrix} 3 & 4 \\ 6 & 2 \end{bmatrix}$ and $C = \begin{bmatrix} 2 & 8 \\ 9 & 4 \end{bmatrix}$. Then the given matrix equation is

$$AB = C$$

Now $|B| = 6 - 24 = -18 \neq 0$. Thus B is non-singular and hence B^{-1} exists. Post multiplying both sides of Equation (1) by B^{-1} gives

$$A = CB^{-1}$$

But $$B^{-1} = \frac{1}{|B|} adj\ B = -\frac{1}{18}\begin{bmatrix} 2 & -4 \\ -6 & 3 \end{bmatrix} = \begin{bmatrix} -1/9 & 2/9 \\ 1/3 & -1/6 \end{bmatrix}$$

Therefore $$A = CB^{-1} = \begin{bmatrix} 2 & 8 \\ 9 & 4 \end{bmatrix}\begin{bmatrix} -1/9 & 2/9 \\ 1/3 & -1/6 \end{bmatrix} = \begin{bmatrix} 22/9 & -8/9 \\ 1/3 & 4/3 \end{bmatrix}$$

Type I : Solving the given system of linear equations when the coefficient matrix is non-singular

Example 22. **Use matrix method to solve the following system of equations :**

$$5x - 7y = 2,\ 7x - 5y = 3$$

Solution. The given system of equations can be written as

$$5x - 7y = 2$$

$7x - 5y = 3$

or $\begin{bmatrix} 5 & -7 \\ 7 & -5 \end{bmatrix}\begin{bmatrix} x \\ y \end{bmatrix} = \begin{bmatrix} 2 \\ 3 \end{bmatrix}$ or $AX = B$

where $A = \begin{bmatrix} 5 & -7 \\ 7 & -5 \end{bmatrix}$, $X = \begin{bmatrix} x \\ y \end{bmatrix}$ and $B = \begin{bmatrix} 2 \\ 3 \end{bmatrix}$

Now, $|A| = \begin{bmatrix} 5 & -7 \\ 7 & -5 \end{bmatrix} = -25 + 49 = 24 \neq 0$

So, the given system has a unique solution, given by $X = A^{-1} B$.

Let C_{ij} be the cofactors of elements a_{ij} in $A = [a_{ij}]$. Then

$C_{11} = (-1)^{1+1} (-5) = -5$, $C_{12} = (-1)^{1+2}\, 7 = -7$, $C_{21} = (-1)^{2+1} (-7) = 7$

and $C_{22} = (-1)^{2+2}\, 5 = 5$.

$\therefore$ $adj\ A = \begin{bmatrix} -5 & -7 \\ 7 & -5 \end{bmatrix}^T = \begin{bmatrix} -5 & 7 \\ -7 & 5 \end{bmatrix}$ So, $A^{-1} = \frac{1}{|A|}\ adj\ A = \frac{1}{24}\begin{bmatrix} -5 & 7 \\ -7 & 5 \end{bmatrix}$

$$X = A^{-1}B = \frac{1}{24}\begin{bmatrix} -5 & 7 \\ -7 & 5 \end{bmatrix}\begin{bmatrix} 2 \\ 3 \end{bmatrix} = \frac{1}{24}\begin{bmatrix} -10 + 21 \\ -14 + 15 \end{bmatrix} = \begin{bmatrix} 11/24 \\ 1/24 \end{bmatrix}$$

$\therefore$ $\begin{bmatrix} x \\ y \end{bmatrix} = \begin{bmatrix} 11/24 \\ 1/24 \end{bmatrix} = x = \frac{11}{24}$ and $y = \frac{1}{24}$

Hence, $x = 11/24$ and $y = 1/24$ is the required solution.

***Example 23.* Solve the following system of equations, using matrix method :**

$$\mathbf{x + 2y + z = 7,\ x + 3z = 11,\ 2x - 3y = 1}$$

Solution. The given system of equations is

$$x + 2y + z = 7$$
$$x\ 0y + 3z = 11$$
$$2x - 3y + 0z = 1$$

or $\begin{bmatrix} 1 & 2 & 1 \\ 1 & 0 & 3 \\ 2 & -3 & 0 \end{bmatrix}\begin{bmatrix} x \\ y \\ z \end{bmatrix} = \begin{bmatrix} 7 \\ 11 \\ 1 \end{bmatrix}$ or $AX = B$,

where $A = \begin{bmatrix} 1 & 2 & 1 \\ 1 & 0 & 3 \\ 2 & -3 & 0 \end{bmatrix}$, $X = \begin{bmatrix} x \\ y \\ z \end{bmatrix}$ and $B = \begin{bmatrix} 7 \\ 11 \\ 1 \end{bmatrix}$

Now $$|A| = \begin{vmatrix} 1 & 2 & 1 \\ 1 & 0 & 3 \\ 2 & -3 & 0 \end{vmatrix} = 1(0+9) - 2(0-6) + 1(-3-0) = 9 + 12 - 3 = 18 \neq 0$$

So, the given system of equations has a unique solution given by $X = A^{-1} B$.

Let C_{ij} be the co-factors of elements a_{ij} in $A = [a_{ij}]$. Then

$$C_{11} = (-1)^{1+1} \begin{vmatrix} 0 & 3 \\ -3 & 0 \end{vmatrix} = 9, \qquad C_{12} = (-1)^{1+2} \begin{vmatrix} 1 & 3 \\ 2 & 0 \end{vmatrix} = -6,$$

$$C_{13} = (-1)^{1+3} \begin{vmatrix} 1 & 0 \\ 2 & -3 \end{vmatrix} = -3, \qquad C_{21} = (-1)^{2+1} \begin{vmatrix} 2 & 1 \\ -3 & 0 \end{vmatrix} = 3,$$

$$C_{22} = (-1)^{2+2} \begin{vmatrix} 1 & 1 \\ 2 & 0 \end{vmatrix} = -2, \qquad C_{23} = (-1)^{2+3} \begin{vmatrix} 1 & 2 \\ 2 & -3 \end{vmatrix} = 7,$$

$$C_{31} = (-1)^{3+1} \begin{vmatrix} 2 & 1 \\ 0 & 3 \end{vmatrix} = 6, \qquad C_{32} = (-1)^{3+2} \begin{vmatrix} 1 & 1 \\ 1 & 3 \end{vmatrix} = -2$$

and $$C_{33} = (-1)^{3+3} \begin{vmatrix} 1 & 1 \\ 1 & 0 \end{vmatrix} = -2.$$

$$\therefore \quad adj\ A = \begin{bmatrix} 9 & 6 & -3 \\ -3 & -2 & 7 \\ 6 & -2 & -2 \end{bmatrix}^T = \begin{bmatrix} 9 & -3 & 6 \\ 6 & -2 & -2 \\ -3 & 7 & -2 \end{bmatrix}$$

$$\Rightarrow \quad A^{-1} = \frac{1}{|A|}\ adj\ A = \frac{1}{18} \begin{bmatrix} 9 & -3 & 6 \\ 6 & -2 & -2 \\ -3 & -7 & -2 \end{bmatrix}$$

Now, $$X = A^{-1}B \Rightarrow X = \frac{1}{18} \begin{bmatrix} 9 & -3 & 6 \\ 6 & -2 & -2 \\ -3 & 7 & -2 \end{bmatrix} \begin{bmatrix} 7 \\ 11 \\ 1 \end{bmatrix} = \frac{1}{18} \begin{bmatrix} 63 - 33 + 6 \\ 42 - 22 - 2 \\ -21 + 77 - 2 \end{bmatrix}$$

$$\Rightarrow \quad \begin{bmatrix} x \\ y \\ z \end{bmatrix} = \frac{1}{18} \begin{bmatrix} 36 \\ 18 \\ 54 \end{bmatrix} = \begin{bmatrix} 2 \\ 1 \\ 3 \end{bmatrix} \Rightarrow x = 2,\ y = 1 \text{ and } z = 3$$

Hence, $x = 2$, $y = 1$ and $z = 3$ is the required solution.

Type II: **Solving the given system of equations when the coefficient matrix is singular**

Example 24. **Use matrix method to examine the following system of equations for consistency or inconsistency :**

$$4x - 2y = 3,\ 6x - 3y = 5$$

Solution. The given system of equations can be written as

$$AX = B, \text{ where } A = \begin{bmatrix} 4 & -2 \\ 6 & -3 \end{bmatrix},\ X = \begin{bmatrix} x \\ y \end{bmatrix} \text{ and } B = \begin{bmatrix} 3 \\ 5 \end{bmatrix}$$

Now, $$|A| = \begin{bmatrix} 4 & -2 \\ 6 & -3 \end{bmatrix} = -12 + 12 = 0.$$

So, the given system of equations is inconsistent or it has infinitely many solutions according as (adj A) $B \neq 0$ or (adj A) $B = 0$ respectively.

Let C_{ij} be the co-factors of elements a_{ij} in $A = [a_{ij}]$. Then

$C_{ij} = (-1)^{1+1}(-3) = -3,\ C_{12} = (-1)^{1+2}\ 6 = -6,\ C_{21} = (-2)^{2+1}(-2) = 2$ and $C_{22} = (-1)^{2+2}(4) = 4$

$$\therefore \quad adj\ A = \begin{bmatrix} -3 & -6 \\ 2 & 4 \end{bmatrix}^T = \begin{bmatrix} -3 & 2 \\ -6 & 4 \end{bmatrix}$$

So, $$(adj\ A)B = \begin{bmatrix} -3 & 2 \\ -6 & 4 \end{bmatrix}\begin{bmatrix} 3 \\ 5 \end{bmatrix} = \begin{bmatrix} -9 + 10 \\ -18 + 20 \end{bmatrix} = \begin{bmatrix} 1 \\ 2 \end{bmatrix} \neq 0$$

Hence, the given system of equations is inconsistent.

Type III: **Solving a system or linear equations when the inverse of the coefficient matrix is obtained from some given relation**

Example 25. **Find A^{-1}, where $A = \begin{bmatrix} 1 & 2 & -3 \\ 2 & 3 & 2 \\ 3 & -3 & -4 \end{bmatrix}$. Hence solve the system of equations**

$$x + 2y + 3z = -4,\ 2x + 3y + 2z = 2,\ 3x - 3y - 4z = 11.$$

Solution. We have $A = \begin{bmatrix} 1 & 2 & -3 \\ 2 & 3 & 2 \\ 3 & -3 & -4 \end{bmatrix}$.

$$\therefore \quad |A| = \begin{vmatrix} 1 & 2 & -3 \\ 2 & 3 & 2 \\ 3 & -3 & -4 \end{vmatrix} = 1(-12 + 6) - 2(-8 - 6) - 3(-6 - 9)$$

$$= -6 + 28 + 45 = 67 \neq 0$$

So, A is invertible.

Let C be the co-factors of a_{ij} in $A = [a_{ij}]$. Then

$\therefore \quad C_{11} = (-1)^{1+1}\begin{vmatrix} 3 & 2 \\ -3 & -4 \end{vmatrix} = -6, \qquad C_{12} = (-1)^{1+2}\begin{vmatrix} 2 & 2 \\ 3 & -4 \end{vmatrix} = 14,$

$C_{13} = (-1)^{1+3}\begin{vmatrix} 2 & 2 \\ 3 & -4 \end{vmatrix} = 14, \qquad C_{21} = (-1)^{2+1}\begin{vmatrix} 2 & -3 \\ -3 & -4 \end{vmatrix} = 17,$

$C_{22} = (-1)^{2+1}\begin{vmatrix} 2 & -3 \\ -3 & -4 \end{vmatrix} = 5, \qquad C_{23} = (-1)^{2+3}\begin{vmatrix} 1 & 2 \\ 3 & -3 \end{vmatrix} = 9,$

$C_{31} = (-1)^{3+1}\begin{vmatrix} 2 & -3 \\ 3 & 2 \end{vmatrix} = 13, \qquad C_{32} = (-1)^{3+2}\begin{vmatrix} 1 & -3 \\ 2 & 2 \end{vmatrix} = -8.$

and $\quad C_{33} = (-1)^{3+3}\begin{vmatrix} 1 & 2 \\ 2 & 3 \end{vmatrix} = -1.$

$$\therefore \quad adj\ A = \begin{bmatrix} -6 & 14 & -15 \\ 17 & 5 & 9 \\ 13 & -8 & -1 \end{bmatrix}^T = \begin{bmatrix} -6 & 17 & 13 \\ 14 & 5 & -8 \\ -15 & 9 & -1 \end{bmatrix}$$

$$\Rightarrow \quad A^{-1} = \frac{1}{|A|}\ adj\ A = \frac{1}{67}\begin{bmatrix} -6 & 17 & 13 \\ 14 & 5 & -8 \\ -15 & 9 & -1 \end{bmatrix} \qquad .....(i)$$

Now, the given system of equations is

$$x + y - 3z = -4$$
$$2x + 3y + 2z = 2$$
$$3x - 3y - 4z = 11$$

or $\quad AX = B$, where $A = \begin{bmatrix} 1 & 1 & -3 \\ 2 & 3 & 2 \\ 3 & -3 & -4 \end{bmatrix}$, $X = \begin{bmatrix} x \\ y \\ z \end{bmatrix}$ and $B = \begin{bmatrix} -4 \\ 2 \\ 11 \end{bmatrix}$.

As discussed above A is non-singular and so invertible. The inverse of A is given by (i).

The solution of the given system of equations is given by

$$X = A^{-1} B$$

or $$\begin{bmatrix} x \\ y \\ z \end{bmatrix} = \frac{1}{67}\begin{bmatrix} -6 & 17 & 13 \\ 14 & 5 & -8 \\ -15 & 9 & -1 \end{bmatrix}\begin{bmatrix} -4 \\ 2 \\ 11 \end{bmatrix} = \frac{1}{67}\begin{bmatrix} 24 + 34 + 143 \\ -56 + 10 - 88 \\ 60 + 18 - 11 \end{bmatrix} = \begin{bmatrix} 3 \\ -2 \\ 1 \end{bmatrix}$$

$\therefore$ $x = 3$, $y = -2$ and $z = 1$ is the required solution.

Exercise 1.3

1. Find the inverse of each of the following matrices :

(*i*) $\begin{bmatrix} 1 & 2 & 3 \\ 2 & 3 & 1 \\ 3 & 1 & 2 \end{bmatrix}$ $\left(\text{Solution : } \frac{1}{18}\begin{bmatrix} -5 & 1 & 7 \\ 1 & 7 & -5 \\ 7 & -5 & 1 \end{bmatrix}\right)$

(*ii*) $\begin{bmatrix} 1 & 2 & 5 \\ 1 & -1 & -1 \\ 2 & 3 & -1 \end{bmatrix}$ $\left(\text{Solution : } \frac{1}{27}\begin{bmatrix} 4 & 17 & 3 \\ -1 & 11 & 6 \\ 5 & 1 & -3 \end{bmatrix}\right)$

(*iii*) $\begin{bmatrix} 2 & -1 & 1 \\ -1 & 2 & -1 \\ 1 & -1 & 2 \end{bmatrix}$ $\left(\text{Solution : } \frac{1}{4}\begin{bmatrix} 3 & 1 & -1 \\ 1 & 3 & 1 \\ -1 & 1 & 3 \end{bmatrix}\right)$

(*iv*) $\begin{bmatrix} 2 & 0 & -1 \\ 5 & 1 & 0 \\ 0 & 1 & 3 \end{bmatrix}$ $\left(\text{Solution : } \begin{bmatrix} 3 & -1 & 1 \\ -15 & 6 & -5 \\ 5 & -2 & 2 \end{bmatrix}\right)$

2

Applications of Matrices

HIGHLIGHTS OF THE CHAPTER

- **Introduction**
- **Matrix Addition and Subtraction – Applications**
- **Multiplication of Matrices – Applications**
- **System of Linear Equations**
- **Leontif Input – Output Model**
- **Hawkins – Simon Conditions**

INTRODUCTION

In the previous chapter, we have discussed the basic concepts of matrices and determinant. The present chapter discusses the application of matrices. Some of the areas, where, matrices are used for analysis and decision making are discussed below.

Representation of Data in the Compact Manner : This is illustrated below with few examples,

(*a*) Distribution of job among different members.

$$\text{Members} = \begin{matrix} \\ M_1 \\ M_2 \\ M_3 \end{matrix} \overset{\textit{Job}}{\begin{matrix} J_1 & J_2 & J_3 \\ \left|\begin{matrix} 2 & 5 & 3 \\ 6 & 2 & 4 \\ 3 & 4 & 4 \end{matrix}\right| \end{matrix}}$$

(*b*) Sale of products in different markets.

$$\begin{matrix} & M_1 & M_2 & M_3 \\ P_1 & 8 & 4 & 5 \\ P_2 & 6 & 3 & 2 \\ P_3 & 2 & 1 & 2 \end{matrix}$$

(*c*) Consumption of Food by different families.

$$\text{Food} = F \overset{\text{Families}}{\overset{\begin{matrix} F_1 & F_2 & F_3 & F_4 \end{matrix}}{\begin{bmatrix} 20 & 30 & 15 & 40 \end{bmatrix}}}$$

MATRIX ADDITION AND SUBTRACTION – APPLICATIONS

The following example illustrates application of matrix addition and subtraction.

Example 1. **Quarterly sales of Jute, Cotton and yarn for the year 2002 and 2003 are given below:**

Year 2002

	QI	*QII*	*QIII*	*QIV*
Jute	20	25	22	20
Cotton	10	20	18	10
Yarn	15	20	15	15

Year 2003

	QI	*QII*	*QIII*	*QIV*
Jute	10	15	20	20
Cotton	5	20	15	30
Yarn	8	30	15	10

Find the total Quarterly sales of Jute, Cotton and Yarn for the two years.

Solution. The total sales of jute, Cotton and Yarn will be obtained as under

$$\begin{array}{l} \\ \text{Jute} \\ \text{Cotton} \\ \text{Yarn} \end{array} \begin{array}{c} \begin{matrix} QI & QII & QIII & QIV \end{matrix} \\ \begin{vmatrix} 20 & 25 & 22 & 20 \\ 10 & 20 & 18 & 10 \\ 15 & 20 & 15 & 15 \end{vmatrix} \end{array} + \begin{array}{l} \\ \text{Jute} \\ \text{Cotton} \\ \text{Yarn} \end{array} \begin{array}{c} \begin{matrix} QI & QII & QIII & QIV \end{matrix} \\ \begin{vmatrix} 10 & 15 & 20 & 20 \\ 5 & 20 & 15 & 30 \\ 8 & 30 & 15 & 10 \end{vmatrix} \end{array}$$

$$= \begin{array}{l} \text{Jute} \\ \text{Cotton} \\ \text{Yarn} \end{array} \begin{vmatrix} 30 & 40 & 42 & 40 \\ 15 & 40 & 33 & 40 \\ 23 & 50 & 30 & 25 \end{vmatrix}$$

Example 2. ***X*** **Ltd. has following sales position of its product *A* and *B* at its two centres *P* and *Q* at the end of the year**

$$\begin{array}{c} \\ A \\ B \end{array} \begin{array}{c} \begin{matrix} P & Q \end{matrix} \\ \begin{vmatrix} 50 & 45 \\ 60 & 70 \end{vmatrix} \end{array}$$

If the sales position for first three months is given as

$$\begin{array}{c} \\ A \\ B \end{array} \begin{array}{c} \begin{matrix} P & Q \end{matrix} \\ \begin{vmatrix} 30 & 15 \\ 20 & 20 \end{vmatrix} \end{array}$$

Find the sales position for the remaining nine months.

Solution. Given

$$\text{Yearly sales position} = \begin{array}{c} \\ A \\ B \end{array} \begin{array}{c} \begin{array}{cc} P & Q \end{array} \\ \begin{vmatrix} 50 & 45 \\ 60 & 70 \end{vmatrix} \end{array}$$

$$\text{Sales position for first three months} = \begin{array}{c} \\ A \\ B \end{array} \begin{array}{c} \begin{array}{cc} P & Q \end{array} \\ \begin{vmatrix} 30 & 15 \\ 20 & 20 \end{vmatrix} \end{array}$$

∴ Sales position for the remaining nine months,

$$= \begin{array}{c} \\ A \\ B \end{array} \begin{array}{c} \begin{array}{cc} P & Q \end{array} \\ \begin{vmatrix} 50 & 45 \\ 60 & 70 \end{vmatrix} \end{array} - \begin{array}{c} \\ A \\ B \end{array} \begin{array}{c} \begin{array}{cc} P & Q \end{array} \\ \begin{vmatrix} 30 & 15 \\ 20 & 20 \end{vmatrix} \end{array}$$

$$= \begin{array}{c} \\ A \\ B \end{array} \begin{array}{c} \begin{array}{cc} P & Q \end{array} \\ \begin{vmatrix} 20 & 30 \\ 40 & 50 \end{vmatrix} \end{array}$$

MULTIPLICATION OF MATRICES – APPLICATIONS

It is very important to note that two matrices can be multiplied if and only if number of columns of the first matrix equals the number of rows of the second. The resultant matrix will have number of rows of the first and number of columns of the second matrix.

For example,

1. $[a \times b]$ matrix can only be multiplied with $[b \times c]$ matrix.
2. The resultant matrix would be $[a \times c]$

Students must exercise following cautions while solving problem based on matrix multiplication

1. Always try to estimate the order of matrix which would represent solution of the problem.
2. The problem is generally framed which gives relationship among three variables in such a manner that one of the variable is common among these variables. The resultant matrix is desired between the remaining two variables. Keeping in view this fact, always formulate your problem in such a manner that the common variable appears as column in the first matrix and row in the second. The concept of matrix multiplication would become more clear from the following examples.

***Example 3.* A man buys 12 kg of sugar, 10 kg of pulses and 5 kg of salt. Sugar cost Rs. 17 per kg., pulses cost Rs. 15 per kg and salt Rs. 12 per kg. Using matrix multiplication, determine the total amount spent by the man.**

Solution. In this case, we will have two matrix. One matrix would represent quantity and other would represent cost per kg.

Since, we are required to calculate total amount spent by the man, it would be represented by (1×1) matrix. Therefore, we must multiply the two matrix in such a way that we finally get $[1 \times 1]$.

The two matrix mentioned above would be given as

$$Q = [12, 10, 5]$$

$$C = \begin{bmatrix} 17 \\ 15 \\ 12 \end{bmatrix}$$

We know that matrix multiplication is possible if number of rows of one matrix is equal to number of columns of other matrix *i.e.* why, we have written the above matrix in the manner 1×3 and 3×1.

$$[1 \times 3]\ [3 \times 1] = [1 \times 1]$$

$$\therefore \qquad \begin{bmatrix} 12 & 10 & 5 \end{bmatrix} \begin{bmatrix} 17 \\ 15 \\ 12 \end{bmatrix} = \begin{bmatrix} 414 \end{bmatrix}$$

$\therefore$ Total amount spent by the man is Rs. 414.

Example 4. **Ram, Shyam and Mohan purchased biscuits of different brand *P, Q* and *R*. Ram purchased 10 packets of *P*, 7 packets of *Q* and 3 packets of *R*. Shyam purchased 4 packets of *P*, 8 packets of *Q* and 10 packets of *R*. Mohan purchased 4 packets of *P*, 7 packets of *Q* and 8 packets of *R*. If brand *P* cost Rs. 4 each, *Q* cost Rs 5 and *R* cost Rs. 6, then using matrix operation, find the amount of money spent by these person individually.**

Solution. In this case we will have two matrix. One would represent number of packets of each brand purchased by these person separately and other would be the cost of each brand. They are given as under.

$$\text{Matrix I} = \begin{matrix} \text{Ram} \\ \text{Shyam} \\ \text{Mohan} \end{matrix} \overset{\begin{matrix} P & Q & R \end{matrix}}{\begin{bmatrix} 10 & 7 & 3 \\ 4 & 8 & 10 \\ 4 & 7 & 8 \end{bmatrix}_{3\times 3}}$$

$$\text{Matrix II} = \begin{matrix} P \\ Q \\ R \end{matrix} \overset{\text{cost}}{\begin{bmatrix} 4 \\ 5 \\ 6 \end{bmatrix}_{3\times 1}}$$

Since, number of rows of one matrix shall be equal to the number of columns of the other matrix for matrix multiplication therefore, we will have to multiply these matrix in the following number

$$= \begin{bmatrix} 10 & 7 & 3 \\ 4 & 8 & 10 \\ 4 & 7 & 8 \end{bmatrix} \begin{bmatrix} 4 \\ 5 \\ 6 \end{bmatrix}$$

$$= \begin{bmatrix} 10 \times 4 + & 7 \times 5 + & 3 \times 6 \\ 4 \times 4 + & 8 \times 5 + & 10 \times 6 \\ 4 \times 4 + & 7 \times 5 + & 8 \times 6 \end{bmatrix} = \begin{bmatrix} 40 + 35 + 18 \\ 16 + 40 + 60 \\ 16 + 35 + 48 \end{bmatrix} = \begin{bmatrix} 93 \\ 116 \\ 99 \end{bmatrix}$$

Amount spent by Ram, Shyam and Mohan is Rs. 99 Rs. 116 and Rs. 99 respectively.

Example 5. **Mr. X has Rs. 100000 as investible fund. The fund is to be invested in two kind of securities offering return of 10% and 20% p.a. Determine the amount to be invested in each securities, if the return of Rs. 12000 is to be earned.**

Solution. Let 'x' be the part of investible fund to be invested in securities offering 10% p.a.

$\therefore$ (100000–x) will be invested in securities offering 20% p.a.

$\therefore$ If the required return is Rs. 12000, therefore we have

$$\begin{bmatrix} x(100000-x) \end{bmatrix}\begin{bmatrix} 10/100 \\ 20/100 \end{bmatrix} = \begin{bmatrix} 12000 \end{bmatrix}$$

$$\therefore \quad \frac{10x}{100} + \frac{20}{100}(100000 - x) = [12000]$$

$$\therefore \quad \frac{10x}{100} + 20000 = -\frac{20x}{100} = 12000$$

$$-\frac{10x}{100} + 12000 - 20000 = -8000$$

$$\therefore \quad x = 80000$$

and $100000 - x = 100000 - 80000 = 20000$

Thus, Rs. 80000 shall be invested @ 10% p.a. and remaining part *i.e.* Rs. 20000 shall be invested @ 20% p.a. to earn a return of Rs. 12000.

Example 6. **A student has 4 places where he can eat lunch. The college canteen charges Rs. 8 for a Dosa, Rs. 3 for French fries and Rs. 5 for a soft drink. The campus coffee house charges Rs. 10 for a Dosa, Rs. 2 for French Fries and Rs. 4.50 for a soft drink. A fast food place charges Rs. 8 for a Dosa, Rs. 4 for French fries and Rs. 5 for a soft drink. A nearby restaurant serves Dosa for Rs. 12, French fries for Rs. 5 and a free soft drink for any order.**

Express the above information in a 4 × 3 matrix. The student wishes to buy 1 Dosa, 2 orders of French fries and a soft drink. Find, using matrix algebra, the cost of lunch at each place. Assuming that the student has no preference for any of the places, decide where he should eat to spend the least amount of money.

Solution. First of all we should form a matrix to represent the eating places and the food required to be purchased.

$$\begin{array}{l} \\ \\ \text{College canteen} \\ \text{Coffee house} \\ \text{Fast food place} \\ \text{Restaurant} \end{array} \begin{array}{ccc} \text{Dosa} & \text{French fries} & \text{Soft drink} \\ \left[\begin{array}{c} 8 \\ 10 \\ 8 \\ 12 \end{array}\right. & \begin{array}{c} 3 \\ 2 \\ 4 \\ 5 \end{array} & \left.\begin{array}{c} 5 \\ 4.50 \\ 5 \\ 0 \end{array}\right] \end{array}$$

The order can be represented by the column matrix

$$\begin{array}{l} \text{Dosa} \\ \text{French Fries} \\ \text{Soft drink} \end{array} \begin{bmatrix} 1 \\ 2 \\ 1 \end{bmatrix}$$

Since, we required final relationship between places and the cost, therefore, we shall place food articles as column in the first matrix and row in the second matrix.

Using matrix multiplication, the cost of lunch at each place can be determined as under :

$$\begin{bmatrix} 8 & 3 & .5 \\ 10 & 2 & 4.50 \\ 8 & 4 & 5 \\ 12 & 5 & 0 \end{bmatrix} \begin{bmatrix} 1 \\ 2 \\ 1 \end{bmatrix} = \begin{bmatrix} Rs.\ 19 \\ Rs.\ 18.50 \\ Rs.\ 21 \\ Rs.\ 22 \end{bmatrix} \begin{matrix} \text{College canteen} \\ \text{Coffee house} \\ \text{Fast food place} \\ \text{Restaurant} \end{matrix}$$

Hence the student would spend the least amount of money by eating at coffee house.

Example 7. **A firm produces three products P_1, P_2 and P_3 requiring the mix up of four materials M_1, M_2, M_3 and M_4. The matrix below gives the amount of material needed for each product:**

$$\begin{matrix} & M_1 & M_2 & M_3 & M_4 \end{matrix}$$
$$= \begin{matrix} P_1 \\ P_2 \\ P_3 \end{matrix} \begin{bmatrix} 2 & 3 & 1 & 12 \\ 7 & 9 & 5 & 20 \\ 8 & 12 & 6 & 15 \end{bmatrix}$$

Find

(*i*) The total requirement to each material if the firm produces 70 units of P_1, 120 units of P_2 and 50 units of P_3.

(*ii*) The per unit cost of production of each product, if the per unit costs of material M_1, M_2, M_3, and M_4 are Rs. 10, Rs. 12, Rs. 15 and Rs. 20 respectively.

(*iii*) The total cost of production.

Solution.

(*i*) We are already given relationship between product and material required for manufacturing the product. From the given information, we can formulate other matrix representing relationship between product and number of units, as under

$$\begin{matrix} & P_1 & P_2 & P_3 \\ \text{Units} & [70 & 120 & 50] \end{matrix}$$

Since, we require relationship between material and units, therefore we should multiply the two matrix in such a manner that products P_1, P_2, P_3 become common variable.

$$= \begin{matrix} \\ M_1 \\ M_2 \\ M_3 \\ M_4 \end{matrix} \begin{matrix} P_1 & P_2 & P_3 \\ \begin{bmatrix} 2 & 7 & 8 \\ 3 & 9 & 12 \\ 1 & 5 & 6 \\ 12 & 20 & 15 \end{bmatrix}_{4\times 3} \end{matrix} \begin{matrix} \text{No. of units} \\ \begin{matrix} P_1 \\ P_2 \\ P_3 \end{matrix} \begin{bmatrix} 70 \\ 120 \\ 50 \end{bmatrix}_{3\times 1} \end{matrix} = \begin{matrix} \text{units} \\ \begin{matrix} M_1 \\ M_2 \\ M_3 \\ M_4 \end{matrix} \begin{bmatrix} 1380 \\ 1890 \\ 970 \\ 3990 \end{bmatrix} \end{matrix}$$

∴ Total requirement of materials M_1, M_2, M_3 and M_4 is 1380, 1890, 970 and 3990 respectively.

(*ii*) Let the relationship between cost of each material and material be represented by the following matrix

$$\begin{matrix} & M_1 & M_2 & M_3 & M_4 \\ \text{cost} & [10 & 12 & 15 & 20] \end{matrix}$$

Since, finally we require relationship between cost and the product, therefore we shall multiply the given matrix and the formulated matrix in such a manner that finally we get relation between cost and product. Keep material as common variable.

$$\begin{matrix} & M_1 & M_2 & M_3 & M_4 \\ \text{cost} & [10 & 12 & 15 & 20]_{(1\times4)} \end{matrix} \begin{matrix} \\ M_1 \\ M_2 \\ M_3 \\ M_4 \end{matrix} \begin{matrix} P_1 & P_2 & P_3 \\ \begin{bmatrix} 2 & 7 & 8 \\ 3 & 9 & 12 \\ 1 & 5 & 6 \\ 12 & 20 & 15 \end{bmatrix}_{(4\times3)} \end{matrix}$$

$$= \begin{bmatrix} 311 & 653 & 614 \end{bmatrix}$$

∴ Per unit cost of production of P_1, P_2, P_4 and P_3 is Rs. 311, Rs. 653 and Rs. 614 respectively.

(*iii*) In order to find total cost of production, we need to multiply matrices showing relationship between products and number of units to be manufactured with the matrix showing relationship between product and cost of production of each product.

The two matrix would be

$$M_1 = \text{Number of units} \begin{matrix} P_1 & P_2 & P_3 \\ [70 & 120 & 50]_{1\times3} \end{matrix}$$

cost of production

$$M_2 = \begin{matrix} P_1 \\ P_2 \\ P_3 \end{matrix} \begin{bmatrix} 311 \\ 653 \\ 614 \end{bmatrix}_{3\times1}$$

∴ since total cost of production would be [1 × 1] matrix

∴ we shall multiply these matrices accordingly.

$$\begin{bmatrix} 70 & 120 & 50 \end{bmatrix} \begin{bmatrix} 311 \\ 653 \\ 614 \end{bmatrix} = \begin{bmatrix} 130830 \end{bmatrix}$$

∴ Total cost of production = 130830

Example 8. **The matrix given below shows the proportionate mix of chemicals used for three type of paints.**

Chemicals

$$\textbf{Paint} \begin{matrix} \\ 1 \\ 2 \\ 3 \end{matrix} \begin{matrix} A & B & C & D \\ \begin{bmatrix} 0.3 & 0 & 0.7 & 0 \\ 0.2 & 0.3 & 0 & 0.5 \\ 0.3 & 0.1 & 0.2 & 0.4 \end{bmatrix} \end{matrix}$$

(*a*) If sales are 600 tins (of one kilogram) per week, 50% (of the total sales) being paint 1,100 tins of paint 2 and remaining of paint 3, how much of each constituent is used.

(*b*) If the cost of each constituent *A, B, C, D* is 20 paise, 30 paise, 50 paise and 80 paise for 100 gram, respectively, how much does a one kilogram tin of each paint cost.

(c) What is the total cost per week.

Solution.

(*a*) Given total Sales = 600 tins.

$$\text{Sales of Paint 1} = \frac{50}{100} \times 600 = 300$$

$$\text{Paint 2} = 100 \text{ (given)}$$

$$\text{Paint 3} = 600 - (300 + 100) = 200$$

$$\therefore \quad \text{Sales Matrix} = \begin{matrix} \text{Paint 1} \\ \text{Paint 2} \\ \text{Paint 3} \end{matrix} \begin{bmatrix} 300 \\ 100 \\ 200 \end{bmatrix}$$

Total quantity of each constituent used would be given as product of following two matrix, as under :

$$= \begin{bmatrix} 0.3 & 0.2 & 0.3 \\ 0 & 0.3 & 0.1 \\ 0.7 & 0 & 0.2 \\ 0 & 0.5 & 0.4 \end{bmatrix} \begin{bmatrix} 300 \\ 100 \\ 200 \end{bmatrix}$$

$$= \begin{bmatrix} 0.3 \times 300 & + & 0.2 \times 100 & + & 0.3 \times 200 \\ 0 \times 300 & + & 0.3 \times 100 & + & 0.1 \times 200 \\ 0.7 \times 300 & + & 0 \times 100 & + & 0.2 \times 200 \\ 0 \times 300 & + & 0.5 \times 100 & + & 0.4 \times 200 \end{bmatrix}$$

$$= \begin{bmatrix} 170 \\ 50 \\ 250 \\ 130 \end{bmatrix}$$

$\therefore \quad A = 170,\ B = 50.\ C = 250$ and $D = 130$.

(*b*) In order to find out the cost of a kilogram of each paint, the following two matrix would be multiplied.

$$\text{Cost} = \begin{bmatrix} 2 & 3 & 5 & 8 \end{bmatrix}$$

[Since cost per 100 gram is given, it has been converted into cost per kilogram]

$$\therefore \quad \text{Cost of Kilogram} = \begin{bmatrix} 2 & 3 & 5 & 8 \end{bmatrix} \begin{vmatrix} 0.3 & 0.2 & 0.3 \\ 0 & 0.3 & 0.1 \\ 0.7 & 0 & 0.2 \\ 0 & 0.5 & 0.4 \end{vmatrix}$$

$$= \begin{bmatrix} 4.1 & 5.3 & 5.1 \end{bmatrix}$$

$$(c) \text{ Total cost per} = \begin{bmatrix} 2 & 3 & 5 & 8 \end{bmatrix} \begin{bmatrix} 170 \\ 50 \\ 250 \\ 130 \end{bmatrix} = \begin{bmatrix} 2780 \end{bmatrix}$$

Exercise 2.1

1. Mr. A purchased equal quantity of sharpener, pencil and rubber aggregating to 15 units. Notebook pencil and rubber costs Rs. 12, Rs. 12 and Rs. 13 respectively. Using matrix multiplication, determine the total amount spent by Mr. A. **[Ans. :** Rs. 185]
2. Sarita purchased 10 greeting cars, 12 keyrings and 18 showpieces. The cost of a greeting card, keyring and show pieces are Rs. 10, Rs. 12 and Rs. 13 respectively. Determine the total amount spent by Sarita using matrix multiplication. **[Ans.** Rs. 478]
3. X, Y and Z went to a market and purchased same type of products but in different quantities. X purchased 5 spoons, 7 bowls and 3 plates. Y purchased the three things in equal quantities aggregating to 12. Z purchased 2 spoons, 7 bowls and 8 plates. If cost of each spoon, bowls and plate is Rs. 1, Rs. 2 and Rs. 3 respectively, find the total amount spent by X, Y and Z individually. **[Ans.** X = Rs. 28, Y = Rs. 24, Z = 40]
4. The cost of a banana, an orange and a papaya is Rs. 2, Rs. 4 and Rs. 8 respectively. If A purchased 9 bananas, 8 oranges, 7 papaya; B purchased 4 bananas, 5 oranges and 6 papaya; C purchased 8 banana, 9 orange, 6 papaya, find the total amount spent by A, B and C respectively. [A = 106, B = 76, C = 100]
5. 'A' capable of making 4 units of X or 7 units of Y per hour. 'B' can make 7 units of X or 6 units of Y in the same time whereas 'C' can make 8 units of X or 7 units of Y in the same time. If the time allotted for making X is 5 hours and 6 hours for Y. Using matrix multiplication, find the total number of units manufactured by A, B and C.

   [A = 62 units, B = 71 units, C = 82 units].
6. A company has two plants. Plant I can manufacture 5 units of X, 7 units of Y and 8 units of Z per hour. Plant II can manufacture 7 units of X, 7 units of Y and 9 units of Z at the same time. Using matrix multiplication find the number of items X, Y and Z produced if plant I is operated for 8 hours and plant II is operated for 9 hours. [X = 103, Y = 1149, Z = 145]
7. A factory produces, three varieties of Alcohol-Methanol, Proponal and Ethanol. The proportion of constituents A, B, C and D used for manufacturing these products is given below :

	Constituents			
	A	*B*	*C*	*D*
Methanol	0.4	0	0.6	0
Proponol	0.1	0.3	0	0.6
Ethanol	0.2	0.2	0.1	0.5

(*a*) If the sales are 700 bottles. 100 bottles of methanol, 200 bottles of Proponal and 400 bottles of Ethanol, how much of each constituent used.

(*b*) If the cost of each constituent is Rs. 4, 6, 8 and 8 per kilogram respectively, how much does each alcohol cost.

(*c*) What is the total cost per week.

Solve using matrix method of multiplication. [(*a*) 140, 140, 100, 320 (*b*) 6.4, 7, 6.8 (*c*) 4760].

8. Company to employ 60 labourers from either of the Party *A* and *B*, comprising of persons in different age groups as under :

Category	*I (20–25 years)*	*II (26–30 years)*	*III (31–40 years)*
Part A	25	20	15
Party B	20	30	10

Rate of labour applicable to categories I, II and III are Rs. 1200, Rs. 1000 and Rs. 600 respectively. Using matrices, find which party is economically preferable over the other.

[Party *A* : More economical]

9. A manufacturer produces three products *X*, *Y* and *Z* which he sells in three market I, II and III. Monthly Sales and Sale prices are given as follows :

Market	*Item Sold*			*Sales Price in Rs.*		
I	*X*	*Y*	*Z*	*X*	*Y*	*Z*
I	1000	1500	2000	2.00	3.00	4.00
II	2000	2800	3000	2.50	2.80	3.70
III	3000	3500	4000	2.30	3.10	4.20

If the cost per items for the three products *X*, *Y* and *Z* are Rs. 1.80, Rs. 2.50 and Rs. 3.40 respectively, find the matrix algebra his total profit. [Rs. 12090]

10. A firm has projected demand of its products *A*, *B* and *C* under different circumstances. The details are given below in the matrix form

$$\begin{array}{l} \\ \text{Optimistic} \\ \text{Mostlikely} \\ \text{Pessimistic} \end{array} \begin{array}{c} \begin{array}{ccc} A & B & C \end{array} \\ \left|\begin{array}{ccc} 20 & 10 & 5 \\ 30 & 12 & 1 \\ 35 & 5 & 2 \end{array}\right| \end{array}$$

If the matrix vector [1 2 4] represent the profit per unit for the goods *A*, *B*, *C* in that order. Using matrix multiplication, find the profit under the different circumstances.

[Optimistic 60, Most likely 58, Pessimistic 53]

SYSTEM OF LINEAR EQUATIONS

Example 9. **A amount of Rs. 5,000 is put into three investments at the rates of interest of 6%, 7% and 8% per annum respectively. The total annual income is Rs. 358. If the combined income from the first two investments is Rs. 70 more than the income from the third, find the amount of each investment by using matrix algebra.**

Solution. Let x, y and z represent the investments at the rates of interest of 6%, 7% and 8% per annum respectively. Based on the information given, we have following three equations.

$$x + y + z = 5000$$

$$0.06x + 0.07y + 0.08z = 358 \text{ or } 6x + 7y + 8z = 35800$$

$$0.06x + 0.07y = 0.08z + 70 \text{ or } 6x + 7y - 8z = 7000$$

The above system can be expressed in the matrix form as

$$\begin{bmatrix} 1 & 1 & 1 \\ 6 & 7 & 8 \\ 6 & 7 & -8 \end{bmatrix} \begin{bmatrix} x \\ y \\ z \end{bmatrix} = \begin{bmatrix} 5000 \\ 25800 \\ 7000 \end{bmatrix}$$

$$A \qquad X = \qquad B$$

The determinant of the coefficient matrix A is

$$|A| = \begin{vmatrix} 1 & 1 & 7 \\ 6 & 7 & 8 \\ 6 & 7 & -8 \end{vmatrix} = -16$$

Since $|A| \neq 0$, A^{-1} exists and the solution is given by $X = A^{-1} B$.

$$A^{-1} = \text{adj } A/|A|$$

$$A^{-1} = -\frac{1}{16} \begin{bmatrix} -112 & 15 & 1 \\ 96 & -14 & -2 \\ 0 & -1 & 1 \end{bmatrix}$$

Hence the solution is

$$X = A^{-1} B = -\frac{1}{16} \begin{bmatrix} -112 & 15 & 1 \\ 96 & -14 & -2 \\ 0 & -1 & 1 \end{bmatrix} \begin{bmatrix} 5000 \\ 35800 \\ 7000 \end{bmatrix}$$

$$= -\frac{1}{16} \begin{bmatrix} -16000 \\ -35200 \\ -28800 \end{bmatrix} = \begin{bmatrix} 1000 \\ 2200 \\ 1800 \end{bmatrix}$$

Hence $x = 1000$, $y = 2200$ and $z = 1800$.

Example 10. **The equilibrium conditions for two substitute good are given by**

$$5P_1 - 2P_2 = 15, \; -P_1 + 8P_2 = 16$$

Using matrix algebra, find the equilibrium prices.

Solution. We have

$$5P_1 \quad 2P_2 = 15$$

$$-p_1 + 8P_2 = 16$$

Using matrix method, we have

$$\begin{vmatrix} 5 & -2 \\ -1 & +8 \end{vmatrix} \begin{vmatrix} P_1 \\ P_2 \end{vmatrix} = \begin{vmatrix} 15 \\ 16 \end{vmatrix}$$

$$\therefore \quad |A| = (5 \times 8 - (-2) \times (-1) = (40 - 2) = 38$$

$$\therefore \quad (A)^C = \begin{vmatrix} 8 & 1 \\ 2 & 5 \end{vmatrix}$$

$$\text{adj } A = \begin{vmatrix} 8 & 2 \\ 1 & 5 \end{vmatrix}$$

$$\therefore \quad A^{-1} = \frac{1}{38} \begin{vmatrix} 8 & 2 \\ 1 & 5 \end{vmatrix}$$

$$X = A^{-1}.B = \frac{1}{38} \begin{vmatrix} 8 & 2 \\ 1 & 5 \end{vmatrix} \begin{vmatrix} 15 \\ 16 \end{vmatrix}$$

$$= \frac{1}{38} \begin{vmatrix} 152 \\ 95 \end{vmatrix} = \begin{vmatrix} 4 \\ 2.5 \end{vmatrix}$$

$\therefore$ $P_1 - 4$ and $P_2 = 2.5$

***Example 11.* A person has his Current Account and Saving Account in a nationalised bank and a multipurpose account in ICICI Bank. Initial credit balance in all these three accounts was Rs. 10,000. During the month, the first withdrew a sum of Rs. 500 from the current account and then the balance in his savings bank account was half of his current account balance. He made the next withdrawal from his ICICI Bank account of Rs. 1,000 and then the balance in his ICICI Bank account was double the difference between his current account and savings account. By using the concept of matrix, find his initial balance at the beginning of the month in these accounts. Assume that there is no interest given by the banks.**

Solution. Let x, y and z be the initial balance in the current account, savings account and ICICI bank account. Then we have following equations.

$$x + y + z = 10{,}000 \qquad \text{....(1)}$$

$$\frac{1}{2}(x - 500) = y \quad \Rightarrow \quad x - 2y + 0z = 500 \qquad \text{....(2)}$$

$$z - 1000 = 2(x - y) \quad \Rightarrow \quad -2x + 2y + z = 1000 \qquad \text{....(3)}$$

Writing the above system of equations in matrix form, we obtain

$$\begin{bmatrix} 1 & 1 & 1 \\ 1 & -2 & 0 \\ -2 & 2 & 1 \end{bmatrix} \begin{bmatrix} x \\ y \\ z \end{bmatrix} = \begin{bmatrix} 10,000 \\ 500 \\ 1,000 \end{bmatrix}$$

Since |**A**| = – 5 ≠ 0, $\mathbf{A}^{-1}$ exists and it can be verified that

$$A^{-1} = \frac{1}{|A|} \text{adj } A = \frac{1}{-5}\begin{bmatrix} -2 & 1 & 2 \\ -1 & 3 & 1 \\ -2 & -4 & -3 \end{bmatrix}$$

$$\text{Now } X\ A^{-1}\ B \Rightarrow \begin{bmatrix} x \\ y \\ z \end{bmatrix} = \frac{1}{-5}\begin{bmatrix} -2 & 1 & 2 \\ -1 & 3 & 1 \\ -2 & -4 & -3 \end{bmatrix}\begin{bmatrix} 10,000 \\ 500 \\ 1,000 \end{bmatrix} = \begin{bmatrix} 3,500 \\ 500 \\ 1,000 \end{bmatrix}$$

Hence x Rs. 3,5000; y = Rs. 500 and z = Rs. 1,000.

Example 12(a). **To control a crop disease it is necessary to use 8 units of chemical *A*, 14 units of chemical *B* and 13 units of chemical *C*. One barel of spray *P* contains one unit of *A*, 2 units of *B* and 3 units of *C*. One barrel of spray *Q* contains 2 units of *A*, 3 units of *B* and 2 units of *C*. One barrel of spray *R* contains 1 unit of *A*, 2 units of *B* and 2 units of *C*. Find how many barrels of each spray be used to just meet the requirement. (Solve by Matrix Algebra).**

Solution : Let x barrels of spray *P*, y barrels of spray *Z* and z barrels of spray *R* be used to just meet the requirements. Then according to the given data :

$$x + 2y + z = 8$$

$$2x + 3y + 2z = 14$$

$$3x = 2y + 2z = 13$$

In matrix from, we have

$$\begin{bmatrix} 1 & 2 & 1 \\ 2 & 3 & 2 \\ 3 & 2 & 2 \end{bmatrix}\begin{bmatrix} x \\ y \\ z \end{bmatrix} = \begin{bmatrix} 8 \\ 14 \\ 13 \end{bmatrix} \quad i.e., \ \boldsymbol{AX} = \boldsymbol{B}$$

Since $|A| = 1 \neq 0$, A^{-1} exists and the solution is given by $\boldsymbol{X} = \boldsymbol{A}^{-1}\boldsymbol{B}$.

$$A^{-1} = \begin{bmatrix} 2 & -2 & 1 \\ 2 & -1 & 0 \\ -5 & 4 & -1 \end{bmatrix}$$

The solution of the given system of equation will be

$$\begin{bmatrix} x \\ y \\ z \end{bmatrix} = \begin{bmatrix} 2 & -2 & 1 \\ 2 & -1 & 0 \\ -5 & 4 & -1 \end{bmatrix}\begin{bmatrix} 8 \\ 14 \\ 13 \end{bmatrix} = \begin{bmatrix} 1 \\ 2 \\ 3 \end{bmatrix} \Rightarrow x = 1,\ y = 2 \text{ and } z = 3.$$

Hence 1 barrel of *P*, 2 barrels of *Q* and 3 barrels of *R* must be used to just meet the requirements.

Example 12(b). ***X*** **Ltd. is engaged in manufacturing of product *X* and *Y*. The cost function has a linear relationship, given as under :**

$C = a + bX + cY$. Data for 3-days is given below :

	Day 1	*Day 2*	*Day 3*
Cost	**6950**	**6725**	**7100**
X (Units)	**10**	**9**	**12**
U (Units)	**40**	**35**	**40**

Find the value of *a*, *b*, and *c*.

Solution. The above in information can be expressed in matrix from as under *i.e.*, $AX = B$.

$$\begin{bmatrix} 1 & 10 & 40 \\ 1 & 9 & 30 \\ 1 & 12 & 40 \end{bmatrix}\begin{bmatrix} a \\ b \\ c \end{bmatrix} = \begin{bmatrix} 6950 \\ 6725 \\ 7100 \end{bmatrix}$$

$$\therefore \quad A^{-1} = \frac{1}{10}\begin{bmatrix} -60 & 80 & -10 \\ -5 & 0 & 5 \\ 3 & -2 & -1 \end{bmatrix}$$

$$X = A^{-1}B = \frac{1}{10}\begin{bmatrix} -60 & 80 & -10 \\ -5 & 0 & 5 \\ 3 & -2 & -1 \end{bmatrix}\begin{bmatrix} 6950 \\ 6725 \\ 7100 \end{bmatrix} = \begin{bmatrix} 5000 \\ 75 \\ 30 \end{bmatrix}$$

$\therefore \quad a = 5000,\ b = 75$ and $c = 30$.

***Example 13.* A company produces three products everyday. Their total production on a certain day in 45 tons. It is found that the production of third product exceeds the production of first product by 8 tons while the total production of first and third product is twice the production of second product. Determine the production level of each product using Cramer's rule.**

Solution. Let the production level of the three products be *x*, *y* and *z* respectively. Therefore, we will have following equations

$$x + y + z = 45 \qquad ....(1)$$

$$z = x + 8$$

i.e. $\quad -x + 0y + z = 8 \qquad ....(2)$

Likewise $\quad x + z = 2y$

i.e. $\quad x - 2y + z = 0 \qquad ....(3)$

$\therefore$ We have, using (1) (2) and (3)

$$\begin{vmatrix} 1 & 1 & 1 \\ -1 & 0 & 1 \\ 1 & -2 & 1 \end{vmatrix}\begin{vmatrix} x \\ y \\ z \end{vmatrix} = \begin{vmatrix} 45 \\ 8 \\ 0 \end{vmatrix}$$

$$\therefore \quad \Delta = \begin{vmatrix} 1 & 1 & 1 \\ -1 & 0 & 1 \\ 1 & -2 & 1 \end{vmatrix} = 6$$

Since $\Delta \neq 0$, there is a unique solution

$$\Delta_1 = \begin{vmatrix} 45 & 1 & 1 \\ 8 & 0 & 1 \\ 0 & -2 & 1 \end{vmatrix} = 66$$

$$\Delta_2 = \begin{vmatrix} 1 & 45 & 1 \\ -1 & 8 & 1 \\ 1 & 0 & 1 \end{vmatrix} = 90$$

$$\Delta_3 = \begin{vmatrix} 1 & 1 & 45 \\ -1 & 0 & 8 \\ 1 & -2 & 0 \end{vmatrix} = 114$$

$$\therefore \quad x = \frac{66}{6} = 11$$

$$y = \frac{90}{6} = 15$$

$$z = \frac{114}{6} = 19$$

Example 14. **The equilibrium conditions for three related markets are given by**

$$11P_1 - P_2 - P_3 = 31$$

$$-P_1 + 6P_2 - 2P_3 = 26$$

$$-P_1 - 2P_2 + 7P_3 = 24$$

Using matrix algebra, find the equilibrium price for each market.

Solution. Using matrix algebra, the above equation can be written as

$$\begin{vmatrix} 11 & -1 & -1 \\ -1 & +6 & -2 \\ -1 & -2 & 7 \end{vmatrix} \begin{vmatrix} P_1 \\ P_2 \\ P_3 \end{vmatrix} = \begin{vmatrix} 31 \\ 26 \\ 24 \end{vmatrix}$$

$$\therefore \quad AX = B$$

$$X = A^{-1}B$$

Since $|A| = 401 \neq 0$, therefore A^{-1} exists.

$$\therefore \quad A^{-1} = \frac{1}{401} \begin{vmatrix} 38 & 9 & 8 \\ 9 & 76 & 23 \\ 8 & 23 & 65 \end{vmatrix}$$

$$\therefore \quad X = \frac{1}{401} \begin{vmatrix} 38 & 9 & 8 \\ 9 & 76 & 23 \\ 8 & 23 & 65 \end{vmatrix} \begin{vmatrix} 31 \\ 26 \\ 24 \end{vmatrix} = \frac{1}{401} \begin{vmatrix} 1604 \\ 2807 \\ 2406 \end{vmatrix} = \begin{vmatrix} 4 \\ 7 \\ 6 \end{vmatrix}$$

Thus $P_1 = 4$, $P_2 = 7$ and $P_3 = 6$.

Example 15. **A holding company *H* has two subsidiaries S_1 and S_2. The subsidiaries also own a portion of the share capital of *H*. The percentage ownership of the group is given below :**

Owner of Shares	*Percentage of Share Capital Held in Company*		
	H	S_1	S_2
H	**0**	**60**	**80**
S_1	**3**	**0**	**10**
S_2	**6**	**10**	**0**
Outside Shareholders	**91**	**30**	**10**
Total	**100**	**100**	**100**

If the separately earned profits of *H*, S_1 and S_2 are Rs. 30,000, Rs. 17,500 and Rs. 5,000 respectively; find the total net profit of each company (separately earned profit plus share in the profits of the other companies) by using matrix algebra. Also, verify that sum of the profits allocated to the outside shareholders equals the sum of the separately earned profits of all the companies.

Solution. Let the total net profit of H, S_1 and S_2 be x, y and z respectively. Using the information given, we obtain the following equations :

$$\begin{aligned} x &= 30{,}000 + 0{,}6y + 0.8z & & x - 0.6y - 0.8z = 30{,}000 \\ y &= 17{,}500 + 0.03x + 0.1z & \Rightarrow \quad & -0.03x + y - 0.1z = 17{,}500 \\ z &= 5{,}000 + 0.06x + 0.1y & & -0.06x - 0.1y + z = 5{,}000 \end{aligned}$$

The above system can be expressed in the matrix form as :

$$\begin{bmatrix} 1 & -0.6 & -0.8 \\ -0.03 & 1 & -0.1 \\ -0.06 & -0.1 & 1 \end{bmatrix} \begin{bmatrix} x \\ y \\ z \end{bmatrix} = \begin{bmatrix} 30000 \\ 17500 \\ 5000 \end{bmatrix}$$

i.e. $\qquad A \qquad X = B$

We have

$$|A| = 1\,(1 - 0.01) + 0.6\,(-0.03 - 0.006) - 0.8\,(0.003 + 0.06)$$

$$\Rightarrow \quad |A| = 0.99 - 0.0216 \cdot 0.0504 = 0.918$$

$$1(1 - 0.01) + 0.6\,(-0.03 - 0.006) - 0.8(0.003 + 0.06)$$

$$0.99 + 0.6\,(-0.036) - 0.8(0.63)$$

$$0.99 - 0.0216 - 0.0504 = 0.918$$

Since $|A| \neq 0$, A^{-1} exists and the solution is given by $X = A^{-1} B$. It can be verified that

$$A^{-1} = \frac{1}{0.918} \begin{bmatrix} 0.99 & 0.68 & 0.86 \\ 0.036 & 0.952 & 0.124 \\ 0.063 & 0.136 & 0.982 \end{bmatrix}$$

$$\therefore \quad X = A^{-1}B = \frac{1}{0.918}\begin{bmatrix} 0.99 & 0.68 & 0.86 \\ 0.036 & 0.952 & 0.124 \\ 0.063 & 0.136 & 0.982 \end{bmatrix}\begin{bmatrix} 30000 \\ 17500 \\ 5000 \end{bmatrix}$$

$$= \frac{1}{0.918}\begin{bmatrix} 45900 \\ 18360 \\ 9180 \end{bmatrix} = \begin{bmatrix} 50,000 \\ 20,000 \\ 10,000 \end{bmatrix}$$

Hence x = Rs. 50,000, y = Rs. 20,000 and z = Rs. 10,000.

The sum of the profits allocated to the outside share holders would be calculated as

$$= \begin{bmatrix} 0.91 & 0.3 & 0.1 \end{bmatrix}\begin{bmatrix} 50,000 \\ 20,000 \\ 10,000 \end{bmatrix} = \begin{bmatrix} 52,500 \end{bmatrix}$$

It is already given that sum of the separately earned profits of all the companies

$$= 30,000 + 17,500 + 5,000 = 52,500$$

Therefore the sum of the profits allocated to the outside shareholders equals the sum of the separately earned profits of all the companies.

***Example 16(a).* A transport company uses 3 types of trucks T_1, T_2 and T_3, to transport 3 types of vehicles V_1, V_2 and V_3. The capacity of each truck in terms of 3 types of vehicles is given below:**

	V_1	V_2	V_3
T_1	1	3	2
T_2	2	2	3
T_3	3	2	2

Using the matrix method, find :

(*i*) The number of trucks of each type required to transport 85, 105 and 110 vehicles of V_1, V_2 and V_3 types respectively.

(*ii*) Find the number of vehicles of each type which can be transport if company has 10, 20 and 30 trucks of each type respectively.

Solution.

(*i*) Let x_1, x_2 and x_3 be the number of trucks of type T_1, T_2 and T_3 respectively. Then we have

$$x_1 + 2x_2 + 3x_3 = 85,\ 3x_1 + 2x_3 = 105,\ 2x_1 + 3x_2 + 2x_3 = 110$$

The above information can be written in the matrix form, as under

$$\begin{bmatrix} 1 & 2 & 3 \\ 3 & 2 & 2 \\ 2 & 3 & 2 \end{bmatrix}\begin{bmatrix} x_1 \\ x_2 \\ x_3 \end{bmatrix} = \begin{bmatrix} 85 \\ 105 \\ 110 \end{bmatrix} \text{ or precisely } AX = B$$

$|A| = 9$. since $|A| \neq 0$, A^{-1} exists and hence the solution is given by :

$$X = A^{-1}B = \frac{1}{9}\begin{bmatrix} -2 & 5 & -2 \\ -2 & -4 & 7 \\ 5 & 1 & -4 \end{bmatrix}\begin{bmatrix} 85 \\ 105 \\ 110 \end{bmatrix} = \begin{bmatrix} 15 \\ 20 \\ 10 \end{bmatrix} \therefore x = 15,\ y = 20,\ z = 10$$

(ii) $$\begin{matrix} T_1 & T_2 & T_3 \end{matrix} \qquad \begin{matrix} V_1 & V_2 & V_3 \end{matrix}$$
$$[10 \quad 20 \quad 30]\begin{bmatrix} 1 & 3 & 2 \\ 2 & 2 & 3 \\ 3 & 2 & 2 \end{bmatrix}\begin{matrix} T_1 \\ T_2 \\ T_3 \end{matrix} = \overset{\begin{matrix} V_1 & V_2 & V_3 \end{matrix}}{[140 \quad 130 \quad 140]}$$

Exercise 2.2

1. A company produces three products everyday. Their total production on a certain day is 45 tons. It is found that the production of third product exceeds the production of first product by 8 tons while the total production of first and third product is twice the production of second product. Determine the production level of each product using cramer's rule. [11, 15, 19]

2. A salesman has the following record of sales during three weeks for the three items *X*, *Y* and *Z* which have different rates of commission.

Weeks	*Units sold*			*Total Commission*
	X	*Y*	*Z*	
I	40	30	20	270
II	50	50	40	450
III	60	30	10	260

Find out, using matrix method, the rates of commission on items *X*, *Y* and *Z*.

[*X* = Rs. 2, *Y* = Rs. 3, *Z* = Rs. 5]

3. Three products *X*, *Y* and *Z* are produced after being processed through three departments D_1, D_2 and D_3. The following data are available :

Products	*Hours Required for a Unit Products*		
	In D_1	*In* D_2	*In* D_3
X	2	5	1
Y	1	2	3
Z	2	2	3
Max, time available in hours	1100	1800	1400

Find by matrix method the number of units produced for each product to have full utilization of capacity. [*X* = 200, *Y* = 100, *Z* = 300]

4. The equilibrium condition for two substitute goods is given by :

$$5p_1 - 2p_2 = 15$$
$$-p_1 + 8p_2 = 16$$

Using matrix algebra, find the equilibrium prices. [$p_1 = 4$, $p_2 = 2.5$]

5. The equilibrium condition for three related markets is given by :

$$11p_1 - p_2 - p_3 = 31$$
$$-p_1 + 6p_2 - 2p_3 = 26$$
$$-p_1 - 2p_2 + 7p_3 = 24$$

Using matrix inversion, find the equilibrium price for each market. [$p_1 = 4$, $p_2 = 7$, $p_3 = 6$]

6. The total cost C for a manufacturer producing two items X and Y is given as $C = p + q.X + rY$. Data for three weeks is as follows :

Week	*Cost*	*Number of Items Produced*	
		X	*Y*
1.	6950	40	10
2.	6725	35	9
3.	7100	40	12

Determine p, q and r using determinant method. [$p = 5000$, $q = 30$, $r = 75$]

7. One unit of food I contains 100 units of vitamins, 60 units of minerals and 80 calories. One unit of food II contains 150 units of vitamins, 60 units of minerals and 180 calories. One unit of food III contains 90 units of vitamins, 40 units of minerals and 100 calories. Diet requirement for a patient is 1100 units of vitamins, 500 units of minerals and 1200 calories. Find out either by matrix method or by determinant method how many units of each food be mixed to form the diet which would meet the requirement exactly.

$$\left[x = \frac{(3-k)}{5},\ y = (80 - 7k),\ z = k,\ 0 \le k \le 80/7 \right]$$

8. The equilibrium for three related markets are given by the equations :

$$p_1 = \frac{2}{3}p_2 - p_3 + \frac{2}{3},\ p_2 = \frac{17}{6}p_1 + \frac{5}{6}p_3 - \frac{1}{3},\ p_3 = p_2 - p_1 - 4.$$

Find the equilibrium price for each market by Cramer's rule. [$p_1 = 3$, $p_2 = 14$, $p_3 = 7$]

9. The total sales(s) in thousands or rupees of a firm selling two products X and Y is given by the relationship :

$$S = a + bX + cY.$$

Data for the first three months are given as under :

Months	*Total Sales*	*X*	*Y*
1.	12	2	3
2.	13	6	2
3.	15	5	3

Using determinant method, determine the sales in the next month when he sells 4 units of X and 5 units of Y. [$S = 20$]

10. The prices per ton of wheat and rice are p_1 and p_2 respectively. The market demand for wheat is given by $x_1 = 4 - 10\,p_1 + 7p_2$ and for rice by $x_2 = 3 + 7\,p_1 - 5p_2$. The supply of wheat is related to prices by the relation $x_1 = 7 + p_1 - p_2$ and supply of rice by $x_2 = -27 - p_1 + 2p_2$.

(*i*) Write down the relevant simultaneous equations for determining the equilibrium prices in matrix form.

(*ii*) Find equilibrium prices and quantities using Cramer's rule.

$$\left[\begin{array}{l}(i)\ 11p_1 - 8p_2 = -3,\ 8p_1 = -7p_2 = -30 \\ (ii)\ p_1 = 219/13,\ p_2 = 306/13,\ x_1 = 4/13,\ x_2 = 42/13\end{array}\right]$$

Leontief Input-Output Model

Leontief input-output model discusses the interdependence of industries on each other. The model was developed by Wassily Leontif who received Nobel Prize in Economics in 1973 for it.

Input-Output are of two types :

(*a*) *Closed input-output model*

In this kind of model, entire production made by various industries are consumed among themselves. Only the participative industries are benefited. For example, consider two industries *A* & *B* producing 100 units and 150 units respectively. Now, out of 100 units produced by *A*. 30 units are consumed by *A* it self whereas 70 units of *A* are consumed by B. Likewise, out of 150 units produced by *B*, 80 units of *B* are consumed by *A* and 70 units are consumed by *B* itself. The above information can be represented in the form of matrix, as under :

$$\text{Producers}\begin{array}{c} \\ A \\ B\end{array}\overset{\text{Consumers}}{\begin{array}{cc} A & B \\ \end{array}}\!\!\!\!\!\!\!\!\!\!\!\!\!\!\begin{array}{c} \\ \begin{bmatrix}30 & 70\\ 80 & 70\end{bmatrix}\end{array}$$

Thus, it can be concluded that the entire production of any industry is consumer by participating industries. Part of the production is consumed by producing industries itself and remaining part is consumed by other participating industries.

(*b*) *Open Input-Output Model*

In this kind of model, the production made by participating industries is not only consumed among themselves but also by the external bodies such as households, Government etc.

Using this model, we try to find out the amount of production needed so that an expected demand of future is fulfilled when the present demand is known.

Assumptions of Input-Output Analysis

1. There are '*n*' industries is an economy. Each industry is producing only one product.
2. The output of any industry becomes either the input of another industry or the final consumption of external bodies.
3. The entire production of each sector is just sufficient to meet the final demand as well as the demands of other industries.

4. One of the very important assumption of the model is that all inputs are used in fixed proportions. This implies, if industry A is using 40% of output of industry B then this proportion will always remain same *i.e.*, if A is producing 120 units, A will use 48 units of B. Likewise, when A will produce 200 units, it will use 80 units of B. This indicates that output of B sector is consumed by the A sector in a linear homogeneous function of total output of the A sector.

The following input-output table called input-output transaction table shows the interdependence of industries during same time period :

Consumer *Producer*	*Industry* *1*	*Industry* *2*	...	*Industry* *x*	*Final* *Demand*	*Total* *Output*
Industry 1	x_{11}	x_{12}	...	x_1n	C_1	x_1
Industry 2	x_{21}	x_{22}	...	x_{2n}	C_2	x_2
⋮						
Industry 3	x_{n1}	x_{n2}	...	x_nn	C_n	x_n

In the above table :

1. The industries appearing in the row 1 shows the consumers.

2. The industries appearing in the column 1 shows the producer.

3. Last Column entitled. 'Total Output' shows total output produced by each respective industries. For example, 'x_1', represent total output of industry 1.

Likewise, 'x_2' represent total output of industry 2. It can also be said that

$$x_1 = x_{11} + x_{12} + x_{13} \cdots = x_{1n} + c_1$$

Here x_{11} represent that part of production of Industry 1 which is consumed by itself x_{12} represent that part of production of industry 1 which is consumed by Industry 2. Likewise x_{1n} represent that part of production of industry 1 which is consumed by n^{th} industry.

C_1 represent that part of production of industry 1 which is consumed by direct consumers.

Thus, it can be summarized that rows represent the sales which each industry makes to the other industry and the column shows the purchases which each industry makes from others.

4. The column entitled, 'Final Demand' shows the consumption of production of various industries by external bodies such as household, government etc.

With the help of Input-Output analysis, one can estimate the total production of each industry if there is change in final demand. However, this is feasible as long as the basic structure of economy remains the same which means that the amount of input required from each industry to produce one unit worth of output of a given industry must remain fixed.

For example, the value of final demand changes from c_1 to d_1 for industry 1, c_2 to d_2 for industry 2 and so on. Now, one would like to estimate how much should each industry now produce to cope up with the changes in final demand.

The input requirement per unit worth of output for each industry can be obtained by setting.

$$\frac{x_{ij}}{x_j} = \frac{\text{Rupee Value of the product of industry } i \text{ used by Industry } j}{\text{Rupee value of the total product of industry } j}$$

$= a_{ij}$ (*i.e.*, Rupees value of output of industry i^{th} that j^{th} industry must purchase to produce one rupee worth of its own product).

Here a_{ij} is known as technological coefficient. a_{ij} can be calculated for different industries and the matrix A **constituted of various technological coefficient is known as input-output coefficient matrix or technology matrix** as shown below :

$$A = \begin{vmatrix} a_{11} & a_{12} & \cdots & a_{1n} \\ a_{21} & a_{22} & \cdots & a_{2n} \\ \vdots & & & \\ a_{n1} & a_{n2} & \cdots & a_{nn} \end{vmatrix}$$

Let
$$D = \begin{vmatrix} d_1 \\ d_2 \\ \vdots \\ d_n \end{vmatrix}$$

represent final demand vector, and

$$X = \begin{vmatrix} X_1 \\ X_2 \\ \vdots \\ X_n \end{vmatrix}$$

represent gross output vector

Now, under the conditions that production is equal to consumption, we have Internal Consumption + Consumer demand = Total Output

This can be represented in the form of balancing equations as under :

$$a_{11}\, x_1 + a_{12}\, x_2 + \ldots + a_{1n}\, x_n + d_1 = x_1$$
$$a_{21}\, x_1 + a_{22}\, x_2 + \ldots + a_{22}\, x_n + d_2 = x_2$$
$$\vdots$$
$$a_{n1}\, x_1 + a_{n2}\, x_2 + \ldots + a_{nn}\, x_n + d_n = x_n$$

In the matrix form, it can be given as

$$\begin{vmatrix} a_{11} & a_{12} & \ldots & a_{1n} \\ a_{21} & a_{22} & \ldots & a_{2n} \\ \vdots & & & \\ a_{n1} & a_{n2} & \ldots & a_{nn} \end{vmatrix} \begin{vmatrix} x_1 \\ x_2 \\ \vdots \\ x_n \end{vmatrix} + \begin{vmatrix} d_1 \\ d_2 \\ \vdots \\ x_n \end{vmatrix} = \begin{vmatrix} x_1 \\ x_2 \\ \vdots \\ x_n \end{vmatrix}$$

i.e., $$AX + D = X$$

$$D = X - XA = (I - A)\ X$$

$$X = (I - A)^{-1}\ D$$

Here $[I - A]$ matrix is called the Leontief matrix and $(I - A)^{-1}$ is known as transaction matrix.

Hawkins – Simon Conditions of viability of the System

Leontief model helps in formulation of Input-Output model with the use of which the new output levels to satisfy changes in final demand can be estimated. Since the system is required to give new output levels which cannot be negative therefore certain conditions were given by D. Hawkins and H.A. Simon to ensure that the system does not give negative outputs : These conditions are

(*i*) The determinant $|I - A|$ of the Leotief matrix must be positive; and

(*ii*) The diagonal elements $(1 - a_{11})$, $(1 - a_{22})$...., $(1 - a_{nm})$

Should all be positive or we can say that a_{11}, a_{22} ..... a_{mn} should all be less than one.

***Example* 16(*b*). Convert the following technology matrix into input-output table for the two sector economy.**

	Sector I	***Sector II***
Sector I	**0.7**	**0.3**
Sector II	**0.2**	**0.5**

The final demand for the two sectors are 10 and 20 respectively.

Solution. We know that

$$x_{ij} = a_{ij} x_j$$

where x_{ij} = Output of the ith industry consumed by the jth industry

x_j = Total output of the jth industry

a_{ij} = Technology coefficient (given)

$\therefore$ first of all, we should determine x_j using the equation

$$X = (I - A)^{-1} D$$

where $$A = \begin{bmatrix} 0.7 & 0.3 \\ 0.2 & 0.5 \end{bmatrix} \text{ and } D = \begin{vmatrix} 10 \\ 20 \end{vmatrix}$$

$$(I - A) = \begin{vmatrix} 1 & 0 \\ 0 & 1 \end{vmatrix} - \begin{vmatrix} 0.7 & 0.3 \\ 0.2 & 0.5 \end{vmatrix} = \begin{vmatrix} 0.3 & -0.3 \\ -0.2 & 0.5 \end{vmatrix}$$

$$\therefore \quad |I - A| = (0.3 \times 0.5) - (-0.3 \times -0.2)$$

$$= (0.15 - 0.06) = 0.09$$

$$|I - A|^C = \begin{vmatrix} 0.5 & 0.2 \\ 0.3 & 0.3 \end{vmatrix}$$

Transpose of the cofactor matrix

$$adj(I - A) = \left[(I - A)^c\right]' = \begin{vmatrix} 0.5 & 0.3 \\ 0.2 & 0.3 \end{vmatrix}$$

$$\therefore \quad (I-A)^{-1} = \frac{\text{adj}(I-A)}{|I-A|} = \frac{1}{0.09}\begin{vmatrix} 0.5 & 0.3 \\ 0.2 & 0.3 \end{vmatrix}$$

$$\therefore \quad X = \frac{1}{0.09}\begin{vmatrix} 0.5 & 0.3 \\ 0.2 & 0.3 \end{vmatrix}\begin{vmatrix} 10 \\ 20 \end{vmatrix}$$

$$= \frac{1}{0.09}\begin{vmatrix} 11 \\ 8 \end{vmatrix} = \begin{vmatrix} 122.22 \\ 88.88 \end{vmatrix}$$

$\therefore \quad X_1 = 122.22 \; X_2 = 88.88$

$\therefore$ Using equation (1). we have

$$X_{11} = 0.7 \times 122.22 = 85.55$$

$$X_{12} = 0.3 \times 88.88 = 26.66$$

$$X_{21} = 0.2 \times 122.22 = 24.44$$

$$X_{22} = 0.5 \times 88.88 = 44.44$$

$\therefore$ Input output table

	Sector I	*Sector II*	*Final Demand*	*Total Output*
Sector I	85.55	26.66	10	1222.21
Sector II	24.44	44.44	20	88.88

Example 17. **For the following transaction matrix, find the gross output for each industry for the final demands 18 and 44 units respectively.**

Industry	***Input to***		***Final Demand***
	I	***II***	
I	**16**	**20**	**4**
II	**8**	**40**	**32**

Solution. First of all, make input-output coefficient matrix. The total output of industry I is the sum of industrial demand and final demand : 16 + 20 + 4 = 40. Similarly, the total output of industry II is 8 + 40 + 32 = 80.

In order to find the input-output coefficient matrix, we divide the industry entries in each industry column by the total value of output for that industry. Thus, the input-output coefficient matrix is

$$A = \begin{bmatrix} \frac{16}{40} & \frac{20}{80} \\ \frac{8}{40} & \frac{40}{80} \end{bmatrix} = \begin{bmatrix} \frac{2}{5} & \frac{1}{4} \\ \frac{1}{5} & \frac{1}{2} \end{bmatrix}$$

If $X = \begin{bmatrix} x_1 \\ x_2 \end{bmatrix}$ is the output matrix representing the gross output of each industry to meet the final demand $D=\begin{bmatrix}18\\44\end{bmatrix}$, then the condition that production equals consumption implies that

$$X = AX + D$$

or $$(I - A)\, X = D.$$

where I is the identity matrix of order 2. Now

$$I - A = \begin{bmatrix}1 & 0\\0 & 1\end{bmatrix} - \begin{bmatrix}\frac{2}{5} & \frac{1}{4}\\\frac{1}{5} & \frac{1}{2}\end{bmatrix} = \begin{bmatrix}\frac{3}{5} & -\frac{1}{4}\\-\frac{1}{5} & \frac{1}{2}\end{bmatrix}$$

$$|I - A| = \frac{3}{10} - \frac{1}{20} = \frac{2}{5} = \frac{1}{4}$$

Since $|I - A| \neq 0$, the output X is given by

$$X = (I - A)^{-1}\, D.$$

We have

$$(I - A)^{-1} = 4\begin{bmatrix}\frac{1}{2} & \frac{1}{4}\\\frac{1}{5} & \frac{3}{5}\end{bmatrix}$$

$\therefore$ $$X = (I - A)^{-1}\, D$$

$$= 4\begin{bmatrix}\frac{1}{2} & \frac{1}{4}\\\frac{1}{5} & \frac{3}{5}\end{bmatrix}\begin{bmatrix}18\\44\end{bmatrix} = \begin{bmatrix}80\\120\end{bmatrix}$$

Hence the gross output of two industries. I and II, for the given final demand, are 80 and 120 units respectively.

Example 18. **Two industries input-output relationships are given below in A with final demand vector B (in units) :**

$$A = \begin{matrix}I\\II\end{matrix}\begin{pmatrix}50 & 75\\100 & 50\end{pmatrix} \quad B = \begin{matrix}I\\II\end{matrix}\begin{pmatrix}75\\50\end{pmatrix}$$

If the gross output increases to $\begin{matrix}I\\II\end{matrix}\begin{pmatrix}400\\600\end{pmatrix}$, **determine the final demand which can be satisfied.**

Also test the Hawkinds-Simon conditions.

Solution. The inter-relationship between the production of two industries in the form of input output table is shown below .

Producer Industry	*Consumer I*	*Industries II*	*Final Demand*	*Total Output*
I	50	75	75	200
II	100	50	50	200

Let A denote the input-output coefficient matrix. Then

$$A = \begin{bmatrix} 50/200 & 75/200 \\ 100/200 & 50/200 \end{bmatrix} = \begin{bmatrix} 1/4 & 3/8 \\ 1/2 & 1/4 \end{bmatrix}$$

Let $D = \begin{bmatrix} d_1 \\ d_2 \end{bmatrix}$ denote the final demand which can be satisfied, if the gross output increases to $X = \begin{bmatrix} 400 \\ 600 \end{bmatrix}$. Then the condition

$$AX + D = X$$

implies that $$D = X - AX = (I - A)\ X.$$

Now

$$I - A = \begin{bmatrix} 1 & 0 \\ 0 & 1 \end{bmatrix} - \begin{bmatrix} 1/4 & 3/8 \\ 1/2 & 1/4 \end{bmatrix} = \begin{bmatrix} 3/4 & -3/8 \\ -1/2 & 3/4 \end{bmatrix}$$

$$\therefore \quad D = \begin{bmatrix} 3/4 & -3/8 \\ -1/2 & 3/4 \end{bmatrix} \begin{bmatrix} 400 \\ 600 \end{bmatrix} = \begin{bmatrix} 75 \\ 250 \end{bmatrix}$$

To test Hawkins-Simon conditions, we have $|I - A| = 3/8 > 0$.

Since each entry on the main diagonal of the input-output matrix A is less than 1.

Hence the Hawkins-Simon conditions are satisfied.

Example 19. **Find the demand vector which is consistent with input-output matrix.**

$$A = \begin{bmatrix} 0.2 & 0.3 & 0.2 \\ 0.4 & 0.1 & 0.2 \\ 0.1 & 0.3 & 0.2 \end{bmatrix} \text{ and the output vector } X = \begin{bmatrix} 25 \\ 21 \\ 18 \end{bmatrix}$$

Also test Hawkins-Simon conditions for the viability of the system.

Solution. As already explained, production equals consumption, therefore we have

$$AX + D = X$$

where $$D = \begin{bmatrix} d_1 \\ d_2 \\ d_3 \end{bmatrix} \text{ is the demand vector.}$$

$$D = (I - A)\, X.$$

Now

$$I - A = \begin{bmatrix} 1 & 0 & 0 \\ 0 & 1 & 0 \\ 0 & 0 & 1 \end{bmatrix} - \begin{bmatrix} 0.2 & 0.3 & 0.2 \\ 0.4 & 0.1 & 0.2 \\ 0.1 & 0.3 & 0.2 \end{bmatrix} = \begin{bmatrix} 0.8 & -0.3 & -0.2 \\ -0.4 & 0.9 & -0.2 \\ -0.1 & -0.3 & 0.8 \end{bmatrix}$$

$$\therefore \qquad D = (I - A)X = \begin{bmatrix} 0.8 & -0.3 & -0.2 \\ -0.4 & 0.9 & -0.2 \\ -0.1 & -0.3 & 0.8 \end{bmatrix} \begin{bmatrix} 25 \\ 21 \\ 18 \end{bmatrix} = \begin{bmatrix} 10.1 \\ 5.3 \\ 5.6 \end{bmatrix}$$

Testing of Hawkins-Simon conditions.

We have $\qquad |I - A| = 0.384 > 0$

The diagonal element of $|I - A|$ are 0.8, 0.9, 0.8.

Since each entry in the main diagonal of the input-output matrix A is less than one. Therefore the Hawkins-Simon conditions are satisfied and the system is viable.

Example 20. **Given the input-output matrix and final demand vector :**

$$A = \begin{bmatrix} 0.05 & 0.25 & 0.34 \\ 0.33 & 0.10 & 0.72 \\ 0.19 & 0.38 & 0.00 \end{bmatrix}, \quad D = \begin{bmatrix} 1800 \\ 200 \\ 900 \end{bmatrix}$$

(*i*) Explain the economic meaning of the elements 0.33, 0.00 and 200.

(*ii*) Explain the economic meaning (if any) of the third-column sum.

(*iii*) Explain the economic meaning (if any) of the third-row sum.

Solution. In the given model :

(*i*) $0.33 = a_{21}$. This means that industry I uses 33 paise worth of the output produced in industry II to produce a rupee worth of its product.

$0.00 = a_{33}$. This means that industry III does not require its own product or producing its output.

$200 = d_2$. This means that the economy needs 200 units of the output of industry II.

(*ii*) The third-column sum : $0.34 + 0.72 + 0.00 = 1.06$ shows that Rs. 1.06 worth of output is required from all the industries to produce a rupee worth of output in industry III. Since, the sum is greater than one unit implies that the system is not feasible.

(*iii*) The third row sum has no economic meaning. Similarly, any other row does not have any economic meaning.

Example 21. **For a three-sector economy, input-output coefficients, a_{ij}'s are as given below :**

$a_{11} = 0.5$, $a_{21} = 0.2$, $a_{31} = 0.1$, $a_{12} = 0.1$, $a_{22} = 0.6$, $a_{32} = 0.2$, $a_{13} = 0.1$, $a_{23} = 0.2$, **and** $a_{33} = 0.6$.

(*i*) Using Simon-Hawkins conditions, test whether the system is viable.

(*ii*) Determine the gross output for the three sectors when the final demand values for them are 21,000; 42000 and 63000 units respectively.

(iii) Determine the new level of output if the final demand increases by : 1,500 3,000 and 4,500 units.

Solution : Let A denote the input-output coefficient matrix. Then

$$A=\begin{bmatrix}0.5 & 0.1 & 0.1\\ 0.2 & 0.6 & 0.2\\ 0.1 & 0.2 & 0.6\end{bmatrix} \text{ and } I-A=\begin{bmatrix}0.5 & -0.1 & -0.1\\ -0.2 & 0.4 & -0.2\\ -0.1 & -0.2 & 0.4\end{bmatrix}$$

We have $|I-A|=0.042$. Since $|I-A|$ is positive and all the elements on the main diagonal of A are less than 1, Hawkins-Simon conditions are satisfied and the system is viable.

Let $X=\begin{bmatrix}x_1\\ x_2\\ x_3\end{bmatrix}$ be the gross output required to meet the final demand $D=\begin{bmatrix}21000\\ 42000\\ 63000\end{bmatrix}$

Then $X = [I - A]^{-1} D$. We have

$$[I-A]^{-1}=\frac{1}{0.042}\begin{bmatrix}0.12 & 0.06 & 0.06\\ 0.10 & 0.19 & 0.12\\ 0.08 & 0.11 & 0.18\end{bmatrix}$$

$$X=[I-A]^{-1}=\frac{1}{0.042}\begin{bmatrix}0.12 & 0.06 & 0.06\\ 0.10 & 0.19 & 0.12\\ 0.08 & 0.11 & 0.18\end{bmatrix}\begin{bmatrix}21000\\ 42000\\ 63000\end{bmatrix}=\begin{bmatrix}210000\\ 420000\\ 420000\end{bmatrix}$$

(*iii*) If the demand increases by 1500; 3000 and 4500 units respectively, the new level of output is $X = [I - A]^{-1} D$.

$$\therefore \quad X_N=[I-A]^{-1}\begin{bmatrix}22500\\ 45000\\ 67500\end{bmatrix}=\begin{bmatrix}225000\\ 450000\\ 450000\end{bmatrix}$$

***Example 22.* Consider an economy consisting of three sectors; agriculture, manufacturers and services. The hypothetical flow of goods and services in physical units is summarised in the following table :**

	Agriculture	*Manufacturers*	*Services*	*Final Demand*
Agriculture	**60**	**180**	**0**	**120**
Manufacturers	**30**	**60**	**30**	**180**
Services	**0**	**40**	**10**	**100**

If the demand changes to [150, 160, 180], what will be the new output? (Calculate upto two decimals).

Solution : The matrix of input-output coefficients would be given by :

$$A = \begin{bmatrix} 60/360 & 180/300 & 0/150 \\ 30/360 & 60/300 & 30/150 \\ 0/360 & 40/300 & 10/150 \end{bmatrix} = \begin{bmatrix} 1/6 & 3/5 & 0 \\ 1/12 & 1/5 & 1/5 \\ 0 & 2/15 & 1/15 \end{bmatrix}$$

Let $X = \begin{bmatrix} x_1 \\ x_2 \\ x_3 \end{bmatrix}$ denote the new output and $D = \begin{bmatrix} 150 \\ 160 \\ 180 \end{bmatrix}$ denote the demand vector.

Then $AX + D = X$

Therefore, $X = (I - A)^{-1} D.$

Now
$$I - A = \begin{bmatrix} 1 & 0 & 0 \\ 0 & 1 & 0 \\ 0 & 0 & 1 \end{bmatrix} - \begin{bmatrix} 1/6 & 3/5 & 0 \\ 1/12 & 1/5 & 1/5 \\ 0 & 2/15 & 1/15 \end{bmatrix} = \begin{bmatrix} 5/6 & -3/5 & 0 \\ -1/12 & 4/5 & -1/5 \\ 0 & -2/15 & 14/15 \end{bmatrix}$$

$\therefore$
$$|I - A| = \frac{5}{6}\left(\frac{56}{75} - \frac{2}{75}\right) + \frac{3}{5}\left(-\frac{14}{180} - 0\right) = \frac{83}{150} = 0$$

Further, we have

$$|I - A|^{-1} = \frac{1}{|I - A|} \text{adj}(I - A) = \frac{150}{83} \begin{bmatrix} 18/25 & 14/25 & 1/25 \\ 7/90 & 7/9 & 1/6 \\ 1/90 & 1/9 & 37/60 \end{bmatrix}$$

Thus $X = [I - A]^{-1} D \Rightarrow \begin{bmatrix} x_1 \\ x_2 \\ x_3 \end{bmatrix} = \frac{150}{83} \begin{bmatrix} 18/25 & 14/25 & 1/25 \\ 7/90 & 7/9 & 1/6 \\ 1/90 & 1/9 & 37/60 \end{bmatrix} \begin{bmatrix} 150 \\ 160 \\ 180 \end{bmatrix} = \begin{bmatrix} 396.14 \\ 300.13 \\ 235.75 \end{bmatrix}$

Therefore, the new output for three sectors is : $x_1 = 396.14$, $x_2 = 300.13$ and $x_3 = 235.75$.

Example 23. **Suppose the inter-industry flow of the products of two industries is given as under:**

	Consumption X	*Consumption* Y	*Domestic Demand*	*Gross Output*
Production X	**30**	**40**	**50**	**120**
Production Y	**20**	**10**	**30**	**60**

Determine the technology matrix and test Hawkins-Simon conditions for the viability of the system. Compute the equilibrium level of output of the products when the domestic demand vector is $\begin{bmatrix} 80 \\ 40 \end{bmatrix}$.

Solution. The technology matrix in this case would be

$$A = \begin{bmatrix} \frac{30}{120} & \frac{40}{60} \\ \frac{20}{120} & \frac{10}{60} \end{bmatrix} = \begin{bmatrix} \frac{1}{4} & \frac{2}{3} \\ \frac{1}{6} & \frac{1}{6} \end{bmatrix}$$

In order to test Hawkins-Simon conditions, we calculate

$$I - A = \begin{bmatrix} 1 & 0 \\ 0 & 1 \end{bmatrix} - \begin{bmatrix} 1/4 & 2/3 \\ 1/6 & 1/6 \end{bmatrix} = \begin{bmatrix} 3/4 & -2/3 \\ -1/6 & 5/6 \end{bmatrix}$$

$$|I - A| = \frac{15}{24} - \frac{2}{18} = \frac{37}{72} > 0$$

Further the diagonal elements, $\frac{1}{4}$ and $\frac{1}{6}$, of the technology matrix are both less than 1. **Hence Hawkins-Simon conditions are satisfied and the system is viable.**

Let $X = \begin{bmatrix} x \\ y \end{bmatrix}$ denote the total output and $D = \begin{bmatrix} 80 \\ 40 \end{bmatrix}$ denote the demand vector. Then

$$AX + D = X$$

$$(I - A)\, X = D$$

$$X = (I - A)^{-1}\, D$$

We have $$(I - A)^{-1} = \frac{1}{|I \quad A|} \operatorname{adj}(I - A) = \frac{72}{37} \begin{bmatrix} \frac{5}{6} & \frac{2}{3} \\ \frac{1}{6} & \frac{3}{4} \end{bmatrix}$$

$$\therefore \qquad X = \frac{72}{37} \begin{bmatrix} \frac{5}{6} & \frac{2}{3} \\ \frac{1}{6} & \frac{3}{4} \end{bmatrix} \begin{bmatrix} 80 \\ 40 \end{bmatrix} = \frac{72}{37} \begin{bmatrix} \frac{280}{3} \\ \frac{130}{3} \end{bmatrix} = \begin{bmatrix} \frac{6720}{37} \\ \frac{3120}{37} \end{bmatrix}$$

Thus the equilibrium level of output of the product is $\frac{6720}{37}$ and $\frac{3120}{37}$ units respectively.

Determination of Equilibrium Prices

In order to find out equilibrium prices, the input-output coefficients matrix which is in quantity terms needs to be converted into value terms. Let the prices of commodities 1 and 2 be p_1 and p_2 respectively and the labour days required per unit of output of the two sectors be l_1 and l_2 . Let the price of the primary input be w, then the technology matrix, in value terms, would be given as under

Sector	*1*	*2*	*Final Demand*
1	$a_{11}x_1p_1$	$a_{12}x_2p_1$	d_1p_1
2	$a_{21}x_1p_2$	$a_{22}x_2p_2$	d_2p_2
Primary Input	l_1x_1w	l_2x_2w	
Total Cost	$a_{11}x_1p_1+a_{21}x_1p_2+l_1x_1w$	$a_{12}x_2p_1+a_{22}x_2p_2+l_2x_2w$	

Under pure competition, revenue equals cost. Therefore, for equilibrium.

$$p_1\, x_1 = a_{11}x_1p_1+a_{21}x_1p_2+l_1x_1w$$

$$p_2\, x_2 = a_{12}x_2p_1+a_{22}x_2p_2+l_2x_2w$$

The above equations can be written as

$$(1-a_{11})\, p_1 - a_{21}\, p_2 = l_1\, w$$

$$a_{12}\, p_1 + (1-a_{22})\, p_2 = l_2\, w$$

This can be put in matrix form as :

$$\begin{bmatrix} 1-a_{11} & -a_{21} \\ -a_{12} & 1-a_{22} \end{bmatrix}\begin{bmatrix} p_1 \\ p_2 \end{bmatrix} = \begin{bmatrix} l_1w \\ l_2w \end{bmatrix}$$

$$\therefore \qquad (I-A)'\, P = \begin{bmatrix} l_1w \\ l_1w \end{bmatrix}$$

$$\therefore \qquad P = \left[(I-A)'\right]^{-1}\begin{bmatrix} l_1w \\ l_2w \end{bmatrix}$$

***Example 24*. For a two sector economy, the input-output coefficient matrix is**

$$A = \begin{vmatrix} \mathbf{0.5} & \mathbf{0.3} \\ \mathbf{0.2} & \mathbf{0.4} \end{vmatrix}$$

If the final demands of the two sectors are 10 and 30, find the gross output

Land and labour are used as two primary inputs. Their coefficients for the two sectors are given as

Labour	**0.4**	**0.3**
Land	**0.5**	**0.4**

If the wage rate and rent are Rs. 40 and Rs. 100 respectively find the equilibrium prices for the two sectors.

Solution. Let $X = \begin{bmatrix} x_1 \\ x_2 \end{bmatrix}$ be the gross output

Given $\qquad A = \begin{bmatrix} 0.5 & 0.3 \\ 0.2 & 0.4 \end{bmatrix} D = \begin{bmatrix} 10 \\ 30 \end{bmatrix}$

$$\therefore \quad |I-A| = \begin{bmatrix} 1-0.5 & -0.3 \\ -0.2 & 1-0.4 \end{bmatrix} = \begin{bmatrix} 0.5 & -0.3 \\ -0.2 & 0.6 \end{bmatrix}$$

$$= (0.5 \times 0.6) - (-0.3 \times -0.2)$$

$$\therefore \quad |I-A| = 0.3 - 0.06 = 0.24$$

$$(I-A)^C = \begin{vmatrix} 0.6 & 0.2 \\ 0.3 & 0.5 \end{vmatrix}$$

$$\therefore \quad \text{adj } (I-A) = \begin{vmatrix} 0.6 & 0.3 \\ 0.2 & 0.5 \end{vmatrix}$$

$$\therefore \quad (I-A)^{-1} = \frac{1}{0.24}\begin{vmatrix} 0.6 & 0.3 \\ 0.2 & 0.5 \end{vmatrix}$$

$$X = \frac{1}{0.24}\begin{vmatrix} 0.6 & 0.3 \\ 0.2 & 0.5 \end{vmatrix}\begin{vmatrix} 10 \\ 30 \end{vmatrix}$$

$$= \frac{1}{0.24}\begin{vmatrix} 6 & + & 9 \\ 2 & + & 15 \end{vmatrix} = \frac{1}{25}\begin{vmatrix} 15 \\ 17 \end{vmatrix} = \begin{vmatrix} 62.5 \\ 70.83 \end{vmatrix}$$

$\therefore$ Gross output of two sectors are

$$X_1 = 62.5 \; X_2 = 70.83$$

Cost of primary inputs for each unit of two sectors is

$$[40 \quad 100]\begin{bmatrix} 0.4 & 0.3 \\ 0.5 & 0.4 \end{bmatrix} = \begin{bmatrix} 16 & + & 50 \\ 12 & + & 40 \end{bmatrix} = \begin{bmatrix} 66 \\ 52 \end{bmatrix}$$

If p_1 and p_2 are the equilibrium prices for sectors I and II respectively, then we have

$$\begin{vmatrix} p_1 \\ p_2 \end{vmatrix} = \left[(I-A)^{-1}\right]' \begin{bmatrix} 66 \\ 52 \end{bmatrix}$$

$$= \frac{1}{0.24}\begin{bmatrix} 0.6 & 0.2 \\ 0.3 & 0.5 \end{bmatrix}\begin{bmatrix} 66 \\ 52 \end{bmatrix}$$

$$= \frac{1}{0.24}\begin{bmatrix} 39.6 & + & 10.4 \\ 19,8 & + & 26 \end{bmatrix} = \frac{1}{0.24}\begin{bmatrix} 50 \\ 45.8 \end{bmatrix}$$

$$\begin{bmatrix} p_1 \\ p_2 \end{bmatrix} = \begin{bmatrix} 208.33 \\ 190.83 \end{bmatrix}$$

$\therefore$ Equilibrium prices are p_1 = Rs. 208.33 and p_2 = 190.83

Example 25. **A hypothetical economy produces only two commodities. *X* and *Y*. The two commodities serve as intermediate inputs in each other's production. To produce a unit of *X*, 0.6 unit of *X* and 0.1 unit of *Y* are needed. Similarly, to produce a unit of *Y*, 0.7 unit of *X* and 0.4 unit of *Y* are needed, Two and five labour-days are required to produce a unit of *X* and a unit of *Y* respectively. The wage rate is Rs. 70 per man-day. The economy needs 100 units of *X* and 50 units of *Y* for final consumption. Your are required to :**

(i) Examine the viability of input-output system using Hawkins-Simon conditions;

(ii) Calculate the gross output of each of the two commodities in tones;

(iii) Determine the equilibrium prices;

(iv) Find the total value added.

Solution. Let A denote technology coefficient matrix. X the gross output matrix, F the final demand vector and V the value added coefficient matrix, as defined below :

$$A = \begin{matrix} & X & Y \\ X & 0.6 & 0.7 \\ Y & 0.1 & 0.4 \end{matrix}, \quad X = \begin{bmatrix} x_1 \\ x_2 \end{bmatrix}, \quad F = \begin{bmatrix} 100 \\ 50 \end{bmatrix}, \quad P = \begin{bmatrix} P_1 \\ P_2 \end{bmatrix}, \text{ and } \quad V = \begin{bmatrix} 2 \times 70 \\ 5 \times 70 \end{bmatrix} = \begin{bmatrix} 140 \\ 350 \end{bmatrix}$$

(i) The system is viable because $|I - A| > 0$ and all elements on the prime diagonal of $[I - A]$ are positive as shown below :

$$I - A = \begin{bmatrix} 1 & 0 \\ 0 & 1 \end{bmatrix} - \begin{bmatrix} 0.6 & 0.7 \\ 0.1 & 0.4 \end{bmatrix} = \begin{bmatrix} 0.4 & -0.7 \\ -0.1 & 0.6 \end{bmatrix} \text{ and } |I - A| = \begin{vmatrix} 0.4 & -0.7 \\ -0.1 & 0.6 \end{vmatrix} = 0.17 > 0$$

(ii) Gross output would be given by : $[I - A]\ X = F$

$$\Rightarrow \begin{bmatrix} 0.4 & -0.7 \\ -0.1 & 0.6 \end{bmatrix} \begin{bmatrix} x_1 \\ x_2 \end{bmatrix} = \begin{bmatrix} 100 \\ 50 \end{bmatrix}$$

We have

$$\begin{vmatrix} 0.4 & -0.7 \\ -0.1 & 0.6 \end{vmatrix} = 0.17$$

Now, using cramer's rule

$$x_1 = \frac{1}{0.17} \begin{bmatrix} 100 & -0.7 \\ 60 & 0.6 \end{bmatrix} = 558.62 \text{ and } x_2 = \frac{1}{0.17} \begin{vmatrix} 0.4 & 100 \\ -0.1 & 50 \end{vmatrix} = 176.47$$

(iii) Equilibrium process is given by : $[I - A]'\ P = V$

$$\Rightarrow \begin{bmatrix} 0.4 & -0.1 \\ -0.7 & 0.6 \end{bmatrix} \begin{bmatrix} p_1 \\ p_2 \end{bmatrix} = \begin{bmatrix} 140 \\ 350 \end{bmatrix}, \text{ Using Cramer's Rule,}$$

We have

$$\begin{vmatrix} 0.4 & -0.1 \\ -0.7 & 0.6 \end{vmatrix} = 0.17$$

Now using cramer's rule

$$p_1 = \frac{1}{0.17} \begin{bmatrix} 140 & -0.10 \\ 350 & 0.6 \end{bmatrix} = 700, \quad p_2 = \frac{1}{0.17} \begin{bmatrix} 0.4 & 140 \\ -0.7 & 350 \end{bmatrix} = 1400$$

(*v*) Total value added = [Given output] [Primary Input]

$$=\begin{bmatrix}100 & 50\end{bmatrix}\begin{bmatrix}700\\1400\end{bmatrix}=1,40,000$$

Example 26. **A three sector economy has the following input-output coefficient matrix (in quantity):**

$$A=\begin{bmatrix}0 & 0.5 & 0\\0.2 & 0 & 0.5\\0.4 & 0 & 0\end{bmatrix}$$

The labour days required per unit of output of the three sectors are 0.4, 0.7 and 1.2 respectively and their consumer output targets are 1000, 5000 and 4000 units respectively. The wage rate is Rs. 10 per labour day. By using matrix algebra, you are required to find.

(*i*) The gross output of each sector

(*ii*) Total labour days required

(*iii*) Equilibrium prices and

(*iv*) Total value added.

Solution.

(*i*) Given technology matrix

$$A=\begin{bmatrix}0 & 0.5 & 0\\0.2 & 0 & 0.5\\0.4 & 0 & 0\end{bmatrix}$$

and final demand matrix $D=\begin{vmatrix}1000\\5000\\4000\end{vmatrix}$

Let the gross output vector be $X=\begin{vmatrix}x_1\\x_2\\x_3\end{vmatrix}$

$$\begin{bmatrix}0 & 0.5 & 0\\0.2 & 0 & 0.5\\0.4 & 0 & 0\end{bmatrix}\begin{bmatrix}x_1\\x_2\\x_3\end{bmatrix}+\begin{bmatrix}1000\\5000\\4000\end{bmatrix}=\begin{bmatrix}x_1\\x_2\\x_3\end{bmatrix}$$

$\therefore \quad AX + D = X$

$\therefore \quad X = (I - A)^{-1} D$

$$\therefore \quad I-A=\begin{vmatrix}1 & 0 & 0\\0 & 1 & 0\\0 & 0 & 1\end{vmatrix}-\begin{vmatrix}0 & 0.5 & 0\\0.2 & 0 & 0.5\\0.4 & 0 & 0\end{vmatrix}=\begin{vmatrix}1 & -0.5 & 0\\-0.2 & 1 & -0.5\\-0.4 & 0 & 1\end{vmatrix}$$

$$|I - A| = 0.8$$

Since $|I - A| \neq 0, (I - A)^{-1}$ exists

$$[I - A]^{-1} = \frac{1}{0.8}\begin{bmatrix} 1 & 0.5 & 0.25 \\ 0.4 & 1 & 0.5 \\ 0.4 & 0.2 & 0.9 \end{bmatrix}$$

$$\therefore \qquad X = \frac{1}{0.8}\begin{vmatrix} 1 & 0.5 & 0.25 \\ 0.4 & 1 & 0.5 \\ 0.4 & 0.2 & 0.9 \end{vmatrix}\begin{vmatrix} 1000 \\ 5000 \\ 4000 \end{vmatrix}$$

$$X = \begin{vmatrix} 5625 \\ 9250 \\ 6250 \end{vmatrix}$$

$\therefore X_1 = 5625, X_2 = 9250$ and $X_3 = 6250$

(*ii*) Total labour days required

$$= \begin{bmatrix} 0.4 & 0.7 & 1.2 \end{bmatrix}\begin{bmatrix} 5625 \\ 9250 \\ 6250 \end{bmatrix}$$

$$= [2250 + 6475 + 7500]$$

$$= 16225$$

(*iii*) Equilibrium prices when the wage rate is Rs. 10 per labour day are given by

$$\begin{bmatrix} p_1 \\ o_2 \\ p_3 \end{bmatrix} = \left((I - A)^{-1}\right)' \begin{bmatrix} l_1 w \\ l_2 w \\ l_3 w \end{bmatrix}$$

$$= \frac{1}{0.8}\begin{bmatrix} 1 & 0.4 & 0.4 \\ 0.5 & 1 & 0.2 \\ 0.25 & 0.5 & 0.9 \end{bmatrix}\begin{bmatrix} 4 \\ 7 \\ 12 \end{bmatrix}$$

$$= \frac{1}{0.8}\begin{bmatrix} 1 & 0.4 & 0.4 \\ 0.5 & 1 & 0.2 \\ 0.25 & 0.5 & 0.9 \end{bmatrix}\begin{bmatrix} 4 \\ 7 \\ 12 \end{bmatrix} = \frac{1}{0.8}\begin{bmatrix} 11.6 \\ 11.4 \\ 15.3 \end{bmatrix} = \begin{bmatrix} 14.5 \\ 14.25 \\ 19.12 \end{bmatrix}$$

Thus, the equilibrium prices are Rs. 14.5, Rs. 14.25 and Rs. 19.12 respectively.

(*iv*) Total value added or cost of primary input

$$= 16225 \times 10 = 162250$$

Example 27. **Given below is technology matrix for a two sector economy.**

	Sector A	*Sector B*
Sector A	**0.4**	**0.2**
Sector B	**0.5**	**0.4**
Labour	**0.4**	**0.6**

Find the gross output of each sector to meet the final demand of 20 and 25 for sector *A* and *B* respectively. Also find the total labour requirement. If the total labour available is 85 units, Is the solution feasible.

Solution. Given technology matrix of the two sector

$$A=\begin{vmatrix}0.4 & 0.2\\0.5 & 0.4\end{vmatrix} \text{ and demand } D=\begin{vmatrix}20\\25\end{vmatrix}$$

Let $D=\begin{vmatrix}20\\25\end{vmatrix}$ *be the gross output vector.*

∴ We have $AX + D = X$

$(I - A)\, X = D$

$$I-A=\begin{vmatrix}1 & 0\\0 & 1\end{vmatrix}-\begin{vmatrix}0.4 & 0.2\\0.5 & 0.4\end{vmatrix}=\begin{vmatrix}0.6 & -0.2\\-0.5 & 0.6\end{vmatrix}$$

$$|I-A|=(0.06\times 0.6)-(-0.2\times -0.5)=0.36-0.10$$

$$= 0.26$$

$$\text{Cofactor matrix of } (I-A)=\begin{vmatrix}0.6 & 0.5\\+0.2 & 0.6\end{vmatrix}$$

$$adj\ (I-A)=\begin{vmatrix}0.6 & 0.2\\0.5 & 0.6\end{vmatrix}$$

$$\therefore \quad (I-A)^{-1}=\frac{1}{0.26}\begin{vmatrix}0.6 & 0.2\\0.5 & 0.6\end{vmatrix}$$

$$\therefore \quad X=\frac{1}{0.26}\begin{vmatrix}0.6 & 0.2\\0.5 & 0.6\end{vmatrix}\begin{vmatrix}20\\25\end{vmatrix}$$

$$=\frac{1}{0.26}\begin{vmatrix}12+5\\10+15\end{vmatrix}=\frac{1}{0.26}\begin{bmatrix}17\\25\end{bmatrix}$$

$$X=\begin{vmatrix}65.38\\96.15\end{vmatrix}$$

After having assessed the gross output required to meet the final demand, total labour requirement can be calculated, as under :

$$[0.4 \quad 0.6]\begin{vmatrix}65.38\\96.15\end{vmatrix} = [0.4 \times 65.38 + 0.6 \times 96.15]$$

$$= [26.152 + 57.69] = [83.84]$$

Since the total labour required is less than total labour available, the system is feasible.

Closed Input-Output Model

In case of this system, any production made by given set of industries in consumed among themselves. Thus, there is no part of gross output which is consumed by external users. Therefore, if 'X' is gross output matrix and 'A' is input output coefficient matrix, we have

$$X = AX$$

or $$[I - A]\ X = 0$$

This can be understood from the following examples.

Example 28. **The Input-output matrix of a closed model with three industries is given below:**

$$\begin{array}{cc} & \begin{array}{ccc}\textbf{I} & \textbf{II} & \textbf{III}\end{array} \\ A = \begin{array}{r} I \\ II \\ III \end{array} & \begin{bmatrix} \mathbf{0.3} & \mathbf{0.2} & \mathbf{0.4} \\ \mathbf{0.4} & \mathbf{0.6} & \mathbf{0.5} \\ \mathbf{0.3} & \mathbf{0.2} & \mathbf{0.1} \end{bmatrix} \end{array}$$

Find the equilibrium level of outputs of the first sectors if the output of the third sector is given to be 120 lakhs.

Solution. For the closed model, we have

$$[I - A]\ X = 0$$

Let x_1, x_2 and x_3 be gross output of Industry I, II and III respectively.

$$\begin{bmatrix} 0.7 & -0.2 & -0.4 \\ -0.4 & 0.4 & -0.5 \\ -0.3 & -0.2 & 0.9 \end{bmatrix}\begin{bmatrix} x_1 \\ x_2 \\ x_3 \end{bmatrix} = 0$$

$$0.7x_1 - 0.2x_2 - 0.4x_3 = 0$$

$$-0.4x_1 - 0.4x_2 - 0.5x_3 = 0$$

$$-0.3x_1 - 0.2x_2 - 0.9x_3 = 0$$

Substituting $x_3 = 120$ in the above equations, we have :

$$0.7x_1 - 0.2x_2 = 48$$
$$-0.4x_1 + 0.4x_2 = 60$$
$$-0.3x_1 - 0.2x_2 = 108$$

Using first two equations, we have

$$\begin{bmatrix} 0.7 & -0.2 \\ -0.4 & +0.4 \end{bmatrix}\begin{bmatrix} x_1 \\ x_2 \end{bmatrix} = \begin{bmatrix} 48 \\ 60 \end{bmatrix}$$

$$AX = B$$

$$A = \begin{bmatrix} 0.7 & -0.2 \\ -0.4 & 0.4 \end{bmatrix}$$

$$|A| = 0.28 - 0.08 = 0.20$$

$$A^C = \begin{bmatrix} -0.4 & +0.4 \\ +0.2 & -0.7 \end{bmatrix}$$

$$\therefore \quad \text{Adj } A = \begin{bmatrix} -0.4 & 0.2 \\ 0.4 & -0.7 \end{bmatrix}$$

$$A^{-1} = \frac{1}{0.20}\begin{bmatrix} -0.4 & 0.2 \\ 0.4 & -0.7 \end{bmatrix} = \begin{bmatrix} -2 & 1 \\ 2 & -3.5 \end{bmatrix}$$

$$\begin{bmatrix} x_1 \\ x_2 \end{bmatrix} = \begin{bmatrix} -2 & 1 \\ 2 & -3.5 \end{bmatrix}\begin{bmatrix} 48 \\ 60 \end{bmatrix}$$

$$\Rightarrow \quad \begin{bmatrix} -96 & +60 \\ 96 & +210 \end{bmatrix} = \begin{bmatrix} 156 \\ 306 \end{bmatrix}$$

$\therefore$ Gross output of Industry I and II shall be 156 and 306 respectively.

Measurement of Change in Gross Output when there is change in demand

According to Leontief Input/Output Model, the gross output is related to demand through the following equation :

$$X - [I - A]^{-1} D$$

If X_1 and X_2 represent old and new gross output and D_1 and D_2 are corresponding demands, we have

$$X_1 = [I - A]^{-1} D_1$$

and $$X_2 = [I - A]^{-1} D_2$$

Then, change in gross output *i.e.*, $(X_2 - X_1)$ will be

$$\therefore \quad \Delta X = [I - A]^{-1} [\Delta D]$$

Example 29. **For a two sector economy, the input-out coefficient matrix is given below :**

$$A = \begin{bmatrix} 0.6 & 0.3 \\ 0.4 & 0.5 \end{bmatrix}$$

The final demand or external demand of goods I increase by 10 units and goods II by 4 units, find the change in output of two sectors.

Solution. We have

$$\Delta X = [I - A]^{1} \Delta D$$

$$[I-A]=\begin{bmatrix} 0.4 & -0.3 \\ -0.4 & 0.5 \end{bmatrix}$$

$$\therefore \quad |I-A| = 0.20 - 0.12 = 0.08$$

$$[I-A]=\begin{bmatrix} 0.5 & +0.4 \\ +0.3 & 0.4 \end{bmatrix}$$

$$Adj[I-A]=\begin{bmatrix} 0.5 & 0.3 \\ 0.4 & 0.4 \end{bmatrix}$$

$$[I-A]^{1} = \frac{1}{0.08}\begin{bmatrix} 0.5 & 0.3 \\ 0.4 & 0.4 \end{bmatrix}$$

$$\Delta X = \frac{1}{0.08}\begin{bmatrix} 0.5 & 0.3 \\ 0.4 & 0.4 \end{bmatrix}\begin{bmatrix} 10 \\ 4 \end{bmatrix}$$

$$= \frac{1}{0.08}\begin{bmatrix} 3.8 \\ 2.4 \end{bmatrix} = \begin{bmatrix} 47.5 \\ 30 \end{bmatrix}$$

***Example 30.* In a two sector economy, the input-output coefficient matrix is given as under:**

$$A=\begin{bmatrix} \mathbf{0.4} & \mathbf{0.4} \\ \mathbf{0.6} & \mathbf{0.2} \end{bmatrix}$$

The final demand of goods *I* increases by 20 units and that of goods II decreases by 6 units. Find the change in the output of the two sectors. If the labour coefficients for the two sectors are $|0.4 \quad 0.3|$, find the change in labour requirement.

Solution. We have

$$\Delta X = [I - A]^{1} AD$$

$$\therefore \quad [I-A]=\begin{bmatrix} 0.6 & -0.4 \\ -0.6 & 0.8 \end{bmatrix}$$

$$= 0.48 - 0.24 = 0.24$$

$$[I-A]=\begin{bmatrix} 0.8 & +0.6 \\ +0.4 & 0.6 \end{bmatrix}$$

$$\text{Adj } [I-A]=\begin{bmatrix} 0.8 & 0.4 \\ 0.6 & 0.6 \end{bmatrix}$$

$$[I-A]^{-1} = \frac{1}{0.24}\begin{bmatrix} 0.8 & 0.4 \\ 0.6 & 0.6 \end{bmatrix}$$

$$\therefore \quad \Delta X = \frac{1}{0.24}\begin{bmatrix} 0.8 & 0.4 \\ 0.6 & 0.6 \end{bmatrix}\begin{bmatrix} 20 \\ -6 \end{bmatrix} = \frac{1}{0.24}\begin{bmatrix} 13.6 \\ 8.4 \end{bmatrix} = \begin{bmatrix} 56.66 \\ 35 \end{bmatrix}$$

$$= [141.65 + 116.66] = [1258.31]$$

Example 31. **For a there sector economy, the input-output coefficient matrix**

$$A = \begin{bmatrix} 0.2 & 0.3 & 0.2 \\ 0.4 & 0.1 & 0.2 \\ 0.1 & 0.3 & 0.2 \end{bmatrix}$$

The final demand of the there sectors are 20, 10 and 5 respectively. Land and Labour are used as two primary inputs. Their Coefficient for the there sectors are given as under :

$$\begin{matrix} \textit{land} \\ \textit{labour} \end{matrix}\begin{bmatrix} 0.2 & 0.5 & 0.3 \\ 0.3 & 0.3 & 0.4 \end{bmatrix}$$

If the rent and wage rate are Rs. 10 and Rs. 50 respectively, find the following:

(*i*) **Gross output for the three sectors**

(*ii*) **Number of labours required.**

(*iii*) **Equilibrium prices for the three sector.**

(*iv*) **Total value added.**

Solution. Let X_1, X_2, X_3 represent gross output of the three Sectors

$$\begin{bmatrix} X_1 \\ X_2 \\ X_3 \end{bmatrix} = [I - A]^{-1}\begin{bmatrix} 20 \\ 10 \\ 5 \end{bmatrix}$$

$$[I - A] = \begin{bmatrix} 0.8 & -0.3 & -0.2 \\ -0.4 & 0.9 & -0.2 \\ -0.1 & -0.3 & 0.8 \end{bmatrix}$$

$$\therefore \quad |I - A| = 0.384$$

$$[I - A]^{-1} = \frac{1}{0.384}\begin{bmatrix} 0.66 & 0.30 & 0.24 \\ 0.34 & 0.62 & 0.24 \\ 0.21 & 0.27 & 0.60 \end{bmatrix}$$

$$X = \frac{1}{0.384}\begin{bmatrix} 0.66 & 0.30 & 0.24 \\ 0.34 & 0.62 & 0.24 \\ 0.21 & 0.27 & 0.60 \end{bmatrix}\begin{bmatrix} 20 \\ 10 \\ 5 \end{bmatrix}$$

$$= \frac{1}{0.384}\begin{bmatrix} 17.4 \\ 14.2 \\ 9.9 \end{bmatrix}$$

$\therefore$ Gross outputs are 45.31, 36.97 and 25.18 respectively.

$$[45.31 \quad 36.97 \quad 25.78]\begin{bmatrix} 0.3 \\ 0.3 \\ 0.4 \end{bmatrix} = [34.99]$$

$\therefore$ approximately 35 labours are required.

(*iii*) To determine equilibrium prices, we need the matrix $\begin{bmatrix} l_1 w \\ l_2 w \\ l_3 w \end{bmatrix}$

$$\begin{bmatrix} l_1 w \\ l_2 w \\ l_3 w \end{bmatrix} = [10 \quad 50] \begin{bmatrix} 0.2 & 0.5 & 0.3 \\ 0.3 & 0.3 & 0.4 \end{bmatrix} = [17 \quad 20 \quad 23]$$

$$\therefore \quad \begin{bmatrix} l_1 w \\ l_2 w \\ l_3 w \end{bmatrix} = \begin{bmatrix} 17 \\ 20 \\ 23 \end{bmatrix}$$

$$\therefore \quad P = \begin{bmatrix} p_1 \\ p_2 \\ p_3 \end{bmatrix} = \left([I - A]^{-1}\right)^{1} \begin{bmatrix} l_1 w \\ l_2 w \\ l_2 w \end{bmatrix}$$

$$= \frac{1}{0.384} \begin{bmatrix} 0.66 & 0.34 & 0.21 \\ 0.30 & 0.62 & 0.27 \\ 0.24 & 0.24 & 0.60 \end{bmatrix} \begin{bmatrix} 17 \\ 20 \\ 23 \end{bmatrix}$$

$$= \frac{1}{0.384} \begin{bmatrix} 22.85 \\ 23.71 \\ 22.68 \end{bmatrix} = \begin{bmatrix} 59.50 \\ 61.74 \\ 59.06 \end{bmatrix}$$

(*iv*) Total value added

= [Gross output] [Cost of Primary input]

$$= [45.31 \quad 36.97 \quad 25.78] \begin{bmatrix} 17 \\ 20 \\ 23 \end{bmatrix} = [2102.61]$$

Example 32. **An economy produces two commodities, Say X and Y, for which the input coefficient matrix is**

$$\begin{bmatrix} \mathbf{0.3} & \mathbf{0.5} \\ \mathbf{0.4} & \mathbf{0.2} \end{bmatrix}$$

The primary input coefficient for the two industries 0.2 and 0.4. The final demands for X and Y are 200 and 150 respectively. The cost of input is Rs. 60 respectively. Find

(*i*) Gross output of each commodity

(*ii*) Equilibrium prices

(*iii*) Value added in each sector

Solution. (*i*) Given Input-Output Coefficient matrix

$$A = \begin{bmatrix} 0.3 & 0.5 \\ 0.4 & 0.2 \end{bmatrix}$$

$$[I - A] = \begin{bmatrix} 0.7 & -0.5 \\ -0.4 & 0.8 \end{bmatrix}$$

$$|I - A| = 0.36$$

$$[I - A]^{-1} = \frac{1}{0.36}\begin{bmatrix} 0.8 & 0.5 \\ 0.4 & 0.7 \end{bmatrix}$$

$\therefore$ Gross output $X = [I - A]^{-1}\ [D]$

$$= \frac{1}{0.36}\begin{bmatrix} 0.8 & 0.5 \\ 0.4 & 0.7 \end{bmatrix}\begin{bmatrix} 200 \\ 150 \end{bmatrix} = \begin{bmatrix} 625.78 \\ 513.89 \end{bmatrix}$$

(*ii*)
$$P = \begin{bmatrix} p_1 \\ p_2 \end{bmatrix} = \left([I - A]^{-1}\right)' \begin{bmatrix} l_1 w \\ l_2 w \end{bmatrix}$$

$\begin{bmatrix} l_1 w \\ l_2 w \end{bmatrix}$ is 2×1 matrix

We have

Coefficient matrix $= [0.2 \quad 0.4]_{1\times 2}$

Rate matrix $= [60]_{1\times 1}$

$$[l_1 w \quad l_1 w]_{2\times 1}$$

$$\therefore \quad = [60][0.2 \quad 0.4]$$

$$= [12 \quad 24]$$

$$\therefore \quad \begin{bmatrix} l_1 w \\ l_2 w \end{bmatrix} = \begin{bmatrix} 12 \\ 24 \end{bmatrix}$$

$$\therefore \quad \begin{bmatrix} p_1 \\ p_2 \end{bmatrix} = \frac{1}{0.36}\begin{bmatrix} 0.8 & 0.4 \\ 0.5 & 0.7 \end{bmatrix}\begin{bmatrix} 12 \\ 24 \end{bmatrix}$$

$$= \frac{1}{0.36}\begin{bmatrix} 9.6 + 9.6 \\ 6 + 16.8 \end{bmatrix}$$

$$= \frac{1}{0.36}\begin{bmatrix} 19.2 \\ 22.8 \end{bmatrix} = \begin{bmatrix} 53.33 \\ 63.33 \end{bmatrix}$$

(*iii*) Value added is $X = 652.78X600.2 = 7833.6$

$Y = 513.89X60X0.4 = 12333.36$

Example 33. **Based on the past marketing trends and his own experience, marketing expert suggested to the concerned company the segments of market for their product as follows : The first segment consisted of lower income class, the second segment that of middle income and the third segment that of high income. The data based on the income of the customers was readily available. During a particular month in a particular area, the agent reported that for the three products of the company the following were the sales. There were 200 customers who bought all the three products, 240 customers bought only products I and II, 60 customers only products II and III and 80 customers only products I and II. There were 120 persons who bought only product I; 220 persons only product II and 80 persons only II regardless of the market segmentation groups. Based on the market segmentation analysis, for product I, the percentage for the income groups are given as (40%, 20% and 40%), for product II (30%, 20% and 50%) for product III (10%, 50% and 40%). Using matrix method, find out the number of persons in the lower income, middle income and higher income class in the region referred.**

Solution.

Let Number of persons purchasing product I = 200 + 240 + 80 + 120 = 640

Number of persons purchasing product II = 200 + 60 + 80 + 220 = 560

Number of persons purchasing product III = 200 + 60 + 240 + 80 = 580

and x, y, z denote the number of persons in the lower income groups, middle income group and higher income group, respectively.

On the basis of above information, we have

$$\frac{40}{100}x + \frac{20}{100}y + \frac{40}{100}z = 640 \qquad 4x + 2y + 4z = 6400$$

$$\frac{30}{100}x + \frac{20}{100}y + \frac{50}{100}z = 560 \quad \Leftrightarrow \quad 3x + 2y + 5z = 5600$$

$$\frac{10}{100}x + \frac{50}{100}y + \frac{40}{100}z = 580 \qquad x + 5y + 4z = 5800$$

The equations can be written in the matrix form as

$$\underset{A}{\begin{bmatrix} 4 & 3 & 4 \\ 3 & 2 & 5 \\ 1 & 5 & 4 \end{bmatrix}} \underset{X}{\begin{bmatrix} x \\ y \\ z \end{bmatrix}} = \underset{B}{\begin{bmatrix} 6400 \\ 5600 \\ 58000 \end{bmatrix}}$$

Now, we have

$$|A| = 4(8 - 25) - 2(12 - 5) + 4(15 - 2) = 30$$

$$A^{-1} = -\frac{1}{3}\begin{bmatrix} -17 & 12 & 2 \\ -7 & 12 & -8 \\ 13 & 18 & 2 \end{bmatrix}$$

$$\therefore \quad X = A^{-1}B = -\frac{1}{3}\begin{bmatrix} -17 & 12 & 2 \\ -7 & 12 & -8 \\ 13 & 18 & 2 \end{bmatrix}\begin{bmatrix} 6400 \\ 5600 \\ 5800 \end{bmatrix} \begin{bmatrix} 1000 \\ 800 \\ 200 \end{bmatrix}$$

There $x = 1000$, $y = 800$ and $z = 200$

Example 34. **ABC Co. has two service departments S_1 and S_2 and four production departments P_1, P_2, P_3, and P_4. Overhead is allocated to production department for inclusion in the stock valuation. The analysis of benefits received by each department during the last quarter and the direct overhead expenses incurred by each department were :**

Service Deptt	***Percentage to be allocated to Deptts.***						
	S_1	S_2	P_1	P_2	P_3	P_4	
S_1	**0**	**20**	**30**	**25**	**15**	**10**	
S_2	**30**	**0**	**10**	**35**	**30**	**6**	
Direct Overhead Exp.							
(In thousand of Rs.)	**20**	**40**	**25**	**30**	**20**	**1**	**0**

(*i*) Express the total overhead of the service departments in the form of simultaneous equations.

(*ii*) Express these equations in a matrix form and solve for total overhead of service departments using matrix-inverse method.

(*iii*) determine total overhead to be allocated from each S_1 and S_2 to the production departments.
[*Delhi University, B.Com., (Hons.), 2003*]

Solution.

(*i*) Let $\quad x$ = Total overhead expenses of service department S_1

$\quad y$ = Total overhead expenses of service department S_s.

From the given data, we have following equations :

$$\left.\begin{aligned} x &= 20,000 + 0.3y \\ y &= 40,000 + 0.2x \end{aligned}\right\} \Leftrightarrow \left\{\begin{aligned} x - 0.3y &= 20,000 \\ -0.2x + y &= 40,000 \end{aligned}\right.$$

$$\begin{bmatrix} 1 & -0.3 \\ -0.2 & 1 \end{bmatrix}\begin{bmatrix} x \\ y \end{bmatrix} = \begin{bmatrix} 20,000 \\ 40,000 \end{bmatrix}$$

Now $\quad A = 1 - 0.06 = 0.94 \neq 0$

Thus A^{-1} exist and the solution is given by $X = A^{-1}B$.

$$A^{-1} = \frac{1}{0.94}\begin{bmatrix} 1 & 0.3 \\ 0.2 & 1 \end{bmatrix}$$

Q.5. A three sector economy has the following input output coefficient matrix A and final demand vector F :

$$A = \begin{bmatrix} 0.3 & 0.2 & 0.2 \\ 0.2 & 0.1 & 0.5 \\ 0.2 & 0.4 & 0.2 \end{bmatrix}, \ F = \begin{bmatrix} 80 \\ 30 \\ 50 \end{bmatrix}$$

Find the gross output of each sector to meet the final demand.

Q.6. A three sector economy has the following input output coefficient matrix:

$$A = \begin{bmatrix} 0 & 0.5 & 0 \\ 0.2 & 0 & 0.5 \\ 0.4 & 0 & 0 \end{bmatrix}$$

The labour days required per unit of output of the three sectors are 0.4, 0.7 and 1.2 respectively and their consumer output targets are 1000, 5000 and 4000 units respectively. The wage rate is Rs. 10 per labour day. By using matrix algebra, you are required to find :

(*i*) The gross output of each sector.

(*ii*) Total labour days required.

(*iii*) Equilibrium prices, and

(*iv*) Total valued added.

Q.7. The input-out technology matrix for three industries is :

$$\begin{bmatrix} 0.2 & 0.3 & 0.1 \\ 0 & 0.5 & 0.2 \\ 0 & 0 & 0.5 \end{bmatrix}$$

If the final demand for three industries is $\begin{bmatrix} 100 \\ 200 \\ 300 \end{bmatrix}$, find the gross output.

Q.8. Given the technology matrix of a Leontief input-output matrix is

$$A = \begin{bmatrix} 0.4 & 0.1 & 0.2 \\ 0.1 & 0.3 & 0.3 \\ 0.2 & 0.1 & 0.2 \end{bmatrix}$$

and the domestic consumption vector $D = \begin{bmatrix} 10 \\ 20 \\ 10 \end{bmatrix}$

(*i*) Test Simon-Hawkins conditions for the viability of the system.

(*ii*) Write the balancing equation.

(*iii*) Obtain gross output vector X consistent with the given vector D.

Q.9. In a two sector economy, it is known that industry *I* uses 10 paise worth of its own product and 60 paise worth of commodity *II* to produce a rupee worth of commodity *I*. Industry *II* uses 30 paise worth of its own product and 50 paise worth of commodity I in producing a rupee worth of commodity *II*. The final demands are Rs. 1,100 billion worth of commodity *I* and Rs. 2,200 billion worth of commodity *II*.

(*i*) Write down the input-output matrix for the economy.

(*ii*) Find the solution output levels using matrix inversion method.

Q.10. Suppose that the final demand for steel, coal and electricity in an economy consisting only of three sectors are Rs. 10 crores, Rs. 5 crores and Rs. 6 crores, respectively. A rupee worth of steel requires 20 paise, 40 paise and 10 paise worth of steel, coal and electricity respectively as inputs; a rupee worth of coal requires 30 paise, 10 paise and 30 paise worth of steel, coal and electricity respectively as inputs and a rupee worth of electricity requires 20 paise worth each of steel, coal and electricity respectively as inputs. How much of steel, coal and electricity should be produced to satisfy both final and intermediate demands?

Q.11. A country produces only two goods *X* and *Y*. The input-output coefficient matrix is

$$A = \begin{bmatrix} 0.3 & 0.6 \\ 0.5 & 0.0 \end{bmatrix}$$

and the primary input coefficients are (0.2, 0.4). The final demand for *X* is 10 and for *Y* is 5.

(*i*) Write down the open input-output model as a set of simultaneous linear equations.

(*ii*) Determine the output solution by finding the inverse of the relevant matrix.

Q 12. You are given the following transaction matrix for a two sector economy.

	Sector	*Purchases*		*Final Demand*	*Gross output*
		1	2		
Sales	1	4	3	13	20
	2	5	4	3	12
Primary input		11	5		

(*i*) Write the technology matrix.

(*ii*) Rewrite the new transaction matrix when the final demand for the output of sector 1 increases to 22 units.

Q 13. You are given the following technology matrix for a two industry economy :

	Steel	*Coal*
Steel	0.2	0.2
Coal	0.4	0.1

Write down the input-output table for the economy, when the final demand targets are Rs. 100 crore in steel and Rs. 20 core in coal.

Q 14. You are given a three industry economy which produces coal, steel and services of Rail Road transportation. Each of these is measured in rupees. Each of these industries employs the products of the others in its manufacture, in proportions shown in the following table. The last row indicates labour coefficients.

		Users of input		
		Steel	*Coal*	*R.R.*
Producers of input	Steel	.2	.2	.1
	Coal	.4	.1	.3
	RR	.2	.5	.1
	Labour	.2	.2	.5

The final demands for steel, coal and Rail Road transportation are Rs. 100 million. Rs. 20 million and Rs. 40 million respectively.

(*i*) Write down the specific input-output matrix equation for the economy.

(*ii*) Find the output levels of these commodities consistent with the model.

Q 15 For a three-sector economy, the input-output co-efficients, *aij's* are as given below:

$a_{11} = 0.5,\ a_{21} = 0.2,\ a_{31} = 0.1,\ a_{12} = 0.1,\ a_{22} = 0.6,\ a_{32} = 0.2,\ a_{13} = 0.1,\ a_{23} = 0.2\ \&\ a_{33} = 0.6$

(*i*) Using Simon-Hawkins conditions, test whether the system is viable.

(*ii*) Determine the gross output for the three sectors when the final demand values for them are 21,000, 42,000 and 63,000 units respectively.

(*iii*) Determine the new level of output if the final demand increases by 1500, 3000 and 4500 units.

Q.16. Consider an economy consisting of three sectors; agriculture, manufacturers and services. The hypothetical flow of goods and services in physical units is summarized in the following table:

Agriculture	*Manufacturers*	*Services*	*Final Demand*	*Final*
Agriculture	60	180	0	120
Manufacturers	30	60	30	180
Services	0	40	10	100

If the demand changes to [150, 160, 180], what will be the new output? Calculate upto two decimals.

Q.17. A hypothetical economy produces only two commodities, *X* and *Y*. The two commodities serve as intermediate inputs in each other's production. To produce a unit of *X*, 0.6 unit of *X* and 0.1 units of *Y* are needed. Similarly, to produce a unit of *Y*, 0.7 unit of *X* and 0.4 unit of *Y* are needed. Two and five labour-days are required to produce a unit of *X* and a unit of *Y* respectively.

The wage rate is Rs. 70 per man-day. The economy needs 100 units of *X* and 50 units of *Y* for final consumption.

You are required to :

(*i*) Examine the viability of input-output system using Hawkins-Simon conditions;

(*ii*) Calculate the gross output of each of the two commodities in tons;

(*iii*) Determine the equilibrium process; and

(*iv*) Find the total value added.

Q. 18. An economy consists of two sectors- manufacturing and agriculture. To produce one unit of manufacturing output, 0.1 unit of manufacturing goods and 0.01 unit of agriculture goods are required as inputs. One unit of agriculture output requires 40 units of manufacturing goods and nil unit of agricultural goods as inputs. A unit of manufacturing goods requires 4 man-hours of labour and unit of agricultural output requires 100 man-hours of labour. Calculate the total labour requirement if 50 million units of manufacturing goods and 2 million units of agricultural goods need to be produced for final consumption.

Supposing the wage rate is Rs. 10 per man-hour, calculate the equilibrium prices of manufacturing goods and agricultural output.

Q. 19. Suppose there are two sector *A, B* and the final demand *F.* The input-output table is given as follows :

Sectors	*A*	*B*	*Final Demand*	*Final*
A	15	20	45	80
B	5	20	15	40
Primary Input	30	25	5	90

What will be the level of output it the final demand becomes 65 for *A* and 25 for *B*. What will happen it the final demand is (*i*) doubled, (*ii*) halved?

Q.20. In an economy there are two industries *A* and *B* and the following table gives the supply and demand position of these in million rupees :

	Users			
	A	*B*	*Final Demand*	*Total Output*
Producer A	15	10	10	35
Producer B	20	30	15	65

Determine the total output if the final demand changes to 12 for A and 18 for B.

Q.21. Let $A=\begin{bmatrix}1/8 & 1/3 & 1/4\\ 1/2 & 1/6 & 1/4\\ 1/4 & 1/6 & 1/4\end{bmatrix}$ and the final demand vector be $\begin{bmatrix}10\\ 28\\ 14\end{bmatrix}$, Find the total output of the three sectors. What will be the total outputs if the final demand for sector 1 has increased by 1?

ANSWERS

1. Agriculture = 2,000, Industry = 4,000
2. A = 220, B = 640
3. P: 417.391, Q: 455.652, R: 417.391
4. 21,000, 42,000 42,000
5. 241.54, 201.54, 230.38
6. (*i*) 5,625, 9,250, 6,250; (*ii*) 16,625; (*iii*) 14.5, 14.125, 19.125; (*iv*) 1,62,250

$$\therefore \quad X = A^{-1}B = \frac{1}{0.94}\begin{bmatrix} 1 & 0.3 \\ 0.2 & 1 \end{bmatrix}\begin{bmatrix} 20,000 \\ 40,000 \end{bmatrix} = \frac{1}{0.94}\begin{bmatrix} 32,000 \\ 44,000 \end{bmatrix} = \begin{bmatrix} 34,043 \\ 46,809 \end{bmatrix}$$

x = Rs. 34,43 and y = 46,809

Total overhead expenses of S_1 allocated to production departments

$$= 34,043[0.3 \quad 0.25 \quad 0.15 \quad 0.10] = [10,213 \quad 8,511 \quad 5,106 \quad 3,404]$$

Total overhead expenses of S_2 allocated to production departments

$$= 46,809[0.10 \quad 0.5 \quad 0.20 \quad 0.05] = [4,681 \quad 16,383 \quad 9,362 \quad 2,304]$$

***Example 35.* Two companies *A* and *B* are holding shares in each other. *A* is holding 20% shares of *B* and *B* is holding 10% shares of *A*. If the separately earned profits of the two companies are Rs. 98,000 and Rs. 49,000 respectively. find total profit of each company using matrix notations. Also show that the total of the profits allocated to outside shareholders is equal to the total of separately earned profits.** *[Delhi University, B.Com. (Hons.) 2004]*

Solution.

Let x and y be total profit of the companies. A and B respectively. From the given data, we obtain the following equations:

$$x = 98,000 + 0.20y \quad \Rightarrow \quad x - 0.20y = 98,000 \quad ...(1)$$

$$y = 49,000 + 0.10y \quad \Rightarrow \quad -0.10x + y = 49,000 \quad ...(2)$$

In matrix form, we have

$$\begin{bmatrix} 1 & -0.20 \\ -0.10 & 1 \end{bmatrix}\begin{bmatrix} x \\ y \end{bmatrix} = \begin{bmatrix} 98,000 \\ 49,000 \end{bmatrix}$$

Since $\quad |A| = \begin{vmatrix} 1 & -0.20 \\ -0.10 & 1 \end{vmatrix} = 0.98 \neq 0, A^{-1}\text{exists}:$

$$A^{-1} = \frac{1}{|A|}\text{adj } A = \frac{1}{0.98}\begin{bmatrix} 1 & -0.20 \\ -0.10 & 1 \end{bmatrix}$$

There $\quad X = A^{-1}\,B \text{ or } \begin{bmatrix} x \\ y \end{bmatrix} = \begin{bmatrix} 1 & -0.20 \\ -0.10 & 1 \end{bmatrix}\begin{bmatrix} 98,000 \\ 49,000 \end{bmatrix} = \begin{bmatrix} 1,10,000 \\ 60,000 \end{bmatrix}$

x = 1,10,000 and y = 60,000

Now, sum of the profits allocated to the outside shareholders

$$= [0.9 \quad 0.8]\begin{bmatrix} 1,10,000 \\ 60,000 \end{bmatrix} = 1,47,000$$

and the sum of separately earned profits = 98,000 + 49,000 = 1.47,000

This proves that the sum of the profits allocated to the outside shareholders is equal to the sum of separately earned profits of all the companies.

Example 36. **A company earns before-tax profit of Rs. 1,00,000. It is committed to making a donation to the Red Cross 10% of its after-tax profits. The Central Government levels corporate taxes of 50% of profits after deducting charitable donations and any local taxes. The company musty also pay local taxes of 10% of its profits less the donation to the Red Cross. Compute how much the company pays in corporate taxes, local taxes and as a donation to the Red Cross, using Cramer's rule.**

Solution.

Let : x = the amount donated to the Red Cross

y = the amount paid in corporate taxes

z = the amount paid in local taxes

On the basis of above information, we have

$$x = 0.10\,(1{,}00{,}000 - y - x) \quad \Leftrightarrow \quad 10x + y + z = 1{,}00{,}00$$

$$y = 0.50\,(1{,}00{,}000 - x - z) \quad \Leftrightarrow \quad x + 2y + z = 1{,}00{,}000$$

$$z = 0.10(1{,}00{,}000 - x) \quad \Leftrightarrow \quad x + 0y + 10z = 1{,}00{,}000$$

Let D be the determinant of the coefficient matrix

$$D = \begin{vmatrix} 10 & 1 & 1 \\ 1 & 2 & 1 \\ 1 & 0 & 10 \end{vmatrix} = 10(20) - 1(10-1) + 1(0-2) = 189$$

Since $D \neq 0$. therefore by Cramer's Rule, the solution is given by

$$x = \frac{D_1}{D}, y = \frac{D_2}{D}, z = \frac{D_3}{D},$$

where $$D_1 = \begin{vmatrix} 1{,}00{,}000 & 1 & 1 \\ 1{,}00{,}000 & 2 & 1 \\ 1{,}00{,}000 & 0 & 10 \end{vmatrix} = 1{,}00{,}000 \begin{vmatrix} 1 & 1 & 1 \\ 1 & 2 & 1 \\ 1 & 0 & 10 \end{vmatrix}$$

$$= 1{,}00{,}000\{1(20) - (10 - 1) + 1\,(-2)\}$$

$$= 1{,}00{,}000\ \{(20) - 1\ (10 - 1) + 1\ (-2)\}$$

$$= 1{,}00{,}000\ (9) = 9{,}00{,}000$$

$$D_2 = \begin{vmatrix} 10 & 1{,}00{,}000 & 1 \\ 1 & 1{,}00{,}000 & 1 \\ 1 & 1{,}00{,}000 & 10 \end{vmatrix} = 1{,}00{,}000 \begin{vmatrix} 10 & 1 & 1 \\ 1 & 1 & 1 \\ 1 & 1 & 10 \end{vmatrix}$$

$$= 1{,}00{,}000\ \{10\ (10 - 1) - 1\ (10 - 1) + 1\ (10)\}$$

$$= 1{,}00{,}000\ (81) = 81{,}00{,}000$$

$$D_3 = \begin{vmatrix} 10 & 1 & 1,00,000 \\ 1 & 2 & 1,00,000 \\ 1 & 0 & 1,00,000 \end{vmatrix} = 1,00,000 \begin{vmatrix} 10 & 1 & 1 \\ 1 & 2 & 1 \\ 1 & 0 & 1 \end{vmatrix}$$

$$= 1,00,000\{10(2) - 1\ (0) + 1\ (-2)\}$$

$$= 1,00,000\ (18) = 18,00,000$$

$$\therefore \quad x = \frac{D_1}{D} = \frac{9,00,000}{189},\ y = \frac{D_2}{D} = \frac{81,00,000}{189},\ z = \frac{D_3}{D} = \frac{18,00,000}{189}$$

Example 37. **A greeting card dealer has three kinds of packets. Packet *A* contains 3 get well cards; 1 birthday card, and 7 anniversary cards, packet *B* contains 2, 3 and 1 respectively and packet contains 5, 4 and 2 respectively. He wishes to merge these so as to form new packets, each containing one get well card, one birthday card and one anniversary card.**

What is the least number of packets *A, B,* and *C* that must be used to accomplish this? How many new packets will be made? (Use matrix method).

Solution. Let *x, y z* packets of A, B, C respectively are used to make t' packets of new mixture.

Therefore, we will have following equations

$$3x + 2y + 5z = t$$

$$x + 3y + 4z = t$$

$$7z + y + 2z = t$$

$$\therefore \quad \begin{bmatrix} 3 & 2 & 5 \\ 1 & 3 & 4 \\ 7 & 1 & 2 \end{bmatrix} \begin{bmatrix} x \\ y \\ z \end{bmatrix} = \begin{bmatrix} t \\ t \\ t \end{bmatrix}$$

$$A \times B = B$$

$$|A| = 3(6-4) - 2(2-28) + 5(1-21) = -42$$

$$\text{Adj } A = \begin{bmatrix} 2 & 26 & -20 \\ 1 & -29 & 11 \\ -7 & -7 & 7 \end{bmatrix}$$

$$A^{-1} = \frac{Adj A}{|A|} = -\frac{1}{42} \begin{bmatrix} 2 & 26 & -20 \\ 1 & -29 & 11 \\ -7 & -7 & 7 \end{bmatrix}$$

$$\begin{bmatrix} x \\ y \\ z \end{bmatrix} = \begin{bmatrix} -\frac{2}{42} & -\frac{1}{42} & \frac{7}{42} \\ -\frac{26}{42} & \frac{29}{42} & \frac{2}{42} \\ \frac{20}{42} & -\frac{11}{42} & -\frac{7}{42} \end{bmatrix} \begin{bmatrix} t \\ t \\ t \end{bmatrix}$$

Solving the above, we have

$$x = \frac{2t}{21}, y = \frac{5t}{21}. z = \frac{t}{21}$$

Since $t = 21$ is the smallest value for which x, y and z are integers. Thus implies 21 new packets are made by in using 2, 5 and 1 packet of A, B and C respectively.

Exercise 2.3

Q.1. Given the following transaction matrix, find the gross output to meet the final demand of 200 units of Agriculture and 800 units of Industry.

Producing Sector	*Purchasing Sector*		*Final Demand*
	Agriculture	*Industry*	
Agriculture	300	600	100
Industry	400	1200	400

Q.2. Two commodities A and B are produced such that 0.4 ton of A and 0.7 ton of B are required to produce a ton of A. Similarly 0.1 ton of A and 0.6 ton of B are needed to produce a ton of B. Write down the technology matrix. If 68 tons of A and 102 tons of B are required, find out the gross production of both of them.

Q.3. In an economy of three industries P. Q, R, the data given below (all figures in millions of Rs.) are available :

Producers	*Users*			*Final Demand*	*Output*
	P	*Q*	*R*		
P	80	100	100	40	320
Q	80	200	60	60	400
R	80	100	100	20	300

Determine the output if the final demand changes to 60 for P, 40 for Q and 60 for R.

Q.4. Given the following technology matrix :

$$A = \begin{bmatrix} 0.5 & 0.1 & 0.1 \\ 0.2 & 0.6 & 0.2 \\ 0.1 & 0.2 & 0.6 \end{bmatrix}$$

Required :

(*i*) Test Simon-Hawkins conditions for the viability of the system.

(*ii*) Determine the gross output vector X, given the demand vector.

$$D = \begin{bmatrix} 2100 \\ 4200 \\ 6300 \end{bmatrix}$$

3. *Divisibility* : According to this assumption, the solution given by Linear programming may take any fractional value. The decision variable need not necessarily be a whole numbers.

4. *Certainty* : It is assumed that the coefficients of the objective function and constraints do not change during the period under study. This implies that resource requirement and profit per unit remain constant.

5. *Finiteness* : It is necessary that there should be finite number of constraints or resource restriction. In case, there would be infinite number of constraints, it would not be feasible to arrive at optimal solution.

6. *Optimality* : In case of Linear programming problem, the optimal solution always occur at a corner point of the set of feasible solution.

General Model of Linear Programming Problem

Let us consider a Linear programming problem involving 'n' decision variables *i.e.*, $x_1, x_2 \ldots\ldots x_n$

$\therefore$ the objective function 'z' would be given as

$$z = C_1x_1 + C_2x_2 + C_3x_3 + \ldots\ldots + C_nx_n \qquad (1)$$

Let there be m constraint, therefore, we will have following constraints.

$$\left.\begin{aligned} &a_{11}x_1 + a_{12}x_2 + \ldots a_{1n}x_n\ (\le, =, \ge)\ b_1 \\ &a_{21}x_1 + a_{22}x_2 + \ldots a_{2n}x_n\ (\le, =, \ge)\ b_2 \\ &\vdots \\ &a_{m1}x_1 + a_{m2}x_2 + \ldots a_{mn}x_n\ (\le, =, \ge)\ b_m \end{aligned}\right\} \qquad (2)$$

and $x_1, x_2, \ldots x_n \ge 0$ (Non negative restrictions)

Rule

(*i*) $x_1, x_2 \ldots, x_n$ are called decision variables.

(*ii*) Linear function z is known as objective function. It is either to be maximized or minimized depending upon the objective.

(*iii*) Conditions given by set of equations (2) are called as constraints.

(*iv*) Thy set of inequalities (3) is known as the set of the non-negative restriction of the Linear programming problem.

(*v*) $C_1, C_2, C_3 \ldots C_n$ *are called per unit contribution to the objective function.*

(*vi*) a_{ij}, where $i = 1, 2 \ldots m$, $j = 1, 2 \ldots, n$, are called substitution coefficients *i.e.*, exchange coefficient of the jth variable in the ith constraint.

(*vii*) $b_1, b_2, \ldots b_n$ *represents requirement of m constraint.*

(*viii*) The expression $(\le, =, \ge)$ means that each constraint may take only one of the three possible forms. (*a*) less than equal to ($\le$), (b) equal to ($=$), (c) greater than or equal to ($\ge$).

Formulation of LP Problem

Formulation of LP problem means converting verbal description of the given problem into mathematical form in terms of objective function, constrains and non negative restriction. It basically involves the following steps :

1. Identification of the decision variables whose values is to be determined.
2. Formation of an objective function as a linear function of the decision variable.
3. Identification of the set of constraints or restrictions. Express them as linear equations with appropriate equality or inequality sign against a given resource.
4. Mention the non negative restrictions for the decision variables.

The technique of formulation of LP problems would become more clear from the following examples.

Example 1 : **A city hospital has the following minimal daily requirement for nurses :**

Period	*Clock time (24 hours day)*	*Minimal Number of Nurses Required*
1.	**6 a.m. – 10 a.m.**	**2**
2.	**10.a.m. – 2 p.m.**	**7**
3.	**2 p.m – 6 p.m.**	**15**
4.	**6 p.m. – 10 p.m.**	**8**
5.	**10 p.m. – 2 a.m.**	**20**
6.	**2 a.m. – 6 a.m.**	**6**

Nurses report to the hospital at the beginning of each period and work for 8 consecutive hours. The hospital wants to determine the minimal number of nurses to be employed so that there will be sufficient number of nurses available for each period. Formulate this as a Linear Programming Problem by setting up appropriate constraints and objective function. Do not solve.

Solution : Let x_i ($i = 1, 2, ..., 6$) be the number of nurses who report at the beginning of ith period. The objective is to minimize the total number of nurses employed in the hospital :

Minimize $Z = x_1 + x_2 + ... + x_6$

It shall be observed that each period is of 4-hour duration and nurses are required to report at the hospital at the beginning of each period and work for 8 consecutive hours. The first nurse x_1 who reports at the beginning of first period shall be on duty when second period starts. Thus, during the second period there will be $x_1 + x_2$ nurses. But the minimal number of nurses required during the second period is specified to be 7.

Therefore, we have

$$x_1 + x_2 \geq 7$$

Similarly, the other constraints of the problem can be found as shown below :

$$x_2 + x_3 \geq 15$$

$$x_3 + x_4 \geq 8$$

$$x_4 + x_5 \geq 20$$

$x_5 + x_6 \geq 6$

$x_6 + x_1 \geq 2$

(Since, number of nurses cannot be negative, therefore) $x_1, x_2, ... x_6 \geq 0$.

Example 2 : **A Pharmaceutical company manufacturers three type of medicines *A, B* and *C*. The processing is done through two plants, Plant *I* and Plant *II*. The number of medicines produced per day in each plant is given as under**

Medicine	***A***	***B***	***C***
Plant *I*	**100**	**75**	**80**
Plant *II*	**150**	**90**	**100**

The monthly demand for type *A, B,* and *C* is 2000, 4000 and 600 respectively. If Plant *I* costs Rs. 2000 per day and Plant *II* costs Rs. 3000 per day to operate, how many days should each be run per month to minimize cost. Formulate the problem as LPP.

Solution : Let x_1 be the number of days for when Plant *I* should be run and x_2 be the number of days which Plant *II* should be run to minimize cost.

$\therefore$ Minimize $z = 2000x_1 + 3000x_2$ (objective function)

It is further given that PLant *I* can manufacture 100 units of *A* and Plant *II* can manufacture 150 units of *A* per day and the monthly demand is 2000 units.

$100x_1 + 150x_2 \geq 2000$ (Constraint)

Likewise, for product *B* and *C*, we have

$75x_1 + 90x_2 \geq 4000$ (Constraint)

and $80x_1 + 100x_2 \geq 6000$ (Constraint)

Since x_1 and x_2 cannot be negative.

$\therefore$ $x_1, x_2 \geq 0$ (Non negative restructions)

Example 3 : **Food *I* contains 10 units of Vitamin *A* and 12 unit of vitamin *B* per gram and cost 20 paise per gram. Food *II* contains 7 unit of vitamin *A* and 15 units of vitamin *B* and costs 18 paise per gram. The daily requirement of vitamin *A* and *B* are atleast 80 units and 90 units respectively. Formulate the above as an LPP to minimize the cost.**

Solution : Let x_1 and x_2 be units of Food *I* and Food *II* respectively to be consumed

$\therefore$ Since cost per gram of *A* and *B* are 20 paise and 18 paise respectively.

$\therefore$ Total Cost $= 20x_1 + 18x_2$

Our objective is to minimize the cost

$\therefore$ Minimize $z = 20x_1 + 18x_2$ (Objective functions)

Further, atleast 80 units of *A* is required

$\therefore$ $10x_1 + 7x_2 \geq 80$ (Constraint)

Likewise

$12x_1 + 15x_2 \geq 90$ (Constraint)

Further x_1 and x_2 cannot be negative

$\therefore$ $x_1, x_2 \geq 0$ (Non negative restriction)

Example 4 : **A person is interested in investing Rs. 50,00,000 in a mix of investments. The investment choices and expected rates of returns on each one of them are:**

Investment	*Expected Rate of Return*
Mutual Fund A	**0.12**
Mutual Fund B	**0.09**
Money Market Fund	**0.08**
Government Bonds	**0.085**
Share Y	**0.16**
Share X	**0.18**

The investor wants at least 35 per cent of his investment in government bonds. Because of the higher perceived risk of the two shares, he was specified that the combined investment in these not to exceed Rs. 80,000. The investor also has specified that at least 20 per cent of the investment should be in the money market fund and that the amount of money invested in shares should not exceed the amount invested in mutual funds. His final investment condition is that the amount invested in mutual fund *A* should not be more than the amount invested in mutual fund *B*. The problem is to decide the amount of money to be invest in each alternative so as to obtain the highest annual total return. Formulate the problem as a linear programming problem.

Solution : Let

x_1 = the amount of money invested in Mutual Fund A.

x_2 = the amount of money invested in Mutual Fund B.

x_3 = the amount of money invested in Money Market Fund.

x_4 = the amount of money invested in Government Bonds

x_5 = the amount of money invested in Share Y.

x_6 = the amount of money invested in Share X.

Since the objective is to maximize total return from the investment.

Therefore, we have

Maximize $= 0.12x_1 + 0.09x_2 + 0.8x_3 + 0.85x_4 + 0.16.x_5 + 0.18x_6$

subject to the constraints

$$x_1 + x_2 + x_3 + x_4 + x_5 + x_6 = 50{,}00{,}000$$

$$x_4 \geq 17{,}50{,}000$$

$$x_5 + x_6 \leq 80{,}000$$

$$x_3 \geq 10{,}00{,}000$$

$$x_5 + x_6 \leq x_1 + x_2$$

$$x_1 \leq x_2$$

$$x_1, x_2, x_3, x_4, x_5, x_6, \geq 0$$

7. 440, 640, 600

8. (*ii*) Balancing Equations :

$0.6x_1 - 0.1x_2 - 0.2x_3 = 10$

$-0.1x_1 + 0.7x_2 - 0.3x_3 = 20$

$-0.2x_1 - 0.1x_2 + 0.8x_3 = 10$

9. (*i*) $\begin{bmatrix} 0.1 & 0.5 \\ 0.6 & 0.3 \end{bmatrix}$ (*ii*) Industry I = 5666.67, Industry II = 8000

10. Steel = 24.84, Coal = 20.68, Electricity = 18.36

11. (*i*) $7x - 0.6y = 10$; (*ii*) $x = 32.5$, $y = 21.25$

$-0.5x + y = 5$

12. (*i*) $\begin{bmatrix} \frac{1}{5} & \frac{1}{4} \\ \frac{1}{4} & \frac{1}{3} \end{bmatrix}$

(*ii*) The new transaction matrix is

		Sector *1*	*Sales* *2*	*Final Demand*	*Gross Output*
Purchaser	1	6.83	4.32	23	34.16
	2	8.54	5.77	3	17.31
Primary Inputs		18.77	7.23		

13. The input-output table is :

Industry	*Steel*	*Coal*	*Final Demand*	*Total Output*
Steel	29.375	17.5	100	146.875
Coal	58.75	8.75	20	87.50

14. (*i*) $\begin{bmatrix} 0.2 & 0.2 & 0.1 \\ 0.4 & 0.1 & 0.3 \\ 0.2 & 0.5 & 0.1 \end{bmatrix}$

(*ii*) Steel = 188.669, Coal = 167.669, Rail Road = 178.325

15. (*i*) The system is viable

(*ii*) 2,10,000; 4,20,000; 4,20,000

(*iii*) 2,25,000; 4,50,000; 4,50,000

16. Agriculture : 396.14, Manufactures : 300.13, Services : 235.75

17. (*i*) X = 558.82 Units, Y = 176.47 Units

    (*ii*) p_1 = Rs. 700, p_2 = 1400

    (*iii*) 139999.3

18. Manufacturing : 260 million units, Agriculture : 4.6 millions units, Total labour requirement : 1500 million man-hours p_1 = Rs. 100, p_2 = Rs. 5000.

19. $\begin{bmatrix} 120 \\ 65 \end{bmatrix}$ (*i*) $\begin{bmatrix} 160 \\ 80 \end{bmatrix}$ (*ii*) $\begin{bmatrix} 40 \\ 20 \end{bmatrix}$

20. (42.78)

21. (62, 88.5 and 59; 64, 90 and 60)

3

LINEAR PROGRAMMING FORMULATION & GRAPHICAL METHOD

HIGHLIGHTS OF THE CHAPTER

- ❖ **Introduction**
- ❖ **Structure of LP Problem**
- ❖ **Formulation LP Problem**
- ❖ **Extreme Point Theorem**
- ❖ **Graphical Method of Solving LP Problem**
- ❖ **Special Cases of Linear Programming Problems**

INTRODUCTION

As we all know that business objectives involve optimal utilization of available resources besides other objectives. Linear programming techniques help in achieving such objectives. For example, a firm manufacturing different products with varying profit margins may face resource constraint in terms of available working hours or raw material. Now the firm may be interested in knowing as to how many units of each product shall be manufactured so that profit can be maximised with the given resources. The operation of the firm is to be confined within the given resources and the profit is to be maximized. **Thus the use of resources is referred as constraint whereas achieving maximum profit is said to be objective of the firm.** Linear Programming helps in dealing with such situations.

Linear programming is a mathematical technique to find value of objective function subject to certain constraints.

Structure of Linear Programming Problem

The structure of a Linear Programming problem can be understood from the following problem:

Let x_1 = quantity of product 1

x_2 = quantity of product 2

The x_1 and x_2 are the decision variables.

Let profit on each unit of product 1 and product 2 be Rs. 10 and Rs. 15 respectively

$\therefore$ Aggregate profit = $10x_1 + 15x_2$

Since the objective is to maximise the profit, it can be stated as

$$\text{Maximize} = 10x_1 + 15x_2$$

This is called the objective function. It is indicated by the symbol 'z'

$$\text{Maximize } z = 10x_1 + 15x_2$$

Let us assume that x_1 requires 3 man-hours to product each unit and x_2 requires 4 man-hours and the total available man hours are 100. This requirement can be mathematically stated as :

$$3x_1 + 4x_2 \leq 100$$

It is further assumed that product x_1 need 5 Kg of material A and 3 Kg of Material B. And x_2 need 6 Kg of material A and 2 Kg of material B. Now, if total material A available is 70 Kg and material B available is 90 Kg then we have following equations:

$$5x_1 + 6x_2 \leq 70$$

$$3x_1 + 2x_2 \leq 60$$

The above problem can now be mathematically summarized in the form of a linear programming model as follows :

Objective Function Maximize $z = 10x_1 + 15z_2$ (1)

Subject to **Constraints**

$3x_1 + 4x_2 \leq 100$ (2)

$5x_1 + 6x_2 \leq 70$ (3)

$3x_1 + 2x_2 \leq 90$ (4)

Besides the above, the number of units of x_1 and x_2 can not be negative

$\therefore$ $x_1 \leq 0$ $x_2 \leq 0$ (5)

Here, equation (1) is **objective functions**

Equation (2) to (4) are **constraint functions**

Equation (5) is **non negative constrain.**

Thus, the structure of a Linear programming problem comprises of three main parts which are

1. Objective Function
2. Constraint Function
3. Non-Negative Constraints

Basic Assumptions of Linear Programming

1. *Proportionality* : According to this assumption, objective function is proportional to resource function. If the resources are doubled, the output would also get doubled.
2. *Additivity* : This assumption means that the sum of resources used by different activities/product is equal to the total resources available for the complete activity. This implies that there is no interaction between the decision variables.

Example 5 : **A firm manufacturers three items *A*, *B*, and *C*. The time required for finishing and polishing alongwith the other necessary details are given below :**

Product	*Time Required in Hours*		*Profit in Rs.*
	Assembly	*Finishing*	
A	**20**	**12**	**80**
B	**14**	**15**	**60**
C	**15**	**14**	**30**
Firms Capacity	**2000**	**1500**	

Express the above data in the form of a Linear programming problem to maximise profit from the production.

Solution : Let x_1, x_2 and x_3 be the number of units of *A, B,* and *C* respectively to be manufactured by a firm.

Since profit per unit is Rs. 80, Rs. 60 and Rs. 30 for x_1, x_2 and x_3 respectively

$\therefore$ Total Profit $= 80x_1 + 60x_2 + 30x_3$

Our objective is to maximise total profit

$\therefore$ Maximise $z = 80x_1 + 60x_2 + 30x_3$ (1)

It is further given that total available polishing hours are 2000 and the product *A, B,* and *C* requires 20, 14 and 15 hours per unit. Since the total activity is required to be confined within the given time.

We have

$$20x_1 + 14x_2 + 15x_3 \leq 2000 \quad (2)$$

Here $20x_1$ represent total time of polishing x_1 units *A*. $14x_2$ represent total time of polishing x_2 units of *B*. $15x_3$ represent total time of polishing x_3 units of *C*.

Similarly we have

$$12x_1 + 15x_2 + 14x_3 \leq 1500 \quad (3)$$

Further x_1, x_2 and x_3 cannot be negative

$\therefore$ We have

$$x_1, x_2, x_3 \leq 0 \quad (4)$$

Thus equation (1) is objective function.

Equation (2) and (3) are constraint.

Equation (4) is non negative restriction.

Example 6 : **A company manufactures two models of car—X(800) and X(1000). The contribution per model is Rs. 50,000 and Rs. 65,000 on X(800) and X(1000) respectively. The material required for X(800) is in short supply and company can only produce maximum of 150 units per week. Each car manufactured has to undergo activity of assembling and painting. However, there are limitation on capacity of these activities. The details are given as under.**

Model	Assembling (per week)	Painting (per week)
X (800)	150	80
X (1000)	200	90

Formulate this problem as an LP model to determine the optimal combination of output.

Solution : Given contribution per model of X(800) and X(1000) of Rs. 50,000 and Rs. 65,000 respectively.

Let x_1, and x_2, be the number of model X(800) and X(1000) unmanufactured to have optimal combination of output.

$\therefore$ Maximum profit $z = 50000x_1 + 65000x_2$ (objective function)

Further there are constrains on assembling and printing

$\therefore$ we have $\frac{x_1}{150} + \frac{x_2}{200} \leq 1$

and $\frac{x_1}{80} + \frac{x_2}{90} \leq 1$

Also $x_1 \leq 150$

and $x_1, x_2 \geq 0$ (Non negative restrictions).

Example 7 : **A media specialist plans to allocate advertising expenditure in three media where unit costs of a message are Rs. 1,500, Rs. 1,250 and Rs. 1,000 respectively. The total advertising budget available for the year is Rs. 50,000. The first medium is a monthly magazine and it is desired to advertise not more than once in one issue. At least five advertisement should appear in the second medium and the number of advertisements in the third medium should strictly lie between 6 and 10. The effective audience for unit advertisement in the three media is given below :**

Medium	:	**1**	**2**	**3**
Expected effective audience :		**50,000**	**40,000**	**25,000**

Formulate a linear programming problem to find the optimum allocation of advertisements in three media that would maximize the total effective audience.

Solution : Let x_1, x_2 and x_3 be the number of advertisements in media 1, 2 and 3 respectively. Since our objective is to maximize total effective audience, therefore mathematical formulation of the problem would be

Maximize $Z = 50,000x_1 + 40,000x_2 + 25,000x_3$

Subjective to the constraints :

$$1500x_1 + 1250x_2 + 1000x_1 \leq 50,000$$

$$x_1 \leq 12$$

$$x_2 \geq 5$$

$$6 \leq x_3 \leq 10$$

$$x_1, x_2, x_3 \geq 0$$

***Example* 8 : A company has two plants, *A* & *B*, each designed for manufacturing 10 biscuit packet and 15 biscuit packet of biscuits. The details of production is given below :**

Machine	*10 Biscuit Packet*	*15 Biscuit Packet*
A	**50 per Minute**	**35 per Minute**
B	**30 per Minute**	**55 per Minute**

Each machine can be run 8-hours per day, 5 days per week. Profit on small packet is 50 paisa and on the 15 biscuit packet, it is 75 paisa. Weekly production of the biscuit cannot exceed 1,00,000 and the market can absorb 30,000 small packets biscuits and 10,000 big packet biscuits per week. Formulate this as a Linear programming problem with a view to maximize profit.

Solution : Let x_1 and x_2 be the number of small packet and large packet biscuits manufactured by the company.

∴ Objective function is to maximise profit

$$z = 0.50x_1 + 0.75x_2 \text{ (Maximise)}$$

(Since manufacturing capacity is given per minute whereas operating capacity is given in hours ∴ operating capacity (in minutes) = 8 × 5 × 60 = 2400)

Constrains

$$\frac{x_1}{50} + \frac{x_2}{35} \leq 2400$$

Likewise $$\frac{x_1}{30} + \frac{x_2}{55} \leq 2400$$

Further demand for total number of biscuits cannot exceed 100000 biscuits

$$10x_1 + 15x_2 \leq 100000$$

(it shall be noted demand has been expressed in terms of number of biscuits)

Also $$x_1 \leq 30000$$

$$x_2 \leq 10000$$

and $x_1, x_2, \leq 0.$

***Example* 9 : A company produce three type of electric components- Resistance, Capacitor and Inductor whose selling price per unit are Rs 5,7, and 10 respectively. All the components can be sold. The cost of raw form resistance, capacitor and inductor are Rs. 3, Rs. 4 and Rs. 6 respectively. Before selling these components, the company is required to polish, charge and shape them. The company possesses only of each type of machine. Cost per hour to run each of the three machines are Rs 15 for polishing, Rs 20 for charging and Rs 25 for shaping. The capacities (parts per hour) for each part on each machine are shown in the following table.**

	Capacity per hour		
Machine	*Resistance*	*Capacitor*	*Inductor*
Polishing	**35**	**25**	**30**
Charging	**15**	**30**	**30**
Shaping	**50**	**45**	**40**

The company wants to know number of each type of product to be produced per hour in order to maximise profit in one hour of operation. Formulate the above problem as a Linear programming problem.

Solution : Let x_1, x_2 and x_3 denote the number of three types of parts to be produced per hour.

Total cost involved in manufacturers of one resistance =

$$\left[3+\left(\frac{15}{35}+\frac{20}{15}+\frac{25}{50}\right)\right] \quad \left(\begin{array}{l}\text{If 35 resistance are polished isRs. 15} \\ \therefore \text{1 resistance is polished in Rs.}\frac{15}{35}\end{array}\right)$$

$\therefore$ Profit per unit of resistance $=\left[5-\left(3+\frac{15}{35}+\frac{20}{15}+\frac{25}{50}\right)\right]$

$\therefore$ Total profit from resistance $=\left[5-\left(3+\frac{15}{35}+\frac{20}{15}+\frac{25}{50}\right)\right]x_1$

Likewise Total Profit from Capacitors $=\left[7-\left(4+\frac{15}{25}+\frac{20}{30}+\frac{25}{45}\right)\right]x_2$

and Total Profit from Inductance $=\left[10-\left(6+\frac{15}{30}+\frac{20}{30}+\frac{25}{40}\right)\right]x_3$

$$\therefore \text{ Combined Profit } z=\left[5-\left(3+\frac{15}{35}+\frac{20}{15}+\frac{25}{50}\right)\right]x_1+\left[7-\left(4+\frac{15}{25}+\frac{20}{30}+\frac{25}{25}\right)\right]x_2$$

$$-\left[10-\left(6+\frac{15}{30}+\frac{20}{30}+\frac{25}{40}\right)\right]x_3$$

Further, there is only one machine for a particular work which implies all the components are to be polished with one machine.

$\therefore \quad \frac{x_1}{35}+\frac{x_2}{25}+\frac{x_3}{30}\leq 1$ (Constraint)

Likewise $\quad \frac{x_1}{15}+\frac{x_2}{30}+\frac{x_3}{30}\leq 1$ (Constraint)

and $\quad \frac{x_1}{50}+\frac{x_2}{45}+\frac{x_3}{40}\leq 1$ (Constraint)

and $\quad x_1, x_2, x_3 \geq 0$ (Non negative restrictions).

Example 10 : **Shyam, an Agriculturist, has a farm with 125 acres. He produces radish, peas and potato. Whatever he raises is fully sold in the market. He gets Rs.5 for radish per kg, Rs. 4 for peas per kg and Rs. 5 for potato per kg. The average yield is 1500 kg of radish per acre, 1800**

kg of peas per acre and 1200 kg of potato per acre. To produce each 100 kg of radish and peas and to produce each 80 kg of potato a sum of Rs. 12.50 has to be used for manure. Labour required for each acre to raise the crop is 6 man days for radish and potato each and 5 days for peas. A total of 500 man days of labour at a rate of Rs. 40 per man day are available. Formulate this as a linear programming model to maximize the Agriculturist's total profit.

Solution : The required data of above problem has been summarised below in the tabular form.

	Radish	*Peas*	*Potato*
Revenue/	Rs. (1500 × 5)	Rs. (1,800 × 4)	Rs. (1,200 × 5)
acre	= Rs. 7,500	= Rs. 7,200	= Rs. 6,000
Cost of	Rs. (40 × 6)	Rs. (40 × 5)	Rs. (400 × 6)
Labour/acre	= Rs. 240	= Rs. 200	= Rs. 240
Cost of Manure	Rs. $\left(\frac{12.50}{100}\times 1500\right)$	Rs. $\left(\frac{12.50}{100}\times 1800\right)$	Rs. $\left(\frac{12.50}{80}\times 1200\right)$
	= Rs. 1,875	= Rs. 225	= Rs. 187.50
Net Profit per	Rs. (7,500 – 240 – 187.50)	Rs. (7,200 – 200 – 225)	Rs. (6,000 – 240 – 187.50)
Acre	= Rs. 7,072.50	= Rs. 6,775	Rs. 5,572.50

Let x_1, x_2 and x_3 acres of farm be used to produce radish, peas and potato, respectively. Since our objective is to maximize profit, therefore objective function would be given as

Maximize $Z = 7072.5x_1 + 6775x_2 + 5572.5x_3$

Subject to constraints

$$x_1 + x_2 + x_3 \le 125$$

$$6x_1 + 5x_2 + 6x_3 \le 500$$

$$x_1, x_2, x_3 \ge 0$$

Example 11 : **Three type of shaping tools are produced in a factory using Activity I, Activity II and Activity III. The duration in hours required to produce one batch of tools in each of these activities are given in the following tables along with the cost and selling prices of each batch of tools and the minimum number of hours available on each machine per week.**

Total	***Processing time (hrs.) Per batch in***			***Cost Per***	***Selling Price***
Type	***Activity I***	***Activity II***	***Activity III***	***Batch (Rs.)***	***(Rs. Per Batch)***
P	**8**	**1**	**7**	**75**	**110**
Q	**2**	**5**	**9**	**60**	**90**
R	**4**	**3**	**3**	**75**	**130**
Max, hours.	**35**	**40**	**50**		

Formulate this problem as an LP model so as to maximise the total profit.

Solution : Given Profit for P product = 110 – 75 = 35 (Per Batch)

Profit for Q Product = 90 – 60 = 30 (Per Batch)

Profit for R Product = 130 − 75 = 55 (Per Batch)

Let x_1, x_2 and x_3 *be the number of batch manufactured of each type P, Q* and *R* respectively,

$\therefore$ Total Profit $z = 35x_1 + 30x_2 + 55x_3$

Our objective is to maximise z.

$\therefore$ Maximize $z = 35x_1 + 30x_2 + 55x_3$

Since the total time available for Activity I is 35 hours and each batch of P. Q and R requires 8, 2 and 4 hours respectively.

$\therefore$ there is a constraint given as $8x_1 + 2x_2 + 4x_3 \leq 35$

Likewise, we have

$$x_1 + 5x_2 + 3x_3 \leq 40$$

$$7x_1 + 9x_2 + 3x_3 \leq 50$$

along with $x_1, x_2, x_3 \geq 0$ (Non negative restrictions)

EXERCISE 3.1

1. A plastic company is producing two products *A* and *B*. The processing times are 3 hours and 4 hours per unit of *A* operations one and two respectively and 4 hours and 5 hours per unit for *B* on operations on one and two respectively. The available times are 18 hours and 21 hours for operation one and two respectively. The product *A* and *B* can be sold at a profit of Rs. 30 per unit and Rs. 80 per unit. Formulate this problem as a LP model so as to maximize the total profit.

2. A person is interested in investing Rs. 5,00,000 in a mix of investments. The investments choices and expected return on each one of them are :

Investment	*Expected Rate of Returned*
Mutual Fund A	0.12
Mutual Fund B	0.09
Money Market Fund	0.08
Government Bonds	0.085
Share Y	0.16
Share X	0.18

The investor wants at least 35 per cent of his investment in government bonds. Because of the higher perceived risk of the two shares, he has specified that the combined investment in these not to exceed Rs. 80,000. The investor also has specified that at least 20 per cent of the investment should be in the money market fund and that amount of money invested in shares should not exceed the amount invested in mutual funds. His final investment condition is that the amount invested in mutual fund *A* should not be more than the amount invested in mutual fund *B*. The problem is to decide the amount of money to be invested in each alternative so as to obtain the highest annual total return. Formulate the problem as a linear programming problem.

3. A media specialist plans to allocate advertising expenditure in three media where unit costs of a message are Rs. 1,500, Rs. 1,250 and 1,000 respectively. The total advertising budget available for the year is Rs. 50,000. The first medium is a monthly magazine and it is desired to advertise not more than once in one issue. At least five advertisements should appear in the second medium and the number of advertisements in the third medium should strictly lie between 6 and 10. The effective audience for unit advertisement in the three media is given below :

Medium	:	1	2	3
Expected effective audience	:	50,000	40,000	25,000

Formulate a linear programming problem to find the optimum allocation of advertisement in three media that would maximize the total effective audience.

4. A firm is planning to advertise a special sale on radio and television during a particular week, A maximum budget of Rs. 16,000 is approved for this purpose. It is known that radio commercials cost Rs. 1,000 per 30-second spot with a minimum contract of four spots, which the firm intends to enter. Television commercials, on the other hand, cost Rs. 4,000 per spot. Because of heavy demand, at the most 4 television spots are available in the week. Also, it is believed that a TV spot is five times as effective as a radio spot in reaching consumers. How should the firm allocate its advertising to attract the largest number of buyers? How will the optimal solution be affected if the availability of TV spots is not constrained?

5. A steel manufacturer products two types of steel. Type I requires 2 hours of melting, 4 hours of rolling and 10 hours of cutting. Type II requires 5 hours of melting, rolling and 60 for cutting. Forty hours are available for melting, 20 for rolling and 60 for cutting. The profit margin for type I is 24 and for type II it is 8. Formulate the above as LPP.

6. A toy manufacturers products two types of dolls, a basic version doll *A* and a deluxe version doll *B*. Each doll of type *B* takes twice as long to product as a doll of type *A*. The company has time to make a maximum of 2000 dolls of type *A* per day. The supply of plastic is sufficient to produce 1500 dolls per day and each type requires equal amount of it. The deluxe version *i.e.*, type *B* requires a fancy dress of which there are only 600 per day available. The company makes a profit of Rs. 3 and Rs. 5 per doll, respectively, on doll *A* and *B*. Formulate the above as LPP.

7. A company makes two kinds of leather belts. Belts *A* is a high quality belt and belt *B* of lower quality. The respective profits are Rs. 0.40 and Rs. 0.30 per belt. Each belt of type *A* requires twice as much time as a belt of type *B* and if all belts were of types *B*, the company could make 1000 per day. The supply of leather is sufficient for only 800 belts per day (both *A* and *B* combined). Belt *A* requires a fancy buckle and only 400 per day are available. There are only 700 buckles a day available for belt *B*. Formulate the above as linear programming problem.

8. Three types of cakes are manufactured by a bakery. The different types C_1, C_2, and C_3, give a contribution of Rs. 1, Rs. 1 and Rs. 3 respectively. The maximum time available at the two stages of manufacture is 3 and 2 hours respectively. The three cake varieties take 3, 2 and 1 hours at the first stage and 2, 1 and 2 hours respectively at the second stage respectively. It is required to find out the optimal product mix for maximum contribution. Formulate the above as linear programming problem.

9. Write a note on the business applications of linear programming.

Answers

1. Maximize $Z = 30x_1 + 80x_2$

   Subject to $30x_1 + 4x_2 \le 18$

   $4x_1 + 5x_2 \le 21,\ x_1\ x_2 \ge 0$

2. Maximize $Z = 0.12x_1 + 0.09x_2 + 0.08x_3 + 0.085x_4 + 0.16x_5 + 0.18x_6$

   Subject to $x_1 + x_2 + x_3 + x_4 + x_5 + x_6 \le 500000$

   $x_4 \le 175000$

   $x_5 + x_6 \le 80000$

   $x_3 \ge 100000$

   $x_5 + x_6 \le x_1 + x_2$

   $x_1 \le x_2$

   $x_1, x_2, x_3, x_4, x_5, x_6, \ge 0$

3. Maximize $Z = 50000x_1 + 40000x_2 + 25000x_3$

   Subject to $1500x_1 + 1250x_2 + 1000x_3 \le 50000$

   $x_1 \le 12,\ x_2 \ge 5,\ 6 \le x_3 \le 10$

   $x_1.\ x_2,\ x_3 \ge 10$

4. Maximize $Z = x_1 + 5x_1$

   Subject to $1000x_1 + 4000x_2 \le 16000$

   $x_1 \le 4$

   $x_2 \le 4$

   $x_1, x_2, \ge 0$

5. Maximize $Z = 24x_1 + 8x_2$

   Subject to $2x_1 + 5x_2 \le 40$

   $4x_1 + x_2 \le 20$

   $10x_1 + 5x_2 \le 60$

   $x_1, x_2 \ge 0$

6. Maximize $Z = 3x_1 + 5x_2$

   Subject to $x_1 + 2x_2 \le 2000$

   $x_1 + x_2 \le 1500$

   $x_2 \le 600$

   $x_1, x_2 \ge 0$

7. Maximize $Z = 0.40x_1 + 0.30x_2$

Subject to $2x_1 + x_2 \leq 1000$

$x_1 + x_2 \leq 800$

$x_2 \leq 700$

$x_1, x_2 \geq 0$

8. Maximize $Z = x_1 + x_2 + 3x_3$

Subject to $3x_1 + 2x_2 + x_3 \leq 3$

$2x_1 + x_2 + 2x_3 \leq 2$

$x_1, x_2, x_3 \geq 0$

Linear Programming Graphical Approach

In order to understand graphical method of Linear programming the students must know how to draw graph of inequation, such as $ax + by + c \geq 0$ or $ax + by + c \leq 0$.

The following steps shall be followed in drawing graph of $ax + by + c \geq 0$ or $ax + by + c \leq 0$

(*a*) Draw the graph of straight line equation $ax + by + c = 0$. (ignoring inequality).

(*b*) Substitute $x = 0$ and $y = 0$ is the given equation. If the inequity is satisfied, shade the portion from the line towards the origin (0,0), otherwise shade the portion from the line on the opposite side. The above concept would become more clear from the following examples.

Example 12 : **Given $2x + 4y \geq 20$, draw a line and shade the relevant area.**

Solution : Assume $2x + 4y \geq 20$

as $2x + 4y = 20$

$\therefore$ $4y = 20 - 2x$

$$y = \frac{(20-2x)}{4}$$

x	0	1	–1	10
y	5	4.5	5.5	0

$\therefore$ Ploting the above coordinates on X – Y graph, we have figure 1.

Put $x = 0$, $y = 0$ in the given inequation we have

$2(0) + 4(0) \geq 20$

$0 \geq 20$

This is false, therefore, we have shaded opposite side of the line *i.e.*, side away from the origin.

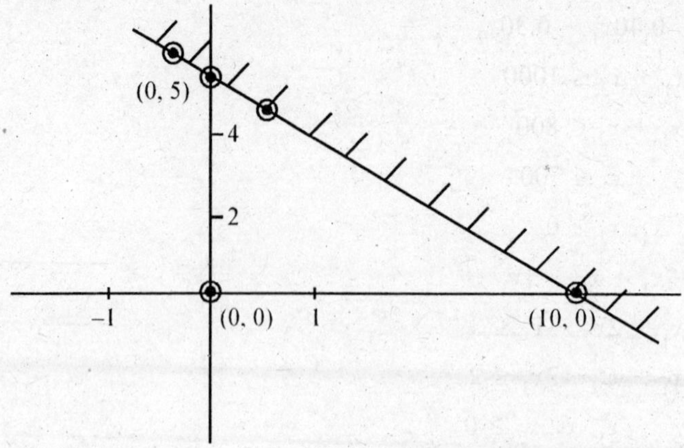

Fig. 1

***Example 13 :* Given $x + 2y \leq 7$, draw a line and shade the relevant area.**

Solution : Assume $x + 2y \leq 7$

as $x + 2y = 7$

$$\therefore \quad y = \frac{(7-x)}{2}$$

x	0	1	-1	7
y	3.5	3	4	0

Ploting the above coordinates on X - Y plane, we have figure 2.

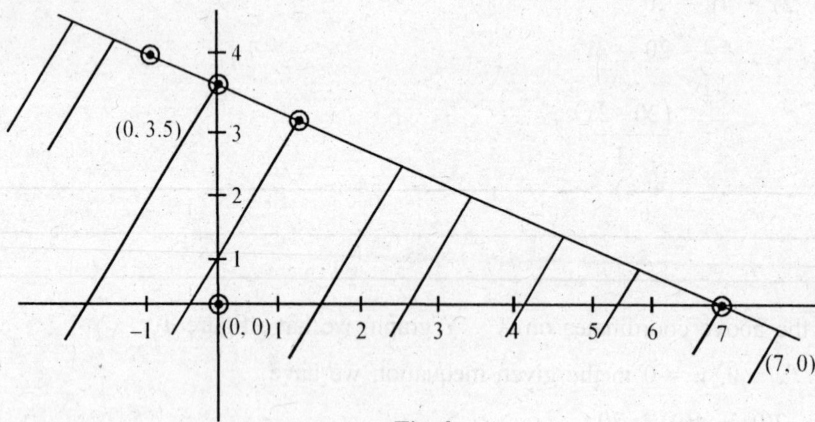

Fig. 2

Put $x = 0$ $y = 0$ in the above equation, we have

$$(0) + 2(0) \leq 7$$

$$0 \leq 7$$

It is true, therefore the area from the line towards origin has been shaded.

When we have two or more linear inequalities in two variables, we should graph them and shade the relevant area. The area which is common to both graphs gives the required result.

The following example would help in understanding the concept properly :

***Example 14* : Exhibit graphically the following :**

$$2x + 2y \leq 4$$

$$-x + y \leq 1$$

***Solution* :** Assume $2x + 2y \leq 4$

as $2x + 2y = 4$ and find coordinates

x	0	2	0.5
y	+2	0	1.5

Put $x = 0$, $y = 0$ in the inequality

$\therefore$ $0 \leq 4$, true

$\therefore$ Shade towards the origin

Likewise find coordinates for

$-x + y \leq 1$

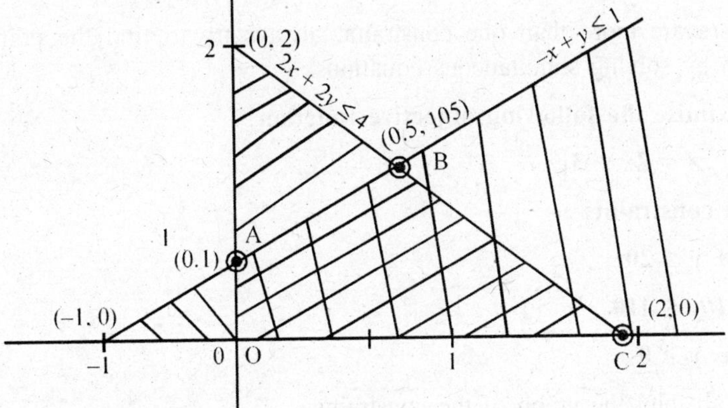

Fig. 3

x	0	–1	0.5
y	1	0	1.5

Put $x = 0$, $y = 0$ in the inequality we have

$\therefore$ $0 \leq 1$, true

$\therefore$ Shade towards the origin.

$\therefore$ Common Shaded Portion is the required area as shown in figure 3. It is observed that common area is OABC.

Using the above concept, graphic method of linear programming can be explained.

Following steps shall be followed in order to graphically solve the Linear Programming problem.

(*a*) First of all formulate the given problem in terms of mathematical constraints and an objective function.

(*b*) The constraints would be inequations which shall be plotted and relevant area shall be shaded.

(*c*) The corner points of common shaded area shall be identified and the coordinates corresponding to these points shall be subsituted in the objective function.

(*d*) The value which maximizes the objective function or minimizes the objective function, as the case may be, shall be optimal solution of the given problem.

This method is based on a theorem, called extreme point theorem, which is given as under.

Extreme Point Theorem

An optimal solution to a linear programming problem, if it exists, occurs at one of the corner or extreme points of the area of feasible region.

Important Points

(*a*) Students shall always try to find the coordinates where the given equation intersects X-axis and Y-axis by substituting $y = 0$ and $x = 0$ respectively in the given equation

(*b*) Whenever there are more than one constraint, always try to find the points of intersection between them by solving simultaneous equations.

Example 15 : **Maximise the following objective function**

$$Z = 2x + 3y$$

Subject to the constraints :

$$x + y \leq 20$$

$$x + 10y \leq 110$$

$$x, y \geq 0$$

Solution : First of all, plot the graph of the constraints

i.e., $x + y \leq 20$

and $x + 10y \leq 110$

and shade the relevant area, as under

Given $x + y \leq 20$

Put $x + y = 20$ $\therefore y = 20 - x$

x	0	10	−10	20
y	20	10	30	0

Put $x = 0$ and $y = 0$ in the given inequation, we have

$$0 \leq 20$$

which is true, therefore, area covering the origin shall be shaded.

Further we have

$$x + 10y \leq 110$$

Put $\quad x + 10y = 110$

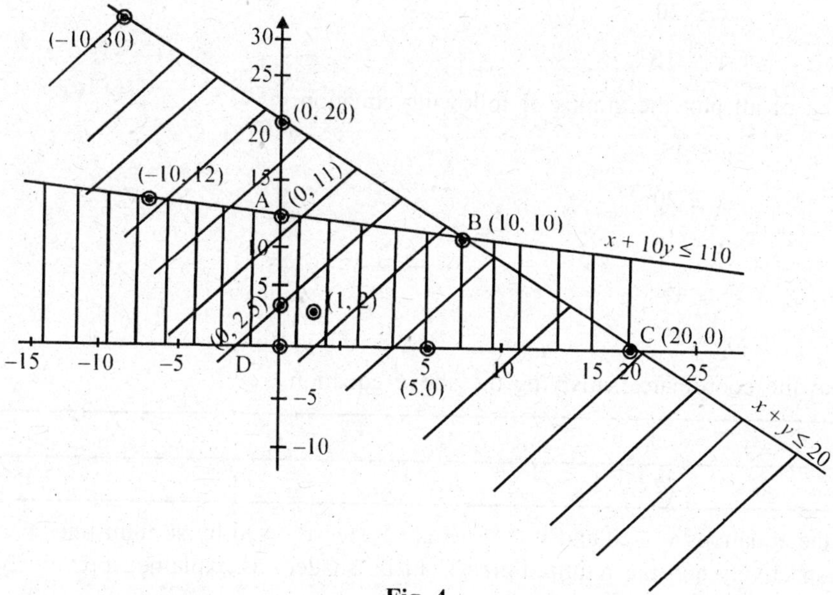

Fig. 4

$\therefore \quad y = \dfrac{(110-x)}{10}$

x	0	10	−10	20
y	11	10	12	9

Put $x = 0$, $y = 0$ in the above equation, we have

$(0) + 10(0) = 0 \leq 110$

which is true, therefore, shade the area covering origin.

The inequalities are satisfied by the common shaded area; ABCD as shown in figure 1.4.

The extreme points of ABCD are

A (0,11), B (10,10), C (20,0) and D (0,0)

Substituting these values in the objective function

$$Z = 2x = 3y$$

we have $\quad Z(0,11) = 2(0) + 3(11) = 33$

$$Z(10,10) = 2(10) + 3(10) = 50$$

$$Z(20,0) = 2(20) + 3(0) = 40$$

$$Z(0,0) = 2(0) + 3(0) = 0$$

The optimum solution is $x = 10$, $y = 10$.

Example 16 : **Solve the following graphically**

Maximize $z = 4x + 3y$

Subject to $x + 2y \leq 45$

$x \leq 20$

$y \leq 15$

Solution : First of all plot the graphs of following equation.

$x + 2y \leq 45$

$x \leq 20$

$y \leq 15$

Assume $x + 2y \leq 45$

as $x + 2y = 45$

we have following coordinates satisfying the above equation

x	0	45	20	15
y	22.5	0	12.5	15

Further, the equations $x \leq 20$ and $y \leq 15$ would be represented by straight lines parallel to y-axis and x-axis respectively and the required area shall be shaded, as explained previously

The above equations are shown graphically in figure 1.5.

$\therefore$ Required Area = OABCD.

The points corresponding to OABCD are (0,0); (2,0); (20,0); (20,12.5); (15,15) and (0,15)

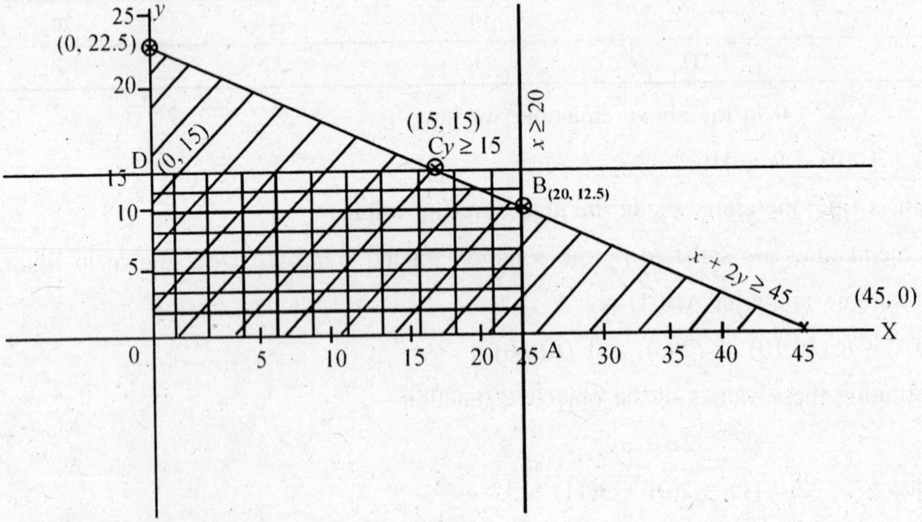

Fig. 5

Substituting the value of corner points in the given objective function, we have

Z at (0,0) = 4(0) + 3(0) = 0

Z at (20,0) = 4(20) + 3(0) = 80

$$Z \text{ at } (20,12.5) = 4(20) + 3(12.5) = 117.5$$

$$Z \text{ at } (15,15) = 4(15) + 3(15) = 105$$

$$Z \text{ at } (0,15) = 4(0) + 3(15) = 45$$

∴ *Z achieves maximum value when* $x = 20$ *and* $y = 12.5$.

Example 17 : **Solve the following graphically.**

Maximize $Z = 2x + 5y$ **(Objective function)**

Subject to $x + 3y \leq 90$

$3x + y \leq 120$

$x \leq 30$

Solution : First of all plot the given constraint functions and shade the relevant area, as under

Given $x + 3y \leq 90$

$3x + y \leq 120$

$x \leq 30$

Assume $x + 3y = 90$ and find set of coordinates

x	0	90	30	33.75
y	30	0	20	18.75

Similarly for $3x + y \leq 120$

assume $3x + y = 120$ and find the set of coordinates as under.

x	0	40	30	33.75
y	120	0	30	18.75

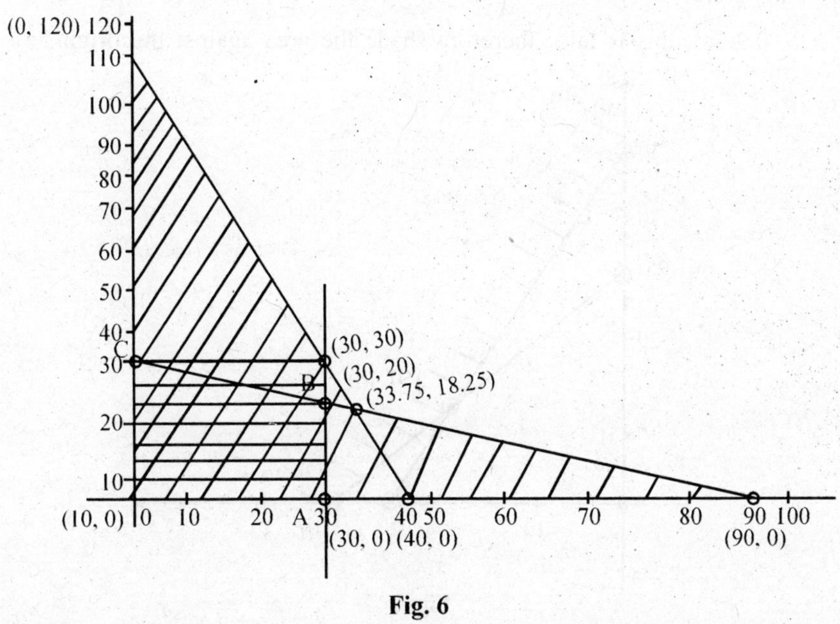

Fig. 6

$x \le 30$ would be represented by a straight line parallel to Y-axis.

The graph of the above equation and relevant area is shown in Figure 1.6.

∴ Corner points of the required area O, A, B, C are (0, 0); (30, 0); (30, 20) and (0, 30).

Substituting these points in the objective function

$$Z_{(0,0)} = 2(0) + 5(0) = 0$$
$$Z_{(30,0)} = 2(30) + 5(0) = 60$$
$$Z_{(30,20)} = 2(30) + 5(20) = 160$$
$$Z_{(0,30)} = 2(0) + 5(30) = 150$$

Thus the maximum point of the function exist at $x = 30$ and $y = 20$.

Example 18 **: Solve the following Linear problem graphically,**

Minimize $z = 2x + 3y$

Subject to

$$2x + y \ge 40$$
$$2x + 2y \ge 50$$
$$x, y \ge 0$$

Solution : First of all plot the given constraint equation and shade the relevant area, as under

$2x + y \le 40$ (1)

x	0	20	15
y	40	0	10

Put $x = 0$, $y = 0$ in equation (1), we have

$2(0) + (0) \ge 40$

$0 \ge 40$, this is false therefore shade the area against the origin.

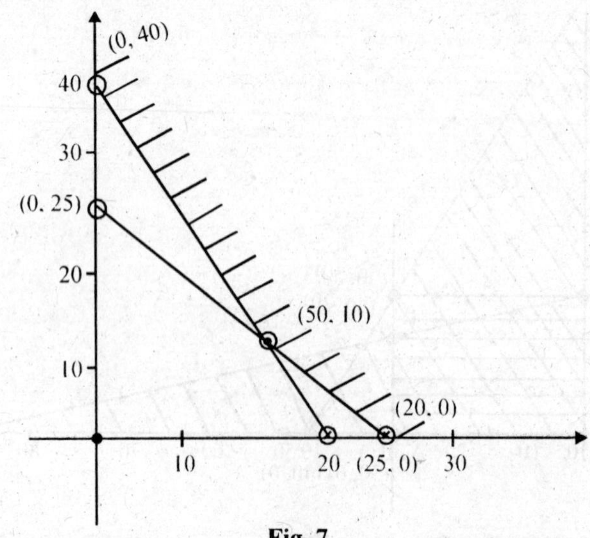

Fig. 7

Similarly, we can solve the other equation and shade the relevant area.

Corresponding to $2x + 2y \le 50$, we have following coordinates

x	0	25	15
y	25	0	10

The corner points are (0,40); (15,10) and (20,0) The value of objective function at these points would be

$$Z_{(0,40)} = 2(0) + 3(40) = 120$$
$$Z_{(15,10)} = 2(15) + 3(10) = 60$$
$$Z_{(20,0)} = 2(20) + 3(0) = 40$$

Thus, Minima of objective function occurs at (20,0)

Example 19 : **Maximize Z = 10*x* + 6*y***

Subject $\quad 3x + y \le 12$

$$2x + 5y \le 34$$
$$x, y \le 0$$

by graphic method.

Solution : We first plot the lines corresponding to the given constraints

$$3x + y \le 12 \quad ....(1)$$
$$2x + 5y \le 34 \quad ....(2)$$

Corresponding to $3x + y = 12$, and $2x + 5y = 34$, we have following coordinates

$3x + y = 12$ $\qquad$ $2x + 5y = 34$

x	0	4	2	x	0	17	2
y	12	0	6	y	34/5	0	6

Note that the line (1) meets the axis at the points (0, 12) and (4,0) and the line (2) at (0, 34/5) and (17,0). The shaded area corresponding to the above constraints is shown in Fig 8.

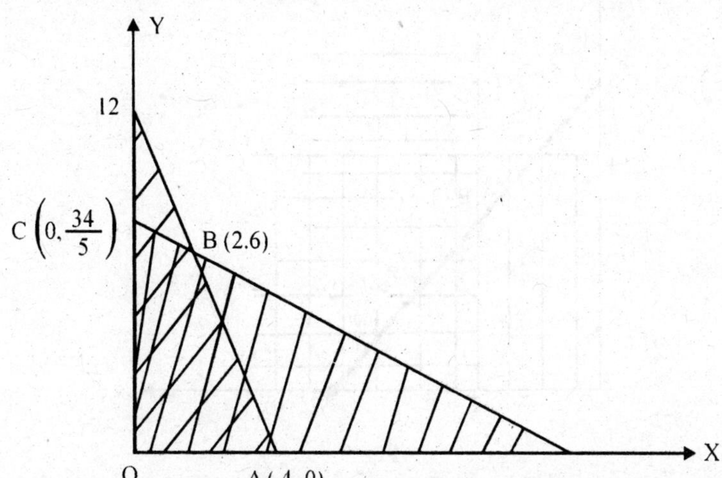

Fig. 8

The corner points of the feasible region are O (0,0), A (4,0), B (2,6) and C (0,34/5). The values of the objective function at these corner points are summarized as follows :

Corner Point (x, y)	*Value of the Objective Function* $Z = 10x + 6y$
O (0,0)	$10(0) + 6(0) = 0$
A (4,0)	$10 (4) + 6 (0) = 40$
B (2,6)	$10 (2) + 6 (6) = 56$
C (0.34/5)	$10(0)+6\left(\frac{34}{5}\right)=\frac{204}{5}$

Since objective function is maximum at B, the optimum solution occurs at $x = 2$ and $y = 6$, yielding the maximum value of Z as 56.

***Example 20* : Solve the following linear programming problem graphically :**

Maximize $Z = 4x + 6y$

Subject to the constraints :

$$x + y = 5$$
$$x \geq 2$$
$$y \leq 4$$
$$x, y \geq 0$$

***Solution* :** In this case, the first constraint $x + y = 5$ is an equality. This meets the x-axis at (5,0) and y-axis at (0, 5). The constraint $x \geq 2$ is the line parallel to y-axis at a distance 2 and the constraint $y \leq 4$ is the line parallel to x-axis at a distance 4. A feasible point (x,y) must have $x \geq 0, y \leq 0$, must lie on the line $x + y = 5$. Therefore the feasible area in this case is the dark line segment AB as shown in figure 1.9. Thus, Z is maximum at one of the two extreme points of AB. The coordinates of A are (5,0). In order to find value of B, we solve the equations $x + y = 5$ *and* $x = 2$ *simultaneously, which gives* $x = 2, y = 3$.

Evaluating Z at these points, we obtain

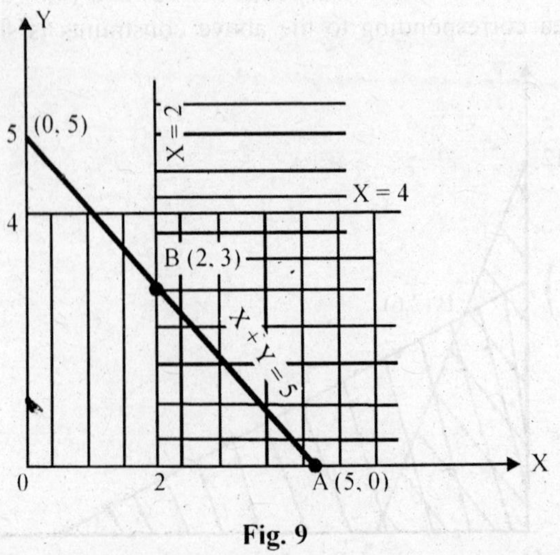

Fig. 9

$$Z(A) = 4(5) + 6\,(0) = 20,$$

$$Z(B) = 4(2) + 6\,(3) = 26.$$

Therefore the maximum value of Z, subject to the constraints, is 26 and it occurs when $x = 2$ and $y = 3$.

Example 21 : **Using graphic method, find the maximum value of**

$$\mathbf{Z = 7x + 10y}$$

subject to $x + y \leq 30000$

$y \leq 12000$

$x \geq 16000$

$x \geq y$

$x, y \geq 0$

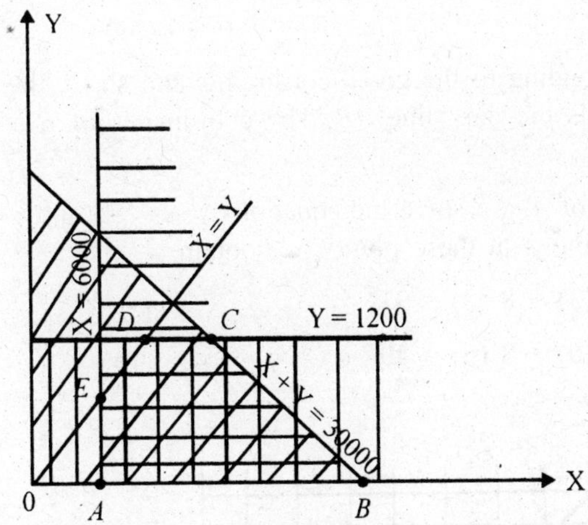

Fig. 10

Solution : Plot the graphs of the given constraints and shade the relevant area. The shaded portion in the above figure 10 represents the feasible region. The corner points of the feasible region are A (6,000, 0), B (30000, 0), C (18000, 12,000), D (12,000, 12000) and E (6000, 6000).

The values of the objective function at these corner points are summarized in the table given below :

Corner Point (x, y)	*The value of the objective function* $Z = 7x + 10y$	
A (6000, 0)	7(6000) + 0	= 42000
B (30000, 0)	7 (30000) + 0	= 210000
C (18000, 12000)	7 (18000) + 10 (12000)	= 246000
D (12000, 12000)	7 (12000) + 10 (12000)	= 204000
E (6000, 6000)	7 (6000) + 10 (6000)	= 102000

Thus the maximum value of Z is 246000 and it occurs when $x = 18000$ and $y = 12000$.

Example 22 : **The standard weight of a special purpose brick is 5 kg and it contains two basic ingredients B_1 and B_2, B_1 costs Rs. 5 per kg and B_2 costs Rs. 8 per kg. Strength considerations dictate that the brick contains not more than 4 kg of B_1 and minimum of 2 kg of B_2. Since the demand for the product is likely to be related to the price of the brick, find the minimum cost of brick satisfying the above conditions.**

Solution.

Let x be the amount of ingredient B_1 (in kg) in the brick and

y be the amount of ingredient B_2 (in kg) in the brick

The appropriate mathematical formulation of the problem will be given as Minimize $Z = 5x + 8y$

subject to $x + y = 5$

$$x \leq 4$$

$$y \geq 2$$

$$x, y \geq 0$$

Plot the graphs corresponding to the given constraints and shade the relevant area as shown in Fig. 11. The required area is the dark line AB. The coordinates of B are (0,5) as can be directly observed.

To find the coordinates of A, we solve the equations $x + y = 5$ and $y = 2$ simultaneously, which gives $x = 3$, $y = 2$. Evaluating Z at these points, we obtain

$$Z(A) = 5(3) + 8(2) = 31$$

$$Z(B) = 5(0) + 8(5) = 40$$

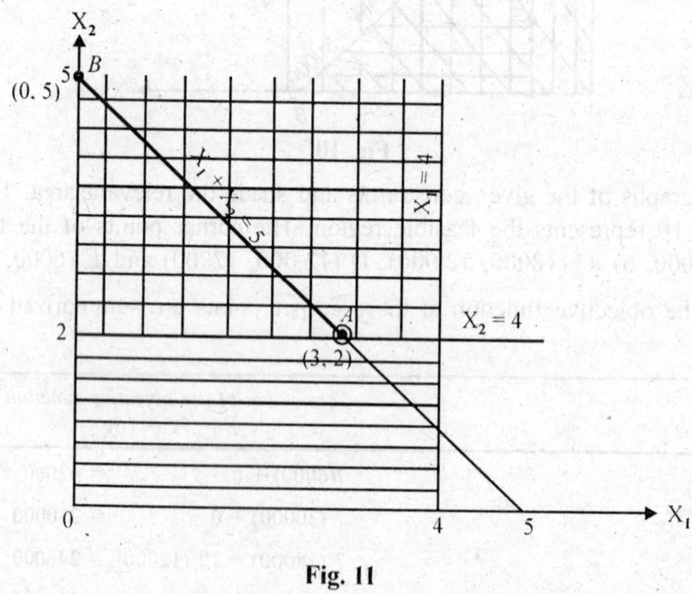

Fig. 11

Therefore, the minimum value of Z occurs at A (3,2). Hence the optimum product mix is : 3 kg of ingredient B_1 and 2 kg of ingredient B_2 so as to achieve the minimum cost of Rs. 31.

Example 23 : **Alpha Heavy Engineering Company produces earthmovers and harvesters. Each product passes through two assembly departments A and B, which, respectively, have 300 hours**

and 320 hours of available time fore the next month's production. Each earthmover requires 20 hours in department *A* and 40 in department *B* and each harvester requires 30 hours in department *A* and 20 in department *B*. The two products are tested in a third department. Each earthmover is given 60 hours of testing and each harvester 20, and as per the agreement with the labour union, the total labours hours devoted to testing cannot fall below 270. The management has the operating policy of manufacturing at least one harvester for every two earthmovers produced. A major customer has placed an order for a minimum of 5 earthmovers and harvesters (in any combination, whatever) for next month, and so, at least that many must be produced. Each earthmovers gives a profit of Rs. 10,000 and each harvester Rs. 8,000.

Solution : Let x denote the number of earthmovers and y denote the number of harvesters produced. Therefore the mathematical formulation of the problem would be given as :

Maximize $Z = 10000x + 8000y$

Subject to $20x + 30y \leq 300$

$40x + 20y \leq 320$

$60x + 20y \geq 270$

Further $y \leq \frac{1}{2}x$ or $x - 2y \leq 0$

$x + y \geq 5$

$x, y, \geq 0$

Plot the graphs corresponding to the above constraints and shade the relevant area. The relevant area would be ABCD as shown in the figure 12.

The corner points of the required area are $A\left(\frac{27}{7}, \frac{27}{14}\right)$, $B\left(\frac{32}{5}, \frac{32}{10}\right)$, $C\left(\frac{9}{2}, 7\right)$ and $D\left(\frac{3}{2}, 9\right)$. The values of the objective function corresponding to these corner points are summarized below :

Corner Point (x,y)	*The value of the objective function* $Z = 10000\,x + 8000\,y$
$A\left(\frac{27}{7}, \frac{27}{14}\right)$	54,000
$B\left(\frac{32}{5}, \frac{32}{10}\right)$	89,600
$C\left(\frac{9}{2}, 7\right)$	1,01,000
$D\left(\frac{3}{2}, 9\right)$	87,000

Thus, the maximum value of Z is Rs. 1,01,000 and it occurs when $x = \frac{9}{2}$ and $y = 7$.

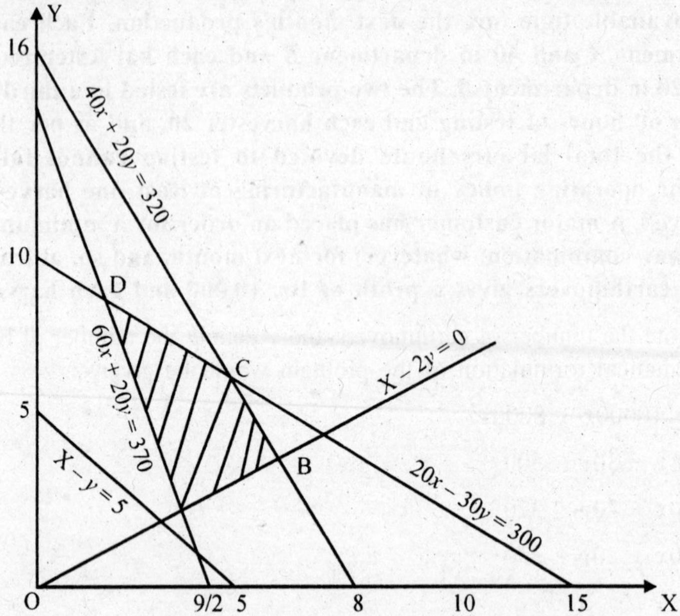

Fig. 12

Example 24 : **Maximize Z = 4*x* + 3*y***

Subject to $3x + 4y \leq 24$

$8x + 6y \leq 48$

$x \leq 5$

$y \leq 6$

$x, y \leq 0$

Solution : As explained in the previous solution, plot the graph corresponding to the given constraints and shade the relevant area. The required area would be OABCD as shown in the Figure 13.

The corner points of the feasible region are O (0,0), A (5,0), $B\left(5,\frac{4}{3}\right), C\left(\frac{24}{7},\frac{24}{7}\right)$ and D (0,6).

Evaluating the objective function at these points, we obtain

$$Z(O) = 4(0) + 3(0) = 0$$

$$Z(O) = 4(5) + 3(0) = 20$$

$$Z(B) = 4(5) + 3\left(\frac{4}{3}\right) = 24$$

$$Z(C) = 4\left(\frac{24}{7}\right) + 3\left(\frac{24}{7}\right) = 24$$

$$Z(D) = 4(0) + 3(6) = 18$$

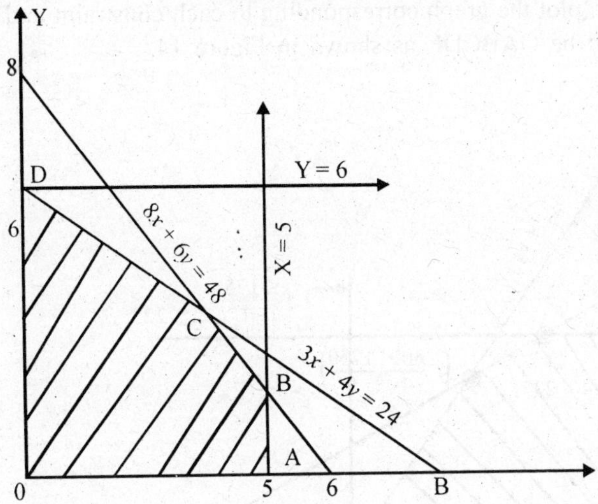

Fig. 13

Since the maximum value of Z is 24 and it occurs at two corner points. B and C, In fact, this maximum value also occurs at all points on the line segment joining B and C. Therefore, we have an infinite number of optimal solutions.

Example 25 : **A firm assembles and sells two different types of outboard motor, *A* and *B* using four resources. The production process can be described as follows :**

Resources	***Capacity per month***
Motor unit shop resource	**400 Type A units or 250 Type *B* units or any linear combination of the two**
Type *A* gear and drive shop resource	**175 Type A units.**
Type *B* gear and drive shop resource	**225 Type *B* units.**
Final assembly resource	**200 Type *A* units or 350 Type *B* units or any linear combination of the two.**

Type *A* units bring in a profit of Rs. 90 and type *B* units, Rs. 60 each. What should be the optimum product mix?

Solution : Let the firm produce x_1 units of A and x_2 units of B. Then, the appropriate mathematical formulation of the problem will be :

Maximize $Z = 90x_1 + 60x_2$

Subject to $\frac{1}{400}x_1 + \frac{1}{250}x_2 \le 1$ or $5x_1 + 8x_2 \le 2000$

$x_1 \le 175$

$x_2 \le 225$

$\frac{1}{200}x_1 + \frac{1}{350}x_2 \le 1$ or $7x_1 + 4x_2 \le 1400$

$x_1, x_2 \ge 0$

As explained earlier, plot the graph corresponding to each constraint and shade the required area. The required area would be OABCDE as shown in Figure 14.

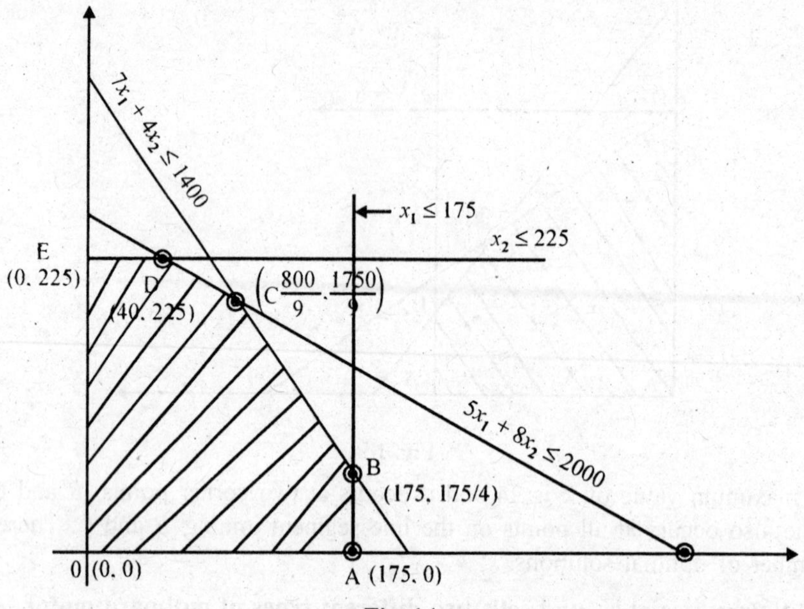

Fig. 14

Let us evaluate the value of objective function at these corner points

Corner Point	*Objective Function*
0 (0,0)	0
A (175, 0)	15750
B (175, 175/4)	18275
C (800/9, 1750/9)	19666.67
D (40, 225)	17100
E (0, 225)	13500

$\therefore$ Maximum value of Z occurs at $x_1 = \frac{800}{9}, x_2 = \frac{1750}{9}$

Maximum value of Z is 19666.67.

Special cases of Linear Programming-Graphical Approach

Sometimes, we come across special cases of linear programming problems, where we may have following situations.

(*a*) Multiple optimal solutions.

(*b*) Infeasible solutions.

(*c*) Unbounded solutions.

(*d*) Redundancy constraints.

Let us explain each of these special cases briefly :

(a) *Multiple Optimal Solutions*

So far, we have in all linear programming problems a unique corner point where optimal solution is obtained. However, in certain situations, we may have more than one such combination of decision variables at which the objective function acquires optimal solution.

For Example

Maximise $Z = 15x + 20y$

Subject to $3x + 4y \leq 12$

$x, y, \geq 0$

In this case we have shaded portion and corner points as shown in figure 15.

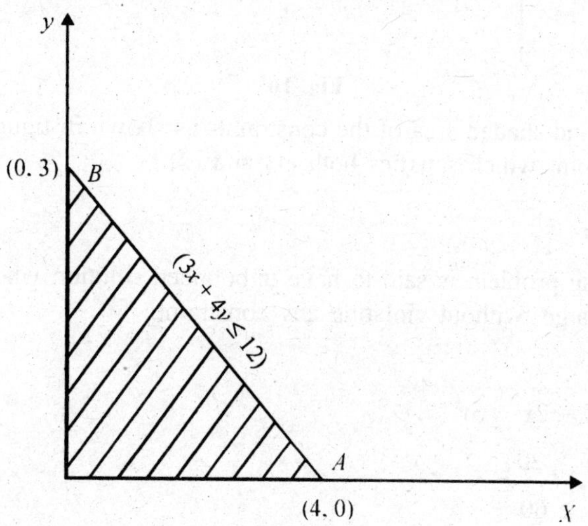

Fig. 15

Value of Z at $A = 15(4) + 20(0)$

$= 60$

Value of Z at $B = 15(0) + 20(3)$

$= 60$

Any point of on the line, say (3, 3/4) would also given same value of Z.

(b) *Infeasible Solution*

This situation is arrived when we have no feasible solution or there is no point which satisfies the system of constraints involved is the given LPP.

For example

Maximize $Z = 2x + y$

Subject to the constraints

$x + y \geq 6$ .....(1)

$2x + 4y \geq 60$ .....(2)

$x, y \geq 0$

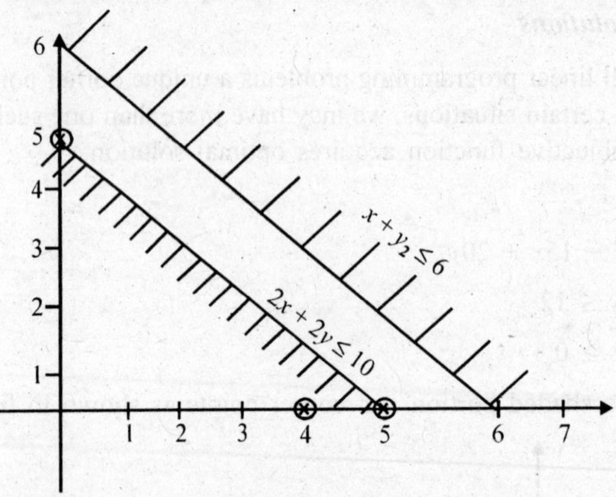

Fig. 16

We will have graph and shaded area of the constraints as shown in figure 16. It is clear from the figure that there is no point which satisfies both (1) and (2).

(c) *Unbounded Solution*

A linear programming problem is said to have unbounded solution when the objective function can be made infinitely large, without violating any constraint.

For example

Maximize $Z = 2x + 5y$

Subject to $x + y \geq 20$

$2x + 4y \geq 60$

$x, y \geq 0$

When we plot the graph and shade relevant area corresponding to the equations, we have 17 figure

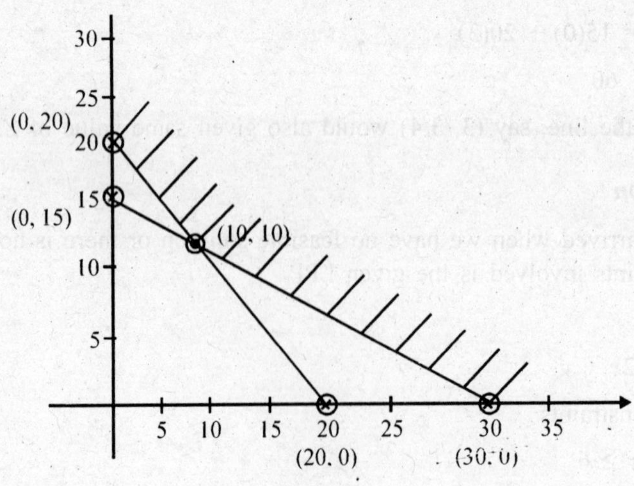

Fig. 17

The corner points are (0,20); (10,10); and (30,0) The value of objective functions at these points would be

$$Z_{(0,20)} = 2(0) + 5(20) = 100$$
$$Z_{(10,10)} = 2(10) + 5(10) = 70$$
$$Z_{(30,0)} = 2(30) + 5(0) = 60$$

∴ The objective functions acquires maximum value at (0,20). However, this is not true because the shaded area would have number of points where the value of the objectives function would be more than 100.

(d) Redundancy Constraint

As the name itself suggest, the constraint under this case is redundant in nature and it does not affect the feasible solution region.

For example

Maximize $Z = 2x + 3y$

Subject to $x \geq 10$

$y \geq 5$

$x + y \geq 4$

$x, y \geq 0$

The graph for the above constraint would be given as under, in figure 1.18.

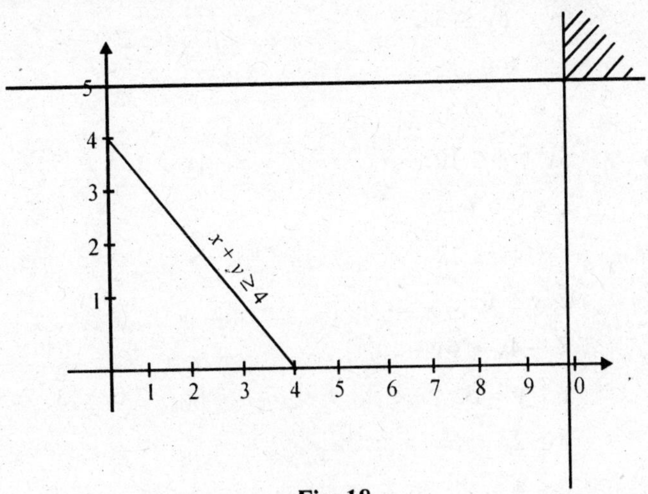

Fig. 18

The constraint $x + y \geq 4$ is redundant because its presence is not affecting the solution.

$x = 1800$

$y = 12000$

Exercise 3.2

1. Explain how you would identify the cases of redundant constraint, no solution, multiple solution and unbounded solution from the graph of linear programming problems involving two variables. Give a rough sketch of each case.

2. Show the solution zone of the following inequalities on a graph paper :

   $5x + y \geq 10,\ x + y \geq 6,\ x + 4y \geq 12,\ x \geq 0,\ y \geq 0$

   Find x and y for which $3x + 2y$ is minimum subject to these inequalities. Use graphic method. [$x = 1$, $y = 5$ and $Z = 13$]

3. Solve the following L.P.P. by graphic method :

   Maximize $Z = 2.75x_1 + 4.15x_1$

   Subject to $2x_1 + 2.5x_2 \leq 100$

   $4x_1 + 8x_2 \geq 160$

   $7.5x_1 + 5x_2 \geq 150$

   $x_1, x_2 \geq 0$ [$x_1 = 0$, $x_2 = 40$ and $Z = 166$]

4. Use graphical method to solve the following linear problems.

   (*a*) Maximize $Z = 10x + 6y$

   Subject to $3x + y \leq 12$ [$x = 2$, $y = 6$, $Z = 56$]

   $2x + 5y \leq 34$

   $x, y \geq 0$

   (*b*) Minimize $Z = 3x + 2y$

   Subject to $5x + y \leq 10$ [$x = 1$, $y = 5$, $Z = 13$]

   $x + y \geq 6$

   $x + 4y \geq 12$

   $x, y \geq 0$

   (*c*) Maximize $Z = 4x + 6y$

   Subject to $x + y = 5$ [$x = 2$, $y = 3$, $Z = 26$]

   $x \geq 2$

   $y \leq 4$

   $x, y \geq 0$

   (*d*) Minimize $Z = 18x + 10y$

   Subject to $4x + y \geq 20$ [$x = 3$, $y = 8$. $Z = 134$]

   $2x + 3y \geq 30$

   $x, y \geq 0$

(e) Maximize $Z = 7x + 10y$

Subject to $x + y \leq 30000$ $[x = 3, y = 8, Z = 134]$

$y \leq 12000$

$x \geq 6000$

$x \geq y$

$x, y \geq 0$ $[x = 18000, y = 12000, Z = 246000]$

5. Consider a firm that produces two products X_1 and X_2 with three fixed resources Z_1, Z_2, Z_3. The profit contribution is Rs. 20 per unit of X_1 and Rs. 25 per unit of X_2 sold. Production of a unit of X_1 requires 10 units of Z_1 and 15 units of Z_2, while that of X_2 requires 10 units of Z_2 and 30 units of Z_3, Z_1, Z_2 and Z_3 available in amounts of 5000, 9000 and 12000 respectively. Find the profit maximizing product mix. $[x_1 = 200, x_2 = 400]$

6. A carpenter has 90, 80 and 50 running feet respectively of teak, plywood and rosewood. The product *A* requires 2, 1 and 1 running feet and product *B* requires 1, 2 and 1 running feet of teak, plywood and rosewood respectively. If *A* would sell for Rs. 48 and *B* would sell for Rs. 40 per unit, how much of each should he make and sell in order to obtain the maximum gross income out of his stock of wood? Use graphical method to solve the problem. $[A = 40$ units, $B = 10$ units, $Z = 2320]$

7. A firm makes two types of furniture : Chairs and Tables. The contribution for each product as calculated by the accounting department is Rs. 20 per Chair and Rs. 30 per Table. Both products are processed on three machines M_1, M_2 and M_3. The time required in hours by each product and the total time available in hours per week on each machine are as follows :

Machine	*Chair*	*Table*	*Available Time*
M_1	3	3	36
M_2	5	2	50
M_3	2	6	60

How should the manufacturer schedule his production in order to maximize contribution? (Use graphical method only) $[x = 3, y = 9, Z = 330]$

8. A retired person wants to invest upto an amount of Rs. 30,000 in the fixed income securities. His broker recommends investing in two bonds-bond *A* yielding 7% per annum and bond *B* yielding 10% per annum. After some consideration he decides to invest at the most Rs. 12,000 in bond *B* and at least Rs. 6,000 in bond *A*. He also wants that the amount invested in bond *A* must be at least equal to the amount invested in bond *B*. What should the broker recommend if the investor wants to maximize his return on investment? Solve graphically.

$[A = 18{,}000, B = 12{,}000, Z = 2{,}460]$

9. The *ABC* company has been a producer of picture tubes for television sets and certain printed circuits for radios. The company has just expanded into full scale production and marketing of *AM* and *AM-FM* radio. It has built a new plant that can operate 48 hours per week. Production of an AM radio in the new plant will require 2 hours and production of an *AM-FM* radio will require 3 hours. Each *AM* radio will contribute Rs. 40/- to profits while an *AM-FM* radio will contribute Rs. 80/- to profits. The marketing department, after extensive research has determined that a maximum of 15 *AM* radios and 10 *AM-FM* radios can be sold each week.

(*i*) Formulate a linear programming model to determine the optimal production mix of *AM* and *AM-FM* radios that will maximize profits.

(*ii*) Solve the above problem using the graphical method. $[x_1 = 9, y = 10, Z = 1160]$

10. A firm is engaged in breeding pigs. The pigs are fed on various products grown on the farm. In view of the need to ensure certain nutrient constituents, it is necessary to buy two additional products, say *A* and *B*.

The content of the various products (per unit) in nutrient constituent (*e.g.* vitamins, proteins, etc.) are given in the following table :

Nutrient	*Nutrient content in product*		*Minimum amount of nutrient*
	A	*B*	
M_1	36	6	108
M_2	3	12	36
M_3	20	10	100

The last column of the above table gives the minimum amounts of nutrient constituents M_1, M_2, and M_3 which must be given to the pigs. If products *A* and *B* cost Rs. 20 and Rs 40 per unit respectively, how much of each of these two products should be bought so that the total cost is minimized? (Use graphical method). $[x = 4, y = 2, Z = 160]$

11. The manager of an oil refinery must decide on the optimal mix of two possible blending processes of which the inputs and outputs per production run are as follows :

Process	*Input (Units)*		*Output (Units)*	
	Crude A	*Crude B*	*Gasoline X*	*Gasoline Y*
1	5	3	5	8
2	4	5	4	4

The maximum quantities available of crudes *A* and *B* are 200 units and 150 units respectively. Market requirements show that at least 100 units of gasoline *X* and 80 units of gasoline *Y* must be produced. The profit per production run from process 1 and process 2 are Rs.300 and Rs.400 respectively. Formulate the problem as linear programming problem and solve it by graphical method.

$$\left[x = 400/3, y = 150/13, \text{Profit} = \frac{180000}{13}\right]$$

12. A firm is planning to advertise a special sale on radio and television during a particular week. A maximum budget of Rs. 16,000 is approved for this purpose. It is known that radio commercials cost Rs. 1000 per 30-second spot with a minimum contract of four spots, which the firm intends to enter. Television commercials on the other hand cost Rs.4000 per spot. Because of heavy demand at the most 4 television spots are available in the week. Also, it is believed that a TV spot is five times as effective as a radio spot in reaching consumers. How should the firm allocate its advertising to attract the largest number of buyers? How will be optimal solution be affected if the availability of TV spot is not constrained? $[x = 4, y = 3, Z = 19]$ (Not affected)

13. A firm has two kinds of fruit juices available *viz.* pineapple and orange juice. These are mixed and two types of mixtures are obtained. These are sold as soft drinks A and B. 1 tin of A needs 4 pounds of pine apple juice and 1 pound of orange juice. 1 tin of B needs 2 pounds of pine apple and 3 pounds of orange juice. Each tin of A and B is sold at a profit of Rs. 4 and Rs.3 respectively. How many tins of A and B should the firm produce to maximize profit?

Formulate the problem mathematically. Solve it graphically. [$x = 9$, $y = 5$, $z = 51$]

4

LINEAR PROGRAMMING - SIMPLEX METHOD

HIGHLIGHTS OF THE CHAPTER

- **Introduction**
- **Simplex Method – Concept**
- **Uses of Index Row**
- **Economic Interpretation of Optimal Table**
- **Duality**
- **Practical Problems – Maximisation and Minimization.**

INTRODUCTION

Linear programming problems, involving more than two decision variables cannot be solved through graphical approach of Linear programming. In such cases, simplex method is used. The present chapter deals with simplex method of Linear programming. Keeping in view the complexity involved in simplex method, utmost care has been taken to present the entire chapter in a very simplified manner. The problems have been divided into various categories depending upon their types, namely.

(*a*) Maximization Problem

(*b*) Minimization Problems

(*c*) Mixed constraint Problems

(*d*) Duality

(*e*) Comprehensive Problems

Besides the above the economic interpretation of various involved in the problem has been provided in a lucid language.

Simplex Method-Concept

The graphical method of linear programming is generally useful is the situations where the number of decisions variable is two. When the number of decision variable is more than two simplex method is used. In order to understand the simplex method, certain basic definitions shall be understood.

(*a*) *Slack Variable*

It is a variable added to convert the inequality into equality. It is used in the situations when we have inequality of the type 'less than or equal to' type. For example, if we have inequality

$$3x + 2y \leq 15$$

then this inequality can be converted into equality as

$$3x + 2y + s_1 = 15$$

where s_1 is a slack variable.

In economic terms, this variable represents unused capacity. For example, if 2 units of x and 4 units of y are produced, then $s_1 = 15 - 3\ (2) - 2(4) = 1$ *i.e.*, unused capacity is 1 unit. In other words, we may say that we require 15 units but we have produced 14 units.

(b) Surplus Variable

It is a variable subtracted from inequations to convert it into equations. It is used in the situations when we have inequality of the type 'more than or equal to' type

For example if we have inequality

$$5x + 3y \geq 28$$

then this inequality can be converted into equality as

$$5x + 3y - s_2 = 28$$

s_2 is always non-negative number. If 4 units of x and 3 units of y are produced

Thus $\quad S_2 = 5(4) + 3(3) - 28$

$$= 20 + 9 - 28 = 1$$

∴ Surplus variable = 1 unit. This implies that our requirement was 28 units but we have produced 29 units.

Therefore we can conclude that slack variable represent unused capacity [Slack = Requirement – Production] and surplus variable represent excess capacity [Surplus = Production– requirement].

(c) Basic Solution

In linear programming problems we have 'n' decision variables and 'm' simultaneous linear equations ($n > m$). If we set ($n - m$) variables equal to zero and solve for remaining 'm' variables, the solution obtained in such case is called a basic solution. The variables ($n - m$) which are set equal to zero in any solution are called non-basic variables. The other 'm' variables whose values are obtained are called basic variables. A basic solution which happens to be feasible is called a basic feasible solution.

(d) Optimal Solution

In case of graphical approach, we can easily find extreme points which are then placed in the given objective function. That value of extreme points which maximizes or minimizes (as the case may be) the value of objective function is called on optimal solution. Analogues to extreme points we get basic feasible solutions in case of simplex method and that value of basic feasible solution which will maximize or minimize the objective function is known as optimal basic feasible solution.

The following example would explain the concept of basic feasible solution.

Example 1

Maximize $Z = 2x + 3y$

Subject to constraints

$$3x + 2y \leq 40$$

$$x + 5y \leq 90$$

$$x, y \geq 0$$

Solution

First of all, convert inequality into equality as under

$$3x + 2y + s_1 = 40$$

$$x + 5y + s_2 = 90$$

Now there are *four* variables and *two* equations.

i.e., $m = 2$ and $n = 4$

∴ We should set $n - m = 4 - 2 = 2$ variables equal to zero and we should solve for the remaining variables.

Let as put $x = 0$, $y = 0$ is the above equation, we have $S_1 = 40$, $S_2 = 90$

If we put $x = 0$, $S_1 = 0$, we have

$y = 20$, $S_2 = -10$

If we put $x = 0$, $S_2 = 0$, we have

$y = 18$, $S_2 = 4$

If we put $y = 0$, $S_1 = 0$, we have

$$x = 40/3 \text{ and } S_2 = \frac{230}{3}$$

If we put $y = 0$, $S_2 = 0$, we have

$y = 90$, $S_2 = -230$

If we put $S_1 = 0$, $S_2 = 0$, we have

$x = 20/13$, $y = 230/13$

The above solutions can be summarised in the following table.

S.No	*Basic Variable*	*Non Basic Variable*
1.	$s_1 = 40$ and $s_2 = 90$	$x = 0, y = 0$
2.	$y = 20$ and $s_2 = -10$	$x = 0, s_1 = 0$
3.	$y = 18$ and $s_1 = 4$	$x = 0, s_2 = 0$
4.	$x = 40/3$ and $s_2 = 230/13$	$y = 0, s_1 = 0$
5.	$x = 90$ and $s_2 = -230$	$y = 0, s_2 = 0$
6.	$y = 20/13$ and $y = 230/13$	$s_1 = 0, s_2 = 0.$

Since, S_1 and S_2 are non-negative, ∴ solution 2 and 5 cannot be accepted in any case. However, solution 1, 3, 4 and 6 are basic feasible solutions.

Simplex Method

Steps for Computation

Step 1. Formulate a given problem in the following form

Maximize $Z = C_1 x_1 + C_2 x_2 + ,, + C_n x_n$ (Objective function)

Subject to the following constraints.

$$\left.\begin{array}{l} a_{11}x_1 + a_{12}x_2 + ... a_{1n}x_n \leq b_1 \\ a_{21}x_1 + a_{22}x_2 + ... a_{2n}x_n \leq b_2 \\ \vdots \\ a_{m1}x_1 + a_{m2}x_2 + ... + a_{mn}x_n \leq b_m \end{array}\right] \text{Constraints}$$

$x_1, x_2, x_3, ...x_n \geq 0$ (Non-Negative restrictions)

Step II. Introduce slack variables $s_1, s_2, ... s_m$ (one for each constraint) to convert inequalities to equation. The slack variable are added to the constraint as well as to the objective function. However, they are assigned zero coefficients in the objective function because they contribute nothing to the value of the objective function.

Step III. Now, the initial basic feasible solution is obtained. In order to obtain initial basic feasible solution, we take *m* slack variables and therefore they are assigned zero values. As a result of this, we get $s_1 = b_1, s_2 = b_2, ..., S_m = bm$.

Step IV. The above equations, so obtained are summarized in a tableau 1 and thereafter, attempts are made to reach at optimal solution which are explained in the next steps. **The structure of the table is shown and explained below :**

Initial Simplex Tableau

C_j (Contribution per unit)			*c_1*	*c_2*	...	*c_n*	*0*	*0*	....	*0*	*Minimum ratio*
C_B	*Basic Variable*	*Solution Values*	*Coefficient Matrix*				*Identity Matrix*				
			x_1	x_2	...	x_n	s_1	s_2	...	s_m	
0	S_1	b_1	a_{11}	a_{12}	...	a_{1n}	1	0	...	0	
0	S_2	b_2	a_{21}	a_{22}	...	a_{2n}	0	1	...	0	
⋮	⋮	⋮	⋮								
0	S_m	b_m	a_{m1}	a_{m2}	...	a_{mn}	0	0	...	1	
Contribution Loss per unit	$Z_j = 0$ $\Sigma C_B a_{ij}$	0	...	0	0	0	...	0			
Net Contribution per unit	$C_j - Z_j$	C_1	C_2	...	C_n	0	0	0	...	0	

(*a*) The first row C_j, is called as objective row. It shows the coefficient of variables in the objective function. These value would remain same in the succeeding tables.

(*b*) The second row shows major column headings for the table and they would also remain unchanged in the succeeding tables of the simplex method.

(*c*) The first column C_B is known as **objective column**. It gives the coefficient of the current basic variables. The second column, known as **'Basic variables'** indicates basic variable. It is also known as **product Mix column.** In the initial simplex tableau, the basic variables are slack variables (for maximisation problems). The third column is known as **'solution values'**. It is also known as **quantity column.**

When we reach to an optimal solution, the values under basic variables and solution values indicates the product to be manufactured along with the respective quantity.

(*d*) The body matrix shows the coefficient of the decision variables in the constraint set. The coefficient basically reflects physical rate of substitution. The **coefficient** (a_{ij}) lies at the intersection of a basic variable (s_i) and a non basic variable (x_j). This implies that if we wish to produce x_j units then a_{ij} units of s_i must be sacrificed.

(*e*) The identity matrix in the initial simplex tableau represent coefficient of the slack variables which have been added to the constraints to make them equations.

(*f*) The Z_j row shows the contribution loss per units. It is obtained by multiplying entries of a given column with the entries in the C_B column and adding them *i.e.*, $\Sigma C_B\ a_{ij}$. The Z_j entry gives current value of the objective function. The entries will be equal to zero in the initial simplex tableau.

(*g*) The final or last row labelled $C_j - Z_j$ is known **as net evaluation row.** The values in this row represent the net contribution to the objective function which occurs by introducing one unit of the respective column.

Uses of row '$C_j - Z_j$'

(*i*) *In case of maximization problem, if all the elements in the index row are negative then the current solution is optimal. If some positive number exists, the current solution can be further improved by removing one basic variable from the basis and replacing it with non basic variable.*

(*ii*) *The values in the $C_j - Z_j$ row under a given slack variable reflects shadow price for the resource of that constraint in which this slack variable is introduced. For example, if the value under a given slack variable in $C_j - Z_j$ row is –7, it implies shadow price for the resource constraint in which the respective slack variable has been introduced to convert inequality into equality is +7. This means we can increase the contribution to the objective function by +7 units if we can have additional unit of that resource. Thus, if one unit of that resource is available at a price less than 7, the manager can pay for it because the net benefit would be more.*

Step V : After having set up initial simplex tableau the next step is to observe the values in the index row $C_j - Z_j$. *As long as any positive value remains in the* $C_j - Z_j$ row, there is scope for improvement in the solution (for maximization problem).

Step VI : Further improvement in the basic feasible solution can be done by replacing one current basic variable (called the departing variable) by a new non basic variable (called the entering variable). In order to find the entering variable and departing variable, the following steps shall be followed.

Step VII : Identify the largest positive entry in $C_j - Z_j$ row. The column in which entry is lying is referred as key column. This column helps in identifying the non basic variable which will replace a particular basic variable. The non basic variable of this column is known as entering variable.

Step VIII : In order to find out which basic variable is to be replaced *i.e.,* departing variable, the entries of the solution column are to be divided by corresponding entry in the key column and the ratios are calculated. The row that corresponds to the smallest non negative quotient is called the key row. The number that lies at the inter sections of the key column and the key row of a given tableau is called the **key number/key element.**

Step IX : After having identified the key element, a new tableau is designed by replacing the old values with new values.

In order to change the numbers in the key row, the following formula is used.

$$\text{New key row elements} = \frac{\text{old key row elements}}{\text{key number}}$$

To change the non-key rows, the following formula is used.

New non-key row = old non key row – (key column entry) x new key row.

Step X : Calculate Z_j *and finally* $C_j - Z_j$. If any positive number exists in this row, again key column shall be identified and replacement of non basic variable with basic variable shall be done after calculating minimum ratio and finding key element. This process is repeated till we get an optimal solution.

The above steps would become more clear from the following example.

Example 2 : **A company makes two types of product, PI and PII. Profit per PI is Rs. 2 and profit per PII is Rs. 3. These product are manufactured using three machines M_1, M_2 and M_3. The time required for each product in hours and total time available in hours per week on each machine are as follows :**

Machine	*PI*	*PII*	*Available Time*
M_1	2	2	20
M_2	3	4	50
M_3	1	3	10

How may units of each product shall be manufactured to maximize profit.

Solution.

Step 1. Let x and y be the number of product *PI* and *PII* to be produced per week respectively. The mathematical formulation of the given problem is :

Maximize $Z = 2x + 3y$

Subject to $2x + 2y \le 20$

$3x + 4y \le 50$

$x + 3y \le 10$

$x, y \ge 0$

Step 2. **Introduce Slack Variable :** In order to convert the constraints into equality, we need to introduce slask variable s_1, s_2 and s_3. Now, we have above equations as

Maximize $Z = 2x + 3y + 0s_1 + 0s_2 + 0s_3$

Subject to $2x + 2y + s_1 = 20$

$$3x + 4y + s_2 = 50$$

$$x + 3y + s_3 = 10$$

$$x, y, s_1, s_2, s_3 \geq 0$$

Step 3. The next step is to find initial basic feasible solution. We have 3 equations and 5 variable. Therefore we have to set $(n - m)$ *i.e.*, $(5 - 3) = 2$ variables as zero.

Put $x = 0$ and $y = 0$, we have initial basic feasible solution as

$x = 0, y = 0, s_1 = 20, s_2 = 50, s_3 = 10.$

[*Student may note that in case of simple maximization problem, equate such variable as zero which can make objective function Z = 0*].

The initial basic feasible solution is summarised below

Simplex Table I

$C_j \rightarrow$	*Basic*	*Solution*	*2*	*3*	*0*	*0*	*0*	*Ratio*
↓	*Variable*		x	y	s_1	s_2	s_3	
0	s_1	20	2	2	1	0	0	10
0	s_2	50	3	4	0	1	0	12.5
0	s_3	10	1	(3)	0	0	1	3.33
	Z_j	0	0	0	0	0	0	
	$C_j - Z_j$		2	3 ↑	0	0	0	

Step 4. $C_j - Z_j$ has non negative elements therefore further scope of improvement is possible. Since $C_j - Z_j$ has highest non negative element as 3 therefore 'Y-column' is key column. The elements in the 'solution' column would be divided by the corresponding elements in Y-Column. The minimum ratio computed is 3.33. The row corresponding to minimum ratio and the column corresponding to the highest positive element intersect at the key element **3.**

Step 5. The above facts indicate that s_3 is departing variable and y is entering variable. Now the simplex table would be rewritten with following changes.

(*a*) 's_3' would be replaced with 'y' and C_j *will have coefficient as* 3, i.e., *coefficient of* y.

(*b*) The element in the key row would be replaced by new elements, which are calculated using the formula.

$$\text{New element} = \frac{\text{old element in key row}}{\text{key element}}$$

(*c*) The element in the non key row are also replaced by new elements, which are calculated by using the formula.

New element = Old non key row element – (key column entry) X (new key row)

∴ In the given situation

New element in the key row would be

10/3, 1/3 1, 0, 0, 1/3

and new element in the non key row would be

Row S_1	***Row*** S_2
$20 - 2 \times 10/3 = 40/3$	$50 - 4 \times 10/3 = 110/3$
$2 - 2 \times 1/3 = 4/3$	$3 - 4 \times 1/3 = 5/3$
$2 - 2 / 1 = 0$	$4 - 4 \times 1 = 0$
$1 - 2 \times 0 = 1$	$0 - 4 \times 0 = 0$
$0 - 2 \times 0 = 0$	$1 - 4 \times 0 = 1$
$0 - 2 \times 1/3 = -2/3$	$0 - 4 / 1/3 = -4/3$

Using the calculated elements, the new table would be

Simplex Table II

$C_j \rightarrow$	*Basic*	*Solution*	*2*	*3*	*0*	*0*	*0*	*Ratio*
↓	*Variable*		*x*	*y*	s_1	s_2	s_3	
0	s_1	40/3	(4/3)	0	1	0	–2/3	10
0	s_2	110/3	5/3	0	0	1	–4/3	22
3	*y*	10/3	1/3	1	0	0	1/3	10
	Z_j	10	1	3	0	0	+1	
	$C_j - Z_j$		1 ↑	0	0		–1	

Since $C_j - Z_j$ has non negative element which indicates further scope of improvement. The highest non negative element is 1 therefore '*x*' is a key column. In order to find key row, divide value under solution by the corresponding elements under *x*. Though, we aregetting minimum ratio as 10 in two cases but row S_1 would be taken as key row because in other case, both departing variable and entering variable are non-basic variables and the replacement of basic variable with non-basic variables is preferred against replacement of a non basic variable against another non-basic variable. The point of intersection of key row and key column is 4/3, which is key element.

Step 6. The next step is to determine new element in the key row and non key row which will be calculated in the same manner as above. Similarly, we will make simplex tableau-III

Simplex Table III

$C_j \rightarrow$	*Basic*	*Solution*	*2*	*3*	*0*	*0*	*0*	*Ratio*
↓	*Variable*		*x*	*y*	s_1	s_2	s_3	
2	*x*	10	1	0	3/4	0	–1/2	
0	s_2	20	0	0	–5/4	1	–1/2	
3	*y*	0	0	(1)	–1/4	0	1/2	
	Z_j	20	2	3	3/4	0	1/2	
	$C_j - Z_j$		0	0 ↑	–3/4	0	–1/2	

In the above table since no element in the row $C_j - Z_j$ is non-negative, it indicates that optimal solution has been arrived.

Economic Interpretation of the Optimal Solution

The optimal solution obtained in the form of table III provides many useful information for decision making, which are briefly discussed.

1. First of all, the second and third column should be interpreted *i.e.*,

Basic Variable	*Solution*
x	10
s_2	20
y	0

These two columns when studied simultaneously, shows the type and number of units to be manufactured. It can be observed, according to the above table, firm should manufacture 10 units of x and no units of y. Appearance of slack variable in the table indicates that there is some unutilized capacity. Since we have s_2 equal to 20, it shows that there is unutilized capacity.

2. The numbers appearing under the slack variables helps is analysing change in contribution due to increase in resources. For example, refer column 's_1' of the final table. Study, this column in conjuction with basic variable and solution, as under:–

Bacis Variable	*Solution*	S_1
x	10	3/4
s_2	20	–19/4
y	0	–1/4

Now, corresponding to intersection of x-row and s_1 column, we have positive number 3/4. This means if 1 unit of resource 1 *i.e.* one units of usage on machine I is increased, it would increase the production of x by 3/4 units but it would decrease the production of y by 1/4 units, as we have negative value (-1/4) at the intersection of s_1 and y. In order to ascertain change in contribution due to any change in resource I, we will have to focus contribution column as well, along with the above facts.

Contribution	*B.V.*	*Solution*	S_1
2	x	10	3/4
0	s_2	20	–19/4
3	y	0	–1/4

Contribution due to x is 2 and due to y is 3. Therefore change in contribution due to increase in one unit of s_1 will be

$$\text{Change in contribution} = 2 \times 3/4 + 3 \times (-1/4) = \frac{6}{4} - \frac{3}{4} = \frac{3}{4}$$

∴ Contribution will increase by 3/4 for every unit increase of S_1.

3. **The number under the slack variable in index row *i.e.* $(C_j - Z_j)$ row are known as shadow prices or accounting prices.** A positive number in the index row indicates a reduction in the objective function due to increase in one unit of resource in which the slack variable was introduced and vice versa. For example, in the given case, we have numbers –3/4, 0 and –1/2 under s_1, s_2 and s_3 respectively. Thus, the shadow prices of resource I, II and III are –3/4, 0 and –1/2 respectively. Since, negative number *i.e.* –3/4 exist at the intersection of s_1 and the index row $C_j - Z_j$, it indicates if one unit of S_1 is increased, the value of objective function would increase by 3/4. This has also been proved in the previous step. Thus, a manager can make use of this information by comparing the cost of one unit of additional resource with net increase in the objective function. **A manager**

shall attempt to *increase* additional resources only when the values under slack variable in the index row are negative. In this case, if the cost of one unit of s_1 is less than 3/4, then only it is beneficial to increase the resource corresponding to s_1.

4. The table also helps in studying change due to change in product mix. For example, we have coefficient matrix along with Basic variable (B. V.). and solution as under

B.V.	*Solution*	*x*	*y*
x	10	1	0
s_2	20	0	–5/3
y	0	0	1

If one unit of product PI is produced, it would reduce production of x, s_2, y by 1, 0, 0 respectively. Likewise, if one unit of PII is produced, it would reduce production of x, s_2, y by 0, 0, 1 respectively.

***Example 3* : Given the simplex tableau for a maximum problem of linear programming :**

C_j	*Product Mix*	x_1	x_2	s_1	s_2	*Quantity*
4	x_2	**1**	**1**	**1**	**0**	**6**
0	s_2	**1**	**0**	**–1**	**1**	**2**
	C_j		**3**	**4**	**0**	**0**

(i) Test whether the above table gives optimum solution. If not, improve it and find the optimum solution.

(ii) If s_1 and s_2 are slack variables at machine I and machine II, what is the maximum price you will like to pay for 1 hour of each machine?

***Solution* :** The table to be assessed is given below:

$C_j \rightarrow$ ↓	*Product Mix*	*Quantity*	*3* x_1	*4* x_2	*0* s_1	*0* s_2
4	x_2	6	1	1	1	0
0	s_2	2	1	0	–1	1
	Z_j	24	4	4	4	0
	$C_j - Z_j$		–1	0	–4	0

(i) Since in the $C_j - Z_j$ row, all entries are zero or negative; it shows that the above table gives optimum solution. The optimum solution is: $x_1 = 0$, $x_2 = 6$ and maximum value is $Z = 24$.

(ii) The slack variable s_1 corresponding to the first constraint in $C_j - Z_j$ row has –4 in the final table. It indicates that the shadow price for machine 1 is +4. This means that we could increase the objective function by 4 if we had an additional unit of machine I. It is the maximum price one should pay for 1 hour of this machine. Likewise, the shadow price of machine II is nil. An additional unit of the second machine won't help, since this machine is not being fully utilised.

***Example 4* : Given below is a table obtained after few iterations using simplex method, to solve a linear programming problem to maximise total contribution from product *A* and product *B*.**

Basic Variable	x_1	x_2	s_1	s_2	s_3	Quantity
x_2	**0**	**1**	**3/5**	**–2/5**	**0**	**300**
x_1	1	0	–2/5	3/5	0	300
s_3	0	0	–1/5	–1/5	1	400
C_j		8.5	10.5	0	0	0

Give short answers to the following giving reasons :

(i) Is the above solution optimal?

(ii) Is the above solution feasible?

(iii) Does the problem have alternative solution? If so, find the other solution.

(iv) What are the shadow prices of the resources?

Solution : In order to answer the given question, let us first rewrite the given table in the normal way, as under:

$C_j \rightarrow$ ↓	Basic Variable	Quantity	8.5 x_1	10.5 x_2	0 s_1	0 s_2	0 s_3
10.5	x_2	300	0	1	3/5	–2/5	0
8.5	x_1	300	1	0	–2/5	3/5	0
0	s_3	400	0	0	–1/5	–1/5	1
	Z_j	5700	8.5	10.5	2.9	0.9	0
	C_j Z_j		0	0	–2.9	–2.9	0

(i) In case of maximisation problem, optimal solution occurs when there is no non-negative number in the $C_j - Z_j$ row. Thus, the given solution is an optimal solution because all the entries in $C_j - Z_j$ row are negative or zero.

(ii) Yes, it is feasible because optimal solution is always feasible.

(iii) Since none of the non-basic variables has a zero $C_j - Z_j$ entry in the final simplex table, therefore, it does not have any alternative solution.

(iv) Shadow prices of the resources are 2.0, 0.9, and 0 respectively.

Example 5 : **Two materials *A* and *B* are required to construct tables and book cases. For one table 12 units of *A* and 16 units of *B* are needed while for a book case 16 units of *A* and of *B* are required. The profit on a book case is Rs. 25 and Rs. 20 on a table. 100 units of material *A* and 80 units of *B* are available. How many book cases and tables be produced to have maximum profit?**

Formulate this is a linear programming problem and solve by simplex method.

Solution : Let x denote the number of tables and y denote the number of book cases produced. Now, the above problem can be mathematically formulated as under :

Maximize $Z = 20x + 25y$

Subject to the constraints :

$$12x + 16y \leq 100$$

$$16x + 18y \le 80$$

$$x, y \ge 0$$

Introducing slack variables s_1 and s_2 to convert inequality into equality, we can restate the problem in terms of equations :

Maximize $Z = 20x + 25y + 0s_1 + 0s_2$

subject to the constraints :

$$12x + 16y + s_1 = 100$$

$$16x + 8y + s_2 = 80$$

$$x, y, s_1, s_2 \ge 0$$

Since there are 4 variables and 2 equations,

∴ We have to set $(n - m) = (4 - 2) = 2$ variables as zero to get initial feasible solution.

An initial basic feasible solution is

$$x = 0, y = 0, s_1 = 100 \text{ and } s_2 = 80$$

at which Z = 0. The initial simplex tableau corresponding to this solution is Tableau 1.

Simplex Tableau I

$C_j \rightarrow$ ↓	*Basic Variable*	*Solution*	*20* x	*25* y	*0* s_1	*0* s_2	*Ratio*
0	s_1	100	12	(16)	1	0	←100/16 = 25/4
0	s_2	80	16	8	0	1	80/8 = 10
	Z_j	0	0	0	0	0	
	$C_j - Z_j$		20	25↑	0	0	

You may recall that the optimal solutions in case of maximisation problem is achieved when there is no non negative number in the $(C_j - Z_j)$ row. Since there is a positive $C_j - Z_j$ entry, we must repeat the previous steps. The largest positive entry is 25. Thus y is the entering variable and y-column is the key column. To find the departing variable, we divide each entry of the "solution" column by the corresponding positive entry of the key column. The smallest nonnegative ratio is $\frac{25}{4}$. Therefore, s_1 is the departing variable. The key number, 16, is circled. We obtain second tableau using elementary row operations, as above.

Simplex Tableau II

$C_j \rightarrow$ ↓	*Basic Variable*	*Solution*	*20* x	*25* y	*0* s_1	*0* s_2	*Ratio*
25	y	25/4	3/4	1	1/16	0	25/3
0	s_2	30	(10)	0	–1/2	1	←3
	Z_j	625/4	75/4	25	25/16	0	
	$C_j - Z_j$		5/4↑	0	–25/16	0	

Again there is a positive entry in the $C_j - Z_j$ row, therefore current solution is not optimal and we must continue our process. The entering variable is now x. The smallest nonnegative ratio is 3. Thus s_2 is the departing variable and the key number, 10, is circled. Using elementary row operations, we have Tableau III.

Simplex Tableau III

$C_j \rightarrow$ ↓	Basic Variable	Solution	20 x	25 y	0 s_1	0 s_2
25	y	4	0	1	1/10	–3/40
20	x	3	1	0	–1/20	1/10
	Z_j	160	20	25	3/2	1/8
	$C_j - Z_j$		0	0	–3/2	–1/8

Now all $C_j - Z_j$ entries in Tableau III are zero or negative. This implies optimal solution has been obtained. Maximum value of Z is 160 which occurs when $x = 3$ and $y = 4$.

Example 6 : **A company produces 2 types of leather belts - Type A and B. Contribution per belt is Rs. 4 for type *A* and Rs. 3 for type *B*. The time requirements of one belt of type *A* and *B* are in the ratio 2:3. Time available is sufficient to produce 500 belts of type *A*. The leather is sufficient for only 400 belts. Belt *A* required a fancy buckles and only 200 fancy buckles are available.**

(*i*) Formulate above as a linear programming problem.

(*ii*) Solve it by simplex method and comment on this optimum solution.

Solution : Let x donote the number of belts of type A and y denote the number of belts of type B produced per unit time. Then the appropriate mathematical formulation of the problem is :

Maximize $Z = 4x + 3y$

Subject to the constraints : $2x + 3y \leq 1000$

$$x + y \leq 400$$

$$x \leq 200$$

$$x, y \geq 0.$$

Introduce slack variables s_1, s_2 and s_3 to convert the constraint inequalities into equation, the given problem can be restated as follows:

Maximize $Z = 4x + 3y + 0s_1 + 0s_2 + 0s_3$

Subject to $2x + 3y + s_1 = 1000$

$$x + y + s_2 = 400$$

$$x + s_3 = 200$$

$$x, y, s_1, s_2, s_3 \geq 0.$$

Since there are five variables and three equations, set (5-3) = 2 variables as zero to get initial basic feasible solution

An initial basic feasible solution will be

$$x = 0,\ y = 0,\ s_1 = 1000,\ s_2 = 400,\ s_3 = 200$$

at which Z = 0. The initial simplex tableau corresponding to this solution is:

Simplex Tableau I

$C_j \rightarrow$	Basic	Solution	4	3	0	0	0	Ratio
↓	Variable		x	y	s_1	s_2	s_3	
0	s_1	1000	2	3	1	0	0	500
0	s_2	400	1	1	0	1	0	400
0	s_3	200	(1)	0	0	0	1	←200
	Z_j	0	0	0	0	0	0	
	$C_j - Z_j$		4↑	3	0	0	0	

Since, 4 is the largest positive number in the $C_j - Z_j$ row therefore x is the entering variable. The smallest nonnegative quotient in the ratio column is 200 therefore s_3 is the departing variable and the key number, 1, is circled. Using elementary row operation, we get Tableau II.

Simplex Tableau II

$C_j \rightarrow$	Basic	Solution	4	3	0	0	0	Ratio
↓	Variable		x	y	s_1	s_2	s_3	
0	s_1	600	0	(3)	1	0	–2	←200
0	s_2	200	0	1	0	1	–1	200
4	x	200	1	0	0	0	1	–
	Z_j	800	4	0	0	0	4	
	$C_j - Z_j$		0	3↑	0	0	–4	

Now y is the entering variable. Since there is a tie for the smallest quotient, we can choose either s_1 or s_2 as the departing variable. We should give preference to s_1 as it will provide higher contribution 3 than 1 by s_2. The key number, 3, is circled. Now the simplex tableau III will be obtained as under.

Simplex Tableau III

$C_j \rightarrow$	Basic	Solution	4	3	0	0	0
↓	Variable		x	y	s_1	s_2	s_3
3	y	200	0	1	1/3	0	–2/3
0	s_2	0	0	0	–1/3	1	–1/3
4	x	200	1	0	0	0	1
	Z_j	1400	4	3	1	0	2
	$C_j - Z_j$		0	0	–1	0	–2

Now it can be observed that all $C_j - Z_j$ entries in Tableau III are zero or negative therefore optimal solution has been obtained. The maximum value of Z is 1400 which occurs when $x = 200$ and $y = 200$. It shall be observed that optimal solution is ***degenerate*** because Tableau III corresponds to a basic feasible solution, in which a basic variable s_2 is zero.

Example 7 : **Following data are available for a firm which manufactures three items *A, B* and *C*:**

Product	*Time Required in Hours*		*Profit*
	Assembly	*Finishing*	*In Rs.*
A	*10*	*2*	*80*
B	*4*	*5*	*60*
C	*5*	*4*	*30*
Firm's Capacity	*2000*	*1009*	

Express the above data in the form of linear programming problem to maximize the profit from the production and solve it by simplex method.

Solution : Let x_1, x_2, x_3 denote number of units of product *A, B* an *C* respectively to be manufactured. Therefore, the above problem would be formulated as under:

Maximize $Z = 80x_1 + 60x_2 + 30x_3$

Subject to the constraints $10x_1 + 4x_2 + 5x_3 \leq 2000$

$$2x_1 + 5x_2 + 4x_3 \leq 1009$$

$$x_1, x_2, x_3 \geq 0$$

Introduce slack variables s_1 and s_2 to convert the constraint inequalities into equations. The given problem can be restated as follows:

Maximize $Z = 80x_1 + 60x_2 + 30x_3 + 0s_1 + 0s_2$

Subject to $10x_1 + 4x_2 + 5x_3 + s_1 = 2000$

$$2x_1 + 5x_2 + 4x_3 + s_2 = 1009$$

$$x_1, x_2, x_3, s_1, s_2 \geq 0.$$

Since there are 5 variables and two equations, therefore, set (5–2) = 3 variables as zero to get initial basic feasible solution.

The initial simplex tableau is Tableau I.

Simplex Tableau I

$C_j \rightarrow$ ↓	*Basic Variable*	*Solution*	*80* x	*60* y	*30* s_1	*0* s_2	*0* s_3	*Ratio*
0	s_1	2000	(10)	4	5	1	0	←200
0	s_2	1009	2	5	4	0	1	1009/2
	Z_j	0	0	0	0	0	0	
	$C_j - Z_j$		80↑	60	0	0	0	

Since $C_j - Z_j$ has non negative numbers, it shows that this is not an optimal solution. The highest value in $C_j - Z_j$ row is 80, therefore, x_1 is the entering variable The smallest nonnegative quotient in the ratio column is 200, so s_1 is the departing variable and the key number, 10, is circled. Using elementary row operations, we get Tableau II.

Simplex Tableau II

$C_j \rightarrow$	Basic	Solution	80	60	30	0	0	Ratio
$\downarrow$	Variable		x_1	x_2	x_3	s_1	s_2	
80	x_1	200	1	2/5	1/2	1/10	0	500
0	s_2	609	0	(21/5)	3	–1/5	1	←145
	Z_j	16000	80	32	40	8	0	
	$C_j - Z_j$		0	28↑	–10	–8	0	

Again, there is a positive entry in the $C_j - Z_j$ row, hence the current solution is not optimal. The entering variable is now x_2. The smallest nonnegative quotient in the ratio column is 145. Thus s_2 is the departing variable and 21/5 is the key number. Using elementary row operations, we have Tableau III.

Simplex Tableau III

$C_j \rightarrow$	Basic	Solution	80	60	30	0	0
$\downarrow$	Variable		x_1	x_2	x_3	s_1	s_2
80	x_1	142	1	0	3/14	5/42	–2/21
60	x_2	145	0	1	5/7	–1/21	5/21
	Z_j	20060	80	60	60	20/3	20/3
	$C_j - Z_j$		0	0	–30	–20/3	–20/3

Now, it can be observed that all entries in $C_j - Z_j$ row of tableau III are zero or negative. This implies optimum solution has been obtained and the maximum value of Z is 20060 which occurs when $x_1 = 142$, $x_2 = 145$ and $x_3 = 0$.

Special situations in case of Simplex Method

Unbounded Solutions. Sometimes, while solving LP problem through simplex method, we may come across a situation when all the entries in the minimum ratio column are either infinite or negative. Logically, it implies that there is a decision variable which can be increased indefinitely without violating a constraint on the solution.

Consider the example given below.

Maximize $Z = 4x + 6y + z$

Subject to $9x + 2y - 2z \leq 5$

$4x + 2y - z \leq 2$

$x - 4y + z \leq 3$

$x, y, z \geq 0$

Introduce slack variables in the constraints to convert inequality to equation.

We have

Maximize $Z = 4x + 6y + z + 0s_1 + 0s_2 + 0s_3$

Subject to $9x + 2y - 2z + s_1 = 5$

$$4x + 2y - z + s_2 = 2$$

$$x - 4y + z + s_3 = 3$$

$$x, y, z, s_1, s_2, s_3 \geq 0$$

Initial basic feasible solution would be

C	B	S	4	6	1	0	0	0	Ratio
			x	y	z	s_1	s_2	s_3	
0	s_1	5	9	2	–2	1	0	0	2.5
0	s_2	2	4	(2)	–1	0	1	0	1
0	s_3	3	1	–4	1	0	0	1	–3/4
	Z_j		0	0	0	0	0	0	
	$C_j - Z_j$		4	↑6	1	0	0	0	

Key element 2 has been circled. Now table II will be obtained using the same steps as explained earlier.

Simplex Tableau II

C	B	S	4	6	1	0	0	0	Ratio
			x	y	z	s_1	s_2	s_3	
0	s_1	1	3	0	–1/3	1	–3/2	0	–3
6	y	1	2	1	–1/2	0	1/2	0	–2
0	s_3	7	9	0	–1	0	2	1	–7
	Z_j	6	12	6	–3	0	3	0	
	$C_j - Z_j$		–8	0	4↑	0	–3	0	

Thus, it can be observed that all value in the minimum ratio column are negative. This is a case of unbounded solution.

Multiple Optimal Solution

When we have zero entry in the $C_j - Z_j$ row under non basic variable of the final simplex tableau, it shows that other alternative optimal solutions are feasible which can be achieved by reiterating the steps. However, we should choose a non basic variable with a zero $C_j - Z_j$ entry as entering variable.

Consider the following example

Maximize $Z = 3x_1 + 2x_2 + 5x_3$

Subject to $x_1 + 2x_2 + 2x_3 \leq 8$

$$3x_1 + 2x_2 + 6x_3 \leq 12$$

$$2x_1 + 3x_2 + 3x_3 \leq 12$$

$$x_1, x_2, x_3 \geq 0$$

Introduce slack variables s_1, s_2, s_3 to convert constraint inequality to equality, we have above equations as

Maximize $Z = 3x_1 + 2x_2 + 5x_3 + 0s_1 + 0s_2 + 0s_3$

Subject to $x_1 + 2x_2 + 2x_3 + s_1 = 8$

$$3x_1 + 2x_2 + 6x_3 + s_2 = 12$$

$$2x_1 + 3x_2 + 3x_3 + s_3 = 12$$

$$x_1, x_2, x_3, s_1, s_2, s_3 \geq 0$$

An initial basic feasible solution is

$x_1 = x_2 = x_3 = 0$ and $s_1 = 8$, $s_2 = 12$, $s_3 = 12$.

We get the following simplex tables

Table I

$C_j \rightarrow$	Basic	Solution	3	2	5	0	0	0	Ratio
↓	Variable		x_1	x_2	x_3	s_1	s_2	s_3	
0	s_1	8	1	2	2	1	0	0	4
0	s_2	12	3	2	(6)	0	1	0	2←
0	s_3	12	2	3	4	0	0	1	3
	Z_j	0	0	0	0	0	0	0	
	$C_j - Z_j$		3	2	↑5	0	0	0	

Table II

$C_j \rightarrow$	Basic	Solution	3	2	5	0	0	0	Ratio
↓	Variable		x_1	x_2	x_3	s_1	s_2	s_3	
0	s_1	4	0	4/3	0	1	–1/3	0	–
5	x_3	2	(1/2)	1/3	1	0	1/6	0	4←
0	s_3	4	0	5/3	0	0	–2/3	1	–
	Z_j	10	5/2	5/3	5	0	5/6	0	
	$C_j - Z_j$		1/2↑	1/3	0	0	–5/6	0	

Table III

$C_j \rightarrow$	Basic	Solution	3	2	5	0	0	0	Ratio
↓	Variable		x_1	x_2	x_3	s_1	s_2	s_3	
0	s_1	4	0	4/3	0	1	–1/3	0	3
3	x_1	4	1	2/3	2	0	1/3	0	6
0	s_3	4	0	5/3	0	0	–2/3	1	12/5
	Z_j	12	3	2	6	0	1	0	
	$C_j - Z_j$		0	0	–1	0	–1	0	

In the above table, all $C_j - Z_j \leq 0$, hence it gives optimal solution with $x_1 = 4$, $x_2 = 0$ and $x_3 = 0$. The maximum value of Z is 12. However, this optimal solution is not unique because x_2 is a non-basic variable and the corresponding entry in $C_j - Z_j$ is 0. In order to get an alternative optimal solution, we shall perform one more iteration treating x_2 as an entering variable.

Thus, the next table would be given as :

Table IV

$C_j \rightarrow$	Basic	Solution	3	2	5	0	0	0	Ratio
$\downarrow$	Variable		x_1	x_2	x_3	s_1	s_2	s_3	
0	s_1	4/5	0	0	0	1	–1/5	–4/5	
3	x_1	12/5	1	0	2	0	3/5	–2/5	
0	x_2	12/5	0	1	0	0	–2/5	3/5	
	Z_j	12	3	2	6	0	1	0	
	$C_j - Z_j$		0	0	–1	0	–1	0	

The above table gives the optimal solution.

Degeneracy

Degeneracy is a situation which arise while solving linear problem when a tie is observed between two values in $C_j - Z_j$ row for deciding entering variable of departing variable. In order to find entering variable in case of maximization problem, we try to observe largest positive entry in $C_j - Z_j$ row. In this case, we may have two equal largest positive number in $C_j - Z_j$ row. Likewise, while deciding departing values, we may across a situation where there are two ratios of equal value. Thus, there may be tie in terms of minimum ratio. In such cases, selection is made on arbitrary basis. As a result of this, we may reach back to the first table. This is called cycling. When cycling occurs, we may achieve optimum solution. However, it shall be noted, when there is tie between a slack and artificial variables to leave the basic variable, the preference shall be given to artificial variable.

Consider the example

Maximize $Z = 2x + 3y$

Subject to constraint

$$2x + 2y \leq 20$$
$$3x + 4y \leq 50$$
$$x + 3y \leq 10$$
$$x, y \geq 0$$

The initial simplex table would be given as

Simplex Tableau I

C	B	S	2	3	0	0	0	Ratio
			x	y	s_1	s_2	s_3	
0	s_1	20	2	2	1	0	0	10
0	s_2	50	3	4	0	1	0	12.5
0	s_3	10	1	**3**	0	0	1	3.3←
	Z_j	0		0	0	0	0	
	$C_j - Z_j$		2	3↑	0	0	0	

Simpex Tableau II

C	B	S	2	3	0	0	0	Ratio
			x	y	s_1	s_2	s_3	
0	s_1	20	2	2	1	0	0	10
0	s_1	40/3	4/3	0	1	0	–2/3	10
0	s_2	110/3	5/3	0	–4	1	–4/3	22
3	y	10/3	1/3	1	0	0	1/3	10
	Z_j	10	1	3	0	0	1	
	$C_j - Z_j$		1	0	0	0	–1	

It can be observed from the above table, row s_1 and y have same minimum ratio, 10. Thus, it is a case of degeneracy.

NON FEASIBLE SOLUTION

A solution is called feasible if it satisfies all the constraints and non-negative conditions. However, we may come across a situation where the constraints may be inconsistent and there may be no feasible solution to the problem. Such a situation is called infeasibility. Further, if an artificial variable appears in the basis of the solution, the solution is also non-feasible.

Exercise 4.1

Solve the following using simplex method

Q. 1 Maximize $Z = 2x + 5y$

Subject to $x + 4y \leq 24$

$3x + y \leq 21$

$x + y \leq 9$

$x, y \geq 0$ $[z = 33,\ x = 4,\ y = 5]$

Q. 2 Maximize $Z = 3x + 6y + 2z$

Subject to $3x + 4y + 2z \leq 2$

$x + 3y + 2z \leq 1$

$x, y, z \geq 0$ $[Z = 12/5,\ x = 3/5,\ y = 6/5]$

Q. 3 Maximize $Z = 25x_1 + 25x_2$

Subject to $10x_1 \leq 5000$

$15x_1 + 10x_2 \leq 9000$

$30x_2 \leq 12000$

$x_1, x_2 \geq 0$ $[Z = 15000,\ x_1 = 200,\ x_2 = 400]$

Q. 4 Maximize $Z = 4x_1 + 6x_2$

Subject to $x_1 + 3x_1 \leq 240$

$$3x_1 + 4x_2 \leq 370$$
$$2x_1 + x_2 \leq 180$$
$$x_1, x_2 \geq 0 \qquad [Z = 540,\ x_1 = 30,\ x_2 = 70]$$

Q. 5 Maximize $Z = 8y_1 + 12y_2 + 9y_3$

Subject to $2y_1 + 6y_2 + y_3 \leq 8.50$

$$y_1 + y_2 + 3y_3 \leq 4$$

and $y_1, y_2, y_3 \geq 0 \qquad [Z = 65/2;\ y_1 = 31/8,\ y_2 = 1/3,\ y_3 = 0]$

Q. 6 Maximize $Z = 30x_1 + 40x_2 + 20x_3$

Subject to $100x_1 + 120x_2 + 70x_3 \leq 10{,}0000$

$$7x_1 + 10x_2 + 8x_3 \leq 8000$$
$$x_1 + x_2 + x_3 \leq 1000$$
$$x_1, x_2, x_3 \geq 0 \qquad [Z = 32500;\ x_1 = 250,\ x_2 = 650,\ x_3 = 0]$$

Q. 7 A toy manufacturer produces two type of dolls; a basic version-doll *A* and a deluxe version doll *B*. Each doll of type *B* takes twice as long as to produce as one doll of type *A*. The company has time to make maximum of 2000 doll of type *A* per day. The supply of plastic is sufficient to produce 1,500 dolls per day and each type requires equal amount of it. The deluxe version, *i.e.*, type *B* requires a fancy dress of which there are 600 per day available. If the company makes a profit of Rs. 3 and Rs. 5 per doll, respectively, on doll *A* and *B*, how many of each should be produced per day in order to maximize profit? Solve it by simplex method.

[Type *A* = 1000. Type *B* = 500, Max. Profit = Rs 5500]

Q. 8 A firm has available 240, 370 and 180 kilos of wood, plastic and steel respectively. The firm produces two products *A* and *B*. Each unit of product *A* requires 1, 3 and 2 kilos of wood, plastic and steel respectively. The corresponding requirements for each unit of *B* are 3, 4 and 1 respectively. If *A* sells for Rs. 4 and *B* for Rs. 6, determine how many units of *A* and *B* should be produced to obtain the maximum gross income.

Formulate the problem mathematically. Solve the problem by simplex method.

$[x = 30,\ y = 70,\ z = 540]$

Q. 9 Hens of two types are available. Type *A* costs Rs. 8/- per hen and type *B*, Rs. 10/ per hen. Type *A* lays on an average 4 eggs per week and type *B*, 5 eggs per week. Eggs sell at 50 paise each. The feeding cost of type *A* hen is Rs. 1.50 per week and of type *B* is Rs. 1.90 per week. Maximum of Rs. 180/- is to be spent on purchasing hens. How many of each type are to be bought to have maximum profit? Assume that it is not possible to house more than 20 hens at a time.

(*i*) Formulate this as a linear programming problem.

(*ii*) Solve it by simplex method. $[x = 10,\ y = 10,\ Z = 11]$

Q. 10 A farmer has 1000 acres of land on which he can grow corn, wheat or soyabeans. Each acre of corn costs Rs. 100 for preparation, requires 7 man-days of work and yields a profit of Rs. 30. An acre of wheat costs Rs. 120 to prepare, requires 10 man days of work and yields a profit of Rs. 40. An acre of soyabeans costs Rs. 70 to prepare, requires 8 man-days of work and yields a profit of Rs. 20. If the farmer has Rs. 1,00,000 for preparation and can count on 8,000 man-days of work, how many acres should be allocated to each crop to maximize profits?

Formulate this as a problem in linear programming, and solve it by simplex method.

[x_1 = Rs. 250, x_2 = Rs 625, x_3 = 0; Z = 32,500]

Q. 11 A firm makes two products, chairs (x) and tables (y), which must be processed on two machines, A and B. The following information is available :

Product	*Hours required per unit of product on machine*		*Profit per unit (Rs.)*
	A	*B*	
Chair	2	4	6
Table	4	2	8

The maximum hours available on A and B are 60 and 48 respectively. The optimum simplex tableau for maximizing the profit of the above problem is as under:

$C_j \rightarrow$	*Product*	*Quantity*	*6*	*8*	*0*	*0*
↑	*Mix*		x	y	s_1	s_2
8	y	12	0	1	1/3	–1/6
6	x	6	1	0	–1/6	1/3
	Z_j	132	6	8	5/3	2/3
	$C_j - Z_j$	0	0	–5/3	–2/3	

(s_1 and s_2 are the slack variables of machine A and B respectively.)

You are required to explain, in the context of the given problem, the meaning and justification of all the elements in the above simplex tableau.

Q. 12 A company produces three products P, Q and R whose prices per unit are 3, 5 and 4 respectively. One unit of product P requires 2 units of m_1 and 3 unit of m_2. One unit of product Q requires 2 units of m_2 and 5 units of m_2 and one unit of product R requires 3 units of m_1, 2 units of m_2 and 4 units of m_3. The company has 8 units of material m_1, 10 units of material m_2 and 15 units of material m_3 available to it.

(*i*) Formulate the problem mathematically.

(*ii*) Use simplex method to find how many units of each product should be produced to maximize revenue?

Hint : Maximize $Z = 3x_1 + 5x_2 + 4x_3$

Subject to $2x_1 + 3x_3 \leq 8$

$3x_1 + 2x_2 + 2x_3 \leq 10$

$5x_2 + 4x_3 \leq 15$

$x_1, x_2, x_3 \geq 0$ [x = 4/3, x_2 = 3, x_3 = 0; Z = 19]

Q. 13 Consider a firm that produces two products P and Q with resources A, B, C. The profit per unit of P and Q is Rs 20 and Rs 25 respectively. P requires 10 units of A and 15 units of B whereas Q requires 10 units of B and 30 units of C. A, B and C are available in amounts of 5000, 9000 and 12000 respectively. Find number of units of P and Q to be manufactured to maximize profits, using simplex method. [P = 200, Q = 400]

Q. 14 A steel manufacturer produces two types of steel x_1 and x_2. Type 1 needs 2 hours of melting, 4 hours of rolling and 10 hours of cutting. Type II requires 5 hours of melting, 1 hour of rolling and 5 hour of cutting. Forty hours are available for melting, 20 for rolling and 60 for cutting. The profit per unit of x_1 is Rs 24 and Rs 24 and Rs 8 for x_2. Find the profit maximizing output mix.

Q. 15 Explain the concept of slack variables and dual of a given linear programming problem from the business point of view.

Artificial Variable

In the previous section, we have discussed the problem of maximisation of an objective functions involving sign of '≤'. However, we may come across situation, where constraints may have sign of the type '≥' or '='. In such a case, the technique of solving linear programming problem needs some modifications. These are discussed below.

Consider the problem, involving '≥' sign, as under.

Minimize $Z = C_1x_1 + C_2x_2 ..... + C_nn_n$ (objective function)

Subject to constraints

$$\left.\begin{array}{l} a_{11}x_1 + a_{12}x_2 + ... + a_{1n}x_n \geq b_1 \\ a_{12}x_1 + a_{22}x_2 + ... + a_{2n}x_n \geq b_2 \\ a_{m1}x_1 + a_{m2}x_2 + ... + a_{mn}x_n \geq b_n \end{array}\right] \text{constraints}$$

$x_1, x_2, ..., x_n \geq 0$ (Non negative constraint)

Now, in order to convert inequality to equality, we subtract surplus variables from each constraints. We will have the above equation in the following form.

Minimize $Z = C_1x_1 + C_2x_2 + ... + C_nn_n + 0s_1 + 0s_2 + ... + 0s_n$.

Subject to following

$$a_{11}x_1 + a_{12}x_2 + ... + a_{1n}x_n - s_1 = b_1$$

$$a_{12}x_1 + a_{22}x_2 + ... + a_{2n}x_n - s_2 = b_2$$

$$a_{1n}x_1 + a_{2n}x_2 + ... + a_{mn}x_n - s_m = b_m$$

Thus, there are '*m*' equations and '*n*' variables. We should set $(n - m)$ variables *i.e.*, $x_1 = x_2 = ... x_n = 0$ to get initial basic feasible solution. But we will get

$$s_1 = -b_1$$

$$s_2 = -b_2$$

$$s_m = -b_m$$

The above solution is not feasible because surplus variable cannot be negative.

Thus, there is requirement of modifying the simplex method. This is done by introducing '*m*' new variables $A_1, A_2, A_3 ...... A_m$ which are known as artificial variables.

The above constraints would be written as.

$$a_{11}x_1 + a_{12}x_2 + ... + a_{1n}x_n - s_1 + A_1 = b_1$$

$$a_{12}x_1 + a_{22}x_2 + ... + a_{2n}x_n - s_2 + A_2 = b_2$$

$$a_{m1}x_1 + a_{m2}x_2 + ... + a_{mn}x_n - s_m + A_m = b_m$$

Now there are '*n* decision variables,' '*m* surplus variable' and '*m* artificial variable'. An initial basic feasible solution can be obtained by setting $(n + 2m - m)$ variable equal to zero *i.e.*, $(n + m)$ variable shall be put equal to zero.

Hence, we set

$\therefore$ $x_1 = x_2 = x_3 = ... = x_n = 0$ (*n* decision variables)

$s_1 = s_2 = s_3 = ... = s_m = 0$ (*m* surplus variables)

$\therefore$ We will have

$$A_1 = b_1, A_2 = b_2, ... A_m = b_m$$

However, the above is not a solution to the original equation. The appearance of artificial variable is required to be made in the original equation. This is done by adding or subtracting the artificial variable (with very high coefficient) to the objective function.

The reason for assigning very large value to the artificial variable in the objective function is that they will be automatically excluded from the final solution or as soon as they become non basic. However, it shall be ensured that in case of maximisation problem, coefficient of $-M$ is assigned to the artificial variable in the objective function and in case of minimisations problem, coefficient of $+M$ is assigned to the artificial variable in the objective function. This method of solving *LP* problem is known as Charle's *M*– method or the 'highest penalty method'.

Students while solving LP problem shall also ensure the following points.

(a) In case of constraints with ≥ sign, surplus variable as well as artificial variable are required.

(b) In case of equality, only artificial variable is required.

The minimisation problem would become more clear from the following example.

These examples are also covering mixed-type constraints *i.e.*, constraints with different inequality signs.

Example 8. **The standard weight of a special purpose brick is 5 kg and it contains two basic ingredients B_1 and B_2. B_1 costs Rs. 5 per kg. and B_2 costs Rs. 8 per kg. Strength Considerations indicate that the brick contains not more than 4 kg of B_1 and minimum 2 kg. of B_2. Since the demand for the product is likely to be related to the price of the brick, find the minimum cost of brick satisfying the above conditions.**

Solution. Let *x* and *y* denote the amount of ingredient B_1 and B_2 respectively used in the brick. The above problem would be formulated as under:

Minimize $Z = 5x + 8y$

Subject to the constraints :

$x + y = 5$

$x \leq 4$ ....(1)

$y \geq 2$ ....(2)

$x, y \geq 0$ .....(3)

Steps 1 : First of all, convert each of the constraints into equations by introducing slack, surplus and artificial variables as the case may be. Therefore we will have

Minimize $Z = 5x + 8y + 0s_1 + 0s_2 + MA_1 + MA_2$

Subject to $x + y + A_1 = 5$

$x + s_1 = 4$

$y - s_2 + A_2 = 2$

$x, y, s_1, s_2, A_1, A_2 \geq 0.$

where s_1 and s_2 are, respectively, slack and surplus variables and A_1 and A_2 are artificial variables, An initial basic feasible solution to the problem would be given as

$$x = 0, y = 0, s_2 = 0, A_1 = 5, s_1 = 4, A_2 = 2.$$

The initial simplex tableau corresponding to the above solution will be given as under :

Simplex Tableau I

$C_j \rightarrow$	Basic	Solution	5	8	0	0	M	M	Ratio
$\downarrow$	Variable		x	y	s_1	s_2	A_1	A_2	
M	A_1	5	1	1	0	0	1	0	5
0	s_1	4	1	0	1	0	0	0	–
M	A_2	2	0	(1)	0	–1	0	1	←2
	Z_j	7M	M	2M	0	–M	M	M	
	$C_j - Z_j$		5–M	8–2M↑	0	M	0	0	

Step 2 : Test for optimality. We have computed $C_j - Z_j$ .Since all $C_j - Z_j$ are not non negative, it implies further scope of improvement in the solution exist. The highest negative value in the $(C_j - Z_j)$ row help in identifying entering variable. Since variable '*M*' has been used, students may face difficulty in identifying highest negative number in the $C_j - Z_j$. Therefore, students are advised to put arbitrary value of *M* but that value shall be highest among the numbers appearing in the $C_j - Z_j$ row.

For example, in this case the numbers are 5, 8, 2, 0 therefore assume $M = 9$.

Now we have, $C_j - Z_j$ row as.

$C_j - Z_j$	5 – (9)	8 – 2(9)	0	9	0	0
$C_j - Z_j$	–4	–10	0	9	0	0

It can be identified (8 – 2*M*) is a highest negative number.

It can be observed that *y* is the entering variable. The smallest nonnegative quotient in the ratio column is 2 therefore A_2 is the departing variable and the key number, 1, is circled. The elements in key row and non key row are recalculated using the formula discussed above and a second simplex table is designed.

Simplex Tableau II

$C_j \rightarrow$ ↓	Basic Variable	Solution	5 x	8 y	0 s_1	0 s_2	M A_1	M A_2	Ratio
M	A_1	3	(1)	0	0	1	1	–1	←3
0	s_1	4	1	0	1	0	0	0	4
8	y	2	0	1	0	–1	0	1	–
	Z_j	16+3M	M	8	0	–8+M	M	8–M	
	$C_j - Z_j$		5–M↑	0	0	8–M	0	–8 + 2M	

Since there are negative values in $C_j - Z_j$ row, this solution is not optimal and we will continue as in previous step. We obtain Tableau III.

Simplex Tableau III

$C_j \rightarrow$ ↓	Basic Variable	Solution	5 x	8 y	0 s_1	0 s_2	M A_1	M A_2
5	x	3	1	0	0	1	1	–1
0	s_1	1	0	0	1	–1	–1	1
8	y	2	0	1	0	–1	0	1
	Z_j	31	5	8	0	–3	5	3
	$C_j - Z_j$		0	0	0	3	M –5	M–3

In this case all values in $C_j - Z_j$ row are now zero or positive. Thus the optimal solution is obtained. The solution is $x = 3$, $y = 2$ at which minimum value of Z = 31.

Example 9 : ***XYZ*** **chemical corporation must produce exactly 1000 kgs. of a special mixture of chemical** ***A*** **and chemical** ***B*** **for a customer. Chemical** ***A*** **costs Rs 50 per kg and chemical** ***B*** **costs Rs 60 per kg. Not more than 300 kgs. of chemical** ***A*** **can be used and atleast 150 kg of chemical** ***B*** **must be used. Using Simplex method, determine the least cost blend of the two ingredients.**

Solution : Let 'x' and 'y' be the number of kg. of chemical A and B respectively.

Minimize $Z = 50x + 60y$

Subject to

$$x + y = 1000$$
$$x \leq 300$$
$$y \geq 150$$

and $x, y \geq 0.$

Introducing slack, surplus and artificial variable, we have

Minimize $Z = 50x + 60y + 0s_1 + 0s_2 + MA_1 + MA_2$

Subject to

$$x + y + 0s_1 + 0s_2 + A_1 + 0A_2 = 1000$$
$$1x + 0y + 1s_1 + 0s_2 + 0A_1 + 0A_2 = 300$$
$$0x + y + 0s_1 - 1s_2 + 0A_1 + 1A_2 = 150$$
$$x, y, s_1, s_2, A_1, A_2 \geq 0.$$

There are 3 equations and 6 variables, therefore, in order to get initial basic feasible solution, set three variables as zero.

The initial simplex table is given below :

Table I

$C_j \rightarrow$	Basic	Solution	50	60	0	0	M	M	Ratio
$\downarrow$	Variable		x	y	s_1	s_2	A_1	A_2	
M	A_1	1000	1	1	0	0	1	0	1000
0	S_1	300	1	0	1	0	0	0	–
M	A_2	150	0	(1)	0	–1	0	1	$\leftarrow$ 150
		Z_j	M	2M	0	–M	M	M	
		$C_j - Z_j$	50–M	60–2M$\uparrow$	0	+M	0	0	

To facilitate identification of highest negative number.

[Assume M = 61 in the above case, then the values in the $C_j - Z_j$ row will be –11, –62, 0, 61, 0,0.]

Table II

$C_j \rightarrow$	Basic	Solution	50	60	0	0	M	M	Ratio
$\downarrow$	Variable		x	y	s_1	s_2	A_1	A_2	
M	A_1	850	1	0	0	(1)	1	–1	850
0	S_1	300	1	0	1	0	0	0	$\leftarrow$300
60	y	150	0	1	0	–1	0	1	–
		Z_j	M	60	0	–60+M	M	60–M	
		$C_j - Z_j$	50–M$\uparrow$	0	0	60–M	0	–60+2M	

Table III

$C_j \rightarrow$	Basic	Solution	50	60	0	0	M	M	Ratio
$\downarrow$	Variable		x	y	s_1	s_2	A_1	A_2	
M	A_1	550	0	0	–1	(1)	1	–1	$\leftarrow$550
50	x	300	1	0	1	0	0	0	–
60	y	150	0	1	0	–1	0	1	–150
		Z_j	50	60	(–M+50)	(M–60)	M	60–M	
		$C_j - Z_j$	0	0	(–50+M)	(60–M)$\uparrow$	0	2M+60	

Table IV

$C_j \rightarrow$	Basic	Solution	50	60	0	0	M	M	Ratio
$\downarrow$	Variable		x	y	s_1	s_2	A_1	A_2	
0	S_2	550	0	0	–1	1	1	–1	
50	x	300	1	0	1	0	0	0	
60	y	700	0	1	–1	0	+1	–1	

Z_j	57000	50	60	–10	0	60	–60
$C_j - Z_j$		0	0	+10	0	(M–60)	(M+60)

Since all elements in the index row $C_j - Z_j$ are greater than or equal to zero, this implies that we have reached optimal solution.

The solutions is $x = 300$ kg, $y = 700$ kg. There would be surplus of 550 kg of chemical *B*. The cost of solution is Rs. 57000.

Example 10. XYZ **company during the festival season combines two items *A* and *B* to form gift packs. Each pack must weight 5 kg and should contain atleast 2kg of *A* and not more than 4kg of *B*. The company wants to determine the optimum mix. Formulate the above as a linear programming problem to maximise net contribution per pack and solve the same by using simplex method.**

Solution : Let x kg of item *A* be mixed with y kg of item *B*.

Thus, we have

Maximize $Z = 10x + 12y$

Subject to $x + y = 5$

$x \geq 2$

$y \leq 4$

$x, y \geq 0$

Adding slack and surplus variables, the above equations would be written as

Maximize $Z = 10x + 12y + 0s_1 + 0s_2 - MA_1 - MA_2$

Subject to $x + y + A_1 = 5$

$x - s_1 + A_2 = 2$

$y + s_2 = 4$

There are three equations and six variables

∴ Set (6–3) = 3 variable as zero to get initial basic feasible solution, which is presented below in a tabular form.

Table I

$C_j \rightarrow$	Basic	Solution	10	12	0	0	–M	–M	Ratio
↓	Variable		x	y	s_1	s_2	A_1	A_2	
–M	A_1	5	1	1	0	0	1	0	5
–M	A_2	2	(1)	0	–1	0	0	1	←2
0	S_2	4	0	1	0	1	0	0	
	Z_j	–7M	–2M	–M	M	M	–M	–M	
	$C_j - Z_j$		↑(10+2M)	(12+M)	–M	–M	0	0	

[*Assume M as 13 in this case, then the values in the* $C_j - Z_j$ *row would be 36, 25, –13, 13,0, 0 and 0*]

Table II

$C_j \rightarrow$ ↓	Basic Variable	Solution	10 x	12 y	0 s_1	0 s_2	M A_1	M A_2	Ratio
–M	A_1	3	0	(1)	1	0	1	–1	←3
10	x	2	1	0	–1	0	0	1	–
0	S_2	4	0	1	0	1	0	0	4
	Z_j	(20–3M)	10	–M	–(M+10)	0	–M	(10+M)	
	$C_j - Z_j$		0	(12+M)	(M+10)	0	0	–(10-2M)	

Table III

$C_j \rightarrow$ ↓	Basic Variable	Solution	10 x	12 y	0 s_1	0 s_2	M A_1	M A_2	Ratio
12	y	3	0	1	1	0	1	–1	–
10	x	2	1	0	1	0	0	1	–
0	S_2	1	0	0	–1	1	–1	1	1
	Z_j	56	10	12	2	0	12	–2	
	$C_j - Z_j$		0	0	–2	0	M–12	M–2	

The optimal solution has reached as there is no positive number in the index row. The solution is $y = 3$, $x = 2$ and profit corresponding to this solution is 56.

Example 11. **A carpenter has started a workshop in which he manufactures handcarts. Each cart consists of a frame and two wheels. A frame uses 3 hours and a wheel 2 hours of labour of which 90 hours per week are available. The carpenter wants that he should manufacture atleast 10 carts during a week. The cost of the frame is Rs 500 and that of a wheel is Rs 200. Formulate this as a linear programming model and using simplex method, determine an optimum production plan.**

Solution : Let x_1 and x_2 be the no. of frame and wheel respectively. The appropriate mathematical formula of the given problem would be then given as:

Minimize $Z = 500x_1 + 200x_2$

Subject to $3x_1 + 2x_2 \le 90$

$x_1 \ge 10$

$x_2 = 2x_1$

$x_1, x_2 \ge 0$

Using surplus, slack and artificial variables, the problem can be restated as:

Minimize $Z = 500x_1 + 200x_2 + 0s_1 + 0s_2 + MA_1 + MA_2$

Subject to $3x_1 + 2x_2 + S_1 = 90$

$x_1 - S_2 + A_1 = 10$

$-2x_1 + x_2 + A_2 = 0$

$x_1, x_2, s_1, s_2, A_1, A_2 \geq 0$

There are 3 equations and 6 variables.

$\therefore$ set (6-3) = 3 variable as zero to find basic feasible solution. We will have

$S_1 = 90$, $A_1 = 10$ and $A_2 = 0$

The Initial basic feasible solution would be summarised in table form, as under.

Initial Simplex Tableau I

$C_j \rightarrow$ ↓	Basic Variable	Solution	500 x_1	200 x_2	0 s_1	0 s_2	M A_1	M A_2	Ratio
0	S_1	90	3	2	1	0	0	0	45
M	A_1	10	1	0	0	–1	1	0	–
M	A_2	0	–2	(1)	0	0	0	1	← 0
	Z_j		–M	M	0	–M	M	M	
	$C_j - Z_j$		(500+M)	(200–M)↑	0	M	0	0	

Simplex Tableau II

$C_j \rightarrow$ ↓	Basic Variable	Solution	500 x_1	200 x_2	0 s_1	0 s_2	M A_1	M A_2	Ratio
0	S_1	90	7	0	1	0	0	–2	(900/7)
M	A_1	10	(1)	0	0	–1	1	–1	←10
200	x_2	0	–2	1	0	0	0	1	
	Z_j		(M–400)	200	0	–M	M	(–M+200)	
	$C_j - Z_j$		(900–M)↑	0	0	M	0	2M-200	

Simplex Tableau III

$C_j \rightarrow$ ↓	Basic Variable	Solution	500 x_1	200 x_2	0 x_1	0 s_2	M A_1	M A_2	Ratio
0	S_1	20	0	0	1	7			
500	x_1	10	1	0	0	–1			
200	x_2	20	0	1	0	–2			
	Z_j	9000	500	200	0	–900			
	$C_j - Z_j$		0	0	0	+900			

Since there are all non negative numbers in the $C_j - Z_j$ row, thus, it shows that optimal solution has reached. The optimal solution is $x_1 = 10$, $x_2 = 20$ with minimum cost of 9000. Thus, 10 frames and 20 wheels shall be manufactured.

Difference between–Maximization and Minimization Problems

Maximization Problem	*Minimization Problem*
1. These problem have sign "≤" in the constraints.	These problem have sign "≥" in the constraints.
2. 'Slack variables' are added to convert inequality to equality.	"Surplus variables" are subtracted to convert inequality to equality. "Artificial variables" are added to get appropriate initial basic feasible solution.
3. The variables with the greatest positive value in $C_j - Z_j$ row is the entering variable.	The variable with the largest negative value in the $C_j - Z_j$ row is the entering variable.
4. An optimal solution is reached when there are no $C_j - Z_j$ number that are greater than zero.	An optimal solution is reached when all $C_j - Z_j$ are greater than or equal to zero.

Exercise 4.2

Solve the following using simplex method

Q. 1 Minimize $Z = 60x_1 + 80x_2$

Subject to $20x_1 + 30x_2 \geq 900$

$40x_1 + 30x_2 \geq 1200$

$x_1, x_2 \geq 0$ [$x_1 = 15$, $x_2 = 20$, $Z = 25$]

Q. 2 Minimize $Z = 3x_1 + 8x_2$

Subject to $x_1 + x_2 = 200$

$x_1 \leq 80$

$x_2 \geq 60$

$x_1, x_2 \geq 0$ [$x_1 = 80$, $x_2 = 120$, $Z = 1200$]

Q. 3 Minimize $Z = 1200x_1 + 800x_2$

Subject to $30x_1 + 30x_2 \geq 400$

$60x_1 + 20x_2 \geq 800$

$40x_1 + 100x_2 \geq 820$

$x_1, x_2 \geq 0$ [$x_1 = 12$, $x_2 = 4$, $Z = 17600$]

Q. 4 Minimize $Z = 4x_1 + 3x_2$

Subject to $200x_1 + 100x_2 \geq 4000$

$x_1 + 2x_2 \geq 50$

$40x_1 + 40x_2 \geq 1400$

$x_1, x_2 \geq 0$ [$x_1 = 5$, $x_2 = 30$, $Z = 110$]

Q. 5 Minimize $Z = 2x_1 + x_2 + 3x_3$

Subject to $2x_1 + 3x_2 + 4x_3 \geq 20$

$4x_1 + 2x_2 + 2x_3 \geq 15$

$x_1 + x_2 + x_3 \geq 0$ $\left[x_1 = \frac{5}{8}, x_2 = \frac{75}{12}, x_3 = 0; Z = \frac{15}{2}\right]$

Q. 6 A paint company is required to produce 10000 kg of metallic paint which is formed of three ingredients *P, Q, R*. The cost of *P, Q* and *R* per kg is Rs 8, Rs 10 and Rs 11 respectively. The supply of ingredient *P* is limited to 3000 kg whereas *Q* and *R* must be used atleast 1500 kg and 2000 kg respectively. Find the number of kg for each ingredient to minimize total cost for 10000 kg of mixture. [P = 3000, Q = 5000, R = 2000,. Cost = Rs 96000]

Q. 7 A diet for a sick person must contain atleast 4000 units of vitamins, 50 units of minerals and 1400 units of calorie. Two foods *A* and *B* are available at a cost of Rs 4 and Rs 3 per unit respectively. If one unit of *A* contain 200 units of vitamins, 1 units of mineral and 40 units of calories, find by simplex method, what combination of food be used to have least cost?

[Z = 110, A = 5, B = 30]

Q. 8 A firm produces three items *A, B* and *C* at two plants X and Y. The number of items produced and operating cost per hour are as follows :

Plants	*Items Produced per Hour*			*Operating Cost Per Hour*
	A	*B*	*C*	
X	30	60	40	Rs 1200
Y	30	20	100	Rs 800

It is desired to produce atleast 400 items of type *A*, atleast 800 of type *B* and atleast 800 of type *C* perday. Find, using simplex method, the number of hours each plant be run on a day to minimize cost. [x = 12, y = 4, Z = 17600]

Q.9 A person consume two types of food *A* and *B* everyday to obtain 8 units of protein, 12 units of carbohydrates and 9 units of fats which is his daily minimum requirement. One kilogram of food *A* contain 2, 6 and 1 units of protein, carbohydrates and fats respectively. Food *A* costs Rs. 8.50 per kilo, while *B* costs Rs. 4 per kilo. Determine how many kilos of each food should he buy daily to minimize his cost of food and still meet the minimum requirements. Solve using simplex method.

[x_1 = 1, x_2 = 6, Z = 65/2]

Q.10 Explain the economic interpretation of surplus variables in the linear programming problems.

Linear Programming (Duality)

According to the duality theorem, "For every maximization (or minimization) problem in linear programming, there is a unique similar problem of minimization (or maximization) involving the same data which describes the original problem". The above definition implies that with every Linear Programming problem, there is another problem associated with it. **For example, if a *LP* is regarding minimisation of cost for a given level of profit, the related problem would be maximisation of profit for a given level of cost. Thus, either one may say that the given problem as of minimisation of cost or it may be said maximization of profit. Therefore, minimization of cost is said to be primal and maximization of profit may be said to be dual or vice versa. Thus, we may say that there is inverse relationship between a primal and its dual. If primal is maximization problem, dual is minimization problem.** We can also conclude that a minimisation (or maximisations) problem can be converted into maximisation (or minimisation) problem using dual-primal relationship. **The rules for constructing the dual from primal or primal from the dual are given below :**

(*a*) If the original problem is a maximization, dual will be minimisation. If the original problem is minimisation, dual will be maximization. Therefore, if all constraints in the primal involve $\leq$ ($\geq$), than constraint in the dual will have $\geq$ ($\leq$).

(*b*) Constraints of the original problem are interchanged to decision variables of the dual. The number of variables in the dual problem is equal to the number of constraints in the original problem. The number of constraints in the dual problem is equal to the number of variables in the original problem.

(*c*) The number of constraints in the dual problem is equal to number of decision variables in the primal problem and vice versa.

(*d*) If the ith constraint in the primal is 'equal to' type, then the ith variable in the dual is 'unrestricted' in sign and vice versa.

(*e*) Dual of the dual is the primal itself.

***Example 12* : Find the dual of each of the following problems:**

(*i*) Maximize $Z = 5x_1 + 10x_2 + 8x_3$

Subject to

$$2x_1 + 5x_2 + 2x_3 \leq 7$$
$$x_1 + 3x_2 + 0x_3 \leq 10$$
$$x_1, x_2, x_3 \geq 0$$

(*ii*) Maximize $Z = 3x_1 + 5x_2$

Subject to

$$2x_1 - 3x_2 \leq 5$$
$$2x_1 + x_2 \geq 3$$
$$-5x_1 + x_2 \geq 4$$
$$x_1, x_2 \geq 0$$

(*iii*) Maximize $Z = 7x_1 + 8x_2 + 6x_3$

Subject to

$$x_1 + 4x_2 + 4x_3 = 8$$
$$3x_1 + 5x_2 + 3x_3 \leq 12$$
$$x_1, x_2, x_3 \geq 0$$

***Solution* :** (*i*) Since given problem is maximization, therefore, the dual will be minimisation problem and it will be given as

Minimize $Z^* = 7y_1 + 10y_2$

Subject to

$$2y_1 + y_2 \geq 5$$
$$5y_1 + 3y_2 \geq 10$$
$$2y_1 + 0y_2 \geq 8$$
$$y_1, y_2 \geq 0$$

(*ii*) The given problem is a maximization problem. Therefore, we must convert all the signs of inequality to $\leq$. We shall multiply constraint 2 and 3 with '-1'. Now, the given problem can be restated as

Maximize $Z = 3x_1 + 5x_2$

Subject to $2x_1 - 3x_2 \leq 5$

$-2x_1 - x_2 \leq -3$

$5x_1 - x_2 \leq -4$

$x_1, x_1 \geq 0$

The dual of the above problem will be given as

Minimize $Z = 5y_1 - 3y_2 - 4y_3$

Subject to $2y_1 - 2y_2 + 5y_3 \geq 3$

$-3y_1 - y_2 - y_3 \geq 5$

$y_1, y_2, y_3 \geq 0$

(*iii*) In this problem, there is one constraint having sign of equality. Therefore, we shall convert the equality constraint in terms of two inequalities, one involving ≤ and other involving ≥. Hence, the given problem can be restated as.

Maximize $Z = 7x_1 + 8x_2 + 6x_3$

Subject to $x_1 + 4x_2 + 2x_3 \leq 8$

$x_1 + 4x_2 + 2x_3 \geq 8$

$3x_1 + 5x_2 + 3x_3 \leq 12$

$x_1, x_1, x_3 \geq 0$

Multiply both the sides of constraint 2 with '–1'

Now the problem can be restated as

Maximize $Z = 7x_1 + 8x_2 + 6x_3$

Subject to $x_1 + 4x_2 + x_3 \leq 8$

$-x_1 - 4x_2 - x_3 \leq -8$

$3x_1 + 5x_2 + 3x_3 \leq 12$

$x_1, x_1, x_3 \geq 0$

The dual of the above problem will be

Minimize $Z = 8y_1 - 8y_2 + 12y_2$

Subject to $y_1 - y_2 + 3y_3 \geq 7$

$4y_1 - 4y_2 + 5y_3 \geq 8$

$y_1 - y_2 + 3y_3 \geq 6$

$y_1, y_2, y_3 \geq 0$

Let $y = y_1 - y_2$ (y is unrestricted in sign). We can write above problems as

Minimize $Z^* = 8y + 12y_2$

Subject to $y + 3y_3 \geq 7$

$4y + 5y_3 \geq 8$

$y + 3y_3 \geq 6$

$y_3 \geq 0$; y: unrestricted in sign.

This, shows that if the ith constraint in the primal is of "equal to" type then the ith variable in the dual is "unrestricted" in sign. Similarly, we can also say if the ith variable in the primal is "unrestricted" in sign, then the ith constraint in the dual is "equal to" type.

Example 13 : **Find the dual of each of the following problems:**

(*i*) Minimize $Z = 4x_1 + 5x_2$

Subject to $3x_1 + 2x_2 \geq 2$

$2x_1 + 3x_2 \geq 3$

$x_1, x_2 \geq 0$

(*ii*) Minimize $Z = 7x_1 + 6x_2$

Subject to $-2x_1 + 3x_2 \leq 5$

$3x_1 + 3x_2 \geq 4$

$x_1, x_2 \geq 0$

(*iii*) Minimize $Z = 2x_1 + 5x_2 + 3x_3$

Subject to $2x_1 - 3x_2 + 2x_3 = 5$

$x_1 - 3x_2 \leq 3$

$3x_2 - 2x_3 \geq 4$

$x_1, x_1 \geq 0$; x_3 **: unrestricted in sign.**

Solution : (*i*) Given primal is a minimization problem. Therefore, its dual will be a maximization problem. The dual would be

Maximize $Z = 2y_1 + 3y_2$

Subject to $3y_1 + 2y_2 \leq 4$

$2y_1 + 3y_2 \leq 5$

$y_1, y_2 \geq 0$

(*ii*) Since, the given problem is of minimisation therefore all the constraint shall have inequality sign of '≥' type. Both the sides of constraint I shall be multiplied with '–1' to convert the sign '≤' to '≥'. Now the given problem can be restated as

Minimize $Z = 7x_1 + 6x_2$

$+2x_1 - 3x_2 \geq -5$

$3x_1 + 3x_2 \geq 4$

$x_1, x_2 \geq 0$

The dual of the problem would be

Maximum $Z = -5y_1 + 4y_2$

Subject to $2y_1 + 3y_2 \leq 7$

$-3y_1 + 3y_2 \leq 6$

$y_1, y_2 \geq 0$

(*iii*) Rewrite the problem as

Minimize $Z = 2x_1 + 5x_2 + 3x_3$

Subject to $2x_1 - 3x_2 + 2x_3 \geq 5$

$-2x_1 + 3x_2 - 2x_3 \geq -5$

$-x_1 + 3x_2 \geq -3$

$3x_2 - 2x_3 \geq 4$

The constraint with equality sign has been written twice sign '≤' and '≥' and finally both sign have been convered into '≥' as it is a problem of minima.

Dual of the problem will be

Maximize $Z = 5y_1 - 5y_2 - 3y_3 + 4y_4$

Subject to $2y_1 - 2y_2 - y_3 \leq 2$

$-3y_1 + 3y_2 + 3y_3 + 3y_4 \leq 5$

$2y_1 - 2y_2 - 2y_4 \leq 3$

Replace y_1 y_2 with y and following other rules of conversion of primal to dual, we have

Maximize $Z = 5y - 3y_3 + 4y_4$

Subject to $2y - y_3 \leq 2$

$-3y + 3y_3 + 3y_4 \leq 5$

$2y - 2y_4 = 3$

$y_3, y_4 \geq 0$ y : unrestricted in sign.

Example 14 : **Write the dual to the following LPP :**

Maximize $Z = 20x_1 + 15x_2 + 18x_3 + 10x_4$

Subject to $4x_1 - 3x_2 + 10x_3 + 4x_4 \leq 60$

$-x_1 + x_2 + x_3 = 27$

$x_1 + 4x_3 + 7x_4 \geq 35$

$x_1, x_2, x_3 \geq 0,\ x_4$**: unrestricted in sign**

Solution : The given problem is said to be primal. It is a maximization problem. Therefore, we shall convert each constraint into the type '≤'. Thus multiplying both sides of the third constraint with '–1' we can restate the primal as

Maximize $Z = 20x_1 + 15x_2 + 18x_3 + 10x_4$

Subject to $4x_1 - 3x_2 + 10x_3 + 4x_4 \leq 60$

$x_1 + x_2 + x_3 + ox_4 = 27$

$Ox_1 + x_2 - 4x_3 - 7x_4 \leq -35$

$x_1, x_2, x_3 \geq 0,\ x_4$: unrestricted in sign

Let y_1, y_2 and y_3 be the dual variables corresponding to three primal constraints in given order. As the second constraint of the primal is an equation, therefore second variable y_2 will be unrestricted in sign. Likewise, the fourth variable x_4 of the primal problem is unrestricted in sign, therefore the fourth constraint of the dual will be an equation.

Therefore the dual of the given problem will be given as

$$\text{Minimize} \quad Z^* = 60y_1 + 27y_2 - 35y_3$$

$$\text{Subject to} \quad 4y_1 + y_2 \geq 20$$

$$-3y_1 + y_2 + y_3 \geq 15$$

$$10y_1 + y_2 - 4y_3 \geq 18$$

$$4y_1 - 7y_3 = 10$$

$$y_1, y_3 \geq 0;\ y_2\text{: unrestricted in sign}$$

Since second constraint of primal is of equal to type: y_2 is unrestricted in sign.

Example 15 : **A firm produces three types of biscuits *A, B,* and *C*. It packs them in assortments of two sizes I and II. The size I contains 20 biscuits of type *A*, 50 of type *B* and 10 of type *C*. The size II contains 10 biscuits of type *A*, 80 of type *B* and 60 of type *C*. *A* buyer intends to but at least 120 biscuits of type *A*, 740 of type *B* and 240 of type *C*. Determine the least number of packets he should buy. Use simplex method and concept of dual.**

Solution : Let x_1 and x_2 denote size I and II to be purchased respectively. The appropriate formulation of the given problem is :

$$\text{Minimize} \quad Z = x_1 + x_2$$

$$\text{Subject to} \quad 20x_1 + 10x_2 \geq 120$$

$$50x_1 + 80x_2 \geq 740$$

$$10x_1 + 60x_2 \geq 240$$

$$\text{and} \quad x_1, x_2 \geq 0.$$

The dual problem would be

$$\text{Maximize} \quad Z^* = 120y_1 + 740y_2 + 240y_3$$

$$\text{Subject to} \quad 20y_1 + 50y_2 + 10y_3 \leq 1$$

$$10y_1 + 80y_2 + 60y_3 \leq 1$$

$$y_1, y_2, y_3 \geq 0$$

Let us now solve the dual problem by simplex method. Introducing slack variables s_1, s_2, the dual problem can be restated in terms of equations :

$$\text{Maximize} \quad Z^* = 120y_1 + 740y_2 + 240y_3$$

$$\text{Subject to} \quad 20y_1 + 50y_2 + 10y_3 + s_1 = 1$$

$$10y_1 + 80y_2 + 60y_3 + s_1 = 1$$

$$\text{and} \quad y_1, y_2, y_3, s_1, s_2 \geq 0$$

Since there are 6 variables and 2 equations therefore set (6-2) = 4 variables as zero to get basic feasible solution. The Initial basic feasible solution is summarized below:

$C_j \rightarrow$ ↓	Basic Variable	Solution	120 y_1	740 y_2	240 y_3	0 s_1	0 s_2	Ratio
0	s_1	1	20	50	10	1	0	1/50
0	s_2	1	10	(80)	60	0	1	← 1/80
	Z_j	0	0	0	0	0	0	
	C_j-Z_j		120	740↑	240	0	0	
0	s_1	3/8	(55/4)	0	–55/2	1	–5/8	← 3/110
740	y_2	5/2	1/8	1	3/4	0	1/80	1/10
	Z_j	37/4	185/2	740	555	0	37/4	
	C_j-Z_j		55/2↑	0	–315	0	–37/4	
120	y_1	3/110	1	0	–2	4/55	–1/22	
740	y_2	1/110	0	1	1	–1/110	1/55	
	Z_j	10	120	740	500	2	8	
	C_j-Z_j		0	0	–260	–2	–8	

As can be observed, all the entries in C_j–Z_j row are negative or zero, it implies optimal solution of the dual is obtained. The maximum value of Z^* is 10 and it occurs when $y_1 = \frac{3}{110}$ and $y_2 = \frac{1}{110}$.

Economic Interpretation of the Dual Problem

The economic interpretation of the dual problem can be understood from the following example.

A firm produces three types of biscuits *A, B* and *C*. It packs them in assortments of two sizes I and II. The size I contains 20 biscuits of type *A*, 50 of type *B* and 10 of type *C*. The size II contains 10 biscuits of type *A*, 80 of type *B* and 60 of type *C*. A buyer intends to buy atleast 120 biscuits of type *A*, 740 of type *B* and 240 of type *C*. Determine the least number of packets he should buy.

Let x_1 and x_2 be the number of packets of size I and II respectively. Then, the above problem can be formulated as under.

Minimize $\quad Z = x_1 + x_2$

Subject to $\quad 20x_1 + 10x_2 \geq 120$

$$50x_1 + 80x_2 \geq 740$$

$$10x_1 + 60x_2 \geq 240$$

$$x_1, x_2 \geq 0.$$

Let us know look at the above problem from different perspective. Let y_1, y_2 and y_3 represent biscuit of type *A*, type *B* and type *C* respectively. Since, the buyer intends to buy atleast 120 biscuit of type *A*, 740 of type *B* and 240 of type *C*, therefore, the objective function can be written as

Maximize $\quad Z = 120y_1 + 740y_2 + 240y_3$

This objective function is to be achieved subject to constraints. The constraints are packet of size I contain 20 biscuits of type *A*, 50 of type *B* and 10 of type *C* and size II contains 10 biscuits of type *A*, 80 of type *B* and 60 of type *C*. These constraints can be mathematically expressed as

$$20y_1 + 50y_2 + 10y_3 \le 1$$

$$10y_1 + 80y_2 + 60y_3 \le 1$$

$$y_1, y_2, y_3 \ge 0$$

Thus, is case of primal, we had tried to minimize number of packets to be purchased subject to procurement of atleast (120, 740, and 240 biscuits of type *A*, *B* and *C* respectively) and in case of dual we had tried to maximize the types of biscuit - *A*, *B* and *C* subject to given number of biscuits in each type of packet.

Relationship between solution of a dual problem and primal problem

Consider the example

Maximize $Z = 2x + 3y$

Subject to

$$2x + 2y \le 20$$

$$3x + 4y \le 50$$

$$x + 3y \le 10$$

$$x, y \ge 0$$

The problem has already been solved in the beginning.

The optimal solution of the above problem was obtained, as under :

$C_j \rightarrow$	Basic	Solution	2	3	0	0	0	Ratio
$\downarrow$	Variable		x	y	s_1	s_2	s_3	
2	x	10	1	0	3/4	0	–1/2	
0	s_2	20	0	–5/3	–19/4	1	–1/2	
3	y	0	0	1	–1/4	0	1/2	
	Z_j	20	2	3	3/4	0	1/2	
	$C_j - Z_j$		0	0	–3/4	0	–1/2	

Now, we can easily obtain dual of the problem and its solution can be easily worked out from the above table.

The dual of the above problem will be

Minimize $Z^* = 20y_1 + 50u_2 + 10u_3$

Subject to $2y_1 + 3y_2 + y_3 \ge 2$

$$2y_1 + 4y_2 + 3y_3 \ge 3$$

$$y_1 . y_2, y_3 \ge 0$$

The solution of the dual problem can be worked out directly from final table of primal. The values in $C_j - Z_j$ row under the basic variables s_1, s_2 and s_3 shall be observed. It can be observed that value corresponding so s_1, s_2 and s_3 are –3/4, 0 and –1/2, s_1, s_2 and s_3 represents slack variables for constraint 1,2 and 3 respectively. Since constraint of primal corresponds to structured variables of dual. Therefore, s_1, s_2 and s_3 would correspond to structured variables y_1, y_2 and y_3 and their value with opposite signs would be treated as values of y_1, y_2 and y_3 for optimal solution.

$\therefore$ optimal solution of the dual would be $y_1 = 3/4$, $y_2 = 0$ and $y_3 = 1/2$. Minimum value of $Z = 20$.

Thus it can be concluded that the optimal solution of dual problem can be ascertained from final table showing optimal solution of primal by observing values of slack/surplus variables in the $C_j - Z_j$ *row.*

Example 16 : **A company produces 2 types of leather belts Type *A* and *B*. Contribution per belt is Rs. 4 for type *A* and Rs. 3 for type *B*. The time requirements of one belt of type *A* and type *B* are in the ratio of 2:3. Time available is sufficient to produce 500 belts of type *A*. The leather is sufficient for only 400 belts. Belt *A* requires a fancy buckle and only 200 fancy buckles are available.**

(*i*) Formulate above as a linear programming problem.

(*ii*) Solve it by simplex method and comment on this optimal solution.

(*iii*) Write its dual and read the optimal solution of the dual.

Solution : Let the firm produce x_1 belts of Type *A* and x_2 belts of Type *B*.

Then the appropriate mathematical formulation of the given problem will be given as

Maximize $Z = 4x_1 + 3x_2$

Subject to $2x_1 + 3x_2 \le 1000$

$$x_1 + x_2 \le 400$$

$$x_1 \le 200$$

$$x_1, x_2 \ge 0$$

[Time taken to produce 2 belts of type A = time taken to produce 3 belts of type B $\therefore$ if $2x_1$ can be produced in 500 units of times, $3x_2$ would also be produced in the same time $\therefore$ $2x_1 + 3x_2 \le 500 + 500 \Rightarrow 2x_1 + 3x_2 \le 1000$]

Introduce slack variables s_1, s_2 and s_3 to convert inequality of equality. The problem can be written as shown below :

Maximize $Z = 4x_1 + 3x_2 + 0.s_1 + 0.s_2 + 0.s_3$

Subject to $2x_1 + 3x_2 + s_1 = 1000$

$$x_1 + x_2 + s_2 = 400$$

$$x_1 + s_3 = 200$$

$$x_1, x_2, s_1, s_2, s_3 \ge 0$$

Since, there are five variables and three equations, therefore, set (5 – 3) = 2 variables as zero.

We start with an initial basic feasible solution and reiterate the same steps till we got optimal solution as shown below :

$C_j \rightarrow$ ↓	*Basic Variable*	*Solution*	*4* x_1	*3* x_2	*0* s_1	*0* s_2	*0* s_3	*Ratio*
0	s_1	1000	2	3	1	0	0	500
0	s_2	400	1	1	0	1	0	400
0	s_3	200	(1)	0	0	0	1	←200

	Z_j	0	0	0	0	0	0	
	$C_j - Z_j$		4↑	3	0	0	0	
0	s_1	600	0	(3)	1	0	–2	←200
0	s_2	200	0	1	0	1	–1	400
4	x_1	200	1	0	0	0	1	–
	Z_j	800	4	0	0	0	4	
	$C_j - Z_j$		0	3↑	0	0	–4	
3	x_2	200	0	1	1/3	0	–2/3	
0	s_2	0	0	0	–1/3	1	–1/3	
4	x_1	200	1	0	0	0	1	
	Z_j	1400	4	3	1	0	2	
	$C_j - Z_j$		0	0	–1	0	–2	

As all entries in the $C_j - Z_j$ row are either negative or zero, it implies optimal solution has been obtained. The maximum value of Z is 1400 and it occurs when $x_1 = 200$ and $x_2 = 200$. **The optimal solution is *degenerate*.**

(*iii*) The dual problem is :

Minimize $\quad Z^* = 1000y_1 + 400y_2 + 200y_3$

Subject to $2y_1 + y_2 + y_3 \geq 4;\ 3y_1 + y_2 \geq 3;\ y_1, y_2, y_3 \geq 0$

Observe the values in the $C_j - Z_j$ row under slack variables in the final simplex table. Corresponding to s_1, s_2 and s_3 we have –1, 0 and –2. Therefore, the dual solution is $y_1 = 1$, $y_2 = 0$, $y_3 = 2$ and minimum $Z = 1400$.

Example 17 : **A firm uses three machines in the manufacture of three products. Each unit of product *A* requires 3 hours on machine 1, 2 hours on machine II and one hour on machine III. Each unit of product *B* requires 4 hours on machine I one hour on machine II and 3 hours on machine III, while each unit of product *C* requires 2 hours on each of the three machines. The contribution margin of the three product is Rs. 30, Rs. 40 and Rs. 35 per unit respectively. The machine hours available on the three machines are 90, 54 and 93 respectively.**

(*i*) **Formulate the above as a linear programming problem and solve for maximum profit, using simplex method.**

(*ii*) **Write the dual to the LPP.**

(*iii*) **Obtain the optimum values of the dual variables and verify that the primal and the dual problems have the same objective function values.**

Solution : Let x_1, x_2 and x_3 denote the number of units produced of products *A, B* and *C* respectively. The appropriate mathematical formulation would be given as

Maximize $\quad Z = 30x_1 + 40x_2 + 35x_3$

Subject to $\quad 3x_1 + 4x_2 + 2x_3 \leq 90$

$$2x_1 + x_2 + 2x_3 \leq 54$$

$$x_1 + 3x_2 + 2x_3 \leq 93$$

$$x_1, x_2\ x_3 \leq 0$$

Introducing slcak variables s_1, s_2 and s_3 in the given problem to convert inequality to equality, we have

Maximize $Z = 30x_1 + 40x_2 + 35x_3 + 0s_1 + 0s_2 + s_3$

Subject to $3x_1 + 4x_2 + 2x_3 + s_1 = 90$

$$2x_1 + x_2 + 2x_3 + s_2 = 54$$

$$x_1 + 3x_2 + 2x_3 + s_3 = 93$$

$$x_1, x_2\ x_3, s_1, s_2 \text{ and } s_3 \leq 0$$

Since there are 6 variables and 3 equations, set (6 – 3) = 3 variables as zero to get initial basic feasible solution.

An initial basic feasible solution is

$$x_1 = x_2 = x_3 = 0;\ s_1 = 90,\ s_2 = 54 \text{ and } s_3 = 93.$$

We start with this solution and we reiterate the same steps till we get optimal solution.

$C_j \rightarrow$	*Basic*	*Solution*	*30*	*40*	*35*	*0*	*0*	*0*	*Ratio*
↓	*Variable*		x_1	x_2	x_3	s_1	s_2	s_3	
0	s_1	90	3	(4)	2	1	0	0	←45/2
0	s_2	54	2	1	2	0	1	0	54
0	s_3	93	1	3	2	0	0	1	31
	Z_j	0	0	0	0	0	0	0	
	$C_j - Z_j$		30	40↑	35	0	0	0	
40	x_2	45/2	3/4	1	1/2	1/4	0	0	45
0	s_2	63/2	5/4	0	(3/2)	–1/4	1	0	←21
0	s_3	51/2	–5/4	0	1/2	–3/4	0	1	·51
	Z_j	900	30	40	20	10	0	0	
	$C_j - Z_j$		0	0	15↑	–10	0	0	
40	x_2	12	1/3	1	0	1/3	–1/3	0	
35	s_2	21	5/6	0	1	–1/6	2/3	0	
0	s_3	15	–5/3	0	0	–2/3	–1/3	1	
	Z_j	1215	85/2	40	35	15/2	10	0	
	$C_j - Z_j$		–25/2	0	0	–15/2	–10	0	

Since, all the values in $C_j - Z_j$ row are negagive or zero, it shows that we have reached optimal solution. Hence the optimal solution is $x_1 = 0$, $x_2 = 12$ and $x_3 = .21$ with maximum value of Z as 1215.

(ii) The dual problem is :

Minimize $Z^* = 90y_1 + 54y_2 + 93y_3$

Subject to $3y_1 + 2y_2 + y_3 \geq 30$

$$4y_1 + y_2 + 3y_3 \geq 40$$

$$2y_1 + 2y_2 + 2y_3 \geq 35$$

$$y_1, y_2, y_3 \geq 0$$

(iii) The optimal values of the dual variables are

$$y_1 = 15/2,\ y_2 = 10 \text{ and } y_3 = 0$$

with minimum value of Z^* as 1215.

Example 18. **'*XYZ*', a boat manufacturing company, makes three different kinds of boats. All can be made profitably in this company, but the company's production is constrained by the limited amount of labour, wood and screws available each month. The director will choose the combination of boats that maximizes his revenue in view of the information given in the following table :**

Input	*Row Boat*	*Canoe*	*Kayak*	*Monthly availability*
Labour	**12**	**7**	**9**	**1,260 hours**
Wood (Board feet)	**22**	**18**	**16**	**19,008**
Screws (kg.)	**2**	**4**	**3**	**396 kg.**
Selling price (in Rs.)	**4,000**	**2,000**	**5,000**	

(i) Formulate the above as a linear programming problem. (ii) Solve it by Simplex method. (iii) Which if any, of the resources are not fully utilized? If so, how much is the spare capacity left? (*iv*) What are the shadow prices? (*v*) State the dual of the formulated problem. (*vi*) How much wood will be used to make all the boats given in the optimal solution.

Solution: Let x_1, x_2 and x_3 denote the number of boats of Row, Canoe and Kayak respectively made every month. Then, the appropriate mathematical formulation of the given problem will be given as

$$\text{Maximize} \quad Z = 4{,}000x_1 + 2{,}000x_2 + 5{,}000x_3$$

$$\text{Subject to} \quad 12x_1 + 7x_2 + 9x_3 \leq 1{,}260$$

$$22x_1 + 18x_2 + 16x_3 \leq 19{,}008$$

$$2x_1 + 4x_2 + 3x_3 \leq 396$$

$$x_1 + x_2 + x_3 \geq 0$$

Introduce slack variables s_1, s_2 and s_3 to convert inequality to equality. The above problem would be written as

$$\text{Maximize} \quad Z = 4{,}000x_1 + 2{,}000x_2 + 5{,}000x_3 + 0.s_1 + 0.s_2 + 0.s_3$$

Subject to

$$12x_1 + 7x_2 + 9x_3 + s_1 + 0.s_2 + 0.s_3 = 1{,}260$$

$$22x_1 + 18x_2 + 16x_3 + 0.s_1 + s_2 + 0.s_3 = 19{,}008$$

$$2x_1 + 4x_2 + 3x_3 + 0.s_1 + 0.s_2 + s_3 = 396$$

$$x_1, x_2, x_3, s_1, s_2, s_3 \geq 0$$

Since there are six variables and three equation, set (6 – 3) = 3 variables as zero to get initial basic feasible solution.

An initial basic feasible solution is: $x_1 = 0$, $x_2 = 0$, $x_3 = 0$, $s_1 = 1260$, $s_2 = 19008$, $s_3 = 396$

We start with this solution and reiterate the same steps till we get optimal solution.

Simplex Tableau I, II, III

$C_j \rightarrow$ ↓	Basic Variable	Solution	4000 x_1	2000 x_2	5000 x_3	0 s_1	0 s_2	0 s_3	Ratio
0	s_1	1260	12	7	9	1	0	0	140
0	s_2	19008	22	18	16	0	1	0	1,188
0	s_3	396	2	4	(3)	0	0	1	← 132
	Z_j	0	0	0	0	0	0	0	
	$C_j - Z_j$		4000	2000	5000↑	0	0	0	
0	s_1	72	(6)	−5	0	1	0	−3	←12
0	s_2	16896	34/3	−10/3	0	0	1	−16/3	1,491
5000	x_3	132	2/3	4/3	1	0	0	1/3	198
	Z_j	660000	10000/3	20000/3	5000	0	0	5000/3	
	$C_j - Z_j$		2000/3↑	−1400/3	0	0	0	−5000/3	
400	x_1	12	1	−5/6	0	1/6	0	−3/6	
0	x_2	16760	0	55/9	0	−34/18	1	1/3	
5000	x_3	124	0	17/9	1	−2/18	0	2/3	
	Z_j	668000	4000	55000/9	5000	1000/9	0	4000/3	
	$C_j - Z_j$		0	2000	37000/9	0	−1000/9	−4000/3	

As all entries in $C_j - Z_j$ row are negative or zero, it implies optimal solution has been obtained. The maximum value of Z is 24 it occurs when $x_1 = 12$, $x_2 = 0$ and $x_3 = 124$.

(*iii*) The presence of s_2 in the final simplex table indicates that the second resource, namely, wood has not been fully utilized. It shows that the spare, capacity of wood left is 16,760 feet.

(*iv*) Shadow prices are 1000/9, 0, and 4000/3 respectively.

(*v*) Let y_1, y_2 and y_3 be the three positive dual variable associated with labour hours, wood and screws respectively. Then the dual problem corresponding to the given primal problem will be

Minimize $\quad Z^* = 1260y_1 + 19008y_2 + 396y_3$

Subject to $\quad 12y_1 + 22y_2 + 2y_3 \geq 4000$

$$7y_1 + 18y_2 + 4y_3 \geq 2000$$

$$9y_1 + 16y_2 + 3y_3 \geq 5000; \; y_1, y_2, y_3 \geq 0$$

(*vi*) According to the optimal solution, 12 row boat and 124 kayak boat are required to be manufactured. Therefore total wood used is : $22 \times 12 + 16 \times 224 = 2248$ board feet.

Example 19 : **A firm has two grades of cashew nuts : Grade I – 750 kg and grade II – 1200 kg. These are to be mixed types of packets of 1 kg each-economy and special. The economy pack consists of grade 1 and grade II in the proportion of 1:3, while the special pack combines the two in equal proportion. The contributions of the economy and the special packs are Rs. 5 and Rs. 8 per pack respectively.**

(*i*) **Formulate this as a linear programming problem to maximize contribution and solve it by Simplex method.**

(*ii*) **Write the dual of the above problem, read the optimum solution of the dual and give its economic interpretation.**

Solution : Let x_1 packets of economy type and $x_2$ackets of special type be produced by the firm. Then the appropriate mathematical formulation of the problem would be given as

Maximize $Z = 5x_1 + 8x_2$

Subject to $\frac{1}{4}x_1 + \frac{1}{2}x_2 \leq 750$ or $x_1 + 2x_2 \leq 3{,}000$

$\frac{3}{4}x_1 + \frac{1}{2}x_2 \leq 1{,}200$ or $3x_1 + 2x_2 \leq 4{,}800;\ x_1, x_2 \geq 0$

Add s_1 and s_2 as slack variable to convert inequalities to equality. Now the above problem would be restated as :

Maximize $Z = 5x_1 + 8x_2$

Subject to $x_1 + 2x_2 + s_1 = 3000$

$3x_1 + 2x_2 + s_2 = 4800$

$x_1, x_2, s_1, s_2 \geq 0$

There are four variables and two equations. Therefore, set (4 –2) = 2 variables as zero. Therefore initial feasible solution is obtained by setting $x_1 = x_2 = 0$

i.e., $s_1 = 3000,\ s_2 = 4800$

The initial basic feasible solution is summarized below in the tabular form in table 1. Therefore, sequence of table are framed to get optimal solution.

Simplex Tableau I, II, III

$C_j \rightarrow$ ↓*Variable*	*Basic Values*	*Solution* x_1	5 x_2	8 s_1	0 s_2	0	*Ratio*
0	s_1	3000	1	(2)	1	0	← 3000/2
0	s_2	4800	3	2	0	1	4800/2
	Z_j	0	0	0	0	0	
	$C_j - Z_j$		5	8↑	0	0	
8	x_2	1,500	$\frac{1}{2}$	1	$\frac{1}{2}$	0	3,000
0	s_2	1,800	(2*)	0	–1	1	←900
	Z_j	12,000	4	8	4	0	
	$C_j - Z_j$		1↑	0	– 4	0	
8	x_2	1,050	0	1	$\frac{3}{4}$	$-\frac{1}{4}$	
5	x_1	900	1	0	$-\frac{1}{2}$	$\frac{1}{2}$	
	Z_j	12,900	5	8	$\frac{7}{2}$	$\frac{1}{2}$	
	$C_j - Z_j$		0	0	$-\frac{7}{2}$	$-\frac{1}{2}$	

Since there is no number greater than zero, it implies optimal solution has been obtained.

Thus the optimal solution is : x_1 = 900 packets and x_2 = 1050 packets with maximum profit = Rs. 12,900

Let the dual variables be y_1 and y_2. Then the dual of the above problem will be given as :

Minimize $Z = 750y_1 + 1200y_2$

Subject to $\frac{1}{4}y_1 + \frac{3}{4}y_1 \geq 5\ \frac{2}{4}y_1 + \frac{2}{4}y_2 \geq 8;\ y_1, y_2 \geq 0$

On observing value in the $C_j - Z_j$ row under variables s_1 and s_2, we conclude optimal solution of dual is $\frac{y_1}{4} = 3.5$ or y_1 = Rs. 14 and $\frac{y_2}{4} = 0.5$ or y_2 = Rs. 2

Therefore, economic values of 1 kg. of g Grade *I* and *II* are Rs.14 and Rs. 2 respectively.

Example 20 : **A manufacturer makes three types of decorative tensor lamps: model 1200, model 1201 and model 1202. The requirement of raw materials for all lamps is the same, while the production time for each differs. Each model 1200 lamp requires 0.1 hr. of assembly time, 0.2 hr. of wiring time and 0.1 hr. of packaging time. The model 1201 requirs 0.2 hr. of assembly time, 0.3 hr. of wiring time and 0.1 hr. of packaging time. The model 1202 requires 0.3 hr. of assembly time, 0.4 hr. of wiring time, and 0.1 hr., of packaging time. The manufacturer makes a profit of Rs. 120 on each model 1200 lamp, Rs. 190 on each model 1201 lamp and Rs. 210 on each model 1202 lamp. The manufacturer can schedule upto 80 hr. of assembly labour, 120 hrs. of wiring labour and 100 hrs. of packaging labour.**

Assuming that all lamps can be sold, determine the optimal quantities of each model and the marginal values of each of the resources.

Write the dual of the given problem and obtain optimal values of the dual variables.

Solution : Let x_1, x_2 and x_3 be the number of lamps of model 1200, model 1201 and model 1202 respectively. Then the mathematical formulation of the problem will be given as :

Maximize $Z = 120x_1 + 190x_2 + 210x_3$

Subject to $0.1x_1 + 0.2x_2 + 0.3x_3 \leq 80$

$0.2x_1 + 0.3x_2 + 0.4x_3 \leq 120$

$0.1x_1 + 0.1x_2 + 0.1x_3 \leq 100$

$x_1, x_2, x_3 \geq 0$

Since there are 6 variables and 3 equations, therefore, set 6 – 3 = 3 variables as zero to get initial basic feasible solution.

$$x_1 = x_2 = x_3 = 0;\ s_1 = 80,\ s_2 = 120 \text{ and } s_3 = 100.$$

We start with this solution, and reiterate the same steps till we get optimal solution.

$C_j \rightarrow$	*Basic*	*Solution*	*120*	*190*	*210*	*0*	*0*	*0*	*Ratio*
↓	*Variable*		x_1	x_2	x_3	s_1	s_2	s_3	
0	s_1	80	1/10	2/10	(3/10)	1	0	0	← 800/3
0	s_2	120	2/10	3/10	4/10	0	1	0	300
0	s_3	100	1/10	1/10	1/10	0	0	1	1000

	Z_j	0	0	0	0	0	0	0	
	$C_j - Z_j$		120	190	210↑	0	0	0	
210	x_3	800/3	1/3	2/3	1	10/3	0	0	400
0	s_2	40/3	1/15	(1/30)	0	–4/3	1	0	←400
0	s_3	220/3	1/15	1/30	0	–1/3	0	1	2200
	Z_j	5600	70	140	210	700	0	0	
	$C_j - Z_j$		50	50↑	0	–700	0	0	
210	x_3	0	–1	0	1	(30)	–20	0	← 0
190	x_2	400	2	1	0	–40	30	0	–
0	s_3	60	0	0	0	1	–1	1	60
	Z_j	(76000)	170	190	210	–1,300	1,500	0	
	$C_j - Z_j$		–50	0	0	1,300↑	–1,500	0	
0	s_2	0	–1/30	0	1/30	1	–2/3	0	
190	x_2	400	2/3	1	4/3	0	10/3	0	
0	s_3	60	1/30	0	–1/30	0	–1/3	1	
	Z_j	76,000	380/3	190	760/3	0	1900/3	0	
	$C_j - Z_j$		–20/3	0	–130/3	0	–1900/3	0	

The optimal solution : $x_1 = 0$, $x_2 = 400$, $x_3 = 0$ with maximum value of Z as 76000

[Using slack variables, we can determine marginal values]

The marginal values are : Assembly –Nil; Wiring – Rs. 1900/3 per hour; Packaging – Nil.

The dual problem will be given as :

Minimize $Z^* = 80y_1 + 120y_2 + 100y_3$

Subject to $0.1y_1 + 0.2y_2 + 0.1y_3 \geq 120$

$0.2y_1 + 0.3y_2 + 0.1y_3 \geq 190$

$0.3y_1 + 0.4y_2 + 0.1y_3 \geq 100$; $y_1, y_2, y_3 \geq 0$

Using the values given in $C_j - Z_j$ *row under* s_1, s_2 and s_3 in the optimal solution of the primal problem. The optimal values of dual variables are determined as $y_1 = 0$, $y_2 = 1900/3$ and $y_3 = 0$ with $Z^* = 76000$

Exercise 4.3

Q.1 Write the duals of the following linear programming problems :

(*i*) Maximize Z = 2x + 6y

Subject to

$$4x + 2y \leq 5$$
$$3x + y \leq 7$$
$$x + y \leq 2$$
$$x, y \geq 0$$

[Minimize $Z^* = 5y_1 + 7y_2 + 2y_3$

Subject to

$$4y_1 + 3y_2 + y_3 \geq 2$$
$$2y_1 + y_2 + y_3 \geq 6$$
$$y_1, y_2, y_3 \geq 0]$$

(*ii*) Minimize $Z = 4x + 5y$

Subject to

$$x \geq 4, \quad y \geq 6, \quad x + y \geq 9, \quad x, y \geq 0$$

$$\left[\begin{array}{l}\text{Minimize } Z = 4y_1 + 6y_2 + 9y_3 \\ \text{Subject to} \\ \qquad y_1 + y_3 \leq 4 \\ \qquad y_2 + y_3 \leq 5 \\ \qquad y_1, y_2, y_3 \geq 0\end{array}\right]$$

Q. 2 Vitamins *A, B* and *C* are found in foods F_1 and F_2. One unit of F_1 contains 1 mg of *A* 100 mg of *B* and 10 mg of *C*. One unit of F_2 contains 1 mg of *A*, 10 mg of *B* and 100 mg of *C*. The minimum daily requirements of *A, B,* and *C* are 1 mg, 50 mg and 10 mg respectively. The costs per unit of F_1 and F_2 are Re. 1 and Rs. 1.5 respectively. You are required to (*i*) formulate the above as a linear programming problem minimizing the cost per day, (*ii*) write the dual of the problem and (*iii*) solve the dual by using simplex method and read from there the answer to the primal.

Q.3 Explain the concept of slack variables and dual of a given linear programming problem from the business point of view.

Q.4 A firm produces three items *A, B* and *C* at two plants *X* and *Y*. The number of items produced and operating cost per hour are as follows :

Plants	*Items produced per hour*			*Operating cost per hour*
	A	*B*	*C*	
X	30	60	40	Rs. 1,200
Y	30	20	100	Rs. 800

It is desired to produce atleast 400 items of type A, atleast 800 of type B and atleast 800 of type *C* per day. Find, using simplex method, the number of hours each plant be run on a day to have the minimum cost.

Q.5 A diet is to contain at least 20 ounces of protein and 15 ounces of carbohydrate. There are three foods *A, B,* and *C* available in the market, costing Rs. 2, Re. 1 and Rs. 3 per unit respectively. Each unit of *A* contains 2 ounces of protein and 4 ounces of carbohydrate; each unit of *B* contains 3 ounces of protein and 2 ounces of carbohydrate; each unit of *C* contains 4 ounces of protein and 2 ounces of carbohydrate. Find, by using simplex method, how many units of each food the diet should contain so that the cost per diet is minimum.

Q. 6 A person consume two types of food *A* and *B* everyday to obtain 8 units of protein, 12 units of carbohydrates and 9 units of fats which is his daily minimum requirement. One kilogram of food *A* contain 2, 6 and 1 units of protein, carbohydrates and fats respectively. One kilogram of food *B* contains 1, 1 and 3 units of protein, carbohydrates and facts respectively. Food *A* costs Rs. 8,50 per kilo, while *B* costs Rs. 4 per kilo. determine how many kilos of each food should he buy daily to minimize his cost of food and still meet the minimum requirements.

Formulate the problem mathematically. Write its dual and solve the dual by the simplex method.

Q.7 The following information is available for a firm which manufacturers three products *A, B* and *C,* which are processed in two departments Assembly and Finishing.

Product	Time Required (in hours)		Profit per Unit (Rs.)
	Assembly	Finishing	
A	10	2	80
B	4	5	60
C	5	4	30
Capacity	2000	1009	

(i) Formulate the above problem as a linear programming problem.

(ii) Obtain optimal solution to the problem by using the simplex method. Which of the three products shall not be produced by the firm? Why?

(iii) Write the dual to the above problem and determine the optimal values of the dual variables.

(iv) What are the shadow prices of the resources?

Q.8 Explain the relationship between a primal and its dual in a linear programming problem. Also explain the economic interpretation of slack variables in the problem. Obtain the dual of the following problem and solve it by simplex method.

Minimize $Z = 3x + 4y$

Subject to $5x + 10y \leq 800$

$15x + 10y \leq 1200$

$x, y \geq 0$

Q.9 A firm produces three articles *X, Y* and *Z* at a total cost of Rs. 4, Rs. 3 and Rs. 6 per item respectively. Total number of *X* and *Z* item produced should be at least 2 and number of *U* and *Z* together be at least 5. The firm wants to minimize the cost. Formulate this as a linear programming problem. Write its dual. Solve the dual by the simplex method. Can you point out from here the solution of the primal problem? If yes, what is it?

Solutions

2.(i) Minimize $Z = x_1 + 1.5x_2$

Subject to

$x_1 + x_2 \geq 1$

$100x_1 + 10x_2 \geq 50$

$10x_1 + 100x_2 \geq 10$

$x_1, x_2 \geq 0$

(ii) Minimize $Z^* = y_1 + 50y_2 + 10y_3$

Subject to $y_1 + 50y_2 + 10y_3 \leq 1$

$y_1 + 10y_2 + 100y_3 \leq 1.5$

$y_1, y_2, y_3 \leq 0$

(*iii*) $x_1 = 1, x_2 = 0$ with min Z = 1

4. Plant *X* shall be run for 12 hours. Plant *Y* shall be run for 4 hours with minimum cost = Rs. 17,600.

5. 5/8 units of *A*, 25/4 units of *B*, 0 unit of *C* with minimum cost = Rs.7.50

6. Minimize $Z = 8.50x_1 + 4x_2$

Subject to $2x_1 + x_2 \geq 8$

$6x_1 + x_2 \geq 12$

$x_1 + 3x_2 \geq 9$

$x_1, x_2 \geq 0$

The dual problem is:

Maximize $Z^* = 8y_1 + 12y_2 + 9y_3$

Subject to $2y_1 + 6y_2 + y_3 \leq 8.50$

$y_1 + y_2 + 3y_3 \leq 4$

$y_1, y_2, y_3 \geq 0$

$x_1 = 1, x_2 = 6$ with min $Z = \frac{65}{2}$, $y_1 = \frac{31}{8}$, $y_2 = \frac{1}{8}$, $y_3 = 0$ with max $Z^* = \frac{65}{2}$.

7.(*i*) Maximize $Z^* = 80x_1 + 60x_2 + 30x_3$

Subject to $10x_1 + 4x_2 + 5x_3 \leq 2000$

$2x_1 + 5x_2 + 4x_3 \leq 1009$

$x_1, x_2, x_3 \geq 0$

(*ii*) $x_1 = 142$, $x_2 = 145$, $x_3 = 0$ and max Z = 20060; Product *C*

(*iii*) The dual problem is:

Minimize $Z^* = 2000y_1 + 1009y_2$

Subject to $10y_1 + 2y_2 \geq 80$

$4y_1 + 5y_2 \geq 60$

$5y_1 + 4y_2 \geq 30$

$y_1, y_2 \geq 0$

Optimum solution to the dual is :

$y_1 = 20/3$, $y_2 = 20/3$ and max $Z = 20060$

(*iv*) Shadow prices: 20/3 and 20/3.

8.(*i*) Maximize $Z^* = 800y_1 + 1200y_2$

Subject to $5y_1 + 15y_2 \leq 3$

$10y_1 + 10y_2 \leq 4$

$y_1, y_2 \geq 0$

$y_1 = \frac{1}{10}$, $y_2 = \frac{3}{10}$ with $Z^* = 360$; $x = 40$, $y = 60$ with min Z = 360.

9. Minimize $Z = 4x_1 + 3x_2 + 6x_3$ The dual problem is:

Subject to	$x_1 + x_3 \geq 2$	Minimize $Z^* = 2y_1 + 5y_2$
	$x_2 + x_3 \geq 5$	$y_1 \leq 4$
	$x_1, x_2, x_3 \geq 0$	$y_2 \leq 3$
		$y_1 + y_2 \leq 6$
		$y_1, y_2 \geq 0$

$x_1 = 0, x_2 = 3, x_3 = 2$ with min $Z = 21$; $y_1 = 3, y_2 = 3$, with max $Z^* = 21$.

Additional Solved Exercise

Q. 1 A toy manufacturer produces two types of dolls: a basic version doll *A* and a deluxe version doll *B*. Each doll of type *B* takes twice as long as to produce as one doll of type *A*. The company has time to make maximum of 2000 doll of type *A* per day. The supply of plastic is sufficient to produce 1500 dolls per days and each type requires equal amount of it. The deluxe version *i.e.,* type *B* requires a fancy dress of which there are 600 per day available. If the company makes a profit of Rs. 3 and Rs. 5 per doll, respectively, on doll *A* and *B*, how many of each should be produced per day in order to maximize profit, Solve using.

(*a*) Graphical Method

(*b*) Simplex Method.

Solution : Let *x* number of doll *A* and *y* number of doll *B* be produced per day. Then, we have

Maximize $Z = 3x + 5y$

Subject to constraints

$$x + 2y \leq 2000$$
$$x + y \leq 1500$$
$$y \leq 600$$
$$x, y \geq 0$$

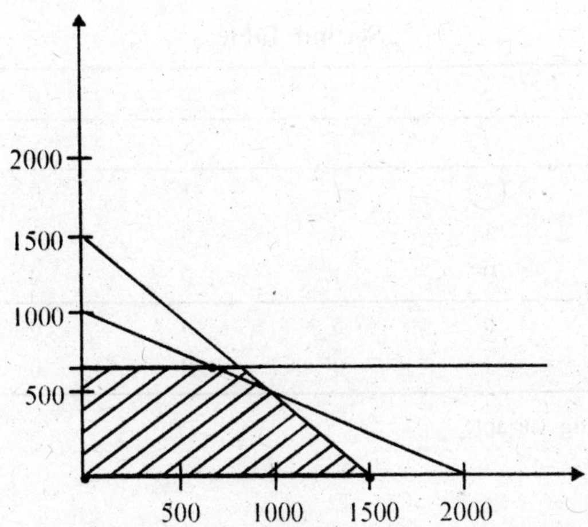

Fig. (A)

Plotting the above constraints, we have common shaded area as shown in figure (A).

Extreme points are (0, 600), (800, 600), (1000, 500), (1500, 0).

Value of Z at these points.

$$Z_{(0,\ 600)} = 3000$$
$$Z_{(800,\ 600)} = 5400$$
$$Z_{(1000,\ 500)} = 5500$$
$$Z_{(1500,\ 0)} = 4500$$

Value of Z is maximum at $x = 1000$ and $y = 500$, therefore 1000 dolls of type A and 500 dolls of type B shall be produced.

(*b*) Solution using Simplex method.

Max. $Z = 3x + 5y + OS_1 + OS_2 + OS_3$

Subject to constraint
$$x + 2y + S_1 = 2000$$
$$x + y + S_2 = 1500$$
$$y + S_3 = 600$$
$$x, y, s_1, s_2, s_3 \geq 0$$

The initial basic feasible solution table would be as under.

$C_j \rightarrow$ ↓	Basic Variable	Solution	3 *x*	5 *y*	0 S_1	0 S_2	0 S_3	Ratio
0	S_1	2000	1	2	1	0	0	1000
0	S_2	1500	1	1	0	1	0	1500
0	S_3	600	0	(1)	0	0	1	600
	Z_j	0	0	0	0	0	0	
	$C_j - Z_j$		3	5	0	0	0	

Y–entering variable; S_3– Departing variable.

Second Table

$C_j \rightarrow$ ↓	Basic Variable	Solution	3 *x*	5 *y*	0 S_1	0 S_2	0 S_3	Ratio
0	S_1	800	(1)	0	1	0	–2	800
0	S_2	900	1	0	0	1	–1	900
5	*y*	600	0	1	0	0	1	–
	Z_j	3000	0	5	0	0	5	
	$C_j - Z_j$		3	0	0	0	–5	

X–entering variable; S_1 –Departing variable.

Third Table

$C_j \rightarrow$ ↓	Basic Variable	Solution	3 x	5 y	0 S_1	0 S_2	0 S_3	Ratio
3	x	800	1	0	1	0	–2	–400
0	S_2	100	0	0	–1	1	(1)	100
5	y	600	0	1	0	0	1	600
	Z_j	5400	3	5	3	0	–1	
	$C_j - Z_j$		0	0	–3	0	+1	

Now S_3 is entering variable and S_2 is departing variable.

$C_j \rightarrow$ ↓	Basic Variable	Solution	3 x	5 y	0 S_1	0 S_2	0 S_3	Ratio
3	x	1000	3	0	–1	2	0	
0	S_3	100	0	0	–1	1	1	
5	y	500	0	1	1	–1	0	
	Z_j	5500	9	5	2	1	0	
	$C_j - Z_j$		–6	0	–2	–1	0	

∴ Solution $X = 1000$, $y = 500$ and Maximum profit = 5500

Q. 2 Satnam Auto Ltd. manufacture two product *A* and *B* using three types of raw material *X, Y, Z*.

The details have been given below in the table :

Material	Product A	Product B	No, of units available
X	5	2	170
Y	4	5	170
Z	3	8	180

The profit from *A* and *B* per unit are Rs. 5 and Rs. 3 respectively. The manager has decided to manufacture 30 units of *A* and 10 units of *B* so as to have optimum product mix for profit maximisation, (using simplex method). the optimal table is partially given below.

$C_j \rightarrow$ ↓	Basic Variable	Solution Values	5 a	3 b	0 s_1	0 s_2	0 s_3
5	a	30	1	0	5/17	–2/17	0
3	b	10	0	1	–4/17	5/17	0
0	S_3	10	0	0	1	–2	1

On the basis of above information.

(*i*) Check it the solution is optimal and what will be the profit in such a case?

(*ii*) What are the shadow prices of material *X, Y,* and *Z*?

(*iii*) If the manager increase the use of material *X* by one unit, what will be the impact on the optimum product portfolio.

(*iv*) If the cost of increasing one additional unit of *Y* is 8/17, shall the manager attempt to increase its use.

(*v*) What will be the change in overall profitability of the company if use of material *X* is decreased by 10 units.

Solution. (*i*) Testing optimal condition.

$C_j \rightarrow$ ↓	*Basic Variable*	*Solution*	*5* *a*	*3* *b*	*0* s_1	*0* s_2	*0* s_3	*Ratio*
5	*a*	30	1	0	5/17	–2/17	0	
3	*b*	10	0	1	–4/17	5/17	0	
0	S_3	10	0	0	1	–2	1	
	Z_j	180	5	3	13/17	5/17	0	
	$C_j - Z_j$		0	0	–13/17	–5/17	0	

Since all the elements in $(C_j - Z_j)$ row are negative it implies optimal solution has reached and the profit in this case is 180.

(*ii*) The shadow prices of material *X*, *Y* and *Z* are 13/17, 5/17 and 0 respectively.

(*iii*) If the use of material *X* is increased by 1 unit, there will be increase in product '*a*' by 5/17, decrease in product '*b*' by 4/17 and increase in unused resource *Z* by 1 unit. As a result of this, profit of the organisation will change as

$$= 5 \times \frac{5}{17} - 3 \times \frac{4}{17} + 0 \times 1 = \frac{13}{17}.$$

This implies the manager shall attempt to increase the use of resource material *X* if its cost is less than 13/17.

(*d*) No, Since one additional unit of *Y* will be able to increase total profit by 5/17 which is less than incremental cost of 8/17.

(*e*) One unit of *X* is impacting the profit by 13/17. Thus, if the use of *X* is decreased by 10 units. the profit will decline by 10 × 13/17 = 130/17.

$$\therefore \quad \text{New Profit} = 180 - \frac{130}{17} = 180 - 7.64 = 172.36.$$

Q. 3 The ABC Company has been a producer of picture tube for television sets and certain printed circuits for radios. The company has just expanded into full scale production and marketing of AM and AM-FM radios. It has built a new plant that can operate 48 hours per week Production of an AM radio in the new plant will require 2 hours and production of an AM-FM radio will require 3 hours. Each AM radio will contribute Rs. 40 to profits while an AM-FM radio will contribute Rs. 80 to profits. The marketing department, after extensive research, has determined that a maximum of 15 AM radios and 10 AM-FM radios can be sold each week.

(*i*) Formulate a linear programming model to determine the optimal production mix of AM and AM-FM radios that will maximize profits.

(*ii*) Solve the above problem using the graphic method.

Solution :

Let x_1 = Number of units of AM Radio

x_2 = Number of units of AM-FM radio.

Therefore the above problem, will be given as:

Maximize (Total profit) $Z = 40x_1 + 80x_2$

Subject to the constraints :

$$2x_1 + 3x_2 \leq 48$$
$$x_1 \leq 15$$
$$x_2 \leq 10$$
$$x_1 \geq 0, x_2 \geq 0$$

The graph of these inequalities is shown in the following figure :

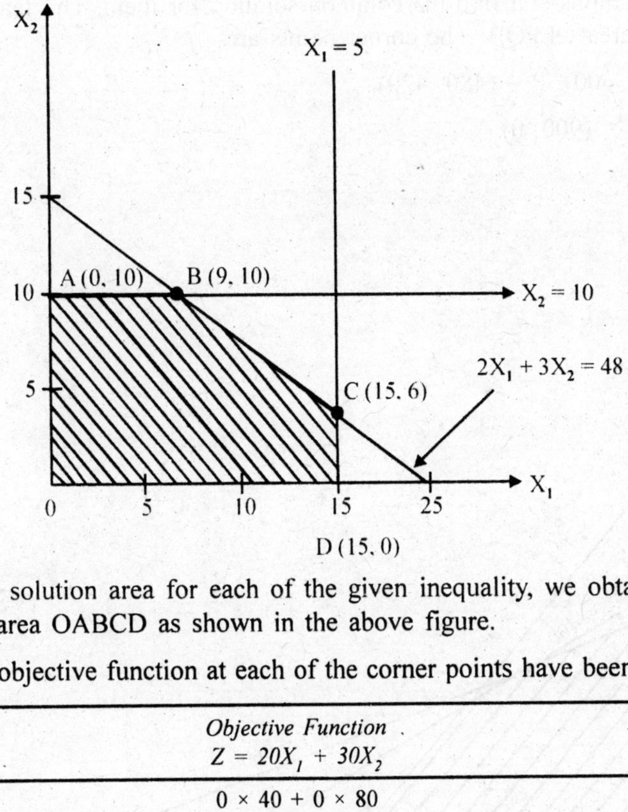

On observing the solution area for each of the given inequality, we obtain the feasible region given by the shaded area OABCD as shown in the above figure.

The value of the objective function at each of the corner points have been tabulated as follows–

Corner Points	*Objective Function* $Z = 20X_1 + 30X_2$	*Value*
O (0, 0)	0 × 40 + 0 × 80	0
A(0, 0)	0 × 40 + 10 × 80	800
B(0, 10)	9 × 40 + 10 × 80	1160
C(15, 6)	15 × 40 + 6 × 80	1080
D(15, 0)	15 × 40 + 0 × 80	600

It can be observed from the above table that the value of Z is maximum at the point B(9, 10). Therefore, the optimum solution will be as follows.

$X_1 = 9$, $X_2 = 10$ and Z = Rs. 1,160.

Q.4 Solve the following problem using graphical method:

Maximize: $Z = 9X + 10Y$

Subject to: $11X + 9Y \leq 9{,}900$

$7X + 12Y \leq 8{,}400$

$6X + 16Y \leq 9{,}600$

$X \geq 0,\ Y \geq 0$

Solution : The equation of equalities corresponding to above constraints are as follows :

$$11X + 9Y = 9{,}900$$

$$7X + 12Y = 8{,}400$$

$$6X + 16Y = 9{,}600$$

Plot the above equations and find the common solution for them. The feasible region has been shown by the shaded area OEPQB. The corner points are–

O = (0, 0) E = (0, 600), P = (480, 420).

Q = (625, 335), B = (900, 0)

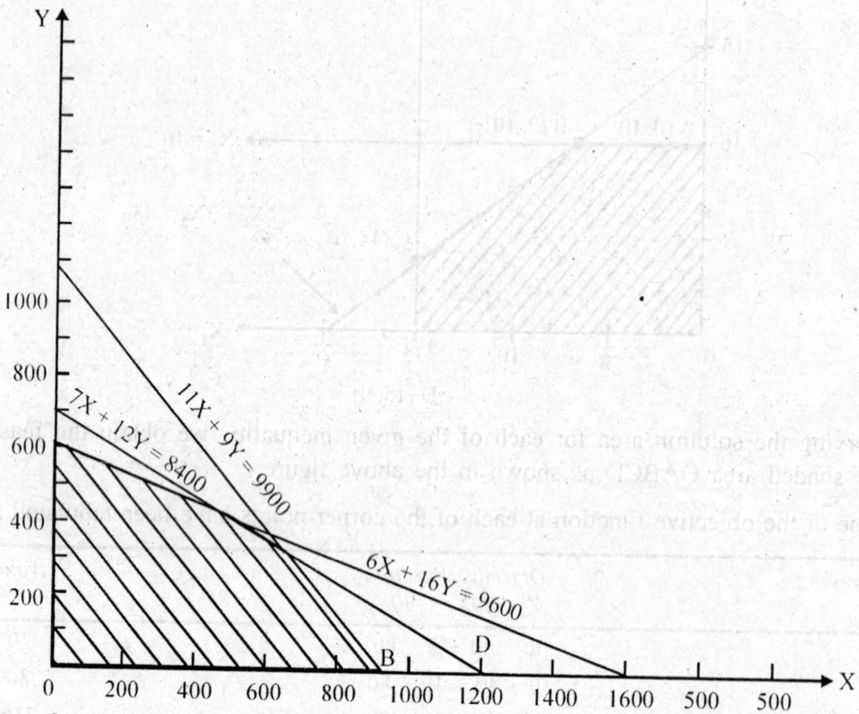

The value of the objective function (Z) at various corner points is tabulated below.

Corner Points	*Objective Function* $Z = 20X_1 + 30X_2$	*Value*
O (0, 0)	$0 \times 9 + 0 \times 10$	0
E(0, 600)	$0 \times 9 + 600 \times 10$	6000

B(480, 420)	480 × 9 + 420 × 10	8520
C(626, 335)	626 × 9 + 335 × 10	8984
D(900, 0)	900 × 9 + 0 × 10	8100

Thus, it is clear that the objective function (Z) is maximum (8984) at Q point. Therefore, X = 626 and Y = 335.

Problem 5

A firm, manufacturing two types of electrical items, A and B, can make a profit of Rs. 20 per unit of A and Rs. 30 per unit of B. Each unit of A requires 3 motors and 2 transformers and each unit of B requires 2 motors and 4 transformers. The total supply of these per month is restricted to 2010 motors and 300 transformers. Type B is an export model requiring a voltage stabilizer, which has a supply restricted to 65 units per month. Formulate the linear programming problem for maximum profit and solve it graphically.

Solution

Let for optimum solution x units of product A and y units of product B be produced. Since the objective of manufacturer is to maximize the profit, thus the objective function will be given as:

Maximize $Z = 20x + 30y$

Each unit of product A and B requires 3 and 2 motors and the supply of motors and the supply of motors is restricted to 210 motors, therefore the inequality constraint will be given as :

$$3x + 2y \leq 210$$

Similarly each unit of product A and B requires 2 and 4 transformers respectively, therefore the inequality constraint will be given as:

$$2x + 4y \leq 300$$

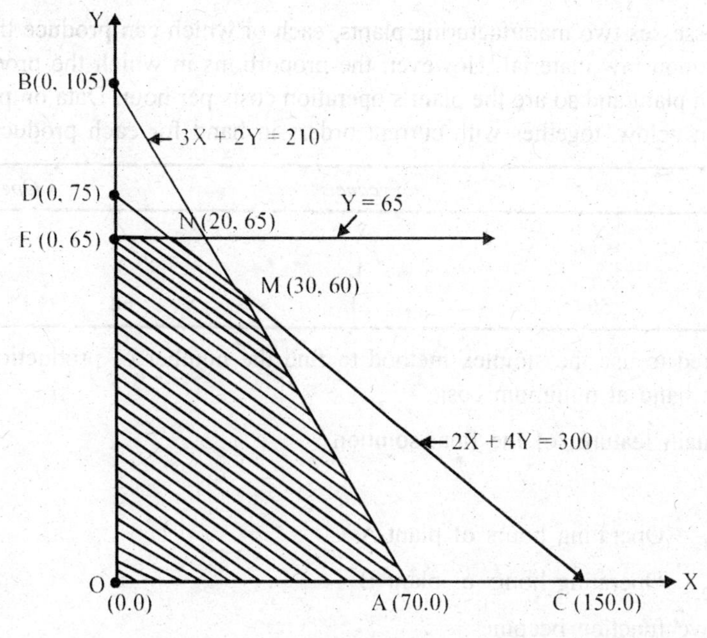

Voltage stabilizer is needed only for product B, therefore the constraint for it will be given as $Y \leq 65$:

Formulating the above problem mathematically, we have

Maximize : $Z = 20X + 30Y$

Subject to : $3X + 2Y \leq 210$

$2X + 4Y \leq 300$

$Y \geq 65$

$X, Y \geq 0$

The shaded area denoted by a OAMNE determines the optimum solution. The corner points of hexagon are O(0, 0), A(70, 0), M(30, 60), N(20, 65), and E(0, 65). The value of objective functions (Z) at various corner points is tabulated as below:

Corner Points	*Objective Function*
20X + 30Y = Z	O (0, 0)
20 × 0 + 30 × 0 = 0	A(70, 0)
20 × 70 + 30 × 0 = 1400	M(30, 60)
20 × 30 + 30 × 60 = 2400	N(20, 65)
20 × 20 + 30 × 65 = 2350	E(0, 65)
20 × 0 + 30 × 65 = 1950	

The value of objective functions (Z) is maximum (2, 400) at M. Therefore, to optimise the profit 30 units of product A and 60 units of product B should be produced. At this level the profit will be Rs. 2,400.

Problem 6

A company possesses two manufacturing plants, each of which can produce three products X, Y and Z, from a common raw material. However, the proportions in which the products are produced are different in each plant and so are the plant's operation costs per hour. Data on production per hour and costs are given below, together with current orders in hand for each product.

		Products		*Operating Cost per Hour*
Plant A	X	Y	Z	Rs.
Plant B	2	4	3	9
Orders on hand	50	24	60	10

You are required to use the simplex method to find the number of production hours needed to fulfil the orders in hand at minimum cost.

Interpret the main features of the final solution.

Solution:

Let, x_1 = Operating hours of plant A

x_2 = Operating hours of plant B

∴ The objective function becomes

Minimize $Z = 9x_1 + 10x_2$

Subject to the constraints

$$2x_1 + 4x_2 \geq 50 \text{ or } x_1 + 2x_2 \geq 25 \quad \text{(Product X)}$$

$$4x_1 + 3x_2 \geq 24 \quad \text{(Product Y)}$$

$$3x_1 + 2x_2 \geq 60 \quad \text{(Product Z)}$$

and $\quad x_1, x_2 \geq 0$

Introducing surplus and artificial variables we get :

Minimize $Z = 9x_1 + 10x_2 + 0s_1 + 0s_2 + MA_1 + MA_2 + MA_3$

Subject to the constraints

$$x_1 + 2x_2 - s_1 + A_1 = 25$$

$$4x_1 + 3x_2 - s_2 + A_2 = 24$$

$$3x_1 + 2x_2 - s_3 + A_3 = 60$$

$$x_1, x_2, s_1, s_2, s_3, A_1, A_2, A_3 \geq 0$$

Simplex Table I

C_j →			9	10	0	0	0	M	M	M		
↓	*Basic Variable*	*Solution value*	x_1	x_2	s_1	s_2	s_3	A_1	A_2	A_3	*Min Ratio*	
M	A_1	25	1	2	–1	0	1	1	0	0	25	
M	A_2	24	4*	3	0	–1	0	0	1	0	6	
M	A_3	64	3	2	0	0	0	0	0	1	26	Key Row
	Z_j		$8M$	$7M$	$-M$	$-M$	$-M$	M	M	$-M$		
	$C_j - Z_j$		$9-8M$↑	$10-7M$	M	M	M	0	0	0		

Table II (Entering variable x_1 Departing variable A_2)

C_j →			9	10	0	0	0	M	M	M	
↓	*Basic Variable*	*Solution value*	x_1	x_2	s_1	s_2	s_3	A_1	A_2	A_3	*Min Ratio*
M	A_1	19		0	$\frac{5}{4}$	–1	$\frac{1}{4}$	0	1	0	76
9	x_1	6		1	$\frac{3}{4}$	0	$-\frac{1}{4}$	0	0	0	–
M	A_3	42		0	$-\frac{3}{4}$	0	$\frac{3}{4}$	–1	0	1	56
	Z_j			9	$M + \frac{27}{4}$	$-M$	$M - \frac{9}{4}$	$-M$	M	M	
	$C_j - Z_j$			0	$-M + \frac{13}{4}$	M	$-M + \frac{9}{4}$ ↑	M	0	0	

Table III (Entering variable S_2, Departing variable A_3)

C_j ↓	→ Basic Variable	Solution value	9 x_1	10 x_2	0 s_1	0 s_2	0 s_3	M A_1	M A_2	M A_3	Min Ratio
M	A_1	5		0	$\frac{4}{3}$	–1	0	$\frac{1}{2}$	1	$\leftarrow \frac{5}{4/3}$	
9	x_1	20		1	$\frac{2}{3}$	0	0	$\frac{1}{3}$	0	$\frac{20}{4/3}$	
0	s_2	56		0	$-\frac{1}{3}$	0	1	$-\frac{4}{3}$	0		
	Zj			9	$\frac{4M}{3}+6$	–M	0	$\frac{M}{3}-3$	M		
	$C_j - Z_j$			0	$-\frac{4M}{3}+4$	M	0	$-\frac{M}{3}+3$	0		

Table IV (Entering variable x_2, Departing variable A_1)

C_j ↓	→ Basic Variable	Solution value	9 x_1	10 x_2	0 s_1	0 s_2	0 s_3
10	x_2	$\frac{15}{4}$	0	1	$-\frac{3}{4}$	0	$\frac{1}{4}$
9	x_1	$\frac{35}{2}$	1	0	$\frac{1}{2}$	0	$-\frac{1}{2}$
0	s_2	$\frac{229}{4}$	0	0	$-\frac{1}{4}$	1	$-\frac{5}{4}$
	Zj		9	10	–3	0	–2
	$C_j - Z_j$		0	0	3	0	2

Since all the entries in the Cj – Zj row are either zero or positive, it implies optimum solution has been obtained *i.e.*, 17.5 hours of plant A and 3.75 hours of plant B are needed to fulfill the orders on hand at minimum cost of Rs. 195.

Problem 7

An animal feed company must produce 200 kgs. of a mixture consisting of ingredients A and B daily. A costs Rs. 3 per kg. and B costs Rs. 8 per kg. No more than 80 kgs. of A can be used and at least 60 kgs. of B must be used. Find how much of each ingredient should be used if the company wants to minimise cost.

Solution

Let A be denoted by X_1 and B by Z_2. The mathematical formulation of the above problem will be given as under:

Minimize $Z = 3X_1 + 8X_2$

Subject to: $X_1 + A_1 = 200$

$X_1 \leq 80$

$X_2 \geq 60$

$X1, X2 \geq 0$

In order to convert the problem of minimization into maximization the objective function shall be changed as follows :

Max $Z = -3X_1 - 8X_2$

Now it, can be solved as the problem of maximization.

$$\text{Max. } Z = -3X_1 - 8X_2 + OS_1 + OS_2 - MA_1 - MA_2$$

Subject to $X_1 + X_2 + A_1 = 200$

$X_1 + S_1 = 80$

$X_2 - S_2 + A_2 = 60$

$X_1 X_2 S_1 S_2 A_1 A_2 \geq 0$

First Simplex Table

C_j		→	-3	-8	0	0	$-M$	M	
↓	*Basic Variable*	*Quality value*	X_1	X_2	S_1	S_2	A_1	A_2	*Ratio*
$-M$	A_1	200	1	1	0	0	1	0	200
0	S_1	80	1	0	1	0	0	0	–
					Key element				
$-M$	A_2	60	0	1	0	–1	0	1	60
								Key Row	
	Zj	*–260M*	*–M*	*–2M*	0	*M*	*–M*	*–M*	
	Cj – Zj		*–3+M*	*–8 – 2M*↑	0	*–M*	0	0	

Second Table

C_j	→		-3	-8	0	0	$-M$
↓	*Basic Variable*	*Quality value*	X_1	X_2	S_1	S_2	A_1
M	A_1	140	1	0	0	1	1
0	S_1	80	1	0	1	0	0
-8	X_2	60	0	1	0	–1	0
	Zj	–480 –140*M*	$-M$	–8	0	8–*M*	$-M$
	$C_j - Z_j$		–3 +*M*↑	0	0	*M* – 8	0

Third Simplex Table

C_j	→		−3	−8	0	0	−M	
↓	*Basic Variable*	*Quality value*	X_1	X_2	S_1	S_2	A_1	*Ratio*
−M	A_1	60	0	0	[−1]	1	1	60
						Key element		
−3	X_1	80	1	0	1	0	0	–
−8	X_2	60	0	1	0	−1	0	–
	Zj	−720−60M	−3	−8	−3 + M	8−M	−M	
	$C_j - Z_j$		0	0	0	M − 8	0	

Fourth Table

C_j	→		−3	−8	0	0
↓	*Basic Variable*	*Quality*	X_1	X_2	S_1	S_2
−M	S_1	60	0	0	−1	1
0	X_1	80	1	0	1	0
−8	X_2	120	0	1	−1	0
	Zj	−1200	−3	−8	5	0
	$C_j - Z_j$		0	0	−5	0

Since all the entries in index row $(C_j - Z_j)$ are negative or zero therefore, the fourth table gives the optimum solution.

Maximize $Z = -1200,\ X_1 = 80,\ X_2 = 120,\ S_2 = 60$

In other words, Minimize $Z = -\text{Maximize } Z$

$$= -(-1200) = 1200$$

Problem 8

A company produced two product A and B, each of which requires three types of processing. The length of time for processing each unit and the profit per unit are given in the following table :

	Product A (hr/unit)	*Product B (hr/unit)*	*Available capacity per day (hr)*
Process I	120	120	8,400
Process II	30	60	3,000
Process III	80	40	4,800
Profit per unit (Rs.)	50	70	4,800

How many units of each product should the company produce per day. In order to maximize the profit?

Solution

Let x_1 be the number of units of product A and x_2 be number of units of product B, produced by the company. The mathematical formulation of the above problem will be given as:

Maximize $Z = 50x_1 + 70x_2$

Subject to the constraints $120x_1 + 120x_2 \leq 8400$

$$x_1 + x_2 \leq 70$$

$$x_1 + 2x_2 \leq 100$$

$$2x_1 + x_2 \leq 120$$

$$x_1, x_2 \geq 0$$

Introducing slack variables s_1, s_2 and s_3 we get

Maximize $Z = 50x_1 + 70x_2 + 0s_1 + 0s_2 + 0s_3$

Subject to the constraints $x_1 + x_2 + s_1 = 70$

$$x_1 + 2x_2 + s_2 = 100$$

$$2x_1 + x_2 + s_3 = 120$$

$$x_1, x_2, s_1, s_2, s_3, \geq 0$$

Table I

$C_j \rightarrow$ ↓	*Basic Variable*	*Solution Values*	50 x_1	70 x_2	0 s_1	0 s_2	0 s_3	*Ratio*
0	s_1	70	1	1	1	0	0	70
0	$\leftarrow s_2$	100	1	2	0	1	0	50←
0	s_3	120	2	1	0	1	1	120
	Z_j	0		0	0	0	0	
	$C_j - Z_j$		50	70↑	0	0	0	

Table II (Introduce and drop s_1)

$C_j \rightarrow$ ↓	*Basic Variable*	*Solution Values*	50 x_1	70 x_2	0 s_1	0 s_2	0. s_3	*Ratio*
0	$\leftarrow s_1$	20	$\frac{1}{2}$	0	1	$-\frac{1}{2}$	0	40←
70	x_2	50	$\frac{1}{2}$	1	0	$\frac{1}{2}$	0	100
0	s_3	70	$\frac{3}{2}$	0	0	$-\frac{1}{2}$	1	46.67
	Z_j	3500	35	70	0	35	0	
	$C_j - Z_j$		15↑	0	0	–35	0	

Table III (Introduce x_1 and s_1)

$C_j \rightarrow$ ↓	Basic Variable	Solution Values	50 x_1	70 x_2	0 s_1	0 s_2	0 s_3
50	x_1	40	1	0	2	–1	0
70	x_2	30	0	1	–1	1	0
0	s_3	10	0	0	–3	1	1
	Z_j	4100	50	70	30	20	0
	$C_j - Z_j$		0	0	–30	–20	0

Since all the elements in the $C_j - Z_j$, row of table–III are either negative or zero. Hence optimal Solution is $x_1 = 40$, $x_2 = 30$ and

$$\text{Max. } Z = \text{Rs } (50\times40) + (70\times30) = \text{Rs. } 4100$$

5

Functions, Limits and Continuity

HIGHLIGHTS OF THE CHAPTER

- **Concept of Functions**
- **Types of Functions**
- **Special Types of Functions**
- **Limit – Concepts**
- **Properties of Limit**
- **Evaluation of Limit**
- **Continuity – Basic Concepts**
- **Cauchy's definition of continuity**
- **Removable Continuity**
- **Applications of Continuity in Business and Economics.**

INTRODUCTION

The present chapter deals with concept of functions, limit and continuity. In business and economics, while making managerial decisions. one must know the relationship among various factors contributing to the growth of the business. One must know, how the demand of his product is related to various components of the market. Keeping in view this fact, one must know basic knowledge of functions, which is discussed in the present chapter along with its relevance in Business Mathematics.

FUNCTIONS–CONCEPT

Function refers to the relationship between two interrelated variables. For example, price and demand. Demand is a function of price. Whenever, there is change in the price, there would be a change in demand. Thus, function may be referred as a model which gives a value to the dependent variable due to any change in independent variable.

For example

$$y = f(x)$$

Here y is a function of x, y is said to be dependent variables of 'x' is said to be independent variable. The set of the values of x belonging to the domains of a function generate another set which consists of values of y. This generated set is called the range of the function $f(x)$.

From the above brief discussion, we conclude that for any given function, the value, which can be taken by independent variable is called **domain** and corresponding to these values, the set of value, generated by dependent variable is called **range.**

The concept of domain and range would because more clear from the following examples.

Example 1 : **Find the domain and range of function** $f(x) = \dfrac{x^2 - 25}{x - 5}$.

Solution : Domain of given function f :

$f(x)$ is not defined for $x - 5 = 0$ *i.e.* $x = 5$

∴ Domain of the given function = $R - \{5\}$

where 'R' is set of real numbers.

Range of function f :

Let $\dfrac{x^2 - 25}{x - 5} = \dfrac{(x+5)(x-5)}{(x-5)} = y$

∴ $x + 5 = y$

Since 'x' cannot be equal to '5'

∴ 'y' cannot be equal to $5 + 5 = 10$

∴ Range of function 'f' = $R - \{6\}$.

Example 2 : Find the domain and range of

$$f(x) = \frac{7 - x}{x - 7}.$$

Solution : Domain of $f(x)$

The function is not defined for $x = 7$ since at $x = 7$ $f(x) = \dfrac{0}{0}$.

∴ Domain = $R - \{7\}$.

Range of $f(x)$

Let $y = \dfrac{7 - x}{x - 7} = -\dfrac{(x-7)}{(x-7)} = -1$

For any value of 'x' range is -1.

Solved Exercise

Example 3 : **Find the domain of each of the following real valued function.**

(*i*) $f(x) = \dfrac{1}{x + 3}$

(*ii*) $f(x) = \dfrac{x - 5}{x - 7}$

(*iii*) $f(x) = \dfrac{5x - 7}{(x^2 - 5x + 5)}$

(*iv*) $f(x) = \dfrac{x^2 - 2x + 9}{x^2 - 7x + 10}$

Solution :

(*i*) Given function

$$f(x) = \frac{1}{x + 3}$$

The function is defined for all values of x except $x = -3$.

$\therefore$ Domain = $R - \{-3\}$.

(*ii*) Given function

$$f(x) = \frac{x - 5}{x - 7}$$

The function is defined for all values of x except $x = 7$.

$\therefore$ Domain = $R - \{7\}$.

(*iii*) Given function

$$f(x) = \frac{5x - 7}{(x^2 - 5x + 5)}$$

Solving for $x^2 - 5x + 5 = 0$, we have

$x = 1$, $x = 5$, therefore, the function is defined for all values of 'x' except $x = 1$, $x = 5$.

$\therefore$ Domain of function = $R - \{1, 5\}$.

(*iv*) Given function

$$f(x) = \frac{x^2 - 2x + 9}{x^2 - 7x + 10}$$

Solving for $x^2 - 7x + 10 = 0$, we have

$x = 2$ and $x = 5$. This implies, the function is defined for all values of 'x' except $x = 2$ and $x = 5$.

$\therefore$ Domain of $f(x) = R - \{2, 5\}$.

***Example 4 :* Find the domain of following functions.**

(*i*) $f(x) = \sqrt{9 - x^2}$

(*ii*) $f(x) = \dfrac{1}{\sqrt{1 - x}}$

Solution :

(*i*) iven function

$$f(x) = \sqrt{9 - x^2}$$

The function will assume real values if

$$9 - x^2 \geq 0$$

$$-(x^2 - 9) \geq 0$$

$$(x^2 - 9) \leq 0$$

$$(x - 3)(x + 3) \leq 0$$

$$x \in [-3, 3]$$

$\therefore$ Domain of $f(x) = [-3, 3]$

(*ii*) Given function $f(x) = \dfrac{1}{\sqrt{1 - x}}$

The function will assume real values if

$1 - x > 0$

$\therefore \quad 1 > x$

$\therefore$ Domain of function $= (-\alpha, 1)$.

Example 5 : Find the domain and range of the following functions :

(*i*) $\dfrac{1}{\sqrt{x - 7}}$

(*ii*) $\sqrt{25 - x^2}$

Solution : (*i*) Given

$$f(x) = \frac{1}{\sqrt{x - 7}}$$

$f(x)$ takes real valves, if $x - 7 > 0$ *i.e.* $x > 7$

$\therefore$ Domain of $f(x) = x \in (7, \alpha)$.

Range for any value of $x < 7$

$$x - 7 > 0$$

$$\therefore \quad \sqrt{x - 7} > 0$$

$$\frac{1}{\sqrt{x - 7}} > 0$$

From the above expression, we conclude that when 'x' will remain in its domain *i.e.* $[7, \alpha]$, 'y' $f(x)$ will remain positive. This implies range of $f(x)$ will be $(0, \alpha)$.

(*ii*) Given function

$$f(x) = \sqrt{25 - x^2}$$

Domain

The function is defined when

$$25 - x^2 \geq 0$$

$$x^2 - 25 \leq 0$$

$$(x - 5)(x + 5) \leq 0$$

Domain of function $f(x) = [-5, 5]$

Finding range

Let $$y = \sqrt{25 - x^2}$$

$\therefore$ $$x = \sqrt{25 - y^2}$$

'x' will take real values when $25 - y^2 \geq 0$

or $$y^2 - 25 \leq 0$$

$\therefore$ $(y - 5)(y + 5) \leq 0$

$y \in [-5, 5]$

However 'y' is positive for $x \in [-5, 5]$

$\therefore$ Range of the gives function is $[0, 5]$.

Note : Range are set of values of $f(x)$ within the domain of x. Since negative values of 'y' are not permissible as per domain of $x \in [-5, 5]$ therefore range has been changed from $y \in [-5, 5]$ to $y \in [0, 5]$.

Example 6 : **Find the domain and range of $f(x) = \sqrt{9 - x^2}$.**

Solution : We have $f(x) = \sqrt{9 - x^2}$.

Domain Clearly, $f(x)$ is not defined for $9 - x^2 < 0$. So, $f(x)$ is defined only when $9 - x^2 \geq 0$.

Now, $9 - x^2 \geq 0 \Rightarrow x^2 - 9 \leq 0 \Rightarrow (x - 3)(x + 3) \leq 0 \Rightarrow -3 \leq x \leq 3 \Rightarrow x \in [-3, 3]$.

So, domain $f(x) = [-3, 3]$.

Range Let $f(x) = y \Rightarrow \sqrt{9 - x^2} = y \Rightarrow x = \pm\sqrt{9 - x^2}$. Clearly, x is defined, when $9 - y^2 \geq 0$. Now $9 - y^2 \geq 0 \Rightarrow y^2 - 9 \leq 0 \Rightarrow (y - 3)(y + 3)$ £ $\leq 0 \Rightarrow -3 \leq y \leq 3$.

But $f(x)$ attains only non-negative values. Therefore, y Î $[0, 3]$.

TYPE OF FUNCTIONS

(i) Constant Function. *Let be a fixed real number. Then a function $f(x)$ given by $f(x) = k$ for all $x \in R$ is called a constant function.*

Clearly, the domain of the constant function $f(x) = k$ is the complete set of real numbers and the range of f is the singleton et $\{k\}$. The graph of a constant function is a straight line parallel to x-axis as shown in Fig. 1. It is above or below x-axis depending on the fact whether k is positive or negative. If $k = 0$, then the straight line coincides with x-axis.

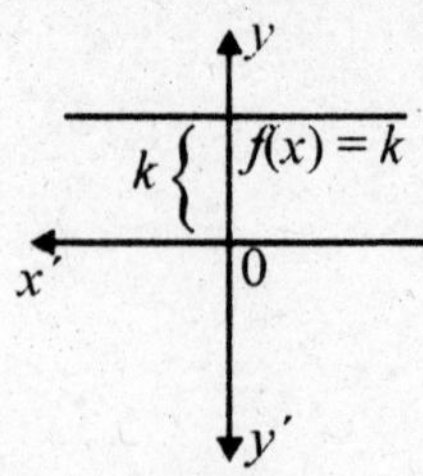

Fig. 1

***(ii)* Identity Function.** *The function defined by I(x) = x for all x ∈ R, is called the identity function on R.*

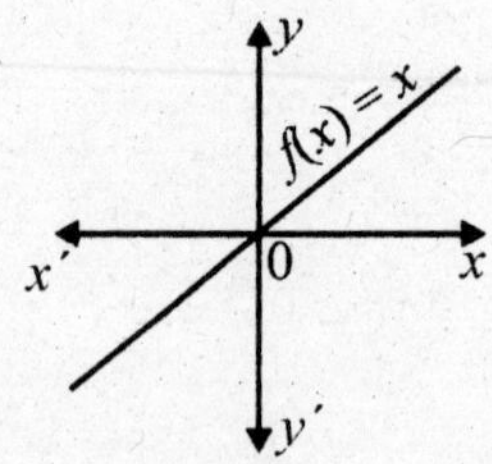

Fig. 2

The domain and range of the identity function are both equal to R. The graph of the identity function is a straight line passing through the origin and inclined at an angle of 45° with x-axis, as shown in figure 2.

***(iii)* Modulus Function.** *The function defined by is called the modulus function.*

$$f(x) = |x| = \begin{cases} x, & \text{when } x \geq 0 \\ -x, & \text{when } x < 0 \end{cases}$$

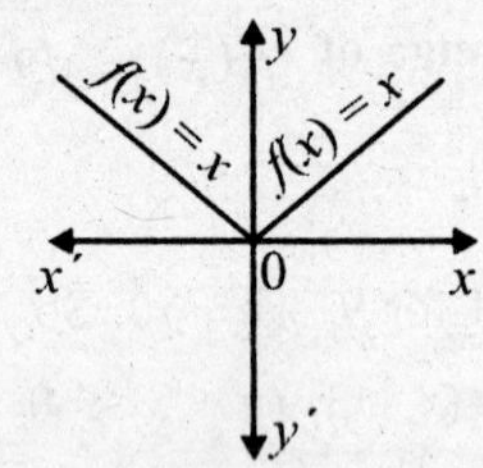

Fig. 3

The domain of the modulus function is the set R of all real numbers and the range is the set of all non-negative real numbers. The graph of the modulus functions is as shown in Fig. 3.

***(iv)* The Greatest Integer Function.** *For any real number x, we denote [x], the greatest integer less than or equal to x.*

The function f defined by f(x) = [x] for all x Î R, is called the greatest integer function.

Clearly, the domain of the greatest integer function is the set R of all real numbers and the range is the set of all integers as it attains only integral values. The graph of the greatest integer function is shown in Fig. 4.

$$f(x) = \begin{cases} \frac{1+1}{x}, & x \neq 0 \\ 0 & x = 0 \end{cases} \quad or \quad f(x) \begin{cases} 1, & x > 0 \\ 0, & x = 0 \\ -1, & x < 0 \end{cases}$$

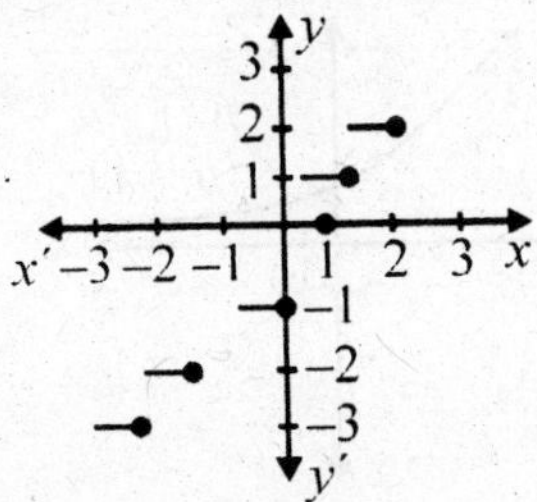

Fig. 4

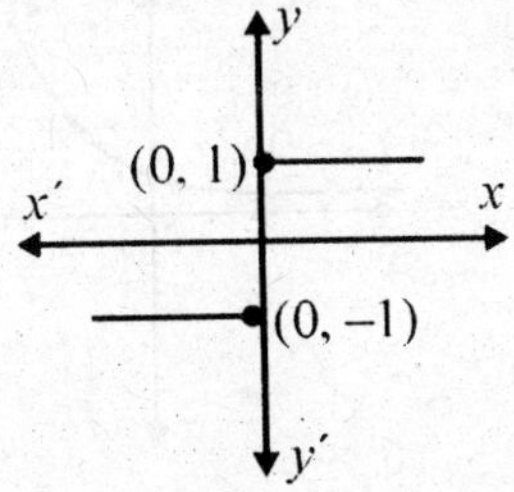

Fig. 5

The domain of the signum function is R and the range is the set $\{-1, 0, 1\}$. The graph of this function is as shown in Fig. 5.

(vi) Reciprocal Function. *The function that associates each non-zero real number x to its reciprocal* $\frac{1}{x}$ *is called the reciprocal function.*

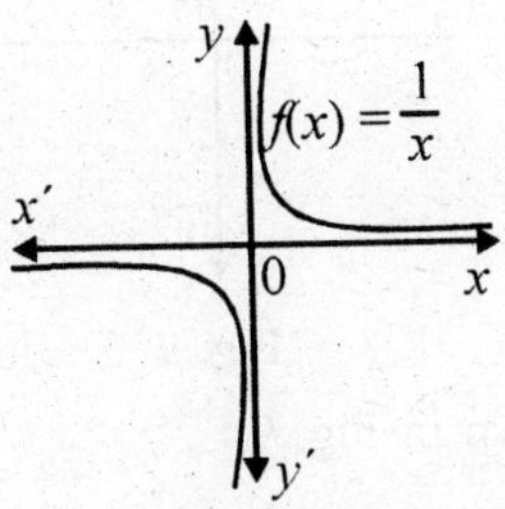

Fig. 6

The domain and range of the reciprocal function are both equal to $R - (0)$ *i.e.*, the set of all non-zero real numbers. The graph is as shown in Fig. 6.

(vii) Logarithmic Function. *If 'a' a positive real number, then the function that associates every positive real number to log x i.e.,* $f(x) = \log_a x$ *is called the logarithmic function. The domain of the logarithmic function is the set of all positive real numbers and the range is the set R of all real numbers. Graph of this function is shown in Fig. 7.*

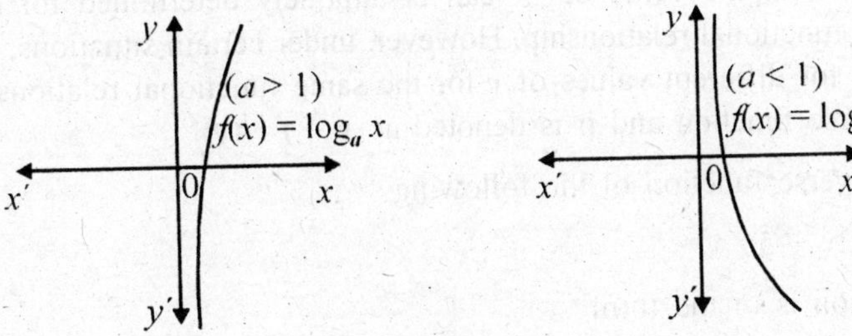

Fig. 7

(viii) Exponential Function. *If a is positive real number, then the function which associates every real number x to* a^x *i.e.,* $f(x) = a^x$ *is called the exponential function.*

Clearly, the domain of the exponential function is R and the range is the set of all positive real numbers. The graph of the exponential function is as shown in Fig. 8.

(ix) Square Root Function. *The function that associates every positive real number x to* $+\sqrt{x}$ *is called the square root function, i.e.,* $f(x) = +\sqrt{x}$.

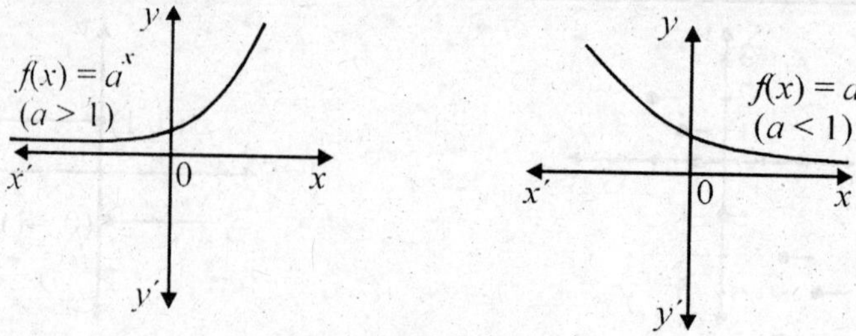

Fig. 8

Since negative real numbers do not have real square roots. Therefore, $f(x)$ is not defined when x is a negative real number. Therefore, domain of f is the set of all non-negative real numbers = $[0, \infty]$. Clearly, range $(f) = \{+ \sqrt{x} | \ x \in [0, \infty] = [0, \infty]$.

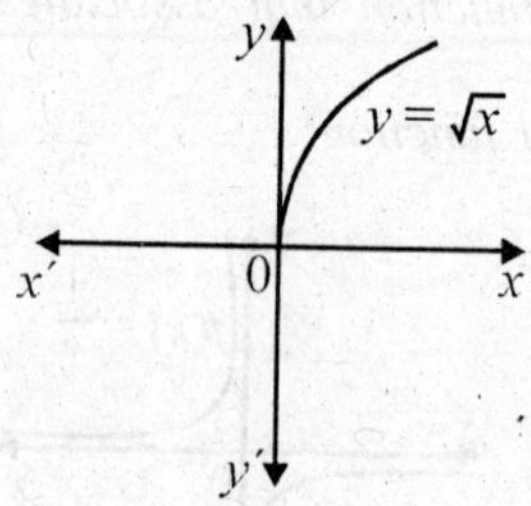

Fig. 9

The graph of $f(x) = + \sqrt{x}$ is shown in Fig. 9.

SPECIAL TYPE OF FUNCTIONS

Inverse Function

Normally, we have function is the form where 'x' is independent variable and 'y' as dependent variable. For example

$$y = f(x)$$

In the above function, the value of 'y' can be uniquely determined for different values of x depending upon their functional relationship. However, under certain situations, we may be interested in finding value of x for different values of y for the same functional relationship. The function so formed is called inverse function and it is denoted as $x = f^{-1}(y)$.

Example 7 : Find inverse function of the following

$$y = 2x + 5$$

Solution : The function is of the form

$$y = f(x)$$

To convert it into inverse function, express 'x' in terms of 'y'.

$$\therefore \quad x = \frac{y}{z} - \frac{5}{2} = \frac{1}{2}(y) - \frac{5}{2} = f(y)$$

Composition of Function

Consider the two function f and g. The composite function is denoted as fog and it is defined as

$f(g(x))$

For example . $f(x) = x^2$ and $g(x) = x + 5$

then $fog(x) = f(g(x)) = (x + 5)^2$

and $gof(x) = g(f(x)) = x^2 + 5$

The domain of *fog* is the set of all numbers x which is in the domain of g such that $g(x)$ is a in the domain of f.

Linear function : A function of the form

$$f(x) = ax + b$$

is said to be linear function.

Here a and b are constant, 'x' is independent variable and $f(x)$ is dependent variable Examples of linear functions are : Supply function and demand function.

***Example 8 :* A manufacturer earn Rs. 4500 in the first month and Rs. 6000 in the second month. On ploting these point, the manufacturer observes a linear function may fit the data:**

(*i*) Find the linear function that fit the data.

(*ii*) Using your model make a prediction of the earning for the third month.

Solution : Given

Time	*Earnings*
First month	4500
Second month	6000

Here time is independent variable and 'earning' is dependent variable.

Expressed in learn of linear function, we have

$$4500 = 1(a) + b \quad \text{...(1)}$$

$$6500 = 2(a) + b \quad \text{...(2)}$$

Substracting (1) firm, (2), we have

$$1500 = a$$

Substracting this value of 'a' in (1), we have

$$b = 3000$$

∴ Linear function is

$$y = 3000 + 1500(x)$$

∴ Earning for third month is

$$y = 3000 + 1500\ (3)$$

$$y = 7500$$

***Example 9 :* A survey shows that there is a linear function between population of a country and time. In the year 1980, population was 84 crores and in the year 1990 population was 93 crores.**

(*i*) Find the linear function between population and time.

(*ii*) Calculate from the obtained linear function, the population in the century that would be in the year 2000.

Solution : Let the linear function be $y = ax + b$, where h stands for the population and x for time. Let 1980 be base year. Then the two points satisfying the linear equation between x and y are (0, 84) and (10, 93). Therefore, we have

$$84 = b$$

$$93 = 10a + b.$$

substituting the value of b in the second equation, we get $a = 0.9$. Thus the required linear function is:

$$y = 0.9x + 84$$

(*ii*) In the year 2000, *i.e.*, when $x = 2000 - 1980 = 20$, population is : $y = 0.9(20) + 84 = 102$ crores.

Quadratic Functions. A function of the form

$$f(x) = ax^2 + bx + c$$

where a, b and c are constants and $a \neq 0$, is called a *quadratic* function. For example, the function $f(x) = x^2 - 5x + 6$ is quadratic function.

The graph of quadratic function $y = f(x) = ax^2 + bx + c$ show below in fig. 10.

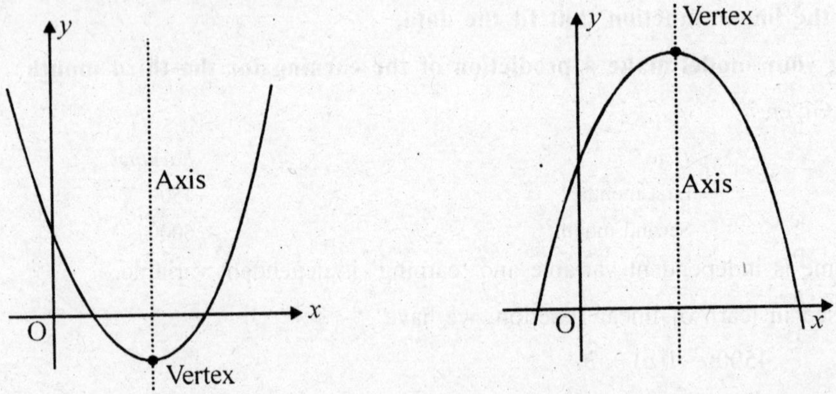

$a < 0$, opens upward $\qquad$ $a < 0$, opens downward

Fig. 10

The graph are parabola that opens upward or downward according as $a > 0$ or $a < 0$.

Example 10 : **A shopkeeper earns Rs. 380 in the first week, Rs. 660 in the second week and Rs. 860 in the third week. On plotting the points (1,380), (2,660) and (3,860), the shopkeeper feels that a quadratic function may fit the data.**

(*i*) Find the quadratic function that fits the data.

(*ii*) Using your model make a prediction of the earning for the fourth week.

Solution : (*i*) Let the quadratic function be

$$y = ax^2 + bx + c$$

where y represent earnings and x represent weeks. Using the given information we have following equations.

$$380 = a.1^2 + b.1 + c \qquad a + b + c = 380 \quad ...(i)$$

$$660 = a.2^2 + b.2 + c \quad \text{or} \quad 4a + 2b + c = 660 \quad ...(ii)$$

$$860 = a.3^2 + b.3 + c \qquad 9a + 3b + c = 860 \quad ...(iii)$$

Substracting (*i*) from (*ii*), and (*ii*) from (*iii*), we have following simultaneous equations

$$3a + b = 280 \quad ...(iv)$$

$$5a + b = 200 \quad ...(v)$$

Substracting (*iv*) from (*v*) gives

$$2a = -80 \quad \therefore \quad a = -40.$$

Substituting this value of a in (*iv*), we get $b = 280 - 3(-40) = 400$.

Substituting the values of a and b in (*i*), we get $c = 20$. Thus the required quadratic function is:

$$y = -40x^2 + 400x + 20 \quad ...(vi)$$

(*ii*) Substituting $x = 4$ in equation (*vi*)

we have $y = -40 \times 16 + 400 \times 4 + 20 =$ Rs. 980.

$\therefore$ Projected earning for fourth week is Rs. 980.

FUNCTIONS RELATED TO BUSINESS AND ECONOMICS

1. *Demand Function.* The demand of a particular commodity is based on its price. Lower the price, higher will be the demand. Similarly, as we increase the price, the demand keeps on decreasing. Thus, the relationship between demand and price would be given as

$$x = f(p)$$

where x is the demand function. The graph of the demand function is known as demand curve. It has negative slope.

2. *Supply Function.* As the price increases, the producers tend to supply more. Therefore, there is direct relationship between supply and price of a commodity. Mathematically, the relationship can be given as

$$s = f(p)$$

The graph of the supply function is known as supply curve. It has a positive slope.

3. *Cost Function.* The total cost incurred in manufacturing any commodity bears a relationship with its quantity. However, cost does not increase in direct proportion to the number of units manufactured because it comprises of two different components – Fixed costs and variable costs. It is only the variable cost which causes increases in the total cost whereas fixed cost remain fixed upto a certain level. Thus, cost function can be expressed as

$$C(x) = V(x) + F(x)$$

The graph of cost functions is known as cost curves. It is generally increasing curves.

4. *Total Revenue Function.* Revenue is amount of money derived by a firm by sellings its product. It has direct relationship with the sales turnover of a firm. Higher the sales turnover, more would be the revenue of the firm. Thus, in mathematical form, it can be given as.

$$R = f(x)$$

where x is the number of units sold.

5. *Profit Function.* Profit is a function of number of units sold and depend upon its cost and sale price. Thus, profit function can be derived by substracting cost function from revenue function, as under : $P(x) = R(x) - C(x)$

Example 11 : **It is that the demand of a particular commodity is 50 units when it is priced at Rs. 10. The demand increases to 64 units when price is decreased by Rs. 2. Find the demand function.**

Solution : Let the demand function be $p = a - bx$

$\therefore \quad 10 = a - 50b$ (Original relation)

$8 = a - 64b$ (New relation)

$2 = 14b$ (Substracting New relation from the original relation)

$\therefore \quad b = 1/7$

Substituting the above value of b in original relation, we have

$10 = a - 50(1/7)$

$70 = 7a - 50$

$7a = 70 + 50 = 120$

$\therefore \quad a = 120/7$

$\therefore$ Demand function

$$p = \frac{120}{7} + \frac{1}{7}x$$

Example 12 : **When the units price is Rs. 4, the daily supply 4was found to 50 units. When the price is increased to Rs. 5, the supply is increased to 60 units. Find the supply function.**

Solution : Let the supply function be $p = a + bx$

$\therefore \quad 4 = a + b(50)$ (Original relation)

$5 = a + b(60)$ (New relation)

$-1 = -10b)$ (substracting New relation from the original relation)

$\therefore \quad b = 1/10)$

Substituting this value of 'b' in original relation, we have

$\therefore \quad 4 = a + \frac{1}{10}(50)$

$\therefore \quad a = 4 - = -1$

Required Supply function

$$\therefore \quad f = -1 + \left(\frac{1}{10}\right)x$$

BREAK – EVEN ANALYSIS

Break even point is defined as the point at which revenue is equal to the cost.

$\therefore$ At break even point.

$R(x) = C(x)$

(*a*) when $R(x) = C(x)$, no profit- no loss.

(*b*) when $R(x) > C(x)$, profit is earned.

(*c*) when $R(x) < C(x)$, Loss is increased.

***Example 13* : X Ltd. has set up *a* manufacturing unit involving fixed cost of Rs. 50000 and the additional cost *i.e.,* variable cost for producing each unit is Rs. 150 per unit. Each unit can be sold at Rs. 500. What would be the profit when 400 units are sold. Also determine,**

(*a*) Cost function.

(*b*) Revenue function

(*c*) Profit function and profit on sale of 400 units.

(*d*) Break even point

***Solution* :** (*a*) Cost function

$$C(x) = 50000 + 150x$$

where x is the number of units sold.

(*b*) Revenue function

$$R(x) = 500x$$

(*c*) Profit function

$$P(x) = -50000 + 350x$$

$$P(400) = -50000 + 350(400)$$

$$= -50000 + 140000$$

$$= 90000$$

(*iv*) Break Even Point

$$R(x) = C(x)$$

$$500x = 5000 + 150x$$

$$\therefore \quad 350x = 50000$$

$$x = \frac{50000}{350}$$

$$x = \frac{1000}{7}$$

Exercise 5.3

Q. 1 A company has a cost function $C(x) = 50 + 20x$ and demand function $p = 75 - 3x$. Find

(*i*) Revenue function

(*ii*) Profit function

[(*i*) Revenue function $= 75x - 3x^2$, (*ii*) Profit function $= -3x^2 + 55x - 50$]

Q. 2 Find the cost as a function of output it costs are Rs. 1000 for 100 units and Rs. 1500 for 200 units. It is further given that cost is a linear function of output. **[Ans.** $C(x) = 500 + 5x$]

Q. 3 The daily supply is 50 units when price Rs. 10 per unit. When the prices per unit is increased to Rs. 12, supply increased to 70. Express the above as a linear function. Also find the supply when price is increased to Rs. 15 per unit. [$s = -50 + 10x$, New supply = 100]

Q. 4 Suppers the consumer will demand 40 units of a product when the price is Rs. 12 per unit and 25 units when the price is Rs. 18 each. Find the demand function, assuming that it is linear. Also determine the total revenue function, the average revenue function and the marginal revenue function.

[Demand function: $p = 28 - \frac{2}{5}x$, Revenue functions: $28x - \frac{2}{5}x^2$

Average revenue function $= 28x - \frac{2}{5}x$, $MR = 28 - \frac{4}{5}x$]

Q. 5 Determine the numbers a, b, c such that the function $y = ax^2 + bx + c$ fits to the data points (–1, 7), (0, 4) and (2, 6). Hence express the quadratic function.

$$\left[a = 4/3, b = -\frac{5}{3}, c = 4 \text{ and } y = 4/3\,x^2 - \frac{5}{3}x + 4\right]$$

Q. 6 A garment manufacturer is planning production of new variety of shirts. It involves initially a fixed cost of Rs. 1.5 lacs and a variable cost of Rs. 150 for producing each shirt. If each shirt can be sold at Rs. 350, then find

(*i*) the cost function,

(*ii*) the revenue function,

(*iii*) the profit function and

(*iv*) the break-even point.

[(*i*) $C(x) = 150000 + 150x$, (*ii*) $R(x) = 350x$, (*iii*) $P(x) = 200x - 150000$, (*iv*) 750]

Q. 7 For a new product, a manufacturer sets up an infrastructure which costs him Rs. 1,50,000. The variable cost (labour, material etc.) is estimated as Rs. 125 for each unit of the product. The sale price per unit is fixed at Rs. 160. Write down the cost function $C(x)$. Revenue function $R(x)$ and Profit function $P(x)$ for x units of the product. How many minimum number of units are to be produced in the first year of production so that there may be no loss during that year?

[(*i*) $C(x) = 150000 + 125x$, (*ii*) $R(x) = 160x$, (*iii*) $P(x) = 35x - 150000$, (*iv*) 4286]

Q. 8 The cost function $C(x)$ for x bread is given by

$C(x) =$ Rs. $3.5x$ + Rs. 12,000.

Each bread is put to a special levy of 20 paise for Andhra Pradesh cyclone victims. Then

(*i*) if each breads is sold for Rs. 6, determine the minimum number of breads that would be produced and sold to ensure no loss,

(*ii*) if the selling price is increased by 70 paise per bread, what would be the break-even point,

(*iii*) if 6,000 breads are sold only, what price per bread should be charged to guarantee no loss.

[(*i*) 5128, (*ii*) 4000, (*iii*) Rs. 5.70]

Q. 9 The total cost and the total revenue of a company that produces and sells x units of a particular product are respectively.

$C(x) = 5x + 350$ and $R(x) = 50x - x^2$

Find

(*i*) the break-even values

(*ii*) the values of x that produce a profit,

(*iii*) the values of x that result in a loss.

[(*i*) $x = 10$ or 35, (*ii*) $10 < x < 35$, (*iii*) $x < 10$ or $x > 35$]

LIMIT – CONCEPT

Limit may be defined as a particular value to which a function approaches as the variable approaches a given value. For example, the value of function $f(x)$ at value c is l. Now, as x approaches c, $f(s)$ approaches l.

***Limits may be defined as** "The limit of f(x), as x approaches a, is l," written as* $\lim_{x \to a} f(x) = l$, *means that f(x) will be as close to the number l as we please for all x sufficiently close to the number a but not equal to a.*

Properties of Limits

Assume that $\lim_{x \to a} f(x)$ and $\lim_{x \to a} g(x)$ exist. Let c be any real number. Then the following relations hold good :

1. $\lim_{x \to a} [f(x) \pm g(x)] = \lim_{x \to a} f(x) \pm \lim_{x \to a} g(x)$
   That is, the limit of a sum or difference is the sum or difference of the limits.

2. $\lim_{x \to a} [f(x)\, g(x)] = \lim_{x \to a} f(x) \,.\, \lim_{x \to a} g(x)$
   That is, the limit of a product is the product of limits.

3. $\lim_{x \to a} \dfrac{f(x)}{g(x)} = \dfrac{\lim_{x \to a} f(x)}{\lim_{x \to a} g(x)}$, provided $\lim_{x \to a} g(x) \neq 0$.
   That is, the limit of a quotient is the quotient of the limits, provided the denominator does not have a limit of 0.

4. $\lim_{x \to a} [cf(x)] = c \,.\, \lim_{x \to a} f(x)$
   That is, the limit of a constant times a function is the constant times the limit.

5. If $h(x) = c$ for all x, then $\lim_{x \to a} h(x) = c$.
   That is, the limit of a constant function is a constant. This is usually abbreviated by writing
   $\lim_{x \to a} c = c$.

6. $\lim_{\to a} \sqrt[n]{f(x)} = \sqrt[n]{\lim_{x \to a} f(x)}$, for any positive integer n.

7. $\lim_{x \to a} x^n = a^n$ for any positive integer n.

In order to solve numericals on limits, one must know the following important limits

(*i*) $\lim_{x \to a} \frac{x^n - a^n}{x - a} = na^{n-1}$, n being a positive integer.

(*ii*) $\lim_{x \to 0} (a + x)^{1/x} = e.$

(*iii*) $\lim_{x \to 0} \frac{a^x - 1}{x} = \log_e a \, (a > 0)$

(*iv*) $\lim_{x \to 0} \frac{e^x - 1}{x} = 1.$

(*v*) $\lim_{x \to 0} \frac{\log(1 + x)}{x} = 1.$

Evaluation of Limits

To evaluate algebraic limits we have the following methods :

(*i*) Direct Substitution

(*ii*) Factorisation Method

(*iii*) Rationalisation Method

(*iv*) Using some standard results

(*v*) Method of evaluating algebric limit when $x \to \infty$.

We shall now discuss these methods with suitable illustrations in the following sections.

Evaluation of Algebraic Limits by Direct Substitution

Direct Substitution method. First of all, we shall directly place the limiting value of 'x' in the given function. If we get a finite number, then the finite number is the limit of the given expression. The following examples will illustrate the procedure.

Solved Examples

Example 14 : **Evaluate** $\lim_{x \to 1} 6x^2 + 4x + 5.$

Solution : We have, $\lim_{x \to 1} 6x^2 + 4x + 5 = 6(1)^2 + 4(1) + 5 = 15.$

Example 15 : **Evaluate** $\lim_{x \to 2} \frac{x^2 - 4}{x + 3}.$

Solution : We have, $\lim_{x \to 2} \frac{x^2 - 4}{x + 3} = \frac{4 - 4}{2 + 3} = \frac{0}{5} = 0..$

Example 16 : $\underset{x \to 1}{Lt} \left(3x^2 + 2\right)$

Solution : $\underset{x \to 1}{Lt} \left(3x^2 + 2\right) = 3(1)^2 + 2$

$= 5$

EVALUATION OF ALGEBRAIC LIMITS BY FACTORIZATION

Consider $\lim\limits_{x \to a} \frac{f(x)}{g(x)}$. If by putting $x = a$ the rational function $\frac{f(x)}{g(x)}$ takes the form $\frac{0}{0}, \frac{\infty}{\infty}$ etc. then we proceed for factorisation of the numerator and denominator. Then we identify common factor $(x - a)$ and cancel them. After cancelling out the common factor $(x - a)$ we again put $x = a$ in the given expression and we try to find whether it is a finite number or not. Repeat the process till we get a finite number.

Example 17 : **Find** $\underset{x \to 1}{Lt} \frac{x^2 + x - 2}{x^2 + 2x - 3}$

Solution : When $x = 1$, we have $\frac{x^2 + x - 2}{x^2 + 2x - 3} = \frac{0}{0}$

Factorizing Nr. and Dr, we have

$$\underset{x \to 1}{Lt} \frac{(x-1)(x+2)}{(x-1)(x+3)} = \underset{x \to 1}{Lt} \frac{(x+2)}{(x+3)} = \frac{3}{4}.$$

Example 18 : **Evaluate** $\lim\limits_{x \to 2} \frac{x^2 - 5x + 6}{x^2 - 4}$.

Solution : When $x = 2$ the expression $\frac{x^2 - 5x + 6}{x^2 - 4}$, We will get $\frac{0}{0}$.

On factorizing Numerator, we have

Now, $$\lim_{x \to 2} \frac{x^2 - 5x + 6}{x^2 - 4} = \lim_{x \to 2} \frac{(x-2)(x-3)}{(x+2)(x-2)} = \lim_{x \to 2} \frac{x-3}{x+2} = \frac{2-3}{2+2} = -\frac{1}{4}.$$

Example 19 : **Evaluate** $\lim\limits_{x \to 1} \frac{x^3 - 1}{x - 1}$.

Solution : When $x = 1$ the expression $\frac{x^3 - 1}{x - 1}$ assumes the indeterminate form $\frac{0}{0}$.

Now, $\lim_{x \to 1} \frac{x^3 - 1}{x - 1} \left(\text{form } \frac{0}{0} \right) = \lim_{x \to 1} \frac{(x-1)(x^2 + x + 1)}{(x-1)}$

$$= \lim_{x \to 1} x^2 + x + 1 = 1^2 + 1 + 1 = 3.$$

***Example 20 :* Find** $\underset{x \to 9}{Lt} \frac{(x^2 - 9x)}{(x^2 - 10x + 9)}$.

Solution : When $x = 9$, we have $\frac{(x^2 - 9x)}{(x^2 - 10x + 9)} = \frac{0}{0}$

Factorizing Nr and Dr, we have

$$\frac{(x^2 - 9x)}{(x^2 - 10x + 9)} = \frac{x(x-9)}{(x-9)(x-1)} = \frac{x}{(x-1)}$$

Taking limit, we have

$$\underset{x \to 9}{Lt} \frac{x}{(x-1)} = \frac{9}{(9-1)} = \frac{9}{8}.$$

Example 21 : $\underset{x \to 1/2}{Lt} \frac{(4x^2 - 1)}{(2x - 1)}$

Solution : $\underset{x \to 1/2}{Lt} \frac{(4x^2 - 1)}{(2x - 1)} = \underset{x \to 1/2}{Lt} \frac{(2x-1)(2x+1)}{(2x-1)} = \underset{x \to 1/2}{Lt} (2x + 1)$

$$= 2.$$

Example 22 : $\underset{x \to 3}{Lt} \left(\frac{1}{x - 3} - \frac{3}{x^2 - 3x} \right)$

Solution : $\underset{x \to 3}{Lt} \left(\frac{1}{x - 3} - \frac{3}{x^2 - 3x} \right)$

$$= \underset{x \to 3}{Lt} \left(\frac{1}{(x-3)} - \frac{3}{x(x-3)} \right)$$

$$= \underset{x \to 3}{Lt} \left(\frac{x-3}{x(x-3)} \right) = \underset{x \to 3}{Lt} \frac{1}{x} = \frac{1}{3}.$$

EVALUATION OF ALGEBRAIC LIMITS BY RATIONALIZATION

This method is used when either the numerator or denominator or both involve expression consisting of square roots and substituting the value of x the rational expression takes the form $\frac{0}{0}, \frac{\infty}{\infty}$ etc.

Following examples illustrate the procedure.

Solved Examples

Example 23 : **Evaluate** $\lim\limits_{x\to 0} \dfrac{\sqrt{2+x}-\sqrt{2}}{x}$.

Solution : When $x = 0$, the expression $\dfrac{\sqrt{2+x}-\sqrt{2}}{x}$ would be of form $\dfrac{0}{0}$.

Now, $\lim\limits_{x\to 0} \dfrac{\sqrt{2+x}-\sqrt{2}}{x}$

$$= \lim_{x\to 0} \frac{\left(\sqrt{2+x}-\sqrt{2}\right)\left(\sqrt{2+2}+\sqrt{2}\right)}{x\left(\sqrt{2+x}+\sqrt{2}\right)}$$

$$= \lim_{x\to 0} \frac{2+x-2}{x\left(\sqrt{2+x}+\sqrt{2}\right)}$$

$$= \lim_{x\to 0} \frac{2+x-2}{\sqrt{2+x}+\sqrt{2}} = \frac{1}{2\sqrt{2}}$$

Example 24 : **Evaluate** $\lim\limits_{x\to 0} \dfrac{x}{\sqrt{a+x}-\sqrt{a-x}}$.

Solution : When $x = 0$, the expression $\dfrac{x}{\sqrt{a+x}-\sqrt{a-x}}$ would be of the form $\dfrac{0}{0}$.

Now, $\lim\limits_{x\to 0} \dfrac{x}{\sqrt{a+x}-\sqrt{a-x}}$

$$= \lim_{x\to 0} \frac{x}{\left(\sqrt{a+x}-\sqrt{a-x}\right)} \cdot \frac{\left(\sqrt{a+x}+\sqrt{a-x}\right)}{\left(\sqrt{a+x}+\sqrt{a-x}\right)}$$

$$= \lim_{x\to 0} \frac{x\left(\sqrt{a+x}+\sqrt{a-x}\right)}{(a+x-a-x)}$$

$$= \lim_{x\to 0} \frac{\left(\sqrt{a}+x+\sqrt{a-x}\right)}{2} = \frac{2\sqrt{a}}{2} = \sqrt{a}$$

Example 25 : **Evaluate** $\lim\limits_{x\to 0} \dfrac{\sqrt{a^2+x^2}-\sqrt{a^2-x^2}}{x^2}$.

Solution : When $x = 0$, the expression $\dfrac{\sqrt{a^2+x^2}-\sqrt{a^2-x^2}}{x^2}$ would be of form $\dfrac{0}{0}$.

Now, $\lim_{x\to 0} \dfrac{\sqrt{a^2+x^2}-\sqrt{a^2-x^2}}{x^2}$

$$= \lim_{x\to 0} \frac{\left(\sqrt{a^2+x^2}-\sqrt{a^2-x^2}\right)}{x^2} \frac{\left(\sqrt{a^2+x^2}+\sqrt{a^2-x^2}\right)}{\left(\sqrt{a^2+x^2}+\sqrt{a^2-x^2}\right)}$$

$$= \lim_{x\to 0} \frac{a^2+x^2-a^2+x^2}{x^2\left(\sqrt{a^2+x^2}+\sqrt{a^2-x^2}\right)}$$

$$= \lim_{x\to 0} \frac{2}{\left(\sqrt{a^2+x^2}+\sqrt{a^2-x^2}\right)} = \frac{2}{\sqrt{a^2}+\sqrt{a^2}} = \frac{1}{a}.$$

***Example 26 :* Evaluate** $\lim_{x\to 4} \dfrac{x^2-16}{\sqrt{(x^2+9)}-5}$.

Solution : When $x = 4$, the expression $\dfrac{x^2-16}{\sqrt{(x^2+9)}-5}$ would be of the form $\dfrac{0}{0}$.

Now, $\lim_{x\to 4} \dfrac{x^2-16}{\sqrt{(x^2+9)}-5}$

$$= \lim_{x\to 4} \frac{(x^2-16)}{\sqrt{(x^2+9)}-5} \frac{\left(\sqrt{(x^2+9+5)}\right)}{\left(\sqrt{(x^2+9)}+5\right)}$$

$$= \lim_{x\to 4} \frac{(x^2-16)\left(\sqrt{x^2+9-5}\right)}{\sqrt{(x^2+9-25)}}$$

$$= \lim_{x\to 4} \sqrt{x^2+9}+5 = 10.$$

Evaluation of Algebraic Limits by using Standard Results

Result If $n \in Q$, then $\lim_{x\to a} \dfrac{x^n-a^n}{x-a} = na^{n-1}$

Solved Examples

***Example 27 :* Evaluate** $\lim_{x\to 2} \dfrac{x^{10}-1024}{x-2}$.

Solution : When $x = 2$, the expression $\dfrac{x^{10}-1024}{x-2}$ would be of the form $\dfrac{0}{0}$.

Now, $\lim\limits_{x\to2}\dfrac{x^{10}-1024}{x-2}=\lim\limits_{x\to2}\dfrac{x^{10}-2^{10}}{x-2}=10.2^{10-1}=5120$

Example 28 : **Evaluate** $\lim\limits_{x\to2}\dfrac{x^{10}-1024}{x^5-32}$

Solution : When $x = 2$, the expression $\dfrac{x^{10}-1024}{x^5-32}$ would be of the indeterminate form $\dfrac{0}{0}$.

Now,
$$\lim_{x\to2}\frac{x^{10}-1024}{x^5-32}=\lim_{x\to2}\frac{x^{10}-2^{10}}{x^5-2^5}$$

$$=\lim_{x\to2}\frac{\dfrac{x^{10}-2^{10}}{x-2}}{\dfrac{x^5-2^5}{x-2}}=\lim_{x\to2}\frac{x^{10}-2^{10}}{x^5-2^5}\div\lim_{x\to2}\frac{x^5-2^5}{x-2}=10.2^{10-1}\div5.2^{5-1}=64.$$

Example 29 : **Evaluate** $\lim\limits_{x\to9}\dfrac{x^{3/2}-27}{x-9}$.

Solution : When $x = 9$, the expression $\dfrac{x^{3/2}-27}{x-9}$ would be of the form $\dfrac{0}{0}$.

Now,
$$\lim_{x\to9}\frac{x^{3/2}-27}{x-9}$$

$$=\lim_{x\to9}\frac{x^{3/2}-9^{3/2}}{x-9}=\frac{3}{2}(9)^{3/2-1}=\frac{3}{2}(3)=\frac{9}{2}.$$

Evaluation of Algebraic Limits when $x\to\infty$

To evaluate this type of limits, the following procedure is adopted :

Step I *Write down the given expression in form of a rational function, i.e.,* $\dfrac{f(x)}{g(x)}$, *if it is not so.*

Step II *If k is the highest power of x in numerator and denominator both, then divide each term in numerator and denominator by* x^k.

Step III *Use the result* $\lim\limits_{x\to\infty}\dfrac{1}{x^n}=0$, *where* $n>0$.

Solved Examples

Example 30 : **Evaluate** $\lim\limits_{x\to\infty}\dfrac{ax^2+bx+c}{dx^2+ex+f}$

Solution : In the given problem, the expression assumes the form $\frac{\infty}{\infty}$. The highest power of x in both the numerator and denominator is 2. So we divide each term in both the numerator and denominator by x^2.

$$\therefore \quad \lim_{x\to\infty} \frac{ax^2 + bx + c}{dx^2 + ex + f} = \lim_{x\to\infty} \frac{a + \frac{b}{x} + \frac{c}{x^2}}{d + \frac{e}{x} + \frac{f}{x^2}} = \frac{a+0+0}{d+0+0} = \frac{a}{d}.$$

Example 31 : **Evaluate** $\lim_{x\to\infty} \frac{5x-6}{\sqrt{4x^2+9}}$.

Solution : $\lim_{x\to\infty} \frac{5x-6}{\sqrt{4x^2+9}} = \lim_{x\to\infty} \frac{5-6/x}{\sqrt{4x^2+9/x^2}}$ (Dividing each term in N^r *and* D^r by x)

$$= \frac{5-0}{\sqrt{4+0}} = \frac{5}{2}.$$

Example 32 : $\underset{x\to l}{Lt} \frac{4x^2+5x+6}{3x^2+4x+5}$.

Solution. Dividing the numerator and denominator by x^2

We have $\underset{x\to l}{Lt} \frac{4 + \frac{5}{x} + \frac{6}{x^2}}{3 + \frac{4}{x} + \frac{5}{x^2}}$

Taking $\underset{x\to l}{Lt}$, we have

$$\underset{x\to l}{Lt}\, \frac{4 + 5/x + 6/x^2}{3 + 4x + 5/x^2} = 4/3.$$

Example 33 : **Evaluate** $\lim_{m\to\infty} P\left(1+\frac{i}{m}\right)^{mn}$.

Solution. $\lim_{m\to\infty} P\left(1+\frac{i}{m}\right)^{mn} = P\left[\lim_{m\to\infty}\left(1+\frac{i}{m}\right)^{mn}\right]$

$$= P\left[\lim_{m\to\infty}\left(1+\frac{i}{m}\right)^{m/i}\right]^{in}$$

Let $x = \frac{i}{m}$. we see that as $m \to \infty$ then $x \to 0$. Thus, the above problem can be restated as

$$\lim_{m\to\infty} P\left(1+\frac{i}{m}\right)^{mn} = P\left[\lim_{m\to\infty} (1+x)^{1/x}\right]^{in}$$

$$= Pe^{in}.\left(\sin ce \lim_{x\to 0} (1+x)^{1/x} = e\right)$$

Example 34 : **For the demand function $p = \dfrac{a}{x+b}$, where p is price, x is quantity demanded and a and b are positive constants, show by using the concept of limit, that the demand increase to infinitely large amount as the price falls. Also, show that total revenue reached a limiting value as the quantity demanded increases.**

Solution : We have $p = \dfrac{a}{x+b}$

$$x = \frac{a}{p} - b$$

Hence $\lim_{p\to 0} x = \lim_{p\to 0} x\left(\frac{a}{p} - b\right) \to \infty - b = \infty$

Thus the demand increases to infinitely large amount as the price falls. Further, the revenue function, $R(x)$, is given by

$$R(x) = px = \frac{ax}{x+b}$$

$$\Rightarrow \lim_{x\to\infty} R(x) = \lim_{x\to\infty} = \frac{ax}{x+b} = \lim_{x\to\infty} \frac{a}{1+\frac{b}{x}} = a$$

Hence the total revenue reaches a limiting value 'a' as the quantity demand increases.

Example 35 : **A right angled triangle has two equal sides of 1 unit each. One of these sides is drawn horizontally and divided into $(n + 1)$ equal portion. On each of the portions, after the first, a rectangle is formed with height equal to the vertical distance from the left hand end of the portion to the hypotenuse of the triangle. Find a expression for the sum of the rectangle areas and evaluate the limit of the sum as n→∞. What is the meaning of the limiting value?**

Solution : ABC is a right-angled triangle in which AB = BC = 1 unit. The triangle is right angled at B. AB is divided into $(n + 1)$ equal portions, each portion being equal to $\dfrac{1}{n+1}$ unit. If we assume rectangles on each portion after the first, then n rectangles are formed, each of width $\dfrac{1}{n+1}$ unit. The length of the first rectangle $= \dfrac{1}{n+1}$, length of the second rectangle $= \dfrac{2}{n+1}$, length of the $(n - 1)$ the rectangle $= \dfrac{n-1}{n+1}$ and length of the nth rectangle $= \dfrac{n}{n+1}$. Thus the sum of the areas of these n rectangles is given by

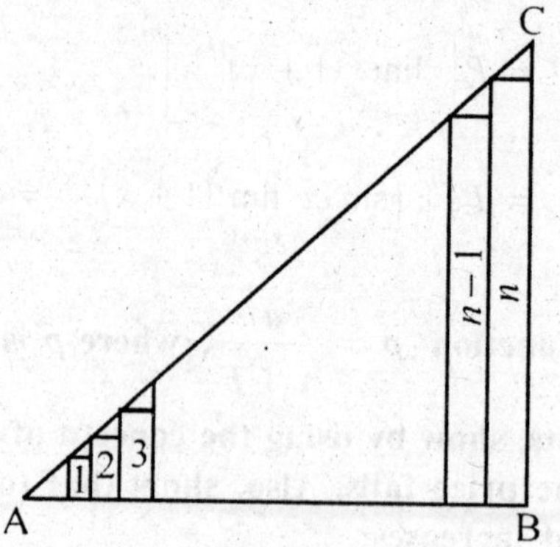

Fig. 11

$$A = \left(+ \frac{1}{n+1} \cdot \frac{1}{n+1} \cdot \frac{1}{n+1} \cdot \frac{2}{n+1} + \ldots + \frac{1}{n+1} \cdot \frac{n}{n+1} \right)$$

Taking $\frac{1}{(n+1)^2}$ as common, we have

$$A = \frac{1}{(n+1)^2}[1 + 2 + \ldots + n]$$

$$= \frac{1}{(n+1)^2} \frac{n(n+1)}{2}$$

$$= \frac{n}{2(n+1)}$$

Taking $\underset{n\to\infty}{Lt}$ we have

$$= \lim_{n\to\infty} = \lim_{n\to\infty} \frac{n}{2n+2} = \lim_{n\to\infty} \frac{1}{2 + \frac{2}{n}} = \frac{1}{2}$$

The limiting value represents the area of the triangle ABC whole height and breadth is 1 unit.

Example 36 : **Show that** $\underset{x\to 2}{Lt} \frac{|x-2|}{(x-2)}$ **does not exist.**

Solution : Let $f(x) = \frac{|x-2|}{(x-2)}$

$$\underset{x\to 2^-}{Lt} f(x) = \underset{h\to 0}{Lt} f(2-h) = \underset{h\to 0}{Lt} \frac{|2-h-2|}{(2-h)-2}$$

$$= \underset{x\to 0}{Lt} \frac{|-h|}{-h} = \underset{x\to 0}{Lt} \frac{h}{-h} = \underset{x\to 0}{Lt} (-1) = -1$$

Also $\underset{x\to 2^+}{Lt} f(x) = \underset{h\to 0}{Lt} f(2+h)$

$$= \lim_{h\to 0} \frac{|2+h-2|}{(2+h-2)} = \lim_{h\to 0} \frac{|h|}{h} = \lim_{h\to 0} \frac{h}{h}$$

$$= \lim_{h\to 0} 1 = 1$$

since $\lim_{x\to 2^-} f(x) \neq \lim_{x\to 2^+} f(x)$, limit does not exist.

Exercise 5.2

1. Evaluate the following limit

(i) $\lim_{x\to 0} \frac{\sqrt{1+x}-\sqrt{1-x}}{2x}$ **Ans.** (1/2)

(ii) $\lim_{x\to 0} \frac{\sqrt{1+x}-1}{x}$ **Ans.** (1/2)

(iii) $\lim_{x\to 0} \frac{\sqrt{2-x}-\sqrt{2+x}}{x}$ **Ans.** $\left(-\frac{1}{\sqrt{2}}\right)$

(iv) $\lim_{x\to 2} \frac{x^2-4}{\sqrt{3x-2}-\sqrt{x+2}}$ **Ans.** (8)

(v) $\lim_{x\to 0} \frac{2x}{\sqrt{a+x}-\sqrt{a-x}}$ **Ans.** $(2\sqrt{a})$

(vi) $\lim_{x\to a} \frac{(x+2)^{3/2}-(a+2)^{3/2}}{(x-a)}$ **Ans.** $\left(\frac{3}{x}(a+2)^{1/2}\right)$

(vii) $\lim_{x\to 0} \frac{(1+x)^6-1}{(1+x)^2-1}$ **Ans.** (3)

(viii) $\lim_{x\to a} \frac{x^6-a^9}{(x-a)} = 9$, find all possible value of a **Ans.** (1, –1)

(ix) $\lim_{x\to 1} \frac{6-5x^2}{4x+15x^2}$ **Ans.** (– 1/3)

(x) $\lim_{x\to 1} \frac{4x^3-2x^2+5x+7}{8x^3+6x^2-3x+11}$ **Ans.** (1/2)

2. A lead shot is allowed to fall in a vacuum. It is known that the shot falls $16x^2$ feet in x seconds. Find an expression for the average numbér of feet fallen per second between then a^{th} and $(a + x)^{th}$ second. Find the limit of the expression as $x \to 0$ and give a meaning to this limit.

3. Show that the following limits does not exist.

(i) $\lim\limits_{x \to 0} \dfrac{x}{|x| + x^2}$ (ii) $\lim\limits_{x \to 1} \dfrac{|x-1|}{(x-1)}$

(iii) $\underset{x \to 0}{Lt} \dfrac{x}{|x|}$ (iv) $\lim\limits_{x \to 0} \dfrac{3x + 2|x|}{5x - 3|x|}$

(v) $\lim\limits_{x \to 0} \dfrac{x - |x|}{x}$

4. Prove that $\lim\limits_{x \to 0} \dfrac{x^2}{|x|} = \lim\limits_{x \to 0} \dfrac{|x|^2}{x}$.

5. State whether the following statement is true or false: The limit of the difference of two functions equals the difference of their limits.

6. For the demand function $p = \dfrac{a}{x+b}$ (where p is price, x is quantity demanded and a and b are positive constants), show, by using the concept of limit, that the demand increases to infinitely large amount as the price falls. Also, show that total revenue reaches a limiting value as the quantity increases.

CONTINUITY AT A POINT

A function $f(x)$ is said to be continuous at a point $x = a$ of its domain, if $\lim\limits_{x \to a} f(x) = f(a)$.

Thus, ($f(x)$ is continuous at $x = a$) if $\lim\limits_{x \to a} f(x) = f(a)$.

and $$\lim_{x \to a^-} f(x) = \lim_{x \to a^+} f(x) = f(a)$$

If $f(x)$ is not continuous at a point $x = a$, then it is said to be discontinuous at $x = a$.

Example 37 : **Discuss the continuity of the function $f(x)$ at $x = 1/2$, where**

$$f(x) = \begin{cases} 1/2 - x & \le x < 1/2 \\ 1 ; & x = 1/2 \\ 3/2 - x; & 1/2 < x \le 1 \end{cases}$$

Solution :. We have :

(LHL at $x = 1/2$) $= \lim\limits_{x \to 1/2^-} f(x) = \lim\limits_{x \to 1/2} (1/2 - x)$ $\left[\because f(x) = 1/2 - x \text{ for } 0 \le x < \dfrac{1}{2}\right]$

$= 1/2 - 1/2 = 0,$ [using direct substitution method]

(RHL at $x = 1/2$) $= \lim\limits_{x \to 1/2^+} f(x) = \lim\limits_{x \to 1/2} (3/2 - x)$ $\left[\because f(x) = 3/2 - x \text{ for } \dfrac{1}{2} < x \le 1\right]$

$= 3/2 - 1/2 = 1$ [using direct substitution method]

$$\therefore \quad \lim_{x \to 1/2^-} f(x) \neq \lim_{x \to 1/2^+} f(x)$$

Hence, $f(x)$ is not continuous at $x = 1/2$.

Example 38 : **Discuss the continuity of the function $f(x)$ at $x = 2$.**

$$f(x) = \begin{cases} 2 - x, & x < 2 \\ 2 + x, & x \geq 2 \end{cases}$$

Solution : We have :

$$\text{(LHL at } x = 2) = \lim_{x \to 2^-} f(x) = \lim_{x \to 2} 2 - x \qquad [\because f(x) = 2 - x \text{ for } x < 2)$$

$$= 2 - 2 = 0$$

$$\text{(RHL at } x = 2) = \lim_{x \to 2^+} f(x) = \lim_{x \to 2} 2 + x \qquad [\because f(x) = 2 + x = \text{ for } x \geq 2]$$

$\therefore \quad \lim_{x \to 2^-} f(x) \neq \lim_{x \to 2^+} f(x)$. Hence, $f(x)$ is not continuous at $x = 2$.

Example 39 : **Show that** $f(x) = \begin{cases} 5x - 4, & \text{when } 0 < x \leq 1 \\ 4x^3 - 3x, & \text{when } 1 < x < 2 \end{cases}$ **is continuous at $x = 1$.**

Solution : We have :

$$\text{(LHL at } x = 1) = \lim_{x \to 1^-} f(x) = \lim_{x \to 1} 5x - 4 \qquad [\because f(x) = 5x - 4 \text{ when } x \leq 1]$$

$$= 5 \times 1 - 4 = 1$$

$$\text{(RHL at } x = 1) = \lim_{x \to 1^+} f(x) = \lim_{x \to 1} 4x^3 - 3x \qquad [\because f(x) = 4x^3 - 3x, x > 1]$$

$$= 4(1)^3 - 3(1) = 1$$

and $\quad f(1) = 5 \times 1 - 4 = 1$

$\therefore \quad \lim_{x \to 1^-} f(x) = f(1) = \lim_{x \to 1^+} f(x)$. So, $f(x)$ is continuous at $x = 1$.

Example 40 : **Determine the value of k for which the following function is continuous at $x = 3$.**

$$f(x) = \begin{cases} \dfrac{x^2 - 9}{x - 3}, & x \neq 3 \\ k, & x = 3 \end{cases}$$

Solution : Since $f(x)$ is continuous at $x = 3$, therefore

$$\lim_{x \to 3} f(x) = f(3) \Rightarrow \lim_{x \to 3} f(x) = k \qquad [\because f(3) = k]$$

$$\Rightarrow \lim_{x \to 3} \frac{x^2 - 9}{x - 3} = k \Rightarrow \lim_{x \to 3} \frac{(x-3)(x+3)}{x - 3} = k \Rightarrow \lim_{x \to 3} (x + 3) = k \Rightarrow 6 = k$$

Thus, $f(x)$ is continuous at $x = 3$, if $k = 6$.

Exercise 5.3

1. Test the continuity of the function on $f(x)$ at the origin :

$$f(x) = \begin{cases} \dfrac{x}{|x|}, & x \neq 0 \\ 1, & x = 0 \end{cases}$$

2. A function $f(x)$ is defined as,

$$f(x) = \begin{cases} \dfrac{x^2 - x - 6}{x - 3}; & \text{if } x \neq 3 \\ 5, & \text{if } x = 3 \end{cases}$$

Show that $f(x)$ is continuous at $x = 3$.

3. A function $f(x)$ is defined as

$$f(x) = \begin{cases} \dfrac{x^2 - 9}{x - 3}; & \text{if } x \neq 3 \\ 6 & \text{if } x = 3 \end{cases}$$

Since that $f(x)$ is continuous at $x = 3$.

4. If $f(x) = \begin{cases} \dfrac{x^2 - 1}{x - 1}; & \text{for } x \neq 1 \\ 2, & \text{for } x = 1 \end{cases}$

Find whether $f(x)$ is continuous at $x = 1$.

5. If $f(x) = \begin{cases} e^{1/x}; & \text{if } x \neq 0 \\ 1, & \text{if } x = 0 \end{cases}$ find whether f is continuous at $x = 0$.

6. Show that $f(x) = \begin{cases} \dfrac{x - |x|}{2}; & \text{when } x \neq 0 \\ 2, & \text{when } x = 0 \end{cases}$ is discontinuous at $x = 0$.

7. Show that $f(x) = \begin{cases} \dfrac{|x - a|}{x - a}; & \text{when } x \neq a \\ 1. & \text{when } x = a \end{cases}$ is discontinuous at $x = a$.

APPLICATION OF CONTINUITY IS BUSINESS AND ECONOMICS

The continuity of a function at a given point is necessary to ensure its differentiation. The derivative of functions helps in studying important relations between various dependent and independent variables such as price and demand, price and supply, etc.

Example 41 : **A company charges Rs. 5 per unit on sales of first 25 units. If an order is placed for above 25 units but upto 50 units, Rs. 4 per unit would be charged. Above 50 units, Rs. 3 per unit would be charged. Determine continuity of the function at $x = 25$ and 50.**

Solution : From the information given, we may say that revenue is a function of number of units sold.

$$R(x) = 5x \quad 0 < x \le 25$$
$$4x \quad 25 < x \le 50$$
$$3x \quad 50 < x$$

Continuity at $x = 25$

when $x < 25$

$$R(x) = 5x$$
$$= 5(25) = 125$$

when $x = 25$

$$R(x) = 5x$$
$$= 5(25) = 125$$

when $x > 25$

$$R(x) = 4(x) = 4(25)$$
$$= 100$$

Function is discontinuous at $x = 25$.

Continuity at $x = 50$

when $x < 50$

$$R = 4x = 4(50) = 200$$

when $x = 50$

$$R = 4(50) = 200$$

when $x > 50$

$$R = 3x = 3(50) = 150$$

$\therefore$ Function at discontinuous at $x = 50$.

Exercise 5.4

Q. 1 What are the discontinuities, if any of the function

$$f(x) = \frac{2x^2 + 3x + 1}{3x^2 - 4x + 1}$$

[Ans. ($x = 1/3$ and $x = 1$)]

Q. 2 Given $y = f(x) = \dfrac{x^2 - x - 12}{x - 4}$ **Ans.** ((*i*) 7; (*ii*) No., if is not defined of $x = 4$)

(*i*) Evaluate the limit of y as $x \to 4$.

(*ii*) Is this function continuous at $x = 4$? Why?

Q. 3 Find the values of a and b, if the function f given below is continuous in the interval $[-1, 2]$,

$$f(x) = \begin{cases} x + 1, & \text{for } -1 \le x \le 0 \\ ax + b, & \text{for } 0 \le x \le 1 \\ -1\ , & \text{for } 1 \le x \le 2 \end{cases}$$

[Ans. ($a = -2$, $6 = 1$)]

Q. 4 A shopkeeper charges Rs. 25 per item for purchasing 20 or less items. He gives some rebate it items bought are more. If the items bought are 50 or less, then a rebate of Re 1 per item and for purchase of more than 50 items, rebate of Rs. 2 per item is given. Find the cost function. What are the points at which this is not continues.

Ans. $$C(x) = \begin{cases} 25x \text{ it } x \le 20 \\ 24x \text{ it } 20 < x \le 50 \\ 23x \text{ it } x > 50 \end{cases}$$

Q. 5 A firm has four plants and operates them as they are needed to person available row material. Each plant has a fixed cost of Rs. 3000 per month whether operating or not. In addition each plant, it in operation, will insure an additional fixed cost of Rs. 50000 per month. The row material cost is fixed at Rs. 5 per units of output, and each plant can produce at the most 10000 units of output per month. Find the total cost function and examine the points of discontinuity there of

$$C'(x) = \begin{cases} 12000 & x = 0 \\ 5x + 17000 & 0 < x \le 10000 \\ 5x + 22000 & 10000 < x \le 20000 \\ 5x + 27000 & 20000 < x \le 30000 \\ 5x + 32000 & 30000 < x \le 40000 \end{cases}$$

Ans. [The function is discontinues at $x = 0$, $x = 10,000$, $x = 20000$, $x = 30000$ and $x = 40000$]

CONTINUITY

Cauchy's definition of Continuity

A function $f(x)$ is said to be continuous at $x = a$ if $f(a)$ exists and corresponding to an arbitrary positive number $\in$ however small, we can find δ such that

$$| f(x) - f(a) | < \in, \text{ whenever } |x - a| < \delta$$

A function is discontinuous at $x = a$ if

$$\underset{x \to a}{\text{Lt}}\ f(x) \ne f(a).$$

Basic concept of Continuity

A function is said to be continuous at a given point or in a given interval if there is no break in its curve at that point or during the given interval. The needs for assessing continuity of a function arises because sometimes on the basis of given of set of values, we may be interested in finding estimated values. For example, the relationship between $f(x)$ and x has been studied and after deriving relationship between them at some points, the following relation is obtained.

$$f(x) = 3x^2 + 7$$

Now, we may find $f(x)$ just by substituting different values of x. This substitution process will hold good only when we have ensured that $f(x)$ is continuous either for all values of x or for a given interval of x. In case it is not so, the function $f(x)$ would be referred as **discontinuous.** A function can be discontinuous in number of ways namely

1. Removable discontinuity
2. Jumped Disc discontinuity
3. Infinity discontinuity.

Removable Discontinuity

Consider a function $f(x)$ which when plotted for different values of x, has figure as shown below.

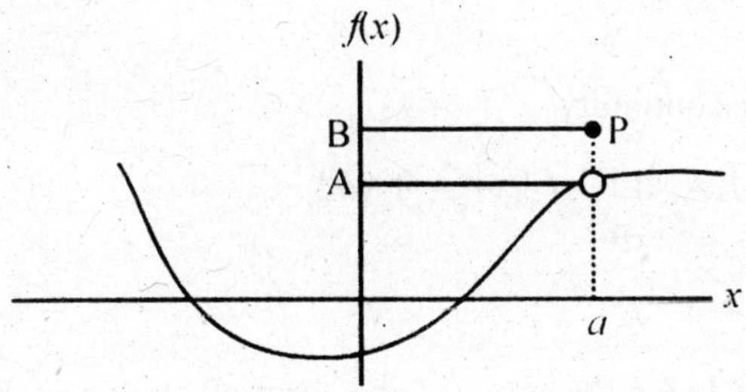

It can be observed when x moves towards a from left hand side as well as right hand side, $f(x)$ moves towards A but at $x = a$, $f(x) = B$. Thus, discontinuity occurs at $x = a$.

In other words,

$$\underset{x \to a^+}{\text{Lt}} f(x) = \underset{x \to a}{\text{Lt}} f(x) = A$$

But $f(a) \neq$ A.

Thus, in a case of removable discontinuity at a given point

(*i*) Limits of function exist

(*ii*) L.H.L. = R.H.L., but

(*iii*) Function is not defined at that point.

If somehow, we can place point P in the gap, the function would be continuous because in that case $f(a) = A$.

Jump Disc Discontinuity

Consider a function $f(x)$ having a curve of the form as shown in figure below.

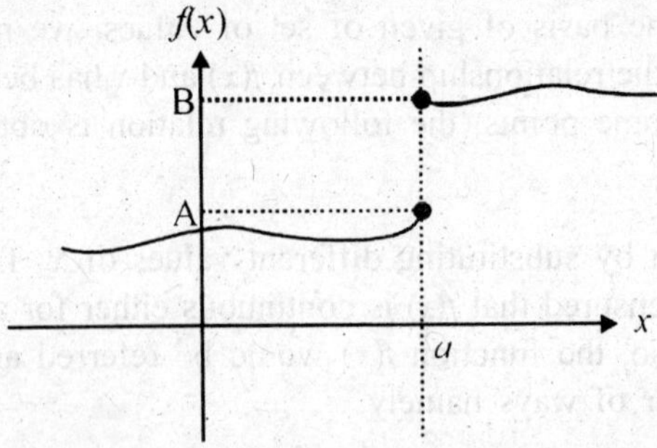

In this case of discontinuity, when x move towards a from left hand side and right hand side, we have different values of $f(x)$, therefore

$$\operatorname*{Lt}_{x \to a} f(x) = A$$

$$\operatorname*{Lt}_{x \to a^+} f(x) = B$$

Since we have different values of $f(x)$ for L.H.L. and R.H.L., therefore, it is known as jump disc discontinuity.

Thus, in this kind of discontinuity

$$\operatorname*{Lt}_{x \to a^-} f(x) \neq \operatorname*{Lt}_{x \to a^+} f(x) \neq f(a)$$

Infinite Discontinuity

Consider a function $f(x)$ having a curve of the form as shown in figure below.

In this case of discontinuity, when x move towards a from left hand side and right hand side, we have infinite values of $f(x)$, therefore

$$\operatorname*{Lt}_{x \to a^-} f(x) = \alpha$$

$$\operatorname*{Lt}_{x \to a^+} f(x) = \alpha$$

Thus, in this kind of discontinuity

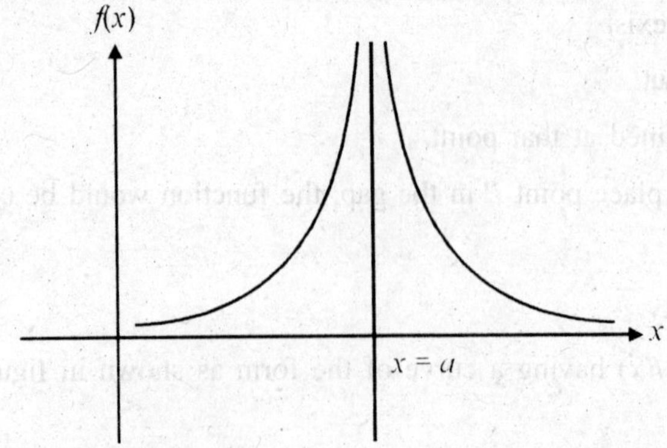

$\operatorname*{Lt}_{x \to a} f(x)$ may or may not be equal to $\operatorname*{Lt}_{x \to a^+} f(x)$ but they are not finite numbers.

CONTINUOUS IN AN INTERVAL

A function $f(x)$ is said to be continuous in the interval $a < x < b$ if $f(x)$ is continuous at each and every point of the interval.

Mathematically,

$$f(a) = \underset{x \to a^+}{\text{Lt}} f(x) \quad \text{and} \quad f(b) = \underset{x \to b^-}{\text{Lt}} f(x).$$

then $f(x)$ is said to be continuous in the closed interval $a \le x \le b$.

PROPERTIES OF CONTINUOUS FUNCTION

1. Every polynomial function is continuous at every number.
2. Every rational function is continuous at every number in its domain.
3. If $f(x)$ is continuous at $x = a$ and $f(a) \neq 0$, then $1/f(x)$ is also continuous at $x = a$.
4. If $f(x)$ is continuous at $x = a$, then $|f(x)|$ is also continuous at $x = a$.
5. The sum, difference and product of two functions which are continuous at that point (or in that interval) are continuous at that point (or in that interval).
6. If $f(x) = \sqrt[n]{x}$, where n is any positive integer then f is continuous at a if either.
   (*i*) a is any positive number, or
   (*ii*) a is a negative number or zero, and n is odd.
7. If the function g is continuous at a and function f is continuous at $g(a)$, then the composite function fog is continuous at a.

CONTINUITY AT A POINT

A function $f(x)$ is said to be continuous at a point $x = a$ of its domain, if $\lim_{x \to a} f(x) = f(a)$.

Thus, ($f(x)$ is continuous at $x = a$) if $\lim_{x \to a} f(x) = f(a)$.

and $$\lim_{x \to a^-} f(x) = \lim_{x \to a^+} f(x) = f(a)$$

If $f(x)$ is not continuous at a point $x = a$, then it is said to be discontinuous at $x = a$.

Example 1 : **Discuss the continuity of the function $f(x)$ at $x = 1/2$, where**

$$f(x) = \begin{cases} 1/2 - x & \le x < 1/2 \\ 1\,; & x = 1/2 \\ 3/2 - x; & 1/2 < x \le 1 \end{cases}$$

Solution :. We have :

$$(\text{LHL at } x = 1/2) = \lim_{x \to 1/2^-} f(x) = \lim_{x \to 1/2} (1/2 - x) \qquad \left[\because f(x) = 1/2 - x \text{ for } 0 \le x < \frac{1}{2}\right]$$

$$= 1/2 - 1/2 = 0, \qquad \text{[using direct substitution method]}$$

$$(\text{RHL at } x = 1/2) = \lim_{x \to 1/2^+} f(x) = \lim_{x \to 1/2} (3/2 - x) \qquad \left[\because f(x) = 3/2 - x \text{ for } \frac{1}{2} < x \leq 1\right]$$

$$= 3/2 - 1/2 = 1 \qquad \text{[using direct substitution method]}$$

$$\therefore \quad \lim_{x \to 1/2^-} f(x) \neq \lim_{x \to 1/2^+} f(x)$$

Hence, $f(x)$ is not continuous at $x = 1/2$.

Example 2 : **Discuss the continuity of the function $f(x)$ at $x = 2$.**

$$f(x) = \begin{cases} 2 - x, & x < 2 \\ 2 + x, & x \geq 2 \end{cases}$$

Solution : We have :

$$(\text{LHL at } x = 2) = \lim_{x \to 2^-} f(x) = \lim_{x \to 2} 2 - x \qquad [\because f(x) = 2 - x \text{ for } x < 2)$$

$$= 2 - 2 = 0$$

$$(\text{RHL at } x = 2) = \lim_{x \to 2^+} f(x) = \lim_{x \to 2} 2 + x \qquad [\because f(x) = 2 + x = \text{ for } x \geq 2]$$

$\therefore \quad \lim_{x \to 2^-} f(x) \neq \lim_{x \to 2^+} f(x)$. Hence, $f(x)$ is not continuous at $x = 2$.

Example 3 : **Show that $f(x) = \begin{cases} 5x - 4, & \text{when } 0 < x \leq 1 \\ 4x^3 - 3x, & \text{when } 1 < x < 2 \end{cases}$ is continuous at $x = 1$.**

Solution : We have :

$$(\text{LHL at } x = 1) = \lim_{x \to 1^-} f(x) = \lim_{x \to 1} 5x - 4 \qquad [\because f(x) = 5x - 4 \text{ when } x \leq 1]$$

$$= 5 \times 1 - 4 = 1$$

$$(\text{RHL at } x = 1) = \lim_{x \to 1^+} f(x) = \lim_{x \to 1} 4x^3 - 3x \qquad [\because f(x) = 4x^3 - 3x, x > 1]$$

$$= 4(1)^3 - 3(1) = 1$$

and $\quad f(1) = 5 \times 1 - 4 = 1$

$\therefore \quad \lim_{x \to 1^-} f(x) = f(1) = \lim_{x \to 1^+} f(x)$. So, $f(x)$ is continuous at $x = 1$.

Example 4 : **Determine the value of k for which the following function is continuous at $x = 3$.**

$$f(x) = \begin{cases} \dfrac{x^2 - 9}{x - 3}, & x \neq 3 \\ k, & x = 3 \end{cases}$$

Solution : Since $f(x)$ is continuous at $x = 3$, therefore

$$\lim_{x \to 3} f(x) = f(3) \Rightarrow \lim_{x \to 3} f(x) = k \qquad [\because f(3) = k]$$

$$\Rightarrow \quad \lim_{x \to 3} \frac{x^2 - 9}{x - 3} = k \Rightarrow \lim_{x \to 3} \frac{(x-3)(x+3)}{x-3} = k \Rightarrow \lim_{x \to 3} (x+3) = k \Rightarrow 6 = k$$

Thus, $f(x)$ is continuous at $x = 3$, if $k = 6$.

Exercise 5.5

1. Test the continuity of the function on $f(x)$ at the origin :

$$f(x) = \begin{cases} \dfrac{x}{|x|}, & x \neq 0 \\ 1, & x = 0 \end{cases}$$

2. A function $f(x)$ is defined as,

$$f(x) = \begin{cases} \dfrac{x^2 - x - 6}{x - 3}; & \text{if } x \neq 3 \\ 5, & \text{if } x = 3 \end{cases}$$

Show that $f(x)$ is continuous at $x = 3$.

3. A function $f(x)$ is defined as

$$f(x) = \begin{cases} \dfrac{x^2 - 9}{x - 3}; & \text{if } x \neq 3 \\ 6, & \text{if } x = 3 \end{cases}$$

Since that $f(x)$ is continuous at $x = 3$.

4. If $f(x) = \begin{cases} \dfrac{x^2 - 1}{x - 1}; & \text{for } x \neq 1 \\ 2, & \text{for } x = 1 \end{cases}$

Find whether $f(x)$ is continuous at $x = 1$.

5. If $f(x) = \begin{cases} e^{1/x}; & \text{if } x \neq 0 \\ 1, & \text{if } x = 0 \end{cases}$ find whether f is continuous at $x = 0$.

6. Show that $f(x) = \begin{cases} \dfrac{x - |x|}{2}; & \text{when } x \neq 0 \\ 2, & \text{when } x = 0 \end{cases}$ is discontinuous at $x = 0$.

7. Show that $f(x) = \begin{cases} \dfrac{|x - a|}{x - a}; & \text{when } x \neq a \\ 1, & \text{when } x = a \end{cases}$ is discontinuous at $x = a$.

APPLICATION OF CONTINUITY IS BUSINESS AND ECONOMICS

The continuity of a function at a given point is necessary to ensure its differentiation. The derivative of functions helps in studying important relations between various dependent and independent variables such as price and demand, price and supply, etc.

Example 5 : **A company charges Rs. 5 per unit on sales of first 25 units. If an order is placed for above 25 units but upto 50 units, Rs. 4 per unit would be charged. Above 50 units, Rs. 3 per unit would be charged. Determine continuity of the function at x = 25 and 50.**

Solution : From the information given, we may say that revenue is a function of number of units sold.

$$R(x) = 5x \quad 0 < x \le 25$$
$$4x \quad 25 < x \le 50$$
$$3x \quad 50 < x$$

Continuity at $x = 25$

when $x < 25$

$$R(x) = 5x$$
$$= 5(25) = 125$$

when $x = 25$

$$R(x) = 5x$$
$$= 5(25) = 125$$

when $x > 25$

$$R(x) = 4(x) = 4(25)$$
$$= 100$$

Function is discontinuous at $x = 25$.

Continuity at $x = 50$

when $x < 50$

$$R = 4x = 4(50) = 200$$

when $x = 50$

$$R = 4(50) = 200$$

when $x > 50$

$$R = 3x = 3(50) = 150$$

∴ Function at discontinuous at $x = 50$.

Exercise 5.6

Q. 1 What are the discontinuities, if any of the function

$$f(x) = \frac{2x^2 + 3x + 1}{3x^2 - 4x + 1}$$

[Ans. ($x = 1/3$ and $x = 1$)]

Q. 2 Given $y = f(x) = \dfrac{x^2 - x - 12}{x - 4}$ *Solution.* ((*i*) 7; (*ii*) No., if is not defined of $x = 4$)

(*i*) Evaluate the limit of y as $x \to 4$.

(*ii*) Is this function continuous at $x = 4$? Why?

Q. 3 Find the values of a and b, if the function f given below is continuous in the interval $[-1, 2]$,

$$f(x) = \begin{cases} x + 1, & \text{for } -1 \le x \le 0 \\ ax + b, & \text{for } 0 \le x \le 1 \\ -1\ , & \text{for } 1 \le x \le 2 \end{cases}$$

[**Ans.** ($a = -2$, $6 = 1$)]

Q. 4 A shopkeeper charges Rs. 25 per item for purchasing 20 or less items. He gives some rebate it items bought are more. If the items bought are 50 or less, then a rebate of Re 1 per item and for purchase of more than 50 items, rebate of Rs. 2 per item is given. Find the cost function. What are the points at which this is not continues.

Ans. $\left[C(x) = \begin{matrix} 25x \text{ it } x \le 20 \\ 24x \text{ it } 20 < x \le 50 \\ 23x \text{ it } x > 50 \end{matrix} \right]$

Q. 5 A firm has four plants and operates them as they are needed to person available row material. Each plant has a fixed cost of Rs. 3000 per month whether operating or not. In addition each plant, it in operation, will insure an additional fixed cost of Rs. 50000 per month. The row material cost is fixed at Rs. 5 per units of output, and each plant can produce at the most 10000 units of output per month. Find the total cost function and examine the points of discontinuity there of

$$C(x) = \begin{cases} 12000 & x = 0 \\ 5x + 17000 & 0 < x \le 10000 \\ 5x + 22000 & 10000 < x \le 20000 \\ 5x + 27000 & 20000 < x \le 30000 \\ 5x + 32000 & 30000 < x \le 40000 \end{cases}$$

Ans. [The function is discontinues at $x = 0$, $x = 10{,}000$, $x = 20000$, $x = 30000$ and $x = 40000$]

6

Derivatives – Concepts

HIGHLIGHTS OF THE CHAPTER

- **Introduction**
- **Increasing and Decreasing Functions**
- **Maxima and Minima**
- **Concavity and Convexity**

INTRODUCTION

In the previous chapter, we have discussed the concepts of limits and continuity which serves as basic tools for understanding the concept of derivative. The present chapter deals with the basic concepts of differentiation and other related issues like increasing and decreasing functions along with the concept of maxima and minima.

The derivative of function f at a point $x = a$, represented by $f'(a)$ is defined as

$$f'(a) = \lim_{h \to 0} \frac{f(a-h) - f(x)}{h} \qquad \text{....(1)}$$

provided the limit exists.

The derivative of a function is also called as differential coefficient.

Explanation of the Term Derivative

Let x be the variable.

Let x receive a certain increment Δx. Then the variable becomes $x + \Delta x$.

The value of f also changes from $f(x)$ to $f(x + \Delta x)$

The difference in the value of f is $f(x + \Delta x) - f(x)$.

This change has taken place for a change Δx in the variable x.

Therefore the rate of change is $\dfrac{f(x+\Delta x) - f(x)}{\Delta x}$

When $\Delta x \Rightarrow 0$, we have

$$\lim_{\Delta x \to 0} \frac{f(x+\Delta x) - f(x)}{\Delta x}$$

This limit, when it exists, is the rate of change of f at a. Replacing Δx in h, this is the same as

$$\lim_{h\to 0}\frac{f(a+h)-f(a)}{h}$$

This is how we define the derivative of $f(x)$ at a.

i.e. Derivative of $f(x)$ at $a = \lim_{h\to 0}\dfrac{f(a+h)-f(a)}{h}$

Physical Meaning : The derivative is related to a function, just as velocity is related to the distance travelled by a moving particle.

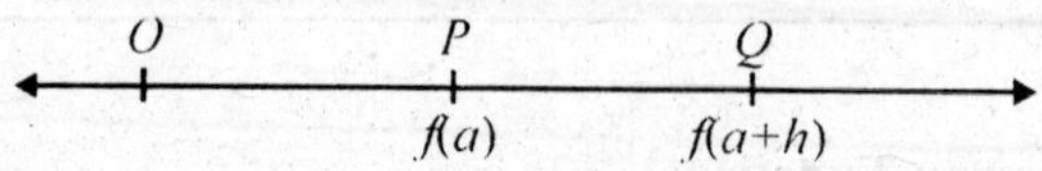

Consider a particle moving along a line and we measure its distance x from a point O in the line. Clearly the displacement depends upon time 'a'.

Let its displacement at time a be $f(a)$. Then its displacement at time $(a + h)$ is $f(a + h)$.

∴ Average velocity of the particle in this interval is

$$\frac{f(a+h)-f(a)}{h}$$

Now if we make h smaller and smaller, we will obtain the *velocity* of the particle at time t.

∴ Velocity at time a is $\lim_{h\to 0}\dfrac{f(a+h)-f(a)}{h}$

Thus, the derivative is related to a function, in the same way as values related to the distance travelled by a moving particle.

Geometrical Meaning : Let $y = f(x)$ be a function and 'a' be a point in the domain. The function has a graph as shown in figure 1.1 and let the point $P(a, f(a))$ lie on it. Let Q be another point on the graph close to the point P. Its co-ordinates $(a + h, f(a + h))$ where $h \neq 0$.

The slope of the line PQ will be $\left[\therefore \text{ slope } = \dfrac{y_2 - y_1}{x_2 - x_1}\right]$

$$PQ = \frac{f(a+h)-f(a)}{a+h-a}$$

$$= \frac{f(a+h)-f(a)}{h}$$

As $Q \to P$ along the curve, $h \to 0$

Therefore, $\lim_{h\to 0}\dfrac{f(a+h)-f(a)}{h} = \lim_{Q\to P}(\text{Slope of } PQ)$

$= \text{Slope of the tangent at } P$

Thus the derivative of function at a is the slope of the tangent to the curve $y = f(x)$ at the point $(a, f(a))$.

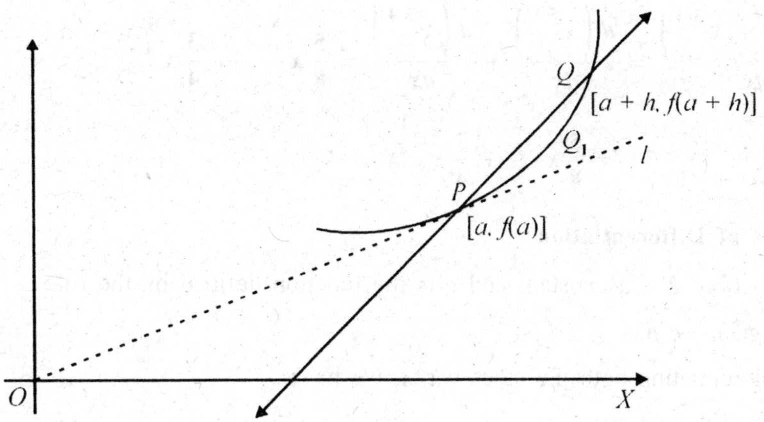

Fig. 1.1

List of Important Formulae

1. $\frac{d}{dx}\left(x^n\right) = nx^{n-1}$

   (where n is fixed number)

2. $\frac{d}{dx}(c) = 0$, where c is constant.

3. $\frac{d}{dx}\left(\log f(x) = \frac{1}{f(x)} \times f'(x)\right)$

4. $\frac{d}{dx}\left(e^{f(x)}\right) = e^{f(x)} \times f'(x)$.

   Where $f'(x) = \frac{d}{dx}[f(x)]$.

   Using the above formulae, the following problem can be solved.

Example 1. **Find the derivative of the following functions w.r.tx.**

(i) $\frac{d\left(x^8\right)}{dx} = 8x^{8-1} = 8x^7$

(ii) $\frac{d\left(3x^2 + 5x + 7\right)}{dx} = \frac{d\left(3x^2\right)}{dx} + \frac{d(5x)}{dx} + \frac{d(7)}{dx} = 6x + 5 + 0 = 6x + 5$

(iii) $\frac{d\left(ax^4 + bx^2 + cx + d\right)}{dx} = \frac{d\left(ax^4\right)}{dx} + \frac{d\left(bx^2\right)}{dx} + \frac{d(cx)}{dx} + \frac{d(d)}{dx}$

$= 4ax^3 + 2bx + c + 0$

(iv) $= \dfrac{d\left(\sqrt{x}+3\right)}{dx} = \dfrac{d\left(x^{1/2}+3\right)}{dx} = \dfrac{1}{2}x^{\frac{1}{2}-1} + 0 = \dfrac{1}{2\sqrt{x}}$

(v) $= \dfrac{d\left(x^{5/8}+x^{3/4}\right)}{dx} = \dfrac{d\left(x^{5/8}\right)}{dx} + \dfrac{d\left(x^{3/4}\right)}{dx} = \dfrac{5}{8}x^{\frac{5}{8}-1} + \dfrac{3}{4}x^{\frac{1}{4}-1}$

$$= \frac{5}{8}x^{-\frac{3}{8}} + \frac{3}{4}x^{-\frac{1}{4}}$$

Important Rules of Differentiation

1. If f is a function, c is a constant and g is the function defined by the rule.

$$g(x) = c\, f(x)$$

then, differentiating both the sides w.r.tx, we have.

$$g'(x) = c\, f'(x)$$

2. If f and g are derivable functions of x, then $y = f\,g$ is also derivating function of x. The derivative of y will be given as

$$y'(x) = f'(x).g(x) + g'(x).f(x)$$

i.e. The derivative of the product of two functions = First function × derivative of the Second + Second Function × Derivative of the First.

This is also known as **product rule**.

3. If f and g are differentiable function then $y = f/g$ is also differentiable at x and it is given as.

$$y'(x) = \frac{f'(x).g(x) - f(x).g'(x)}{\left(g(x)\right)^2}$$

$$\text{Derivative of}\left(\frac{\text{Numerator}}{\text{Denominator}}\right) = \frac{\text{Deno} \times \text{Derivative of Num.} - \text{Num. Derivative of Deno}}{(\text{Deno})^2}$$

This is also known as **quotient rule**.

The examples based on above formulae and rules are given as under.

***Example** 2.* **Differentiate x^{x^x} w.r.t. x.**

Solution.

$$y = x^{x^x}$$

Taking long repeatedly are have

$$\log y = x \log x + \log x$$

Differentiating w.r.t.x.

$$\frac{1}{\log y}.\frac{1}{y}\frac{dy}{dx} = x \times \frac{1}{x} + \log x \times 1 + \frac{1}{\log x} \times \frac{1}{x}$$

$$\frac{dy}{dx} = y \log y\left[1 + \log x + \frac{1}{x \log x}\right]$$

$$= x^{\left(x^x\right)}.x^x \log x\left[1 + \log x + \frac{1}{x \log x}\right]$$

$$= x^{\left(x^x\right)}.x^x\left[\log x + (\log x)^2 + \frac{1}{x}\right]$$

Example 3. **Differentiate $x^{1/x}$ w.r.t.x.**

Solution.

Let $y = x^{1/x}$. $\therefore \log y = \log x^{1/x}$

$$\log y = \frac{1}{x}\log x = \frac{\log x}{x}$$

Differentiating w.r.t.x.

$$\frac{1}{y}.\frac{dy}{dx} = \frac{x.\frac{1}{x} - 1.\log x}{x^2} = \frac{1 - \log x}{x^2}$$

$$\therefore \quad \frac{dy}{dx} = y\left(\frac{1 - \log x}{x^2}\right) = x^{1/x}\left(\frac{1 - \log x}{x^2}\right)$$

Example 4. **Differentiate $x^{\sqrt{x}}$ w.r.t.x.**

Solution.

Let $y = x^{\sqrt{x}}$

$$\log y = \log x^{\sqrt{x}} = \sqrt{x}\log x$$

Differentiating w.r.t.x.

$$\frac{1}{y}.\frac{dy}{dx} = \sqrt{x}.\frac{1}{x} + \log x.\frac{1}{2\sqrt{x}}$$

$$= \frac{1}{\sqrt{x}} + \frac{1}{2\sqrt{x}}\log x = \frac{2 + \log x}{2\sqrt{x}}$$

$$\frac{dy}{dx} = y\left(\frac{2 + \log x}{2\sqrt{x}}\right) = x^{\sqrt{x}}\left(\frac{2 + \log x}{2\sqrt{x}}\right)$$

Example 5. **Differentiate $(1 + x)^{\log x}$, $x > 0$ w.r.t.x.**

Solution.

Let $y = (1 + x)^{\log x}$, $x > 0$

Taking logarithms of both sides, we get

$$\log y = \log (1 + x)^{\log x} = \log x \log (1 + x)$$

Differentiating both sides w.r.t. x, we have

$$\frac{1}{y}\cdot\frac{dy}{dx} = \frac{d}{dx}(\log x).\log(1+x) + \log x.\frac{d}{dx}(1+x)$$

$$= \frac{1}{x}\log(1+x) + \log x.\frac{1}{1+x}$$

$$\frac{dy}{dx} = y\left[\frac{\log(1+x)}{x} + \frac{\log x}{1+x}\right]$$

$$= (1+x)^{\log x}\left[\frac{\log(1+x)}{x} + \frac{\log x}{1+x}\right]$$

Example 6.

(a) If $y = \dfrac{x\left(1-x^2\right)^{1/2}}{1-x}$, **find** $\dfrac{dy}{dx}$

(b) Find the differential coefficient of

$$\log\frac{1+\sqrt{x}}{1-\sqrt{x}} \text{ w.r.t.x}$$

(c) Find the differential coefficient of

$$\frac{x^3\sqrt{x+4}}{(2x-3)^3}$$

(d) If $\log\left[e^x\left(\dfrac{x-2}{x+2}\right)^{3/2}\right]$ **find** $\dfrac{dy}{dx}$

(e) Differentiate w.r.t.x. $\dfrac{\sqrt{x}\,(2x-3)^2}{\sqrt{x+1}}$

Solution.

(*a*) Given $y = \dfrac{x\left(1-x^2\right)^{1/2}}{(1-x)}$

$$\log y = \log x + \frac{1}{2}\log\left(1-x^2\right) - \log(1-x)$$

Differentiating above equation w.r.t.x. we get

$$\frac{1}{y}\cdot\frac{dy}{dx} = \frac{1}{x} + \frac{1}{2}\left(\frac{-2x}{1-x^2}\right) + \frac{1}{1-x}$$

$$\frac{dy}{dx} = y\left[\frac{1}{x} - \frac{x}{1-x^2} + \frac{1}{1-x}\right]$$

$$= \frac{x\left(1-x^2\right)^{1/2}}{1-x}\left[\frac{1-x^2-x^2+(1+x)x}{x(1-x)^2}\right]$$

$$= \frac{1+x-x^2}{(1-x)\left(1-x^2\right)^{1/2}} = \frac{1+x-x^2}{(1-x)^{3/2}(1+x)^{1/2}}$$

(*b*) Let $\quad y = \log\frac{1+\sqrt{x}}{1-\sqrt{x}}$

$$= \log\left(1+\sqrt{x}\right) - \log\left(1-\sqrt{x}\right)$$

$$\frac{dy}{dx} = \frac{1}{1+\sqrt{x}} \times \frac{d}{dx}\left(1+\sqrt{x}\right) - \frac{1}{1-\sqrt{x}} \times \frac{d}{dx}\left(1-\sqrt{x}\right)$$

$$= \frac{1}{1+\sqrt{x}} \times \frac{1}{2}x^{-1/2} + \frac{1}{1-\sqrt{x}} \times \frac{1}{2}x^{-1/2}$$

$$= \frac{1}{2+\sqrt{x}}\left[\frac{1}{1+\sqrt{x}} + \frac{1}{1-\sqrt{x}}\right]$$

$$= \frac{1}{2\sqrt{x}}\left[\frac{1-\sqrt{x}+1+\sqrt{x}}{\left(1+\sqrt{x}\right)\left(1-\sqrt{x}\right)}\right]$$

$$= \frac{1}{2\sqrt{x}}\left(\frac{2}{1-x}\right) = \frac{1}{\sqrt{x}(1-x)}$$

(*c*) Let $\quad y = \frac{x^3\sqrt{x+4}}{(2x+3)^3}$

Taking log both sides, we get

$$\log y = 3\log x + \frac{1}{2}\log(x+4) - 3\log(2x+3)$$

$$\frac{1}{y}\cdot\frac{dy}{dx} = 3 \times \frac{1}{x} + \frac{1}{2} \times \frac{1}{x+4} - 3 \times \frac{1}{2x+3} \times 2$$

$$\frac{dy}{dx} = y\left[\frac{3}{x} + \frac{1}{2(x+4)} - \frac{6}{2x+3}\right]$$

***Example* 7. Find $\frac{dy}{dx}$ when x and y are connected by the relations :**

(*i*) $x^2 + y^2 = r^2$

(*ii*) $xy = c^2$

(*iii*) $\dfrac{x^2}{a^2} + \dfrac{y^2}{b^2} = 1$

Solution.

(*i*) $x^2 + y^2 = r^2$

Differentiating both sides w.r.t. x, we get

$$\frac{d}{dx}\left(x^2\right) + \frac{d}{dx}\left(y^2\right) = \frac{d}{dx}\left(r^2\right)$$

$$2x + 2y\frac{d}{dx} = 0$$

or $$x + y\frac{dy}{dx} = 0$$

Hence $$\frac{dy}{dx} = -\frac{x}{y}$$

(*iii*) $\dfrac{x^2}{a^2} + \dfrac{y^2}{b^2} = 1$

Differentiating both sides w.r.t. x we get

$$\frac{d}{dx}\left(\frac{x^2}{a^2}\right) + \frac{d}{dx}\left(\frac{y^2}{b^2}\right) = 1$$

or $$\frac{2x}{a^2} + \frac{2y}{b^2}\frac{dy}{dx} = 0$$

or $$\frac{y}{b^2}\frac{dy}{dx} = -\frac{x}{a^2}$$

INCREASING AND DECREASING FUNCTIONS

Consider the graph of any function, say $y = f(x)$ as shown in the Fig. 1.2 and tangents are drawn at the points A, B, C and D. If we think of a point as moving along the curve from left to right, we notice that the moving point would be rising at some positions and falling at others. At points on the curve where the moving point is rising, we say that $y = f(x)$ is an *increasing function.* At these points, y increase as x increases. At points where the moving point is falling, $y = f(x)$ is a *decreasing function.*

As already explained, that the derivative yields the slope of the tangent, it can be observed that a function is increasing at points where the slope is positive, and decreasing at points where the slope is negative.

It can be concluded that same function can be an increasing function in a certain interval and a decreasing function in certain other interval.

Certain functions are neither increasing nor decreasing in a given interval.

A differential real function is increasing when $f(x) > 0$ and decreasing when $f'(x) < 0$.

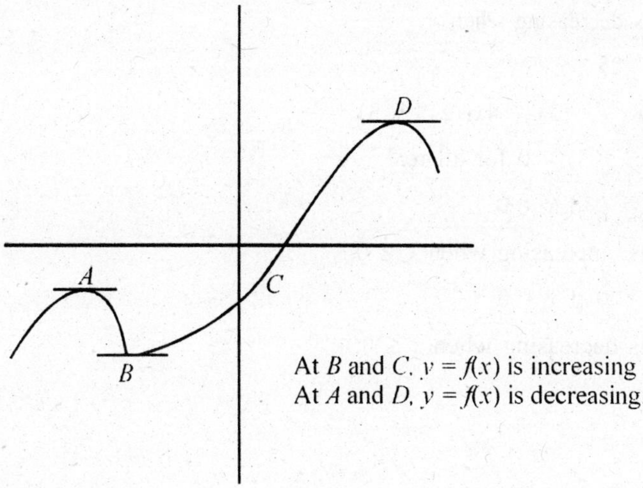

Fig. 1.2

Example 8. **Determine for which values of x the following functions are increasing and for which values they are decreasing.**

(*i*) $f(x) = 6x^2 - 2x + 12$

(*ii*) $f(x) = -3x^2 + 12x + 8$

(*iii*) $y = x + \frac{1}{x}, \neq 0.$

Solution.

(*i*) $f(x) = 6x^2 - 2x + 12$

$\therefore \quad f(x) = 12x - 2$

$f'(x) > 0$ *if* $12x - 2 > 0$ *or if* $x > \frac{1}{6}$

$f'(x)$ is increasing when $x > \frac{1}{6}$

Again $\quad f'(x) < 0$ if $12x - 2 < 0$ or if $x < \frac{1}{6}$

$\therefore \quad f'(x)$ is decreasing when $x < \frac{1}{6}$

(*ii*) $f'(x) = -3x^2 + 12x + 8$

$\therefore \quad f'(x) = -6x + 12$

$f'(x) > 0$ if $-6x + 12 > 0$

or $\quad -6x > -12$ *i.e.,* if $x < 2$.

$f(x)$ is increasing when $x < 2$

Also $\quad f'(x) < 0$ if $-6x + 12 < 0$ *i.e.,* $-6x < -12$.

or $\quad x > 2$.

$f(x)$ is decreasing when $x > 2$.

(*iii*) $f(x) - x^8 + 6x^2 + 25$

$f'(x) 8x^7 + 12x = 4x(2x^6 + 3)$

Since $4x(2x^6 + 3) > 0$ for all real x.

$\therefore$ $f'(x) > 0$ if $x > 0$

$\therefore$ $f(x)$ is increasing when $x \geq 0$.

Also $f'(x) < 0$ if $x < 0$

$\therefore$ $f(x)$ is decreasing when $x \leq 0$.

(*iv*) $y = x + \frac{1}{x}, x \neq 0.$

$\therefore$ $\frac{dy}{dx} = 1 - \frac{1}{x^2} = \frac{x^2 - 1}{x^2}.$

But $x^2 > 0 \quad \forall \quad x \neq 0$

$\therefore$ $\frac{dy}{dx} > 0$ if $x^2 - 1 > 0$

i.e., $x^2 > 1$

i.e., if $x > 1$ or $x < -1$ $\qquad [\therefore x^2 > a^2 \Rightarrow x > a \text{ or } x < -a]$

$\therefore$ y is increasing when x ³ 1 or $x < -1$

Also $\frac{dy}{dx} < 0$ if $x^2 < 1$

i.e., if $-1 < x < 1, x \neq 0$

$\therefore$ y is decreasing when $-1 \leq x \leq 1, x \neq 0$.

Example 9. **Determine the value of x for which the function**

$$f(x) = 5x^{3/2} - 3x^{5/2}, x > 0$$

Solution. $f(x) = 5x^{3/2} - 3x^{5/2}, x > 0$

$$\therefore \quad f'(x) = 5\left(\frac{3}{2}x^{1/2}\right) - 3\left(\frac{5}{2}x^{3/2}\right)$$

$$= \frac{15}{2}x^{1/2} - \frac{15}{2}x^{3/2} = \frac{15}{2}x^{1/2}(1 - x)$$

$$= \frac{15}{2}\sqrt{x}(1 - x)$$

As $\sqrt{x} > 0 \ \forall \ x > 0$

$\therefore$ $f'(x) > 0$ if $1 - x > 0$ *i.e.*, $x < 1$

$\therefore$ $f(x)$ is increasing when $0 < x < 1$

Again $f'(x) < 0$ if $1 - x < 0$ *i.e.*, $x > 1$

$\therefore$ $f(x)$ is decreasing when $x \geq 1$.

Example 10. **Determine the intervals in which the following : function is increasing or decreasing.**

$$f(x) = 2x^3 - 24x + 7.$$

Solution. $f(x) = 2x^3 - 24x + 7$

$\therefore$ $f(x) = 6x^2 - 24 = 6(x^2 - 4) = 6(x - 2)(x + 2)$

$f'(x) > 0$, for the function to be increasing which implies either

$(x - 2) > 0$ and $(x + 2) > 0$

i.e., $x > 2$ and $x > -2$

which gives $x > 2$.

(*ii*) or $x - 2 < 0$ and $x + 2 < 0$

$x < 2$ and $x < /0\ 2$

which gives $x < -2$.

$\therefore$ $f(x)$ is increasing for $x \geq 2$ and for $x \leq -2$.

$f'(x) < 0$, for the function to be decreasing which

implies either $x - 2 > 0$ and $x + 2 < 0$

$x > 2$ and $x < -2$

which is not possible.

or $x - 2 < 0$ and $x + 2 > 0$

$x - 2$ and $x > -2$

which gives $-2 < x < 2$.

$\therefore$ $f(x)$ is decreasing function for $-2 \leq x \leq 2$.

MAXIMA AND MINIMA

Definition

A function $f(x)$ is said to have a minimum value in an internal I at a, if a is in I and $f(a) \geq f(x)$ for all x in I. The number of $f(a)$ is called maximum value of $f(x)$ in I and $f(a)$ is called a (point of) maximum of $f(x)$.

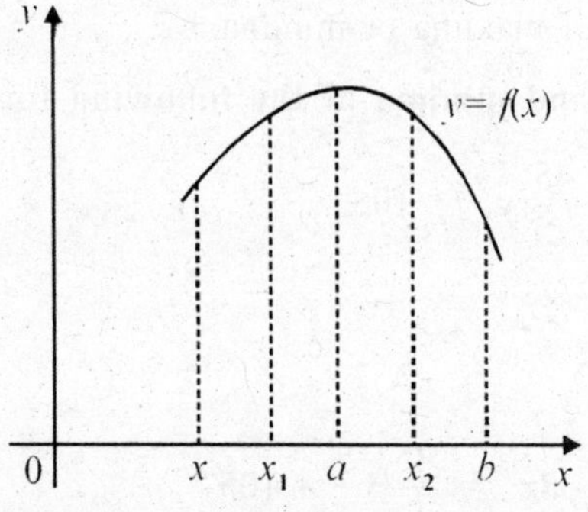

Fig. 1.3

In above Fig. 1.3, $x = a$ is a point of maximum of $f(x)$

Definition. A function $f(x)$ is said to have a minimum value in an interval I at a, if a is in I and if $f(a) \leq f(x)$ for all x in I. The number $f(a)$ is called minimum value of $f(x)$ in I and a is called a point of minimum of $f(x)$.

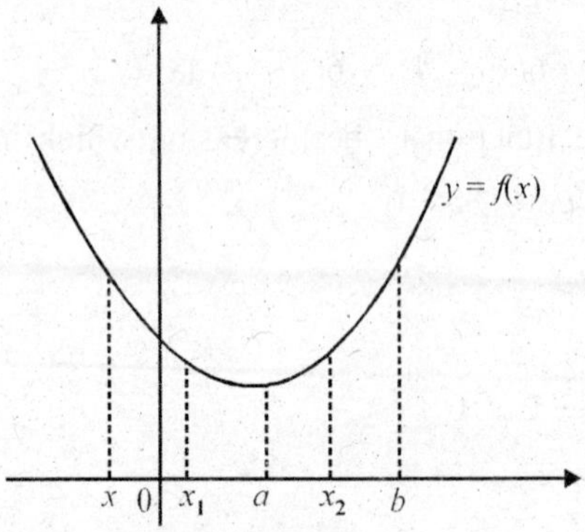

Fig. 1.4

In above fig. 1.4, $x = a$ is a point of minimum of $f(x)$.

Maximum and minimum values are also called as extreme values.

Steps to find maximum and minimum

Step I. Put $y = f(x)$

Step II. Find $\frac{dy}{dx}$

Step III. Put $\frac{dy}{dx} = 0$ to get stationary values or critical values of x and the corresponding values of $f(x)$ are called stationary or turning values of $f(x)$.

Step IV. In order to find whether the value obtained in Step III are representing maxima or minima, find $\frac{d^2y}{dx^2}$ and substitute these values in $\frac{d^2y}{dx^2}$.

Step V. If the resultant is + *ve*, it is point of minima. If the resultant is *–ve* it is point of maxima.

In case the result is zero, if reflects point of inflextion and in that case further exercise is to be done to find whether it is point of maxima or minima.

Example 11. **Find the maxima and minima of the following functions.**

(*i*) $f(x) = -\frac{3}{4}x^4 - 8x^3 - \frac{45}{2}x^2 + 105$

(*ii*) $f(x) = 41 + 24x - 18x^2$.

Solution.

(*i*) We have $f(x) = -\frac{3}{4}x^4 - 8x^3 - \frac{45}{2}x^2 + 105$

$\therefore \quad f'(x) = -3x^3 - 24x^2 - 45x$

Put $f'(x) = 0$

$\therefore \quad -3x^3 - 24x^2 - 45x = 0$

$\therefore \quad -3x\ (x + 3)\ (x + 5) = 0$

$\therefore \quad x = 0,\ x = -3,\ x = -5.$

In order to find whether these points are representing point of maxima or minima, we shall find $f''(x)$ and substitute these values in it.

$\therefore \quad f''(x) = -9x^2 - 48x - 45x = 0$

$\therefore \quad f''(00 = -45 < 0 \quad \therefore \quad x = 0$ is point of maxima.

$f''(-3) = 18 > 0 \quad \therefore \quad x = -3$ is point of minima.

$f''(-5) = -30 < 0\ x = -5$ is point of maxima.

(*ii*) $f(x) = 41 + 24x - 18x$

Find $f'(x)$ and put it equal to zero.

$f'(x) = 24 - 36x$

$x = 2/3$

In order to find whether it is point of maxima or minima, find $f''(x)$ and substitute $x = 2/3$ in it.

$\therefore \quad f''(x) = -36$

since $f''(x) < 0$, therefore $x = 2/3$ is point of maxima.

CONCAVITY AND CONVEXITY

A function $f(x)$ is concave from below at a point $x = x_1$ when the graph lies completely below the tangent line, as shown below.

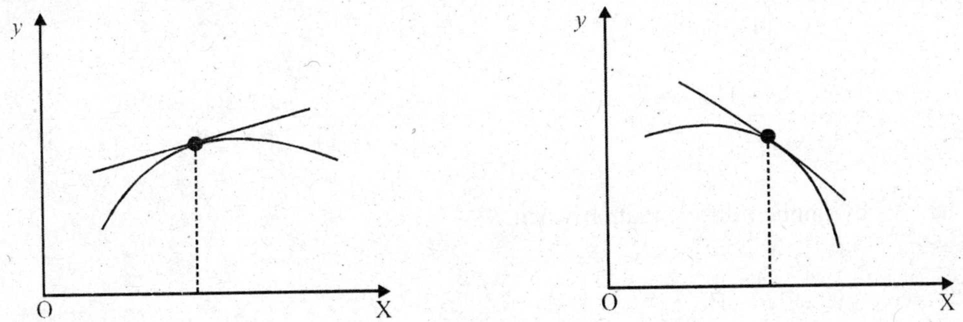

Fig. 1.5

Condition for Concavity

(*i*) $f'(x_1) > 0$ or $f'(x_1) < 0$

(*ii*) $f''(x_1) < 0$

A function is convex from below at a point $x = x_1$ when the graph lies completely above the tangent line, as show below.

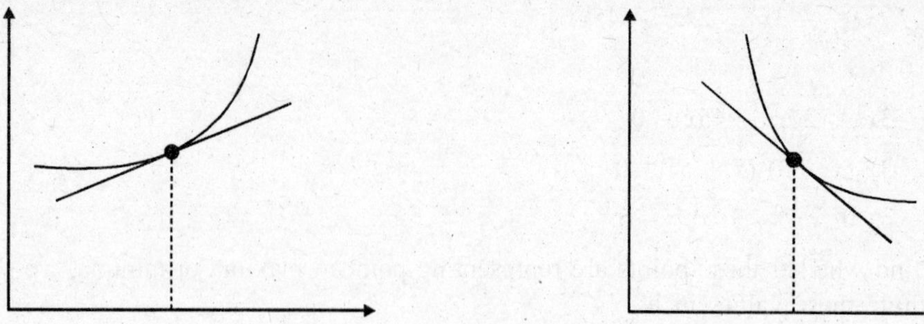

Fig. 1.6

Conditions for Convexity

(*i*) $f'(x_1) > 0$ or $f(\acute{x}_1) < 0$

(*ii*) $f''(x_1) > 0$

Exercise 6.1

1. Find dy/dx of the following function

(*i*) $x^x + x^{1/x}$ $\left(x^x(1 + \log x) + x^{1/x}\left(\frac{1 - \log x}{x}\right)\right)$

(*ii*) $x^y + y^x$ $\left(\frac{y(x \log y - y)}{x(y \log x - y)}\right)$

(*iii*) $x^{\log x}$

(*iv*) $y = \frac{(x+3)^{3/2}(3-x)^{5/2}}{(x-4)^{7/2}(4-x)^{9/2}}$ $\left[y\left(\frac{3}{2} \cdot \frac{1}{(x+3)} - \frac{5}{2(3-x)} - \frac{7}{2(3-x)} + \frac{9}{2(4-x)}\right)\right]$

(*v*) $y = \frac{x\sqrt{x^2+1}}{(x+1)^{2/3}}$ $\left[\frac{x\sqrt{x^2+1}}{(x+1)^{2/3}}\left[\frac{1}{x} + \frac{x}{(x^2+1)} - \frac{2}{3(x+1)}\right]\right]$

2. Find $\frac{dy}{dx}$ by implicit differentiation when.

(*i*) $x^2 + y^2 + 2y = 15$ $\left(-\frac{x}{y+1}\right)$

(*ii*) $x^{2/3} + y^{2/3} = a^{2/3}$ $\left(-(y/x)^{1/3}\right)$

(*iii*) $x^y + y^x = a^b$ $-\left[\frac{x^{y-1}y + y^x \log y}{x^y \log x + xy^{x-1}}\right]$

(*iv*) $x^y = a^{x-y}$ $\left(\frac{\log x}{(1 + \log x)^2}\right)$

(v) If $x^m = a^n = (x + y)^{m+n}$, prove that $\frac{dy}{dx} = \frac{y}{x}$.

3. Find dy/dx in the following cases :

(i) If $x = at^2$ and $y = 2at$, find $\frac{dy}{dx}$ $(1/t)$

(ii) If $x = \frac{a(1-t^2)}{(1+t^2)}$ and $y = \frac{2bt}{1+t^2}$, find $\frac{dy}{dx}$ $\left(-\frac{b}{2a}\left(\frac{1-t^2}{t}\right)\right)$

4. Find the intervals for which the following functions are increasing or decreasing.

(i) $f(x) = x^4 - 8x^3 + 33x^2 - 24x + 21$ (Increasing : $1 < x2$ or $3 < x < 8$ Decreasing : $2 < x < 3$ or $x <$)

(ii) $f(x) = x^4 - 2x^2$ (Increasing : $-1 < x < 0$, $x > 1$ Decreasing : $x < -1$ or $0 < x < 1$)

(iii) $f(x) = \frac{x}{2} + \frac{2}{x}$ (Increasing : $x < -.2$ or $x > 2$ Decreasing : $(-2, 2)$)

(iv) $f(x) = x^3 + \frac{x^3}{3}$ (Increasing : $x > 1/4$ Decreasing : $x < 1/4$)

5. Find the maxima and minima of the following functions.

(i) $f(x) = x^4 - 62x^2 + 120x + 9$ (Max (x = `) Min (x = 5, –6)

(ii) $f(x) = \frac{2}{x} - \frac{2}{x^2}$, $x > 0$ (Max $x = 2$)

(iii) $f(x) = (x = 1)(x = 2)^2$ (Max (x = 4/3) Min (x = 2))

(v) $f(x) = x\sqrt{1-x}$, $x \le 1$ (x = 2/3)

(vi) $2x^3 + 3x^2 - 36x + 10$ (Max value: 91, Min. value = –34)

6. Show that the function $f(x) = x^3 - 6x^2 + 9x - 8$ has a maximum value at $x = 1$ and a minimum value at $x = 3$.

7

Application of Derivatives

Highlights of the Chapter

- Introduction
- Market Equilibrium
- Cost Function
- Marginal Propensity to Save & Consume
- Revenue Function
- Marginal Revenue Product
- Elasticity Price, Cost, Income, Supply
- Profit Function – Maximization
- Optimal Trade-in-Time
- Inventory Control

INTRODUCTION

As already explained, derivative basically refers to change in one variable due to a very small change in other variable. The present chapter deals with the application of derivatives in business and economics.

MARKET EQUILIBRIUM

In order to understand market equilibrium, it is necessary to first understand the demand function and supply function. Demand function gives a relationship between the price per unit and quantity demanded at that price, of a certain commodity. It is shown in Fig. 7.1. As can be observed that it usually slopes downwards, as demand decreases when price increases.

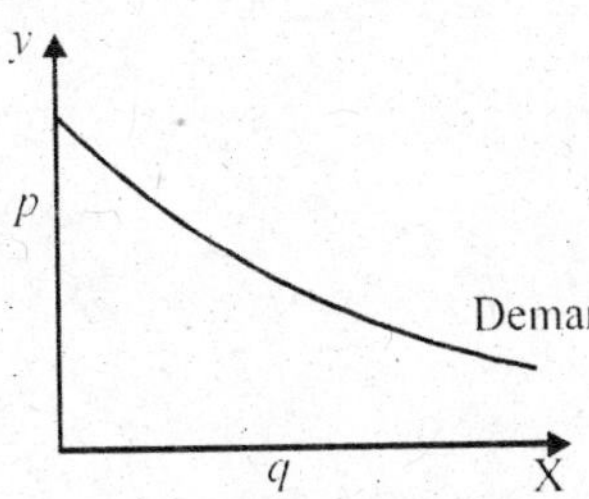

Fig. 7.1

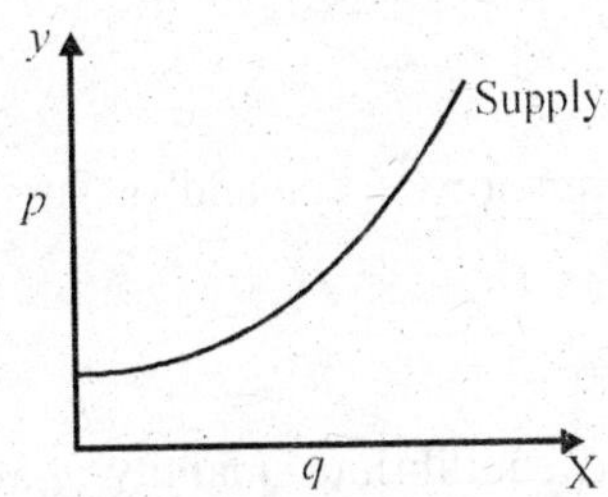

Fig. 7.2

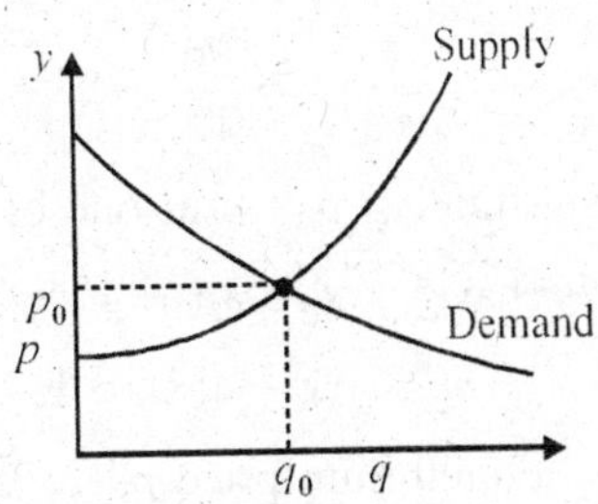

Fig. 7.3

The supply function shown in Fig. 7.2 gives relationship between the price per unit and quantity supplied at that price. The supply function slopes upwards because as the price increases, the producers tend to supply more. The point at which these two curves intersect is known as equilibrium point, as shown in Fig. 7.3 Point 0 represent equilibrium. The price and quantity at equilibrium point are known as equilibrium price and equilibrium quantity respectively. Thus, mathematically, equilibrium point can be achieved by equating demand and supply functions.

The above fact can be understood with the help of following examples.

Example 1. **Find the equilibrium point in the following cases.**

(*a*) **Given supply and demand equations,** $p = \frac{2x}{100} + 2$ **and** $p = -\frac{8x}{100} + 12$ **respectively.**

(*b*) **Given supply and demand equation of a product are** $x_s = 4p + 4$ **and** $x_d = 100 - 8p$ **respectively.**

Solution.

(*a*) At equilibrium point, supply and demand equations intersect, therefore equating the two equations.

$$\therefore \quad \frac{2x}{100} + 2 = -\frac{8x}{100} + 12$$

$$\frac{10x}{100} = 10$$

$$x = 100$$

$\therefore$ Equilibrium quantity = 100

and Equilibrium price $p = \frac{2x}{100} + 2$

$$= \frac{2(100)}{100} + 2$$

$$= 4$$

(*b*) At equilibrium point, both demand and supply equation intersect

$$\therefore \quad x_s = x_d$$

$$4p + 4 = 100 - 8p$$

$$4p + 8p = 96$$

$$12p = 96$$

$$p = \frac{96}{12} = 8$$

Substituting $p = 8$ in one of equation of demand or supply

We have $x_s = 4p + 4$

$$xs = 4(8) + 4 = 36$$

$\therefore$ Equilibrium price $p = 8$ and equilibrium quantity = 36

COST FUNCTION

We know that the total cost associated with the production process comprises of two main components – Fixed cost and variable cost. Fixed cost is that cost which does not directly change with the change in number of units manufactured whereas variable cost do vary with change in number of units manufactured.

$\therefore$ Total cost = Fixed Cost + Variable Cost.

If $C(x)$ represent total cost, then the rate of change of cost with volume *i.e.*, number of unit manufactured is said to be marginal cost, which is given as

$$\text{Marginal Cost} = \frac{d\,C(x)}{dx}$$

It helps in ascertaining the change in total cost when the number of unit manufactured increased by one unit.

When we divide Total Cost $C(x)$ by number of units *i.e.*, volume, we get

$$\text{Average Cost} = \frac{C(x)}{x}.$$

Relationship between Marginal Cost and Average Cost

We have already explained above

$$\text{Marginal Cost}\,(MC) = \frac{dC}{dx}$$

$$\text{Average Cost}\,(AC) = \frac{C}{x}$$

i.e.,
$$AC = \frac{C}{x}$$

Differentiating both the sides of (1) w.r.t. x, we have

$$\frac{d}{dx}(AC) = \frac{d}{dx}\left(\frac{C}{x}\right)$$

$$= \frac{x\dfrac{dC}{dx} - C.1}{x^2} = \frac{1}{x}\left[\frac{dC}{dx} - \frac{C}{x}\right]$$

$$\therefore \quad \frac{d}{dx}(AC) = \frac{1}{x}[MC - AC]$$

When AC is increasing function

$$\frac{d}{dx}(AC) > 0$$

$$\therefore \quad \frac{1}{x}(MC - AC) > 0$$

i.e.,
$$MC > AC$$

When *AC* is decreasing function

$$\frac{d}{dx}(AC) < 0$$

i.e., $$\frac{1}{x}[MC - AC] < 0$$

$$MC < AC$$

When *AC* is minimum,

$$\frac{d}{dx}(AC) = 0$$

i.e., $$\frac{1}{x}[MC - AC] = 0$$

$$MC = AC$$

The above relations are shown in figure drawn below.

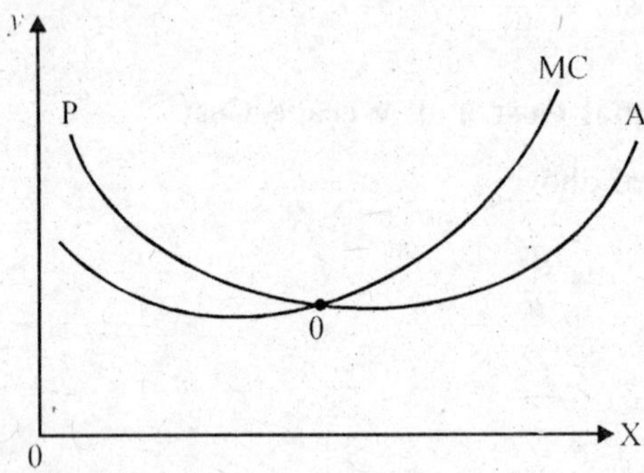

When AC is on the path PO, we have $AC > MC$

At point 0, $MC = AC$

When AC is on the path OR, we have $AC < MC$.

Example 2. **The manufacturer's total cost function is given as $C(x) = 2x^2 + 3x + 1000$**

Find

(*i*) Average cost function

(*ii*) Marginal cost function

(*iii*) Marginal cost when 5 units are produced. Interpret the result.

Solution. Given Cost function

$$C(x) = 2x^2 + 3x + 1000$$

(*a*) Average cost $= \dfrac{C(x)}{x} = \dfrac{(2x^2 + 3x + 1000)}{x}$

$$= 2x + 3 + \frac{1000}{x}$$

(*b*) Marginal cost $= \frac{d[C(x)]}{dx} = \frac{d(2x^2 + 3x + 1000)}{dx}$

$= 4x + 3$

(*c*) Marginal cost when 6 units are produced is

$$(MC)_{x=5} = (4x + 3)_{x=5} = 4(5) + 3 = 23$$

INTERPRETATION

It indicates that the cost of producing 6th unit is Rs. 23 which can be observed from the following equation

$$C(6) - C(5) = [2(6)^2 + 3\,(6) + 1000] - [2(5)^2 + 3\,(5) + 1000]$$
$$= (72 + 18 + 1000) - (50 + 15 + 1000)$$
$$= 25 \text{ i.e., Rs. 23 (approx)}$$

Example 3. **The average cost function (*AC*) for a commodity is given by $AC = x + 20 + \frac{81}{x}$, where *x* is the output. Find the output for which *AC* is increasing and the output for which *AC* is decreasing.**

Solution.

Given $\qquad AC = x + 20 + \frac{81}{x}$

Differentiating both the sides, with respect to x, we have

$$\frac{d}{dx}(AC) = 1 - \frac{81}{x^2}$$

For AC to be increasing, we have

$$\frac{d}{dx}(AC) > 0$$

$\therefore \qquad 1 - \frac{81}{x^2} > 0$

$\Rightarrow \qquad x^2 > 81$

$\Rightarrow \qquad x > 9$

as x cannot be negative

For AC to be decreasing, we have

$$\frac{d}{dx}(AC) < 0$$

$$1 - \frac{81}{x^2} < 0$$

$$x^2 < 81$$

or $\qquad 0 < x < 9$

Hence, when output is upto 9 units. AC is decreasing but beyond 9 units, AC is increasing.

Example 4. **If the total cost function is given by $C = a + bx + cx^2$, where x is the quantity of output, show that**

$$\frac{d}{dx}(AC) = \frac{1}{x}(MC - AC)$$

where MC and AC are marginal and average cost.

Solution. By definition, average cost function is

$$AC = \frac{C}{x} = \frac{a}{x} + b + cx.$$

Also $$MC = \frac{dC}{dx} = \frac{d}{dx}\left(a + bx + cx^2\right) = b + 2cx.$$

$$\therefore \quad \frac{1}{x}(MC - AC) = \frac{1}{x}\left[(b + 2cx) - \left(\frac{a}{x} + b + cx\right)\right]$$

$$= \frac{1}{x}\left[cx - \frac{a}{x}\right] = c - \frac{a}{x^2} \qquad \text{....(1)}$$

Now $$\frac{d}{dx}(AC) = \frac{d}{dx}\left(\frac{a}{x} + b + cx\right) = -\frac{a}{x^2} + c \qquad \text{...(2)}$$

From (1) and (2), we conclude that

$$\frac{d}{dx}(AC) = \frac{1}{x}[MC - AC]$$

Example 5. **A company has cost function for 'x' number of units as**

$$C(x) = x^3 - \frac{15}{2}x^2 + 18x + 10$$

Determine

1. **Number of units for which the Marginal Cost is minimum.**
2. **Total cost and average cost for the number of units which minimise the marginal cost.**

Solution : Marginal Cost $MC = \dfrac{dc}{dx}$

$$\frac{dc}{dx} = \frac{d}{dx}\left(x^3 - \frac{15}{2}x^2 + 18x + 10\right)$$

$$\text{MC} = 3x^2 - 15x + 18$$

To get minimum of MC, find $\dfrac{d(MC)}{dx}$

$$\frac{d}{dx}(3x^2 - 15x + 18) = 6x - 15$$

Put $\frac{d}{dx}(MC)=0$, to get stationary point

$$6x - 15 = 0$$

$$\therefore \quad x=\frac{15}{6}=2.5$$

$\therefore$ Second derivative $=\frac{d^2}{dx^2}(MC)=-6$

Since second derivative is +ve, it implies $x = 2.5$ reflects point of minima for MC (*ii*) Total Cost for minimum MC

$$=C(2.5)=(2.5)^3-\frac{15}{2}(2.5)^2+18(2.5)+10$$

$$= 15.625 - 46.875 + 45 + 10$$

$$= 23.75$$

Average Cost for minimum MC

$$AC=\frac{C(x)}{x}=\frac{23.75}{2.5}=9.5$$

***Example 6.* The rate of change of total cost (Y) of a commodity per unit change of output (X) is called the marginal cost of the commodity. If there exists a relation between Y and X in the form :**

$$Y = 3X\left(\frac{X+7}{X+5}\right) + 5.$$

Prove that the marginal cost falls continuously as the output increases.

Solution. Given

$$Y = 3X\left(\frac{X+7}{X+5}\right) + 5 = 3\left(\frac{X^2+7X}{X+5}\right) + 5 \qquad \text{...(1)}$$

Differentiating (1) with respect to X, we obtain

$$\text{Marginal Cost} = \frac{dY}{dX} = 3\left[\frac{(X+5)(2X+7)-(X^2+7X)}{(X+5)^2}\right]$$

$$3\left[\frac{X^2+10X+35}{(X+5)^2}\right] = 3\left[\frac{(X^2 = 10X+25)+10}{(X+5)^2}\right]$$

$$3\left[\frac{(X+5)^2+10}{(X+5)^2}\right] = 3\left[1+\frac{10}{(X+5)^2}\right]$$

Thus

$$\text{Marginal Cost} = MC = 3\left[1+\frac{10}{(X+5)^2}\right]$$

$$\therefore \quad \frac{d}{dx}(MC) = 3\left[\frac{-20}{(X+5)^3}\right] = \frac{-60}{(X+5)^3} < 0.$$

Since $\frac{d}{dx}(MC) < 0$, therefore the marginal cost falls continuously as the output increases.

REVENUE FUNCTION

Revenue of a firm depends upon its sales. The higher the sale turnover, higher would be the revenue of a firm. Thus, revenue is a function of number of units sold *i.e.*, x and it is given as $R(x)$. It is a product of price per unit, p, and number of unit sold, x.

i.e. $\quad R(x) = px$

$$\text{Average Revenue}(AR) = \frac{R(x)}{x}.$$

Marginal revenue is rate of change of revenue with one additional unit sold.

It is necessary to understand marginal analysis of a firm operating under the two extreme conditions of pure competition and monopoly.

CASE OF PURE COMPETITION

Assumptions

1. There are many firms.
2. Prices are determined by the market. This implies, price per unit, p, does not depend on the will of the firm. Thus 'p' is treated as constant

Now $\quad R = px$

$$\therefore \quad \frac{dR}{dx} = p$$

$$\therefore \quad MR = p$$

CASE OF MONOPOLY

Assumptions

1. There is only one seller and there are no substitutes of the product.
2. Demand changes with price. Therefore, p is treated as variable.
3. Price per unit depends on number of units being sold.

$$\therefore \quad R = px$$

$$\frac{dR}{dx} = p.\frac{dx}{dx} + x.\frac{dp}{dx} = p + x.\frac{dp}{dx}$$

$$\therefore \quad MR = p + x.\frac{dp}{dx}$$

Example 7. **A monopolist has a demand function**

$$x = 5 - 2p$$

Find

1. **Total revenue**
2. **Average revenue**
3. **Marginal revenue**

Solution.

1. Revenue = $p.x$

Given demand function $x = 5 - 2p$ ...(1)

$$\therefore \quad p = \frac{5 - x}{2} \quad ...(2)$$

From (1) and (2), we have

$$\text{Total Revenue} = \left(\frac{5 - x}{2}\right)x = \frac{5x}{2} - \frac{x^2}{2}$$

2. Average revenue $= \dfrac{\text{Total Revenue}}{x}$

$$\therefore \quad AR = \frac{\left(5x - \frac{x^2}{2}\right)}{x} = \frac{5}{2} - \frac{x}{2}$$

3. Marginal revenue $= \dfrac{d\,(TR)}{dx} = \dfrac{d}{dx}\left(\dfrac{5x}{2} - \dfrac{x^2}{2}\right)$

$$= \left(\frac{5}{2} - x\right)$$

Example 8. **A monopolist's demand function is $p = 300 - 5x$, find**

(*i*) the marginal revenue function.

(*ii*) the relationship between the slope of *MR* and *AR*

(*iii*) at what price is the marginal revenue zero

Solution.

(*i*) To find marginal revenue function

$$\text{Revenue} = p.x. = (300 - 5x)\,x$$

$$R = 300x - 5x^2$$

$$\text{Marginal revenue} = \frac{dR}{dx} = \frac{d}{dx}\left(300x - 5x^2\right)$$

$$= 300 - 10x$$

(*ii*) Marginal revenue = $300 - 10x$

$$\text{Average revenue} = \frac{(300x - 5x^2)}{x} = 300 - 5x$$

$$\therefore \quad \text{Slope of Marginal revenue} = \frac{d(300 - 10x)}{dx} = -10$$

Slope of Average revenue = 2 (slope of Average revenue)

(*iii*) To find price at which marginal revenue is zero.

Put $Mr = 0$

i.e. $300 - 10x = 0$

$x = 30$

Substitute this value of x in the equation

$p = 300 - 5x$

$p = 300 - 5(30) = 300 - 150 = 150$

$\therefore$ When price = Rs. 150/-, Marginal revenue is zero

MARGINAL REVENUE PRODUCT

Revenue of a firm though directly depends upon number of units sold but indirectly it also depends on those factors which are associated with the manufacturing activities. For example, if a firm hires more labour, it will be able to produce more and therefore it will sell more which will increase its revenue. Thus, revenue may also said be function of labour, l.

We have $\quad R = px$

$$\frac{dR}{dl} = p.\frac{dx}{dl} + x.\frac{dp}{dl}$$

$$\frac{dR}{dl} = \frac{dx}{dl}\left[p + x.\frac{dp}{dx}\right]$$

Here, $\frac{dR}{dl}$ is said to be marginal revenue product.

Example 8a. **A manufacturer determines that t employees will produce a total of x units of a product per day, where $x = 8t$. If demand equation for the product is $p = -0.5x + 50$, determine the marginal revenue product at $t = 3$. Interpret your result.**

Solution. If r is the total revenue, then

$$R = p.x = (-0.5x + 50).\ x \qquad \text{....(1)}$$

$$= -0.5x^2 + 50x$$

Given $\quad x = 8t$

Substituting $x = 8t$ in (*i*), we have

$$R = -0.5\ (8t)_2 + 50\ (8t)$$

$$R = -0.5 \times 64 \times t^2 + 400t$$

$$\therefore \quad \frac{dR}{dt} = -64t + 400$$

When $t = 3$, $\frac{dR}{dt} = -64(3) + 400 = 208$. This means if fourth employee is hired, the extra revenue generated is approximately 208.

Example 9. **A manufacturing firm faces a demand schedule $p = 1000 - 80x$ and its production functions is $x = t^{1/2}$, where t is labour. Currently the firm employs 25 workers. Find the marginal revenue product of labour.**

Solution. We have Total Revenue $= p.x = (1000 - 80x).\ x$

$$R = 1000x - 80x^2$$

We need to Calculate $\frac{dR}{dt} = \frac{dR}{dx} \times \frac{dx}{dt}$

$$\therefore \quad \frac{dR}{dx} = 1000 - 160x$$

$$\frac{dx}{dt} = \frac{d\left(t^{1/2}\right)}{dt} = \frac{1}{2\sqrt{t}}$$

$$\therefore \quad \frac{dR}{dt} = (1000 - 160x).\ \frac{1}{2\sqrt{t}} = \frac{500}{\sqrt{t}} - \frac{80\,(t)^{1/2}}{\sqrt{t}} \text{ - } \left(Subsituting\ x = \sqrt{t}\right)$$

$$= \frac{500}{\sqrt{t} - 80}$$

Substituting $t = 25$ in the above equation, we have

$$\frac{dR}{dt} = \frac{500}{\sqrt{t}} - 80 = \frac{500}{\sqrt{25}} - 80 = \frac{500}{5} - 80 = 100 - 80 = 20$$

Example 10. **If the demand law is given by $p = \frac{10}{(x+2)}$, show that total revenue increases while marginal revenue decrease as output increases.**

Solution. Revenue $= p.x. = \left(\frac{10}{x+2}\right).x$

$$R = \frac{10x}{(x+2)}$$

Change in revenue *w.r.t.* x will be $\frac{dR}{dx}$

$$\therefore \quad \frac{dR}{dx} = \frac{(x+2).10 - 10x.1}{(x+2)^2}$$

$$= \frac{10x + 20 - 10x}{(x+2)^2} = \frac{20}{(x+2)^2}$$

Since $\frac{dR}{dx}$ is positive for all values of x $\therefore$ revenue is increasing function x.

$$\text{Marginal revenue} = MR = \frac{dR}{dx} = \frac{d}{dx}\left(\frac{20}{(x+2)^2}\right)$$

$$\therefore \quad \frac{d(MR)}{dx} = \frac{(x+2)^2.0 - 20.2(x+2)}{(x+2)^4}$$

$$= \frac{(40x+80)}{(x+2)^3} = -\frac{40(x+2)}{(x+2)^4}$$

$$= -\frac{40}{(x+2)^3}$$

Since $\frac{d(MR)}{dx} < 0$ for all values of x marginal revenue in decreasing function of x.

MARGINAL PROPENSITY TO CONSUME

As we all know that consumption depends upon income. When income increases, consumption also tend to increase and vice versa.

Thus, we may say consumption is a function of income

i.e. $\qquad C = f(I)$

Differentiating both the sides w.r.t. I, we have

$$\frac{dC}{dI} = f'(I)$$

$\frac{dC}{dI}$ measures rate of change of consumption with income and it is known as Marginal propensity to consume.

MARGINAL PROPENSITY TO SAVE

We know that

$$\text{Saving} = \text{Income} - \text{Consumption}$$

i.e. $\qquad S = I - C \qquad$ ...(1)

If we differentiate (1) w.r.t. I, we have

$$\frac{ds}{dI} = 1 - \frac{dC}{dI}$$

where $\frac{ds}{dI}$ is rate of change of saving with Income and it is known as Marginal propensity to Save

Therefore

Marginal Propensity to save = 1 – Marginal propensity to consume.

***Example 11.* If the Consumption function is given by $C = 8 + \frac{4y}{5} - \frac{\sqrt{y}}{2}$, determine the marginal propensity to consume and marginal propensity to save when $y = 100$.**

Solution.

$$\text{Marginal propensity to consume} = \frac{dC}{dy} = 0 + \frac{4}{5} - \frac{1}{4\sqrt{y}}$$

$$\therefore \quad \frac{dC}{dy} = 0 + \frac{4}{5} - \frac{1}{4\sqrt{100}} = \frac{4}{5} - \frac{1}{40} = \frac{31}{40}$$

$\therefore$ Marginal propensity to save when $y = 100$

$$= 1 - \frac{31}{40} = \frac{9}{40} \left(\text{since } MPS = 1 - MPC\right)$$

Exercise 7.1

1. Find the equilibrium point from the following supply and demand equations

(*a*) $p = \frac{2x}{35} + 5,\ p = -\frac{3x}{35} + 10$, respectively. $[x = 35, p = 7]$

(*b*) $x = 20 - 3p - p^2,\ x = p - 1$, respectively. $[x = 2, p = 3]$

2. The manufacturer's total cost function is

$$C = 500 + 25x + x^2$$

Find

(*a*) Average cost function.

(*b*) Marginal cost function.

(*c*) Marginal cost when 10 units are produced.

(*d*) Actual cost of producing eleventh unit.

$$\left[(a)\frac{500}{x} + 25 + x \ (b)\,25 + 2x \ (c)\,45 \ (d)\,46\right]$$

3. Total cost is given by $C = 5000 + 1000q - 500q^2 + \frac{2}{3}q^3$

(*i*) Find the *MC* function.

(*ii*) Find the expression for the slope of the *MC* curve.

(*iii*) Find the average total cost function.

(iv) At what value of q does MC equal AVC.

$$\left[\begin{array}{l}(i)\ 1000 - 1000q + 2q^2 \quad (ii)\ -1000 + 4q \\ (iii)\ \dfrac{5000}{q} + 1000 - 500q + \dfrac{2}{3}q^2 \quad (iv)\ q = 375\end{array}\right]$$

4. The total cost $C(x)$ of a firm is

$$C(x) = 0.25x^3 - 0.01x^2 - 80x + 1000$$

where x is the output. Determine

(a) The average cost.

(b) The Marginal average cost.

(c) The Marginal cost.

(d) The rate of change of MC w.r.t. x

(e) The value of x for which $MVC = AVC$.

$$\left[\begin{array}{l}(a)\ 0.25x^2 - 0.01x - 80 + \dfrac{1000}{x} \quad (b)\ 0.5x - 0.01 - \dfrac{1000}{x} \\ (c)\ 0.75x^2 - 0.02x - 80 \quad (d)\ 1.5x - 0.02 \quad (e)\ x = 1/50\end{array}\right]$$

5. The total cost function is $C = 2x^3 - 5x^2 + 7x$, find the marginal average cost function (MAC). What type of curve is the MAC? Find the points where it cut the axis.

6. The average cost function for a product is given by the equation.

$AC = 0.004x^2 - 0.07x + \dfrac{500}{x}$, where x is the output, find the marginal cost function. What is the marginal cost when 100 units are produced.

[$MC = 0.012x^2 - 0.14x$, for 100 units $MC = 106$]

7. If the total cost function is given as $C(x) = a + bx + cx^2$, where x is the quantity of output, show that $\dfrac{d}{dx}(AC) = \dfrac{1}{x}(MC - AC)$. (Where MC and AC are marginal and average cost.)

8. Given demand function

$$p = a - bx$$

Find

(a) Total revenue

(b) Average revenue

(c) Marginal revenue

[(a) $R = ax - bx^2$ (b) $AR = a - bx$ (c) $MR = a - 2bx$]

9. The total revenue received is a function of number of units sold (x), as

$$R(x) = 500 + \frac{x^2}{10}$$

Find

(*i*) Average Revenue

(*ii*) Marginal Revenue

(*iii*) Marginal Revenue, when $x = 20$

(*iv*) Actual revenue from the sale of twenty first unit.

$$\left[(i)\ \frac{500}{x} + \frac{x}{10}\ (ii)\ x/5\ (iii)\ 4\ (iv)\ 4.1\right]$$

10. Show that demand curve $p = a/(x + b)$ is downward sloping and convex from below (a and b are positive constants). Does the same property hold for marginal revenue curve?

11. A manufacturer has following cost and demand functions.

$$C(x) = 500 + 14x + \frac{x^2}{2}$$

and $$p = 500 - \frac{3x}{2}$$

respectively. Find

(*a*) Marginal Cost

(*b*) Average Cost

(*c*) Marginal Average cost.

(*d*) Show that $MAC = \dfrac{x(MC) - C(x)}{x^2}$

(*e*) For what value of x, AC is decreasing.

(*f*) When is demand function increasing or decreasing.

$$\left[(a)\ x + 14,\ (b)\ \frac{500}{x} + 14 + \frac{x}{2}\ (c) - \frac{500}{x^2} + \frac{1}{2}\ (e)\ 0 < x < 10\sqrt{10}\right]$$

12. The total cost function $C(x) = \sqrt{ax + b} + c$. Find an expression for marginal cost and show that it decreases as the output increases.

13. The rate of change of total cost (y) of a commodity per unit change of output (x) is called the marginal cost of a commodity. If there exist a relation between y and x in the form

$$y = 3x\left[\frac{x + 7}{x + 5}\right] + 5$$

Prove that marginal cost falls continuously as the output increases.

14. The cost function of a firm is given by $C(x) = 300x - 10x^2 + \frac{x^3}{3}$. Calculate the output at which the marginal cost is minimum. Will it be the same for the output at which average cost is minimum? [$x = 15$]

15. If the consumption function is $C = 0.01y^2 + 0.2y + 50$, Calculate marginal propensity to save and marginal propensity to consume when $y = 10$.

$$\left[MPS = \frac{6}{10}, MPC = 4/10\right]$$

16. If the consumption function is

$$C = 60I = \frac{I^2}{20}$$

Find Marginal propensity to consume. $\left[MPC = 60 - \frac{I}{10}\right]$

17. A manufacturer has a demand function $p = 12000 - 900x$ and its production function is $x = l^{1/3}$. where l is labour. Currently the firm employs 27 labourers. Find the marginal revenue product of labour.

$$\left[MRP_L = \frac{2200}{9}\right]$$

POINT ELASTICITY OF DEMAND

Elasticity, in simple words, means degree of responsiveness of one variable due to change is another variable. It may also be defined as the ratio of the percentage change in the dependent variable due to percentage change in the independent variable.

It is denoted by a Greek Letter 'η'. The expression of elasticity is derived as under.

Let y be any variable dependent on x.

$$y = f(x)$$

If x changes to $x + \Delta x$, we have

$$y + \Delta y = f(x + \Delta x)$$

where Δy is corresponding change in y.

Now the percentage change in y would be given as

$$\frac{(y + \Delta y) - y}{y} = \frac{f(x + \Delta x) - f(x)}{f(x)} \times 100$$

and the percentage in x would be given as

$$\frac{x + \Delta x - x}{x} \times 100$$

By def, Elasticity $= \dfrac{\text{\% change in dependent variable}}{\text{\% change in independent variable}}$

$$\eta = \frac{\dfrac{f(x + \Delta x) - f(x)}{f(x)}}{\dfrac{(x + \Delta x - x)}{x}}$$

$$= \frac{x}{f(x)} \frac{f(x + \Delta x) - f(x)}{\Delta x}$$

As $\Delta x \to 0$, $\underset{\Delta x \to 0}{Lt} \frac{f(x + \Delta x) - f(x)}{\Delta x} = \frac{dy}{dx}$

$$\therefore \qquad \eta = \frac{x}{f(x)} \cdot \frac{dy}{dx}$$

This can be written as

$$\eta_x = \frac{x}{f(x)} f'(x)$$

This is known as point elasticity of the function $y = f(x)$ at the point x.

Example 12. **Find the elasticities of**

(*i*) $x^2 e^x$ (*ii*) $(x + 1) e^{x^2}$

Solution.

(*i*) Elasticity of any function $f(x)$

$$= \frac{x}{f(x)} . f'(x)$$

Give $\qquad f(x) = x^2 e^x$

$$f'(x) = x^2 e^x + 2xe^x = xe^x (x + 2)$$

$$\therefore \qquad \text{Elasticity} = \frac{x}{x^2 e^x} . xe^x (x + 2) = x + 2$$

(*ii*) Given $f(x) = (x + 1) e^{x^2}$

$$\therefore \qquad f'(x) = (x + 1) e^{x^2} .2x + e^{x^2} .$$

$$\text{Elasticity} = \frac{x}{(x + 1) e^{x^2}} . \left[(x + 1) e^{x^2} .2x + e^{x^2} . \right]$$

$$= 2x^2 + \frac{x}{(x + 1)} .$$

PRICE ELASTICITY OF DEMAND

As we know demand depends on the price, therefore keeping in view the definition of elasticity explained above, price elasticity of demand may be defined as ratio of percentage change in quantity demanded to a percentage change in price. It is given by the relation

$$\eta_d = - \frac{P}{x} . \frac{dx}{dp}$$

Significance of '–ve' sign

Negative sign has been placed because there exist inverse relationship between quantity demanded and price for most of the goods.

Other Important Results

(*a*) When $1 < |n_d| < \infty$, demand is said to be elastic. This implies, for a given percentage change in price, there is a greater percentage change in quantity demanded.

(*b*) When $|n_d| = 1$, demand is said to be unit elasticity. This means for a given percentage change in price, there is equal amount of percentage change in quantity demanded.

(*c*) When $0 < |n_d| < 1$, demand is said to be inelastic. It implies, for a given change in price, there is smaller percentage change in quantity demanded.

(*d*) When $|n_d| = 0$, demand is said to be perfectly inelastic. It implies, a change in price is accompanied by no change at all in the quantity demanded.

(*e*) When $|n_d| = \infty$, demand is said to be perfectly elastic. In this case, a reduction, in price increases the quantity demanded infinitely.

Price Elasticity of Demand in Logarithms

We know that price elasticity of demand is given as.

$$\eta_d = -\frac{P}{x} \cdot \frac{dx}{dp}$$

$$= -\frac{1}{x} \cdot \frac{dx}{dp} \times \frac{1}{1/p}$$

$$\eta_d = \frac{-\frac{1}{x} \cdot \frac{dx}{dp}}{1/p} = \frac{-\frac{d}{dp}(\log x)}{\frac{d}{dp}(\log p)}.$$

$$= -\frac{d(\log x)}{d(\log p)}$$

since $-\dfrac{d}{dp}(\log x) = -\dfrac{1}{x} \cdot \dfrac{dx}{dp}$

and $\dfrac{d}{dp}(\log p) = \dfrac{1}{p} \cdot \dfrac{dp}{dp} = \dfrac{1}{p}$

$$\eta_d = -\frac{d(\log x)}{d(\log p)}$$

Relationship between Marginal Revenue, Average Revenue and Point Elasticity of Demand

We have, Total Revenue $= R = p\,x$

$$\text{Average revenue} = \frac{R}{x} = p \qquad \text{...(1)}$$

$$\text{Marginal Revenue} = \frac{dR}{dx} = \frac{d}{dx}(px)$$

$$= p.\frac{dx}{dx} + x.\frac{dp}{dx}$$

$$= p + x.\frac{dp}{dx}$$

$$= p\left(1 + \frac{x}{p}.\frac{dp}{dx}\right)$$

$$\eta_d = -\frac{p}{x}.\frac{dx}{dp}$$

$$\therefore \quad MR = p\left[1 - \frac{1}{\eta_d}\right]$$

Using (1) and (2), we have

$$MR = AR\left[1 - \frac{1}{\eta_d}\right]$$

On simplification, we have

$$\eta_d = \frac{AR}{AR - MR}$$

Example 13. **The demand function for a product is given by $p = 6 - 3x^2$. Find value of x at which demand will have unit price elasticity of demand.**

Solution. Given

$$p = 6 - 3x^2$$

Differentiating both the sides w.r.t. x.

$$\therefore \quad \frac{dp}{dx} = 0 - 6x$$

$$\therefore \quad \frac{dx}{dp} = -\frac{1}{6x}$$

$$n_d = \frac{-p}{x}.\frac{dx}{dp} = -\frac{(6 - 3x^2)}{x}.\left(-\frac{1}{6x}\right)$$

$$= \frac{6 - 3x^2}{6x^2}$$

Equating $\quad n_d = 1$

$$\therefore \quad = \frac{6 - 3x^2}{6x^2} = 1$$

$$6 - 3x^2 = 6x^2$$

$$6 = 9x^2$$

$$x^2 = \frac{6}{9}$$

$$x = \pm\sqrt{\frac{6}{9}}$$

$$\therefore \quad x = +\sqrt{\frac{6}{9}},$$ (negative sign is not feasible as quantity can never be negative)

Example 14 : **Adlab Films Ltd. charges Rs. 50 per person as movie ticket. A study conducted by is marketing team determined that with a price of 'p' rupees, 'x' persons will turn up for a movie where $x = 80,000\ e^{-0.5p}$.**

(*i*) Compute the elasticity of demand at $p = 50$

(*ii*) Is demand elastic or inelastic at $p = 50$.

(*iii*) Determine the value of 'p' for which values of $n_d = 1$.

Solution. (*i*) Elasticity of demand $= \eta_d$

$$\eta_d = \frac{-p}{x}\cdot\frac{dx}{dp}$$

$$= \frac{-p}{80000\ e^{-0.5p}}(-40000)e^{-0.5p} = \frac{p}{2}$$

Since $p = 50$, therefore $\eta_d = \frac{50}{2} = 25.$

(*ii*) Since $\eta_d > 1$, therefore demand is elastic at Rs. 50. Any increase in price would result in decline in revenues.

(*iii*) Elasticity would be unity when

$$\frac{p}{2} = 1$$

i.e., $p = 2.$

Example 15.

(*a*) The demand for a commodity is given by $x = 200 - 6p^2$. Find the price elasticity of demand when $p = 5$.

(*b*) If the price of 5 is decreased by 20%, determine the relative increase in demand and hence an approximate elasticity of demand.

Solution.

(*a*) Given $x = 200 - 6p^2$

$$\therefore \quad \frac{dx}{dp} = -12p$$

$$\therefore \quad \eta_d = -\frac{p}{x}\cdot\frac{dx}{dp} = \frac{-p}{dp} = \frac{-p}{\left(200 - 6p^2\right)}.(-12p)$$

Substitute $p = 5$ is the above equation, we have

$$\eta_d = \frac{-5}{\left(200 - 6(5)^2\right)}(-12 \times 5) = \frac{300}{(200 - 150)} = \frac{300}{50}$$

$$\eta_d = 6$$

(*b*) When price is decreased by 20%

New price = 5 – (20% of 5) = 4

∴ Old Demand = x = 200 – 6(5)² = 50

New Demand = x' = 200 – 96 = 104

$$\therefore \ \% \text{ increase in demand} = \frac{\text{New Demand} - \text{Old demand}}{\text{Old demand}} \times 100$$

$$= \frac{104 - 50}{50} \times 100 = \frac{54}{50} \times 100 = 108$$

$$\therefore \ \text{New Elasticity} = \frac{\text{Percentage Change in Quantity demanded}}{\text{Percentage change in Price}}$$

$$\therefore \ \text{New Elasticity} = \frac{108}{20} = 5.4$$

Example 16. **If the elasticity of a function $f(x)$ of x is defined to be $\eta = \frac{x}{f(x)}\cdot\frac{d}{dx}[f(x)]$. Show that the elasticities of $xf(x)$ and $f(x)/x$ are, respectively, $(\eta + 1)$ and $(\eta - 1)$.**

Solution. By definition, the elasticity of the function $xf(x)$ is

$$\frac{x}{xf(x)}\cdot\frac{d}{dx}[xf(x)]$$

$$= \frac{1}{f(x)}\left[x\frac{d}{dx}(f(x)) + f(x).1\right]$$

$$= \frac{x}{f(x)}\frac{d}{dx}(f(x)) + 1$$

$$= \eta + 1.$$

Similarly, the elasticity of the function $f(x)/x$ is

$$\frac{x}{f(x)/x}\cdot\frac{d}{dx}[f(x)/x]$$

$$= \frac{x^2}{f(x)}\left[\frac{x\frac{d}{dx}(f(x)) - f(x).1}{x^2}\right]$$

$$= \frac{x}{f(x)} \frac{d}{dx}(f(x)) - 1$$

$$= \eta - 1.$$

Example 17. **Suppose the demand q and price p for a product are related by the equation**

$$q = 1200 - 60p, \text{ for } 0 \le p \le 25$$

(*i*) Determine where the demand is elastic, inelastic and of unit elasticity w.r.t. price.

(*ii*) Use the result of part (*i*) to determine the intervals of increase and decrease of the revenue function and the price at which revenue is maximized.

(*iii*) Find the total revenue function explicitly and use its first derivative to determine its intervals of increase and decrease and the price at which revenue is maximized.

Solution.

(*i*) Elasticity of demand is

$$n_d = \frac{p}{q} \cdot \frac{dq}{dp} = \frac{-p}{(1200 - 60p)} \cdot (-60) = \frac{60p}{1200 - 60p}$$

The demand is of unit elasticity when $n_d = 1$, *i.e.*

when

$$\frac{60p}{1200 - 60p} = 1$$

$$60p = 1200 - 60p$$

$$120p = 1200$$

$$p = \frac{1200}{120} = 10$$

If $0 \le p < 10$, $n_d < 1$

Let us take $p = 9$, then $n_d = \frac{60(9)}{1200 - 60(9)} = \frac{540}{660} = 0.8181$

i.e. $n_d < 1$

If $10 < p \le 25$, $n_d > 1$

Let us take $p = 11$, then $n_d = \frac{60(11)}{1200 - 60(11)} = \frac{660}{1200 - 660}$

$$= \frac{660}{540} = 1.22$$

$\therefore$ $n_d > 1$.

(*ii*) The total revenue is an increasing function of p when demand is inelastic *i.e.* on the interval $0 \le p < 10$ and a decreasing function of 'p' when demand is elastic *i.e.* on the interval $10 < p \le 25$. At the price $p = 10$ of unit elasticity, the revenue function has a relative maximum.

(*iii*) The revenue function is $R(p) = p.q. = p.(1200–60p)$. First derivative of revenue function is Marginal revenue which is given as

$$MR = \frac{dR}{dp} = 1200 - 120p, \text{ which is zero when } p = 10$$

On the interval $0 \le p < 10$, $\frac{dR}{dp}$ is positive, which implies $R(p)$ is increasing.

On is interval $10 < p \le 25$, $\frac{dR}{dp}$ is negative, which implies $R(p)$ is decreasing. At the critical value $p = 10$, $R(p)$. Stops increasing and starts decreasing and hence has a relative maximum.

Example 18. **For the demand curve $aQ + bP - K = 0$, where a, b and K are positive constants. Determine the point elasticity of demand when marginal revenue is zero.**

Solution : The demand function is given by

$$aQ + bP - K = 0 \Rightarrow P = \frac{K - aQ}{b}$$

Let R denote the revenue function. Then

$$R = PQ = \frac{K - aQ}{b} . Q = \frac{KQ - aQ^2}{b}$$

$$\Rightarrow \qquad MR = \frac{dR}{dQ} = \frac{K - 2aQ}{b}$$

Setting $MR = 0$ gives $= \frac{K}{2a}$.

Further, differentiating the demand function $P = \frac{K - aQ}{b}$ w.r.t. Q.

we obtain

$$\frac{dp}{dQ} = -\frac{a}{b} \Rightarrow \frac{dQ}{dP} = -\frac{b}{a}$$

Thus $\qquad \eta_Q = -\frac{P}{Q}\frac{dQ}{dP} = \frac{K - aQ}{bQ} . \frac{b}{a} = \frac{K - aQ}{aQ}$

At $\qquad MR.Q = k/2a$

$$\therefore \qquad \eta_Q = \frac{2Qa - aQ}{aQ}$$

$$\frac{aQ}{aQ} = 1$$

Hence demand has unit elasticity when $MR = 0$.

PRICE ELASTICITY OF SUPPLY

As already mentioned, as the price increases, the producers tend to increase supply so as to earn more profits. Thus, price elasticity of supply is the ratio of the percentage change in the supply of a commodity to a given percentage change in price.

It is given as

$$\eta_S = \frac{p}{x} \cdot \frac{dx}{dp}$$

η_S always have positive sign.

Example 19. **A product has supply function**

$q = m\sqrt{p-n}$, **where q is the quantity demanded, p is price and m and n are positive constants. (p is greater than n)**

(a) Find elasticity of supply as a function of price.

(b) Show that elasticity decreases as price increases.

(c) Show that elasticity becomes unity at the price equal to $2n$.

Solution.

(a) $$n_s = \frac{d}{q} \cdot \frac{dq}{dp} = \frac{p}{m\sqrt{p-n}} \cdot \frac{m}{2\sqrt{p-n}} = \frac{p}{(p-n)}$$

$\therefore$ Elasticity of supply $= \dfrac{p}{2(p-n)}$

(b) In order to show that elasticity decreases as price increases, we need to calculate first derivative of n_s w.r.t. price.

$$\frac{d(n_s)}{dp} = \frac{d}{dp}\left(\frac{p}{2(p-n)}\right) = \frac{2(p-n).1 - p.2}{4(p-n)^2}$$

$$= \frac{2p - 2n - 2p}{4(p-n)^2} = \frac{-2n}{4(p-n)^2} = \frac{-n}{2(p-n)^2}$$

Since $n > 0$ and $(p-n)^2 > 0$ therefore $\dfrac{dn_s}{dp} < 0$. Thus, n_s is a decreasing function of p.

(c) To show that elasticity becomes unity at a price equal to $2n$

Put $\quad n = 1$

$\therefore \quad \dfrac{p}{2(p-n)} = 1$

$\therefore \quad p = 2p - 2n$

$\Rightarrow \quad p = 2n$, Hence proved.

Example 20. **If η_1 and η_2 be the price elasticities of supply laws : $p = e^x$ and $p = e^x/x$, respectively, show that $\eta_1\eta_2 = \eta_2 - \eta_1$.**

Solution : To find η_1, we differentiate both sides of the equation $p = e^x$ to obtain

$$\frac{dp}{dx} = e^x$$

$$\therefore \quad \frac{dx}{dp} = \frac{1}{e^x}$$

$$\Rightarrow \quad \eta_1 = \frac{p}{x}\frac{dx}{dp} = \frac{e^x}{x}\cdot\frac{1}{e^x} = \frac{1}{x}$$

Similarly, to find η_2, we differentiate both sides of the equation $p = e^x/x$ to obtain

$$\frac{dx}{dp} = \frac{xe^x - e^x.1}{x^2} = \frac{e^x(x-1)}{x^2}$$

$$\therefore \quad \frac{dx}{dp} = \frac{x^2}{e^x(x-1)}$$

$$\Rightarrow \quad \eta_2 = \frac{p}{x}\frac{dx}{dp} = \frac{e^x}{x^2}\cdot\frac{x^2}{e^x(x-1)} = \frac{1}{x-1}$$

Using the above values of η_1 and η_2, we have

$$\eta_1\eta_2 = \left(\frac{1}{x}\right)\left(\frac{1}{x-1}\right) = \frac{1}{x(x-1)} \qquad ...(1)$$

$$\eta_2 - \eta_1 = \frac{1}{x-1} - \frac{1}{x} = \frac{x-(x-1)}{x(x-1)} = \frac{1}{x(x-1)} \qquad ...(2)$$

From Equations (1) and (2), it is proved that

$$\eta_1\eta_2 = \eta_2 - \eta_1$$

Example 21. **The supply of a certain good is given by $x = a\sqrt{p-b}$,, where x is quantity supplied, p (which is greater than b) is price and a and b are positive constants. Find the expression for the elasticity of supply as a function of price and, by using calculus, show that the elasticity decreases as price increases and becomes unity at the price equal to $2b$.**

Solution.

Given $\quad x = a\sqrt{p-b}$

$$\therefore \quad \frac{dx}{dp} = a.\frac{1}{2}(p-b)^{-1/2}.1 = \frac{a}{2\sqrt{p-b}}$$

$$\therefore \quad \eta_s = \frac{p}{x}\frac{dx}{dp}$$

$$\frac{p}{a\sqrt{p-b}}\cdot\frac{a}{2\sqrt{p-b}} = \frac{p}{2(p-b)}$$

Differentiating η. with respect to p, we obtain

$$\frac{d}{dp}(\eta_s) = \frac{1}{2}\left[\frac{(p-b).1 - p.1}{(p-b)^2}\right] = -\frac{b}{2(p-b)^2}$$

Since $b > 0$, therefore above value will always be negative. Hence η_s is a decreasing function of p. In other words, elasticity decreases as price increases.

Further when $p = 2b$, $\eta_s = \dfrac{2b}{2(2b-b)} = 1$.

$\therefore$ η_s becomes unity when price equal to $2b$.

INCOME ELASTICITY TO DEMAND

In the previous section, we have price elasticity of demand which means that the demand depends upon the price of a commodity. The demand of a product also depends upon the income and varies with the change in income. In other words, demand is income elastic. By definition, it is a ratio of percentage change in demand to a given percentage change in income.

$\therefore$ Income elasticity of demand $\eta_i = \dfrac{I}{x}.\dfrac{dx}{dI}$

The sign income elasticity would depend on the nature of commodity.

In case of normal commodities, income is directly proportional to the quantity demanded therefore $\dfrac{dx}{dI}$ is positive. Hence, elasticity is positive. In case of inferior commodity, income is inversely proportional to quantity demanded therefore $\dfrac{dx}{dI}$ is negative. Hence, elasticity is negative.

Example 22. **The demand x as a function of income y is given by the equation $x = 2 + 7y$. Find income elasticity of demand and its value when $y = 50$.**

Solution. We have

$$n_s = \frac{y}{x}.\frac{dx}{dy}$$

Given $\quad x = 2 + 7y$

$$\therefore \quad \frac{dx}{dy} = 0 + 7$$

$$\therefore \quad n_s = \frac{y}{(2+7y)}.(7) = \frac{7y}{2+7y}$$

Put $y = 50$, in the above equation, we have

$$n_s = \frac{7y}{2+7y} = \frac{(7 \times 50)}{2 + (7 \times 50)} = \frac{350}{352}$$

ELASTICITY OF COST

It measures the relationship between change in cost due to change in output. It is defined as the ratio of percentage change in total cost due to percentage change in number of units manufactured *i.e.* output

It is given as

$$\eta_C = \frac{x}{C} \cdot \frac{dC}{dx}$$

similarly, elasticity of average cost would be given as

$$\eta_{AC} = \frac{x}{AC} \cdot \frac{d}{dx}(AC)$$

$$= \frac{x}{AC} \frac{d}{dx}\left(\frac{C}{x}\right) = \frac{x}{C/x}\left(\frac{x.\frac{dC}{dx} - C.1}{x^2}\right)$$

$$\eta_{AC} = \frac{\frac{x^3}{C}\frac{dC}{dx.} - x^2}{x^2} = C$$

$$\therefore \qquad \eta_{AC} = \frac{x}{c}\frac{dc}{dx} - 1$$

i.e. $\eta_{AC} = \eta_C - 1$

Example 22a. **Given Cost function $C(x) = 7x^2 + 5x + 4$. Find elasticity of total cost and of average cost.**

Solution. $TC = 7x^2 + 5x = 4$

$$\therefore \qquad n_{TC} = \frac{x}{TC} \cdot \frac{d(TC)}{dx} = \frac{x}{(7x^2 + 5x + 4)}.(14x + 5)$$

$$= \frac{(14x^2 + 5x)}{(7x^2 + 5x + 4)}$$

$$\text{Average Cost } (AC) = \frac{TC}{x} = 7x + 5 + 4/x$$

$$\therefore \qquad n_{AC} = \frac{x}{AC} \cdot \frac{d(AC)}{dx} = \frac{(7x^2 - 4)}{(7x^2 + 5x + 4)}$$

Example 23. **Find the elasticity of total cost and elasticity of average cost of the function $C = ax^2 + bx + C$.**

Solution : Elasticity of total cost

$$n_{TC} = \frac{x}{TC} \cdot \frac{d(TC)}{dx} = \frac{x}{(ax^2 + bx + c)} \cdot \frac{d(ax^2 + bx + c)}{dx}$$

$$= \frac{x(2ax + b)}{(ax^2 + bx + c)} = \frac{(2ax^2 + bx)}{(ax^2 + bx + c)} = \frac{x(2ax + b)}{(ax^2 + bx + c)}$$

Elasticity of Average cost

$$AC = \frac{ax^2 + bx + c}{x} = ax + b + \frac{c}{x}$$

$$\therefore \quad n_{AC} = \frac{x}{AC} \cdot \frac{d(AC)}{dx}$$

$$= \frac{x^2}{ax^2 + bx + c} \cdot \left(a - \frac{c}{x^2} \right)$$

$$\therefore \quad \frac{x^2}{ax^2 + bx + c} \cdot \left(\frac{ax^2 - c}{x^2} \right) = \frac{(ax^2 - c)}{(ax^2 + bx + c)}$$

Example 24. **A manufacturer total cost function is defined as**

$$C(x) = \frac{1}{6}x^3 + 642x + 400$$

Find

(*i*) Elasticity of Cost when level of production is 4 units.

(*ii*) The amount by which the manufacturer should decrease the production to reduce total cost by 5%.

Solution : We have cost function as

$$C(x) = \frac{1}{6}x^3 + 642x + 400$$

$$\text{Elasticity of Cost, } \eta_c = \frac{x}{(C_x)} \times \frac{dc}{dx}$$

$$\eta_c = \frac{x}{\frac{1}{6}x^3 + 642x + 400} \times \left(\frac{x^2}{2} + 642 \right)$$

Substituting $x = 4$ in the above equation, we have,

$$= \frac{4}{\frac{1}{6}(4)^3 + 642(4) + 400} \times \left(\frac{(4)^2}{2} + 642 \right)$$

$$= \frac{4}{2978.66} \times 650 = 0.8728$$

$$\therefore \quad 0.8728 = \frac{\%\text{ change in cost}}{\%\text{ change in output}}$$

$$0.8728 = \frac{(-5\%)}{\%\text{ change in output}} \text{(–ve sign indicates decrease)}$$

$\therefore$ % change in output $= \dfrac{(-5\%)}{0.8728}$

$= -5.72\%$

$\therefore$ New Output should be

$$= 4(100 - 5.72\%) = 3.77 \text{ units}$$

***Example 25.* Show that for the total cost function $C = \sqrt{ax + b}$, where a and b are positive constants, the elasticity of total cost increases but remains less than unity as x increases.**

Solution. Elasticity of total cost function is

$$n_{TC} = \frac{x}{TC} \cdot \frac{d(TC)}{dx} = \frac{x}{(ax^2 + bx + c)} \cdot \frac{d(ax^2 + bx + c)}{dx}$$

$$= \frac{x(2ax + b)}{(ax^2 + bx + c)} = \frac{(2ax^2 + bx)}{(ax^2 + bx + c)} = \frac{x(2ax + b)}{(ax^2 + bx + c)}$$

Elasticity of Average cost

$$AC = \frac{ax^2 + bx + c}{x} = ax + b + \frac{c}{x}$$

$$\therefore \quad n_{AC} = \frac{x}{AC} \cdot \frac{d(AC)}{dx}$$

$$= \frac{x^2}{ax^2 + bx + c} \cdot \left(a - \frac{c}{x^2}\right)$$

$$\therefore \quad \frac{x^2}{ax^2 + bx + c} \cdot \left(\frac{ax^2 - c}{x^2}\right) = \frac{(ax^2 - c)}{(ax^2 + bx + c)}$$

***Example 26.* Show that for the total cost function $C = \sqrt{ax + b}$, where a and b are positive constants, the elasticity of total cost increases but remains less than unity as x increases.**

Solution. Elasticity of total cost function is

$$\eta_C = \frac{x}{C}\frac{dC}{dx} = \frac{x}{\sqrt{ax + b}} \cdot \frac{d}{dx}(\sqrt{ax + b})$$

$$= \frac{x}{\sqrt{ax + b}} \cdot \left(\frac{1}{2}\frac{1}{\sqrt{ax + b}}.a\right)$$

$$= \frac{ax}{2(ax + b)}$$

Differentiating η_C with respect to x, we have

$$\frac{d}{dx}(\eta_C) = \frac{a}{2}\left[\frac{(ax + b) \cdot 1 - x \cdot a}{(ax + b)^2}\right]$$

$$= \frac{ab}{2(ax+b)^2}$$

Since $\frac{d}{dx}(\eta_C)$ is always positive as 'a' and 'b' are both positive constants, therefore η_C is an increasing function of x. It is further proved that η_C always remain less than unity as the 'x' increases.

$$\eta_C = \frac{ax}{2(ax+b)} = \frac{1}{2}\left[\frac{(ax+b)-b}{(ax+b)}\right]$$

$$= \frac{1}{2}\left[1 - \frac{b}{(ax+b)}\right] < 1.$$

Exercise 7.2

1. If η_1 and η_2 be the price elasticities of supply $p = e$ and $\frac{e}{x}$ respectively show that $\eta_1 \eta_2 - \eta_2 - \eta_1$.
2. Calculate the price elasticity of demand for the demand functions.

   (*i*) $\frac{16}{p} = x^{2/5}$ (*ii*) $q = bp^{-a}$

   (*iii*) $p = ae^{-kx}$ (*iv*) $q = 60000e^{-0.5p}$

   (*v*) $x = 15p^{-0.75}$

   $\left[(i)\ \frac{5}{2}\ (ii)\ a\ (iii)\ \frac{1}{kx}\ (iv)\ p/2\ (v)\ 0.75\right]$
3. The demand function for a commodity is $p = 10 + 5x - 2x^2$. Find the elasticity of demand when $x = 2$. **[Ans.** 2]
4. If the demand law is $x = 20/(p + 1)$, find the elasticity of demand at the point $p = 3$. What type of curve is the demand function? What is its economic importance?

   [Ans. 3/4, rectangular hyperbola]
5. Find the elasticities of demand and supply at equilibrium price for the demand function $p = \sqrt{100 - x^2}$ and supply function $x = 2p - 10$, where p is price and x is quantity.

   $[\eta_d = 16/9,\ \eta_s = 8/3]$
6. Using calculus, show that

   $$MR = AR\left(1 - \frac{1}{\eta_d}\right)$$

   and verify this for the demand function $x = \frac{a-p}{b}$, $b \neq 0$.
7. Show that for the total cost function $C = \sqrt{ax+b}$, where a and b are positive constants, the elasticity of total cost increases but remain less than unity as x increases.

8. Find the elasticity of cost for the following functions :

(a) $C = 2x^2 + 3x$

(b) $C = x^2 + 4x$

$$\left[(a)\ (4x^2 + 3x)\Big/(2x^2 + 3x) \quad (b)\ \frac{(2x^2 + 4x)}{(x^2 + 4x)}\right]$$

9. Given the manufacturer cost functions as

$$C = ax^2 + bx + c$$

Find the elasticity of average cost and total cost. Also prove that

$$\eta_{AC} = \eta_C - 1 \qquad \left[\eta_{AC} = \frac{ax^2 - c}{ax^2 - bx + c},\ \eta_C = \frac{2ax^2 + bx}{ax^2 + bx + c}\right]$$

10. If the demand function is $p = 4 - 5x$, for what value of x will the elasticity of demand be unitary? [x 2/5]

11. For the demand function $aQ + bp - k = 0$, where a, b are k are positive constants. Determine the point elasticity of demand when marginal revenue is zero. [$\eta = 1$]

12. Find the elasticity of demand w.r.t. price for the demand function $x = \dfrac{8}{p^{3/2}}$. [$\eta = 3/2$]

13. The demand function for a commodity is given by $x = 48 - 3p^2$ at $p = 3$, $x = 21$. If the price (p) decreases by 4%, determine the relative increase in demand (x) and hence an approximation to the elasticity of demand at $p = 3$. Compare this with the elasticity of demand at $p = 3$.

[Relative increase in demand = 2.10, η_d at $p = 3$ is 2.57, η_d at $p = 2.88$ is 2.15]

14. If the demand curve is given by $p = x^a.e^{b(x + c)}$ show that the demand increases as the price decreases become large as the price approaches the value a/b. Find the effect of any price greater than a/b, on the elasticity of demand. [$\eta_d = bp - a$]

15. If a firm produces an output x at a total cost of $C = ax^2 + bx$, find an expression for elasticity of total cost. Show that elasticity is always greater than unity and increases as x increases.

16. A firm's demand function is $p = \sqrt{a - bx}$, show that demand curve is downward sloping and concave from below. Does the corresponding marginal revenue function also satisfy these conditions.

17. If demand equation for a certain commodity is $q = 500 - 2p$ (for $0 \le p \le 250$)

(i) Determine where the demand is elastic, inelastic and of unit elasticity w.r.t. price.

(ii) Use the result of part (i) to determine the intervals of increase and decrease of the revenue function and the price at which revenue is maximized.

[(i) elastic when $p > 125$, inelastic when $p < 125$, unit elastic when $p = 125$]

18. The supply function of a product is $x = a\sqrt{p - b}$, where x is quantity demanded, p (which is greater than b) is price and a and b are positive constants. Find the expression for the elasticity of supply as a function of price and, by using calculus, show that the elasticity decreases as price increases, and becomes unity at the price equal to $2b$.

19. For a liner demand function, show that price elasticity of demand increases and decreases as the quantity increases, using calculus.

PROFIT FUNCTION – MAXIMIZATION

As we have already studied that revenue as well cost depends upon the output. Profit by definition, is excess of revenue over cost.

It is given as

$$\text{Profit} = R(x) - C(x)$$

$$\therefore \quad p(x) = R(x) - C(x)$$

The aim of any business firm is to maximise profit which can be achieved in either of the following two ways :

1. Keep price per unit as constant and find the number of units maximising profit.
2. Keep number of units as constant and find the price per unit which can maximise the profit.

The above methods are feasible in case of **Monopoly situation. In case of pure competition,** a firm cannot dictate the price per unit. It has only one way to maximize its profit *i.e.* by finding number of units to be sold to maximise profit.

Thus, in case of pure competition,

$$\text{Find } \frac{dp}{dx}$$

Equate it to zero to get stationary points. Test whether stationary points represents maxima or minima by calculating second derivative and substituting the values of stationary point in the same. If the result is positive, it represent maxima and if it is negative, the stationary point is a Maxima.

The above discussion is summarised below and the facts have also been explained in the context of marginal analysis.

As explained above, profit is maximum, when

(*i*) $\frac{dP}{dx} = 0$ *i.e.* $\frac{dR}{dx} = \frac{dC}{dx}$

This implies $MR = MC$.

(*ii*) $\frac{d^2P}{dx^2} < 0$

i.e. $\frac{d}{dx}(MR) < \frac{d}{dx}(MC)$

Slope of MR < Slope of MC.

Thus, for maximisation of profit, Marginal revenue is equal to marginal cost and slope of marginal revenue is less than slope of marginal cost.

The conditions of profit maximization would differ in case of monopoly and perfect competition because price per unit *i.e.* 'p' is treated as constant in case of perfect competition. The conditions have been summarized below :

	Monopoly	Perfect Competition
First Order Condition	$MR = MC$	$MC = p\left(\because \frac{d}{dx}(R) = \frac{d}{dx}(px) = p\right)$
Second Order Condition	$\frac{d}{dx}(MR) < \frac{d}{dx}(MC)$	$0 - \frac{d^2C}{dx^2} < 0$

Example 27. **The demand function for a particular commodity is $y = 15\,e^{-x/3}$ for $0 \le x \le 8$, where y is the price per unit and x is the number of units demanded. Determine the price and quantity for which total revenue is maximum.**

Solution. Let R be the total revenue, then

$$R = \text{(price per unit) (number of units sold)}$$

$$= y\,.\,x = 15\,e^{-x/3}\,x.$$

In order to maximize R, we differentiate. 'R' w.x.t. x, as under

$$\frac{dR}{dx} = 15\left[e^{-x/3}.1 + xe^{-x/3}\left(-\frac{1}{3}\right)\right]$$

$$= 15e^{-x/3}\left[1 - \frac{x}{3}\right]$$

To get the stationary points, we put $\frac{dR}{dx} = 0$. Thus

$$15e^{-x/3}\left(1 - \frac{x}{3}\right) = 0$$

$\therefore$ $x = 3$ (*since* $e^x > 0$)

Further, $$\frac{d^2R}{dx^2} = \left[15e^{-x/3}\left(-\frac{1}{3}\right) + \left(1 - \frac{x}{3}\right)15e^{-x/3}\left(-\frac{1}{3}\right)\right]$$

$$= -15e^{-x/3}\left[2 - \frac{x}{3}\right]$$

When $x = 3,\ \frac{d^2R}{dx^2} = -5e^{-1} < 0,$

Since $\frac{d^2R}{dx^2}$ is negative

therefore R is maximum when $x = 3$. Substituting this value of x in the demand function $y = 15e^{-x/3}$, we get price $y = 15\,e^{-1} = 15/e$.

Example 28. **A company charges Rs. 550 for a transistor set on orders of 50 or less sets. The charge is reduced by Rs. 5 per set for each set ordered in excess of 50. Find the largest size order company should allow so as to receive a maximum revenue.**

Solution. Let x be the number of transistor sets ordered in excess of 50. Thus the total number of transistor sets ordered is $50 + x$. Further, we are given for each set ordered in excess of 50, the charge is reduced by Rs. 5 per set, therefore for each x sets ordered in excess of 50, the charge is reduced by $5x$ per set. Therefore, the new charge per set is $550 - 5x$.

Let R be the revenue of the company, then

$$R = \text{(order size) (charge per set)}$$
$$= (50 + x)(550 - 5x)$$
$$= 27500 + 300x - 5x^2$$
$$\frac{dR}{dx} = 300 - 10x$$

For R to be maximum, $\frac{dR}{dx} = 0.$

i.e. $300 - 10x = 0$

$$x = 300/10 = 30$$

Also $\frac{d^2R}{dx^2} = -10 < 0$. Thus the maximum revenue is obtained when $(50 + 30) = 80$ sets are ordered.

Example 29. **A firm's demand function is :**

$$x = 400 \ln\left(\frac{10}{p}\right)$$

Find the price and quantity where total revenue is maximum. Also, find price elasticity of demand at that price.

Solution. Given

$$x = 400.\, ln\left(\frac{10}{p}\right)$$

$$\therefore \quad \frac{x}{400} = ln\left(\frac{10}{p}\right)$$

$$\frac{10}{p} = e^{x/400}$$

$$p = 10\, e^{-x/400}$$

$$\therefore \quad R = px = 10\, xe^{-x/400} \qquad \text{(where } R \text{ is the total revenue)}$$

Differentiating R w.r.t. x, we obtain

$$\frac{dR}{dx} = 10\left[xe^{-x/400}\left(-\frac{1}{400}\right) + e^{-x/400}.1\right]$$

$$= 10\, e^{-x/400}\left[-\frac{x}{400} + 1\right]$$

For R to be maximum

$$\frac{dR}{dx} = 0$$

i.e. $$-\frac{x}{400} + 1 = 0 \qquad (\because\ 10\ e^{-x/400} \neq 0)$$

$\therefore$ $$x = 400$$

Also $$\frac{d^2R}{dx^2} = 10\left[e^{-x/400}\left(-\frac{1}{400}\right) + \left(-\frac{x}{400} + 1\right)e^{-x/400}\left(-\frac{1}{400}\right)\right]$$

$$= \frac{1}{40}e^{-x/400}\left[2 - \frac{x}{400}\right]$$

At $x = 400$, $\frac{d^3R}{dx^2} = -\frac{1}{40}e^{e-1} < 0$. Therefore R is maximum when $x = 400$. Substituting $x = 400$ in $p = 10\ e^{-x/400}$, we obtain price $p = 10\ e^{-1}$.

In order to find, price elasticity of demand, we differentiate the demand function w.r.t. p

$$x = 400\ ln\left(\frac{10}{p}\right) = 400\left(\ln 10 - \ln p\right)$$

$$\frac{dx}{dp} = -\frac{400}{p}$$

$\therefore$ $$\eta_d = -\frac{p}{x}\frac{dx}{dp}$$

$$= -\frac{p}{400 \ln\left(\frac{10}{p}\right)}\left(-\frac{400}{p}\right)$$

$$= \frac{1}{\ln\left(\frac{10}{p}\right)} = \frac{400}{x}$$

Evaluating η_d at $p = 10e^{-1}$ or at $x = 400$, we obtain $\eta_d = 1$.

***Example 30.* Tour operator charges Rs. 136 per passenger for 100 passengers with a refund of Rs. 4 for each 10 passengers in excess of 100. Determine the number of passengers that will maximise the amount of money the tour operator receives.**

Solution. We have

Current revenue = 136×100

When number of passengers will increase to $(100 + 10) = 110$, Charges per passengers would be $(136 - 4)$.

i.e. Revenue = 132×100

Likewise when number of passengers increase to 120, charges per passenger will decrease to 128 *i.e.* (132 – 4)

$\therefore \quad R = 128 \times 120$

Since decline in revenue is taking place in multiples of 4 whereas increase in passenger is taking place in multiple of 10, therefore generalizing the above equation, we have

$$R = (136 - 4x)(100 + 10x).$$

$$R = 13600 + 1360x - 400x - 40x^2$$

$$\therefore \quad R = 13600 + 960x - 40x^2$$

Alternately. Let $10x$ be the passengers in excess of 100 therefore, $4x$ will be the refund

$$\therefore \quad \text{Revenue} = (100 + 10x)(136 - 4x)$$

$$\therefore \quad R = 13600 - 400x + 1360x - 40x^2 = 13600 + 960x - 40x^2$$

In order to find maxima of R, we calculate $\frac{dR}{dx}$ and equate it to zero to get stationary points.

$$\therefore \quad \frac{dR}{dx} = 960 - 80x$$

Put $\frac{dR}{dx} = 0$ and find x

$$\therefore \quad 960 - 80x = 0$$

$$\therefore \quad x = \frac{960}{80} = 12$$

$$\therefore \quad x = 12$$

In order to know whether $x = 12$ reflects points of maxima, find $\frac{d^2R}{dx^2}$ and substitute $x = 12$.

$$\therefore \quad \frac{d^2R}{dx^2} = -80$$

Thus, $x = 12$ reflects point of maxima.

It implies revenue will be maximum when number of passenger is (100 + 10(12)) – 220.

***Example 31.* Given Cost function $C(x) = \frac{x^2}{4}$ and demand function $x = 10 - p$ for a firm. (where x and p denote quantity and price respectively). Find number of units to be sold the maximize profit when ..... firm is operating under**

(*i*) Monopoly

(*ii*) Perfect competition.

Solution (*i*) Under Monopoly, price can be changed.

$\therefore$ We have $x = 10 - p$

$\therefore \quad p = 10 - x$

$\therefore$ Revenue 'R' $= p.x. = (10 - x).x = 10x - x^2$

$$\therefore \quad \text{Profit} = \text{Revenue} - \text{cost} = 10x - x^2 - \left(\frac{x^2}{4}\right)$$

$$= 10x - x^2 - \frac{x^2}{4}$$

The maximize profit, find $\frac{dP}{dx}$ and equate it to zero to get stationary points

$$\frac{dP}{dx} = 10 - 2x - \frac{2x}{4}$$

Put $\quad \frac{dP}{dx} = 0$

$$\therefore \; 10 - 2x - \frac{2x}{4} = 0$$

$$\therefore \quad 40 - 10x = 0$$

$$x = 4$$

we have $\quad \frac{d^2P}{dx^2} = -10$

Since $\quad \frac{d^2R}{dx^2} < 0$

$\therefore$ $x - 4$ is a point of maxima

$$\therefore \text{ Maximum Profit } = 10(4) - (4)^2 - \frac{1}{4}(4)^2$$

$$= 20$$

Under perfect competition, price remain constant

Revenue $= p.x.$ (where p is constant)

$\therefore \quad$ Profit = Revenue − Cost

$$= px - \frac{1}{4}x^2$$

To find maximum profit, find $\frac{dP}{dx}$ and equate it to zero.

$$\therefore \quad \frac{dP}{dx} = p - \frac{x}{2}$$

$$\therefore \quad p - \frac{x}{2} = 0$$

$$\therefore \quad x = 2p$$

To conclude $x = 2p$ represent maxima, find $\frac{d^2P}{dx^2}$

$$\therefore \quad \frac{d^2P}{dx^2} = -\frac{1}{2} < 0$$

Since $\frac{d^2P}{dx^2} < 0$, $x = 2p$ is a point of maxima.

We have $\quad x = 2p$

and $\quad x = 10 - p$

Using (1) and (2), we have

$$p = \frac{10}{3} \text{ and } x = \frac{20}{3}.$$

***Example 32.* Birla Hotel Ltd. has 40 rooms which can be given at the rate of Rs. 1000 per day. However, for each Rs. 100 per day increase in rent, 2 units will be vacant with no possibility of filling them. How many rooms should be rent per day and at what rate to maximize daily income?**

Solution.

Increase in rent takes place in multiples of 100 and decrease in rented room takes place in multiples of 2.

Therefore, let '$2x$' be the number of vacant rooms for every $100x$ increase in rent.

$$\therefore \quad \text{Revenue} = (40 - 2x)(1000 + 100x)$$

$$\therefore \quad R = 40000 + 4000x - 2000x - 200x^2$$

$$R = 40000 + 2000x - 200x^2$$

$$\therefore \quad \frac{dR}{dx} = 2000 - 400x$$

To find maxima of R, equate $\frac{dR}{dx} = 0$ to get stationary points

$\therefore$ $2000 - 400x = 0$

$$\therefore \quad x = 5$$

In order to know whether $x = 5$ represent maxima or minima, find $\frac{d^2R}{dx^2}$

$$\therefore \quad \frac{d^2R}{dx^2} = -400$$

Since $\quad \frac{d^2R}{dx^2} < 0$

$\therefore$ $x = 5$ represent point of maxima.

$\therefore$ Number of rooms to be given on rent $= 40 - 2x$

per night $= 40 - 2(5) = 30$

and Rate of Rent per night $= 1000 + 100(5)$

$= 1500$

Example 33. **A financial institution has determined that the proportion of account receivable P (in rupees) collected 't' months after the credit was issued is given by $P = 0.95\ (1 - e^{-0.7t})$. The average credit issue in any months is Rs. 100 million. The financial institution estimates that for each Rs. 100 million in new credit issued in any month, collection efforts cost Rs. 1 million per month. Determine the number of months that collection efforts should be continued if the objectives is to maximize the net collections (*i.e.,* rupees collected minus collection costs). [Given $e^{-42} = 0.0153$].**

Solution. Let 't' be number of months for maximizing net collections.

$\therefore$ Amount collected during 't' months $= 100\ (0.95)\ (1 - e^{-0.7t})$

collection cost $= 1.t$ [where '100' and '1' are in millions]

$\therefore$ Net collection $= 100\ (0.95)\ (1 - e^{-0.7t}) - 1.t$

$$N = 95 - 95e^{-0.7t} - t.$$

Differentiating both sides *w.r.t.* time 't', we have

$$\frac{dN}{dt} = 66.5\, e^{-0.7t} - 1$$

Putting $\frac{dN}{dt} = 0$ and solving for 't' we have

$$e^{-0.7t} = \frac{1}{66.5}$$

$$66.5 = e^{0.7t}$$

$$\log 66.5 = 0.7t \log e$$

$$1.8228 = 0.7t\ (0.4343)$$

$$t = \frac{1.8228}{0.7 \times 0.4343} = 5.99 \approx 6 \text{ months.}$$

Second derivative $\frac{d^2N}{dt^2} = 46.55\, e^{-0.7t}$ is positive for $t = 6$, therefore, the number of months for maximising net collections is 6.

Example 34. **The proportion of people responding to an advertisement of a new product in a certain marketing area is given by $(1 - e^{-0.3t})$ where t is the number of days the advertisement runs. The marketing area contains 4,00,000 potential customer and each response to the advertisement results in an average profit of Rs. 2. The profit is exclusive of advertisement cost. The fixed cost of producing the advertising is Rs. 30000 and the variable cost is Rs. 4000 for each day the advertisement runs. How many days should the advertisement run to maximize total net profit?**

Solution. Let 't' be the number of days for which advertisement runs.

Therefore, revenue earned during this time

$$R = 4,00,000\ (1 - e^{-0.3t}).2$$

Cost of running the advertisement

$$C = 30000 + 4000\ t$$

$\therefore$ Profit = Revenue – cost

$$= 8,00,000\ (1 - e^{-0.3t}) - (30,000 + 4,000\ t)$$

$$P = 8,00,000 - 8,00,000\ e^{-0.3t} - 30,000 - 4,000\ t$$

Differentiating both the sides with respect to time

$$\frac{dP}{dt} = +\ 240000\ e^{-0.3t} - 4000$$

Put $\frac{dP}{dt} = 0$ to get stationary points.

$$\therefore \quad e^{-0.3t} = +\frac{4000}{240000} = +\frac{1}{60}$$

$$\therefore \quad 60 = \frac{1}{e^{-0.3t}} = e^{+0.3t}$$

Taking log both the sides

$$\log 60 = 0.3t \log e$$

$$1.7782 = 0.3t\ (0.4343)$$

$$t = \frac{1.7782}{(0.3 \times 0.4343)} = 13.64 \text{ days.}$$

i.e., time = 14 days (approximately).

Example 35. **A manufacturer of water tank has noticed that each tank cost Rs. 500 alongwith over head cost of Rs. 2 per unit. The demand function observed by the manufacturer is**

$$p = 202 - 2x \text{ for '}x\text{' number of unit.}$$

How many tanks shall be produced to maximise profit. What will be the maximum profit.

Solution : Let 'x' be number of tanks manufactured to maximise profit

$\therefore$ Cost function $C(x) = 500 + 2x$

Revenue function $R(x) = p \cdot x$

$$= (202 - 2x) \cdot x$$

$$= 202x - 2x^2$$

$$\text{Profit} = 202x - 2x^2 - 500 - 2x$$

$$= 200x - 2x^2 - 500$$

∴ Calculate $\frac{dp}{dx}$ and equate it to zero to get stationary points.

$$\therefore \quad \frac{dp}{dx} = \frac{d}{dx}\left(200x - 2x^2 - 500\right)$$

$\Rightarrow 200 - 4x = 0$

$\therefore \quad x = 50$

Second derivative $\frac{d^2p}{dx^2} = -4$ (negative)

∴ $x = 50$ represent point of maxima.

Maximum Profit $= 200\ (50) - 2(50)^2 - 500$

$= 10{,}000 - 5000 - 500$

$= 4500$

Example 36. **A company makes a profit of Rs. 5 on each unit of its product it sells. If it spends an amount of Rs. A per week on advertising, then the number of items per week it sells is given by $x = 2000\ (1 - e^{-KA})$ where K = 0.001. Find the value of A that will maximise the net profit.**

Solution : Given Profit per unit = Rs. 5

∴ if 'x' units will be sold per week, total profit $= 5x$

However, this profit will be available after spending Rs. A per week.

∴ Net Profit $P = 5x - A$

$P = 5[2000\ (1 - e^{KA})] - A$

$P = 10000\ (1 - e^{KA})] - A$

Applying maxima conditions.

Substituting $k = 0.001$, we have $\frac{dp}{dA} = +K(10{,}000)e^{KA} - 1 = 0$

$\therefore\ 0.001\ (10{,}000)e^{-(0.001)A} - 1 = 0$

$$\therefore\ 10{,}000e^{-0.001A} = \frac{1}{0.001}$$

$e^{\ (0.001)A} = 0.1$

$\therefore \quad e^{(0.001)A} = 10$

Taking log both the sides

$(0.001)\ A \log e = \log 10$

$\Rightarrow \quad (0.001)\ A\ (0.4343) = 1$

$$A = \frac{1}{(0.001)\times(0.4242)} = 2302.55$$

Second derivative

$$\therefore \quad \frac{d^2p}{dA^2} = -0.001e^{-0.001A} < 0$$

Since, Second derivative is negative, it implies maxima at A = 2302.55

$\therefore$ Profit = 10000 $\{1 - e^{-(0.001)(2302.55)}\}$ – 2302.55

P = 10000 $(1 - e^{-2.3})$ – 2302.55

= 10000 (0.89974) – 2302.55

= 8997.4 – 2302.55 = 6694.85

Example 37. **A manufacturer of a product finds that for the 500 units that are produced and sold, the profit is Rs. 50 per unit. The profit on each of the units beyond 500 is decreased by Rs. 0.10 times the number of additional units produced. What level of output will maximise profit.**

Solution. Let 'x' be the number of additional units produced beyond 500 units.

$\therefore$ Total Profit P = $(500 \times 50) + (50 - 0.10x) \cdot x$

Differentiating both the sides *w.r.t.* 'x'

$$\therefore \quad \frac{dP}{dx} = 0 + 50 - 0.20x$$

$$\therefore \quad 50 - 0.20\,x = 0$$

$$x = \frac{50}{0.20} = \frac{5000}{20} = 250$$

Find $\frac{d^2P}{dx^2}$ to confirm x = 250 is point of maxima.

$$\therefore \quad \frac{d^2P}{dx^2} = -\,0.20$$

Since $\frac{d^2P}{dx^2}$ is negative, x = 250 represent point of maxima.

Therefore, the manufacturer shall produce 500 + 250 = 750 units to maximize profits.

Example 38. **From the past experience cricket control board knows that if the average cost of ticket is Rs. 50 per match. 50000 spectators turn up and for an increase of Rs. 5 per ticket in the average cost they lose 5000 spectators. On an average each spectator spends Rs. 4 in buying souvenir etc. which is also the income of cricket control board. The board also has to issue 3000 complimentary passes and has to spend Rs. 17000 in making arrangements. What should be average cost of tickets so as to maximize the profit for the board? What would be the number of spectators expected.**

Solution. Let the demand function be

$$p = a - bx$$

(which 'p' is cost of ticket and 'x' is number of spectators)

Substituting given value we have

$$50 = a - b\,(50000) \qquad (1)$$

$$55 = a - b\,(45000) \qquad (2)$$

Solving for 'a' and 'b', we have

$$5 = 5000\,b$$

$$b = \frac{1}{1000}$$

Substituting this value of 'b' is equation 1, we have

$$50 = a - \frac{1}{1000} \times 50000$$

$$50 = a - 50$$

$$a = 100$$

∴ Demand function will be given as

$$p = 100 - \frac{1}{1000}x$$

Using the above demand function and given information that each spectator could purchase souvenir by paying Rs. 4, the total revenue would be given as

$$\text{Revenue } 'R' = p.x + 4.x$$

$$= \left(100 - \frac{1}{1000}x\right)x + 4x$$

$$= 100x - \frac{x^2}{1000} + 4x$$

Cost to be spent = Rs. 17000

∴ Profit = Revenue − Cost

$$P = 100x - \frac{x^2}{1000} + 4x - 17000$$

Differentiating *w.r.t.* x, we have

$$\frac{dP}{dx} = 100 - \frac{x}{500} + 4$$

Substituting $\frac{dP}{dx} = 0$, we have

$$100 - \frac{x}{500} + 4 = 0$$

$$104 = \frac{x}{500}$$

$$x = 104 \times 500 = 52000$$

∴ No. of spectators = 52000. Since, there are 3000 complimentary passes, hence total number of spectators = 52000 + 3000 = 55000.

Average cost $p = 100 - \frac{1}{100}(x)$

$$= 100 - \frac{1}{100}(52000) = 100 - 52$$

$$= 48.$$

Example 39. **United India Bank has conducted a study and found that amount of deposits it receives from customers is directly proportional to the interest rate offered by it. However, the funds collected by way of deposits can be invested at the rate of 14% p.a. by the bank. What rate should the bank offer to its customers so as to maximize its profit?**

Solution. Let 'A' be the amount deposited and 'r' be the rate offered to the depositors.

$$\therefore \quad A \propto r$$

$$A = kr$$

(where 'k' is constant of proportionality).

Revenue to the bank $= \frac{14}{100} A = \frac{14}{100}(kr)$

Cost to the bank $= \frac{r}{100}(A) = \frac{r}{100}(kr)$

$$\therefore \quad \text{Profit} = \text{Revenue} - \text{Cost}$$

$$= \frac{14}{100}(kr) - \frac{r}{100}(kr)$$

$$P = \frac{14}{100}(kr) - \frac{kr^2}{100}$$

Differentiating P w.r.t. r

$$\frac{dP}{dr} = \frac{14}{100}k - \frac{2kr}{100}$$

Applying first order condition,

$$\frac{14k}{100} = \frac{2kr}{100}$$

$$r = 7.$$

Second order condition

$$\frac{d^2P}{dr^2} = -\frac{2k}{100} \text{ (Negative)}$$

∴ Rate offered to depositor shall be 7% to maximise profit of the bank.

Example 40. **A company makes x kg. of material A ($x \leq 4$) and y kg of material B with $y = \frac{(24-6x)}{(5-x)}$. The profit of material A is Rs. 2000 and B it is Rs. 1000 per kg. How much of material A should be produced per day to maximize profit.**

Solution. Given

Profit margin on material A = Rs. 2000

Profit margin on material B = Rs. 1000

Total Profit P = 2000 (x) + 1000 (y)

$$P = 2000x + 1000\left(\frac{24-6x}{5-x}\right)$$

$$= \frac{2000x \times (5-x) + 1000(24-6x)}{(5-x)}$$

$$= \frac{(10000x - 2000x^2 + 24000 - 6000x)}{(5-x)}$$

$$P = \frac{(4000x - 2000x^2 + 24000)}{(5-x)}$$

∴ Differentiating both the side *w.r.t.* x.

we have

$$\frac{dp}{dx} = \frac{(5-x)(4000-4000x) - (4000x - 2000x^2 + 24000)(-1)}{(5-x)^2}$$

put $\frac{dp}{dx} = 0$ to get stationary point

∴ $x^2 - 10x + 22 = 0$

∴ $x = \frac{10 + \sqrt{100-88}}{2}$ $\left[\therefore x = \frac{-b + \sqrt{b^2 - 4ac}}{2a}\right]$

∴ $x = 5 + \sqrt{3},\ 5 - \sqrt{3}$

∴ $x = 5 + \sqrt{3}$, (Since x cannot be less than 4).

Exercise 7.3

1. A firm's demand function is $x = 400\ ln\ (10/p)$. Find the price and quantity where total revenue is maximum. Also, find the price elasticity of demand at that price. [$\eta_d = 1$ at $x = 400$]
2. Company makes a profit of Rs. 5 on each unit of its product it sells. If it spends an amount of Rs. A per week on advertising, then the number of items per week it sells is given by $x = 2000\ (1 - e^{-kA})$, where $K = 0.001$. Find the value of A that will maximize the net profit. [A = Rs. 2300 and maximum profit = Rs 6700]

3. A firm produces x units of output per week at a total cost of Rs $\left(\frac{x^3}{3} - x^2 + 5x + 3\right)$. Find the output levels at which the marginal cost and the average variable cost attain their respectively minima. [**Ans.** 1 and 3/2]

4. The cost of fuel in running a vehicle is proportional to the square of the speed and is Rs. 45 per hour for a speed of 15 km per hour. Other expenses amount to Rs. 500 per hour. Find the most economical speed for the vehicle and also the minimum cost for a distance of 100 km. [50km/hr, Rs. 2000]

5. Show using calculus that profit of a monopolist is maximum when

   (*i*) $MR = MC$; and

   (*ii*) Slope of MR < Slope of MC

6. A firm has found from past experience that its profit in terms of number of units x produced is given by

$$P(x) = -\frac{x^3}{3} + 729x - 2500, \; 0 \le x \le 35$$

Compute

(*i*) the value of x that maximizes the profit,

(*ii*) the profit per unit of the product when this maximum level is achieved.

[(*i*) $x = 27$, (*ii*) Rs. 393.40]

7. If a monopolist has a total cost of $C = ax^2 + bx + c$ and it the demand law is $p = \beta - lx^2$, show that the output for maximum net revenue is

$$x = \frac{\sqrt{a^2 + 3l(\beta - b)} - a}{3l}$$

8. The proportion of people responding to an advertisement of a new product in a certain marketing area is given by $(1 - e^{-0.3t})$ where t is the number of days the advertisement runs. The marketing area contains 400,000 potential customer and each response to the advertisement result is an average profit of Rs. 2. The profit is exclusive of advertisement cost. The fixed cost of producing the advertising is Rs. 30000 and the variable cost is Rs. 4000 for each day the advertisement runs. How many days should the advertisement run to maximize total net profit? [**Ans.** 14 days]

9. A produces x tonnes of steel per week at total cost of $\frac{1}{10}x^3 + 3x^2 + 50x + 300$. If the market price is fixed as Rs. $33\frac{1}{3}$, find the profit maximizing output of the plant.

[$x = -10/3, -50/30$ (No production shall be done)]

10. The manufacturing cost of an item consist of Rs. 1000 as overheads, material cost Rs. 2 per item and labour cost $x^2/90$ for x items produced. Find how many items be produced to have the average cost as minimum. [$x = 300$]

11. If x be the number of worker's employed, the average cost of production is given by $AC = \dfrac{3}{2(x-4)} + 24x$. Show that $x = 4.25$ will make the expression minimum. In the interest of the management will you then advise to employ four or five workers? Give reasons for you answer. **[Ans.: 5]**

12. The cost function of a firm is given by $C = 300x - 10x^2 + 1/3x^3$. Calculate the output at which the marginal cost is minimum. Will it be the same at which average cost is minimum?

[MC is minimum at $x = 10$, AC is minimum at $x = 15$]

13. From the past experience Cricket Control Board knows that if the average cost of ticket is Rs. 50 per match. 50000 spectators turn up and for an increase of Rs. 5/- per ticket is the average cost they lose 5000 spectators. On an average each spectator spends Rs. 4 in buying souvenir etc. which is also the income of Cricket Control Board. The Board also has to issue 3000 complimentary passes and has to spend Rs. 17000/- in making arrangements. What should be the average cost of tickets so as to maximize the profit for the Board? What would be the number of spectators expected? [Average price 48, spectators expected = 55000]

14. If the cost function of a firm is

$$C = \frac{1}{3}x^3 - 5x^2 + 30x + 10$$

where C is the cost and x is the output, and the price under perfect competition is given as 6, find for what value of x the profit will be maximized. Examine both first and second order conditions. [$x = 6$]

15. The production function of a commodity is given by $Q = 40F + 3F^2 - \frac{1}{3}F^3$, where Q is the total output and F is the units of input.

   (*i*) Find the number of units of input required to give maximum output.

   (*ii*) Find the maximum value of marginal product.

   (*iii*) Verify that when the average product is maximum, it is equal to its marginal product.

[10 units, 49]

EFFECT OF TAXATION AND SUBSIDY ON MONOPOLY

Taxes are one of the source of revenue for a government. Whenever a government wants to raise its revenue, it increases tax. The producers, passes the burden of tax on the consumers by increasing the price of goods or commodities. As we have already discussed that in case of pure competition, the prices per unit cannot be changed by a producer because they have no control over the prices. But, for a monopoly, it is possible to reduce or increase his output, and thereby control the price.

Another issue of concern is whether changes have been made is respect of excise tax or sales tax. This is important because increase in excise tax is based on number of units sold whereas sales tax is based on revenues of a firm. Both the taxes tend to decrease profit of a firm because they are added to the cost, as shown below :

Effect of Excise tax

Consider a Monopolist having following cost and demand functions :

$$C = C(x) \text{ and } p = f(x) \text{ respectively}$$

Let 't' per unit of output be the excise tax imposed by the government.

$\therefore$ New Cost function $C_N(x) = C(x) + tx$

$\therefore$ New Profit function $P_N = R(x) - C_N$

$$\therefore \quad P_N = R(x) - [C(x) + tx]$$

Let us apply, first order condition *i.e.*, calculating first derivative and equating it to zero.

$$\frac{dP_N}{dx} = \frac{dR(x)}{dx} - \frac{dC(x)}{dx} - t$$

When $\frac{dP_N}{dx} = 0$

We have $\frac{dR(x)}{dx} = \frac{dC(x)}{dx} + t$

$$\therefore \quad \boldsymbol{MR = MC + t}$$

We can find x from the above equation. The corresponding price can be calculated using demand equation.

Further second order condition is

$$\frac{d^2R}{dx^2} < \frac{d^2C}{dx^2}$$

Let the 'x' derived from above equation be denoted as x_N. This is the output at which profit of the monopolist under the new situations would be maximum. Now in order to find the tax rate 't', which maximises the revenue of a government, we shall use the equation

$$T = t.X_N$$

Applying, maxima conditions we can find 't' for maximizing tax revenue of the Government.

Effect of Sales Tax

Sales Tax is charged on the revenue. Therefore, if r is the rate of Sales Tax then the amount of Sales Tax would $\frac{r}{100} \times R$

$$\therefore \quad \text{Profit} = \text{Revenue} - (\text{Cost} + \text{Sales Tax})$$

i.e.

$$P_N = R - \left(C + \frac{r}{100}R\right) = R - C_N$$

Now, we can apply conditions of maxima to find output level and therefore corresponding price, using demand function.

Effect of Subsidy

Subsidy is financial assistance given to the producer by a Government which has effect on decreasing the cost price and hence increases the profit of a firm. Let 'S' be the rate of subsidy and 'x' be the output.

$\therefore$ Amount of Subsidy = $S.x$

$$\therefore \quad \text{Profit} = \text{Revenue} - (\text{Cost} - \text{Subsidy})$$

$$P = R - (C - S.x)$$

Using Maxima conditions, we can find the level of output at which P is maximum and using the demand function, we can find the price per unit at the calculated output.

Imposition of Excise Duty

***Example 41* : Consider a cost function and demand function**

$$C(x) = \frac{x^2}{4} + 2x + 50$$

and demand function $x = 10 - 2p$ respectively. Find the Excise Duty/Tax per unit at which profit will be maximum. Also find the maximum profit and rate of Excise Duty per unit.

Solution

Let 'k' be the rate of tax per unit

$$\therefore \text{ New cost } C_N(x) = \frac{x^2}{4} + 2x + 50 + kx$$

$$\text{and Revenue } R = p.x = \left(\frac{10-x}{2}\right).x \left[\therefore p = \frac{(10-x)}{2}\right]$$

$$R = 5x - \frac{x^2}{2}$$

$$R = 5x - \frac{x^2}{2}$$

$$\therefore \quad \text{Profit} = \text{Revenue} - \text{Cost}$$

$$= 5x - \frac{x^2}{2} - \left(\frac{x^2}{4} + 2x + 50 + kx\right)$$

$$P = 5x - \frac{x^2}{2} - \frac{x^2}{4} - 2x - 50 - kx$$

$$= (3-k)x - \frac{3x^2}{4} - 50$$

For maximum profit

$$\text{Set} \quad \frac{dp}{dx} = 0$$

$$\therefore \quad \frac{dP}{dx} = (3-k) - \frac{3x}{2} = 0$$

$$\therefore \quad x = \frac{2(3-k)}{3}$$

To find whether x = 2/3 (3–k) represent maxima. Find $\frac{d^2P}{dx^2}$

$$\frac{d^2P}{dx^2} = -\frac{3}{2}$$

$$\therefore \quad \frac{d^2P}{dx^2} < 0$$

$\therefore \quad x = \frac{2}{3}(3-k)$ is point of maxima.

$\therefore$ Max Profit $p = (3-k)\left[\frac{2}{3}(3-k)\right] - \frac{3}{4}\left(\frac{2}{3}(3-k)\right)^2 - 50$

$$= \frac{2}{3}(3-k)^2 - \frac{3}{4}\left(\frac{2}{3}(3-k)\right)^2 - 50$$

$$= \frac{2}{3}(3-k)^2\left[1 - \frac{1}{2}\right] - 50$$

$$= \frac{1}{3}(3-k)^2 - 50$$

If T denotes the total tax revenue then

$$T = k.x = k\left[\frac{2}{3}(3-k)\right]$$

$$T = 2k - \frac{2}{3}k^2$$

To find maximum value of T. $\frac{dT}{dk} = 0$

$$\therefore \quad \frac{dT}{dk} = 2 - \frac{4}{3}k$$

$$\therefore \quad 2 - \frac{4}{3}k = 0$$

To assess of k = 3/2 represent maxima, find $\frac{d^2T}{dk^2}$

$$\frac{d^2T}{dk^2} = -\frac{4}{3}$$

Since $\frac{d^2T}{dk^2} < 0$

$\therefore\ k = \frac{3}{2}$ represent maxima

Imposition of Sales Tax

Example 42 : **Consider the cost function and demand function as**

$$C(x) = 2x^2 + 3x + 10$$

$p = 100 - 30x$ respectively. If 10% is rate of Sales Tax, find the level of out put at which profit will be maximum.

Solution.

Let 'R' be revenue and 'r' be rate of Sales Tax

$\therefore\quad R = p.x = (100 - 30x)x = 100x - 30x^2$

$\therefore\quad r = 10\%$ of R

$\therefore\quad r = 10x - 3x^2$

Since 'r' would reduce our profits therefore it can be added to the cost.

$P = R - (C + r)$ (Where P is profit)

$\therefore\quad P = 100x - 30x^2 - (2x^2 + 3x + 10 + 10x - 3x^2)$

$100x - 30x^2 - 2x^2 - 3x - 10 - 10x + 3x^2$

$P = 87x - 29x^2 - 10$

To get stationery point find $\frac{dP}{dx}$ and equate ii to zero.

$\therefore\quad \frac{dP}{dx} = 87 - 58x$ $\therefore$ Put $\frac{dP}{dx} = 0$. We have

$$x = \frac{87}{58}$$

Also $\frac{d^2P}{dx^2} = -58 < 0$ $\therefore$ it is point of maxima

Therefore, the profit will be maximum when $x = 87/58$

Offer of Subsidy

Example 43 : **Consider of firm having following details**

$C = 2x^2 + 250x + 2000$ (where 'x' number of units manufactured)

Subsidy = Rs. 50 per unit

Demand = P = 700 − 3x

where C and P are cost and demand functions respectively. Find the level of output at which profit will be maximum.

Solution : Let 'R' be the revenue

New cost $C_N = C + S$ (where 'S' is subsidy per unit)

$$\therefore \quad R = px = (700 - 3x).x = 700x - 3x^2$$

$$P = R - C = 700x - 3x^2 - (2x^2 + 250x + 2000 - 50x)$$

$$= 700x - 3x^2 - 2x^2 - 200x - 2000$$

$$p = -5x^2 + 500x - 2000$$

To find maximum profit

Find $\frac{dP}{dx} = -10x + 500$ and equate it to zero

$$\therefore \quad -10x + 500 = 0$$

$$x = 50$$

To find, if $x = 50$ represent point of maxima, find $\frac{d^2P}{dx^2}$

$$\frac{d^2P}{dx^2} = -10 < 0$$

Since $\frac{d^2P}{dx^2} =< 0, x = 50$ is a profit of maxima.

and Maximum Profit $= -5(50)^2 + 500(50) - 2000$

$$= -5 \times 2500 + 25000 - 2000$$

Profit = 10500

***Example 44* : A monopolist has the following demand and total cost function's $p = 45 - 5x$ and $C = 5x$ respectively**

(*i*) **Determine the optimum level of output and price for profit maximisation.**

(*ii*) **If a tax of Rs.2 per unit is imposed, find the new profit maximizing output and price.**

(*iii*) **If a subsidy of Rs. 2 per unit is given, find the new profit maximizing output and price.**

(*iv*) **If a tax of '*t*' per unit is imposed, find the output and price that correspond to the maximum profit.**

(*v*) **Find the tax that maximizes the tax revenue and determine the maximum tax revenue.**

Solution

(*i*) Given Cost function $C = 5x$

demand function $p = 45 - 5x$

$$\therefore \quad \text{Revenue} = R = p.x. = (45 - 5x) \,.\, x = 45x - 5x^2$$

$\therefore$ Profit $= P = R - C$

$= 45x - 5x^2 - 5x$

$= 40x - 5x^2$

$\therefore$ To find optimum level of output and price for profit maximisation.

Set $\frac{dP}{dx} = 0$

$\therefore$ $\frac{dP}{dx} = 40 - 10x = 0$

$\therefore$ $x = 4$

Since $\frac{d^2P}{dx} = -10 < 0, x = 4$ represents maxima

Substituting $x = 4$ in the demand function $p = 45 - 5x$,

We have $p = 45 - 5(4) = 45 - 20 = 25$

$\therefore$ $p = 25$

(*ii*) If excise tax of Rs. 2/- per unit is imposed

New Cost function $C_n(x) = 5x + 2x$

$\therefore$ $P = R - C$

$= 45x - 5x^2 - (5x + 2x)$

$= 45x - 5x^2 - 7x = 38x - 5x^2$

To find maximum value of P.

Set $\frac{dP}{dx} = 0$

$\frac{d}{dx}(38x - 5x^2) = 38 - 10x = 0$

$x = 3.8$

Since $\frac{d^2P}{dx^2} = -10 < 0, x = 3.8$ represent point of maxima

$\therefore$ Optimum quantity $= 3.8$

Optimum price $p = 45 - 5(3.8) = 26$

(*iii*) If a subsidy of Rs. 2 per unit is imposed.

New cost function $C_N(x) = 5x - 2x = 3x$

$\therefore$ $P = 45x - 5x^2 - (3x)$

$= 42x - 5x^2$

To find maximum profit, set $\frac{dP}{dx} = 0$

$$\therefore \quad \frac{dp}{dx} = 42 - 10x$$

$$\therefore \quad x = 4.2$$

Since $\frac{d^2P}{dx^2} = -10 < 0, x = 4.2$ represent maxima

optimum quantity $= 4.2$

optimum price $p = 45 - 5x = 45 - 5(4.2) = 24$

(*iv*) If '*t*' tax per unit is imposed.

New Cost $C_N(x) = 5x + tx$

$$\therefore \quad \text{Profit} = P = 45x - 5x^2 - 5x - tx$$

To find optimum level of profit, set $\frac{dP}{dx} = 0$

$$\therefore \quad \frac{dP}{dx} = 40 - t - 10x = 0$$

$$\therefore \quad x = \frac{40 - t}{10}$$

Since $\frac{d^2P}{dx^2} = -10 < 0, \therefore x = \frac{40-t}{10}$ represent point of maximum

$$\therefore \quad \text{optimum quantity} = \frac{(40-t)}{10}$$

and optimum price $\quad p = 45 - 5x = 45 - 5\left(\frac{40-t}{10}\right)$

$$\therefore \quad p = 45 - 20 + \frac{t}{2} = 25 + \frac{t}{2}$$

(*v*) To find rate of tax which maximizes tax revenue

$$T = t\,x$$

$T = t\left(\frac{40-t}{10}\right) = t\left(4 - \frac{t}{10}\right) = 4t - \frac{t^2}{10}$ To find maximum value of T, set $\frac{dT}{dt} = 0$

$$\frac{dT}{dt} = 4 - \frac{t}{5} = 0$$

$$\therefore \quad = 20$$

Since $\frac{d^2T}{dt^2} = -\frac{1}{5} < 0. \therefore t = 20$ represent point of maxima.

$\therefore$ Tax shall be charged at the rate of Rs. 20 per unit to maximize tax revenue.

Example 45 : **A monopolist's total cost is $C = ax^2 + bx + c$ and the demand function is $p = \beta - \alpha x$, where x and p *denote the units of output and price respectively and* a, b, c, α and β are positive constants. If the Government imposes tax at the rate of t per unit of output, show that the total tax is maximum when $t = (\beta - b)/2$.**

Solution : The tax of 't' per unit means that for x units the total cost increases by tx. Therefore, the new cost function is

$$C_N = ax^2 + bx + c + \text{tx},$$

and the new profit is given by

$$P_N = R - C_N$$

$$= px - (ax^2 + bx + c + tx)$$

$$= (\beta - \alpha x)x - (ax^2 + bx + c + tx)$$

$$= \beta x - \alpha x^2 - ax^2 - bx - c - tx$$

$$= -(\alpha + a)x^2 + (\beta - b - t)x - c$$

First order condition for maximum profit is

$$\frac{dP_N}{dx} = 0$$

$$\Rightarrow \qquad -2\ (a + a)\ x + (b - b - t) = 0$$

$$\Rightarrow \qquad x = \frac{(\beta - b - t)}{2(\alpha + a)}$$

Second order condition for maximum profit is

$$\frac{d^2P_N}{dx^2} < 0.$$

But $\qquad \dfrac{d^2P_N}{dx^2} = -2(\alpha + a).$

which is always negative, because α and a are positive. Thus, the profit maximizing level of output after the imposition of tax 't', denoted by x_N, is

$$x_N = (\beta - b - t)/2\ (a + \alpha).$$

The total tax revenue, T, of the government for this level of output is

$$T = tx_N = t\left[\frac{(\beta - b - t)}{2(a + \alpha)}\right] = \frac{\beta t - bt - t^2}{2(a + \alpha)}.$$

First order condition for maximum total tax revenue is $\dfrac{dT}{dt} = 0$. Thus gives $\dfrac{\beta - b - 2t}{2(a + \alpha)} = 0$ or $t = \dfrac{\beta - b}{2}$.

Second order condition for maximum total tax revenue requires that

$$\frac{d^2T}{dt^2} < 0.$$

But $$\frac{d^2T}{dt^2} = \frac{-1}{(a+\alpha)}.$$

which is always negative, since a and α are both positive. Thus the tax rate t that maximizes the total tax revenue is $t = (\beta - b)/2$.

Example 46 : **The demand and total cost function for a product facing a monopolist are given as $p = 5(2 - x)$ and $C = 10 + 3x^2 - 2x^3$, respectively (the symbols have their usual meaning). Determine the optimum level of price and output for profit maximization. Also determine the effect on price and output of imposition of sales tax of 20%.**

Solution : The revenue function is

$$R = px = (10 - 5x)\,x = 10x - 5x^2.$$

The cost function is

$$C = 10 + 3x^2 - 2x^3.$$

Hence the profit function P is

$$P = R - C$$

$$= (10x - 5x^2) - (10 + 3x^2 - 2x^3)$$

$$= 2x^3 - 8x^2 + 10x - 10,$$

$$\therefore \quad \frac{dP}{dx} = 6x^2 - 16x + 10 = 2(3x - 5)(x - 1).$$

For maximum profit, set

$$\frac{dP}{dx} = 0$$

i.e., $$2\,(3x - 5)\,(x - 1) = 0$$

$$\Rightarrow \quad \text{either } x = \frac{5}{3} \text{ or } x = 1.$$

The stationary points are $x = \frac{5}{3}$ and $x = 1$.

Further $$\frac{d^2P}{dx^2} = 12x - 16$$

When $x = \frac{5}{3}$, $\frac{d^2P}{dx^2} = 4 > 0$

When $x = 1$, $\frac{d^2P}{dx^2} = -4 < 0$,

Second derivative of P is negative when $x = 1$ $\therefore$ profit is maximum when $x = 1$. In order to get value of 'p', substitute this value of x in the demand function.

i.e. $p = (10 - 5x) = 10 - 5(1)$

$p = 5$

Hence optimum price = 5.

Effect of Sales tax on price and output : As already explained, sales tax is levied on the sales proceeds. i.e., on total revenue, therefore sales tax of 20% will amount to

$\frac{20}{100} \times R = \frac{1}{5}(10x - 5x^2) = 2x - x^2$. Therefore, the new total cost is

$$C_N = C + (2x - x^2)$$
$$= (10 + 3x^2 - 2x^3) + (2x - x^2)$$
$$= -2x^3 + 2x^2 + 2x + 10.$$

Therefore, the new profit function is

$$P_N = R - C_N$$
$$= (10x - 5x^2) - (-2x^3 + 2x^2 + 2x + 10)$$
$$= 2x^3 - 7x^2 + 8x - 10$$

In order to get level of output, which maximizes the profit

Set $$\frac{dP_N}{dx} = 0$$

and test for

$$\frac{d^2P_N}{dx^2} < 0$$

We have

$\Rightarrow$ $$\frac{dP_N}{dx} = 6x^2 - 14x + 8 = 2(3x - 4)(x - 1).$$

and $$\frac{d^2P_N}{dx^2} = 12x - 14.$$

For maximum profit, we get

$$\frac{dP_N}{dx} = 0,$$

i.e. $2(3x - 4)(x - 1) = 0$

$\therefore$ either $x = 4/3$ or $x = 1$

when $x = 4/3, \frac{d^2P_N}{dx^2} = 2 > 0,$

When $x = 1$, $\frac{d^2P_N}{dx^2} = -2 < 0$

Therefore, the profit maximizing level of output after the imposition of sales tax of 20% is x = 1, as calculated earlier. The corresponding price p = 5. It can also be observed that there is no effect on price and quantity of an imposition of sales tax of 20%.

Example 47 : **The cost of producing units of TV sets by a monopolist is given by $TC = \frac{x^2}{25} + 3x + 100$ and the demand function is given by $x = 75 - 3p$ (where p is price). If a tax of k per set is imposed by the government, determine the monopolist's output and price under the new situation. Find the value of k that maximizes tax revenue to the government.**

Solution : Given

$$k = \text{tax per set}$$

$\therefore$ New cost $C_N = C + kx$

i.e. $$C_N = C + kx = \frac{x^2}{25} + 3x + 100 + kx$$

The revenue function is given by

$$R = px = \left(25 - \frac{x}{3}\right)x = \left(25x - \frac{x^2}{3}\right).$$

Let P_N denotes the new profit function, then

$$P_N = R - C_N = 25x - \frac{x^2}{3} - \frac{x^2}{25} - 3x - 100 - kx$$

$$= -\frac{25}{75}x^2 + 22x - kx - 100$$

For maximum profit, we set

$$\frac{dP_N}{dx} = 0$$

$$= \frac{d}{dx}\left(-\frac{28}{75}x^2 + 22x - kx\right)$$

$$= -\frac{56}{75}x + 22 - k$$

$$-\frac{56}{75}x + 22 - k = 0$$

$\therefore$ $$x = \frac{75}{56}(22 - k)$$

Also, $$\frac{d^2P_N}{dx^2} = -\frac{56}{75} < 0$$

Therefore, profit is maximum at $x = \frac{75}{56}(22 - k)$ and price is given by, $p = \frac{75}{3} - \frac{x}{3} = 25 - \frac{x}{3}$

$$\therefore \qquad p = 25 - \frac{25}{56}(22 - k) = \frac{425}{28} + \frac{25}{56}k$$

If 'T' denotes the total tax revenue, then

$$T = kx = \frac{75}{56}(22k - k^2)$$

which is to be maximized. For maxima of T

$$\frac{dT}{dk} = 0 \text{ and } \frac{d^2T}{dk^2} < 0$$

Setting $\qquad \dfrac{dT}{dk} = 0$ gives $\dfrac{75}{56}(22 - 2k) = 0 \Rightarrow k = 11.$

Further $\qquad \dfrac{d^2T}{dk^2} = -\dfrac{150}{56} < 0$, (since $\dfrac{d^2T}{dk^2} < 0$, $k = 11$ represent point of maxima)

Hence total tax is maximum at $k = 11$.

Exercise 7.4

1. The demand and the total cost function for a product facing a monopolist are given as : $p = 5(2 - x)$ and $C = 10 + 2x^2 - 2x^3$, respectively. Determine the optimum level of price and output for profit maximization. Also determine the effect on price and output of imposition of sales tax of 20%. [Profit max when $x = 1$, Price = Rs. 5]

2. A monopolist's total cost is $TC = ax^2 + bx + c$ and the demand function is $p = \beta - lx$, where x and p denote the units of output and price respectively and a, b, c, l and β are positive constants. If the government imposes tax at the rate of t per unit of output, show that the total tax is maximum when $t = (\beta - b)/2$.

3. Suppose the demand and total cost functions of a monopolists are $p = 20 - 4x$ and $TC = 4x + 2$ respectively, where p is a price and x is quantity. If the government imposes a tax of 20% of sales, determine the total tax revenue that the government will be able to collect. [75/16]

4. The demand and total cost functions of a monopolist are :

$$p = 12 - 4x,\ C = 8x + x^2 \text{ respectively.}$$

(*i*) Determine the profit maximizing output and price.

(*ii*) If a tax of 't' per unit-output is imposed, find the output and the price that would correspond to the maximum profit of monopolist. What will be maximum profit.

(*iii*) Determine the tax that maximizes the tax revenue and determine the maximum tax revenue.

(*iv*) Find the total tax revenue if the tax is 10% of the sales.

[(*i*) $x = 2/5$, $p = 52/5$ (*ii*) $x = (4 - t)/10$, $p = (52 + 2t)/5$, Max profit $= (4 - t)^2/20$ (*iii*) $t = 2$, max tax revenue $= 2/5$ (*iv*) Total tax revenue $= 868/2645$]

5. Given the demand function $y = 21 - 4x$ and the average cost function $y = 2$ (where y denotes price per unit and x quantity), determine the profit maximising output of a monopolist. What would be the impact of a tax of Rs. t per unit of output on profit?

[Pre tax profit maximising output = 19/8, Post tax = $(19 - t)/8$]

6. The total cost function of a firm is given by $C = \frac{1}{3}x^3 - 5x^2 + 28x + 10$ and the demand function for its product is given by $p = 2530 - 5x$, where p x denote the price and quantity of the product, respectively. A tax at the rate of Rs. 2 per unit of output is imposed which the manufacturer adds to the cost. Determine the level of output after the tax is imposed and show that post tax output is less than the pre-tax output.
[Before tax $x = 50.02$, After tax $x = 50$]

7. A firm under non-perfect competition has the following total cost and demand function.

$$C = 20 + 2x + 3x^2, \; p = 50 - x$$

(*i*) Find the values of p and x that maximizes profit.

(*ii*) An excise tax, is imposed at Rs. 5 per unit. Compare the profit maximizing levels of p and x with those in pre tax situation.

[(*i*) $x = 6$, $p = 44$ (*ii*) $x = 5.375$, $p = 44.625$]

8. A manufacturer has following revenue and cost function

$$R(x) = q^3 - 20q^2 + 500q + 10$$

and $$C(x) = 7q^2 + 260q + 5 \text{ respectively.}$$

Find the level of output which will maximise the profit of the manufacturer. [$q = 8$]

OPTIMAL TRADE — IN TIME

One of the major decision faced by many organisations is to determine the optimal point of time at which the assets shall be replaced. There are two kind of costs associated with the assets.

1. Capital Cost
2. Operating Cost

Capital cost comprises of purchase cost less salvage value and operating cost includes cost of owning and maintaining an asset. With the passage of time, capital cost decreases over a period of time whereas operating cost increases over a period of time. Therefore, average cost comprises of average capital cost and average operating cost, which moves in opposite directions with time. Hence, one should look for that level of time when the sum of these two costs in minimum.

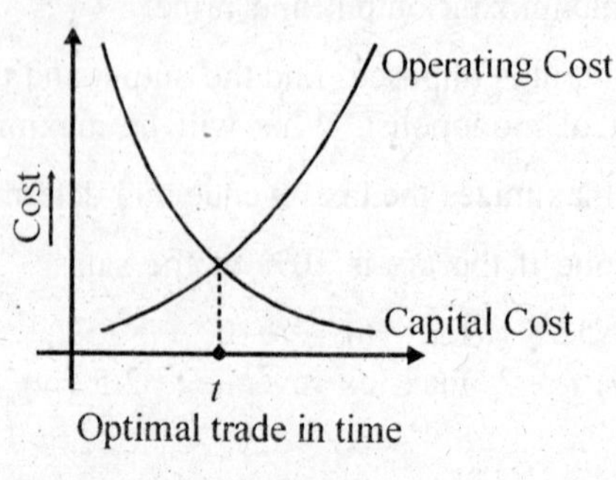

Optimal trade in time

$\therefore$ Average Cost = Average Capital Cost + Average operating cost

We shall differentiate the above function w.r.t. 't' and apply minima conditions to find optimum time of replacement.

Optimal Trade in Time

Example 48 : **The average cost per repair of a scooter is found to be Rs. 50 and the number of repairs is given by $t^{3/2}$, where t is time in months since the purchase of the scooter. The replacement cost is estimated to be Rs. 25000. Find the optimum replacement time.**

Solution.

Let optimum replacement time be 't' months

Total number of repairs = $t^{3/2}$

$$\text{Average number of repairs during time 't'} = \frac{t^{3/2}}{t}$$

Cost per repair = Rs. 50

$$\therefore \text{ Average repairing cost during time } t = \frac{50.t^{3/2}}{t}$$

Cost of replacement = Rs. 25,000

$$\therefore \text{ Average replacement cost per month} = \frac{25000}{t}$$

Average repair and replacement cost per month is given by

$$C(t) = 50\frac{t^{3/2}}{t} + \frac{25000}{t}$$

To find time 't' which minimizes cost

$$\therefore \quad \frac{dC(t)}{dt} = \frac{25}{t^{1/2}} - \frac{25000}{t^2}$$

Put $\frac{dc}{dt} = 0$ to get stationery points

$$\therefore \quad \frac{25}{t^{1/2}} = 1000$$

$$\therefore \quad t^{3/2} = 1000 = 10^3$$

$t^{1/2}$ = 10 (Squaring both the sides, we have)

t = 100 months

$\therefore$ optimum replacement period is t = 100 months.

Example 49: **A piece of machinery cost Rs. 12,000. The total cost of operation from the time of purchase up to time 't' is given by the function $20t^2 + 15t$. If the machine is sold as scrap after t years, the resale value is given by the function $6880 - 60t^2$. Find the optimum time for replacement**

of the machine.

Solution.

Let the machine be replaced after 't' years

Given Original cost = Rs.12,000

Scrap value = $6880 - 60t^2$

$\therefore$ Total Depreciation = $12000 - (6880 - 60t^2)$

$$\therefore \text{ Average Depreciation per year} = \frac{5120+60t^2}{t}$$

$$= \frac{5120}{t} + 60t$$

Total cost of operation = $20t^2 + 15t$

$$\text{Average cost of operation} = \frac{20t^2+15t}{t} = (20t+15)$$

$$\therefore \text{ Total cost} = C(t) = \frac{5120}{t} + 60t + 20t + 15$$

$$= \frac{5120}{t} + 80t + 15$$

Since we want to minimize, total cost, therefore applying minima conditions.

$$\frac{dC}{dt} = -\frac{5120}{t^2} + 80 = 0$$

$$\therefore \qquad t^2 = 64 = 8$$

$$\text{Further } \frac{d^2C}{dt^2} = \frac{10240}{t^3} = \frac{10240}{(8)^3} = 20 > 0$$

$\therefore$ Total cost is minimum when $t = 8$

$\therefore$ optimum time for replacement = 8 years.

Example 50 : **A machine initially costs Rs. 6400 with no scrap value. The cost of operating is Rs. 500 in the first year and increases Rs. 800 in each successive year. Determine,**

(*i*) **the number of years it should be operated for minimising per year average cost;**

(*ii*) **corresponding average cost.**

Solution : Let 'C' be the total cost and 't' be number of years for minimising total cost.

C = Operating Cost + Capital Cost

C = 6400 + [500 + 1300 + 2100 + ... + 't' term

$$= 6400 + \frac{t}{2}[2(500) + (t-1)800]$$ [Using sum of Arithmetic progressio

$$= 6400 + 400\ t^2 + 100t$$

$$\therefore \text{ Average Cost} = \frac{AC}{t} = \frac{6400}{t} + 400t + 100$$

let $y = AC$

$$y = \frac{6400}{t} + 400t + 100$$

Applying Minima conditions

$$\frac{dy}{dt} = 400 - \frac{6400}{t^2} = 0$$

$\therefore$ $t = 4$ years

$$\frac{d^2y}{dt^2} = \frac{12800}{t^3} > 0, \text{ when } t = 4$$

$\therefore$ Hence operating cost is minimum if the machine is operated for 4 years and the corresponding average cost is

$$= \frac{6400}{4} + 400(4) + 100 = \text{Rs. } 3300$$

Example 51 : **The average cost per repair of a car is found to be Rs. 320 and the number of repairs is given by $\frac{1}{2}t^{3/2}$ where 't' is time in months since the purchase of a car. The replacement cost is estimated to be Rs. 80000. Find the optimum replacement period.**

Solution : Let the car be replaced after every 't' months.

The optimum replacement period is given by minimising the average cost, where

Average Cost = Average repair cost + Average Replacement Cost.

$$\text{Average Replacement Cost} = \frac{80000}{t}$$

$$\text{Average repair cost} = \frac{320\left(\frac{1}{2}\right)t^{3/2}}{t}$$

$$\therefore \text{ Average Cost} = C = 160t^{1/2} + \frac{80000}{t}$$

$\therefore$ Differentiating both the sides w.r.t. 't'

$$\frac{dc}{dt} = \frac{80}{t^{1/2}} - \frac{80000}{t^2}$$

Applying Minima Conditions

i.e. $\frac{dc}{dt} = 0$

$$= \frac{80}{t^{1/2}} = \frac{80000}{t^2} = 0$$

$$\therefore \quad \left(t^{3/2}\right) = 1000 = 10^3$$

$$\therefore \quad t^{1/2} = 10$$

Squaring both the sides, we have t = 100

Further,

$$\frac{d^2C}{dt^2} = -\frac{40}{t^{3/2}} + \frac{160000}{t^3} > 0$$

Since second derivative is positive at t = 100 months.

∴ optimum replacement period is 100 months.

INVENTORY CONTROL

There are different type of costs associated with the inventory management. They are briefly discussed below :

1. ***Purchasing Cost :*** It comprises of price to purchase the asset.
2. ***Ordering Cost :*** It is cost incurred for placing the order. It has no relationship with the quantity of items ordered rather it depends on the number of orders placed.
3. ***Carrying Cost :*** It includes cost of maintaining an asset. For example, cost of capital, spoilage etc. If one tends to reduce ordering cost by placing few orders then carrying cost in likely to go up and if one tends to decrease carrying cost, ordering cost goes up as shown below. Therefore, the objective of financial manager is to minimise the sum of these two costs. Purchasing cost has been ignored while developing Economic Order Quantity (EOQ) model because it is constant.

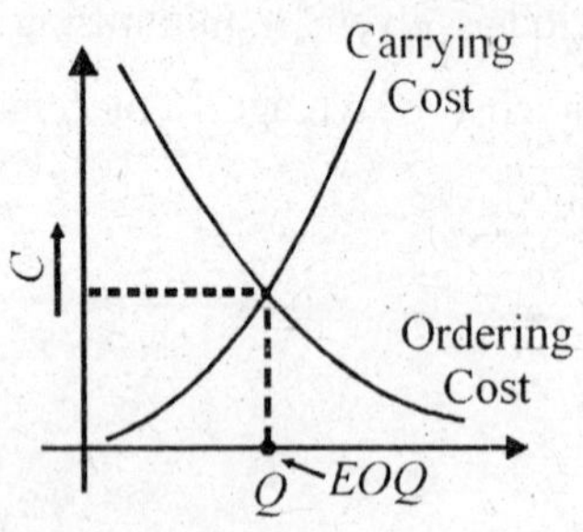

The procedure to derive EOQ is given below :

Let 'A' be the total annual requirement of inventory. If 'Q' inventories are ordered each time.

∴ Number of orders required to be placed in year = $\frac{A}{Q}$

If C_o is the cost per order, then

Annual ordering cost = $\frac{A}{Q}.C_o$

For a given period, the amount of inventory ordered is Q units which gradually decreases to zero level at the end of the period. Thus average inventory may be treated as $\frac{(Q+0)}{2}=\frac{Q}{2}$.

If C_h is the cost of holding in the given period, then annual holding cost $=\frac{Q}{2}C_h$.

$\therefore$ total inventory cost C would be

$$C=\frac{A}{Q}C_o+\frac{Q}{2}C_h$$

To obtain minima in cost,

Calculate $\frac{dC}{dQ}$ and equate it to zero.

$$\frac{dC}{dQ}=-\frac{A}{Q^2}C_o+\frac{C_h}{2}$$

$$\therefore\quad -\frac{A}{Q^2}C_o+\frac{C_h}{2}=0$$

$$Q^2=\frac{2AC_o}{C_h}$$

$$\therefore\quad Q=\sqrt{\frac{2AC_o}{C_h}}$$

Second order condition

$$\frac{d^2C}{dQ^2}=\frac{2AC_o}{Q^3}+0$$

since, second order derivative is positive for any size of order, Q

$\therefore\quad Q=\sqrt{\frac{2AC_o}{C_h}}$ represent point of minima.

Thus, the quantity which minimizes the total cost of maintaining inventory is

$$Q=\sqrt{\frac{2AC_o}{C_h}}$$

Inventory Control

Example 52 : **A company annually produces and sells 6000 units of cards. Sales are uniformly distributed throughout the year. It cost Rs. 30 to set up the machine for operation regardless of the number of units produced in a run. The production cost of each units is Rs. 5 and carrying cost is estimated to be 20% of the value of the average inventory. Find the economic lot size.**

Solution : Let Q be the economic lot size.

Annual requirement = 6000

Number of times machine is required to be set = $\frac{6000}{Q}$

Cost of setting each time = Rs. 30

$\therefore$ Total setting up cost = $\left(\frac{6000}{Q}\right)\times 30$

Carrying cost = $\frac{20}{100}\times$ Average value $=\frac{20}{100}\times 5=1$

Total production cost = 6000 × 5 = 30000

$\therefore$ Total cost = $C=\frac{6000}{Q}(30)+\frac{Q}{2}+30000$

$\therefore$ To find minimum cost, set $\frac{dC}{dQ}=0$

$$\therefore \quad \frac{dC}{dQ}=1\times\frac{1}{2}$$

$$\therefore \quad Q^2=360000\left(\text{Putting } \frac{dC}{dQ}=0\right)$$

$$Q=\sqrt{360000}=600 \text{ unit}$$

Second derivative of 'C' w.r.t. 'θ'

$$=\frac{d^2C}{d\theta^2}=-\frac{360000}{Q^3}$$

Substituting Q = 600 in the second derivative of Q, we will get positive value of the second derivative which means Q = 600 is the economic lot size.

Example 53 **: A firm requires 10,000 units of a material per annum. The cost of purchasing is Re. 1 per unit, the cost of replenishment of stock of material is Rs. 25 and the cost of storing material is 12.5 per cent per annum of the average rupee inventory. Find the optimum order size and the corresponding total cost using calculus.**

Solution : Let the optimum order size be Q units.

Annual demand is 10000 units per year.

$\therefore$ Number of orders per year $=\frac{10000}{Q}$

and hence

Total annual ordering cost $=\frac{10000}{Q}\times 25=\frac{250000}{Q}$

Further

Total annual holding cost = cost of storing per item

× average number of items in stock

$$= (12.5\% \text{ of Re.}1) \times \frac{Q}{2}$$

$$= \frac{125}{1000} \times \frac{Q}{2} = \frac{5Q}{80}$$

Total annual purchasing cost = Total annual demand

× cost of purchasing per item

= 10000 × 1 = 10000

∴ Total annual cost is :

$$C = \frac{250000}{Q} + \frac{5Q}{80} + 10000 \qquad \text{–(1)}$$

Differentiating C w.r.t. Q we obtain

$$\frac{dC}{dQ} = -\frac{250000}{Q^2} + \frac{5}{80}$$

Setting $\frac{dC}{dQ} = 0$ gives $Q^2 = 4000000$ or $Q = 2000$.

Also, $\frac{d^2C}{dQ^2} = \frac{500000}{Q^3}$,

which is positive for $Q = 2000$ and hence C is minimum if the order size is 2000 units. The corresponding cost per annum is obtained by substituting $Q = 2000$ in Eq. (1) :

$$C = \frac{250000}{2000} + \frac{5 \times 2000}{80} + 10000$$

= Rs. 10,250

Example 54 : **A manufacturer has to produce annually 1000 units of a watches that is sold at a uniform rate during the year. The production cost of each unit is Rs. 10 and carrying cost is estimated to be 12.8% of the value of average inventory. Set up cost per production run is Rs. 40. Find the economic lot size.**

Solution. Let Q be the economic lot size.

Annual requirement = 1000

Number of times machine is required to be Set up $= \frac{1000}{Q}$

∴ Total Cost of setting up $= \frac{1000}{Q}(40)$

Total production cost = 10 × 1000 = 10000

Carrying cost per unit $= \frac{12.8}{100} \times 10 = 1.28$

$\therefore$ Total Carrying cost $= 1.28 \times \frac{Q}{2}$

$\therefore$ Total Cost $C = \frac{1000}{Q}(40) + 1.28\frac{Q}{2} + 10000$

To get minimum value of C, set $\frac{dC}{dQ} = 0$

$$\therefore \quad \frac{dC}{dQ} = -\frac{40000}{Q^2} + 0.64 = 0$$

$$\therefore \quad Q = \sqrt{\frac{40000}{0.64}} = \sqrt{62500} = 250 \text{ units}$$

Since $\frac{d^2C}{dQ^2} = +\frac{80000}{Q^3} > 0$, $Q = 250$ unit represent economic lot size.

Example 55 : **A company annually uses 8000 cassettes which are bought at the cost of Rs. 40 each from a supplier. Regardless of the quantity ordered the ordering cost is Rs. 80 per order. The holding cost is estimated to be 20% of the value of average inventory. Determine the order quantity that minimizes total annual cost.**

Solution. Let Q be the order quantity that minimizes total annual cost.

Annual requirement = 8000 units

Number of orders required to be placed $= \frac{8000}{Q}$

$\therefore$ Total ordering cost $= \frac{8000}{Q}(80)$

Holding cost $= \frac{20}{100}$ of average inventory

$$= \frac{20}{100} \times 40 = 8$$

$\therefore$ Total Holding cost $= 8 \times \frac{Q}{2} = \frac{8Q}{2} = 4Q$. (Since $\frac{Q}{2}$ is the average inventory)

Total purchasing cost = 8000 × 40 = 320000

$\therefore$ Total cost $C = \frac{8000}{Q}(80) + 4Q + 320000$

To get minimum value of C, set $\frac{dC}{dQ} = 0$

$$\therefore \quad \frac{dC}{dQ} = -\frac{640000}{Q^2} + 4 = 0$$

$\therefore \quad Q = \sqrt{160000} = 400$

Since $\dfrac{d^2C}{dQ^2} = \dfrac{1280000}{Q^3} > 0$, $\therefore$ Q = 400 units represents point of minima or economic lot size.

***Example 56* : A chemical company acquires its requirement in 20 orders of the size 250 drums each. Each drum costs Rs. 80. The replenishment cost is Rs. 40 irrespective of the order size, and the annual carrying cost is 2% of the average rupee inventory. Find how much can company save if its buys according to economic order quantity using calculus.**

Solution. Let Q be the economic order quantity.

Given Annual Demand : D = 20 × 250 = 5000 units

Purchasing cost : C = Rs. 80 per unit

Ordering cost : C_o = Rs. 40 per order

Holding cost : C_h = (2% of Rs. 80)

= Rs. 1.60 per unit

Substituting the above values in (1), we have

$C(Q)$ = Total ordering cost + Total holding cost + Total purchasing cost

$$= C_o \times \frac{D}{Q} + C_h \times \frac{Q}{2} + c \times D \qquad \text{—(1)}$$

$$= 40 \times \frac{5000}{Q} + 1.60 \times \frac{Q}{2} + 80 \times 5000$$

$$C(Q) = \frac{200000}{Q} + 0.80Q + 400000$$

Differentiating C w.r.t. Q, we obtain

$$\frac{dC}{dQ} = -\frac{200000}{Q^2} + 0.80$$

Setting $\dfrac{dC}{dQ} = 0$ gives $Q^2 = 250000$ or $Q = 500$.

Also $\dfrac{d^2C}{dQ^2} = \dfrac{400000}{Q^3} > 0$.

Since $\dfrac{d^2C}{dQ^2} > 0$, at Q = 500, it implies Q = 500 represent = EOQ.

Determination of Annual Saving

Total cost at EOQ $C(500) = \dfrac{200000}{500} + 0.80(500) + 400000$

$$= \text{Rs. } 400800$$

Total cost under existing policy.

$$C(250) = \frac{200000}{250} + 0.80(250) + 400000$$

$$= \text{Rs. } 401000.$$

Therefore annual saving = Rs. 40100 – Rs. 400800 = Rs. 200.

Example 57 : **Kwality dairy ice-cream Ltd. requires 45000 ice creams every quarter (3 months) based on estimated daily sales of 475 ice creams plus an additional 25 that are consumed by staff members. These ice creams are placed is a packet having capacity to hold 10 ice creams. The manager of the company incurs order charges of Rs. 5 due to handling and delivery for each order. The cost of storing the ice cream is estimated to be 50 paise per box. How many boxes of ice cream should be ordered and how many orders should be placed to minimize the cost of storage and ordering?**

Solution. Let 'Q' be the size of order (number of ice creams)

$$\therefore \quad \text{Total ordering cost } = \left(\frac{45000}{Q}\right).5$$

$$\text{and total carrying cost } = \left(\frac{Q}{2}\right)(0.05)$$

[Since the given product are packets in boxes containing 10 units each and cost of storing is 50 paise per box *i.e.*, 5 paise per ice cream].

$$\therefore \text{ Total cost } C = \left(\frac{45000}{Q}\right).5 + \left(\frac{Q}{z}\right)(0.05)$$

Differentiating both the sides *w.r.t.* 'Q', we have

$$\frac{dC}{dQ} = -\frac{225000}{Q^2} + \frac{0.05}{2}$$

Putting $\frac{dC}{dQ} = 0$ and solving for 'Q' we have

$$Q = 3000$$

Second derivative $\frac{d^2C}{dQ^2} = +\frac{450000}{Q^3}$ is positive for all values of Q, therefore $Q = 3000$ is point of minima.

$\therefore$ Order size for minimizing cost = 3000.

and number of order $= \frac{45000}{3000} = 15.$

Example 58 : **A Television Co. can sell around 2500 television per year. The annual holding cost per T.V. is Rs. 10. To re-order there is a basic Rs. 20 service fee per order plus Rs. 10 insurance charge for each television ordered. What economic lot size should the store re-order to minimise the total inventory cost? Also find the number of orders to be placed.**

Solution : Let Q be the quantity which minimise the total cost.

Given ordering cost = Rs. 20 per order, Annual turnover = 2500

Number of orders to be placed $= \dfrac{2500}{Q}$

$\therefore$ Total ordering cost $= \dfrac{2500}{Q}(20)$

Holding cost per television = Rs. 10

$\therefore$ Total Holding cost = 10 × Average order size

$$= 10 \times \frac{Q}{2}$$

Insurance charge = Rs. 10

$\therefore$ Total cost of Insurance = 2500 × 10 = 25000

$$\therefore \text{ Total Cost} = \frac{2500}{Q}(20) + 10\left(\frac{Q}{2}\right) + 25000$$

To get minimum value of cost,

Set $\dfrac{dC}{dQ} = 0$

$$\frac{dC}{dQ} = -\frac{50,000}{Q^2} + 5 = 0$$

$$\therefore \quad Q = \sqrt{\frac{50000}{5}} = \sqrt{10000}$$

$$\therefore \quad Q = 100$$

$\therefore$ Since $\dfrac{d^2C}{dQ^2} = +\dfrac{100000}{Q^3} > 0, Q = 100$ represent order size that minimizes the total cost,

Number of order $= \dfrac{2500}{100} = 25$

***Example 59 :* A manufacturing firm purchases 2000 units of a particular item per year at a unit cost of Rs. 80. The ordering cost per order is Rs. 50 and the inventory carrying cost is 25% of the value of the average inventory. Find the optimum order quantity and the minimum total cost. If the supplier offers a 5% discount for purchases in lots of 1000, should the offer be accepted?**

Solution : Let Q be the number of units per order.

$\therefore$ Purchasing Cost = 2000 × 80 = 160000

Ordering Cost $= \dfrac{2000}{Q}(50)$

$$\text{Storage Cost } = \frac{Q}{2}\times(80)\times\frac{25}{100} = 10Q$$

$$\therefore \quad \text{Total Cost, } C = \frac{2000}{Q}(50)+10Q+160000$$

Applying Minima Conditions, we have

$$\frac{dC}{dQ} = -\frac{100000}{Q^2}+10$$

Put $\dfrac{dC}{dQ} = 0 \quad \therefore Q^2 = 10000$

i.e. $Q = 100$

Second order condition

$$\frac{d^2C}{dQ^2} = \frac{200000}{Q^3} > 0$$

Since $\dfrac{d^2C}{dQ^2} > 0$ at $Q = 100$ $\therefore Q = 100$ represent economic lot size.

$$\text{Total cost} = \frac{2000}{100}(50)+10(100)+160000$$

$$= 1000 + 1000 + 160000 = 162000$$

When discount of 5% is offered, we have

$$\text{Purchase price } = 80-\left(\frac{5}{100}\times 80\right) = 76, \text{ Also } Q = 1000 \text{ units (given)}$$

$$\therefore \quad \text{Total cost} = \frac{2000}{1000}(50)+\left(\frac{1000}{2}\times 76\times\frac{25}{100}\right)+(2000\times 76)$$

$$= 100 + 9500 + 152000$$

$$= 161600$$

Since, total cost in case of discount is less than total cost in case of *EOQ,* therefore, discount shall be availed.

Example 60: **A firm produces 36,000 items per year. It costs Rs. 250 to make the machine run regardless of the number (x) of items produced in a run. The cost of storage is 50 paise per item per year of average inventory ($x/2$) in hand. The cost of material per item is Rs. 5. Find the economic lot size x.**

Solution : The firm is producing 36,000 items per year at the rate of x items per run, therefore the number of production runs per year is $\dfrac{36000}{x}$.

$$\therefore \text{ Total annual set up cost } = \frac{36000}{x}\times 250 = \frac{9000000}{x}$$

We have

Total annual storage cost = cost of storing per item × average number of items in stock

$$= 0.50 \times \frac{x}{2} = 0.25x$$

Total annual material cost = total annual production × cost of material per item

$$= 36000 \times 5 = 180000$$

Therefore the total annual will be given as

$$C = \frac{9000000}{x} + 0.25x + 180000$$

Differentiating C w.r.t. x, we obtain

$$\frac{dC}{dx} = -\frac{9000000}{x^2} + 0.25$$

Setting $\frac{dC}{dx} = 0$ gives $x^2 = 36000000$ or $x = 6000$.

Also, $\frac{d^2C}{dx^2} = \frac{18000000}{x^3} > 0$ for $x = 6000$. This implies C is minimum if the lot size is 6000 units.

Exercise 7.5

1. A firm requires 10000 units of a material per annual. The cost of purchasing is Re 1 per unit, the cost of replacements of stock of material is Rs. 25 and the cost of storing material is 12.5 percent per annum of the average rupee inventory. Find the optimum order size and the corresponding total cost using calculus. [q = 2000, TC = 10250]

2. A bicycle manufacturer buys 6000 tyres in a year from a distributor. The ordering cost is Rs. 20 per order, the storage cost is 96 paise per tyre per year. Each tyre cost Rs. 25. Suppose that the tyres are used at a constant rate throughout the year. Using calculus, find EOQ. If the tyre requirement increases fourfold and other conditions remain the same, what will be new EOQ. [old EOQ = 500, New EOQ = 1000]

3. A firm requires 2000 units of a material per annum. The cost of ordering is Rs. 10 per order and carrying cost is 4% of the purchase price. If the purchase price is Rs. 100 per units, find EOQ. [EOQ = 100 units]

4. A firm has annual demand of 1000 units. The cost of placing on order is Rs. 40 per order. The holding cost is 4% of the purchase price. If the purchase price is Rs. 50, find the economic lot size. [EOQ = 200 units]

5. A firm has to produce 1,44,000 units of an item per year. The cost of material is Rs. 5 per unit and cost of storing is 50 paise per item per year on the average inventory $x/2$ in hand. If it costs Rs. 90 to make the factory ready for a production run, irrespective of the units x produced in one run, find the economic lot size x. [x = 7200]

8

Partial Differentiation – Concepts

HIGHLIGHTS OF THE CHAPTER

- Introduction
- Partial Derivatives
- Second Order Partial Derivative
- Homogeneous Functions and Euler's Theorem
- Euler's Theorem
- Derivative of an Implicit Function
- Maxima and Minima of Functions of Two Variable

INTRODUCTION

In our previous chapter, we have dealt with the situation where a given function is dependent upon only one variable.

However, in actual situation, we may come across with the cases where a given function is dependent on more than one variable. For example, the cost of production of any commodity depends not only on cost of raw material but also on other factors such as labour, cost of capital, rent etc. Partial differentiation helps in studying such relations.

PARTIAL DERIVATIVES

Generally, in business and economic problems, we are interested in studying the relationship between the dependent and independent variable keeping other independent variables as constant. For example, we may be interested in finding rate of increase in cost of product and cost of labour keeping other factors of production as constant. In such cases, we should use partial differentiation.

i.e., if $z = f(x, y)$

Partial differentiation of z *w.r.t.* x will be calculated presuming y as constant.

$$\therefore \quad \frac{\partial z}{\partial x} = f_x(x, y) \qquad [y \text{ as constant}]$$

Likewise, when partial differentiation of z will be calculated *w.r.t.* y, x will be presumed constant.

$$\therefore \quad \frac{\partial z}{\partial y} = f_y(x, y) \qquad [x \text{ as constant}]$$

The concept of partial differentiation can be understood from the following example.

Example 1 : **Find the first order partial derivatives of the following functions.**

(*a*) $3x^2y + xy + 2x$ (*b*) $x^3y + y^2x^2 + 3xy + 5y$. (*c*) Log $(3x^2 + 2x)$

Solution : (*a*) Let

$$z = 3x^2y + xy + 2x$$

∴ Partial differential of z *w.r.t.* x will be given

as $$\frac{\partial z}{\partial x} = 6xy + y + 2$$ (*i.e.*, we have presumed '*y*' as constant)

Partial differentiation of z *w.r.t.* y will be given

as $$\frac{\partial z}{\partial y} = 3x^2 + x + 0$$ (*i.e.*, we have presumed '*x*' as constant)

(*b*) Let $$z = x^3 y + y^2x^2 + 3xy + 5y$$

Partial differentiation of Z *w.r.t.* x will be

$$\frac{\partial z}{\partial x} = \frac{\partial}{\partial x}\left(x^3 y + y^2 x^2 + 3xy + 5y\right)$$

$$= (3x^2y + 2xy^2 + 3y)$$ (since y is presumed as constant)

∴ Partial differential of Z *w.r.t.* y will be given as

as $$\frac{\partial z}{\partial y} = \frac{\partial}{\partial y}\left(x^3 y + y^2 x^2 + 3xy + 5y\right)$$

$$= x^3 + 2yx^2 + 3x + 5$$ (Since x is presumed as constant)

(*c*) Log $(3x^2 + 2y)$

Given $$z = \log (3x^2 + 2y)$$

∴ Partial differentiation z *w.r.t.* x will be

$$\frac{\partial z}{\partial x} = \frac{\partial}{\partial x}\left[\log\left(3x^2 + 2y\right)\right]$$

$$= \frac{1}{\left(3x^2 + 2y\right)}.(6x + 0) = \frac{(6x + 0)}{\left(3x^2 + 2y\right)}$$

$$\therefore \quad \frac{\partial z}{\partial x} = \frac{6x}{\left(3x^2 + y\right)}$$

Partial differentiation of z *w.r.t.* y will be

$$\frac{\partial z}{\partial y} = \frac{\partial}{\partial y}\left[\log\left(3x^2 + 2y\right)\right]$$

$$= \frac{1}{\left(3x^2 + 2y\right)} \times 2 = \frac{2}{\left(3x^2 + 2y\right)}$$

Total Differential

If $Z = f(x, y)$ is a function of two variable x and y, then

$$dz = \frac{\partial z}{\partial x}.dx + \frac{\partial z}{\partial y}.dy$$

is called total differential of the function z at (x, y).

Example 2: Given $z = x^2 + y^2 + 2xy$

Solution

$$\therefore \quad \frac{\partial z}{\partial x} = 2x + 2y$$

$$\frac{\partial z}{\partial y} = 2y + 2x$$

$$\therefore \quad dz = (2x + 2y) \ . \ dx + (2x + 2y) \ . \ dy.$$

SECOND ORDER PARTIAL DERIVATIVE

The second order partial derivative are derivatives of first order derivatives. However, in case of second order derivatives, we can have successive differentiation as well as mixed or cross partial derivative.

Let $z = f(xy)$

$\therefore$ First order derivatives will be

$$\frac{\partial z}{\partial x} = f_x \quad \text{[Keeping } y \text{ as constant]}$$

$$\frac{\partial z}{\partial y} = f_y \quad \text{[Keeping } x \text{ as constant]}$$

Second order derivatives would be

$$\frac{\partial^2 z}{\partial x^2} = f_{xx} \quad \text{[Keeping } y \text{ as constant]}$$

$$\frac{\partial^2 z}{\partial y \partial x} = f_{yx} \quad \text{[Keeping } x \text{ as constant while taking second derivative of } \frac{\partial z}{\partial x} \text{ w.r.t. } y\text{]}$$

$$\frac{\partial^2 z}{\partial y^2} = f_{yy} \quad \text{[Keeping } x \text{ as constant]}$$

$$\frac{\partial^2 z}{\partial x \partial y} = f_{xy} \quad \text{[Keeping } y \text{ as constant while taking second derivative of } \frac{\partial z}{\partial y} \text{ w.r.t. } x\text{]}$$

Here, $\frac{\partial^2 z}{\partial y \partial z}$ and $\frac{\partial^2 z}{\partial x \partial y}$ are cross or mixed partial derivatives whereas $\frac{\partial^2 z}{\partial x^2}$ and $\frac{\partial^2 z}{\partial y^2}$ are successive differentiation.

This would become more clear from the following example.

Example 2(a) : **Given $z = 5x^2y^3 + 3x^2y + x^3$. Find second order partial derivatives.**

Solution : $$z = 5x^2y^3 + 3x^2y + x^2$$

$$\therefore \quad \frac{\partial z}{\partial x} = 10xy^3 + 6xy + 3x^2$$

and $$\frac{\partial z}{\partial y} = 15x^2y^3 + 3x^2 + 0$$

Second order derivative will be

$$\frac{\partial^2 z}{\partial x^2} = \frac{\partial}{\partial x}\left(10xy^3 + 6xy + 3x^2\right) = 10y^3 + 6y + 6x$$

$$\frac{\partial}{\partial y}\left(\frac{\partial z}{\partial x}\right) = \frac{\partial}{\partial y}\left(10xy^3 + 6xy + 3x^2\right) = 30y^2 + 6x + 0$$

$$\therefore \quad \frac{\partial^2 z}{\partial y \partial x} = 30xy^2 + 6x.$$

Second order derivatives $\frac{\partial z}{\partial y}$ will be

$$\frac{\partial^2 z}{\partial y^2} = \frac{\partial}{\partial y}\left(15x^2y^2 + 3x^2 + 0\right) = 30x^2y$$

$$\therefore \quad \frac{\partial}{\partial x}\left(\frac{\partial z}{\partial y}\right) = \frac{\partial}{\partial x}\left(15x^2y^2 + 3x^2\right) = 30xy^2 + 6x$$

$$\frac{\partial^2 z}{\partial x \partial y} = 30xy^2 + 6x.$$

Example 2(b) : **Find the first and second order total differentials of the function**

$$z = f(x, y) = 7y \log (1 + x).$$

Solution : We have

$$f_x = \frac{\partial z}{\partial x} = \frac{7y}{1 + x},$$

$$f_x = \frac{\partial z}{\partial y} = 7 \log (1 + x)$$

Thus the first order total differential of z will be

$$dz = f_x\, dx + f_y\, dy$$

$$= \frac{7y}{1 + x} dy + 7 \log (1 + x)\, dy.$$

Also $$f_{xx} = \frac{\partial^2 z}{ax^2} = \frac{7y}{(1 + x)^2}$$

$$f_{xy} = \frac{\partial^2 z}{\partial y \partial x} = \frac{7}{1+x}$$

$$f_{yy} = \frac{\partial^2 z}{\partial y^2} = 0.$$

Therefore the second-order total differential of z will be

$$d^2z = f_{xx}\,(dx)^2 + 2f_{xy}\,dx\,dy + f_{yy}\,(dy)^2$$

$$= -\frac{7y}{(1+x)^2}(dx)^2 + 2\left(\frac{7}{1+x}\right)dx\,dy + (0)(dy)^2$$

$$= -\frac{7y}{(1+x)^2}(dx)^2 + \frac{14}{(1+x)}dx\,dy.$$

Example 2(c) : **Calculate the first and second order total differentials :**

$$\boldsymbol{Z = 3x^2 + xy - 2y^2}$$

Solution :

$$Z = 3x^2 + xy - 2y^2$$

$$\frac{\partial Z}{\partial x} = 6x + y \quad \text{and} \quad \frac{\partial Z}{\partial y} = x - 4y$$

The first-order total differential of Z will be

$$dZ = \frac{\partial Z}{\partial x}dx + \frac{\partial Z}{\partial y}dy$$

$$= (6x + y)\,dx + (x - 4y)\,dy.$$

Further,

$$\frac{\partial^2 Z}{\partial x^2} = 6, \quad \frac{\partial^2 Z}{\partial x \partial y} = 1, \quad \frac{\partial^2 Z}{\partial y^2} = -4$$

The second-order total differential of Z will be

$$d^2Z = \frac{\partial^2 Z}{\partial x^2}(dx)^2 + 2\frac{\partial^2 Z}{\partial x \partial y}dxdy + \frac{\partial^2 Z}{\partial y^2}(dy)^2$$

$$= 6(dx)^2 + 2dxdy - 4(dy)^2.$$

HOMOGENEOUS FUNCTIONS AND EULER'S THEOREM

Definition : Any function $z = f(x, y)$ is said to be homogeneous function. if

$$f(\lambda x, \lambda y) = \lambda^n f(x, y)$$

where λ = real number

and n = degree of homogeneous function.

For example,

if $f(x, y) = 3x^3y + x^4 + 2x^2y^2 + 6y^3x;$

then $f(\lambda x, \lambda y) = 3(\lambda x)^3 (\lambda y) + (\lambda x)^4 + 2(\lambda x)^2 (\lambda y)^2 + 6(\lambda y)^3(\lambda x)$

$= 3\lambda^3x^3\lambda y + \lambda^4x^4 + 2\lambda^2x^2\lambda^2y^2 + 6\lambda^3y^3\lambda x$

$= \lambda^4(3x^3y + x^4 + 2x^2y^2 + 6y^2x)$

i.e., $f(\lambda x, \lambda y) = \lambda^4 f(x, y)$

Example 3 **: Find the degree of homogeneous function in the following cases.**

(*i*) $\sqrt{3x^2 + 2axy + 5y^2}$ **(*ii*)** $5x^2y^2 + 3y^2x + y^4$ **(*iii*)** $(5x^{-5} + 6y^{-5})^{-1/5}$

Solution : (*i*) we have

$$f(x, y) = \sqrt{3x^2 + 2axy + 5y^2}$$

$$\therefore \quad f(\lambda x, \lambda y) = \sqrt{3(\lambda x)^2 + 2a\ \lambda x\lambda y + 5(\lambda y)^2}$$

$$= \sqrt{3\lambda^2 x^2 + 2a\lambda^2 xy + 5\lambda^2 y^2}$$

$$= \sqrt{\lambda^2\left(3x^2 + 2axy + 5y^2\right)}$$

$$= \lambda\sqrt{3x^2 + 2axy + 5y^2} = \lambda\ f(x, y)$$

$$\therefore \quad f(\lambda x, \lambda y) = \lambda^1 f(x, y)$$

Hence degree of homogenous function is 1.

(*ii*) We have

$$f(x, y) = 5x^2y^2 + 3y^3x + y^4$$

$$\therefore \quad f(\lambda x, \lambda y) = 5(\lambda x)^2 (\lambda y)^2 + 3(\lambda y)^3 (\lambda x) + (\lambda y)^4$$

$$= 5\lambda^2x^2\ \lambda^2y^2 + 3\ \lambda^3y^3\ \lambda x + \lambda^4y^4$$

$$= \lambda^4\ (5x^2y^2 + 3y^3x + y^4)$$

$$= \lambda^4\ f(x, y)$$

Hence, degree of homogenous function is 14.

$$f(x, y) = (5x^{-5} + 6y^{-5})^{-1/5}$$

$$\therefore \quad f(\lambda x, \lambda y) = [5(\lambda x)^{-5} + 6(\lambda y)^{-5}]^{-1/5}$$

$$= [5\lambda^{-5}x^{-5} + 6\lambda^{-5}\ y^{-5}]^{-1/5}$$

$$= (\lambda^{-5})^{-1/5}\ [5x^{-5} + 6y^{-5}]^{-1/5}$$

$$= \lambda^1\ [5x^{-5} + 6y^{-5}]^{-1/5}$$

$$= \lambda\ f(x, y)$$

Hence degree of homogenous function is 1.

EULER'S THEOREM

If $z = f(x, y)$ is a homogeneous function in x and y of degree n, then

$$x\frac{\partial z}{\partial x} + y\frac{\partial z}{\partial y} = nz.$$

Proof. Since $z = f(x, y)$ is a homogeneous function of degree n, we can write

$$f(\lambda x, \lambda y) = \lambda^n f(x, y) \text{ for all } \lambda.$$

Substituting $\lambda = \frac{1}{x}$ in the above equation, we get

$$f\left(1, \frac{y}{x}\right) = \frac{1}{x^n} f(x, y) \text{ or } f(x, y) = x^n f\left(1, \frac{y}{x}\right).$$

Since $f\left(1, \frac{y}{x}\right)$ is a function of $\frac{y}{x}$ only, we can also write it as $\Phi\left(\frac{y}{x}\right)$.

$$\therefore \quad f(x, y) = x^n\, \Phi\left(\frac{y}{x}\right) \text{ or } x^n\, \Phi\left(\frac{y}{x}\right)$$

Now
$$\frac{\partial z}{\partial x} = x^n\, \Phi'\left(\frac{y}{x}\right) \cdot \left(\frac{-y}{x^2}\right) + nx^{n-1}\, \Phi\left(\frac{y}{x}\right)$$

$$= -x^{n-2}\, y\, \Phi'\left(\frac{y}{x}\right) + nx^{n-1}\, \Phi\left(\frac{y}{x}\right)$$

Also
$$\frac{\partial z}{\partial y} = x^n\, \Phi'\left(\frac{y}{x}\right) \cdot \frac{1}{x} = x^{n-1}\, \Phi'\left(\frac{y}{x}\right).$$

Therefore

$$x\frac{\partial z}{\partial x} + y\frac{\partial z}{\partial y} = x\left[-x^{n-2} y\, \Phi'\left(\frac{y}{x}\right) + n\, x^{n-1}\, \Phi\left(\frac{y}{x}\right)\right] + y\, x^{n-1} \Phi'\left(\frac{y}{x}\right)$$

$$= -x^{n-1} y\, \Phi'\left(\frac{y}{x}\right) + n\, x^n\, \Phi\left(\frac{y}{x}\right) + y\, x^{n-1} \Phi'\left(\frac{y}{x}\right)$$

$$= n\, x^n\, \Phi\left(\frac{y}{x}\right)$$

$$= nz.$$

Hence $x\frac{\partial z}{\partial x} + y\frac{\partial z}{\partial y} = nz.$

Example 4 : **If $z = f(x, y)$ is a homogeneous function in x and y of degree n, then**

$$x^2 \frac{\partial^2 z}{\partial x^2} + 2xy\frac{\partial^2 z}{\partial x \partial y} + y^2 \frac{\partial^2 z}{\partial y^2} = n(n-1)\, z.$$

Solution : Given z is a homogeneous function of degree n, we have by Euler's theorem.

$$x\frac{\partial z}{\partial x} + y\frac{\partial z}{\partial y} = nz \qquad \text{...(1)}$$

Differentiating (1) *w.r.t.* x treating y as a constant, we get

$$x\frac{\partial^2 z}{\partial x^2} + \frac{\partial z}{\partial x} + y\frac{\partial^2 z}{\partial x\partial y} = n\frac{\partial z}{\partial x}$$

$$x\frac{\partial^2 z}{\partial x^2} + y\frac{\partial^2 z}{\partial x\partial y} = (n-1)\frac{\partial z}{\partial x} \quad ...(2)$$

Now, differentiating (1) *w.r.t.* y treating x as a constant, we get

$$x\frac{\partial^2 z}{\partial x\partial y} + y\frac{\partial^2 z}{\partial y^2} + \frac{\partial z}{\partial y} = n\frac{\partial z}{\partial y}$$

$$x\frac{\partial^2 z}{\partial x\partial y} + y\frac{\partial^2 z}{\partial y^2} = (n-1)\frac{\partial z}{\partial y} \quad ...(3)$$

Multiply (2) by x and (3) by y and then add, we have

$$x^2\frac{\partial^2 z}{\partial x^2} + xy\frac{\partial^2 z}{\partial x\partial y^2} + xy\frac{\partial^2 z}{\partial x\partial y} + y^2\frac{\partial^2 z}{\partial y^2} = (n-1)\times\left[x\frac{\partial z}{\partial x} + y\frac{\partial z}{\partial y}\right]$$

or $$x^2\frac{\partial^2 z}{\partial x^2} + 2xy\frac{\partial^2 z}{\partial x\partial y} + y^2\frac{\partial^2 z}{\partial y^2} = n(n-1)z \text{ by using (1).}$$

Hence degree of homogenous function is 4.

Example 5 : **Verify Euler's Theorem in case of following function**

(*i*) $Z = x^2 + y^2$ **(*ii*)** $Z = ax^{\lambda} y^{1-\lambda}$

(*iii*) $Z = xe^{y/x}$ **(*iv*)** $Z = ax^2y^3$

Solution : (*i*) Given $Z = x^2 + y^2$

In order to verify Euler's Theorem, first of all we are required to find the degree of the homogenous function.

$$f(\lambda x, \lambda y) = (\lambda x)^2 + (\lambda y)^2 + \lambda^2x^2 + \lambda^2y^2$$
$$= \lambda^2(x^2 + y^2) = \lambda^2 f(x, y)$$

∴ Degree of the given homogenous function is 2.

∴ According to Euler theorem, we should have

$$x\frac{\partial z}{\partial x} + y\frac{\partial z}{\partial y} = nz$$

∴ $$\frac{\partial z}{\partial x} = \frac{\partial}{\partial y}\left(x^2 + y^2\right) = 2x$$

∴ $$\frac{\partial z}{\partial x} = \frac{\partial}{\partial y}\left(x^2 + y^2\right) = 2y$$

∴ $$x\,.\,(2x) + y(2y) = 2x^2 + 2y^2 = 2(x^2 + y^2) = 2Z.$$

Hence proved.

(*ii*) $Z = ax^{\lambda}\, y^{1-\lambda}$

$$f(\lambda x, \lambda y) = a(\lambda x)^{\lambda}\, (\lambda y)^{1-\lambda}$$
$$= a\, \lambda^{\lambda} x^{\lambda}\, \lambda^{(1-\lambda)}\, y^{(1-\lambda)}$$
$$= \lambda^{\lambda+1-\lambda}\, .\, a\, x^{1}\, y^{(1-\lambda)}$$
$$= \lambda\, f(x, y)$$

∴ Degree of the homogeneous function is one. According to Euler's Theorem.

$$x\frac{\partial z}{\partial x} + y\,.\frac{\partial z}{\partial y} = nz \qquad \text{(where } n = 1 \text{ in this case)} - (1)$$

$$\therefore \qquad \frac{\partial z}{\partial x} = \lambda a x^{\lambda-1} y^{1-\lambda}$$

$$\frac{\partial z}{\partial y} = (1-\lambda)\, a x^{\lambda} y^{(1-\lambda-1)}$$
$$= (1-\lambda)\, a x^{\lambda}\, y^{-\lambda}$$

Substituting these values in (1), we have

$$x\,(\lambda a x^{\lambda-1}\, y^{1-\lambda}) + y\,.\,[(1-l)\, a x^{l}\, y^{-l}] = 1(Z)$$
$$= \lambda a x^{\lambda}\, y^{1-\lambda} + (1-\lambda)\, a\, x^{\lambda}\, y^{(1-\lambda)}$$
$$= (\lambda + 1 - \lambda)\, a x^{\lambda}\, y^{1-\lambda} = 1\,.\, a x^{\lambda}\, y^{1-\lambda} = n.Z.$$

(*iii*) $Z = xe^{y/x}$

$$f(\lambda x, \lambda y) = (\lambda x)\, e^{(Ly/Lx)}$$
$$= \lambda\, x\, e^{y/x} = \lambda\, f(x, y)$$

∴ Degree of homogenous function is one.

$$\therefore \qquad \frac{\partial z}{\partial y} = e^{y/x} - \frac{xye^{y/x}}{x^{2}} = e^{y/x} - \frac{ye^{y/x}}{x}$$

$$\frac{\partial z}{\partial y} = xe^{y/x}.\left(\frac{1}{x}\right) = e^{y/x}$$

According to Euler Theorem.

$$\therefore \qquad x\,.\frac{\partial z}{\partial y} + y\,.\frac{\partial z}{\partial y} = n.z$$

$$\therefore \qquad x\left(e^{y/x} - \frac{ye^{y/x}}{x}\right) + y.\left(e^{y/x}\right) = 1.(z)$$

$$\therefore \qquad x\, e^{y/x} - ye^{y/x} + ye^{y/x} = xe^{y/x}$$

Hence Proved.

(*iv*) $\qquad Z = ax^{2}y^{3}$

$$\therefore \qquad f(\lambda x, \lambda y) = a(\lambda x)^{2}\, (\lambda y)^{3} = a\, \lambda^{2}x^{2}\lambda^{3}y^{3} = \lambda^{5}ax^{2}y^{3}$$

$\therefore$ degree of homogenous function is 5.

According to Euler's Theorem.

$$x.\left(\frac{\partial z}{\partial x}\right) + y.\frac{\partial z}{\partial y} = 5z \qquad \text{(Since } n = 5 \text{ in this case)}$$

$$\therefore \quad \frac{\partial z}{\partial x} = 2axy^3 \qquad \frac{\partial z}{\partial y} = 3ax^2y^2$$

$$\therefore \quad = x\,(2axy^3) + y\,(3ax^2y^2)$$

$$= 2ax^2y^3 + 3ax^2y^3 = 5ax^2y^3 = 5z$$

Hence Proved.

DERIVATIVE OF AN IMPLICIT FUNCTION

A function in which y is not directly expressed in terms of x, is known as implicit function of x and y.

In order to find derivative, $\frac{dy}{dx}$ of such functions, we proceed in the following manner:

Let $\quad z = f(x, y)$, where $z = 0$ for all (x, y)

$$\therefore \quad dz = \frac{\partial z}{\partial x}.dx + \frac{\partial z}{\partial y}.dy \text{ or}$$

Since $\quad z = 0$ for all (x, y)

$$\therefore \quad dz = 0$$

Thus,

$$\frac{\partial z}{\partial x}.dx + \frac{\partial z}{\partial y}.dy = 0$$

$$= fx\,.\,dx + fy\,.\,dy = 0$$

$$\therefore \quad \frac{dy}{dx} = -\frac{fx}{fy}.$$

***Example 6* : Find $\frac{dy}{dx}$ for the following implicit function :**

(*i*) $x^3 + y^3 - 2x^2y = 0$ $\qquad$ **(*ii*) $x^y + y^x - a^b$**

***Solution* :** (*i*) $f(x, y) = x^3 + y^3 - 2x^2y$

$$fx = \frac{\partial f}{\partial x} = 3x^2 - 4xy$$

$$fy = \frac{\partial f}{\partial y} = 3y^2 - 2x^2$$

$$\therefore \quad \frac{dy}{dx} = -\frac{fx}{fy} = -\frac{\left(3x^2 - 4xy\right)}{\left(3y^2 - 2x^2\right)}$$

(*ii*) Let $f(x, y) = x^y + y^x - a^b = 0$

$$\therefore \quad \frac{\partial f}{\partial x} = fx = yx^{y-1} + y^x \log y$$

$$\frac{\partial f}{\partial y} = fy = x^y \log x + xy^{x-1}$$

$$\therefore \quad \frac{dy}{dx} = -\frac{fx}{fy} = \frac{\left(yx^{y-1} + y^x \log y\right)}{\left(x^y \log x + xy^{x-1}\right)}$$

MAXIMA AND MINIMA OF FUNCTIONS OF TWO VARIABLE

In order to find maxima and minima of a given function $z = f(x, y)$, the following steps shall be followed.

1. Find $f_x(x, y)$ and $f_y(x, y)$
2. Find the critical points by solving.

$$f_x(x, y) = 0$$

and $$f_y(x, y) = 0$$

Let (a, b) be a critical point :

3. Find $f_{xx}(x, y)$, $f_{xy}(x, y)$ and $f_{yy}(x, y)$
4. Let $A = f_{xx}(a, b)$, $B = f_{xy}(a, b)$ and $C = f_{yy}(a, b)$,
5. (*i*) If $AC - B^2 > 0$ and $A < 0$, f has a relative maximum at (a, b).

   (*ii*) If $AC - B^2 > 0$ and $A > 0$, f has a relative minimum at (a, b).

   (*iii*) If $AC - B^2 < 0$, f has a saddle point at (a, b).

   (*iv*) If $AC - B = 0$, the test fails and further analysis is needed.

The concept of maxima and minima would become more clear from the following examples.

***Example 7 :* Find the relative maxima and minima in the following cases**

(*i*) $f(x, y) = x^2 + y^2 - 3y$ **(*ii*) $f(x, y) = x^2 + 3y^2 + 4x - 9y + 7$**

Solution : Given

$$z = f(x, y) = x^2 + y^2 - 3y$$

$$\therefore \quad \frac{\partial z}{\partial x} = 2x \quad \frac{\partial z}{\partial y} = 2y - 3$$

$$\therefore \quad fx = 2x \quad fy = 2y - 3$$

Put $fx = 0$ and $fy = 0$ to find critical points.

$$\therefore \quad fx = 2x = 0 \quad fy = 2y - 3 = 0$$

$$\therefore \quad x = 0 \quad y = 3/2$$

$\therefore$ Critical point is $(0, 3/2)$

At (0, 3/2)

$\therefore \quad f_{xx}$ (0, 3/2) = 2 = A

f_{yy} (0, 3/2) = 2 = C

$$f_{xy} = \frac{\partial^2 z}{\partial y \partial x} = \frac{\partial}{\partial y} = (2x) = 0 = B$$

$\therefore \quad AC - B^2 = (2 \times 2) - (0)^2 = 4 - 0 = 0$

$\therefore \quad AC - B^2 > 0$ and $A > 0 \quad \therefore f$ has

relative minima at (0, 3/2).

(*iii*) Given

$$Z = x^2 + 3y^2 + 4x - 9y + 7$$

$$f_x = \frac{\partial z}{\partial x} = 2x + 4$$

and $\quad f_x = \dfrac{\partial z}{\partial y} = 6y - 9$

Put $fx = 0$ and $fy = 0$ to get critical points

$\therefore$ We have

$$fx = 2x + 4 = 0 \text{ and } fy = 6y - 9 = 0$$

$$\therefore \quad x = -2 \quad \therefore y = \frac{3}{2}$$

Critical Point is (–2, 3/2)

$\therefore$ At the critical point, we have

$$f_{xx} = \frac{\partial z}{\partial x}\left(\frac{\partial z}{\partial x}\right) = 2$$

$$f_{yy} = \frac{\partial z}{\partial y}\left(\frac{\partial z}{\partial y}\right) = 6$$

$$f_{xy} = \frac{\partial}{\partial y}\left(\frac{\partial z}{\partial x}\right) = 0$$

$\therefore \quad A = 2, B = 0$ and $C = 6$

$AC - B^2 = (2)(6) - (0)^2 = 12$

Since $AC - B^2 > 0$ and $A > 0$

$\therefore f$ has relative minima at (–1, 3/2)

Exercise 8.1

Q. 1 Find $\frac{\partial z}{\partial x}$ and $\frac{\partial z}{\partial y}$ in each of the following cases.

(i) $Z = x^2 + y^2 + 5xy$ (ii) $Z = 2x^2 + 3xy^2$

(iii) $Z = 5x^2 + 2y^2 + 3y$ (iv) $Z = x^3 + y^2 + 5x^3y^2$.

$$\begin{bmatrix} (i)\, f_x = 2x + 5y,\ f_y = 2y + 5x & (ii)\, f_x = 4x + 3y^2,\ f_y = 6xy \\ (iii)\, f_x = 10x,\ f_y = 4y + 3 & (iv)\, f_x = 3x^2 + 15x^2y^2,\ f_y = 2y + 10x^3y \end{bmatrix}$$

Q. 2 Find the degree of homogeneity of each of the following functions.

(i) $Z = \sqrt{ax^2 + by^2 + 2hxy}$ (ii) $Z = \frac{(ax^2 + by^2 + 2hxy)}{cx + dy}$

[(i) 1; (ii) 1]

Q. 3 Verify Euler theorem in the following cases

(i) $Z = x^2 + 2xy - y^2$

(ii) $U = \log (x^3 + y^3 + z^3 - 3xyz)$

(iii) $U = \frac{xy}{(x + y)}$

(iv) $U = \log\left(\frac{x^2 + y^2}{x + y}\right)$

(v) $Z = \frac{x^2 + y^2}{(x + y)}$

9

Applications of Partial Differentiation

HIGHLIGHTS OF THE CHAPTER

- **Introduction**
- **Demand Analysis**
- **Partial Elasticities of Demand**
- **Application of Partial Differentiation**
- **The Production Function**
- **Linear Homogeneous Production Function**
- **Cobb–Douglas Production Function**
- **Important Features of the Function**
- **Marginal Rate of Technical Subsitution (MRTS)**
- **Optimization Problems**
- **Discriminating Monopoly**
- **Duopoly**
- **Lagrange's Method & Hessian Determinant**

INTRODUCTION

In the previous chapter we had discussed the cases where a producer is manufacturing only one type of product but in actual situations we may have producer manufacturing number of products. Therefore, we may have number of independent variables corresponding to a given dependent variable. Such type of problem can be solved using the concept of partial differentiation. The present chapter deal with such issues.

DEMAND ANALYSIS

In normal situations, we may have number of commodities which are related to each other in terms of demand and price. For example – ink and pen are related commodities. If the price of ink will increase, demand of pen will decrease.

Let x_1 and x_2 be the two related commodities and their demand be x_1 and x_2 at prices p_1 and p_2 respectively.

Since, these are related commodities therefore demand function of a commodity will be dependent not only on its own price but also on the price of other related commodity.

$\therefore$ we have, demand function of x_1 as

$$x_1 = f(p_1, p_2)$$

and demand function of x_2 as

$$x_2 = f(p_1, p_2)$$

Now, if we want to assess rate of change in demand of one commodity *w.r.t.* its own price then we will have to keep price of other commodity as constant.

Therefore we will have four partial marginal demand of two interrelated commodities as under

(*i*) $\frac{\partial x_1}{\partial p_1}$ with p_2 as constant. This represent rate of change in demand of x_1 with respect its own price p_1 keeping price of other commodity x_1 as constant.

(*ii*) Likewise, we have $\frac{\partial x_1}{\partial p_2}$ with p_1 as constant. This represent rate of change in demand of x_1 with respect to price of other commodity keeping its own price as constant.

Similarly we can calculate

$$\frac{\partial x_2}{\partial p_2}, \text{ keeping } p_1 \text{ as constant}$$

and $$\frac{\partial x_2}{\partial p_1}, \text{ keeping } p_2 \text{ as constant.}$$

Using the above partial derivative we can assess the nature of the two commodities x_1 and x_2.

If both $\frac{\partial x_1}{\partial p_2}$ and $\frac{\partial x_2}{\partial p_1}$ are negative, the commodities x_1 and x_2 are complementary. Two commodities are said to be complementary if increase in price of one causes decrease in demand of other provided price of other commodity is kept constant. For example, diesel and generators.

If $\frac{\partial x_1}{\partial p_2}$ and $\frac{\partial x_2}{\partial p_1}$ are both positive, it implies that the two commodities are substitutes or competitive *i.e.*, increase in price of one commodity cause increase in demand of the other provided price of other commodity remain constant. For example, tea and coffee.

Partial Elasticities of Demand

Partial elasticity refers to percentage change in dependent variable due to percentage change in one independent variable keeping the other independent variable as constant.

When partial elasticity of percentage change in demand of commodity x_1 is calculated with respect to percentage change in price of commodity x_1 keeping price of commodity x_2 as constant, it is known as **direct elasticity.** However, when percentage change in demand of commodity x_1 is calculated with respect to percentage change in price of commodity x_2 keeping price of commodity x_1 as constant, it is known as **cross elasticity.**

Therefore, we have following four kind of elasticities for two commodities x_1 and x_2.

	x_1	x_2
Direct elasticity	$n_{11} = \frac{p_1}{x_1} \frac{\partial x_1}{\partial p_1}$ (p_2 as constant)	$n_{22} = \frac{p_2}{x_2} \frac{\partial x_2}{\partial p_2}$ (p_1 as constant)
Cross elasticity	$n_{12} = \frac{p_2}{x_1} \frac{\partial x_1}{\partial p_2}$ (p_1 as constant)	$n_{21} = \frac{p_1}{x_2} \cdot \frac{\partial x_2}{\partial p_1}$ (p_2 as constant)

Using the four partial elasticities, one can determine the nature of commodities.

(*a*) **When n_{12} and n_{21} are positive, commodities are competitive.**

(*b*) **When n_{12} and n_{21} are negative, commodities are complementary.**

APPLICATION OF PARTIAL DIFFERENTIATION

Example 1 : **The demand function for two commodities X and Y are given by**

$$x = 3q^2 - 2pq \qquad \text{and} \qquad y = 6p^2 - pq$$

respectively, where x and y are the quantities demanded for X and Y respectively, and p and q are their respective prices. Find the four partial marginal demands when $p = 30$ and $q = 45$. Interpret the result.

Solution : Partial marginal demand for x with respect to p

$$\frac{\partial x}{\partial p} = -2q$$

Partial marginal demand for x *w.r.t.* q

$$\frac{\partial x}{\partial q} = 6q - 2p$$

when $p = 30$ and $q = 45$, we have

$$\frac{\partial x}{\partial p} = -90 \quad \text{and} \quad \frac{\partial x}{\partial q} = 6(45) - 2(30)$$

$$= 270 - 60 = 210$$

This implies, if $p = 30$ and $q = 45$, increasing p to 31 and holding q at 45 will **decrease** demand for X by 90. But, if q is increased to 46 while p is held at 30 the demand for X **increase** by 210 units.

Further, partial marginal demand for y with respect to p

$$\frac{\partial y}{\partial p} = 12p - q$$

and partial marginal demand for y *w.r.t.* q

$$\frac{\partial y}{\partial q} = -p$$

At $p = 30$ and $q = 45$, we have $\frac{\partial y}{\partial q} = 315$ and $\frac{\partial y}{\partial q} = -30$.

This implies if p is increased to 31 whereas q is kept constant at 45, demand for y will increase by 315 units whereas if p is kept constant at 30 and q is increased to 46, y will decrease by 30 units.

Example 2 **: Given demand function for two commodities X_1 and X_2 as under**

$$X_1 = \frac{150}{p_1^2 p_2} \quad \text{and} \quad X_2 = \frac{150}{p_1 p_2^2}$$

respectively. Find the four partial marginal demand functions. Also determine whether X_1 and X_2 are complementary or competitive.

Solution : Partial marginal demands have been calculated as under

$$\frac{\partial X_1}{\partial p_1} = -\frac{300}{p_1^3 p_2} \quad \frac{\partial X_1}{\partial p_2} = -\frac{150}{p_1^2 p_2^2}$$

$$\frac{\partial X_2}{\partial p_1} = -\frac{150}{p_1^2 p_2^2} \quad \frac{\partial X_2}{\partial p_2} = -\frac{300}{p_1 p_2^3}$$

Since both $\frac{\partial X_1}{\partial p_2}$ and $\frac{\partial X_2}{\partial p_1}$ are negative,

X_1 and X_2 are complementary.

Example 3 **: Given below are demand function of the products X_1 and X_2.**

(*i*) $x_1 = p_1^{-0.8} e^{0.3p_2}$ and $x_2 = p_2^{-0.9} e^{0.6p_1}$

(*ii*) $x_1 = \frac{20(p_2)^{1/3}}{(p_1)^{1/2}}$ and $x_2 = \frac{60p_1}{(p_2)^{1/4}}$

where x_1, x_2 and price p_1, p_2 are quantities and price of the two products respectively. Calculate four partial marginal demand functions. Determine whether x_1 and x_2 are complementary or substitutes.

Solution : (1) Given

$$x_1 = p_1^{-0.8} e^{0.3p_2}$$

and $$x_x = p_2^{-0.9} e^{0.6p_1}$$

To find both nature of the products, let us calculate their partial marginal demand function.

$$\frac{\partial x_1}{\partial p_1} = -0.8\, p_1^{-1.8} e^{0.3p_2} \qquad \frac{\partial x_1}{\partial p_2} = -0.3\, p_1^{-0.8} e^{0.3p_2}$$

$$\frac{\partial x_2}{\partial p_1} = 0.6\, p_2^{-0.9} e^{0.6p_1} \qquad \frac{\partial x_2}{\partial p_2} = -0.9\, p_9^{-0.9} e^{0.6p_1}$$

since both $\frac{\partial x_1}{\partial p_2}$ and $\frac{\partial x_2}{\partial p_1}$ are positive, X_1 and X_2 are substitute.

(*ii*) Given

$$x_1 = \frac{20(p_2)^{1/3}}{(p_1)^{1/2}} \quad \text{and} \quad x_2 = \frac{60p_1}{(p_2)^{1/4}}$$

$$\therefore \quad \frac{\partial x_1}{\partial p_1} = \frac{1}{2} \cdot \frac{20\,(p_2)^{1/3}}{(p_1)^{3/2}} \qquad \frac{\partial x_1}{\partial p_2} = \frac{20\,(p_2)^{-2/3}}{3\,(p_1)^{1/2}}$$

$$\frac{\partial x_2}{\partial p_1} = \frac{60}{(p_2)^{1/4}} \qquad \frac{\partial x_2}{\partial p_2} = -\frac{1}{4} \cdot \frac{60\,p_1}{(p_2)^{-5/4}}$$

Since both $\frac{\partial x_1}{\partial p_2}$ and $\frac{\partial x_2}{\partial p_1}$ are positive, therefore both X_1 and X_2 are substitutes.

Example 4 : **The demand functions of two commodities, X_1 and X_2, are $x_1 = p_2^{0.6}$ and $x_2 = p_1^{0.5}$ $p_2^{-1.2}$ respectively, where x_1 and x_2 are the quantities demanded of X_1 and X_2 respectively, and p_1 and p_2 are their respective prices. Find the four partial elasticities of demand and determine whether the commodities are competitive or complementary.**

Solution : We have $x_1 = p_1^{-1.5}\, p_2^{0.6}$ and $x_2 = p_1^{0.5}\, p_2^{-1.2}$

therefore

$$\frac{\partial x_2}{\partial p_1} = -1.4\; p_1^{-2.4}\; p_2^{0.6}$$

$$\frac{\partial x_1}{\partial p_2} = 0.6\; p_1^{-1.4}\; p_2^{-0.4}$$

$$\frac{\partial x_2}{\partial p_1} = 0.5\; p_1^{-0.5}\; p_2^{-1.2}$$

$$\frac{\partial x_2}{\partial p_2} = -1.5\; p_1^{0.5}\; p_2^{-2.2}$$

Calculation of direct and cross partial elasticities of demand

The (direct) partial elasticity of demand of X_1 with respect to p_1 is

$$\eta_{11} = \frac{p_1}{x_1}\frac{\partial x_1}{\partial p_1} = \frac{p_1}{p_1^{-1.4}\; p_2^{0.6}}\left(-1.4\; p_1^{-2.4}\; p_2^{0.6}\right) = -1.4$$

The (cross) partial elasticity of demand of X_1 with respect to p_2 is

$$\eta_{12} = \frac{p_2}{x_1}\frac{\partial x_1}{\partial p_2} = \frac{p_2}{p_1^{-1.4}\; p_2^{0.6}}\left(0.6\; p_1^{-1.4}\; p_2^{-0.4}\right) = 0.6$$

The (cross partial elasticity of demand of X_2 with respect to p_1 is

$$\eta_{21} = \frac{p_1}{x_2}\frac{\partial x_2}{\partial p_1} = \frac{p_1}{p_1^{0.5}\; p_2^{-1.2}}\left(0.5\; p_1^{-0.5}\; p_2^{-1.2}\right) = 0.5$$

The (direct) partial elasticity of demand of X_2 with respect to p_2 is

$$\eta_{22} = \frac{p_2}{x_2}\frac{\partial x_2}{\partial p_2} = \frac{p_2}{p_1^{0.5}\; p_2^{-1.2}}\left(-1.2\; p_1^{-0.5}\; p_2^{-2.2}\right) = -1.2$$

X_1 and X_2 are competitive in nature because both η_{12} and η_{21} are positive.

Example 5 : **The demand functions for two related goods are given by**

$$x_1 = \frac{3p_2^3}{p_1^5} \qquad x_2 = \frac{5p_1^3}{p_2^4}$$

Find the four partial marginal demand functions. Also determine whether the goods are competitive or complementary?

Solution : The four partial marginal demand functions are

$$\frac{\partial x_1}{\partial p_1} = \frac{-15p_2^3}{p_1^6} \qquad \frac{\partial x_1}{\partial p_2} = \frac{9p_2^2}{p_1^5}$$

$$\frac{\partial x_2}{\partial p_1} = \frac{15p_1^2}{p_2^4} \qquad \frac{\partial x_2}{\partial p_2} = \frac{-20p_1^3}{p_2^5}$$

Since both $\frac{\partial x_2}{\partial p_1}$ and $\frac{\partial x_1}{\partial p_2}$ are positive, they are competitive products.

Example 6 : **Given the demand function of two commodities as**

$$Q_1 = 2000 + \frac{400}{(p_1 + 3)} - 50p_2$$

and

$$Q_2 = 2000 + -100p_2 \frac{500}{(p_1 + 4)}$$

(*i*) **Find the nature of commodities.**

(*ii*) **Calculate the four partial elasticities of demand at $p_1 = 5$ and $p_2 = 1$.**

Solution : Given demand functions

$$Q_1 = 2000 + \frac{400}{(p_1 + 3)} - 50p_2 \quad \text{and} \quad Q_2 = 2000 - 100p_2 + \frac{500}{(p_1 + 4)}$$

Differentiating both the functions *w.r.t.* p_1 and p_2 partially

$$\therefore \quad \frac{\partial Q_1}{\partial p_1} = -\frac{400}{(p_1 + 3)^2}, \qquad \frac{\partial Q_1}{\partial p_2} = -50$$

$$\frac{\partial Q_2}{\partial p_1} = -\frac{500}{(p_1 + 4)^2}, \qquad \frac{\partial Q_2}{\partial p_2} = -100$$

(*i*) The commodities are *complementary* because both $\frac{\partial Q_1}{\partial p_2}$ and $\frac{\partial Q_2}{\partial p_1}$ are negative.

(*ii*) The (direct) partial elasticity of Q_1 with respect to p_1 is :

$$\eta_{11} = \frac{p_1}{Q_1}\frac{\partial Q_1}{\partial p_1} = \frac{p_1}{2000 + \frac{400}{p_1 + 3} - 50p_2} \times \frac{-400}{(p_1 + 3)^2}$$

$\therefore$ When $p_1 = 5$ and $p_2 = 1$,

$$\eta_{11} = \frac{5}{2000 + \frac{400}{8} - 50} \times \frac{-400}{64} = -\frac{1}{64}.$$

The (cross) partial elasticity of Q_1 with respect to p_2 is :

$$\eta_{12} = \frac{p_2}{Q_1}\frac{\partial Q_1}{\partial p_2} = \frac{p_2}{2000 + \frac{400}{p_1 + 3} - 50p_2} \times -50$$

$\therefore$ When $p_1 = 5$ and $p_2 = 1$.

$$\eta_{12} = \frac{1}{2000 + \frac{400}{8} - 50} \times -50 = -\frac{1}{40}.$$

The (cross) partial elasticity of Q_2 with respect to p_1 is :

$$\eta_{21} = \frac{p_1}{Q_2}\frac{\partial Q_2}{\partial p_1} = \frac{p_1}{2000 - 100p_2 + \frac{500}{p_1 + 4}} \times \frac{-500}{(p_1 + 4)^2}$$

$\therefore$ When $p_1 = 5$ and $p_2 = 1$,

$$\eta_{21} = \frac{5}{2000 - 100 + \frac{500}{9} - 50} \times \frac{-500}{81} = -\frac{25}{1584}.$$

The (direct) partial elasticity of Q_2 with respect to p_2 is

$$\eta_{22} = \frac{p_2}{Q_2}\frac{\partial Q_2}{\partial p_2} = \frac{p_2}{2000 - 100p_2 + \frac{500}{p_1 + 4}} \times -100$$

$\therefore$ When $p_2 = 5$ and $p_2 = 1$,

$$\eta_{22} = \frac{1}{2000 - 100 + \frac{500}{9}} \times -100 = -\frac{9}{176}.$$

Example 7 : **Demand function for a commodity X is given by**

$$D(x) = 300 - \frac{p_x^2}{2} + \frac{p_y}{50} + \frac{Y}{20}$$

where p_x is the price of the commodity, p_y is the price of a related commodity and Y the income of the consumers. Find the cross elasticity and income elasticity of demand for X when $p_x = 10$, $p_y = 15$ and $y = 300$.

Solution : Given demand function $D(x) = 300 - \frac{p_x^2}{2} + \frac{p_y}{50} + \frac{Y}{20}$

$$\therefore \quad \frac{\partial D(x)}{\partial p_y} = \frac{1}{50}$$

Also $$\frac{\partial D(x)}{\partial Y} = \frac{1}{20}$$

The cross partial elasticity of demand for X with respect to p_y is given by

$$\eta_x, p_y = \frac{p_y}{D(x)} \frac{\partial D(x)}{\partial p_y}$$

$$= \frac{p_y}{300 - \frac{p_x^2}{2} + \frac{p_y}{50} + \frac{Y}{20}} \times \frac{1}{50}$$

When $p_x = 10$, $p_y = 15$ and $Y = 300$, we have

$$n_x, p_y = \frac{3}{2653}$$

Income elasticity of demand for X is given by

$$n_x, Y = \frac{Y}{D(x)} \frac{\partial D(x)}{\partial Y}$$

$$= \frac{Y}{300 - \frac{p_x^2}{2} + \frac{p_y}{50} + \frac{Y}{20}} \times \frac{1}{20}$$

Thus evaluating when $p_x = 10$, $p_y = 15$ and $Y = 300$, we obtain

$$n_x, Y = \frac{150}{2653}.$$

Example 8 : **If the supply function $x = f(p_1, p_2, ...p_m)$ is homogeneous of degree n, show that the sum of the partial price elasticities of supply equals n. (x denotes the quantity supplied of a particular commodity and $p_1, p_2, ...\ p_m$ are the prices of the different commodities).**

Solution : Let η denote the partial price elasticity of supply for X with respect to p_i ($i = 1, 2, ...\ m$). Therefore, by definition, we have

$$n_i = \frac{p_i}{x} \frac{\partial x}{\partial p_i}$$

Give $x = f(p_1, p_2, ...p_m)$ is homogeneous of degree n, therefore according to Euler's theorem, we have

$$p_1 = \frac{\partial x}{\partial p_1} + p_2 \frac{\partial x}{\partial p_2} + ... + p_m \frac{\partial x}{\partial p_m} = nx.$$

Dividing both sides of this equation by x, we obtain.

$$\frac{p_1}{x} \frac{\partial x}{\partial p_1} + \frac{p_2}{x} \frac{\partial x}{\partial p_2} + ... + \frac{p_m}{x} \frac{\partial x}{\partial p_m} = n$$

$\therefore \quad \eta_1 + \eta_2 + \ldots + \eta_m = n$

This shows that the sum of the partial elasticities of supply equals n.

Exercise 9.1

1. If the demand laws for two goods are given by

$$x_1 = p_1^{-a_{11}} e^{a_{12}p_2 + a_1}$$

and $\quad x_2 = p_2^{-a_{22}} e^{a_{21}p_1 + a_2}$

Show that the 'direct' price elasticities of demand are independent of the prices while 'cross' price elasticities are determined in sign by the constants a_{12} and a_{21} respectively.

2. The demand function for a commodity x is given by

$$D(x) = 300 - \frac{p_x^2}{2} + \frac{p_y}{50} + \frac{Y}{20}$$

where p_x is the price of the commodity, p_y is the price of a related commodity and y, the income of the consumers. Find the cross elasticity and income elasticity of demand for X when $P_x = 10$, $P_y = 15$ and $Y = 300$. [$h_{xy} = 3/2653$, Income elasticity $= 150/2653$]

3. The demand function for two commodities X and Y are $x = \dfrac{10}{p_1^2 p_2}$ and $y = \dfrac{5}{p_1 p_2^2}$ respectively,

where p_1 and p_2 are the prices of the commodities. Find $\dfrac{\partial x}{\partial p_1}, \dfrac{\partial x}{\partial p_2}, \dfrac{\partial y}{\partial p_1}$ and $\dfrac{\partial y}{\partial p_2}$, and interpret them in economic sense. Examine whether the two commodities are complementary or competitive.

$$\left[-20/p_1^3 p_2, \frac{10}{p_1^2 p_2}, \frac{-5}{p_1^2 p_2^2}, \frac{10}{p_1 p_2^3}, \text{Complementary}\right]$$

4. If x_1 and p_1 are the demand and price of tea, and x_2 and p_2 are demand and price of coffee and the demand functions are given by

$x_1 = p_1^{-1.7} p_2^{0.6}$ and $x_2 = p_1^{0.4} p_2^{-0.8}$,

calculate the two cross elasticities of demand and point out whether the commodities are competitive or complementary. [$\eta_{12} = 0.6$, $\eta_{21} = 0.4$, Competitive]

5. Discuss whether the two goods are substitutes or complementary on the basis of demand functions as given below :

$$x_1 = p_1^{-0.5} e^{0.2p_2}, \qquad x_2 = p_2^{-0.6} e^{0.5p_1},$$

where p_1 and p_2 denote the prices and x_1, x_2 are the quantities of the two goods respectively. [Substitute]

6. The demand functions for two commodities are given below :

$$x_1 = -\frac{p_1}{p_2^2}, \qquad x_2 = \frac{p_1^2}{p_2}.$$

where p_1 and p_2 are prices and x_1, x_2 denote the quantities of the two commodities respectively. Show that the two commodities are substitutes for one another.

7. If the demand laws of two goods are given as:

$$x_1 = p_1^{-a_{11}} e^{a_{12}p_2+a_1} \text{ and } x_2 = p_2^{-a_{22}} e^{a_{21}p_1+a_2}$$

Find the condition that goods are

(*i*) Competitive and (*ii*) complementary.

8. For the demand function of two commodities given below, find the four partial elasticities of demand with respect to price and indicate whether the commodities are competitive or complementary:

$$x_1 = 2p_1^{-0.6}\, p_2^{0.8}$$

$$x_2 = 3p_1^{0.7}\, p_2^{-0.5}$$

(where x_1 and x_2 are the quantities demanded of the two commodities at prices p_1 and p_2 respectively). [$\eta_{11} = -0.6$, $\eta_{12} = 0.8$, $\eta_{21} = 0.7$, $\eta_{22} = -0.5$; Competitive]

9. The demand function for mutton is

$$Q_M = 4850 - 5p_M + 1.5P_C + 0.1Y$$

Find

(*i*) the income elasticity of demand, and

(*ii*) The cross price elasticity of demand for mutton at

Y (income) = Rs. 1000

P_M (price of mutton) = Rs. 200

P_C (price of Chicken) = Rs. 100. [(*i*) 1/41, (*ii*) 3/82]

10. Two commodities joint demand functions are :

$$x_1 = p_1^{-a_{11}} e^{a_{12}p_2+a_1}$$

and

$$x_2 = p_2^{-a_{22}} e^{a_{21}p_1+a_2}$$

where x_1 and x_2 are the units demanded when prices are p_1 and p_2 per unit respectively. Show that direct price elasticities of demand are independent of prices whereas cross price elasticities of demand depend on the price of other commodity. Also find the condition when both the commodities are : (*i*) Competitive and (*ii*) Complementary.

11. The demand D of passenger automobiles is given by $D = 0.90$, $I^{1.1}$, $p^{0.7}$, where is the income and p is price per car. Find (*i*) the price elasticity of demand and (*ii*) the income elasticity of demand.

THE PRODUCTION FUNCTION

There are different factors of production such as land, labour, capital etc. on which the output of a firm depends. In other words, we may say that production is a function of various factors such as land, labour, capital, etc. For simplicity, we may presume that production is a function of labour (L) and capital (K).

Therefore, if P is the Output, we may write

$$P = f(L, K)$$

Now, if we want to assess the change in production due to change in any variable, we will have to keep other variable as constant. Thus, we are required to calculate partial derivative, as under.

$$\frac{\partial P}{\partial L} = MP_L \text{ (keeping '}K\text{' as constant)}$$

It represent the rate of change of P *w.r.t.* L when K is held constant. This is called **Marginal productive of labour.** Likewise we can calculate **marginal productivity of capital,** keeping labour as constant.

$$\frac{\partial P}{\partial K} = MP_K \text{ (keeping '}L\text{' as constant)}$$

It represent the rate of change in production due to change in capital, keeping labour as constant.

In order to assess the amount of production per unit of a given factor, we shall calculate average product of the factor. For example, the **average product of labour,** denoted as AP_L, given by P/L measures amount of production per unit of L. Likewise, the **average product of capital** is calculated as $AP_K = \frac{P}{K}$.

LINEAR HOMOGENEOUS PRODUCTION FUNCTION

The concept of homogeneous function has already been dealt in the previous chapter. A homogeneous production function is the one which satisfies the following condition.

If $\quad P = f(L, K)$

then $\quad f(\lambda L, \lambda K) = \lambda^r f(L, K)$

When degree of homogeneous function is 1, $r = 1$, we have

$$f(\lambda L, \lambda K) = \lambda f(L, K) \qquad ...(1)$$

Equation (1) is referred as linear homogeneous function.

Properties of Linear Homogeneous Production Function

1. We have linear homogeneous function as

$$f(\lambda L, \lambda K) = \lambda f(L, K)$$

when $\lambda = 1$, we have $f(L, K) = 1\ f(L, K)$

when $\lambda = 2$, we have $f(2L, 2K) = 2f(L, K)$

Thus, if both inputs are doubled, the output is doubled.

Linear homogeneous function has constant returns to scale.

2. Linear homogeneous functions satisfy Euler's Theorem. This implies, if $P = f(L, K)$, then according to Euler's Theorem.

$$L\,.\frac{\partial P}{\partial L} + K\,.\frac{\partial P}{\partial K} = P$$

3. In case of Linear homogeneous function, the average and marginal product depend on the ratio of factors used in the production.

For example, consider $P = f(L, K)$, then

$$f(\lambda L, \lambda K) = \lambda f(L, K) \qquad ...(1)$$

Put $\lambda = \frac{1}{K}$ in (1), we have

$$f\left(\frac{L}{K}, 1\right) = \frac{1}{K} f(L, K)$$

$$= \frac{1}{K} P \qquad [\because P = f(L, K)]$$

$$f\left(\frac{L}{K}, 1\right) = \frac{P}{K} = AP_K$$

$$\therefore \qquad AP_K = f\left(\frac{L}{K}, 1\right).$$

Thus, average product of capital is a function of ratio (L/K).

Example 9 : **The production function of a firm is given by $Q = 8\,LK - L^2 - K^2$, $L > 0$, $K > 0$. Find the marginal productivities of labour and capital. Also show that**

$$L\frac{\partial Q}{\partial L} + K\frac{\partial Q}{\partial K} = 2Q.$$

Solution : We have $Q = 8\,LK - L^2 - K^2$, therefore marginal productivity of labour $= \frac{\partial Q}{\partial L} = 8K - 2L$.

and marginal productivity of capital $= \frac{\partial Q}{\partial K} = 8L - 2K$.

Substituting the above value in the equation $L\frac{\partial Q}{\partial L} + K\frac{\partial Q}{\partial K}$ we have

$$L\frac{\partial Q}{\partial L} + K\frac{\partial Q}{\partial K} = L(8K - 2L) + K(8L - 2K)$$

$$= 8LK - 2L^2 + 8LK - 2K^2$$

$$= 2(8LK - L^2 - K^2) = 2Q.$$

Hence proved.

Example 10 : **The production function of a firm is given by**

$$P = 25\, L^{1/5}\, K^{4/5}$$

Find the average and marginal products and evaluate when $L = 32$ and $K = 243$. Interpret the results.

Solution : Average Product of Labour, AP_L, is

$$AP_L = \frac{P}{L} = \frac{25L^{1/3}K^{4/3}}{L} = 25L^{-4/5}K^{4/5}$$

Average Product of capital, AK_K, is

$$AP_K = \frac{P}{K} = \frac{25L^{1/3}K^{4/3}}{K} = 25L^{1/5}K^{-1/5}$$

$$= 25\frac{(3)^4}{(2)^4} = 25 \times \frac{81}{16} = \frac{2025}{16} = 126.56$$

and $$AP_K = 25\,(32)^{1/5}\,(243)^{-1/5} = \frac{25 \times 2}{3} = 16.66$$

Interpretation

If labour is kept constant at 32 units, then output per unit of capital is 16.66. Similarly, if capital is kept constant at 243, the output per unit of labour is 126.56.

Further,

Marginal Product of labour is $MP_L = \dfrac{\partial P}{\partial L} = 5L^{-4/5}.K^{4/5}$

and Marginal product of capital is $MP_K = \dfrac{\partial P}{\partial K} = 20L^{1/5}.K^{-1/5}$

when $L = 32$ and $k = 243$, $MP_L = 5(32)^{-4/5}\,(243)^{4/5}$

$$MP_L = \frac{5\,(3)^4}{(2)^4} = \frac{5\,(81)}{(16)} = 25.31$$

$$MP_K = 20\,(32)^{1/5}\,(243)^{-1/5} = \frac{20\,(2)}{(3)} = \frac{40}{3} = 13.33$$

Interpretation

This implies if $L = 32$ and $K = 243$, and L is increased by one unit to 33 keeping K as constant, it will increase output by 25.31 units. When k is increased to 244 keeping L as constant, it will increase output to 13.33 units.

Example 11 : **For the production function given below, show that the marginal products of the factors depend only on the ratio of factors.**

$$x = f\,(l, k) = \frac{2hlk - al^2 - bk^2}{cl + dk}$$

Also, determine the degree of homogeneity and verify Euler's theorem for the function.

Solution : Given $x = f(l, k) = \dfrac{2hlk - \alpha l^2 - \beta k^2}{cl + dk}$

Differentiating (1) partially *w.r.t.* l

Marginal product of labour is :

$$MP_l = \frac{\partial x}{\partial l} = \frac{(cl + dk)(2hk - 2\alpha l) - \left(2hlk - \alpha l^2 - \beta k^2\right)(c)}{(cl + dk)^2}$$

Dividing numerator and denominator by k^2, we have

$$MP_l = \frac{2\left(c\dfrac{l}{k} + d\right)\left[h - \alpha\left(\dfrac{l}{k}\right)\right] - \left[2h\dfrac{l}{k} - \alpha\left(\dfrac{l}{k}\right)^2 - \beta\right](c)}{\left[c\left(\dfrac{l}{k}\right) + d\right]^2}$$

This shows that MP_1 depends only on the ratio $\dfrac{l}{k}$ of factors.

Differentiating (1) partially *w.r.t.* k, we have

$$MP_k = \frac{\partial x}{\partial k} = \frac{(cl + dk)(2hl - 2\beta k) - \left(2hlk - \alpha l^2 - \beta k^2\right)(d)}{(cl + dk)^2}$$

$$MP_k = \frac{2\left(\dfrac{l}{k} + d\right)\left[h\left(\dfrac{l}{k}\right) - \beta\right] - \left[2h\left(\dfrac{l}{k}\right) - \alpha\left(\dfrac{l}{k}\right)^2 - \beta\right](d)}{\left[c\left(\dfrac{l}{k}\right) + d\right]^2}$$

This shows that MP_k also depends on the ratio $\dfrac{l}{k}$ of factors.

In order to find the degree of homogeneity, substitute l and k as λl and λk in (1), we have

$$f(\lambda l, \lambda k) = \frac{2h(\lambda l)(\lambda k) - \alpha(\lambda l)^2 - \beta(\lambda k)^2}{c(\lambda l) + d(\lambda k)}$$

$$= \frac{\lambda^2\left[2hlk - \alpha l^2 - \beta k^2\right]}{\lambda(cl + dk)}$$

$$= \lambda f(l, k).$$

This shows that $x = f(l, k)$ is homogeneous of degree 1.

In order to verify Euler's theorem, we are required to prove

$$l\frac{\partial x}{\partial l} + k\frac{\partial x}{\partial k} = x$$

We have

$$l\frac{\partial x}{\partial l}+k\frac{\partial x}{\partial k} = k\left\{\frac{(cl+dk)(2hk-2\alpha l)-\left(2hlk-\alpha l^2-\beta k^2\right)(c)}{(cl+dk)^2}\right\}$$

$$+\,k\left\{\frac{(cl+dk)(2hl-2\beta k)-\left(2hlk-\alpha l^2-\beta k^2\right)(d)}{(cl+dk)^2}\right\}$$

$$= \frac{(cl+dk)\left[2hlk-2\alpha l^2+2hlk-2\beta k^2\right]-\left[2hlk-\alpha l^2-\beta k^2\right](cl+dk)}{(cl+dk)^2}$$

$$= \frac{(cl+dk)\left[2hlk-\alpha l^2-\beta k^2\right]}{(cl+dk)^2}$$

$$= \frac{2hlk-\alpha l^2-\beta k^2}{cl+dk} = x.$$

Hence proved.

COBB–DOUGLAS PRODUCTION FUNCTION

One of the linear homogeneous production function which would be used quite often for studying various characteristics is Cobb–Douglas production function.

A production function of the form

$Q = A\,L^{\alpha}\,K^{\beta}$, is called a Cobb-Douglas production function.

where A is a positive constant.

K and L are inputs of capital and labour respectively

Here $0 \le$ a, b ≤ 1.

IMPORTANT FEATURES OF THE FUNCTION

1. It is a homogeneous function of degree ($\alpha + \beta$).
2. The exponent α and β represent the elasticities of output *w.r.t.* labour and capital respectively.

i.e.,

$$\eta_L = \frac{L}{Q}\cdot\frac{\partial Q}{\partial L} = \frac{L}{AL^{\alpha}K^{\beta}}\,.\,A\alpha\,L^{\alpha-1}K^{\beta} = \alpha$$

$$\eta_K = \frac{K}{Q}\cdot\frac{\partial Q}{\partial K} = \frac{K}{AL^{\alpha}K^{\beta}}\,.\,AL^{\alpha}\,.\,\beta\,.\,K^{\beta-1} = \beta$$

3. The sum of exponents also gives information.

   If $\alpha + \beta = 1$, it indicates constant returns to scale.

   If $\alpha + \beta < 1$, it indicates decreasing returns to scale.

   If $\alpha + \beta > 1$, it indicates increasing returns to scale.
4. The marginal productivity of the function are related to the average productivity through the these exponents.

$$MP_L = \frac{\partial Q}{\partial L} = A\alpha\, L^{\alpha-1}\ K^{\beta} = \lambda \frac{AL^{\alpha}K^{\beta}}{L}$$

$$= \lambda \frac{Q}{L} = \lambda\,(AP_L)$$

$\therefore$ $$MP_L = \lambda(AP_L)$$

Similarly, $$MP_K = \beta(AP_K)$$

Example 12 : **Show that the production function**

$$x = f(l, k) = 2\sqrt{lk}$$

(where x, l and k are the units of output, labour and capital respectively) gives constant returns to scale and diminishing returns to inputs.

Solution : Substitute l and k as λl and λk respectively in the given production function, we have

$$f(\lambda l, \lambda k) = 2\sqrt{(\lambda l)(\lambda k)} = 2\sqrt{\lambda^2 lk} = \lambda 2\sqrt{lk} = \lambda f(l, k)$$

$\therefore$ $$f(\lambda l, \lambda k) = \lambda f(l, k).$$

which shows that the given production function is homogeneous function of degree 1 and hence there are constant returns to scale.

In order to prove that the production function gives diminishing returns to inputs, we shall find marginal products of inputs and show them as decreasing function.

We have

$$MP_l = \text{marginal product of input } l = \frac{\partial x}{\partial l} = \sqrt{\frac{k}{l}}, \text{ and}$$

$$MP_k = \text{marginal product of input } k = \frac{\partial x}{\partial k} = \sqrt{\frac{l}{k}}$$

Differentiating MP_l partially with respect to l gives

$$\frac{\partial}{\partial l}(MP_l) = -\frac{1}{2}\frac{\sqrt{k}}{l^{3/2}} < 0.$$

This implies, if l is increased while k is held constant, marginal product of labour will diminish. Likewise, differentiating MP_k partially with respect to k gives

$$\frac{\partial}{\partial k}(MP_k) = -\frac{1}{2}\frac{\sqrt{l}}{k^{3/2}} < 0$$

This implies, if k is increased while l is held constant, marginal product of labour wiil diminish.

Hence it is proved that the product function gives diminishing returns to input.

Example 13 : **For the production function :**

$$Q = f(L, K) = AK^{\alpha}\ L^{\beta}\ e^{a(K/L)}$$

where A, α, β and a are positive constants, find the marginal products of labour and capital. Also verify Euler's theorem.

Solution : Given production function

$$Q = f(L, K) = AK^{\alpha} L^{\beta} e^{a(K/L)} \quad ...(1)$$

Differentiating (1) partially *w.r.t.* L and K to get marginal product of labour and marginal product of capital respectively, we have

Marginal product of labour will be

$$MP_L = \frac{\partial Q}{\partial L} = \beta A K^{\alpha} L^{\beta-1} e^{a(K/L)} + A K^{\alpha} L^{\beta} e^{a(K/L)} \left(-\frac{aK}{L^2}\right)$$

$$= A K^{\alpha} L^{\beta-1} e^{a(K/L)} \left(\beta - \frac{aK}{L}\right)$$

Marginal product of capital will be

$$MP_K = \frac{\partial Q}{\partial K} = \alpha A K^{\alpha-1} L^{\beta} e^{a(K/L)} + A K^{\alpha} L^{\beta} e^{a(K/L)} \left(\frac{a}{L}\right)$$

$$= A K^{\alpha-1} L^{\beta} e^{a(K/L)} \left(\alpha + \frac{aK}{L}\right)$$

In order to verify Euler's theorem, first of all find degree of homogeneity by substituting L and K as λL and λK in the given function.

$$f(\lambda L, \lambda K) = A(\lambda K)^{\alpha} (\lambda L)^{\beta} e^{a(\lambda K/\lambda L)} = \lambda^{\alpha+\beta} AK^{\alpha} L^{\beta} e^{a(K/L)}$$

$$= \lambda^{\alpha+\beta} f(L, K)$$

This shows that $Q = f(L, K)$ is homogeneous function of degree $(\alpha + \beta)$, hence we required to prove that

$$L\frac{\partial Q}{\partial L} + K\frac{\partial Q}{\partial K} = (\alpha + \beta) Q.$$

Substituting values of $\frac{\partial Q}{\partial L}$ and $\frac{\partial Q}{\partial K}$ from above, we have

$$L\frac{\partial Q}{\partial L} + K\frac{\partial Q}{\partial K} = L\left[AK^{\alpha} L^{\beta-1} e^{a(K/L)} \left(\beta - \frac{aK}{L}\right)\right] + K\left[AK^{\alpha-1} L^{\beta} e^{a(K/L)} \left(\alpha - \frac{aK}{L}\right)\right]$$

$$= AK^{\alpha} L^{\beta} e^{a(K/L)} \left(\beta - \frac{aK}{L} + \alpha + \frac{aK}{L}\right)$$

$$= (\alpha + \beta) Q.$$

Example 14 : **A production function is given by**

$$Q = f(L, K) = 25L^{2/5} K^{3/5}$$

where L is labour and K is capital.

(*i*) Find the behaviour of the marginal product of each factor.

(*ii*) What is the nature of returns to scale?

(*iii*) What is the total reward of labour and capital if each factor is paid a price equal to its marginal product?

Solution : We have

$$Q = f(L, K) = 25L^{2/5}\ K^{3/5}$$

Differentiating Q partially *w.r.t.* L

$$MP_L = \frac{\partial Q}{\partial L} = 10L^{-3/5}K^{3/5}$$

Rate of change of marginal product of labour is given by

$$\frac{\partial}{\partial L}(MP_L) = \frac{\partial}{\partial L}\left(10L^{-3/5}K^{3/5}\right) = -6L^{-8/5}K^{3/5} < 0$$

This show that the marginal product of labour decreases as L increases while K is held constant. Similarly

$$MP_K = \frac{\partial Q}{\partial K} = \frac{\partial}{\partial K}\left(25L^{2/5}K^{3/5}\right) = 15L^{2/5}K^{-2/5}$$

Rate of change of marginal product of capital is given by

$$\frac{\partial}{\partial K}(MP_K) = \frac{\partial}{\partial K}\left(15L^{2/5}K^{-2/5}\right) = -6L^{2/5}K^{-7/5} < 0$$

This shows that the marginal product of capital decreases as K increases while L is held constant.

(*b*) since $f(\lambda l, \lambda K) = 25(\lambda L)^{2/5}\ (\lambda K)^{3/5}$

$$= 25\ \lambda^{2/5}\ L^{2/5}\ \lambda^{3/5}\ K^{3/5}$$

$$= l(25\ L^{2/5}.\ K^{3/5})$$

This implies that the production function is homogeneous function of degree one. This reflects that the production function shows constant returns to scale.

(*c*) If each factor is paid a reward equal to its marginal product then we have

$$L.\frac{\partial Q}{\partial L} + \frac{\partial Q}{\partial K} = L\left(10L^{-3/5}K^{3/5}\right) + K.\left(15L^{2/5}K^{-2/5}\right)$$

$$= 10\ L^{2/5}\ K^{3/5} + 15\ .\ L^{2/5}\ K^{3/5}$$

$$= 25\ L^{2/5}\ K^{3/5} = Q$$

This shows that the total product is exhausted.

***Example 15 :* For the linear homogeneous production function**

$$z = \sqrt{x_1 x_2},$$

where z is output and x_1, x_2 are inputs, show that the average and marginal products of inputs depends only on the ratio of the factors and verify Euler's theorem for this production function.

Solution : Given production function

$$z = \sqrt{x_1 x_2},$$

Therefore

Average product of input x will be

$$AP_{x_1} = \frac{z}{x_1} = \frac{\sqrt{x_1 x_2}}{x_1} = \sqrt{\frac{x_2}{x_1}}$$

Average product of input x_2 will be

$$AP_{x_2} = \frac{z}{x_2} = \frac{\sqrt{x_1 x_2}}{x_2} = \sqrt{\frac{x_1}{x_2}}$$

It can be observed from the expressions of AP_{x_1} and AP_{x_2} that they depend on the ratio of factors.

Similarly, we have

Marginal product of input x_1 as

$$MP_{x_1} = \frac{\partial z}{\partial x_1} = \frac{2}{2} = \sqrt{\frac{x_2}{x_1}}$$

Marginal product of input x_2 as

$$MP_{x_2} = \frac{\partial z}{\partial x_2} = \frac{1}{2} = \sqrt{\frac{x_1}{x_2}}$$

It can be observed from the expressions of MP_{x_1} and MP_{x_2} that they depend on the ratio of factors.

Verification of Euler's Theorem

Substitute x_1 and x_2 as λx_1 and λx_2 in the given function

$$\therefore \qquad Z = \sqrt{(\lambda x_1)(\lambda x_2)} = \sqrt{\lambda^2 x_1 x_2} = \lambda \sqrt{x_1 x_1}$$

$\therefore$ degree of homogeneity = 1.

Therefore, we are required to prove $x_1 = \frac{\partial z}{\partial x_1} + x_2 \frac{\partial z}{\partial x_2} = Z$

$$x_1 \frac{\partial z}{\partial x_1} + x_2 \frac{\partial z}{\partial x_2} = x_1 \left(\frac{1}{2} \sqrt{\frac{x_1}{x_2}} + x_2 \right) \left(\frac{1}{2} \sqrt{\frac{x_1}{x_2}} \right)$$

$$= \frac{1}{2} \sqrt{x_1 x_2} + \frac{1}{2} \sqrt{x_1 x_2} = \sqrt{x_1 x_2} = z$$

i.e.,

$$= x_1 \frac{\partial z}{\partial x_1} + x_2 \frac{\partial z}{\partial x_2} = z.$$

Hence proved.

MARGINAL RATE OF TECHNICAL SUBSTITUTION (MRTS)

Marginal rate of technical substitution means substitution of one factor of production with the other so as to maintain same level of production. For example, assume that in order to produce 100 units, currently 8 labours and Rs. 1000 is required. Now, if we decrease number of labours then what should be the increase in capital so to maintain the output level to 100 units. This substitution of capital against labour is called marginal rate of technical substitution.

If the production function is

$$P = f(L, K)$$

then $MRTS = -\frac{dK}{dl}$

$$= \frac{f_L}{f_K}2$$

where f_L and f_K are partial derivatives of P *w.r.t.* L *and* K respectively.

In other words, the marginal rate of technical substitution between labour and capital is equal to the ratio of their marginal productivities.

Example 16(a) : **Show that marginal rate of technical substitution (*MRTS*) between two factors in case of production function.**

$$P = AL^{\lambda} K^{\beta}$$

is given by $\frac{\lambda}{\beta}(K/L)$.

Solution : Marginal product of labour is given as

$$MP_L = \frac{\partial P}{\partial L} = \lambda A\ L^{\lambda-1} K^{\beta}$$

Marginal product of capital is given as

$$MP_K = \frac{\partial P}{\partial K} = \beta\ AL^{\lambda}\ K^{\beta-1}$$

$$\therefore \quad MRTS = \frac{MP_L}{MP_K} = \frac{\lambda\ AL^{\lambda-1}\ K^{\beta}}{\beta\ AL^{\lambda}\ K^{\beta-1}}$$

$$= \frac{\lambda}{\beta} L^{\lambda-1-\lambda}\ K^{\beta-\beta+1}$$

$$= \frac{\lambda}{\beta}\left(\frac{K}{L}\right)$$

Hence proved.

Example 16(b) : **Production function for a commodity is :**

$$x = 2HLK - AL^2 - BK^2$$

find out at any point on constant product curve, the marginal rate of substitution of *L* for *K*.

Solution : We know that

$$MRTS = -\frac{dK}{dL} = \frac{\partial x/\partial L}{\partial x/\partial K}$$

Given

$$x = 2HLK - AL^2 - BK^2$$

$$\therefore \quad \frac{\partial x}{\partial L} = 2HK - 2AL$$

and $$\frac{\partial x}{\partial K} = 2HL - 2BK$$

$$\therefore \quad MRTS = \frac{\partial x/\partial L}{\partial x/\partial K} = \frac{2HK - 2AL}{2HL - 2BK} = \frac{(HK - AL)}{(HL - BK)}$$

OPTIMIZATION PROBLEMS

These problem mainly pertains to maximization of profit in different situations and minimizations of cost. These situations have been separately dealt, as under.

Monopoly and Joint Profit Maximisation

Consider a monopolist producing two commodities X_1 and X_2 which are being sold at a price of p_1 and p_2 per unit respectively. Let x_1 and x_2 be the quantities demanded of X_1 and X_2 respectively. Therefore, the profit of the monopolit would be given as

$$\text{Profit} = \text{Revenue} - \text{Cost}$$

$$P(x_1, x_2) = R - C$$

$$P(x_1, x_2) = p_1x_1 + p_2x_2 - C(x_1, x_2)$$

In order to maximize his profits, he can either keep quantities as constant and may change the price or vice versa. If the prices are kept constant, then the monopolist can find the quantities of each product x_1 and x_2 to maximize his profit, in the following manner.

(*i*) Calculate $\frac{\partial P}{\partial x_1}$ and $\frac{\partial P}{\partial x_2}$. Equate them to zero and find x_1 and x_2 using simultaneous equation.

(*ii*) Find $\frac{\partial^2 P}{\partial x_1^2}$, $\frac{\partial^2 P}{\partial x_2^2}$ and $\frac{\partial^2 P}{\partial x_1\,\partial x_2}$

(*b*) $\left(\frac{\partial^2 P}{\partial x_1^2}\right)\left(\frac{\partial^2 P}{\partial x_2^2}\right) - \left(\frac{\partial^2 P}{\partial x_1\,\partial x_2}\right)^2 > 0$ and $\frac{\partial^2 P}{\partial x_1^2} < 0$, P is maximum.

Example 17 : **The joint cost function of a firm producing two product is**

$$C(x, y) = 5x^2 - 4x - 8xy - 16y + 4y^2 + 150$$

where x and y denote their units. Find the values of x and y which minimises $C(x, y)$. Also find minimum cost.

Solution : First order conditions is

$$\frac{\partial C}{\partial x} = 10x - 4 - 8y = 0 \qquad ...(1)$$

$$\frac{\partial C}{\partial y} = -8x - 16 + 8y = 0 \qquad ...(2)$$

Adding (1) and (2) we have

$$2x - 20 = 0$$

$$\therefore \quad x = 10$$

and $$y = \frac{10(10) - 4}{8} = \frac{96}{8} = 12.$$

$$\therefore \quad x = 10,\ y = 12.$$

Second order condition for minima requires

$$\frac{\partial^2 C}{\partial x^2} > 0 \quad \text{and} \quad \left(\frac{\partial^2 C}{\partial x^2}\right)\left(\frac{\partial^2 C}{\partial y^2}\right) - \left(\frac{\partial^2 C}{\partial x \partial y}\right) > 0$$

$$\frac{\partial^2 C}{\partial x^2} = 10 > 0$$

$$\frac{\partial^2 C}{\partial y^2} = 8 > 0$$

and $$\frac{\partial^2 C}{\partial x \partial y} = -8$$

$$\therefore \quad \left(\frac{\partial^2 C}{\partial x^2}\right)\left(\frac{\partial^2 C}{\partial y^2}\right) - \left(\frac{\partial^2 C}{\partial x \partial y}\right)^2$$

$$= (10)(8) - (-8)^2$$

$$= 80 - 64 = 16 > 0$$

$\therefore$ $x = 10$ and $y = 12$ minimizes total cost.

$\therefore$ Minimum cost

$$= C(10, 12) = 5(10)^2 - 4(10) - 8(10)(12) - 16(12) + 4(12)^2 + 150$$

$$= 5(100) - 4(10) - 8(120) - 16(12) + 4(144) + 150$$

$$= -1000 - 192 + 1076 + 150$$

$$= -1192 + 1226 = 34.$$

Example 18 : **A monopolist firm produces commodities of two types X_1 and X_2 at constant average cost Rs. 2.50 and Rs. 3.00 per item respectively. If p_1 and p_2 are the prices charged and the market demands are $x_1 = 5(p_2 - p_1)$ and $x_2 = 32 + 5p_1 - 10p_2$, find the prices of two commodities for maximum joint monopoly profit.**

Solution : Let R denote the total revenue function, then

$$R = p_1x_1 + p_2x_2$$

$$= p_1(5p_1 - 5p_1) + p_2(32 + 5p_1 - 10p_2)$$

$$= 10\,p_1p_2 - 5p_1^2 - 10p_2^2 + 32p_2$$

Let C_1 denote the cost of producing x_1 units of X_1 and let C_2 denote the cost of producing x_2 units of X_2, then we have

$$AC_1 = \frac{C_1}{x_1} = 2.50 \quad \Rightarrow \quad C_1 = 2.5x_1$$

and $$AC_1 = \frac{C_2}{x_2} = 3.00 \quad \Rightarrow \quad C_2 = 3x_1$$

Thus the joint cost function of the firm is

$$C = C_1 + C_2 = 2.5x_1 + 3x_2$$
$$= 2.5\,(5p_2 - 5p_1) + 3(32 + 5p_1 - 10p_2)$$
$$= 2.5p_1 - 17.5p_2 + 96$$

Hence the joint profit is given by

$$P = R - C = (10p_1p_2 - 5p_1^2 - 10p_2^2 + 32p_2) - (2.5p_1 - 17.5p_2 + 96)$$
$$= 10p_1p_2 - 5p_1^2 - 10p_2^2 - 2.5p_1 + 49.5p_2 - 96$$

Setting (1) and (2) for p_1 and p_2 yield $p_1 = 4.45$ and $p_2 = 4.70$

Now $$\frac{\partial^2 P}{\partial p_1^2} = -10, \quad \frac{\partial^2 P}{\partial p_1 \partial p_2} = 10, \quad \frac{\partial^2 P}{\partial p_2^2} = -20$$

$\therefore$ At (4.45, 4.70)

$$A = -10, \qquad B = 10, \qquad C = -20$$

$\therefore$ $AC - B^2 = 100 > 0$ and since $A = -10 < 0$, we conclude that P is maximum when $p_1 = 4.45$ and $p_2 = 4.70$.

Example 19 : **A firm produces two items X_1 and X_2. The market prices are given by $p_1 = 100 - 2x_1$ and $p_2 = 125 - 3x_2$. The cost of production is $12x_1 + 11x_2 + 4x_1x_2$ for producing X_1 and X_2 items. Find how many items of each should be produced to have the joint profit maximum?**

Solution : Let R_1 and R_2 denote the revenues obtained from X_1 and X_2 respectively.

Then $$R_1 = x_1p_1 = x_1(100 - 2x_1) = 100x_1 - 2x_1^2$$

and $$R_2 = x_2p_2 = x_2(125 - 3x_2) = 125x_2 - 3x_2^2$$

Thus the joint revenue, R is given by

$$R = R_1 + R_2 = 100x_1 - 2x_1^2 + 125x_2 - 3x_2^2$$

Let C denote the total cost function, then

$$C = 12x_1 + 11x_2 + 4x_1x_2$$

Therefore, the profit function of the firm is:

$$P = R - C$$
$$= (100x_1 - 2x_1^2 + 125x_2 - 3x_2^2) - (-12x_1 + 11x_2 + 4x_1x_2)$$
$$= 88x_1 + 114x_2 - 2x_1^2 - 4x_1x_2 - 3x_2^2.$$

$$\therefore \quad \frac{\partial P}{\partial x_1} = 88 - 4x_1 - 4x_2 \quad \text{and} \quad \frac{\partial P}{\partial x_2} = 114 - 4x_1 - 6x_2$$

Setting these equals to zero, we obtain

$$88 - 4x - 4x_2 = 0 \qquad ...(1)$$

$$114 - 4x_1 - 6x_2 = 0 \qquad ...(2)$$

Solving (1) and (2) for x_1 and x_2, we obtain

$$x_1 = 9 \quad \text{and} \quad x_2 = 13$$

Also $$\frac{\partial^2 P}{\partial x_1^2} = -4 \qquad \frac{\partial^2 P}{\partial x_1 \partial x_2} = 4, \qquad \frac{\partial^2 P}{\partial x_2^2} = -6$$

Therefore, at (9, 13), we have

$$A = -4, \qquad B = -4, \qquad C = -6$$

Now $AC - B^2 = 8 > 0$, and since $A = -4 < 0$, we conclude that P is maximum when $x_1 = 9$ and $x_2 = 13$.

Example 20 : **A monopolist is practicing price discrimination by charging different price in two separate markets. In market I, the demand function is $p_1 = 50 - x_1$ and in market II, the demand function is $p_2 = 36 - x_1$, where x_1 and x_2 are the quantities sold per week and p_1 and p_2 are the respective prices per unit. If the monopolist cost function is**

$$C = 200 + 2(x_1 + x_2)$$

how much should be sold in each market to maximize profit? What selling prices give him maximum profit? Find the maximum profit.

Solution : Let R_1 and R_2 be revenue function for the two given markets then.

$$R_1 = p_1x_1 = (50 - x_1)\,x_1 = 50x_1 - x_1^2$$

$$R_2 = p_2x_2 = (36 - x_2)\,x_2 = 36x_2 - x_2^2$$

$\therefore$ Given cost function

$$C(x, y) = 200 + 2(x_1 + x_2)$$

Profit, $$P = (R_1 + R_2) - C$$

$$= 50x_1 - x_1^2 + 36x_2 - x_2^2 - 200 - 2x_1 - 2x_2$$

$$= 48x_1 - x_1^2 + 34x_2 - x_2^2 - 200$$

To maximize P, we set its partial derivatives equal to zero, which implies

$$\frac{\partial P}{\partial x_1} = 48 - 2x_1 = 0 \quad \therefore \quad x_1 = 24$$

and $$\frac{\partial P}{\partial x_2} = 34 - 2x_2 = 0 \quad \therefore \quad x_2 = 17$$

Also $$\frac{\partial^2 P}{\partial x_1^2} = -2 \qquad \frac{\partial^2 P}{\partial x_2^2} = -2$$

and $$\frac{\partial^2 P}{\partial x_1 \partial x_2} = 0$$

Therefore at (24, 17)

$$A = -2 < 0, \qquad B = 0, \qquad C = -2$$

$$\therefore \quad AC - B^2 = (-2)(-2) - (0)^2 = 4 > 0$$

This satisfies the condition of maxima. Substituting $x_1 = 24$ and $x_2 = 17$ in the respective demand functions, we have

For market I : $p_1 = 50 - x_1 = 50 - 24 = 26$

For market II : $p_2 = 36 - x_2 = 36 - 17 = 19$

$\therefore$ Maximum Profit would be

$$P(24, 17) = 48(24) - (24)^2 + 34(17) - (17)^2 - 200$$

$$= 1152 - 576 + 578 + 289 - 200$$

$$= 665.$$

***Example 21* : A multiproduct firm produces two commodities X_1 and X_2 whose prices per unit are 12 and 18 respectively. Assuming the firm's cost function as:**

$$C(x) = 2x_1^2 + x_1x_2 + 2x_2^2$$

Obtain the optimum levels of its products which maximize profit.

***Solution* :** Let x_1 and x_2 denote the number of units produced and sold of each commodity. Then the revenue function of the firm is :

$$R = 12x_1 + 18x_2$$

Also, the total cost function is :

$$C = 2x_1^2 + x_1x_2 + 2x_2^2$$

$\therefore$ The profit function of the firm is given by

$$P = R - C = (12x_1 + 18x_2) - (2x_1^2 + x_1x_2 + 2x_2^2)$$

$$= 12x_1 + 18x_2 - 2x_1^2 - x_1x_2 - 2x_2^2.$$

Differentiating P partially with respect to x_1 and x_2, we obtain

$$\frac{\partial P}{\partial x_1} = 12 - 4x_1 - x_2 \quad \text{and} \quad \frac{\partial P}{\partial x_2} = 18 - x_1 - 4x_2$$

To maximize P we set its partial derivatives equal to zero. Thus,

$$12 - 4x_1 - x_2 = 0 \qquad ...(1)$$

$$18 - x_1 - 4x_2 = 0 \qquad ...(2)$$

Solving (1) and (2) for x_1 and x_2, we obtain

$$x_1 = 2 \qquad \text{and} \qquad x_2 = 4$$

Also $$\frac{\partial^2 P}{\partial x_1^2} = -4, \quad \frac{\partial^2 P}{\partial x_1 \, \partial x_2} = -1, \quad \frac{\partial^2 P}{\partial x_2^2} = -4$$

$\therefore$ At (2, 4)

$$A = -4, \qquad B = -1, \qquad C = -4$$

$\therefore$ $AC - B^2 = 15 > 0$, and since $A = -4 < 0$, we thus conclude that profit is maximum when $x_1 = 2$ and $x_2 = 4$.

DISCRIMINATING MONOPOLY

Sometimes a monopolist may charge different prices from different consumers for the same product. This is known as price discrimination. If x_1 and x_2 be the number of units sold at price p_1 and p_2 then the profit of the monopolist would be given as

$$P = (R_1 + R_2) - C$$

$$P = (p_1x_1 + p_1x_2) - C(x_1, x_2)$$

The profit can be maximised in a similar manner as in the previous case.

Example 22 : **A discriminating monopolist, serving two isolated markets with demand elasticities h$_1$ and h$_2$ sell quantities x_1 and x_2 of his product, at prices p_1 and p_2 respectively. Show that for maximum profits,**

$$\frac{p_1}{p_2} = \frac{(1 - 1/\eta_2)}{(1 - 1/\eta_1)}$$

Hence deduce that the price will be higher in the market where the demand is less elastic.

Solution : Let R_1 and R_2 denote the revenue function in the two markets then

$$R_1 = p_1x_1 \text{ and } R_2 = p_2x_2$$

If $C = C(x)$ denote the cost function for producing $x = (x_1 + x_2)$ units. Then the monopolist's profit P is

$$P = R_1 + R_2 - C.$$

Differentiating P partially with respect to x_1, we obtain

$$\frac{\partial P}{\partial x_1} = \frac{\partial R}{\partial x_1} + 0 - \frac{\partial C}{\partial x_1}$$

$$= \frac{\partial R_1}{\partial x_1} - \frac{\partial C}{\partial x}\frac{\partial x}{\partial x_1} \qquad \textit{(Chain Rule)}$$

$$= \frac{\partial R_1}{\partial x_1} - \frac{\partial C}{\partial x}.1 \qquad \text{(since } x = x_1 + x_2\text{)}$$

$$= MR_1 - MC \qquad \left(\therefore \frac{\partial x}{\partial x_1} = \frac{\partial}{\partial x_1}(x_1 + x_2) = 1\right)$$

Similarly, differentiating P partially with respect to x_2 gives

$$\frac{\partial P}{\partial x_2} = MR_2 - MC.$$

To maximize, P, we set $\frac{\partial P}{\partial x_1}$ and $\frac{\partial P}{\partial x_2}$ equal to zero. Thus, we have

$$\frac{\partial P}{\partial x_1} = MR_1 - MC = 0 \quad \Rightarrow \quad MR_1 = MC \qquad ...(1)$$

and

$$\frac{\partial P}{\partial x_2} = MR_2 - MC = 0 \quad \Rightarrow \quad MR_2 = MC \qquad ...(2)$$

From equations (1) and (2), we get

$$MR_1 = MC = MR_2$$

Hence, to maximize profit it is necessary to charge prices so that the marginal revenues in both markets will be the same.

But $\quad MR_1 = p_1\left(1 - \frac{1}{\eta_1}\right)$ and $MR_2 = p_2\left(1 - \frac{1}{\eta_2}\right)$

$\therefore$ For maximum profit, it is necessary that

$$p_1\left(1 - \frac{1}{\eta_1}\right) = p_2\left(1 - \frac{1}{\eta_2}\right)$$

$$\frac{p_1}{p_2} = \frac{\left(1 - \frac{1}{\eta_2}\right)}{\left(1 - \frac{1}{\eta_1}\right)}$$

Now, assume that the demand is less elastic in market I, *i.e.*, $\eta_1 < \eta_2$.

$$\Rightarrow \quad \frac{1}{\eta_1} > \frac{1}{\eta_2}, \quad i.e., \quad -\frac{1}{\eta_1} < -\frac{1}{\eta_2}$$

or

$$\left(1 - \frac{1}{\eta_1}\right) < \left(1 - \frac{1}{\eta_2}\right)$$

Thus

$$\frac{\left(1 - \frac{1}{\eta_2}\right)}{\left(1 - \frac{1}{\eta_1}\right)} > 1$$

$$\Rightarrow \quad \frac{p_1}{p_2} > 1, \text{ or } p_1 > p_2.$$

Hence the price will be higher in the market where the demand is less elastic.

Example 23 : **A monopolist charges different prices in the two markets where his demand functions are $x_1 = 21 - 0.1\, p_1$ and $x_2 = 50 - 0.4p_2$, p_1 and p_2, being prices and x_1 and x_1 quantities demanded. His total cost function is $TC = 10x + 2000$, where x is total output. Find the prices that the monopolist should charge to maximize his profit. Also, verify that higher price will be charged in the market having the lower price elasticity of demand.**

Solution : Let R_1 and R_2 denote the revenue functions in the two markets, then

$$R_1 = p_1x_2 = p_1(21 - 0.1p_1) = 21p_1 - 0.1p_1^2$$

and
$$R_2 = p_2x_2 = p_2(50 - 0.4p_2) = 50p_2 - 0.4p_1^2$$

The total cost function is

$$\begin{aligned} TC &= 10x + 2000 = 10(x_1 + x_2) + 2000 \\ &= 10\,[(21 - 0.1p_1) + (50 - 0.4p_2)] + 2000 \\ &= 2710 - p_1 - 4p_2 \end{aligned}$$

$\therefore$ The monopolist's profit function is

$$\begin{aligned} P &= R_1 + R_2 - TC \\ &= (21p_1 - 0.1p_1^2) + (50p_2 - 0.4p_2^2) - (2710 - p_1 - 4p_2) \\ &= 22p_1 + 54p_2 - 0.1p_1^2 - 0.4p_2^2 - 2710 \end{aligned}$$

$$\therefore \quad \frac{\partial P}{\partial p_1} = 22 - 0.2p_1 \quad \text{and} \quad \frac{\partial P}{\partial p_2} = 54 - 0.8p_2$$

For maximum profit, it is necessary that

$$\frac{\partial P}{\partial p_1} = 0 \quad \therefore \quad 22 - 0.2p_1 = 0$$

$$\therefore \quad p_1 = 0$$

$$\frac{\partial P}{\partial p_2} = 0 \quad \therefore \quad 54 - 0.8p_2 = 0$$

$$\therefore \quad p_2 = 67.5$$

Further
$$\frac{\partial^2 P}{\partial p_1^2} = -0.2, \quad \frac{\partial^2 P}{\partial p_1 \partial p_2} = 0, \quad \frac{\partial^2 P}{\partial p^2} = -0.8$$

$$\therefore \quad AC - B^2 = (-0.2)\,(-0.8) - (0)^2 = 1.6 > 0$$

Since $A < 0$ and $AC - B^2 > 0$, profit is maximum when price in market is 110 and is market II, 67.5

Calculation of Elasticities

$$\eta_1 = \frac{-p_1}{x_1}\frac{dx_1}{dp_1} = \frac{-110\,(0.1)}{[21 - 0.1(110)]} = \frac{11}{10}$$

$$\eta_2 = \frac{-p_2}{x_2}\frac{dx_2}{dp_2} = \frac{-67.5\,(-0.4)}{[50 - 0.4\,(67.5)]} = \frac{27}{23}$$

$\therefore \qquad \eta_1 < \eta_2$

Thus, price elasticity of demand in the market I is less than the price elasticity of demand in the market II.

DUOPOLY

In case of this situation, there are two firms producing same type of product. Let x_a and x_b be the numbers of units produced by firm A and B contributing to the total demand 'x' of the industry. Let the profit of A and B be given as

$$P_A = R_A - C_A \quad \text{and} \quad P_B = R_B - C_B$$

$$P_A = p_A x_A - C_A \quad \text{and} \quad P_B = p_B x_B - C_B$$

Calculate $\frac{\partial P_A}{\partial x_A}$ and $\frac{\partial P_B}{\partial x_B}$ and equate them to zero. Solve the two simultaneous equation to find x_A and x_B.

Find $\frac{\partial^2 P_A}{\partial x_A^2}$ and $\frac{\partial^2 P_B}{\partial x_B^2}$, for maxima, they should be negative.

Example 24 : **Consider two firms P and Q selling same product in the market. The demand function for the product is $p = 40 - x_1 - x_2$, where x_1 and x_2 denote the outputs produced and sold by P and Q respectively. For firm P, the cost function is $C_1 = 4x_1$ and for firm Q, the cost function is $C_2 = 3x_2^2$. Assume that each firm expects the other to make no adjustments in current output in response to changes in his own output. Determine the equilibrium output of each firm.**

Solution : For firm P, revenue function is

$$R_1 = p\,x_1 = (40 - x_1 - x_2)\,x_1 = 40x_1 - x_1^2 - x_2x_1$$

$\therefore$ Profit of firm $P = P_1 = R_1 - C_1$

$$P_1 = 40x_1 - x_1^2 - x_2x_1 - 4x_1 = 36x_1 - x_2 - x_2x_1$$

For firm Q, revenue function is

$$R_2 = p\,x_2 = (40 - x_1 - x_2)\,x_2 = 40x_2 - x_1x_2 - x_2^2$$

$$\therefore \quad P_2 = R_2 - C_2 = 40x_2 - x_1x_2 - x_2^2 - 3x_2^2 = 40x_2 - x_1x_2 - 4x_2^2$$

For P_1 to be maximum, $\frac{\partial P_1}{\partial x_1} = 0$.

$$\therefore \quad \frac{\partial P_1}{\partial x_1} = 36 - 2x_1 - x_2 = 0$$

$$\therefore \quad 2x_1 + x_2 = 36 \qquad \text{...(1)}$$

and for P_2 to be maximum, $\frac{\partial P_2}{\partial x_2} = 0$

$$\therefore \quad \frac{\partial P_2}{\partial x_2} = 40 - x_1 - 8x_2 = 0$$

$$\therefore \quad = x_1 + 8x_2 = 40 \qquad \text{...(2)}$$

Solving (1) and (2), we have

$$2x_1 + x_2 = 36$$

$$2x_1 + 16x_2 = 80 \text{ (multiplied both sides of (2) with 2)} \qquad ...(3)$$

$$-15x_2 = -44 \text{ (on subtracting (3) from (1)}$$

$$x_2 = \frac{-44}{-15} = \frac{44}{15} = 2.93$$

$$\therefore \quad 2x_1 + \frac{44}{15} = 36$$

$$\therefore \quad 2x_1 = 360 - \frac{44}{15} = \frac{540 - 44}{15} = \frac{496}{15}$$

$$\therefore \quad x_1 = \frac{496}{30} = 16.53$$

Further, we have

$$A = \frac{\partial^2 P}{\partial x_1^2} = -2 < 0 \quad \text{and} \quad \frac{\partial^2 P}{\partial x_2^2} = -8 < 0$$

Thus, second order conditions for maximum profit are satisfied, at $x_1 = 16.53$ and $x_2 = 2.93$. Therefore, equilibrium outputs of firm P and Q are 16.53 and 2.93 respectively.

Example 25 : **In a duopolistic industry the mark demand function is $p = 100 - 2q$, while the cost functions of the two firms are $C_1 = 5q_1$ and $C_2 = 5q_2$ respectively. Write down the profits of the two firms as functions of q_1 and q_2. Both firms are profit maximizers. Both assume zero conjectural variation. Find the two reaction functions and determine the equilibrium output and price in the market.**

Solution : In this case, $q = q_1 + q_2$

Profit of the first firm is :

$$P_1 = pq_1 - C_1 = [100 - 2(q_1 + q_2)]\, q_1 - 5q_1$$

$$= -2q_1^2 - 2q_1.q_2 + 95q_1$$

For maximum profit, we have

$$\frac{\partial P}{\partial q_1} = 0$$

$$\Rightarrow \quad -4q_1 - 2q_2 + 95 = 0$$

$$\text{or,} \quad 4q_1 + 2q_2 = 95 \qquad ...(1)$$

Similarly, profit of the second firm is :

$$P_2 = pq_2 - C_2 = [100 - 2(q_1 + q_2)]\, q_2 - 5q_2$$

$$= -2q_2^2 - 2q_1q_2 + 95q_2$$

For maximum profit, we have

$$\frac{\partial P_2}{\partial q_2} = 0$$

$$\Rightarrow \qquad -4q_2 - 2q_1 + 95 = 0$$

or, $$2q_1 + 4q_2 = 95 \qquad ...(2)$$

Equations (1) and (2) are *reaction functions*. Solving these equations simultaneously for q_1 and q_2, we obtain

$$q_1 = q_2 = 95/6$$

Also $$\frac{\partial^2 P_1}{\partial q_1^2} = -4 < 0 \quad \text{and} \quad \frac{\partial^2 P_2}{\partial q_2^2} = -4 < 0$$

Thus, the second order conditions for maximum profit are also satisfied.

Hence the equilibrium output under duopoly is given by $q = q_1 + q_2 = \frac{95}{6} + \frac{95}{6} = \frac{95}{3}$, and the price is given by $p = 100 - 2q = 100 - 2 \times \frac{95}{3} = \frac{110}{3}$.

Lagrange's Method & Hessian Determinant

This method can also be used for maximizing the utility functions. Consider a function $f(x, y)$ which need to be maximized or minimized subject to the constraint $g(x, y) = 0$. Now the following steps shall be followed.

(1) Let 'λ' be the lagrange multipliers. Construct a new function involving the given function $f(x, y)$, λ and the constraint $g(x, y)$, as shown below.

$$F(x, y, \lambda) = f(x, y) - \lambda\, g(x, y)$$

(2) Differentiating F partially w.r.t. x, y and λ and equate them to zero. These are known as **necessary conditions** for getting optimal value of the function. The order to find out whether this optimal condition represent maxima or minima, or none of these, sufficient conditions are applied by finding Δ.

$$\frac{95}{3} = \frac{110}{3}.$$

Δ is called Hessian determinant. If D is positive, function is maximum. If Δ is negative, function is minimum.

Example 25 : **Find optimal value of the function**

$$f(x, y) = 5xy$$

Subject to the constraint

$$g(x, y) = 3x + 2y - 500 = 0$$

Solution: The new function $F(x)$ would be given as

$$F(x, y, \lambda) = (x, y) - \lambda\, g(x, y)$$

$$= 5xy - \lambda\,(3x + 2y - 500)$$

Necessary conditions.

$$F_x = 5y - 3\lambda = 0 \therefore\ y = \frac{3}{5}\lambda$$

$$F_y = 5x - 2\lambda = 0 \therefore\ x = \frac{2}{5}\lambda$$

$$F_\lambda = -3x - 2y + 500 = 0$$

$$= -3\left(\frac{3}{5}\lambda\right) - 2\left(\frac{2}{5}\lambda\right) + 500 = 0$$

$$\Rightarrow \quad -\frac{9}{5}\lambda - \frac{4}{5}\lambda = -500$$

$$\frac{13}{5}\lambda = 500$$

$$\lambda = \frac{2500}{13}$$

$$\therefore \quad y = \frac{3}{5}\left(\frac{2500}{13}\right) = \frac{1500}{13}$$

$$x = \frac{2}{5}\left(\frac{2500}{13}\right) = \frac{1000}{13}$$

$\therefore$ $f(x, y)$ has optimal value at $y = \frac{1500}{13}$ and $x = \frac{1000}{13}$.

Example 26. **Find the optimum commodity purchases for a consumer whose utility function is $U = f(x, y) = xy$ where prices of x and y are Rs. 1 and Rs. 5 respectively. The income constraint (y) being Rs. 10. Also use the bordered Hessian condition to verify that the solution is indeed a constrained maximum.**

Solution. Given Utility function

$$U = f(x, y) = xy$$

Subject to the constraint

$$g(x, y) = 10 - x - 5y$$

Using lagrangian multiplier:

$$F(x, y, \lambda) = xy + \lambda(10 - x - 5y)$$

For maximum utility

$$\frac{\partial F}{\partial x} = y - \lambda = 0 \qquad \text{...(1)}$$

$$\frac{\partial F}{\partial y} = x - 5\lambda = 0 \qquad \text{...(2)}$$

$$\frac{\partial F}{\partial y} = 10 - x - 5y = 0 \qquad ...(3)$$

From (1) and (2), we have

$$y = \frac{x}{5} \quad \text{or} \quad x = 5y$$

Substituting this value in equation (3), we get

$$10 - 10y = 0$$

$$\therefore \quad y = 1$$

$$\therefore \quad x = 5(1) = 5$$

Second order condition :

We have $F_{xx} = 0, F_{xy} = 1, F_{yy} = 0, g_x = -1, g_y = -5$

$$\Delta = \begin{vmatrix} 0 & -1 & -5 \\ -1 & 0 & 1 \\ -5 & 1 & 0 \end{vmatrix} = 10 > 0$$

since Δ is positive, it indicates maximum.

Exercise 9.2

1. A monopolist sells two products X and Y for which the demand is $x = 50 - 0.5p$ and $y = 75 - p_y$ the combined cost functions is $C = 3x^2 + 2xy + 2y^2 + 55$. Find

   (*i*) the profit maximizing level of output and price for each product, and

   (*ii*) the maximum profit. [(*i*) $x = 8$, $y = 10$, $p_x = 84$, $p_y = 66$, (*ii*) Max. Profit = 725]

2. A monopolist produces two commodities X_1 and X_2 which have the following demand functions:

   $p_1 = 100 - 2x_1$, $p_2 = 80 - x_2$,

   where p_1 and p_2 are their respective prices and x_1 and x_2 are their respective quantities. If the total cost function of the monopolist is $TC = 20\,(x_1 + x_2)$, find the prices and quantities that would maximize his profit. [$x_1 = 20$, $x_2 = 30$, $p_1 = 60$, $p_2 = 50$]

3. A company manufactures two types of typewriters – electrical (E) and manual (M). The revenue function of the company, in units of thousands, is

   $$R = 8E + 5M + 2EM - E^2 - 2M^2 + 20.$$

   where E represents the units of electrical typewriter in thousand and M represents manual typewriter in thousands. Determine the quantity of electrical and manual typewriters which lead to maximum revenue. Also calculate the maximum revenue.

   [$E = 10.5$, $M = 6.5$, Max $R = 78.25$]

4. Given the following least squares function :

   $S = f(a, b) = [50 - (5a + b)^2 + [30 - (10a + b)]^2 + [20 - (15a + b)]^2$

You are required to determine the value of a and b which will minimize the sum of squares, S. Also calculate the minimum values of S.[$a = -3$, $b = 190/3$, Min $S = 50/3$]

5. A discriminating monopolist can separate his consumers into two distinct markets with the following demand functions :

Market I : $Q_1 = 16 - 0.2P_1$

Market II : $Q_2 = 180 - 2P_2$

Assume that the monopolist total cost function takes the form $TC - 20Q - 20 = 0$ where Q is the total output.

Obtain the total profit function and determine the prices he would charge in the two markets to maximize the profit. What is the total profit? Do you agree that the price charged in the market with a higher elasticity of demand would be higher? Show by calculation.

[$P_1 = 50$, $P_2 = 55$, Max Profit = 6138, No]

6. A firm sells two products. The annual total revenue R behaves as a function of the number of units sold. Specifically,

$$R = 400x - 4x^2 + 1960y - 8y^2$$

where x and y equal, respectively, the number of units sold of each product. The cost of producing two products is –

$C = 100 + 2x^2 + 4y^2 + 2xy.$

(*i*) Determine the number of units which should be produced and sold in order to maximise annual profit.

(*ii*) What is total revenue equal to at the output level determined in (*i*)?

(*iii*) What is the maximum profit? [(*i*) $x = 20$, $y = 80$, (*ii*) 112000, (*iii*) 82300]

7. The joint cost function of a firm producing two products is given by

$$C(x, y) = 6x^2 - 9x - 3xy - 7y + 5y^2 + 20$$

where x and y denote their units. Find the values of x and y that minimises the joint cost. Also find the minimum cost. **[Ans. :** $x = 1$, $y = 1$; $C(1, 1) = 12$]

8. Two commodities X and Y are produced by a firm at constant average cost of Rs. 2 and Rs. 4 per item respectively. The market demands are : $x = 50\,(p_y - p_x)$ and $y = 320 + 50p_x - 100p_y$, where p_x, and p_y are the prices charged. If the firm is a monopolist, find the prices of the two commodities for the maximum joint profit. [$p_x = 4.2$, $p_y = 5.2$]

9. Assume that a monopolist sells his product in two separate markets and the demand functions are : $p_1 = 12 - x_1$, $p_2 = 20 - 3x_2$. The total cost function for his product is given by. $C = 3 + 2x$ where $x = x_1 + x_2$. Determine the prices that the monopolist will charge and the quantities he will sell in each of the markets to maximize his profit. [$x_1 = 5$, $x_2 = 3$, $p_1 = 7$, $p_2 = 11$]

10. A multiproduct firm produces two commodities X_1 and X_2 whose prices per unit are 12 and 18 respectively. Assuming the firm's cost function as $C(x_1, x_2) = 2x_1^2 + x_1 x_2 + 2x_2^2$, obtain the optimum levels of its product which maximise profit.

[Ans. : $x_1 = 2$, $x_2 = 4$, Max Profit = 148]

11. The demand functions of two commodities X_1 and X_2 are $p_1 = 14 - x_1^2$ and $p_2 = 8 - x_1$ and the joint cost function is $C = 20 + 2x_1 + 4x_2$. Determine the quantities that maximises the profit of the monopolist, and also find the maximum profit. **[Ans. :** $x_1 = 2, x_2 = 2; P = 15$]

12. Assume that monopolist sells in two isolated markets and demand functions in the two markets are:

$$p_1 = 17 - 2x_1 \text{ and } p_2 = 25 - 3x_2$$

The monopolist's total cost function is $C = 2 + x_1 + x_2$. What are the prices that the monopolist will charge in order to maximize his profits and how much he will sell in each market.

[Ans. : $p_1 = 9, p_2 = 13; x_1 = x_2 = 4$]

13. A firm produces two items X_1 and X_2. The market prices are given by $p_1 = 100 - 2x_1$ and $p_2 = 125 - 3x_2$. The cost of production is $12x_1 + 11x_2 + 4x_1x_2$ for producing x_1 and x_2 items. Find how many items of each should be produced to have the maximum profit.

[Ans. : $x_1 = 9, x_3 = 13$]

14. A monopolist produces cheap razor and blades at a constant average cost of Rs. 2 per razor and Re 1 per dozen blades. The demand of the market per week is $x_1 = 10/p_1 p_2$ thousand razor and $x_2 = 20/p_1 p_2$ thousand dozen blades when the prices for razors and blades are p_1, p_2 respectively. Show that monopoly fixes prices for Rs. 4 per razor and Rs. 2 per dozen blades.

15. A monopolist sells two products x and y for which the demand is $x = 50 - 0.5Px$ and $y = 76 - Py$. The combined cost function is.

$$C = 3x^2 + 2xy + 2y^2 + 55.$$

Find

(*i*) the profit maximizing level of output and price for each product, and

(*ii*) the maximum profit. **[Ans. :** p_x = Rs. 84, $p_y = 66$ Max $P = 725$]

16. Each firm assumes that no matter what changes it makes in the output, the other firm makes no change. Determine the equilibrium output of each firm.

[Ans. : $x_1 = 3980/43, x_2 = 210/43$]

17. The cost functions for two duopolits producing a common article are respectively given by $C_1 = 5x_1$ and $C_2 = 5x_2^2$. The demand function for the article is given by $p = -0.5 (x_1 + x_2)$.

18. An individual's utility function for two goods is given by $U = x^a \cdot y^b$. It is given that p_x and p_y are the fixed prices of two goods X and Y and the individual's fixed income is μ. Using the Lagrange multiplier method, find the demand function for X and Y (you need not use the second order condition). Deduce that the elasticity of demand for either article with respect to income or its price is equal to utility.

$$\left[\begin{array}{l} \text{Demand function fod } X : x = \dfrac{\alpha}{\alpha + \beta} \cdot \dfrac{\mu}{px} \\[2ex] \text{Demand function for } Y : y = \dfrac{\beta}{\alpha + \beta} \cdot \dfrac{\mu}{py} \end{array}\right]$$

19. An individual's utility function for two goods is given below :

$$U = (x + 2)(y + 1).$$

It is given that p_x = Rs. 4, p_y = Rs. 6 and the individual's fixed income is Rs. 130. Using the Lagrange Multiplier method, find the optimum levels of purchase of the two commodities. Is the second order condition for maximum utility satisfied? **[Ans. :** $x = 16, y = 11, D = 48 > 0$]

20. Use Lagrangian multiplier to find optimum commodity purchase for a consumer whose utility function is $u = x_1 x_2 + 2x_1$ and prices of X_1 and X_2 are Rs. 4 and Rs. 2 respectively and his income is Rs. 60. **[Ans. :** $x_1 = 8$, $x_2 = 14$]

21. The demand function and the total cost function of a monopolist are as follows :

$$p = 100 - 3q + 4\sqrt{X} \qquad \text{and} \qquad C = 4q^2 + 10q + X$$

where X is the level of advertisement expenditure. Find the values of X, p and q to maximize profit. **[Ans. :** $X = 900$, $p = 175$, $q = 151$]

10

Integration – Concepts

HIGHLIGHTS OF THE CHAPTER

- Introduction
- Fundamental Formulas of Integration
- Properties of Integration
- Methods of Integration
- Integration by Parts
- Integration by Partial Fraction
- Some Special Integrals
- Some Standard Integrals
- Definite Integrals

INTRODUCTION

In this chapter, we have discussed reverse of differentiation *i.e.* integration. Various techniques of integration has also been discussed in this chapter along with determination of relevant areas using definite integral.

Concept of Integration : If $f(x)$ is a function of x such that

$$\frac{d}{dx}(f(x)) = f(x)$$

$$\therefore \qquad d(f(x)) = f(x).dx$$

$$\therefore \qquad = \int f(x).dx$$

$$F(x) = \int f(x).dx$$

FUNDAMENTAL FORMULAS OF INTEGRATION

(*i*) $\int x^n dx = \dfrac{x^{n+1}}{n+1} + C, \; n \neq -1$

(ii) $\int \frac{1}{x}\, dx = \log|x| + C$

(iii) $\int e^{x} dx = e^{x} + C$

(iv) $\int a^{x} dx = \frac{a^{x}}{\log_e a} + c$

With the help of the above formulas, we can evaluate the following integrals.

***Example 1.* Evaluate**

(i) $\int x^{5} dx$ **(ii)** $\int \sqrt{x} dx$

(iii) $\int \frac{1}{\sqrt{x}} dx$ **(iv)** $\int \frac{2}{x^{3}} dx$

(v) $\int a^{3 \log_a x} dx$

Solution.

(i) $\int x^{5} dx = \frac{x^{5+1}}{5+1} + C = \frac{x^{6}}{6} + C$

(ii) $\int \sqrt{x}\, dx \int x^{1/2} dx = \frac{x^{\frac{1}{2}+1}}{\frac{1}{2}+1} + C = \frac{2}{3} x^{3/2} + C.$

(iii) $\int \frac{1}{\sqrt{x}} dx = \int x^{-1/2} dx = \frac{x^{-\frac{1}{2}+1}}{-\frac{1}{2}+1} + C = 2x^{1/2} + C.$

(iv) $\int \frac{1}{x^{3}} dx = \int x^{-3} dx = \frac{x^{-3+1}}{-3+1} + C = -\frac{\;}{2x^{2}} + C.$

(v) $\int a^{3 \log_a x} dx = \int a^{\log_a x^{3}} dx = \int x^{3} dx = \frac{x^{3+1}}{3+1} + C = \frac{x^{4}}{4} + C.$

PROPERTIES OF INTEGRATION

(i) $\frac{d}{dx}\left(\int f(x)\, dx \right) = f(x)$

i.e. the differentiation of an integral is the integrand itself or differentiation and integration are inverse operations (ii) $\int f(x)\,dx = k\int f(x)\,dx$, *where k is a constant*

i.e., the integral of the product of a constant and a function = the constant × integral of the function.

(iii) $\int |f(x) \pm g(x)|\,dx = \int f(x)\,dx \pm \int g(x)\,dx$

i.e. the integral of the sum or difference of a finite number of functions is equal to the sum or difference of the integrals of the various functions.

Example 2. **Evaluate**

(i) $\int x^3 + 5x^2 - 4 + \frac{7}{x} + \frac{2}{\sqrt{x}}\,dx$

(ii) $\int \frac{x^3 + 5x^2 + 4x + 1}{x^2}\,dx$

(iii) $\int (1 - x)\sqrt{x}\,dx$

(iv) $\int \left(\sqrt{x} + \frac{1}{\sqrt{x}}\right)^2 dx$

Solution.

(i) $\int x^3 + 5x^2 - 4 + \frac{7}{x} + \frac{2}{\sqrt{x}}\,dx$

$$= \int x^3 dx + \int 5x^2 dx - \int 4dx + \frac{7}{x}\,dx + \int \frac{2}{\sqrt{x}}\,dx$$

$$= \int x^3 dx + 5.\int x^2 dx - 4.\int 1.dx + 7.\int \frac{1}{x}\,dx + 2.\int x^{-1/2} dx$$

$$= \frac{x^4}{4} + 5.\frac{x^3}{3} - 4x + 7\log|x| + 2\left(\frac{x^{1/2}}{1/2}\right) + C$$

$$= \frac{x^4}{4} + \frac{5}{3}x^3 - 4x + 7\log|x| + 4\sqrt{x} + C.$$

(ii) $\int \frac{x^3 + 5x^2 + 4x + 1}{x^2}\,dx = \int \left(x + 5 + \frac{4}{x} + \frac{1}{x^2}\right) dx$ [Dividing each term by x^2].

$$= \int x\,dx + \int 5dx + \int \frac{4}{x}\,dx + \int \frac{1}{x^2}\,dx = \int x\,dx + \int 5.dx + 4\int \frac{1}{x}\,dx + \int x^{-2} dx$$

$$= \frac{x^2}{2} + 5x + 4\log|x| + \left(\frac{x^{-1}}{-1}\right) + C = \frac{x^2}{2} + 5x + 4\log|x| - \frac{1}{x} + C.$$

(iii) $\displaystyle\int (1-x)\sqrt{x}\,dx = \int \left(\sqrt{x} - x\sqrt{x}\right)dx = \int \sqrt{x}\,dx - \int x^{3/2}\,dx$

$$= \frac{x^{3/2}}{3/2} - \frac{x^{5/2}}{5/2} + C = \frac{2}{x}\cdot x^{3/2} - \frac{2}{5}x^{5/2} + C.$$

(iv) $\displaystyle\int \left(\sqrt{x} + \frac{1}{\sqrt{x}}\right)^2 dx = \int \left(x + \frac{1}{x} + 2\right)dx = \int x\,dx + \int \frac{1}{x}\,dx + 2\int 1\,dx$

$$= \frac{x^2}{2} + \log|x| + 2x + C.$$

Example 3. **Evaluate**

$$\int \left(\frac{x}{m} + \frac{m}{x} + x^m + m^x\right)dx$$

Solution.

$$\int \left(\frac{x}{m} + \frac{m}{x} + x^m + m^x\right)dx = \frac{1}{m}\int x\,dx + m\int \frac{1}{x}\,dx + \int x^m\,dx + \int m^x\,dx$$

$$= \frac{1}{m}\cdot\frac{x^2}{2} + m.\log|x| + \frac{x^{m+1}}{m+1} + \frac{m^x}{\log m} + C.$$

Example 4. **Evaluate**

(i) $\displaystyle\int \frac{2^x + 3^x}{5^x}\,dx$

(ii) $\displaystyle\int \frac{\left(a^x + b^x\right)}{a^x b^x}\,dx$

(iii) $\displaystyle\int \frac{e^{5\log_e x} - e^{4\log_e x}}{e^{3\log_e x} - e^{2\log_e x}}\,dx$

Solution.

(i) $\displaystyle\int \frac{2^x + 3^x}{5^x}\,dx = \int \left(\frac{2^x}{5^x} + \frac{3^x}{5^x}\right)dx = \int \left[\left(\frac{2}{5}\right)^x + \left(\frac{3}{5}\right)^x\right]dx$

$$= \frac{(2/5)^x}{\log_e 2/5} + \frac{(3/5)^x}{\log_e 3/5} + C$$

(ii) $\displaystyle\int \frac{\left(a^x + b^x\right)^2}{a^x b^x}\,dx = \int \frac{a^{2x} + b^{2x} + 2a^x b^x}{a^x b^x}\,dx = \int \left(\frac{a^x}{b^x} + \frac{b^x}{a^x} + 2\right)dx$

$$= \int \left\{\left(\frac{a}{b}\right)^x + \left(\frac{b}{a}\right)^x + 2\right\}dx = \frac{(a/b)^x}{\log_e (a/b)} + \frac{(b/a)^x}{\log_e (b/a)} + 2x + C$$

(iii) $\int \frac{e^{5\log_e x} - e^{4\log_e x}}{e^{3\log_e x} - e^{2\log_e x}} = \int \frac{x^5 - x^4}{x^3 - x^2} dx$ $\left[\because e^{a\log_e x} = x^a\right]$

$$= \int \frac{x^4(x-1)}{x^2(x-1)} dx = \int x^2 dx = \frac{x^3}{3} + C$$

Exercise 10.1

1. Find the following integration.

(i) $\int \frac{(x+1)^2}{\sqrt{x}} .dx$

(ii) $\int \left(5x + 4/x + 3e^x\right) .dx$

(iii) $\int x(x+2)(x-3) .dx$

(iv) $\int \frac{x^3 - 2}{x^2} .dx$

(v) $\int \left(\sqrt{x} - \frac{1}{\sqrt{x}}\right)^2 .dx$

(vi) $\int \sqrt{x}\left(x^3 - \frac{2}{x}\right) .dx$

$\Big[$ **Ans. :** (i) $\frac{2}{5}x^{5/2} + 2x^{1/2} + 4/3x^{1/2} + c$ (ii) $\frac{5}{2}x^2 + 4\log x + 3e^x + c$

(iii) $\frac{x^4}{4} - \frac{x^3}{3} - 3x^2 + c$ (iv) $\frac{x^2}{2} + \frac{2}{x} + c$

(v) $\frac{x^2}{2} - 2x + \log|x| + c$ (vi) $\frac{2}{9}.x^{9/2} - \sqrt[4]{x} + c$ $\Big]$

2. Find '$f(x)$' in the following cases.

(a) If $f'(x) = x - \frac{1}{x^2}$ and $f(1) = \frac{1}{2}$

(b) If $f'(x) = 8x^3 - 2x$, $f(2) = 8$

(c) If $f'(x) = x\sqrt{x^2 + 1}$, $f(0) = 6$

$\left[\textbf{Ans. :} (a)\ \frac{x^2}{2} + \frac{1}{x} - 1\ (b)\ 2x^4 - x^2 - 20\ (c)\ y = \frac{(x^2+1)^{3/2}}{3} + \frac{17}{3}\right]$

METHODS OF INTEGRATION

Some of the methods which are generally used for solving integral problem are discussed below:

(*i*) Integration by substitution.

(*ii*) Integration by parts.

(*iii*) Integration of rational algebraic functions by using partial fractions. We shall now discuss these methods in the following sections :

Integration by Substitution

We may have three type situation under this method of Integration.

(*a*) Integration of the form $\int f(ax+b).dx$

(*b*) Integrations of the form $\int \frac{f'(x)}{f(x)} \cdot dx$

(*c*) Integrations of the form $\int f(x)^n f'(x) \cdot dx$

(a) Integration of the form $\int f(ax+b).dx$

Some of the formulae which are frequently used are given below :

(*i*) $\int (ax+b)^n dx = \frac{1}{a} \cdot \frac{(ax+b)^{n+1}}{n+1} + C,\ n \neq -1$

(*ii*) $\int \frac{1}{ax+b} dx = \frac{1}{a} \log|ax+b| + C$

(*iii*) $\int e^{ax+b} dx = \frac{1}{a} e^{ax+b} + C$

(*iv*) $\int a^{bx+c} dx = \frac{1}{b} \cdot \frac{a^{bx+c}}{\log a} + C,\ a > 0$ and $a \neq 1$

Example **5. Evaluate the following integrals**

(*i*) $\int (2x-9)^3 \cdot dx$

(*ii*) $\int \frac{1}{(5x+2)} \cdot dx$

(*iii*) $\int (7x+1)^4 \cdot dx$

(*iv*) $\int e^{2x+5}\, dx$

Solution.

(i) $\int (2x-9)^3 \cdot dx$

$$= \frac{(2x-9)^{3+1}}{4 \times 2} + c = \frac{(2x-9)^4}{8} + c$$

(ii) $\int \frac{1}{(5x+2)} \cdot dx = \frac{1}{5} \log(5x+2) + c$

(iii) $\int (7x+1)^4 \cdot dx = \frac{(7x+1)^{4+1}}{7.(4+1)} = \frac{(7x+1)^5}{35} + c$

(iv) $\int e^{2x+5} \cdot dx = \frac{e^{2x+5}}{2} + c$

Example 6. **Evaluate**

(i) $\int (2x-3)^5 + \frac{1}{(7x-5)^3} + \frac{1}{\sqrt{5x-4}} + \frac{1}{2-3x} + \sqrt{3x+2}\, dx$

(ii) $\int \frac{x+2}{(x+1)^2} dx$

(iii) $\int e^{2x-3} dx$

(iv) $\int a^{3x+2} dx.$

Solution.

(i) $\int (2x-3)^5 + \frac{1}{(7x-5)^3} + \frac{1}{\sqrt{5x-4}} + \frac{1}{2-3x} + \sqrt{3x+2}\, dx$

$$= \int (2x-3)^5 dx + \int (7x-5)^{-3} dx + \int (5x-4)^{-1/2} dx$$

$$+ \int \frac{1}{x-3x} dx + \int \sqrt{3x+2}\, dx$$

$$= \frac{(2x-3)^6}{2 \times 6} + \frac{(7x-5)^{-2}}{7 \times -2} + \frac{(5x-4)^{1/2}}{5 \times \frac{1}{2}}$$

$$+ \left(\frac{1}{-3}\right) \log|2-3x| + \frac{(3x+2)^{3/2}}{3 \times \frac{3}{2}} + C$$

$$= \frac{1}{12}(2x-3)^6 - \frac{1}{14}(7x-5)^{-2} + \frac{2}{5}\sqrt{5x-4}$$

$$-\frac{1}{3}\log|2-3x| + \frac{2}{9}(3x+2)^{3/2} + C.$$

(ii) $\displaystyle\int \frac{x+2}{(x+1)^2}\,dx = \int \frac{x+1+1}{(x+1)^2}\,dx = \int \frac{x+1}{(x+1)^2} + \frac{1}{(x+1)^2}\,dx$

$$= \int \frac{1}{x+1}\,dx + \int (x+1)^{-2}\,dx = \log|x+1| + \frac{(x+1)^{-1}}{(-1)} + C$$

$$= \log|x+1| - \frac{1}{x+1} + C.$$

(iii) $\displaystyle\int e^{2x-3}\,dx = \frac{1}{2}\cdot e^{2x-3} + C.$

(iv) $\displaystyle\int a^{3x+2}\,dx = \frac{1}{3\log a}\cdot a^{3x+2} + C.$

***Example 7.* Evaluate**

(i) $\displaystyle\int \frac{1}{\sqrt{3x+4}-\sqrt{3x+1}}\,dx$

(ii) $\displaystyle\int \frac{8x+13}{\sqrt{4x+7}}\,dx$

(iii) $\displaystyle\int (7x-2)\sqrt{3x+2}\,dx$

(iv) $\displaystyle\int \frac{x^3}{x+2}\,dx$

(v) $\displaystyle\int \frac{x^2}{(a+bx)^2}\,dx$

Solution.

(i) $\displaystyle\int \frac{1}{\sqrt{3x+4}-\sqrt{3x+1}}\,dx$

$$= \int \frac{\sqrt{3x+4}+\sqrt{3x+1}}{(3x+4)-(3x+1)}\,dx = \frac{1}{3}\int \sqrt{3x+4}+\sqrt{3x+1}\,dx$$

$$= \frac{1}{3}\int \sqrt{3x+4}\,dx + \frac{1}{3}\int \sqrt{3x+1}\,dx = \frac{1}{3}\left\{\frac{(3x+4)^{3/2}}{3\times\frac{3}{2}}\right\} + \frac{1}{3}\left\{\frac{(3x+1)^{3/2}}{3\times\frac{3}{2}}\right\} + C$$

$$= \frac{2}{27}\left\{(3x+4)^{3/2} + (3x+1)^{3/2}\right\} + C$$

(ii) $$\int \frac{8x+13}{\sqrt{4x+7}}\,dx = \int \frac{9x+14-1}{\sqrt{4x+7}}\,dx = \int \frac{2(4x+7)-1}{\sqrt{4x+7}}\,dx$$

$$= 2\int \sqrt{4x+7}\,dx - \int -\frac{1}{\sqrt{4x+7}}\,dx = 2\left\{\frac{(4x+7)^{3/2}}{4\times\frac{3}{2}}\right\} - \left\{\frac{(4x+7)^{1/2}}{4\times\frac{1}{2}}\right\} + C$$

$$= \frac{1}{3}(4x+7)^{3/2} - \frac{1}{2}(4x+7)^{1/2} + C.$$

(iii) $$\int (7x-2)\sqrt{3x+2}\,dx = 7\int\left(x-\frac{2}{7}\right)\sqrt{3x+2}\,dx$$

$$= \frac{7}{3}\int\left(3x-\frac{6}{7}\right)\sqrt{3x+2}\,dx = \frac{7}{3}\int\left(3x+2-2-\frac{6}{7}\right)\sqrt{3x+2}\,dx$$

$$= \frac{7}{3}\int\left\{(3x+2)-\frac{20}{7}\right\}\sqrt{3x+2}\,dx = \frac{7}{3}\int (3x+2)^{3/2} - \frac{20}{7}(3x+2)^{1/2}\,dx$$

$$= \frac{7}{3}\int (3x+2)^{3/2}dx - \frac{20}{3}\int (3x+2)^{1/2}\,dx$$

$$= \frac{7}{3}\left\{\frac{(3x+2)^{5/2}}{3\times\frac{5}{2}}\right\} - \frac{20}{3}\left\{\frac{(3x+2)^{3/2}}{3\times\frac{3}{2}}\right\} + C$$

$$= \frac{14}{45}(3x+2)^{5/2} - \frac{40}{27}(3x+2)^{3/2} + C.$$

(iv) $$\int \frac{x^3}{x+2}\,dx = \int x^2 - 2x + 4 - \frac{8}{x+2}\,dx = \frac{x^3}{3} - x^2 + 4x - 8\log|x+2| + C.$$

Whenever, the degree of numerator is greater than or equal to the degree of denominator, then always divide the numerator by denominator and use the result.

$$\frac{\text{Numerator}}{\text{Denominator}} = \textit{Quotient} + \frac{\text{Remainder}}{\text{Denominator}}$$

(v) $$\int \frac{x^2}{(a+bx)^2}\,dx = \int \frac{1}{b^2} + \frac{-\frac{2a}{b}x - \frac{a^2}{b^2}}{(bx+a)^2}\,dx = \int \frac{1}{b^2}\,dx - \frac{a}{b^2}\int \frac{2bx+a}{(bx+a)^2}\,dx$$

$$= \frac{1}{b^2}x - \frac{a}{b^2}\int \frac{2bx+2a-a}{(bx+a)^2}\,dx = \frac{1}{b^2}x - \frac{a}{b^2}\left\{\int \frac{2(bx+a)}{(bx+a)^2}\,dx - a\int \frac{1}{(bx+a)^2}\,dx\right\}$$

$$= \frac{1}{b^2}x - \frac{a}{b^2}\left\{\frac{2}{b}\log|bx+a| - a\frac{(bx+a)^{-1}}{(-1)\times b}\right\} + C$$

$$= \frac{1}{b^2}x - \frac{a}{b^2}\left\{\frac{2}{b}\log|bx + a| + \frac{a}{b(bx + a)}\right\} + C$$

$$= \frac{1}{b^3}\left\{bx - 2a\log|bx + a| - \frac{a^2}{(a + bx)}\right\} + C$$

Example 8. **Evaluate**

(i) $\int \frac{x}{\sqrt{x + 2}}\,dx$

(ii) $\int x\sqrt{x + 2}$

(iii) $\int \frac{x + 1}{\sqrt{2x - 1}}\,dx$

Solution.

(i) $$\int \frac{x}{\sqrt{x + 2}}\,dx = \int \frac{x + 2 - 2}{\sqrt{x + 2}}\,dx = \int \frac{x + 2}{\sqrt{x + 2}}\,dx - \int \frac{2}{\sqrt{x + 2}}\,dx$$

$$= \int \sqrt{x + 2}\,dx - 2\int (x + 2)^{-1/2}\,dx = \frac{(x + 2)^{3/2}}{3/2} - 2\frac{(x + 2)^{1/2}}{1/2} + C$$

$$= 2/3\,(x + 2)^{3/2} - 4\sqrt{x + 2} + C$$

(ii) $$\int x\sqrt{x + 2}\,dx = \int (x + 2 - 2)\sqrt{x + 2}\,dx = \int (x + 2)\sqrt{x + 2}\,dx - 2\int \sqrt{x + 2}\,dx$$

$$= \int (x + 2)^{3/2}\,dx - 2\int (x + 2)^{1/2}\,dx = \frac{(x + 2)^{5/2}}{5/2} - 2\frac{(x + 2)^{3/2}}{3/2} + C$$

$$= (2/5)\,(x + 2)^{5/2} - (4/3)\,(x + x)^{3/2} + C$$

(iii) $$\int \frac{x + 1}{\sqrt{2x - 1}}\,dx = \frac{1}{2}\int \frac{2x + 2}{\sqrt{2x - 1}}\,dx = \frac{1}{2}\int \frac{2x - 1 - 3}{\sqrt{2x - 1}}\,dx$$

$$= \frac{1}{2}\left[\int \sqrt{2x - 1}\,dx + 3\int = \frac{1}{\sqrt{2x - 1}}\,dx\right] = \frac{1}{2}\left[\frac{(2x - 1)^{3/2}}{2 \times \frac{3}{2}} + 3\frac{(2x - 1)^{1/2}}{2 \times \frac{1}{2}}\right] + C$$

Example 9. **Find '$f(x)$' in the following cases.**

(*a*) $f'(x) = 2x^3 + 5x^2 + 7,\ f(1) = 7$

(*b*) $f'(x) = 3e^x + 2x + 8,\ f(0) = 2$

Solution.

(*a*) Given $\quad f'(x) = 2x^3 + 5x^2 + 7$

$$\therefore \quad f(x) = \int (2x^3 + 5x^2 + 7) \cdot dx$$

$$f(x) = 2\frac{x^4}{4} + \frac{5x^3}{3} + 7x + k$$

when $x = 1$, we have

$$7 = \frac{1}{2} + \frac{5}{3} + 7 + k$$

$$\therefore \quad k = -\frac{1}{2} - \frac{5}{3} = -\frac{13}{6}$$

$$\therefore \quad f(x) = \frac{x^4}{2} + \frac{5x^3}{3} + 7x - \frac{13}{6}$$

(*b*) Given

$$f'(x) = 3e^x + 2x + 8$$

$$\frac{d}{dx}(f(x)) = 3e^x + 2x + 8$$

$$d(f(x)) = (3e^x + 2x + 8).\ dx$$

Integrating both the sides, we have

$$f(x) = \int (3e^x + 2x + 8) \cdot dx$$

$$= 3e^x + \frac{2x^2}{2} + 8x + k$$

when $x = 0$, $f(0) = 2$

$$\therefore \quad 2 = 3e^0 + 0 + 0 + k$$

$$k = -1$$

$$\therefore \quad f(x) = 3e^x + x^2 + 8x - 1$$

(*b*) Integrals of the form $\int \frac{f'(x)}{f(x)} \cdot dx$

Put $\quad f(x) = t$

$$\therefore \quad f'(x) = \frac{dt}{dx}$$

$$\therefore \quad dt = f'(x).dx$$

$$\therefore \quad \int \frac{f'(x)}{f(x)} \cdot dx = \int \frac{dt}{t} = \log t + c$$

$$= \log f(x) + c$$

Example 10 : **Integrate the following w.r.t. *x***

(*i*) $\int \frac{e^{x} - e^{-x}}{e^{x} + e^{-x}} \cdot dx$

(*ii*) $\int \frac{2x + 7}{x^{2} + 7x + 5} \cdot dx$

(*iii*) $\int \frac{1}{1 + e^{-x}} \cdot dx$

Solution.

(*i*) $\int \frac{\left(e^{x} - e^{-x}\right)}{\left(e^{x} + e^{-x}\right)} \cdot dx$

Put $e^{x} + e^{-x} = t$

$\therefore \quad e^{x} + e^{-x} = \frac{dt}{dx}$

$\therefore \quad dt = (e^{x} - e^{-x}).dx$

$\therefore \quad \int \frac{\left(e^{x} - e^{-x}\right)}{\left(e^{x} + e^{-x}\right)} \cdot dx = \int \frac{dt}{t} = \log t + c$

$\therefore \log (e^{x} + e^{-x}) + c$

(*ii*) $\int \frac{2x + 7}{x^{2} + 7x + 5} \cdot dx$

Put $x^{2} + 7x + 5 = t$

$\therefore \quad 2x + 7 = \frac{dt}{dx}$

$\therefore \quad dt = (2x + 7).dx$

$$\int \frac{dt}{dx} = \log t + c$$

$$= \log (x^{2} + 7x + 5) + c$$

(*iii*) $\int \frac{1}{1 + e^{-x}} \cdot dx$

$$= \int \frac{1}{1 + \frac{1}{e^{x}}} \cdot dx$$

$$= \int \frac{e^{x}}{e^{x} + 1} \cdot dx$$

Put $e^x + 1 = t$

$\therefore \quad e^x = \frac{dt}{dx}$

$e^x.dx = dt$

$\therefore \quad \int \frac{dt}{t} = \log t + c$

$= \log(e^x + 1) + c$

(c) Integrals of the form $\int (f(x))^n f'(x) \cdot dx$

Example 11. **Evaluate the following integrals**

(i) $\int \frac{1}{9x-1} \cdot dx$

(ii) $\int \sqrt{3x^2 + 5} \cdot 6x \cdot dx$

(iii) $\int e^{5x+2} \cdot dx$

(iv) $\int (7x+1)^2 \cdot dx$

Solution.

(i) $\int \frac{1}{9x-1} \cdot dx$

put $9x - ! = t$

$\therefore \quad 9.dx = dt$

$\therefore \quad dx = \frac{dt}{9}$

$\therefore$ Above Integral can be written as

$$\int \frac{1}{(9x-1)} \cdot dx = \frac{1}{9} \int \frac{dt}{t} = \frac{1}{9} \log t + c$$

$$\therefore \quad \frac{1}{9} \log(9x-1) + c$$

(ii) $\int \sqrt{3x^2 + 5} \cdot 6x \cdot dx$

Put $3x^2 + 5 = t$

$6x = \frac{dt}{dx}$

$\therefore \quad dt = 6x \; . \; dx$

$$\therefore \quad \int \sqrt{t}.dt = \frac{t^{1/2+1}}{1/2+1} + c = \frac{2t^{1/2}}{3} + c$$

$$\therefore \quad = \frac{2\left(3x^2+5\right)^{1/2}}{3} + c$$

(*iii*) $\int e^{5x+2} \cdot dx$

Put $t = 5x + 2$

$$\therefore \quad \frac{dt}{dx} = 5$$

$$\therefore \quad dt = 5.dx$$

$$\therefore \quad \int \frac{e^t}{5} \cdot dt = \frac{1}{5} e^t + c$$

$$= \frac{1}{5} e^{5x+2} + c$$

(*iv*) $\int (7x+1)^2 \cdot dx$

Put $t = 7x + 1$

$$\therefore \quad \frac{dt}{dx} = 7$$

$$\therefore \quad \frac{dt}{7} = 7 \cdot dx$$

$$= \frac{1}{7} \int t \cdot dt = \frac{1}{7} \times \frac{t^3}{3} c$$

$$= \frac{(7x+1)^3}{21} + c$$

***Example 12.* Evaluate**

(*i*) $\displaystyle\int \frac{3x+1}{\left(3x^2+2x+1\right)^3} dx$

(*ii*) $\displaystyle\int \frac{(\log x)^3}{x} dx$

Solution.

(*i*) Let $I = \displaystyle\int \frac{3x+1}{\left(3x^2+2x+1\right)^3} dx$. Put $3x^2 + 2x + 1 = t$ so that $(6x + 2)\ dx = dt$ or 2

$$(3x + 1)\, dx = dt \text{ or } dx = \frac{dt}{2(3x+1)}.$$

$$\therefore \qquad I = \frac{3x+1}{t^3} \cdot \frac{dt}{2(3x+1)} = \frac{1}{2}\int t^{-3} dt = \frac{1}{2}\left(\frac{t^{-2}}{-2}\right) + C$$

(*ii*) Let $I = \int \frac{(\log x)^3}{x} dx$. Put $\log x = t$ so that $\frac{1}{x} dx = dt$ or $dx = x\, dt$

$$\therefore \qquad I = \int \frac{t^3}{x} x\, dt = \int t^3 dt = \int \frac{t^4}{4} + C = \frac{(\log x)^4}{4} + C.$$

INTEGRATION BY PARTS

If u and v are two functions of x, then

$$\int uv \cdot dx = u \int v.dx - \int\left[\frac{du}{dx} - \int v \cdot dx\right] \cdot dx$$

Here u is referred as first function and v is referred as second function. In order to find which of the two function shall be taken as first function, we generally use the following rule

I → Inverse of trigonometric function

L → Log functions

A → Algebraic functions

T → Trigonometric function

E → Exponential function

For simplicity, it is called as "I Late". It implies if there is choice between algebric and exponential function, algebric will be taken as first function and exponential as second function.

Example 13. **Evaluate the following integrals.**

(*i*) $\int (\log x) \cdot dx$

(*ii*) $\int (\log x)^2 \cdot dx$

(*iii*) $\int e^x (1 + x) \log (xe^x) \cdot dx$

Solution.

(*i*) $\int \log x \cdot dx = \int \log x \cdot 1\, dx$

$$= \log x \int dx - \int\left[\frac{d}{dx}(\log x) \cdot \int 1 \cdot dx\right] \cdot dx$$

$$= x \log x - \int \left(\frac{1}{x} \cdot x \right) \cdot dx$$

$$= x \log x - x + c$$

$$= x (\log x - 1) + c.$$

(ii) $\int (\log x)^2 \cdot 1\, dx$

$$= x (\log x)^2 - \int \left(2 \log x \frac{1}{x} \cdot x \right) \cdot dx$$

$$= x (\log x)^2 - 2 \int \log x \cdot dx$$

$$= x (\log x)^2 - 2 (x \log x) - x) + c.$$

$$\left[\therefore \int \log x \cdot dx = x (\log x) - x + c \right]$$

(iii) $\int e^x (1 + x) \log (xe^x) \cdot dx$

Put $xe^x = t$

$\therefore \quad e^x (1 + x).dx = dt$

$\therefore \quad \int e^x (1 + x) \log (xe^x) \cdot dx = \int \log t \cdot dt$

since $\int \log t \cdot dt = t \log t - t + c$ (already proved)

$\therefore \quad I = xe^x [\log (xe^x) - 1] + C.$

Integrals of the Form

$$\int e^x \{ f(x) + f'(x) \} dx = e^x f(x) + C.$$

Example 14. **Evaluate**

(i) $\int e^x \left(\frac{1}{x} - \frac{1}{x^2} \right) dx$

(ii) $\int e^x \frac{x}{(x+1)^2} dx$

Solution.

(i) $\int e^x \left(\frac{1}{x} - \frac{1}{x^2} \right) dx = \int e^x \frac{1}{x} dx - \int e^x \frac{1}{x^2} dx$

$$= \frac{1}{x}.e^x \int -\frac{1}{x^2} e^x dx - \int e^x \cdot \frac{1}{x^2} dx + C$$

$$= \frac{1}{x} \cdot e^x + \int \frac{1}{x^2} \cdot e^x dx - \int \frac{1}{x^2} \cdot e^x dx + C = \frac{1}{x} e^x + C.$$

(ii) $$\int e^x \frac{x}{(x+1)^2} dx = \int e^x \cdot \frac{x}{(x+1)^2} dx = \int e^x \frac{x+1-1}{(x+1)^2} dx = \int e^x \left\{ \frac{1}{x+1} + \frac{1}{(x+1)^2} \right\} dx$$

$$= \int e^x \frac{1}{x-1} dx + \int e^x \frac{(-1)}{(x+1)^2} dx$$

$$= \frac{1}{x+1} e^x - \int \frac{-1}{(x+1)^2} e^x dx + \int e^x \frac{(-1)}{(x+1)^2} dx + C = \frac{1}{x+1} \cdot e^x + C.$$

Example 15. **Evaluate**

(*i*) $$\int e^x \frac{x^2+1}{(x+1)^2} dx$$

(*ii*) $$\int \frac{\log x}{(1+\log x)^2} dx.$$

Solution.

(*i*) $$\int e^x \frac{x^2+1}{(x+1)^2} dx = \int e^x \left(1 - \frac{2x}{(x+1)^2}\right) dx = \int e^x dx - 2\int e^x \frac{x}{(x+1)^2} dx$$

$$= e^x - 2\int e^x \cdot \frac{x+1-1}{(x+1)^2} dx = e^x - 2\int e^x \left\{ \frac{1}{x+1} + \frac{-1}{(x+1)^2} \right\} dx$$

$$= e^x - 2\left[\int e^x \cdot \frac{1}{x+1} dx - \int e^x \frac{1}{(x+1)^2} dx \right]$$

$$= e^x - 2\left[\frac{1}{x+1} e^x - \int -\frac{1}{(x+1)^2} e^x dx - \int e^x \frac{1}{(x+1)^2} dx \right]$$

$$= e^x - 2\left[\frac{1}{x+1} \cdot e^x + \int e^x \cdot \frac{1}{(x+1)^2} dx - \int e^x \cdot \frac{1}{(x+1)^2} dx \right] + C$$

$$= e^x - 2\frac{e^x}{x+1} + C.$$

(*ii*) Let $$I = \int \frac{\log x}{(1+\log x)^2} dx.$$

Put $\log x = t$ so that $\frac{1}{x}\,dx = dt$ or $dx = x\,dt$ or $dx = e^t\,dt$ [$\because \log x = t \Rightarrow x = e^t$]

$$\therefore \qquad I = \int \frac{te^t}{(t+1)^2}\,dt.$$

INTEGRATION BY PARTIAL FRACTION

Sometimes, we have algebric functions of the form

$f(x)/g(x)$.

In order to integrate such functions, first of all we should observe relationship between $f(x)$ and $g(x)$.

If degree of $f(x)$ < degree of $g(x)$, then $\frac{f(x)}{g(x)}$ is called a proper rational function otherwise it is called improper rational function.

In case of improper rational function *i.e.* when degree of $f(x) \geq$ degree of $g(x)$, we divide $f(x)$ by $g(x)$ so that we may have the above relation of the form.

$$\frac{f(x)}{g(x)} = R(x) + \frac{S(x)}{g(x)}$$

where $R(x)$ and $S(x)$ are polynomials such that degree of $S(x)$ is less than $g(x)$.

Now, integration of $f(x)/R(x)$ can be easily obtained. However $g(x)$ is to be expressed is term of factor so as to facilitate computation. Depending upon the nature of $g(x)$, we may have number of cases which have been discussed as under.

Case I : When denominator can be expressed as the product of non-repeating linear factors.

Let $g(x) = (x - a_1)(x - a_2) \ldots\ldots (x - a_n)$. Then we assume that

$$\frac{f(x)}{g(x)} = \frac{A_1}{x - a_1} + \frac{A_2}{x - a_2} + \ldots. + \frac{A_n}{x - a_n}$$

where $A_1, A_2 \ldots. A_n$ are constants and can be determined by equating the numerator on RHS to the numerator on LHS and then substituting $x = a_1, a_2, \ldots.. a_n$.

Example 16. **Resolve** $\frac{5x + 2}{x^2 - 6x^2 + 11x - 6}$ **into partial fractions.**

Solution.

We have $$\frac{5x + 2}{x^2 - 6x^2 + 11x - 6} = \frac{5x + 2}{(x-1)(x-2)(x-3)}$$

Let $$\frac{5x + 2}{(x-1)(x-2)(x-3)} = \frac{A}{x-1} + \frac{B}{x-2} + \frac{C}{x-3}.$$

or $3x + 2 = A(x-2)(x-3) + B(x-1)(x-3) + C(x-1)(x-2)$ ...(*i*)

Putting $x - 1 = 0$ or $x = 1$ in (*i*), we get $7 = A(1-2)(1-3) \Rightarrow A = \frac{7}{2}$.

Putting $x - 2 = 0$ or $x = 2$ in (*i*), we obtain $12 = B(2 - 1)(2 - 3) \Rightarrow B = -12$.

Putting $x - 3 = 0$ or $x = 3$ in (*i*), we obtain $17 = C(3 - 1)(3 - 2) \Rightarrow C = \frac{17}{2}$.

Case II : When the denominator contains some repeating linear factors.

Let $g(x) = (x - a)^k (x - a_1)(x - a_2)...(x - a_n)$. Then we assume that

$$\frac{f(x)}{g(x)} = \frac{A_1}{x - a} + \frac{A_2}{(x - a)^2} + \frac{A_3}{(x - a)^3} + ... + \frac{A_k}{(x - a)^k} + \frac{B_1}{x - a} + \frac{B_2}{x - a_2} + ... + \frac{B_r}{(x - a_r)}$$

i.e., corresponding to non-repeating factors we assume as in Case I and for each repeating factor $(x - a)^k$, we assume partial fractions

$$\frac{A_1}{x - a} + \frac{A_2}{(x - a)^2} + \frac{A_3}{(x - a)^3} + ... + \frac{A_k}{(x - a)^k},$$ where $A_1, A_2, ...A_k$ are constants.

Now to determine constants we equate numerators on both sides. Some of the constants are determined by substitution as in case I and remaining are obtained by comparing coefficients of equal powers of x on both sides.

The following example illustrate the procedure.

Example 17. **Resolve** $\frac{5x - 2}{(x - 1)^2 (x + 1)(x + 2)}$ **in partial fractions.**

Solution.

Let $$\frac{5x - 2}{(x - 1)^2 (x + 1)(x + 2)} = \frac{A_1}{x - 1} + \frac{A_2}{(x - 1)} + \frac{A_3}{x + 1} + \frac{A_4}{x + 2}.$$

$$(5x - 2) = A_1 (x - 1)(x + 1)(x + 2) + A_2 (x + 1)(x + 2)$$
$$+ A_3 (x - 1)^2 (x + 2) + A_4 (x - 1)^2 (x + 1)$$

Putting $x - 1 = 0$ or $x = 1$ in (*i*), we get

$$3 = A_2 (1 + 1)(1 + 2) \Rightarrow A_2 = \frac{3}{6} = \frac{1}{2}$$

Putting $x + 1 = 0$ or $x = -1$ in (*i*), we get

$$-7 = A_3 (-2)^2 (-1 + 2) \Rightarrow A_3 = -\frac{7}{4}.$$

Putting $x + 2 = 0$ or $x = -2$ in (*i*), we get

$$-12 = A_4 (-3)^2 (-1) \Rightarrow A_4 = \frac{12}{9} = \frac{4}{3}.$$

Now equating coefficient of x^3 on both sides, we get

$$0 = A_1 + A_3 + A_4 \Rightarrow A_1 = -A_3 - A_4 = +\frac{7}{4} - \frac{4}{3} = \frac{5}{12}.$$

$$\frac{3x - 2}{(x - 1)^2 (x + 1)(x + 2)} = \frac{5}{12(x - 1)} + \frac{1}{2(x - 1)^2} - \frac{7}{4(x + 1)} + \frac{4}{3(x + 2)}$$

Case III : When some of the factors of denominator $g(x)$ are quadratic but non-repeating.

Corresponding to each quadratic factor $ax^2 + bx + c$, we assume partial fraction of the type $\frac{Ax + B}{ax^2 + bx + c}$, where A and B are constants to be determined by comparing coefficients of similar powers of x in the numerator of both sides. In practice it is advisable to assume partial fractions of the type $\frac{A(2ax + b)}{ax^2 + bx + c} + \frac{B}{ax^2 + bx + c}$.

The following example illustrates the procedure.

Example 18. **Resolve** $\frac{5x - 1}{(x+1)(x^2+2)}$ **into partial fractions.**

Solution.

Let
$$\frac{5x - 1}{(x+1)(x^2+2)} = \frac{A}{x+1} + \frac{Bx + C}{x^2 + 2}$$

or
$$\frac{5x - 1}{(x+1)(x^2+2)} = \frac{A(x^2+2) + (Bx + C)(x+1)}{(x+1)(x^2+2)}.$$

$$\Rightarrow \quad 5x - 1 = A(x^2 + 2) + (Bx + C)(x + 1) \qquad \text{...}(i)$$

Putting $x + 1 = 0$ $x = -1$ in (*i*), we get $-6 = A(3) \Rightarrow A = -2$.

Comparing coefficients of like powers of x on both sides of (*i*), we get

$$A + B = 0,\ C + 2A = -1 \text{ and } C + B = 5$$

$$\therefore \quad -2 + B = 0,\ C - 4 = -1 \text{ (Putting } A = -2) \Rightarrow B = 2,\ C = 3.$$

$$\frac{2x - 1}{(x+1)(x^2+2)} = -\frac{2}{x+1} + \frac{2x + 3}{x^2 + 2}.$$

Case IV : When some of the factors of the denominator $g(x)$ are quadratic and repeating.

For every quadratic repeating factor of the type $(ax^2 + bx + c)^k$ we assume

$$\left\{\frac{A_0(2ax + b)}{ax^2 + bx + c} + \frac{A_1}{ax^2 + bx + c}\right\} + \left\{\frac{A_1(2ax + b)}{(ax^2 + bx + c)^2} + \frac{A_2}{(ax^2 + bx + c)^2}\right\}$$
$$+ \ldots + \left\{\frac{A_{2k-1}(2ax + b)}{(ax^2 + bx + c)^k} + \frac{A_{2k}}{(ax^2 + bx + c)^k}\right\}$$

The following example illustrates the procedure.

Example 19. **Resolve** $\dfrac{5x-3}{(x-1)\left(x^2+1\right)^2}$ **into partial fractions.**

Solution.

Let $$\frac{5x-3}{(x-1)\left(x^2+1\right)^2}=\frac{A}{x-1}+\frac{Bx+C}{x^2+1}+\frac{Dx+E}{\left(x^2+1\right)^2}.$$

$$5x-3=A(x^2+1)^2+(Bx+C)(x-1)(x^2+1)+(Dx+E)(x-1) \qquad ...(i)$$

Putting $x=1$ in (i), we get $+2=A(1+1)^2 \Rightarrow A=+\frac{2}{4}=\frac{1}{2}$.

Equating coefficients of like powers of x, we get :

$A+B=0,\ C-B=0,\ 2A+B-C+D-0,\ C+E-B-D=5$ and $A-C-E=-3$.

Putting $A=+\frac{1}{2}$ and solving these equations, we get

$$C=B=-\tfrac{1}{2}\,D=C-A-B=-\frac{1}{2}-\left(-\frac{1}{2}\right)-\frac{1}{2}$$

$$=-\tfrac{1}{2}$$

$$E=5+B+D-C$$

$$=5+\left(-\frac{1}{2}\right)+\left(-\tfrac{1}{2}\right)-\left(-\frac{1}{2}\right)$$

$$=5-\frac{3}{2}=\frac{7}{2}$$

$$B=-\frac{1}{2}\text{ and }E=\frac{5}{2}.$$

$$\therefore\quad \frac{2x-3}{(x-1)\left(x^2+1\right)^2}=\frac{-1}{4(x-1)}+\frac{x+1}{4\left(x^2+1\right)}+\frac{x+5}{2\left(x^2+1\right)^2}.$$

Example 20. **Resolve** $\dfrac{2x}{x^3-1}$ **into partial fractions.**

Solution.

Let $$\frac{2x}{x^3-1}=\frac{2x}{(x-1)\left(x^2+x+1\right)}=\frac{A}{x-1}+\frac{Bx+C}{x^2+x+1}.$$

Then $$2x=A(x^2+x+1)+(Bx+C)(x-1) \qquad ...(i)$$

Putting $x-1=0$ or $x=1$ in (i), we get $2=3A \Rightarrow A=\frac{2}{3}$.

Putting $x=0$ in (i), we get $A-C=0 \Rightarrow C=A=\frac{2}{3}$.

Putting $x = -1$ in (*i*), we get $-2 = A + 2B - 2C$.

$$\Rightarrow \quad -2 = \frac{2}{3} - 2B - \frac{4}{3} \Rightarrow B = \frac{2}{3}$$

$$\therefore \quad \frac{2x}{x^3 - 1} = \frac{2}{3} \cdot \frac{1}{x-1} + \frac{1/3x + 2/3}{x^2 + x + 1} \text{ or } \frac{2x}{x^3 - 1} = \frac{2}{3} \cdot \frac{1}{x-1} + \frac{2}{3} \frac{x+1}{x^2 + x + 1}.$$

Example 21. **Evaluate**

(*i*) $\displaystyle\int \frac{2x}{(x^2+1)(x^2+2)}\, dx$

Solution.

(*i*) $\displaystyle\int \frac{2x}{(x^2+1)(x^2+2)}\, dx$. Put $x^2 = t$ so that $2x\, dx = dt$

$$\therefore \quad I = \int \frac{dt}{(t+1)(t+2)}.$$

Let $\dfrac{1}{(t+1)(t+2)} = \dfrac{A}{t+1} + \dfrac{B}{t+2}$ ...(*i*)

$$\Rightarrow \quad 1 = A(t+2) + B(t+1) \quad \text{...(ii)}$$

Putting $t - 2$ in (*ii*), we obtain $B = -1$. Putting $t = -1$ in (*ii*), we obtain $A = 1$.

Substituting the values of A and B in (*i*), we get.

$$\frac{1}{(t+1)(t+2)} = \frac{1}{t+1} + \frac{1}{t+2}$$

So, $\displaystyle I = \int \frac{1}{(t+1)(t+2)}\, dt = \int \left(\frac{1}{t+1} - \frac{1}{t+2} \right) dt$

$$= \log|t+1| - \log|t+2| + C = \log|x^2+1| - \log|x^2+2| + C.$$

SOME SPECIAL INTEGRALS

(*i*) $\displaystyle\int \frac{1}{x^2 - a^2}\, dx = \frac{1}{2a} \log\left|\frac{x-a}{x+a}\right| + C.$

(*ii*) $\displaystyle\int \frac{1}{x^2 - a^2}\, dx = \frac{1}{2a} \log\left|\frac{a+x}{a-x}\right| + C.$

Solution.

(*i*) $\therefore \quad \dfrac{1}{x^2 - a^2} = \dfrac{1}{(x-a)(x+a)} = \dfrac{1}{2a}\left[\dfrac{1}{x-a} - \dfrac{1}{x+a}\right]$

$$\therefore \int \frac{1}{x^2 - a^2} dx = \frac{1}{2a} \int \left(\frac{1}{x - a} - \frac{1}{x + a} \right) dx = \frac{1}{2a} \left[\int \frac{1}{x - a} dx - \int \frac{1}{x + a} dx \right]$$

$$= \frac{1}{2a} \left[\log |x - a| - \log |x + a| \right] + C = \frac{1}{2a} \log \left| \frac{x - a}{x + a} \right| + C.$$

(*ii*) $\therefore$

$$\frac{1}{a^2 - x^2} = \frac{1}{(a - x)(a + x)} = \frac{1}{2a} \left[\frac{1}{a + x} + \frac{1}{a - x} \right]$$

$$\therefore \int \frac{1}{a^2 - x^2} dx = \frac{1}{2a} \left[\int \frac{1}{a + x} dx + \int \frac{1}{a - x} dx \right]$$

$$= \frac{1}{2a} \left[\log |a + x| - \log |a - x| \right] + C = \frac{1}{2a} \log \left| \frac{a + x}{a - x} \right| + C.$$

SOME STANDARD INTEGRALS

1. $\displaystyle\int \frac{1}{ax^2 + bx + c} \cdot dx$

2. $\displaystyle\int \frac{1}{\sqrt{ax^2 + bx + c}} \cdot dx$

Example 22 : **Evaluate**

(*i*) $\displaystyle\int \frac{1}{(2x^2 + x + 1)} \cdot dx$

(*ii*) $\displaystyle\int \frac{1}{x(x^5 + 1)} \cdot dx$

Solution.

(*i*)
$$\int \frac{1}{(2x^2 + x + 1)} \cdot dx = \frac{1}{2} \int \frac{1}{x^2 + \frac{x}{2} - \frac{1}{2}} \cdot dx$$

$$= \frac{1}{2} \int \frac{1}{x^2 + \frac{x}{2} + \left(\frac{1}{4}\right)^2 - \left(\frac{1}{4}\right)^2 - \frac{1}{2}} \cdot dx = \frac{1}{2} \int \frac{1}{\left(x + \frac{1}{4}\right)^2 - \left(\frac{3}{4}\right)^2} \cdot dx$$

$$= \frac{1}{2} \cdot \frac{1}{2\left(\frac{3}{4}\right)} \log \left| \frac{x + \frac{1}{4} - \frac{3}{4}}{x + \frac{1}{4} + \frac{3}{4}} \right| + C$$

$$= \frac{1}{3} \log \left| \frac{x - \frac{1}{2}}{x + 1} \right| + C$$

(ii) $\int \frac{1}{x\left(x^5+1\right)} \cdot dx$

Put $x^5 + 1 = t$

$\therefore \quad 5x^4 = \frac{dt}{dx} \quad \therefore dt = 5x^4 \cdot dx$

$$\therefore \int \frac{dt}{5x^5(t)} = \int \frac{dt}{5(t-1)t} = \frac{1}{5}\int \frac{dt}{\left(t^2-t\right)}$$

$$= \frac{1}{5}\int \frac{1}{t^2 - t + \frac{1}{4} - \frac{1}{4}} = \frac{1}{5}\int \frac{1}{\left(t-\frac{1}{2}\right)^2 - \left(\frac{1}{2}\right)^2}$$

$$= \frac{1}{5}\cdot\frac{1}{2\left(\frac{1}{2}\right)}\log\frac{\left|t-\frac{1}{2}-\frac{1}{2}\right|}{\left|t-\frac{1}{2}+\frac{1}{2}\right|} + C = \frac{1}{5}\log\frac{|t-1|}{t} + C$$

$$= \frac{1}{5}\log\frac{\left|x^5\right|}{\left|x^5+1\right|} + C$$

***Example 23.* Evaluate the following integrals**

(i) $\int \frac{1}{\sqrt{(x-1)(x-2)}} \cdot dx$

(ii) $\int \frac{1}{\sqrt{x^2-4x+2}} \cdot dx$

Solution.

(i) $$\int \frac{1}{\sqrt{(x-1)(x-2)}} \cdot dx = \int \frac{1}{\sqrt{x^2 - 3x + \frac{9}{4} - \frac{9}{4} + 2}} \cdot dx$$

$$\int \frac{1}{\sqrt{(x-3/2)^2 - (1/2)^2}} \cdot dx = \log\left[(x-3/2) + \sqrt{(x-3/2)^2 - \left(\frac{1}{2}\right)^2}\right]$$

(ii) $$\int \frac{1}{\sqrt{x^2-4x+2}} \cdot dx = \int \frac{1}{\sqrt{x^2-4x+4-4+2}} \cdot dx$$

$$= \int \frac{1}{\sqrt{(x-2)^2 - \left(\sqrt{2}\right)^2}} \cdot dx = \log\left|(x-2) + \sqrt{(x-2)^2 - \left(\sqrt{2}\right)^2}\right| + C$$

$$= \log\left|(x-2) + \sqrt{x^2-4x+2}\right| + C$$

Exercise 10.2

1. Evaluate the following integrals :

(i) $\int \frac{1}{\sqrt{x^2 + 4x + 2}} \cdot dx$ $\left(\textbf{Ans.} = \log\left|(x+2) + \sqrt{x^2 + 4x + 2}\right| + C\right)$

(ii) $\int \frac{1}{x\left(x^n + 1\right)} \cdot dx$ $\left(\textbf{Ans.} = \frac{1}{n}\log\left|\frac{x^n}{x^n + 1}\right| + C\right)$

(iii) $\int \frac{dx}{e^x + e^{-x}}$ $\left(\textbf{Ans.} = \log\left|\frac{e^x + 2}{x^n + 3}\right| + C\right)$

(iv) $\int \frac{(2 + \log x)^3}{x} \cdot dx$ $\left(\textbf{Ans.} = \frac{(2 + \log x)^4}{4} + C\right)$

(v) $\int \frac{x^3}{\left(x^2 + 1\right)^3} \cdot dx$ $\left(-\frac{1}{4}\frac{\left(2x^2 + 1\right)}{\left(x^2 + 1\right)^2} + C\right)$

(vi) $\int \frac{1}{\sqrt{x + a} + \sqrt{x}} \cdot dx$ $\left(\frac{2}{3a}\left[(x + a)^{1/3} - x^{1/3}\right] + C\right)$

2. Resolve the following into partial functions :

(i) $\frac{2x + 3}{x^2 - 2x - 3}$ $\left(\frac{9}{4(x - 3)} - \frac{1}{4(x + 1)}\right)$

(ii) $\frac{x^3 - 2x^2 - 13x - 12}{x^2 - 3x - 10}$ $\left((x + 1) - \frac{2}{7(x - 5)} + \frac{2}{(x + 2)}\right)$

(iii) $\frac{(2x - 3)}{(x - 1)\left(x^2 + 1\right)^2}$ $\left[-\frac{1}{4(x - 1)} + \frac{(x - 1)}{4\left(x^2 + 1\right)} + \frac{(x + 5)}{2\left(x^2 + 1\right)^2}\right]$

3. Integrate using partial fractions.

(i) $\int \frac{(2x + 1)}{(x + 1)(x - 2)} \cdot dx$ $\left(\frac{1}{3}\log|x + 1| + \frac{5}{3}\log|x - 2| + C\right)$

(ii) $\int \frac{2x}{\left(x^2 + 1\right)\left(x^2 + 2\right)} \cdot dx$ $\left(\log\left|x^2 + 1\right| - \log\left|x^2 + 2\right| + C\right)$

(iii) $\int \frac{(3x + 1)}{(x - 2)^2 (x + 2)} \cdot dx$ $\left(\frac{5}{16}\log|x - 2| - \frac{7}{4(x - 2)} - \frac{5}{16}\log|x + 2| + C\right)$

(*iv*) $\displaystyle\int \frac{x^2}{(x-1)(x-2)(x-3)} \cdot dx$ $\left(\frac{1}{2}\log|x-1| - 4\log|x-2| + \frac{9}{2}\log|x-3| + C\right)$

(*v*) $\displaystyle\int \frac{(3+4x-x^2)}{(x+2)(x-1)} \cdot dx$ $(-x + 3\log|x+2| + 2\log|x-1| + C)$

(*vi*) $\displaystyle\int \frac{(x^2+1)}{(x^2-1)} \cdot dx$ $\left(x + \log\left|\frac{x-1}{x+1}\right| + C\right)$

DEFINITE INTEGRALS

Let $f(x)$ be the continuous function which is defined in the interval $[a, b]$. In order to assess the definite integral

$$\int_a^b f(x) \cdot dx$$

The following steps are followed :

Step 1 : Find the value of integral $\int f(x) \cdot dx$. Let this be represented by $g(x)$.

Step 2 : Evaluate $g(a)$ and $g(b)$.

Step 3 : Calculate $g(b) - g(a)$. The resultant would be the required area.

Area of Bounded Regions

If $f(x)$ be a continuous function defined on $[a, b]$. Then, the area bounded by the curve $y = f(x)$, the x-axis and the ordinates $x = a$ and $x = b$ is given by

$$\int_a^b f(x)\,dx \text{ or } \int_a^b y\,dx.$$

Other important points (1) If curve $y = f(x)$ lies below x-axis, then the area bounded by the curve $y = f(x)$, the x-axis and the ordinates $x = a$ and $x = b$ is negative. So, area is given by

$$\left|\int_a^b y\,dx\right|$$

(2) The area bounded by the curve $x = f(y)$, the y axis and the abscissae $y = c$ and $y = d$ is given by

$$\int_c^d f(y)\,dy \text{ or, } \int_c^d x\,dy$$

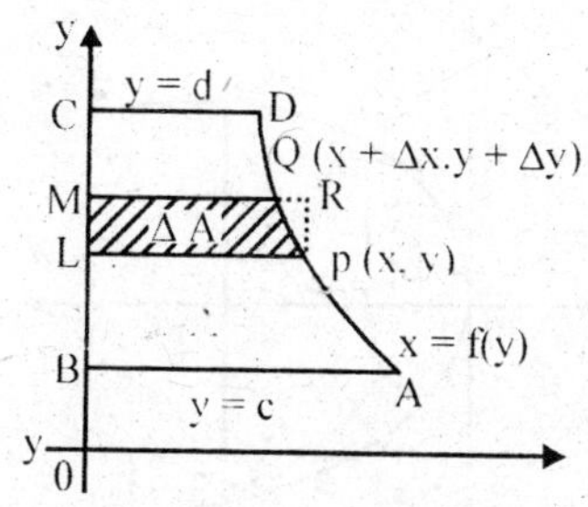

Fig. 1

In order to find the area of bounded regions, we may use the following steps

(*a*) Draw a sketch and shade the relevant area.

(*b*) Divide the area into horizontal or vertical strips depending upon a given situation.

(*c*) The strip would appear like a rectangle.

(*d*) Find the area of the approximating rectangle. If the representative strip is parallel to y-axis, then its width is taken as Δx and if it as parallel to x-axis, then its width is taken as Δy. If it is an erect rectangle, the area would be $y\ \Delta x$. If it is a lateral rectangle, the area would be $x.\Delta y$.

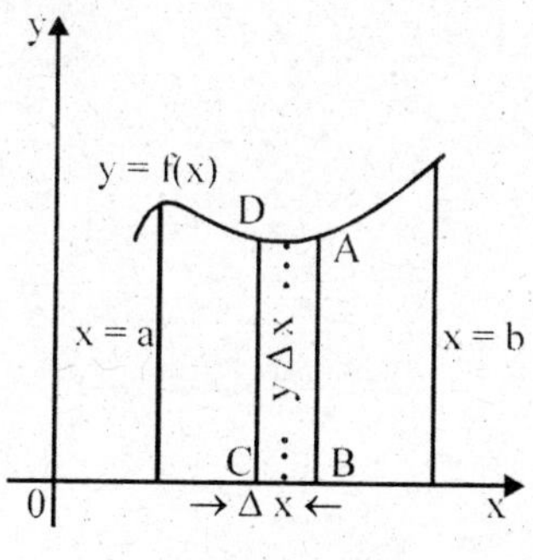

Fig. 2

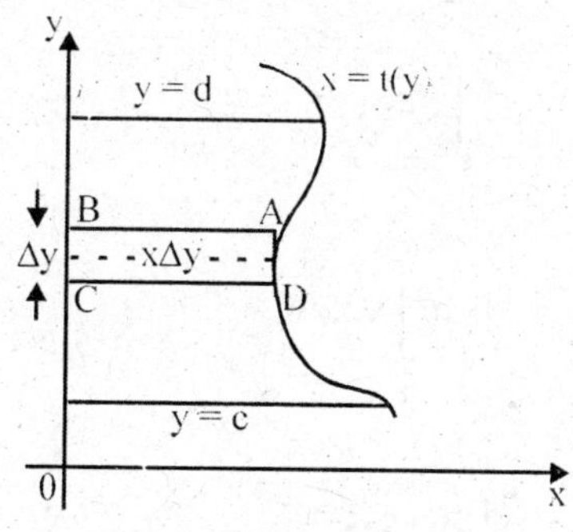

Fig. 3

(*e*) Gradually increase the breadth of the rectangle and find the limits within which the approximating rectangle can move. In Fig. 2, the approximating rectangle of area $y\ \Delta x$ can move between $x = a$ and $x = b$, therefore the area bounded by $y = f(x)$, $y = 0$, $x = a$ and $x = b$ is given by $\int_a^b y\ dx$. In Fig. 3 the rectangle of area $x\ \Delta y$ can move between $y = c$ and $y = d$, therefore area bounded by $x = \phi\ (y)$, $x = 0$, $y = c$ and $y = d$ is given by $\int_c^b x\ dy$.

Example 24. **Find the area bound by the parabola $y^2 = 4ax$ and its latus rectum.**

Solution. A rough sketch of the parabola $y^2 = 4ax$ is shown in Fig. 4.

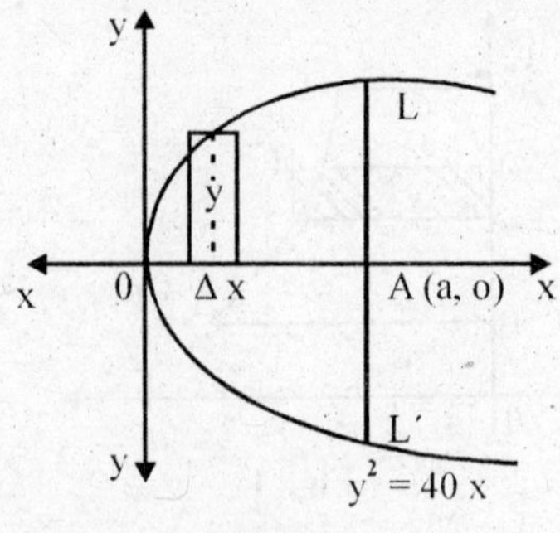

Fig. 4

As can be observed, area of the rectangle

$\therefore$ Area $= y\ \Delta x$

$\Rightarrow$ Area $= \sqrt{4ax}\ \Delta x$ $\left[\because p(x, y) \text{ lies on } y^2 = 4ax \therefore y = \sqrt{4ax}\right]$

Since the rectangle can move between $x = 0$ and $x = a$.

$\therefore$ Required area

$$= 2 \text{ (Area LOSL)}$$

$$= 2\int_0^a \sqrt{4ax}\, dx$$

$$= 4\sqrt{a}\int_0^a \sqrt{x}\, dx$$

$$= 4\sqrt{a}\left[\frac{x^{3/2}}{\frac{3}{2}}\right]_0^a$$

$$= 4\sqrt{a} \times \frac{2}{3}\left(a^{3/2} - 0\right) = \frac{8}{3}a^2 \text{ sq. units}$$

Example 25. **Using integration, find the area of the region bounded between the line $x = 4$ and the parabola $y^2 = 16x$.**

Solution. A rough sketch of the parabola along with interacting points of the line $x = 4$ are shown below in figure 5.

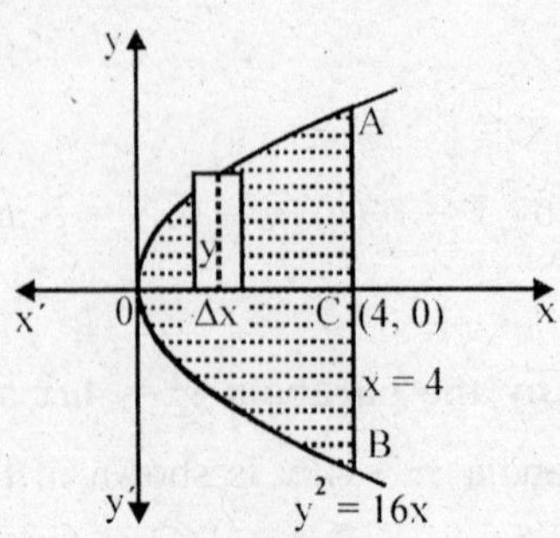

Fig 5

In this case, the area of rectangle would be $= y.\,\Delta x$

The rectangle can move between $x = 0$ and $x = 4$.

$\therefore$ Required area

$$= 2\ (\text{Area } OCAO)$$

$$= 2\int_0^4 y\,dx$$

$$= 2\int_0^4 \sqrt{16x}\,dx$$

$$= 8\int_0^4 \sqrt{x}\,dx$$

$$= 8\left[\frac{x^{3/2}}{\frac{3}{2}}\right]_0^4 = \frac{16}{2}\left(4^{3/2} - 0^{3/2}\right) = \frac{16}{3} \times 8 = \frac{128}{3} \text{ sq. units}$$

Exercise 10.3

1. Find the area lying above the x-axis and under the parabola $y = 4x - x^2$.
2. Find the area of the region bounded by the parabola $y^2 = 4x$ and the line $y = 2x$.
3. Find the area bounded by the curve $y = 4 - x^2$ and the lines $y = 0$, $y = 3$.
4. Find the area of the region bounded between the line $x = 2$ and the parabola $y^2 = 8x$.
5. Find the area of the region bounded by the line $2y = 5x + 7$, x-axis and lines $x = 2$ and $x = 8$.

[**Ans.** : (1) $\frac{32}{3}$ sq units (2) $\frac{1}{3}$ sq units (3) $\frac{28}{3}$ sq units (4) $\frac{32}{3}$ sq units (5) 96 sq units.]

11

Applications of Integration

HIGHLIGHTS OF THE CHAPTER

- ❖ **Introduction**
- ❖ **Marginal Cost to Cost Function**
- ❖ **Marginal Revenue to Revenue Function**
- ❖ **Consumer Surplus and Producer Surplus under Pure Competition**
- ❖ **Consumer Surplus and Producer Surplus under Monopoly**
- ❖ **Finding Profit from MR and MC**
- ❖ **Optimum time for which business be continued**
- ❖ **Rate of Sales**
- ❖ **Learning of Curve**
- ❖ **Investment and Capital Formation**

INTRODUCTION

The present chapter deals with the applications of integration in business and economics. As we know, integration is reverse of differentiation therefore it is required to convert marginal functions to total functions. It is also used for summing up activities etc.

Some of the basic applications of integration are given below.

To convert marginal cost function to cost function

We have $MC = \dfrac{dC}{dx}$

$\therefore \quad dC = MC.dx$

Integrating both the sides of above equation, we have

$$\int dC = \int Mc.\,dx$$

$$C = \int Mc.\,dx + k \text{ (where } k \text{ is constant)}$$

Example 1. **The marginal cost function of a product is given by**

$$MC = 50 - 2x + 3x^2$$

Find the total cost function and average cost function if cost of producing 5 units is 360.

Solution. Given $MC = \frac{dC}{dx} = 50 - 2x + 3x^2$

$\therefore \quad dC = (50 - 2x + 3x^2) \cdot dx$

Integrating both the sides, we have

$$\int dC = \int (50 - 2x + 3x^2) \cdot dx$$

$$C = 50x - \frac{2x^2}{2} + \frac{3x^3}{3} + k$$

Substituting $x = 5$ in the above equation, we have

$$= 50(5) - (5)^2 + (5)^3 + k$$

$$= 250 - 25 + 125 + k$$

$$360 = 350 + k$$

$\therefore \quad k = 360 - 350 = 10$

$\therefore$ Cost function $C = 50x - x^2 + x^3 + 10$

$\therefore$ Average cost $= \frac{C}{x} = 50 - x + x^2 + \frac{10}{x}$.

Example 2. **If the marginal cost of a product is equal to half its average cost, show that fixed cost is zero. If the cost of producing 9 units of the product is Rs. 60, find the cost function.**

Solution. Given marginal cost $= \frac{1}{2}$(Average cost)

$$MC = \frac{dC}{dx} = \frac{1}{2} AC = \frac{1}{2} \frac{C}{x}$$

i.e., $\quad \frac{dC}{dx} = \frac{1}{2} \frac{C}{x}$

$\therefore \quad \frac{dC}{C} = \frac{1}{2} \frac{dx}{x}$

Integrating both the sides, we have

$$\int \frac{dC}{C} = \frac{1}{2} \int \frac{dx}{x}$$

$$\log C = \frac{1}{2} \log x + \log k$$

$\therefore \quad 2 \log C = \log x + 2 \log k$

$$\log C^2 = \log x + \log k^2$$

$$C^2 = x \cdot k^2$$

Fixed cost is incurred even if no units are manufactured $\therefore$ substituting $x = 0$ in the above equation, we have

$$C^2 = 0$$

$$C = 0$$

This implies fixed cost = 0

when $x = 9$, $C = 60$ (given)

$\therefore \quad (60)^2 = 9\,(k)^2$

$= \quad 3600 = 9\,(k)^2$

$\therefore \quad k^2 = 400$

$\therefore$ Cost function $C^2 = x\,.\,k^2 = x.\,(400)$

$\therefore \quad C = 20\sqrt{x}.$

Example 3. **Assume that the marginal cost in lakhs of rupees is given by**

$$MC = 4 + 5x^2 + \frac{3}{2}e^{-x},$$

where x is the quantity produced. Find the total cost of production when $x = 2$, if fixed cost is Rs. 6 lakhs.

Solution. given marginal cost

$$MC = 4 + 5x^2 + \frac{3}{2}e^{-x},$$

$$\therefore \quad \frac{dC}{dx} = 4 + 5x^2 + \frac{3}{2}e^{-x}$$

$$dC = \left(4 + 5x^2 + \frac{3}{2}e^{-x}\right).dx$$

Integrating, both sides, we have

$$C = \int\left(4 + 5x^2 + \frac{3}{2}e^{-x}\right).dx$$

$$= 4x + \frac{5}{2}x^3 - \frac{3}{2}e^{-x} + k.$$

where k is the constant of integration. It is given that fixed cost is 6, this implies when $x = 0$, $c = 6$, therefore

$$6 = -\frac{3}{2} + k \text{ or } k = \frac{15}{2}$$

Therefore $\quad C = 4x + \frac{5}{3}x^3 - \frac{3}{2}e^{-x} + \frac{15}{2},$

which gives the cost of producing x units. When $x = 2$, we have

$$C = 8 + \frac{40}{3} - \frac{3}{2}e^{-x} + \frac{15}{2}$$

$$= \frac{173}{6} - \frac{3}{2} e^{-2}.$$

Example 4. **The marginal cost function of manufacturing x pair of shoes is $6 + 10x - 6x^2$. The total cost of producing a pair of shows is Rs. 12. Find the total and average cost functions.**

Solution. Given

$$MC = 6 + 10x - 6x^2$$

$$\therefore \quad \frac{dC}{dx} = 6 + 10x - 6x^2$$

Integrating both sides with respect to x, we have

$$C = \int (6 + 10x - 6x^2)\, dx$$

$$= 6x + 5x^2 - 2x^3 + k.$$

where k is the constant of integration. It is given that the cost of producing a pair of shoes is /Rs. 12. It implies, when $x = 1$, $C = 12$.

$$12 = 6(1) + 5(1)^2 - 2(1)^3 + k, \qquad \therefore \quad k = 3$$

Therefore, the total cost function is given by

$$C = 6x + 5x^2 - 2x^3 + 3.$$

The average cost function will be given as :

$$AC = \frac{C}{x} = 6 + 5x - 2x^2 + \frac{3}{x}.$$

Example 5. **The marginal cost function of a firm is given by**

$$MC = 3{,}000\, e^{0.3x} + 50,$$

where x is quantity produced. If the fixed cost is Rs. 80,000, find the total cost of the firm.

Solution. It is given that

$$MC = 3{,}000e^{0.3x} + 50$$

Integrating with respect to x, we obtain

$$C = \int (3{,}000e^{0.3x} + 50)\, dx$$

$$= 3{,}000\frac{e^{0.3x}}{0.3} + 50x + k \qquad (k \text{ is a constant})$$

$$= 10{,}000e^{0.3x} + 50x + k,$$

Given fixed cost is 80,000. This implies when $x = 0$, $C = 80000$ (as fixed cost is incurred even if no units are manufactured)

$$\therefore \quad 80{,}000 = 10{,}000e^{(0.3)(0)} + 50\,(0) + k.$$

$$\Rightarrow \quad k = 70{,}000$$

Hence, the total cost function of the firm is given by

$$C = 10{,}000\, e^{0.3x} + 50x + 70{,}000.$$

Example 6. **If the marginal cost function is given by MC = $2(2x + 9)^{-1/2}$ and the fixed cost is Rs. 4, find the average cost for 8 units of output.**

Solution. Given

$$MC = \frac{dC}{dx} = 2(2x+9)^{-1/2}$$

$$\therefore \quad dC = 2(2x + 9)^{-1/2} \cdot dx$$

Integrating both the sides, we have

$$\int dC = \int \frac{2}{(2x+9)^{½}} \cdot dx$$

$$C = \frac{2.2(2x+9)^{½}}{2} + K$$

when $x = 0$, $C = 4$,

$$\therefore \quad 4 = 2(\sqrt{9}) + k$$

$$\therefore \quad K = 4 - 6 = -2$$

Hence cost function will be given as $C = (\sqrt{2x+9}) - 2$

When $\quad x = 8$ units

$$C = 2(\sqrt{2(8)+9}) - 2$$

$$= 2(\sqrt{25}) - 2$$

$$= 2\ (5) - 2 = 8$$

$\therefore$ Average cost $= \frac{C}{x} = \frac{8}{8} = 1.$

Example 7. **The marginal cost function is given by $MC = 2e^{0.001x}$. Find the total cost function is fixed cost is Rs. 2000.**

Solution. Given $MC = 2e^{0.001x}$

$$\therefore \quad dC = 2e^{0.001x} \cdot dx$$

Integrating both the sides, we have

$$\int dC = 2\int e^{0.001x} \cdot dx$$

$$C = \frac{2e^{0.001x}}{0.001} + K$$

Since fixed cost = Rs. 2000

$\therefore$ when $x = 0$, total cost = 2000

$$\therefore \quad 2000 = \frac{2e^0}{0.001} + K$$

$$\Rightarrow \quad 2000 = 2000 + K$$

$\therefore \quad K = 0$

$\therefore$ Cost function $C = 2000\ e^{0.001x}$.

Exercise 11.1

1. The marginal cost of a product is given

$$MC = 0.03x^2 - 0.8x + 50$$

Find the total cost function, given that the fixed cost is 80. $\left[C = \frac{x^3}{100} - \frac{4}{10}x^2 + 50x + 80\right]$

2. The marginal cost of a product is given by

$$MC = 20 - 0.04x + 0.006x^2$$

Find the total cost function and the average cost function if the cost of producing 10 units is given by Rs. 300.

$$\left[\begin{aligned} Tc &= 20x - 0.02x^2 + 0.002x^3 + 100 \\ AC &= 20 - 0.02x + 0.002x^2 + \frac{100x}{} \end{aligned}\right]$$

3. The marginal cost of a product is given by $MC = e^x + 5$

Find the total cost function and average cost function when fixed cost is Rs. 75.

$$\left[C = e^x + 5x + 74,\quad C = \frac{e^x}{x} + \frac{5x}{x} + \frac{74}{x}\right]$$

4. The marginal cost function of given firm is

$$MC = 2 + 3x^2$$

Find the increase in total cost when number of units is increased from 1 to 3. **[Ans.** Rs. 30]

5. The marginal cost of production si found to be $MC = 1000 - 20x + x^2$, where x is the number of units produced. The fixed cost of production is 9000, find the cost function.

$$\left[C = 1000x - 10x^2 + \frac{x^3}{3} + 9000\right]$$

6. If the marginal cost function is $MC = 4 - 2x + x^2$, find the total and the average cost functions, given that the fixed cost is 100.

$$\left[C = 4x - x^2 - x^2/3 + 1000,\quad AC = 4 - x + x^2/3 + \frac{100}{x}\right]$$

7. The Marginal cost of production is found to be $MC = 2000 - 40x + 3x^2$, where x is the number of units produced. The fixed cost of production is Rs. 18000. Find the total cost of function and the average cost function.

$$\left[C = 2000x - 20x^2 - x^3 + 18000,\quad AC = 2000 - 20x + x^2 + \frac{18000}{x}\right]$$

8. The marginal cost function of a firm is $MC = (\log x)^2$. Find the total cost of 100 units if the cost of producing one unit is Rs. 22. [Rs. 220]

9. If the marginal cost function at x units of output is $\frac{a}{\sqrt{ax+b}}$ and if the cost of output is zero, find the total cost as a function of x. $\left[C = 2\sqrt{ax+b} - 2\sqrt{b}\right]$

10. The cot of a truck engine overhauling is Rs. A, and the operating costs are at the rate of Rs. $A + bx$ per km, where the engine has run x kms since the last overhaul. If the engine is overhaulted at M kms, find the total cost function, C. $\left[C = A + a\,M + \frac{b}{2}M^2\right]$

TO CONVERT MARGINAL REVENUE FUNCTION TO TOTAL REVENUE FUNCTION.

We have $$MR = \frac{dR}{dx}$$

$\therefore$ $$MR.dx = dR$$

i.e., $$dR = MR.dx$$

Integrating both the sides, we have

$$\int dR = \int MR.dx$$

$$R = \int MR.dx + k \text{ (where } k \text{ is constant)}$$

with the help of R, we can find demand function by using the equation $R = px$.

To find the total revenue function and the demand function from a given marginal revenue function.

Example 8. **Given marginal revenue function**

$$\mathbf{MR = 100 - 50x.}$$

Find

1. **Total Revenue function**
2. **Demand function**

Solution. Given MR = $100 - 50x$

$$MR = \frac{dR}{dx} = 100 - 50x$$

$\therefore$ $$dR = (100 - 50x).dx$$

Integrating both the sides

$$\int dR = \int (100 - 50x).dx$$

$=$ $$R = 100x - \frac{50x^2}{2} + k$$

However, when $x = 0$, revenue $= 0$

$\therefore \quad 0 = 100(0) - 25(0)^2 + k$

$\therefore \quad k = 0$

$\therefore \quad R = 100x - 25x^2$

$= (100 - 25x) \cdot x \quad ...(1)$

By definition $R = p \cdot x$. (where 'p' is demand function) ... (2)

Using (1) and (2), we have

$$p = 100 - 25x$$

Example 9. **Marginal revenue function of a firm is** $\dfrac{ab}{(x-b)^2} - c$. **Prove that the demand law is**

$$p = \frac{a}{b-c} - c.$$

Solution. Given

$$\frac{ab}{(x-b)^2} - c$$

$$\therefore \quad \frac{dR}{dx} = \frac{ab}{(x-b)^2} - c$$

$$\therefore \quad dR = \left[\frac{ab}{(x-b)^2} - c\right] . dx$$

Integrating both sides with respect to x, we have

$$R = \int\left[\frac{ab}{(x-b)^2} - c\right] dx$$

$$= \frac{ab}{(b-x)} - cx + k,$$

where k is constant. When $x = 0$, $R = 0$

$$0 = \frac{ab}{b} - 0 + k \quad \Rightarrow \quad k = -a.$$

Therefore, the revenue function is

$$R = \frac{ab}{(b-x)} - cx - a$$

Revenue, by def., $R = px$, where p is the price per unit. Therefore

$$px = +\frac{ab}{(b-x)} - cx - a$$

$$\therefore \quad p = \frac{ab}{x(b-x)} - c - \frac{a}{x}$$

$$= \frac{abx - abx + ax^2}{x^2 (b - x)} - c$$

$$= \frac{a}{(b - x)} - c.$$

***Example 10* : A firm's marginal revenue function is given by** $MR = \frac{a}{(x+b)} - \frac{ax}{(x+b)^2} + c.$

Show that its demand function is $p = \frac{a}{(x+b)} + c.$

Solution.

$$MR = \frac{a}{(x+b)} - \frac{ax}{(x+b)^2} + c$$

$$\therefore \quad dR = \left[\frac{a}{(x+b)} - \frac{ax}{(x+b)^2} + c\right].dx$$

Integrating both the sides we have

$$\int dR = \int\left[\frac{a}{(x+b)} - \frac{ax}{(x+b)^2} + c\right].dx$$

$$R = a\log(a+x) - a - a\int\frac{ax}{(x+b)^2} + cx + k$$

Solving $\int \frac{x}{(x+b)^2}.dx$
$= \int \frac{(x+b)\,dx}{(x+b)^2} - \int \frac{b}{(x+b)^2}.dx$
$= \log(x+b) + \frac{b}{(x+b)}$

$$R = a\log(x+b) - a\log(x+b) - \frac{ab}{(x+b)} + cx + k$$

$$R = -\frac{ab}{(x+b)} + cx + k$$

when $x = 0,\ R = 0.$

$$0 = -\frac{ab}{b} + 0 + k$$

$$k = a$$

$$\therefore \quad R = -\frac{ab}{(x+b)} + cx + a$$

Subssituting $R = px$ in the above equation, we have

$$px = \frac{ab}{(x+b)} + cx + a$$

$$p = \frac{ab}{x(x+b)} + \frac{cx}{x} + \frac{a}{x}$$

$$= \frac{a}{x}\left[1 - \frac{b}{(x+b)}\right] + c$$

$$= \frac{a}{x}\left[\frac{x+b-b}{(x+b)}\right] + c$$

$$= \frac{a}{x}\left[\frac{x}{(x+b)}\right] + c$$

$$p = \frac{a}{(x+b)} + c.$$

Example 11: **If the marginal revenue function is $\frac{ab}{(x+b)^2} - c$ find the total revenue function and show that $p = \frac{a}{(x+b)} - c$ is the demand function (where 'p' is price, 'x' is quantity demanded and a, b, and c are contant).**

Solution.

$$MR = \frac{ab}{(x+b)^2} - c$$

$$\frac{dR}{dx} = \frac{ab}{(x+b)^2} - c$$

$$dR = \left[\frac{ab}{(x+b)^2} - c\right].dx$$

Integrating both the sides.

$$\int dR = \int\left[\frac{ab}{(x+b)^2} - c\right].dx$$

$$R = ab\int\frac{dx}{(x+b)^2} - c\int dx$$

$$R = -\frac{ab}{(x+b)} - cx + k$$

when $x = 0,\ R = 0$

$$0 = -\frac{ab}{b} + k$$

$$k = a$$

$$R = \frac{-ab}{(x+b)} - cx + a$$

$$= a\left[1 - \frac{b}{(x+b)}\right] - cx$$

$$= a\left[\frac{x+b-b}{x+b}\right] - cx$$

$$R = \frac{ax}{(x+b)} - cx$$

Substituting $R = p \, . \, x$

$$px = \frac{ax}{(x+b)} - cx$$

$$p = \frac{ax}{(x+b) \, . \, x} - \frac{cx}{x}$$

$$p = \frac{a}{(x+b)} - c$$

Example 12. **A firm's marginal revenue function is $MR = 20e^{-x/10}\left(1 - \frac{x}{10}\right)$. Find the corresponding demand function.**

Solution. Given

$$MR = 20e^{-x/10}\left(1 - \frac{x}{10}\right)$$

$$\frac{dR}{dx} = 20e^{-x/10}\left(1 - \frac{x}{10}\right)$$

$$\therefore \qquad dR = 20e^{-x/10}\left(1 - \frac{x}{10}\right). \, dx$$

Integrating both sides with respect to x, we have

$$R = \int 20e^{-x/10}\left(1 - \frac{x}{10}\right) dx$$

$$= 20\int e^{-x/10} \, dx - 2\int xe^{-x/10} dx$$

$$= 20\int e^{-x/10} \, dx - 2\left[-10xe^{-x/10} - \int -10e^{-x/10} dx\right]$$

$$= 20\int e^{-x/10} \, dx + 20xe^{-x/10} - 20\int e^{-x/10} dx$$

$$= 20xe^{-x/10} + k.$$

where k is constant. When $x = 0$, $R = 0$, therefore

$$0 = 0 + k \quad \Rightarrow \quad k = 0$$

Therefore, the revenue function is given by

$$R = 20xe^{-x/10}$$

Revenue, by def. $R = px$, where p is the price per unit, therefore

$$px = 20xe^{-x/10}$$

$$p = 20e^{-x/10}$$

which is the required demand function.

Example 13. **If the marginal revenue function of a firm is given by $MR = 25e^{-x/400}\left(1-\frac{x}{400}\right)$, show that the corresponding demand function is $p = 25e^{-x/400}$, where p is price and x is quantity.**

Solution. Given

$$MR = 25e^{-x/400}\left(1-\frac{x}{400}\right)$$

$$\therefore \quad \frac{dR}{dx} = 25e^{-x/400}\left(1-\frac{x}{400}\right)$$

$$\therefore \quad dR = 25e^{-x/400}\left(1-\frac{x}{400}\right).dx$$

Integrating both the sides, we have,

$$\int dR = \int 25e^{-x/400}\left(1-\frac{x}{400}\right).dx$$

$$R = -10000e^{-x/400} - \frac{1}{16}\int xe^{-x/400}.dx$$

$$R = -10000e^{-x/400} - \frac{1}{16}[-400xe^{-x/400} + 160000e^{-x/400}] + k$$

$$\therefore \quad R = -10000e^{-x/400} + \frac{400}{16}x.e^{-x/400} + 10000e^{-x/400} + k$$

$$R = \frac{400}{16}x.e^{-x/400} + k$$

when $x = 0$, Revenue $R = 0$

$$\therefore \quad 0 = 0 + k$$

$$\therefore \quad k = 0$$

$$\therefore \quad R = \frac{400}{16}x.e^{-x/400}$$

$$= 25x.e^{-x/400}$$

$$= 25e^{-x/400}.x \qquad ...(1)$$

Since Revenue $= p.x$ (where p is a demand function) ...(2)

Using (1) and (2), we have demand function as

$$p = 25e^{-x/400}.$$

Example 14. **A firm has following marginal revenue and marginal cost function.**

$$MR = 50 - 4x$$

$$MC = -20 + 2x$$

The firm suffers a loss of Rs. 200 when no units are sold.

(*a*) Determine total profit functions

(*b*) Find Break even point

(*c*) Determine the profit enclosed between these two B.E. points.

Solution. (*a*) Given

Marginal Revenue = $MR = 50 - 4x$

Marginal cost = $MC = -20 + 2x$

$$\therefore \quad \frac{dP}{dx} = MR - MC$$

$$= 50 - 4x - (-20 + 2x)$$

$$= 50 - 4x + 20 - 2x$$

$$= 70 - 6x$$

$$\therefore \quad dP = (70 - 6x) \,.\, dx$$

Integrating both the sides, we have

$$\int dP = \int (70 - 6x).dx = 70x - \frac{6x^2}{2} + k$$

$$\therefore \quad p = 70x - 3x^2 + k$$

when $\quad x = 0,\ p = -200$ (Given)

$$\therefore \quad -200 = 70(0) - 3(0)^2 + k$$

$$\therefore \quad K = -200$$

$$P = 70x - 3x^2 - 200 \qquad \text{...(1)}$$

(*b*) In order to find break even points, put $p = 0$ in the equation (1) derived above.

$$70x - 3x^2 - 200 = 0$$

$$\therefore \quad 3x^2 - 70x + 200 = 0$$

$$x = \frac{70 \pm \sqrt{4900 - 2400}}{6} = \frac{70 \pm \sqrt{2500}}{6}$$

$$= \frac{120}{6}, \frac{20}{6}$$

$$x = 20, \frac{20}{6}$$

$\therefore$ Break even point occurs at $x = 20$ and $x = \frac{20}{6}$.

(*c*) $P = \int_{20/6}^{20} (70x - 3x^2 - 200).dx$

$$= \left| 70\frac{x^2}{2} - \frac{3x^3}{3} - 200x \right|_{20/6}^{20}$$

$$= \left| 35x^2 - x^3 - 200x \right|_{20/6}^{20}$$

$$= (14000 - 8000 - 4000) - \left(\frac{14000}{36} - \frac{8000}{216} - \frac{4000}{6} \right)$$

$$= 2000 - (388.88 - 37.03 - 666.66)$$

$$= 2000 - (-314.81) = 2314.81$$

∴ Profit between two break even points is 2314.81.

Exercise 11.2

1. If the marginal revenue function for a commodity $MR = 9 - 4x^2$, find the demand function.
$[p = 9 - 4/3x^2]$

2. If the marginal revenue function for output x is given by $MR = \frac{6}{(x+2)^2} + 5$, find the total revenue function and the demand function. $\left[R = 3x/(x+2) + 5x,\ p = \frac{3}{(x+2)} + 5 \right]$

3. If the marginal revenue function is

$$\frac{ab}{(x+b)^2} - c,$$

Find the total revenue function and show that

$$p = \frac{a}{x+b} - c$$

is the demand function (where p is price, x is quantity demanded and a, b and c are constants).
$\left[R = \frac{ax}{x+b} - cx \right]$

4. A firm has the marginal revenue function given by $MR = \frac{a}{(x+b)^2} - c$, where x is the output and a, b and c are constants. Show that the demand function is given by $x = \frac{a}{b(p+c)} - b$.

5. A firm has a marginal revenue function given by $MR = \frac{a}{x+b} - c$, where x is the output and a, b and c are constants. Show that the demand function is given by $p = \frac{a}{x}\log\left(\frac{x+b}{b}\right) - c$.

6. A firm's marginal revenue function is given by $MR = \dfrac{a}{x+b} - \dfrac{ax}{(x+b)^2} + c$. Show that its demand function is $p = \dfrac{a}{x+b} + c$.

7. If the marginal revenue function of a firm is given by $MR = 25e^{-x/400}\left(1 - \dfrac{x}{400}\right)$, show that the corresponding demand function is $p = 25e^{-x/400}$, where p is price and x is quantity.

8. If the marginal revenue function for a product is MR = $3 + e^{-0.05x}$, where x denotes number of units produced. Determine the total revenue firm the sale of 100 units of the product.

[Ans. Rs. 319.86]

9. The sale producer of a product has determined that the marginal revenue function is $MR = 50 - 3x^2$. Determine the elasticity of demand of the product when $x = 4$. **[Ans.** 17/16]

TO FIND THE CONSUMPTION FUNCTION IF THE MARGINAL PROPENSITY TO CONSUME IS GIVEN

Marginal propensity to consume is defined as the rate of change of consumption with income. If I and C denote national income and national consumption, respectively then

$$MPC = \frac{dC}{dI}$$

$$\therefore \quad MPC.\ dI = dC$$

i.e.,

$$dC = MPC.dI$$

Integrating both the sides, we have

$$\int dC = \int MPC.dI$$

$$C = \int MPC.dI + k \text{ (constant)}$$

Similarly, marginal propensity to save $(MPS) = \dfrac{dS}{dx}$

Also $\quad MPS = (1 - MPC)$

Example 15. **The marginal propensity to consume is given by**

$$\frac{dC}{dI} = \frac{3}{4} - \frac{1}{2\sqrt{3I}}$$

where consumption C is a function of national income?

Determine the consumption function if it is given that consumption is 10 when $I = 12$.

Solution. Given $\dfrac{dC}{dI} = \dfrac{3}{4} - \dfrac{1}{2\sqrt{3I}}$

$$\therefore \quad \int dC = \int \frac{3}{4} - \frac{1}{2\sqrt{3I}} \cdot dI$$

$$\therefore \qquad C = \frac{3}{4}I - \frac{\sqrt{I}}{\sqrt{3}} + K$$

when $I = 12$, $C = 10$

$$\therefore \qquad 10 = \frac{3}{4}(12) - \frac{\sqrt{12}}{\sqrt{3}} + k = 9 - \sqrt{4} + k$$

$$10 = 9 - 2 + k$$

$$\therefore \qquad K = 3$$

Thus, the required consumption function will be given as

$$C = \frac{3}{4}I - \frac{\sqrt{I}}{\sqrt{3}} + 3.$$

***Example 16.* The marginal propensity to save is given**

$$\frac{dS}{dI} = \frac{1}{4} + \frac{1}{6\sqrt{I}}$$

where S is the savings and I is the income. Find the total savings S if $S = 12$ when $I = 25$.

Solution. Given

$$\frac{dS}{dI} = \frac{1}{4} + \frac{1}{6\sqrt{I}}$$

$$\therefore \qquad dS = \left(\frac{1}{4} + \frac{1}{6\sqrt{I}}\right).dI$$

Integrating both the sides, we have

$$S = \int\left(\frac{1}{4} + \frac{1}{6\sqrt{I}}\right).dI$$

$$= \frac{I}{4} + \frac{2\sqrt{I}}{6} + K$$

when $I = 25$, $S = 2$.

Substituting these values is the above equation, we have

$$2 = \frac{25}{4} + \frac{\sqrt{25}}{3} + K$$

$$2 = \frac{25}{4} + \frac{5}{3} + K$$

$$2 = \frac{95}{12} + K$$

$$\therefore \qquad K = 2 - \frac{95}{12} = \frac{24 - 95}{12} = -\frac{71}{12}$$

$$S = \frac{I}{4} + \frac{\sqrt{I}}{3} - \frac{71}{12}$$

Exercise 11.4

1. The marginal propensity to consume is given by $\frac{dC}{dI} = 0.7$, where C is the consumption and I is income. Find the consumption function if $C = 70$ when $I = 2$. $[C = 0.7\ I + 50]$

2. The marginal propensity to consume is given by the equation $\frac{dC}{dI} = 8I + 2$ where C is the consumption and I is income. Find the consumption function if $C = 75$ when $I = 3$.

$[C = 4I^2 + 2k + 75]$

3. The marginal propensity to save is given by $\frac{dS}{dI} = \frac{1}{3} + \frac{1}{2\sqrt{I}}$ where S is the savings and I is the income. Find the total savings s if $S = 10$ when $I = 36$.

$$\left[S = \frac{I}{3} + I^{1/2} - 8\right]$$

TO FIND MAXIMUM PROFIT IF MARGINAL REVENUE AND MARGINAL COST FUNCTIONS ARE GIVEN

We have

$$P = R - C$$

$$\therefore \quad \frac{dP}{dx} = \frac{dR}{dC} - \frac{dC}{dx} = MR - MC.$$

Thus, if MR and MC are given, we can find $\frac{dP}{dx}$.

Equate $\frac{dP}{dx} = 0$ to get stationary points.

Find $\frac{d^2P}{dx^2}$. If it is negative, it confirms maxima of profit at the stationary point.

***Example 17.* The marginal cost $C'(x)$ and the marginal revenue $R'(x)$ are given by**

$$C'(x) = 20 + \frac{x}{20} \text{ and } R'(x) = 30$$

The fixed cost is 200. Determine the maximum profit and the number of items produced for this profit.

Solution. Let P denote the profit function, therefore, as already explained

$$\frac{dP}{dx} = \frac{dR}{dx} - \frac{dC}{dx} = 30 - 20 - \frac{x}{20} = 10 - \frac{x}{20}$$

$$dP = (10 - x/20)\ .\ dx$$

Integrating both sides with respect to x, we get

$$P = \int \left(10 - \frac{x}{20}\right) dx = 10x - \frac{x^2}{40} + k,$$

where k is the constant of integration. Given fixed cost is 200. This implies when $x = 0$, profit $P = -200$. Substituting these values in the above equation, we have

$$\therefore \quad -200 = k$$

Therefore $P = 10x - (x^2/40) - 200$ is the profit function.

For P to be maximum, it is necessary that

$$\frac{dP}{dx} = 0, \text{ i.e., } 10 - \frac{x}{20} = 0 \quad \Rightarrow \quad x = 200.$$

Further $\frac{d^2P}{dx^2} = -\frac{1}{20} < 0$ since second derivative is negative, it implies the output $x = 200$ gives a maximum profit. The maximum profit will be

$$P = 10(200) - \frac{(200)^2}{40} - 200 = 800.$$

Thus, maximum profit is Rs. 800 which is obtained when 200 items are produced.

TO FIND THE OPTIMUM TIME FOR WHICH BUSINESS SHALL BE CONTINUED.

There are certain business sin which revenue keeps on declining with time and cost of operating goes on increasing with time *i.e.*, revenue and cost are functions of time and they move in opposite direction. Thus, we may come across a situation or point of time till which revenue is higher than cost and after which cost is higher than revenue. **The point, after which this change takes place is called optimum time.** At this point

$$R'(t) = C'(t)$$

i.e., rate of change of revenue with time get equal to the rate of change in cost with time, we have profit as long as $R'(t)\ C'(t)$ and we have loss when $R'(t) < C'(t)$. This can be observed from the graph shown in Fig. 11.1

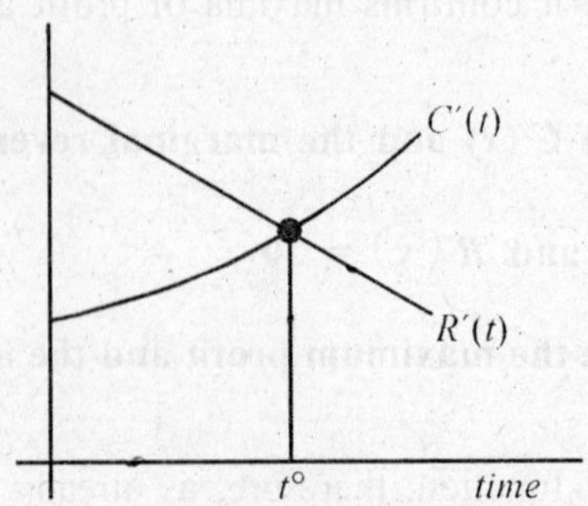

Fig. 11.1

Thus, the business **shall** be continued upto time t_0. The profit till this time would be

$$P = \int_0^{t_0} [R'(t) - C'(t)]\, dt$$

P represent maximum profit.

Example 18. **The revenue and cost rate of a firm, which are dependent on time, are given as under.**

$$R'(t) = 8 - t^{1/2}$$

$$C'(t) = 2 + 2t^{1/2}$$

where t is measured in years and R and C are measured in lakhs of rupees. Determine how long the operation should continue and the profit that can be generated during this period.

Solution. The optimum time till which the business operation should be continued is derive by equating the revenue rate and cost rate

$$\therefore \quad R'(t) = C'(t)$$

$$\Rightarrow \quad 8 - t^{1/2} = 2 + 2t^{1/2}$$

$$\therefore \quad 8 - 2 = 2t^{1/2} + t^{1/2} = 3t^{1/2}$$

$$\therefore \quad t^{1/2} = \frac{6}{3} = 2$$

Squaring both the sides, we have

$$t^* = 4$$

The profit that can be generated during this period is given by

$$p(t)^* = \int_0^4 [R'(t) - C'(t)].\,dt$$

$$= \int_0^4 \left(8 - t^{1/2}\right) - \left(2 + 2t^{1/2}\right).\,dt$$

$$= \int_0^4 \left(6 - 3t^{1/2}\right).\,dt$$

$$= \left| 6t - \frac{3t^{3/2}}{3} \times (2) \right|_0^4$$

$$= \left| 6t - 2t^{3/2} \right|_0^4$$

$$= 6(4) - 2(4)^{3/2} - 0$$

$$= 24 - 2 \times (2)^3 - 0$$

$$= 24 - 16 = 18$$

Thus, optimum time is 4 and profit during this period is 8.

***Example 19.* The marginal cost of producing x units of a commodity in a day is given as $MC = 16x - 1591$. The selling price is fixed at Rs. 9 per unit and the fixed cost is Rs. 1,800 per day. Determine (*i*) Cost function (*ii*) Revenue function, (*iii*) Profit function, and (*iv*) Maximum profit that can be obtained in one day.**

Solution. (*i*) Given marginal cost function as

$$MC = 16x - 1591.$$

$$\therefore \quad \frac{dC}{dx} = 16x - 1591$$

$$\therefore \quad dC = (16x - 1591) \cdot dx$$

Integrating, we obtain

$$C = \int (16x - 1591)\, dx$$

$$= 8x^2 - 1591x + k$$

where k is constant. It is given that the fixed cost is Rs. 1,800, which means, C = 1,800 when $x = 0$.

$$\therefore \quad 1800 = 8(0)^2 - 1591\,(0) + k \quad \Rightarrow \quad k = 1800.$$

Therefore the cost function will be given as :

$$C = 8x^2 - 1591x + 1800$$

(*ii*) The selling price is fixed at Rs. 9 per unit, therefore the revenue function will be given as

$$R = 9x.$$

(*iii*) The profit function is given by substracting the cost function from the revenue function.

$$\therefore \quad P = R - C = 9x - (8x^2 - 1591x + 1800)$$

$$= -8x^2 + 1600x - 1800.$$

(*iv*) For maximum profit, the first order condition is

$$\frac{dP}{dx} = 0$$

i.e., $\quad - 16x + 1600 = 0 \Rightarrow x = 100.$

Also $\dfrac{d^2P}{dx^2} = -16 < 0$. (Second order derivatives is negative)

This shows that profit is maximum when $x = 100$. Corresponding to $x = 100$, maximum profit will be

$$P = (-8)\,(100)^2 + 1600\,(100) - 1800 = \text{Rs. } 78{,}200.$$

***Example 20.* A company suffers a loss of Rs. 560 if one of its product does not sell. Marginal revenue and marginal cost functions for the product are given by**

$$\mathbf{MR = 170 - 25x \text{ and } MC = -50 + 15x}$$

Determine the total profit function, the break even points and the total profit between the break even points.

Solution. Let P denote the profit function, then

$$\frac{dP}{dx} = MR - MC$$

$$= (170 - 25x) - (-50 + 15x)$$

$$\frac{dP}{dx} = 220 - 40x$$

$$P = \int (220 - 40x).dx = 220x - \frac{40x^2}{2} + k$$

when $x = 0$, $P = -560$ (Given)

$$\therefore \quad -560 = 220(0) - \frac{40(0)^2}{2} + k$$

$$-560 = k$$

$$\therefore \quad P = 220x - 20x^2 - 560$$

For breakeven points, $P = 0$

$$\therefore \quad 220x - 20x^2 - 560 = 0$$

$$-20(x^2 + 11x + 28) = 0$$

$$\therefore \quad x^2 + 11x + 28 = 0$$

$x = 4$, $x = 7$

Total profit between these points

$$P = \int_4^7 (220x - 20x^2 - 560).dx$$

$$\left| \frac{220x^2}{2} - \frac{20x^3}{3} - 560x \right|_4^7$$

$$(5390 - 2286.66 - 3920)$$

$$-(1760 - 426.66 - 2240)$$

$$= (-81.66) - (-906.66) = 825.$$

Exercise 11.3

1. At the production level x, the marginal cost of production of a firm is Rs. $(4 + 0.11x)$ and the marginal revenue is Rs. 15. The overhead costs are Rs. 100. Find the maximum profit the firm can earn and the level of production for this profit. [Max Profit = Rs. 450, $x = 100$]

2. The marginal cost of production si found to be

$$MC = 1000 - 20x + x^2,$$

where x is the number of units produced. The fixed cost of production is Rs. 9,000. Find the cost function. If the manufacturer fixes are price per unit at Rs. 3,400, find the profit function and the sales volume that yields maximum profit.

$$\left[\begin{array}{l} C = 1000x - 10x^2 + \dfrac{x^3}{3} + 9000, \text{ Profit function} \\ P = 2400x + 10x^2 - x^{3/3} - 9000, \ x = 60 \end{array}\right]$$

3. The marginal cost (MC) and marginal revenue (MR) of a firm are given as $MC = 4 + .08\,x$ and $MR = 12$, where x denotes the level of output. Compute the total profit of the firm given that the initial fixed cost is Rs. 100. [Max Profit = Rs. 300 and $x = 100$]

4. The *ABC*, Co. Ltd. has approximated the marginal revenue function for one of its products by $MR = 20x - 2x^2$. The marginal cost function is approximated by $MC = 80 - 16x + x^2$.

   Determine the profit maximizing output and the total profit at the optimal output.

   [$x = 9$, Max. profit = 0]

5. A company suffers a loss of Rs. 1,000 if its product does not sell at all. Marginal revenue and Marginal cost functions for the product are given by

$$MR = 50 - 4x, \ MC = -10 + x.$$

   Determine the total profit function, breakeven points and the profit maximizing level of output.

$$\left[(i)\ P = 60x - \frac{5}{2}x^2 - 1000, (ii) \text{ No break even point, } (iii)\ x = 12\right]$$

6. Suppose that when it is t years old, an industrial machine generates revenue at the rate of $R'(t) = 6028 - 8t^2$ rupees per year and results in costs that accumulate at the rate of $C'(t) = 4681 + 13t^2$ rupees per year.

   (*i*) For how many years is the use of the machine profitable?

   (*ii*) What are the net earnings generated by the machine during its period of profitability?

   [(*i*) 8 years, (*ii*) Rs. 7168]

7. The marginal cost $C'(x)$ and marginal revenue, $R'(x)$ are respectively given by $C'(x) = 4x^2 + 30x + 14$ and $R'(x) = 10x^2 - 12x + 50$, x being the number of units produced. Find the level of output at which profit will be maximum. [$x = 1$]

8. Find the maximum profit that a company can make, if the profit function is given by $P(x) = 41 + 24x - 18x^2$. [$x = 2/3$ Max Profit = 49]

9. Obtain the demand function for a commodity for which price elasticity of demand is 'k' throughout. [$x\,p^k = c$]

10. The price elasticity of demand for commodity is

$$Ep = \frac{3p}{(p-1)(p+2)}$$

   Find the corresponding demand function if quantity demanded is 8 units when the price is Rs. 2.

   [$x = 2(p + 2)/(p - 1)$]

DETERMINATION OF DEMAND FUNCTION WHEN PRICE ELASTICITY OF DEMAND IS GIVEN.

We know that price elasticity of demand is given as :

$$\eta_d = \frac{p}{x} \cdot \frac{dx}{dp}$$

Let $\eta_d = a$ (any constant), we have

$$a = -\frac{p}{x} \cdot \frac{dx}{dp}$$

$$\therefore \quad x\,a\,.\,dp = -p\,.\,px$$

$$\frac{adp}{p} = -\frac{dx}{x}$$

$$\therefore \quad \frac{a\,.\,dp}{p} + \frac{dx}{x} = 0$$

Integrating both the sides we have

$$a \log p + \log x = \log k$$

$$\therefore \quad \log p^a + \log x = \log k$$

$$\log (x\,p^a) = \log k$$

$$\therefore \quad k = x\,p^a$$

$$p^a = \frac{x}{k}$$

$$p = \left(\frac{x}{k}\right)^{1/a}$$

Thus, with the help of integration we can find demand function from a given price elasticity of demand.

Example 22. **Derive the demand function which has the unit price elasticity of demand throughout.**

Solution. Given

$$\eta_d = 1$$

$$\therefore \quad -\frac{p}{x}\frac{dx}{dp} = 1$$

i.e.,

$$\frac{dx}{x} + \frac{dp}{p} = 0$$

Integrating, we have

$$\log x + \log p = \log k,$$

where k is an arbitrary constant. Therefore,

$$\log (xp) = \log k$$

$$xp = k,$$

The above equation represent the required demand function.

Example 23. **The elasticity of demand of a commodity with respect to price is calculated to be $\frac{5p}{(p+3)(p-2)}$ (where p is price). Find the demand function, if it is known that the quantity demanded is 5 units at $p = 3$.**

Solution. By definition, the elasticity of demand is given as

$$e_d = -\frac{p}{x}\frac{dx}{dp} \qquad \text{...(1)}$$

Given $$e_d = \frac{5p}{(p+3)(p-2)} \qquad \text{...(2)}$$

Equation (1) and (2), we have

$$\frac{5p}{(p+3)(p-2)} = -\frac{p}{x}\frac{dx}{dp}$$

Integrating both sides, we have

$$\int \frac{5}{(p+3)(p-2)} = -\int \frac{1}{x}\,dx$$

$$\Rightarrow \quad \int \frac{-1}{p+3}\,dp + \int \frac{1}{p-2}\,dp = -\int \frac{1}{x}\,dx$$

$$\Rightarrow \quad -\log(p+3) + \log(p-2) = -\log x + \log k$$

where k is constant. Therefore

$$\log \frac{p-2}{p+3} = \log \frac{k}{x}$$

$$\Rightarrow \quad \frac{p-2}{p+3} = \frac{k}{x} \quad \Rightarrow \quad x = \frac{k(p+3)}{p-2}$$

We are given that $x = 5$ at $p = 3$. Therefore

$$5 = \frac{k(3+3)}{3-2} \quad \Rightarrow \quad k = \frac{5}{6}.$$

Hence the required demand function is given by

$$x = \frac{5(p+3)}{6(p-2)}.$$

Example 24. **A commodity has price elasticity of demand of $\frac{p}{2x^4}$. Find the demand function if the demand is 2 when the price is 1.**

Solution. Given $n_d = -\frac{p}{x}\cdot\frac{dx}{dp} = \frac{p}{2x^4}$

$$\therefore \quad = -\frac{p}{x}\cdot\frac{dx}{dp} = \frac{p}{2x^4}$$

$\therefore \qquad = -2x^3 \ . \ dx = dp$

Integrating both the sides, we have

$$-\int 2x^3 . dx = \int dp$$

$$\therefore \qquad \frac{-2x^4}{4} + k = p$$

$$\therefore \qquad K = p + \frac{x^4}{2}$$

Substituting

when $p = 1, x = 2$

we have $\qquad K = (1) + \frac{(2)^4}{2}$

$$= 1 + \frac{16}{2} = 1 + 8 = 9$$

$$\therefore \qquad k = 9$$

$$\therefore \qquad 9 = p + \frac{x^4}{2}$$

$\therefore$ Required demand function is:

$$\therefore \qquad p = 9 - \frac{x^4}{2}$$

Example 25. **Obtain the demand function for a commodity whose elasticity of demand is given by $e_{xp} = a - bp$, where a, b are constants and p denotes the price per unit of the commodity.**

Solution. Given elasticity of demand as

$$e_{xp} = a - bp$$

$$-\frac{p}{x}\frac{dx}{dp} = a - bp$$

$$\frac{dx}{x} + \left(\frac{a}{p} - b\right) dp = 0$$

Integrating both the sides, we have

$$\log x + a \log p - bp = c,$$

where c is constant. Therefore

$$\log x + \log p^a = bp + c$$

$$\Rightarrow \qquad \log (xp^a) = bp + c$$

$$\Rightarrow \qquad xp^a = e^{bp + c}$$

i.e, $\qquad x = p^{-a} e^{bp + c}$

The above equation represent the required demand function.

Exercise 11.4

1. At the production level x, the marginal cost of production of a firm is Rs. $(4 + 0.11x)$ and the marginal revenue is Rs. 15. The overhead costs are Rs. 100. Find the maximum profit the firm can earn and the level of production for this profit. [Max Profit = Rs. 450, $x = 100$]

2. The marginal cost of production is found to be

   $MC = 1000 - 20x + x^2$,

   where x is the number of units produced. The fixed cost of production is Rs. 9,000. Find the cost function. If the manufacturer fixes the price per unit at Rs. 3,400, find the profit function and the sales volume that yields maximum profit.

   $3400x - 1000x + 10x^2 - x^{3/3}$

   $$\left[\begin{array}{l} C = 1000x - 10x^2 + \dfrac{x^3}{3} + 9000, \text{ Profit function} \\ P = 2400x + 10x^2 - \dfrac{x^3}{3} - 9000, x = 60 \end{array}\right]$$

3. The marginal cost (MC) and marginal revenue (MR) of a firm are given as $MC = 4 + .08x$ and $MR = 12$, where x denotes the level of output. Compute the total profit of the firm given that the initial fixed cost is Rs. 100. [Max Profit = Rs. 300 and $x = 100$]

4. The *ABC* Co. Ltd. has approximated the marginal revenue function for one of its products by $MR = 20x - 2x^2$. The marginal cost function is approximated by $MC = 81 - 16x + x^2$. Determine the profit maximizing output and the total profit at the optimal output.

   [$x = 9$, Max. profit = 0]

5. A company suffers a loss of Rs. 1000, if its product does not sell at all. Marginal revenue and Marginal cost functions for the products are given by

   $MR = 50 - 4x$, $MC = -10 + x$.

   Determine the total profit function, breakeven points and the profit maximizing level of output.

   $$\left[(i)\, P = 60x - \frac{5}{2}x^2 - 1000, \ (ii) \text{ No break even point}, \ (iii)\, x = 12\right]$$

6/ Suppose that when it is t years old, an industrial machine generates revenue at the rate of $R'(t) = 6025 - 8t^2$ rupees per year and results in costs that accumulate at the rate of $C'(t) = 4681 + 13t^2$ rupees per year.

   (*i*) For how many years is the use of the machine profitable?

   (*ii*) What are the net earnings generated by the machine during its period of profitability?

   [(*i*) 8 years, (*ii*) Rs. 7168]

7. The marginal cost $C'(x)$ and marginal revenue, $R'(x)$ are respectively given by $C'(x) = 4x^2 + 30x + 14$ and $R'(x) = 10x^2 - 12x + 50$, x being the number of units produced. Find the level of output at which profit will be maximum. [$x = 1$]

8. Find the maximum profit that x company can make, if the profit function is given by $P(x) = 41 + 24x - 18x^2$. [$x = 2/3$ Max Profit = 49]

RATE OF SALES

We know that sales during a given period changes at a particular rate. Once we know the rate of change of sale with time, we can find sales during a given time frame. For example, if sales function is $S(t)$, then the sales during the time commencing from n^{th} period and ending on $(n + m)^{th}$ period can be calculated using the formula

$$\int_{n}^{(n+m)} S(t).dt$$

Example 26. **After an advertising campaign, a product has a sales rate $f(t)$ given by**

$$f(t) = 1000e^{-0.5t},$$

where t is the number of months since the close of campaign. Find the total (cumulative) sales after three months.

Solution. The total sales after three months will be given as

$$\int_0^3 1000e^{-0.5t}dt = \frac{1000}{-0.5}\left|e^{-0.5t}\right|_0^3$$

$$= 2000\ (1 - e^{-1.5}) = \text{Rs. } 1553.74.$$

Example 27. **The purchase price of a car is Rs. 75,000. The rate of cost for repairs is given by $C = 6000\ (1 - e^{-0.5t})$, where t represents the year of use since purchase. Find the cumulative repair cost at the end of 5 years. Also find the equation to give the time in years at which the cumulative repair cost equals the original cost of the car.**

Solution. Given the rate of cost for repair as

$$C = 6000\ (1 - e^{-0.5t}),$$

hence the cumulative repair cost at the end of 5 years will be given by

$$\int_0^5 6000\left(1 - e^{-0.5t}\right)dt$$

$$= 6000\left|t - \frac{e^{-0.5t}}{-0.5}\right|_0^5$$

$$= 6000\left|t + 2e^{-0.5t}\right|_0^5$$

$$= 6000\ [5 + (2e^{-2.5t}) - 2] = 6000\ (3 + 2e^{-2.5})$$

$$= 6000\ (3 + 2\ (0.08208)]$$

$$= \text{Rs. } 18984.96$$

Let x years be elapsed to make the cumulative repair cost equal to the original cost, then

$$\Rightarrow \quad \int_0^x 6000\left(1 - e^{-0.5t}\right)dt = 75,000$$

$$\Rightarrow \quad 6000\left|t + 2e^{0.5t}\right|_0^x = 75,000$$

$$\Rightarrow \quad \left[\left(x + 2e^{0.5t}\right) - 2\right] = \frac{25}{2}$$

$\Rightarrow \qquad 2x + 4e^{-0.5x} - 29 = 0.$

Above equation is the required relation.

Example 28. **A company has a current sales of Rs. 1000 per month and profit to the company average 10%. The company's past experience with a certain advertising strategy is that sales increase by 2% per month compounded continuously over the length of the advertising campaign (12 months). If the advertisement costs Rs. 130 in a year, determine if the company should embark on a similar campaign when the market rate of interest is 12% per annum.**

Solution. Let $f(t)$ is sales rate per month during the advertising campaign. Therefore $f(t)$ is given by the relation

$$f(t) = 1000\ e^{0.02t}$$

Thus the total sales during the time interval $t = 0$ to $t = 12$ will be given as

$$\text{Total sales} = \int_0^{12} f(t)\,dt = \int_0^{12} 1000e^{0.02t}\,dt$$

$$= \frac{1000}{0.02}\left|e^{0.02t}\right|_0^{12} = 50,000\left(e^{0.24} - 1\right)$$

$$= 50000\ (0.2712) = \text{Rs. } 13560.$$

Since the profit to the company is 10% of sales, therefore the profit due to the increase in sales will be

$$0.10\ (13560 - 12000) = \text{Rs. } 156.$$

This profit of Rs. 156 has been obtained through the expenditure of Rs. 130 in advertising. Therefore, net profit is Rs. (156 – 130) = Rs. 26. As it represents more than 12% return on cost of the advertisement ($Prt = 130 \times 0.12 \times 1$ = Rs. 15.60) the company should continue with the similar campaign.

Example 29. **Assume that in 1990 the annual world use of natural gas was 50 trillion cubic feet. The annual consumption of gas is increasing at a rate of 3% compounded continuously. How long will it take to use all available gas, if it is known that in 1990 there were 2200 trillion cubic feet of proven reserves? Assume that no new discoveries are made.**

Solution. It is given that the annual consumption of gas was 50 trillion cubic feet in the year 1990 and it is increasing at a rate of 3% compounded continuously, therefore the rate of consumption of the gas will be given by the relation :

$$f(t) = 50e^{0.03t},$$

where t is measured in years. Thus the total consumption of the gas in x years is given by

$$\int_0^{x} f(t)\,dt = \int_0^{x} 50e^{0.03t}\,dt$$

$$= \frac{50}{0.03}\left|e^{0.03t}\right|_0^{x}$$

$$= \frac{5000}{3}\left[e^{0.03x} - 1\right].$$

We are required to find the value of x so that

$$\int_0^x f(t)\,dt = 2200$$

i.e., $$\frac{5000}{3}\left(e^{0.03x} - 1\right) = 2200$$

$$\Rightarrow \qquad e^{0.03x} = 2.32$$

$$0.03x \log e = \log 2.32 = 0.3655$$

$$\Rightarrow (0.03)\,(0.4343)\,x = 0.3655$$

$$0.03029\,x = 0.3655$$

$$\Rightarrow \qquad x = \frac{0.3655}{0.013029} = 28 \text{ years (approximately).}$$

Hence it will take about 28 years to use all available gas.

Exercise 11.5

1. After an advertising campaign a product has sales rate $f(t)$ given by $f(t) = 1000e^{-0.5t}$, where t is the number of months since the close of the campaign. Find (*a*) the total cumulative sales after 3 months, (*b*) the sales during the fourth months, (*c*) the total sales as a result of the campaign.

   [(*a*) 1553.74, (*b*) 175.58, (*c*) 2000]

2. After an advertising campaign, a product has a sales rate $f(t)$ given by

   $$f(t) = 5000e^{-0.05t}$$

   where t is number of months since the close of campaign. Find the total sales after three months.

   [Rs. 776.87]

3. The purchase price of scooter is rs. 40,000. The rate of cost for repairs is given by $C = 2000\,(1 - e^{-0.05t})$, where t represents the year of since purchase. Find the cumulative repair cost at the end of 5 years. Also find the equation to give the time in years at which the cumulative repair cost equals the original costs of the car. [6328.32, $2x + 4e^{-0.5x} - 22$]

4. A firm's annual sales are Rs. 10,000. The sales are continuously increasing as the rate of 20% per annum. Find the cumulative sales of first five years using calculus. [Rs. 8591.5]

5. A firm has the current sales of Rs. 50,000 per month. The firm wants to embark on a certain advertising campaign that will increase the sales by 2% per month (compounded continuously) over the period of the campaign which is 12 months. Find the total increase in sales as a result of the campaign. Use calculus.

   [Rs. 78000]

6. A small business is considering buying an energy-saving device which will reduce its consumption of fuel. The device will cost Rs. 32,000. Engineering estimates suggest that savings from using the device will occur at a rate of $s(t)$ rupees per year where $s(t) = 20000\,e^{-0.5t}$ and t equals time measured in years. Determine how long will it take for the firm to recover the cost of device.

   [3.2 years]

7. The purchase price of a car is Rs. 1,75,000. The rate of repairing cost of the car is given by the function

$$C = 8000\,(1 - e^{-0.5t})$$

where t represents the years of úse since purchase and C denote the cost. Determine the cumulative repair cost at the end of 5 years. [25313.28]

8. At $t = 0$, the annual world use of natural gas was 50 trillion cubic feet. The annual consumption of gas is increasing at the rate of 10% continuously. Assume the rate remains the same in future–

   (*i*) How many cubic feet will be consumed in the next 10 years from $t = 0$?

   (*ii*) How long will it take to use all the available gas, if it is known that world reserves are of 2200 trillion cubic feet in the beginning (assume that no new discoveries are made)?
   [(*i*) 859 trillion cubic feet, (*ii*) 16.86 years)]

THE LEARNING CURVE

There are certain industrial operations such as assembly of electric units, assembling of computers where a time required by a labour to perform a unit job keeps on decreasing due to experience gained over a period of time. This rate of reduction in direct labour requirements with time is described by a curve called learning curve.

It is generally represented as

$$f(x) = Ax^{\lambda}, \; -1 \leq \lambda < 0, \; A > 0$$

where $f(x)$ is the number of hours of direct labour required to produce x units of the product. The above function is shown in Figure 11.3

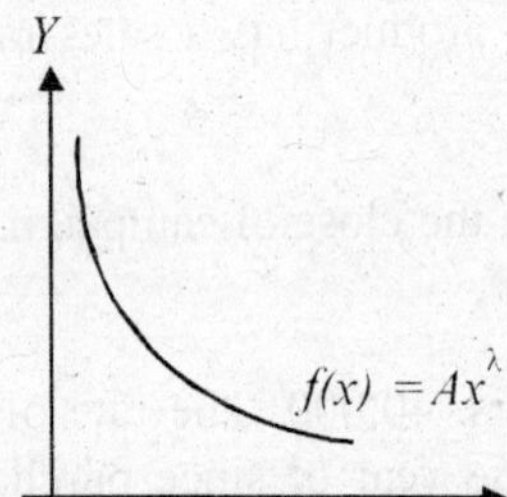

Fig. 11.2

Once we are able to find learning curve of a given production process, we can estimate number of units which can be manufactured within a given time of labour hours, using the formula given below.

$$N = \int_a^b f(x)\,.\,dx = \int_a^b Ax^{\lambda}\,.\,dx$$

Example 30. **A company has learning curve, after producing 50 units of the form**

$$\mathbf{f(x) = 25x^{-1/4}}, \text{ where}$$

$f(x)$ is the number of hours of direct labour required to produce x^{th} unit. How many total labour-hours are required to produce an additional 40 units?

Solution. Total number of labour-hours required to produce an additional 40 units is given by

$$N = \int_{50}^{90} 25x^{-1/4}\,.dx$$

$$= 25\left|\frac{x^{-1/4+1}}{-1/4+1}\right|_{50}^{90}$$

$$= 25\left|\frac{4x^{3/4}}{3}\right|_{50}^{90}$$

$$= 25\left(\frac{4}{3}\right)\left[\left((90)^{3/4} - (50)^{3/4}\right)\right]$$

$$\therefore \quad N = \frac{100}{3}(29.22 - 18.80) = 347.33$$

***Example 31. XYZ* Ltd. after producing 60 units has learning curve of the form**

$$f(x) = 100x^{-2/5}$$

where $f(x)$ is the number of hours of direct labour required to produce x^{th} unit. How many total labour-hour are required to produce an additional 20 units.

Solution. Total number of labour hour required to produce an additional 20 units is given by

$$N = \int_{60}^{80} 100x^{-2/5}.dx = 100\left|\frac{x^{-2/5+1}}{-2/5+1}\right|_{60}^{80} = 100\left|\frac{5x^{3/5}}{3}\right|_{60}^{80}$$

$$= \frac{500}{3}\left[(80)^{3/5} - (60)^{3/5}\right] = \frac{500}{3}(13.86 - 11.66) = 366.66$$

Exercise 11.6

1. A company has learning curve of the form $f(x) = 25x^{-1/3}$. The company has already produced 8 units. How many total labour-hours are required to produce an additional 19 units.

   [Ans. 187.50 hours]

2. A company has learning curve defined by the function

   $$f(x) = 1000x^{-1/2}$$

   Find the total number of labour hours required for producing additional 20 units when 16 units have already been produced. **[Ans.** 4000]

3. After producing 35 units of a product, the production manager determines that the production facility is following the learning curve of the form $f(x) = 300 - 190e^{-2x}$, where $f(x)$ is the rate of labour hours required to produce x^{th} units. How many labour hours would be required to produce additional 25 units. **[Ans.** 7500]

INVESTMENT AND CAPITAL FORMATION

Capital formation refers to the process of adding to a given stock of capital. Since capital formation is a continuous process over time, therefore it can be expressed as a function of time as $k(t)$. The rate of change of capital with time is given as $\frac{dK}{dt}$. This is equivalent to net investment flow at time t.

$$\therefore \quad \frac{dK}{dt} = I(t)$$

$$\therefore \quad dK = I(t) \, . \, dt$$

$$K(t) = \int I(t) \, . \, dt$$

Thus, if we are interested in finding the amount of capital formation during the time interval $[a, b]$, it can be measured as

$$K(t) = \int_a^b I(t) \, . \, dt$$

$$\therefore \quad \int_a^b I(t) \, . \, dt = K(b) - K(a).$$

Example 32. **Investment function is given by $I(t) = 500e^{0.4t}$, where $I(t) = \frac{dK}{dt}$ and K denotes and capital at time t, and the initial stock is $K(o) = 100$. Find**

(*i*) Time path of capital stock.

(*ii*) Capital formation during the first five years.

Solution. (*i*) Time path of capital stock is

$$K(t) = \int I(t) \, . \, dt = \int 500e^{0.4t} \, . \, dt$$

$$= 500 \, e^{0.4t} + k$$

where k is the constant of integration.

At time $t = 0$,

$$K(o) = 100, \text{ we have}$$

$$100 = 500e^{0.4t} + k$$

$$100 = 500e^{0} + k$$

$$\therefore \quad k = -400$$

$\therefore$ The time path of capital stock is

$$K(t) = 500e^{0.4t} - 400$$

(*ii*) Capital formation during the first five years

$$= \int_0^5 I(t) \, . \, dt = \left|500e^{0.4t}\right|_0^5$$

$$= 500 \, (e^2 - 1) = 3194.55$$

Exercise 11.7

1. The rate of investment is described by the function

$$I(t) = 5t^{1/2} \quad \text{and} \quad K(o) = 10$$

(*i*) Find the time path of capital *K*.

(*ii*) The amount of capital formation durint the time interval [1, 4].

$$\left[(i)\frac{10t^{3/2}}{3} + 10 \quad (ii)\ 70/3\right]$$

2. The rate of investment is defined by the function

$$I(t) = 6t^{2/3} \quad \text{and} \quad K(o) = 20$$

Find the time path of capital and the amount of capital formation during the time interval [8, 1].

$$\left[(i)\frac{18t^{3/2}}{5} + 20 \quad (ii)\frac{558}{5}\right]$$

3. If the investment flow is given by $I(t) = 3t^{1/2}$ crore of rupees per year, what will be the capital formation in the time period of 5 years, and during last year of the plan *i.e.*, 5th year? Also, find the capital growth equation from the given rate of capital formation if the initial stock of the capital is 20 crores of rupees. $[2 \times 5^{3/2},\ 2 \times 5^{3/2} - 6,\ k = 2t^{3/2} + 20]$

CONSUMER'S AND PRODUCER'S SURPLUS

We have already discussed under application of differentiate, equilibrium point. It is a point where demand curve intersect supply curve. The price and quantity an equilibrium point is known as equilibrium price and equilibrium quantity. The equilibrium point, 'O' is graphically shown below in figure 11.4.

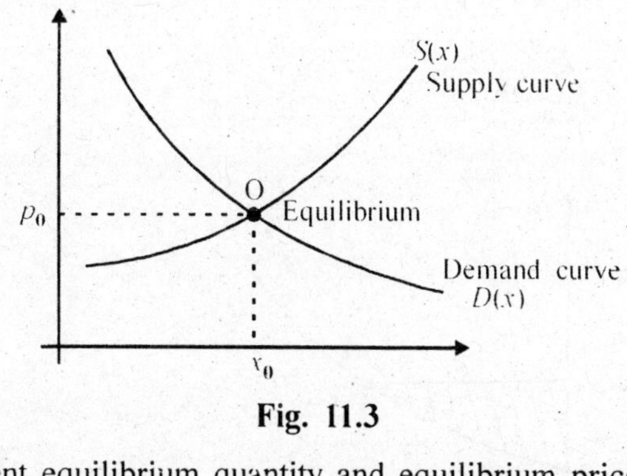

Fig. 11.3

Here x_0 and p_0 represent equilibrium quantity and equilibrium price respectively. Now we can understand the concept of consumer surplus and producer surplus.

CONSUMER SURPLUS

If we refer only the demand curve alongwith the equilibrium point, we will find that there are some consumers who are ready to pay even a price higher than the equilibrium price and thus consumers have been benefitted because of equilibrium points to the extent shown in the diagram drawn below. The consumer are able to get the commodity at a price lower than what they are willing to pay for the same commodity. The benefit received by them is known as consumer surplus and it is shown as shaded are in figure 11.4.

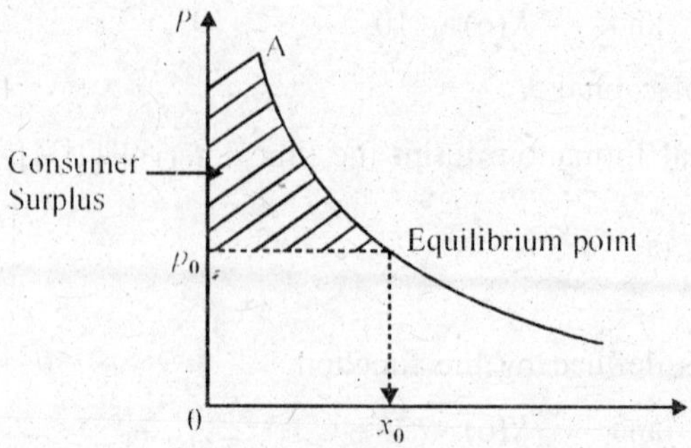

Fig. 11.4

Required Area (Consumer Surplus) = Total area under the curve AE − area of rectangle $p_0\ Ex_0\ O$.

$$CS = \int_0^{x_0} D(x).dx - x_0\ p_0$$

PRODUCER'S SURPLUS

Consider the supply curve alongwith the equilibrium point, as shown below in figure 11.5.

As can be observed from the supply curve, there are certain producer who are willing to sell their goods even at a price lower than the equilibrium price. Thus, due to equilibrium price which is higher than their expected price, they are benefitted. This is known as producer surplus. This is shown in the shaded area.

∴ Required area = Area of Rectangle − Area under the curve AE

$$= x_0 p_0 - \int_0^{x_0} S(x).dx$$

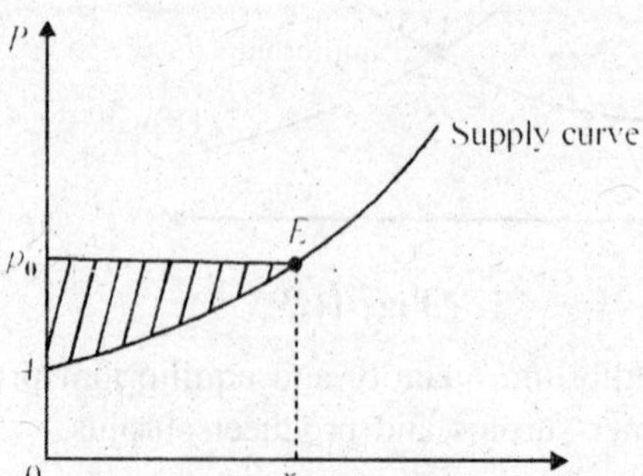

Fig. 11.5

CONSUMER SURPLUS UNDER PURE COMPETITION

In case of pure competition, price is determined by the intersection of demand and supply curve. Using the demand function and the equilibrium quantity, we can find consumer surplus.

Consumer Surplus and Producer Surplus under Monopoly

In case of monopoly, prices depend on the choice of monopolist. Obviously, monopolist would like to fix such a price which would maximize his profits. At maximum profits, we have

$$MR = MC$$

This equation can be used to determine the output level at which profit can be maximised. With the help of the output level obtained and the given demand function, price can be calculated which can be used to find consumer surplus.

CONSUMER SURPLUS

Example 33. **The demand functions for a commodity is given by $p = 75 - 3x$. Find the consumers' surplus corresponding to the equilibrium price = 15**

Solution. Given $p_0 = 15$

$$\therefore \quad x_0 = \frac{75 - p_0}{3} = \frac{75 - 15}{3} = \frac{60}{3}$$

$$x_0 = 20$$

$$\therefore \text{ Consumer Surplus } = \int_0^{x_0} D(x).dx - x_0 p_0$$

$$= \int_0^{20} (75 - 3x).dx - (20 \times 15)$$

$$= \left| 75x - \frac{3x^2}{2} \right|_0^{20} - 300$$

$$= \left[75(20) - \frac{3}{2}(20)^2 - 0 \right] - 300$$

$$= [1500 - 600] - 300$$

$$= 900 - 300 = 600$$

$\therefore$ Consumer Surplus = 600

Example 34. **If the supply function for a particular commodity is $p = 10(x + 3)^2$ and the market price is Rs. 360, find the producer's surplus by two method.**

(*a*) integrate *w.r.t.* x **(*b*) integrate *w.r.t.* p**

Solution : Producer surplus when calculator *w.r.t.* x is given as

$$PS = x_0 p_0 - \int_0^{x_0} S(x).dx \qquad ...(1)$$

Give p_0 = Rs. 360 and supply function $p = 10(x + 3)^2$

Substituting this value of 'p' in the supply function we have

$$360 = 10(x + 3)^2$$

$$\therefore \quad 36 = (x + 3)^2$$

$$\therefore \quad x + 3 = 6$$

$$\therefore \quad x_0 = 3$$

Substituting these value of p_0 and x_0 in (1), we have

$$PS = 3 \times 360 - \int_0^3 10(x+3)^2 .dx$$

$$= 1080 - 10\left|\frac{(x+3)^3}{3}\right|_0^3$$

$$= 1080 - 10\left[\frac{(6)^3}{3} - \frac{(3)^3}{3}\right]$$

$$= 1080 - 10\left[\frac{216 - 27}{3}\right] = 1080 \quad 10(63)$$

$$= 1080 \quad 630 = 450.$$

Calculating of Producer Surplus *w.r.t. p*

$$\therefore \quad PS = \int_{p_1}^{p_0} (\text{Sypply function}).dp$$

p_1 is obtained by substituting $x = 0$ is the supply function.

$$\therefore \quad p = 10(0 + 3)^2 = 90$$

$$p_1 = 90$$

$\therefore$ Expressing the supply function in terms of x, we have

$$x = \sqrt{\frac{p}{1}} - 3$$

$$PS = \int_{90}^{360} \left(\sqrt{\frac{p}{10}} - 3\right).dp.$$

$$PS = \left|\frac{2p^{3/2}}{3\sqrt{10}} - 3p\right|_{90}^{30}$$

$$= \left\{\frac{2(360)^{3/2}}{3\sqrt{10}} - 3(360)\right\} - \left\{\frac{2(90)^{3/2}}{3\sqrt{10}} - 3(90)\right\}$$

$$= (1440.20 - 1080) - 179.7 - 270) = 360.2 - (-90.3)$$

$$= 450.50$$

Example 35. **Find the consumer's surplus and producers' surplus under pure competition for demand function** $p = \frac{8}{x+1} - 2$ **and supply function** $p = \frac{1}{2}(x+3)$, **where** p **is price and** x **is quantity.**

Solution. In case of pure competition, the market demand is obtained by equating the demand and supply functions. Therefore, we have

$$\frac{8}{x+1} - 2 = \frac{1}{2}(x+3)$$

$$16 - 4(x+1) = |(x+3)(x+1)|$$

$$x^2 + 8x - 9 = 0$$

$$\therefore \quad x = 1, -9.$$

Finally we take $x = 1$, as $x = -9$ does not have any meaning.

Substituting $x = 1$ in the demand function, we obtain $p = \frac{8}{1+1} - 2 = 2$. Therefore the equilibrium point is (1, 2).

The consumers' surplus will be given as

$$CS = \int_0^1 \left(\frac{8}{x+1} - 2\right) dx - 1 \times 2$$

$$= \left|\left[8 \log(x+1) - 2x\right]_0^1\right| - 2$$

$$= 8 \log 2 - 4.$$

The producer's surplus will be given as

$$PS = 1 \times 2 - \int_0^1 \frac{1}{2}(x+3)\, dx = 2 - \left[\frac{(x+3)^2}{4}\right]_0^1 = \frac{1}{4}.$$

Example 36. **When the price of a given commodity averaged Rs. 150, the company sold 10 units. When the price dropped to an average of Rs. 80, 20 units were sold by the same company. It has also been observed, when the price was Rs. 80, 20 units were available for sale. When the price reached Rs. 60, 15 units were available for sale. Find the demand and supply functions, assuming both are linear. Also determine consumer's and producer's surplus.**

Solution. Let $p = ax + b$ be the demand function

$\therefore$ We have

$$150 = 10a + b \qquad \text{...(1)}$$

$$80 = 20a + b \qquad ...(2)$$

Substracting (2) from (1), we have

$$70 = -10a$$

$\therefore$ $$a = -7$$

and $$150 = 10(-7) + b$$

$\therefore$ $$b = 220$$

$\therefore$ Demand function $p = -7x + 220$ ...(3)

Similarly, we can solve for the supply function, we have

$$p = 4x \qquad ...(4)$$

At equilibrium point, demand = supply, therefore Equating (3) and (4), we have

$$-7x + 220 = 4x$$

$$220 = 11x$$

$\therefore$ $$x = 20, \ p_0 = 80$$

Now $$CS = \int_0^{20} (-7x + 220).dx - (20 \times 80)$$

$$= \left| -\frac{7x^2}{2} + 220x \right|_0^{20} - 1600$$

$$= (-1400 + 4400) - 1600$$

$$= 1400$$

$$P.S. = (20 \times 80) - \int_0^{20} 4x \ dx$$

$$= (20 \times 80) - \left| \frac{4x^2}{2} \right|_0^{20}$$

$$= 1600 - \left| 2x^2 \right|_0^{20}$$

$$= 1600 - (800 - 0) = 800$$

***Example 37.* For a monopolist, the demand law is $p = 50 - x^2$ and marginal cost $MC = 1 + x^2$. Determine the consumer's surplus at the price which monopolist will like to fix. If there is pure competition in this case, what will be the consumer's surplus at equilibrium price?**

Solution. Given demand function : $p = 50 - x^2$. If R denotes the revenue function, then, we have

$$R = px = (50 - x^2)\,x = 50x - x^3$$

Marginal revenue will be given as

$$MR = \frac{dR}{dx} = 50 - 3x^2 \qquad ...(1)$$

Marginal cost is already given as:

$$MC = 1 + x^2 \qquad ...(2)$$

In case of monopoly, the quantity x_0 is obtained by equating MR and MC. Therefore equating (1) and (2), we have

$$50 \quad 3x^2 = 1 + x^2$$

$$\Rightarrow \qquad 4x^2 = 49, \text{ i.e., } x = \frac{7}{2}, \text{ (negative value is ignored)}$$

Therefore $x_0 = \frac{7}{2}$. Substitute this value in the demand law $p = 50 - x^2$, we get $p_0 = \frac{151}{4}$.

Consumer surplus would be

$$\therefore \qquad Cs = \int_0^{\frac{7}{2}} (50 - x^2)\, dx - \frac{7}{2} \times \frac{151}{4}$$

$$= \left(50x - \frac{x^3}{3}\right)_0^{\frac{7}{2}} - \frac{1057}{8}$$

$$= \left(175 - \frac{343}{24}\right) - \frac{1057}{8} = \frac{343}{12}$$

In case of pure competition, the equilibrium point is obtained by equating demand and supply functions. Using marginal cost function as supply function, we have

$$50 - x^2 = 1 + x^2$$

$$\Rightarrow \qquad 2x^2 = 49 \text{ i.e., } x = \frac{7}{\sqrt{2}} \text{ (ignoring negative value)}$$

Substituting this value of x in the demand function, we have

$$p = 50 - \frac{49}{2} = \frac{51}{2}. \text{ Thus } x_0 = \frac{7}{\sqrt{2}} \text{ and } p_0 = \frac{51}{2}$$

Therefore, consumer surplus will be

$$\therefore \qquad CS = \int_0^{7/\sqrt{2}} (50 - x^2)\, dx - \frac{7}{\sqrt{2}} \times \frac{51}{2}$$

$$= \left(50x - \frac{x^3}{3}\right)_0^{\frac{7}{\sqrt{2}}} - \frac{357}{2\sqrt{2}} = \frac{350}{\sqrt{2}} - \frac{343}{6\sqrt{2}} - \frac{357}{2\sqrt{2}} = \frac{353}{3\sqrt{2}}$$

Example 38. **The supply curve for a commodity is $p = \sqrt{9 + x}$ and the quantity sold is 7 units. Find the producer's surplus. Can you find the consumer's surplus? If yes, find it, if not explain with the help of a diagram why not.**

Solution. Given $x_0 = 7$, substitute this value in the supply function $p = \sqrt{9+x}$, we have

$$p = \sqrt{9+7} = \sqrt{16} = 4.$$ Therefore producer's surplus is

$$PS = 7 \times 4 - \int_0^7 \sqrt{9+x}\,dx$$

$$= 28 - \left[\frac{2}{3}(9+x)^{\frac{3}{2}}\right]_0^7$$

$$= 28 - \frac{2}{3}\left[16^{3/2} - 9^{3/2}\right]$$

$$= 28 - \frac{2}{3}\left[4^3 - 3^3\right] = \frac{10}{3}.$$

We can not find consumer's surplus because demand function is not given. Consider Fig. 11.6 drawn below. Consumers surplus is represented by the area between the line joining y-axis at p_0 and the equilibrium point (x_0, p_0) along with the area under the demand curve $p = D(x)$ from $x = 0$ to $x = x_0$, where (x_0, p_0) is the equilibrium point.

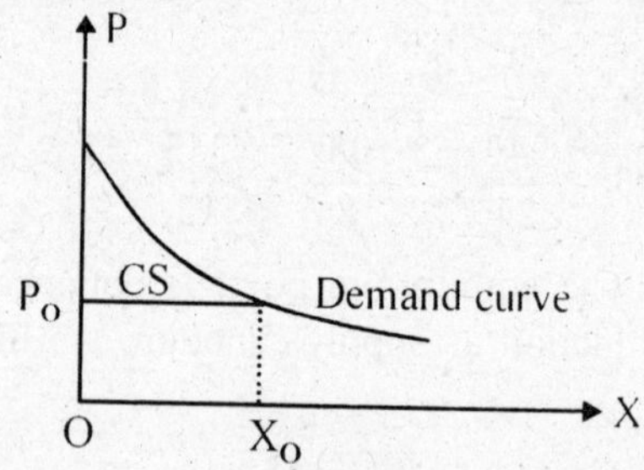

Fig. 11.6

Since, we are not given information about the demand curve, we cannot find consumer surplus.

***Example 39.* The demand equation of a product is $p - 10e^{-x} = 0$. Find the consumer surplus when the market price $p = 1$.**

Solution. Given demand equation

$$p = 10e^{-x}$$

and the market price $p = 1$. Substitute $p = 1$ in the demand equation, we get the quantity demanded, as under

$$1 = 10e^{-x}$$

$$\Rightarrow \qquad e^{-x} = \frac{1}{10} \text{ or } e^{x} = 10$$

$$\Rightarrow \qquad x \log_{10} e = \log_{10} 10 = 1$$

$$\text{or} \qquad x(0.4343) = 1 \quad \Rightarrow \quad x = \frac{1}{0.4343} = 2.30$$

Therefore, consumer's surplus will be given as

$$CS = \int_0^{2.30} 10e^{-x}dx - 1 \times 2.30$$

$$= -10\left|e^{-x}\right|_0^{2.30} \quad 2.30$$

$$= -10\ [e^{\ 2.30} - e^{\ 0}] - 2.30$$

$$= -10\left[\frac{1}{10} - 1\right] - 2.30 = 6.70$$

Since $e^{+2.30} = 9.97 = 10$.

Exercise 11.8

1. The demand equation of a product is $p - 10e^{-x} = 0$. Find the consumer surplus when the market price $p = 0$. [CS = Rs. 6.70]

2. The demand equation of a product is $p = 4 - 2x$. Find the consumer surplus when the market price $p = 2$ **[Ans.** 1]

3. The demand low for a commodity is $p = 9 - x^2$. Find the consumer's surplus when the equilibrium price is Rs. 5. **[Ans.** 16/3]

4. The supply curve for a commodity is $p = \sqrt{4 + x}$ and the quantity sold is 4 units. Find the producer's surplus. **[Ans.** 7/3]

5. If supply function for a particular commodity is $p = \sqrt{9 + x}$ and the equilibrium quantity is 7 units find the producer's surplus by two methods.

(*a*) integrate *w.r.t.* x

(*b*) integrate *w.r.t.* p. [10/3, 10/3]

6. The demand law for a commodity is $p = 35 - 2x - x^2$. Find the consumer's surplus at equilibrium price $p = 20$. **[Ans.** $CS = 27$]

7. The supply function for a commodity is $p = 4 + x$. Determine producer's surplus if 12 units of goods are sold. **[Ans.** $PS = 72$]

8. Demand and supply functions are : $p = D(x) = (12 - 2x)^2$ and $p = S(x) = 56 + 4x$ respectively. Determine CS under monopoly (so as to maximize the profit) and the supply function is identified with the marginal cost function. $\left[\textbf{Ans. } \frac{64}{3}\right]$

9. For a monopolist demand law is $p = (6 - x)^2$ and marginal cost = $14 + x$. Find the consumer's surplus.

10. The demand and supply laws for a commodity are $pd = 18 - 2x - x^2$ and $ps = 2x - 3$. Find the consumer's surplus and producer's surplus at equilibrium price. **[Ans.** $CS = 27$, $PS = 9$]

11. The demand and supply laws for a commodity are $pd = 56 - x^2$ and $Ps = 8 + \frac{x^2}{3}$. Find the consumer's surplus and producer's surplus at equilibrium price. **[Ans.** $CS = 144$, $PS = 48$**]**

12. If the demand function for a commodity is $10p = \sqrt{900 - x}$ and the demand is fixed at 500, find the consumer's surplus by two methods : (*a*) integrate with respect to *x*, (*b*) integrate with respect to *p*. **[Ans.** $CS = 226.66$**]**

13. A supply function is given to be $p = S(x) = 3 + x^2$ and the corresponding demand function is $p = D(x) = -2x + 18$. Find both the consumer's surplus and producer's surplus.

[Ans. $CS = 9$, $PS = 18$**]**

14. Suppose the demand function for a commodity is given by $p = 100 - 2x - 3x^2$. Find the consumer's surplus corresponding to the prices : (*a*) $p = 84$ and (*b*) $p = 15$.

[Ans. (*a*) 20, (*b*) 275**]**

15. The demand equation for a product is $x = \sqrt{100 - p}$ and the supply equation is $x = \frac{p}{2} - 10$. Determine the consumer's surplus and producer's surplus under market equilibrium.

12

Mathematics of Finance

HIGHLIGHTS OF THE CHAPTER

- Introduction
- Interest
- Simple Interest
- Compound Interest
- Compound Interest at Changing Rates
- Nominal and Effective Rates of Interest
- Depreciation
- Nominal and Effective Rate of Discount
- Present Value
- Equation of Value
- Annuity
- Annuity Due
- Perpetuity
- Capital Expenditure, Bonds and Leasing
- Amortization of Loan
- Deferred Anuity

INTRODUCTION

This chapter mainly focuses on the concept of time value of money. As we know, in case of business transactions, there are cash inflows and cash outflows associated with it. These cash flows occur at different point of time. Since the value of time keeps on changing with time therefore sometimes it become necessary to evaluate the value of money at a particular point of time. The present chapter covers such issues.

INTEREST

Interest may be defined as the consideration required to be paid for borrowing a particular amount of money. For example, A borrows Rs. 1000 for B for a year. Since A would be using money owed by B, therefore, he is required to pay interest to B. The amount of interest mainly depends upon the amount of borrowed funds, time for which the money has been borrowed and the rate of interest. Interest can be calculated in two ways.

(*i*) Simple Interest

(*ii*) Compound Interest

SIMPLE INTEREST

Simple Interest is calculator by using the following formula.

$$I = Prt$$

When $\quad I$ = Interest

P = Principal

r = Rate of Interest

t = time (in years)

$\therefore$ Amount = Principal + Interest

The concept of simple interest would become more clear from the following examples.

Example 1 : **Find the simple interest on Rs. 7000 for 4 year at 6% p.a.. Find the amount at the end of 4 years.**

Solution : Simple Interest = SI

Given $P = 700$

$R = 6\%$ p.a.

$t = 4$ years.

$$\therefore \quad SI = \frac{700 \times 6 \times 4}{100} = 168$$

$\therefore$ Amount = Principal + Interest

$= 700 + 168 =$ Rs. 868

Example 2 : **Find the time required to earn Rs. 400 as simple Interest on the principal of 2000 at the rate 10%.**

Solution :

$$\text{Simple Interest} = \frac{PRT}{100}$$

Given $P = 2000$

$R = 10\%$

$t = ?$

$SI = 400$

$$SI = \frac{PRT}{100}$$

$$400 = 2000 \times \frac{10}{100} \times t$$

$$\therefore \quad t = \frac{100 \times 400}{2000 \times 10} = \frac{40000}{20000} = 2 \text{ years}$$

$t = 2$ years.

Example 3 : **At what rate of Interest would the sum Rs. 5000 grow to Rs. 6000 in 2 years at simple interest?**

Solution :

$$I = \frac{PRT}{100}$$

$\therefore \quad I = (6000 - 5000) = 1000$

$T = 2$ years

$P = 5000$

Substituting these values in the above equation, we have

$$1000 = \frac{5000 \times R \times 2}{100}$$

$$R = \frac{1000 \times 100}{5000 \times 2} = 10\%$$

Exercise 12.1

1 Find the simple interest on Rs. 800 for 3 year at 4%. Also find the amount. ($I = 96$, $A = 896$)

2 Find the time required for Rs. 2000 to yield Rs. 900 in simple interest at 9% interest per annum.

[**Ans.** $t = 5$ year]

3 Find the rate of interest at which Rs. 5000 will yield Rs. 750 in simple interest in 3 years.

[Rate = 5%]

4 The simple interest on Rs. 5000 for 6 months in 125. Find the annual rate of interest.

(r = 5%)

COMPOUND INTEREST

In case of compound interest computation, interest calculated for a given period is added to the principal amount. The interest of the subsequent period is calculated not only on the initial principal amount but also on the interest amount of the preceeding annually, quarterly or at any other required periods of time. The number of times interest is compounded in a given year is known as **frequency of conversion.** The time between two successive conversions of interest is called the **conversion period.** The principal amount when added to the interest earned there on is called the **compound amount.**

The formula used for calculating compound interest is given below.

$$\textbf{Amount} = \textbf{Principal}\left(1 + \frac{\textbf{rate}}{\textbf{100}}\right)^{\textbf{time}}$$

Compound Interest = Amount – Principal

Symbolically, the above formula can be written as

$$A = P(1 + r)^t$$

If the principal is compounded on **six monthly basis,** then frequency of conversion is 2. The above formula will be written as

$$A = P\left(1 + \frac{r}{2}\right)^{t \times 2}$$

If the compound is on **quarterly basis,** then frequency of conversion is 4. The above formula will be written as

$$A = P\left(1 + \frac{r}{4}\right)^{t \times 4}$$

Likewise, in case of **monthly** compounding, the above formula will be given as

$$A = P\left(1 + \frac{r}{12}\right)^{t \times 12}$$

Similarly, if the compounding is done 'm' times in a year, we have

$$A = P\left(1 + \frac{r}{m}\right)^{t \times m}$$

When compounding is done continuously *i.e.*, m becomes very large ($\because$ m $\to \infty$) we have

$$A = \underset{m \to \infty}{Lt}\ P\left(1 + \frac{r}{m \times 100}\right)^{t \times m}$$

$$= P\left[\underset{m \to \infty}{Lt}\left(1 + \frac{r}{m}\right)^{m/r}\right]^{rt}$$

If we let $\frac{r}{m} = x$, now when $m \to \infty$, $x \to 0$

$$A = P\left[\underset{x \to 0}{Lt}\ (1 + x)^{1/x}\right]^{rt} = pe^{rt}$$

$$(\because \text{ By def. } \underset{x \to \infty}{Lt}\ (1 + x)^{1/x} = e)$$

Thus, the compound amount A accumulated after t year on depositing 'P' amount at rate of r compounding continuously will be given as

$$A = pe^{rt}$$

COMPOUND INTEREST AT CHANGING RATES

Sometimes, we come across a situation where interest is paid at different rates for different time period. In such cases, the compound amount is the product of original principal and compounding factors of the form $(1 + r)^n$ or e^{rt} depending upon the fact whether compounding is being done at intervals or continuously. For example consider Rs P has been deposited for which interest is paid at the rate of r_1 for t_1 years, at the rate of r_2 for t_2 years and at the rate r_3 compounding continuously for t_3 years, then the amount at the end of period would be given as

$$A = P(1 + r_1)^{t_1}(1 + r_2)^{t_2}e^{r_3 t_3}$$

Compound Interest

Find the compound amount of Rs. 5000 for 3 years at 8% converted

(*a*) Annually (*b*) Semiannually (*c*) Quarterly

(*a*) ***Annually***

$$A = P(1 + r)^n$$

$$= 5000\left(1 + \frac{8}{100}\right)^3 = 6298.56$$

(*b*) ***Semi Annually***

$$A = P\left(1 + \frac{r}{2}\right)^{n \times 2}$$

$$= 5000\left(1 + \frac{4}{100}\right)^6 = 6326.59$$

(*c*) ***Quarterly***

$$A = P\left(1 + \frac{r}{4}\right)^{n \times 4}$$

$$= 5000\left(1 + \frac{r}{4}\right)^{4 \times 4}$$

$$= 5000\left(1 + \frac{2}{100}\right)^{12}$$

$$= 5000 \times 1.26824179 = 6341.20$$

Example 4 : **Find the compound interest and compound amount of Rs. 500 investment for 12 years at 6% compounded semiannually.**

Solution : $P = 5000$

$$r = 6\%$$

Since compounding is done semiannually, we have

$$r = \frac{6}{2} = 3\%$$

and $\quad$ time $= 12 \times 2 = 24$

$\therefore \quad A = 500\ (1 + 3\%)^{24}$

Using table I

$$A = 500 \times 2.032709411$$

$$= 1016.3547$$

∴ Compound interest $= 1016.3547 - 500$

$= 516.3547$

Example 5 : **If interest is compounded continuously at an annual rate of 8%, how much time (in years) would it take for a principal *P* to**

(*i*) Double

(*ii*) Triple

Solution : Let '*t*' be the number of years in which the principal would double itself

$$\therefore \quad 2P = pe^{0.08t}$$

$$2 = e^{0.08t}$$

Taking log of both the sides, we have

$$\log 2 = 0.08t \log e$$

$$\therefore \quad 0.08t\,(0.4343) = 0.3010$$

since $\log 2 = 0.3010$ and $\log e = 0.4343$

$$\therefore \quad t = \frac{0.3010}{0.4343 \times 0.08} = 8.66$$

∴ If will take approximately 9 years.

(*ii*) **Triple**

$$3P = Pe^{0.08t}$$

$$\therefore \quad 3 = e^{0.08t}$$

Taking log of both the sides, we have

$$0.08t \log e = \log 3$$

$$0.08\,(0.4343).\,t = 0.4771$$

$$t = \frac{0.4771}{0.08 \times 0.4343} = 13.731$$

∴ It will take approximately 14 years.

Example 6 : **If the interest is compounded continuously, at what rate the principal would (*i*) double (*ii*) triple itself in 8 years.**

Solution : **Double**

$$A = Pe^{rt}$$

$$\therefore \quad 2P = Pe^{r(0.08)}$$

Taking log of both the sides, we have

$$r.(0.08) \log e = \log 2$$

$$r(0.08)\,(0.4343) = 0.3010$$

$$r = \frac{(0.3010)}{(0.08)(0.4343)}$$

(*b*) *Triple*

$$3P = Pe^{0.08r}$$

$$3 = e^{0.08r}$$

Taking log of both the sides, we have

$$0.08r \,.\, \log e = \log 3$$

$$r = \frac{(0.4771)}{(0.08)(0.4343)} = 13.73\%$$

Example 7 : **A person deposited Rs. 1200 in a saving account. For the first three years, interest was compounded continuously on semiannual basis at the rate of 6% and thereafter for next four years compounding was done on quarterly basis at the rate of 10%. Find the compound amount at the end of seven years.**

Solution : For the first three years

$$r_1 = \frac{6\%}{2} = 3\% \quad t_1 = 3 \times 2 = 6$$

For next four years

$$r_2 = \frac{10\%}{4} = 2.5\% \quad t_2 = 4 \times 4 = 16$$

$$\therefore \quad A = P(1 + r_1)^{t_1}(1 + r_2)^{t_2}$$

$$\therefore \quad A = 1200\,(1 + 0.03)^6\,(1 + 0.025)^{16}$$

$$= 1200 \times 1.19405230 \times 1.48450562 \text{ (Using table I)}$$

$$A = \text{Rs. } 2127.09.$$

Example 8 : **A person deposit Rs. 5000 in a bank which pays an interest of 11% per annum compounding continuously. How much amount will be in his account after 10 years?**

Solution : We have $P = 5000$, $r = 0.11$ and $t = 10$. Substituting these values in the formula $S = Pe^{rt}$, we have amount S after 10 years which is given by

$$S = 5000e^{0.11(10)} = 5000e^{1.1}$$

Taking logarithm of both sides, we obtain

$$\log S = \log 5000 + (1.1) \log e$$

$$= 3.6990 + (1.1)(0.4343)$$

$$= 4.1767$$

$$\Rightarrow \quad S = \text{Antilog } (4.1767) = \text{Rs. } 15020 \; (app.)$$

Example 9 : **A National Savings certificate costs Rs. 15 and realises Rs. 20 after 10 years. Find the rate of interest involved when it is added (*a*) yearly (*b*) continuously.**

Solution : **(*a*) When interest is added yearly**

Given $P = 15$, $S = 20$ and $n = 10$. Substituting these values in the formula $S = P(1 + i)^n$, we have

$$20 = 15\,(1 + i)^{10}$$

$$\Rightarrow \quad \frac{4}{3} = (1 + i)^{10}$$

Taking logarithm of both sides, we have

$$\log(1 + i) = \frac{\log 4 - \log 3}{10} = \frac{0.6021 - 0.4771}{10} = 0.0125$$

$$1 + i = \text{Antilog}\,(0.0125) = 1.0292$$

$$i = 0.0292 \text{ or } 2.92\%$$

(b) When Interest is added continuously

In this case, we will substitute the given value in the formula $S = Pe^{rt}$, we have

$$20 = 15e^{10r} \quad \text{i.e.,} \quad e^{10r} = \frac{4}{3}$$

$$10r \log e = \log 4 - \log 3 = 0.6021 - 0.4771 = 0.125$$

$$r = \frac{0.125}{10 \log e} = \frac{0.125}{10\,(0.4343)} = 0.0288 \text{ or } 2.88\%$$

Example 10 : **(*i*) A certain sum of money is invested at 4% compounded annually. The interest for second year is Rs. 25. Find the interest for the third year.**

(*ii*) A sum of money is put at compound interest for two years at 20% per annum. It would fetch Rs. 482 more, if the interest were payable half yearly than if it were payable yearly. Find the sum.

Solution : (*i*) Let P be the original principal, which is being invested at 4% compound annually.

$\therefore$ The amount at the end of first year $= P\,(1.04)$

The amount at the end of second year $= P\,(1.04)^2$

The amount at the end of third year $= P\,(1.04)^3$

$\Rightarrow$ interest for the second year $= P\,(1.04)^2 - P\,(1.04)^1$

but interest for the second year $= 25$ (given

$\therefore \quad P(1.04)^2 - P\,(1.04) = 25$

$P\,(1.04)\,(1.04 - 1) = 25$

$P\,(1.04)\,(0.04) = 25$

The interest for the third year

$$P\,(1.04)^3 - P\,(1.04)^2$$

$$= P\,(1.04)^2\,(1.04 - 1)$$

$$= P\,(1.04)\,(1.04)\,(0.04)$$

$$= 25 \times 1.04$$

$$= \text{Rs. } 26. \qquad (\because P\,(1.04)\,(1.04) = 25)$$

(*ii*) Let the sum invested be Rs. P. Then the amount of Rs. P at the end of two years at 20% per annum compounded annually

$$= P\,(1.20)^2 = P\,(1.44)$$

Further, the amount of Rs. P at the end of two years at 20% per annum compounded semiannually $= P\,(1.10)^4 = P\,(1.4641)$

Given

$$P\,(1.4641) - P\,(1.44) = 482$$

$$\Rightarrow \quad P\,(0.0241) = 482$$

$$\Rightarrow \quad P = \text{Rs. } 20{,}000.$$

Example 11 : **Mr. X deposited Rs. 10,000 in a bank for 3 years offering interest at the rate of 6% compounded half yearly during first year at the rate of 12% compounded quarterly during second year and at 10% compounded continuously during third year. Find his balance after 3 years.**

Solution : In this case compounding is done at changing rates, therefore, amount 's' would be given as

$$S = 10000\left(1+\frac{0.06}{2}\right)^2\left(1+\frac{0.12}{4}\right)^4 e^{0.10}$$

$$= 1000(1.03)^2\,(1.03)^4\,e^{0.10}$$

$$= 1000(1.03)^6\,e^{0.10} = \text{Rs. } 13196.64.$$

Exercise 12.2

1. Find the compound amount of Rs. 50000 for 4 years at 6% converted
   (*a*) Annually
   (*b*) Semiannually
   (*c*) Quarterly
   (*d*) Monthly [**Ans.** (*a*) 6312.38 (*b*) 6333.85 (*c*) 6344.925 (*d*) 6352.44]
2. A person deposited Rs. 2000 for 8 years at 5% compounded annually. Find the compound amount and compound interest.

   [Compound amount = Rs. 2954.91; compound interest = 954.91]
3. Find the amount if Rs. 3000 is invested at 4% compounded semiannually for 9 years. Find the compound interest also. [Amount = 4284.73 Compound interest = 1284.73]
4. How long will it take for Rs. 2000 to become Rs. 4000 it money is worth 12% compounded monthly? [**Ans.** 5.84 years]
5. Find the time required to convert Rs. 500 to 900 at 6% (*i*) converted semiannually (*ii*) converted quarterly. [**Ans.** (*i*) 19.89 year. (*ii*) 39.88 years]
6. How long will it take to double an investment at 5% converted quarterly? [**Ans.** 57.89 years]

7. A person deposit Rs. 6000 in a bank which pays an interest of 9% per annum compounded continuously. How much amount will be in his account after 10 years. [**Ans.** 15170]

8. A company is offering investment certificates at a discount price of Rs. 150 which would be redeemed by the company at Rs. 200 after 10 years. Find the rate of interest involved when it in added. (*a*) yearly; (*b*) continuously [**Ans.** (*a*) 2.92%; (*b*) 2.88%]

9. Find the approximate time taken for an amount to triple itself if interest is compounded continuously at an annual rate of 9%. [**Ans.** 12.20 years]

10. Mr. X deposited Rs. 20000 in a bank for 3 years offering interest at the rate of 6% compounded half yearly during first year, at the rate of 12% compounded quarterly during second year and at 10% compounded continuously during the third year. Find his balance after 3 years. [**Ans.** 26393.28]

11. A person deposit Rs. 3000 is a saving account. The deposit would grow at 6% compounded quarterly for first five years at 8% compounded semiannually for the next 10 years. Find the compound amount at the end of fifteen years. [**Ans.** 8853.32]

12. Find the amount of Rs. 70000 after 6 years if invested at 6% compounded semiannually for first 2 years and 8% compounded quarterly for next four years. [**Ans.** 10815.44]

13. How long will it take for Rs. 3000 to accumulate to Rs. 4500 at 8% converted quarterly. [**Ans.** 20.01 years]

NOMINAL AND EFFECTIVE RATES OF INTEREST

In case of compound interest, the rate of interest which is specified is known as nominal rate of interest. However, the actual interest which gets accumulated on a given principal amount is called as effective rate of Interest. The concept of nominal and effective rate of interest would be come more clear from the following example.

Let the principal be Rs. 100, rate of interest be 10% p.a. and time be one year. Then the interest would be (100 × 10%) = Rs. 10. However, if the compounding is done on semiannual basis, then the interest for the entire year would be different, as shown below.

Interest for first six months.

$$= 100 \times \frac{10}{100} \times \frac{6}{12} = 5$$

∴ Principal at the beginning for next six months.

= 100 + Interest for last six months = 100 + 5 = 105

∴ Interest for next six months

$$= 105 \times \frac{10}{100} \times \frac{6}{12} = 5.25$$

∴ Total interest = Rs. 5 + Rs. 5.25 = Rs. 10.25.

Thus according to nominal interest, the interest should be Rs. 10 on rupees hundred but due to compounding on semiannual basis the interest is Rs. 10.25. Thus, effective rate of interest is higher than nominal rate of interest. **If the conversion period in taken as one year, nominal rate of interest and effective rate of interest would be equal.**

Effective rates are also called annual yields.

Relationship between Nominal rate and Effective rate of Interest.

Let re denote the effective rate

r denote the nominal rate

P be the principal amount

As we know, the amount at compound interest, at nominal rate r after 1 year is equal to the amount at the effective rate re, after 1 year.

$$\therefore \quad P(1 + re) = P\left(1 + \frac{r}{m}\right)^m$$

$$\therefore \quad 1 + re = \left(1 + \frac{r}{m}\right)^m$$

$$re = (1 + r/m)^m - 1$$

From the above relationship, it can be observed that

Effective rate depends on the nominal rate and the frequency of compounding in a year. Effective rate also helps in evaluation of investment alternatives.

Equation (1) can be used in situations where compounding is done m times a year. Let us see what happens, when $m \to \infty$, *i.e.*, when compounding is done continuously. Thus, we have

$$r_e = \underset{m\to\infty}{Lt}\left[(1 + r/m)^m - 1\right]$$

$$= \underset{m\to\infty}{Lt}(1 + r/m)^m - 1$$

$$= \underset{m\to\infty}{Lt}\left[(1 + r/m)^{\frac{m}{r}}\right]^r - 1$$

$$= \left[\underset{m\to\infty}{Lt}(1 + r/m)^{\frac{m}{r}}\right]^r - 1$$

Let $\frac{r}{m} = x$, when $m \to \infty$, $x \to 0$

$\therefore$ We can restate above relation as

$$= \left[\underset{x\to 0}{Lt}(1 + x)^{1/x}\right]^r - 1 \qquad \left(\text{By definition } \underset{x\to 0}{Lt}(1 + x)^{1/x} = e\right)$$

Effective rate $r_e = e^r - 1$

The nominal rate r compounded continuously and equivalent to a given rate r_e is called force of interest.

Example 12 : **Find the effective rate equivalent to nominal rate of**

(*i*) 6% converted quarterly **(*ii*) 8% converted semiannually**

Solution : (*i*) We have

$$r_e = \left(1 + \frac{r}{m}\right)^m - 1$$

$$= \left(1 + \frac{6\%}{4}\right)^4 - 1$$

$$= (1 + 0.015)^4 - 1$$

$$= (1.0613) - 1 \qquad \text{(Using table I)}$$

$$= 0.0613 = 6.13\%$$

$\therefore$ Effective rate = 6.13%

(*ii*) 8% converted semiannually.

$$r_e = \left(1 + \frac{8\%}{2}\right)^2 - 1$$

$$= (1 + 0.04)^2 - 1$$

$$= 1.0816 - 1 \qquad \text{(Using Table I)}$$

$$r_e = 0.816 = 8.16\%$$

$\therefore$ Effective rate = 8.16%

Example 13 : **Which is better option for an investor compounding at**

(*a*) 3.01% annual rate or 3% on semiannual basis.

(*b*) 8% semiannual basis or 8.10% annual basis.

Solution : (*a*) Let us find effective rate when compounding is done at 3% semiannual basis.

$$r_e = \left(1 + \frac{0.03}{2}\right)^2 - 1 = (1 + 0.015)^2 - 1$$

$$= 1.0302 - 1 = 0.0302 = 3.02\%$$

$\therefore$ It is better to invest at 3% compounding on semiannual basis instead of 3.01 at annual basis.

(*b*) In example no. 12, we have already worked out effective rate corresponding 8% compounding on semiannually basis which come out to 8.16%. Since effective rate is greater than the given 8.10% rate on annual basis. Therefore, investor shall upto 8% compounding on semiannual basis.

Example 14 : **Find the force of interest corresponding to the effective rate (*i*) 6% (*ii*) 5%**

Solution : (*i*) We have

$$r_e = e^r - 1$$

$$0.06 = e^r - 1$$

$$e^r = 1.06$$

Taking log of both the sides, we have

$$r \log e = \log 1.06$$

$$r\,(0.4343) = 0.0253$$

$$r = \frac{0.0253}{0.4343} = 0.05825$$

Thus, the force of interest is 5.825%.

It implies 5.825% compounded continuously and 6% effective rate are equal.

(*ii*) We have

$$r_e = e^r - 1$$

$$0.05 = e^r - 1$$

$$e^r = 1.05$$

Taking log of both the sides, we have

$$r \log e = \log (1.05)$$

$$r\,(0.4343) = 0.0212$$

$$r = \frac{0.0212}{0.4343} = 0.0488$$

$$= 4.88\%$$

Thus, the force of interest is 4.88%

***Example 15 :* A person deposited Rs. 15000 at an effective rate of 6%. What would be the amount after 10 years.**

Solution : Effective rate is basically an actual rate on per annum basis

$$A = P(1 + r)^n$$

$$A = 15000(1 + 6\%)^{10} \qquad ...(1)$$

$$= 1500 \times 1.79084770 \qquad \text{(Using table I)}$$

$$A = 26862.71$$

Alternatively,

Take log of both sides of equation (1), we have

$$\log A = \log 15000 + 10 \log (1.06)$$

$$\log A = 4.1760 + 10 \times 0.0253 = 4.429$$

$$\therefore \quad A = \text{Antilog } (4.429) = 26850.$$

***Example 16 :* A money lender changes 'interest' at the rate of 10 paise per rupee per month, payable in advance. What effective rate of interest does he charges per annum?**

Solution : It is given that money lender charges 10 paise advance per rupee per month therefore it can be concluded that 10 paise is interest on 90 paise per month.

$\therefore$ Interest rate $i = \frac{10}{90} = 1/9$

$\therefore$ Effective rate $r_e = (1 + i)^{12} - 1 = (1 + 1/9)^{12} - 1$

$\therefore$ $(1 + r_e) = (10/9)^{12}$

Taking log of both sides, we have

$$\log(1 + r_e) = 12 \log(10/9)$$
$$= 12(\log 10 - \log 9)$$
$$= 12(1 - 0.9542)$$
$$= 12(0.0458) = 0.5496$$

$\therefore$ $(1 + r_e) = \text{Antilog}(0.5496) = 3.545$

$\therefore$ $r_e = 3.545 - 1 = 2.545 = 254.5\%$

Example 17 : **Find, for each of the following, the amount to which Rs. 100 will accumulate :**

(*i*) at the rate of interest 12% per annum compounded quarterly for 10 years.

(*ii*) at the force of interest 3% per annum, for 3.5 years.

(*iii*) at the effective rate of interest 3% per annum for 10 years, 4% per annum for 4 years and 5% per annum for 2 years.

(*iv*) at the rate of interest corresponding to 3% per annum effective rate of discount for 8 years.

(*v*) What constant force of interest would produce the same amount after 16 years as the rate in (*iii*) above?

Solution : (*i*) The required amount would be

$$= 100(1.03)^{40} = \text{Rs. } 326.20$$

(*ii*) The required amount would be

$$= 100e^{0.03(3.5)} = 100e^{0.105}$$
$$= 100\,[\text{AL}\,(0.105 \times 0.4343)]$$
$$= 100\,[\text{AL}\,(0.04561)]$$
$$= 100 \times 1.111 = \text{Rs. } 111.1$$

(*iii*) The required amount would be

$$= 100\,(1.03)^{10}\,(1.04)^4\,(1.05)^2 = \text{Rs. } 173.33$$

(*iv*) Let i be the rate of interest corresponding to an effective rate of discount of $d = 0.03$ per annum.

We have $1 - d = \frac{1}{1 + i}$

$\Rightarrow$ $1 + i = \frac{1}{(1 - d)}$

$\therefore$ Required amount $= 100\,(1 + i)^8 = 100\left(\frac{1}{0.97}\right)^8$

$= 127.59$

(*v*) Let 'x' be the force of interest

$$\therefore \quad 100\, e^{16x} = 173.33$$

$$e^{16x} = 1.7333$$

Taking log of both the sides, we have

$$16x \log e = \log (1.7333)$$

$$\therefore \quad x = \frac{\log (1.7333)}{16 \times \log e} = 0.0343$$

$$= 3.43\%$$

Exercise 12.3

1. Distinguish between the nominal and effective rate of interest. Also establish the relationship between nominal and effective rate of interest when compounded n times a year and when compounded continuously.
2. Find the effective rate equivalent to nominal rate of 6% converted quarterly. [**Ans.** 6.13%]
3. Find the effective rate equivalent to nominal rate of 8% converted half yearly. [**Ans.** 8.16%]
4. Find the effective rate equivalent to nominal rate of 9% converted (*a*) monthly (*b*) continuously. [**Ans.** (*a*) 9.38% (*b*) 9.42%]
5. Find the force of interest corresponding to the effective rate of 6% [**Ans.** 5.82%]
6. Find the force of interest corresponding to the effective rate of 4%. [**Ans.** 3.9%]
7. Which is better from the investor point of view – 5.5% compounded semiannually or 5% compounded monthly. [**Ans.** 5.5% compounded semiannually]
8. Which is better investment opportunity – 6.2% converted semiannually or 6% converted monthly. [**Ans.** 6.2% converted semiannually]
9. A finance company offers 7% compounded annually to its customer. Another finance company wants to release a scheme offering same benefit to the customer but wants that money should be compounded continuously. Find the rate to be offerred by such company. [**Ans.** 6.76%]
10. A money lender charges 'interest' at the rate of 5 rupees or 100 rupees per quarter, payable in advance. What effective rate of interest does he charge per annum. [**Ans.** 22.7%]
11. To what amount will Rs. 15000 accumulate in 12 years if it is invested at an effective rate of 5%. [**Ans.** 26937]
12. In how many years would the amount double itself at an effective rate of 8%. [**Ans.** 9.14 years]
13. A person deposited Rs. 2500 for nine years. It has to be invested at 5% effective rate for first two years, 6% compounded semiannually for the next three years and thereafter at 7% compounded continuously. [**Ans.** 3529.55]

APPLICATIONS OF MATHEMATICS OF FINANCE

In most of the business, the benefits from any investment arises in number or succeeding years. Thus, cash outflow takes place in the current year whereas benefits of the same amount arises in future years. The present value of these benefits are calculated and compared against the cash outflows and accordingly the decision is taken. This process of calculating present value of future benefits is also called discounting. The present value of any amount can be calculated using the formula given below by taking amount as future benefits and principle as present value.

We have $A = P(1 + r)^n$

When we have to calculate present value of any amount due to be received in future, basically. we are required to find 'P' in the above formula.

For example : if the rate of interest is 10% and Rs. 10000 is to be received at the end of two years, then in this case $A = 10000$, $r = 10\%$ and $n = 2$ and we are required to find P, which is calculated as under :

$$P = \frac{A}{(1+r)^n} = \frac{10000}{(1+10\%)^2} = 10000 \times 0.826 = 8260$$

Thus, present value of Rs. 10000 due to be received after two years is Rs. 8260.

In other words, we may say that Rs. 8260 deposited today at the compound rate of 10% for two years is Rs. 10000.

∴ we may say, present value of A due to be received after t years at the rate r per period is given as

$$\boldsymbol{P = A(1 + r)^{-t}}$$

Here $(1 + r)^{-t}$ is called as **discount factor.** ...(1)

You will recall, when compounding is done continuously, the formula.

$$\boldsymbol{A = P(1 + r)^t \text{ reduces to } A = Pe^{rt}}$$

Likewise, in this case, when discounting is done continuously, the present value formula (1) reduces to

$$\boldsymbol{P = Ae^{-rt}}$$

PRESENT VALUE

Example 18 : **Find the principal to the invested at 8% per annum so that after four years the amount will be Rs. 5000 when the interest is compounded**

(*a*) Annually **(*b*) Quarterly** **(*c*) Continuously.**

Solution : (*a*) When interest is compounded annually.

We have
$$A = P(1 + r)^n$$
$$P = A(1 + r)^{-n}$$
$$= 5000(1 + 0.08)^{-4}$$
$$= 5000(0.7350) \quad \text{(Using table II)}$$
$$= 3675$$

(*b*) When interest in compounded quarterly.

$$P = 500\left(1+\frac{r}{4}\right)^{-n\times 4}$$

$$= 5000(1 + 0.02)^{-16}$$

$$= 5000(0.7284)$$

$$= 3642$$

(*c*) When interest is compounded continuously.

$$P = Ae^{rt}$$

$$= 5000\ e^{(-0.08)(4)}$$

$$= 5000\ e^{-0.32} \qquad \text{(From table V)}$$

$$= 5000\ (0.72615)\ (\text{we have } e^{-0.32} = 0.72615)$$

$$= 3630.75$$

Example 19 : **Ram divided Rs. 70000 between his sons – Shyam and Mohan. Both the sons invested their respective parts at 6% rate of interest compounded annually. Ram had divided his property in such a manner that amount invested by Shyam for 3 years would be equivalent to the amount invested by Mohan for 5 years. Find the share of both sons.**

Solution : Let 'A' be the amount received by Shyam after 3 years, on investment @ of 6% p.a.

∴ Amount received by Mohan = A (Since both would have same amount)

on investment @ 6% for 5 years.

∴ Present value of Shyam + Present value of Mohan = Present value of Ram.

$$\therefore \quad A(1+0.06)^{-3} + A(1+0.06)^{-5} = 70000$$

$$\therefore \quad A\,[(1.06)^{-3} + (1.06)^{-5}] = 70000$$

$$A\,[(0.8396) + (0.7472)] = 70000$$

$$A\,(1.5868) = 70000$$

$$A = \frac{70000}{1.5868} = 44113.94$$

$$\therefore \quad \text{Share of Shyam} = 44113.94\ (0.8396)$$

$$= 37038.06$$

$$\therefore \quad \text{Share of Mohan} = 44113.94\ (0.7472)$$

$$= 32961.93$$

Example 20 : **Find the present value of Rs. 500 due to 10 years hence when interest of 10% is compounded (*i*) half yearly (*ii*) continuously.**

Solution : (*i*) When interest of 10% is compounded half yearly.

We have $P = S(1+i)^{-n}$

Where $S = 500$

$$i = \frac{10}{2} = 5\%$$

$$n = 10 \times 2 = 20$$

$\therefore$ $$P = 500\ (1.05)^{-20} \quad ...(1)$$

Using Table II, $(1.05)^{-20} = 0.37688948$

$\therefore$ $$P = 500\ (0.3768) = 188.40$$

Alternatively

Taking log of both the sides of (1)

$$\text{Log } p = \log 500 - 20 \log (1.05)$$

$$\log p = 2.6990 - 20(0.0212) = 2.275$$

$\therefore$ $$p = \text{Antilog } (2.275) = \text{Rs. } 188.40$$

(*ii*) When interest is compounded continuously

We have $$P = Se^{-rt}$$

$$= 500e^{-1} = 500(0.36788)$$

$\therefore$ $$P = 183.94.$$

Exercise 12.4

1. Find the present value of Rs. 1500 due in 10 years at 5% compounded annually.
   [Ans. Rs. 920.86]
2. Find the present value of Rs. 1800 due after 5 years if the interest rate is 8% compounded semiannually. **[Ans.** 1260.01]
3. Find the present value of Rs. 2000 due 6 years from now if the interest rate is 7% compounded continuously. **[Ans.** Rs. 1314.1]
4. A person desire Rs. 9000 at the end of four years. Find how much he shall invest today, if the interest rate is 6%. **[Ans.** Rs. 7377.71]

EQUATION OF VALUE

In simple words, equation of value equates the sum of the values on a given date of one set of obligations with the sum of the values, of another set of obligations. This could be explained with the help of following example.

Example 21 : ***X* promises to make two payments of Rs. 100 each of *Y*. One payment will be made currently and other at the end of third year. The value of these two payments would be different at various point of time, as shown below.**

Solution : At time $t = 0$, first instalment of Rs. 100 would have same value whereas second instalment of Rs. 100 due to be received at the end of three years will be equal to $100\ (1 + 10\%)^{-3} = 100 \times 0.751 = 75.10$.

∴ Total value of the two instalments = 100 + 75.10 = 175.10

Similarly,

At time t = 1

$$\text{First Instalment} = 100\ (1 + 1\%) = 110$$

$$\text{Second Instalments} = 100\ (1 + 10\%)^{-2} = 82.6$$

$$\therefore \quad \text{Total value} = 110 + 82.6 = 192.6$$

At time t = 2

$$\text{First Instalment} = 100(1 + 10\%)^{+2} = 121$$

$$\text{Second Instalment} = 100(1 + 10\%)^{-1} = 95.1$$

$$\therefore \quad \text{Total value} = \text{Rs. } 216.10$$

At time t = 3

$$\text{First Instalment} = 100(1 + 10\%)^{+3} = 133.10$$

$$\text{Second Instalment} = 100(1 + 10\%)^{0} = 100$$

$$\therefore \quad \text{Total value} = 133.10 + 100 = 233.10$$

The above facts can be summarized as :

Time	$t = 0$	$t = 1$	$t = 2$	$t = 3$
Payment	175.10	192.6	216.10	233.10

It can be concluded from the above that if Y has to make payment to repay the money against these two payments, it will vary with time. The point of time t = 0, 1, 2, 3 is known as **focal date. Focal date may be defined as the benchmark with reference to which compounded and discounted values of various set of obligations are calculated.**

The concept of Equation of value would become more clear from the following examples :

Example 21 : ***X*** **borrowed Rs. 100,000 at the rate of 10% p.a. from** ***Y. Y*** **promised to pay Rs. 30000 at the end of first year and the remaining at the end of second year. What payment should be made at the end of second year to repay the entire debt.**

Solution : It is given that ?X has to make final payment

∴ first of all find payment and Receipts *w.r.t. X.*

	Payment	*Receipt*
1	Rs. 30,000	100,000
2	S	

where S is the final payment to be made to discharge the entire debt

If t = 2 is taken as focal date.

∴ Then receipt of Rs. 100,000 would be $100000\ (1 + 10\%)^2$ and payment of Rs. 30000 would be $30000\ (1 + 10\%)^1$ at the end of 2 years.

∴ we have

$$10000\ (1 + 10\%)^2 = 30000\ (1 + 10\%) + S$$

$$121000 = 33000 + S$$

$$\therefore \quad S = 88000$$

Hence, X shall make payment of Rs. 88000 at the end of second year.

Example 22 : **Mr. X has to make following payments**

(1) Two year hence : Rs. 500

(2) Five year hence : Rs. 800

If the rate of interest is 6%, what are the total value of these payment (*a*) today (*b*) One year hence.

Solution : (*a*) Today *i.e.*, present value.

Let 'x' be the total value of these payments.

$$\therefore \quad \text{Present value of Ist payment} = 500\,(1.06)^{-2}$$
$$= 500(0.8899)$$
$$= 444.95$$

$$\text{Present value IInd payment} = 800(1.06)^{-5}$$
$$= 800(0.7472)$$
$$= 597.76$$

$$\therefore \quad \text{Total value of these payment} = 444.95 + 597.76$$
$$= 1042.71$$

(*b*) Value of these payment one year hence.

$$\text{Present value of Ist Payment} = 500(1.06)^{-1}$$
$$= 471.69$$

$$\text{Present value of IInd Payment} = 800(1.06)^{-4}$$
$$= 800(0.7920)$$
$$= 633.6$$

$$\therefore \quad \text{Total value} = 471.69 + 633.60$$
$$= 1105.29$$

Alternately

$$\text{Value of payment one year hence} = \text{Value of payment today } (1.06) = 1042.71(1.06)$$
$$= 1105.27$$

Example 23 : **Mr. X has received Rs. 500 today and he would receive Rs. 1200 five hence. Mr. X wants to discharge these two debt through a single payment one year hence. If the rate of interest is 6% find the value of the payment.**

Solution : Let 'x' be the value of single payment to be made from X and $t = 1$ year be a focal point. Measuring on time scale, we have

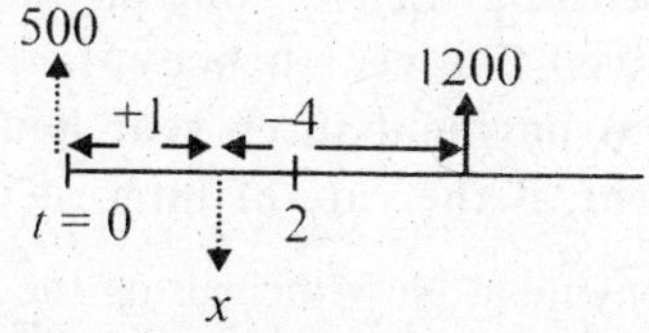

$$x = 500(1.06) + 1200(1.06)^{-4}$$
$$= 500(1.06) + 1200(0.7920)$$
$$= 530 + 950.4 = 1480.4$$
$$x = 1480.4$$

∴ Single payment = 1480.4

Example 24 : **What would your answer for example 23 given above, if *X* decide to discharge the debt**

(*a*) Three year hence

(*b*) Ten year hence

Solution : (*a*) Measuring on time scale we have (focal point t = 3 years)

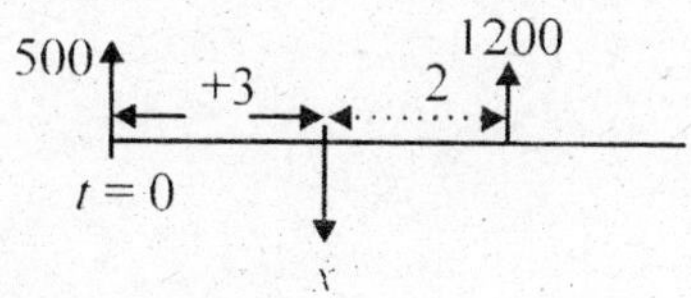

$$x = 500(1.06)^3 + 1200(1.06)^{-2}$$
$$= 500(1.1910) + 1200(0.8899)$$
$$= 595.5 + 1067.88$$
$$= 1663.88$$

(*b*) Let t = 10 years be the focal point, then

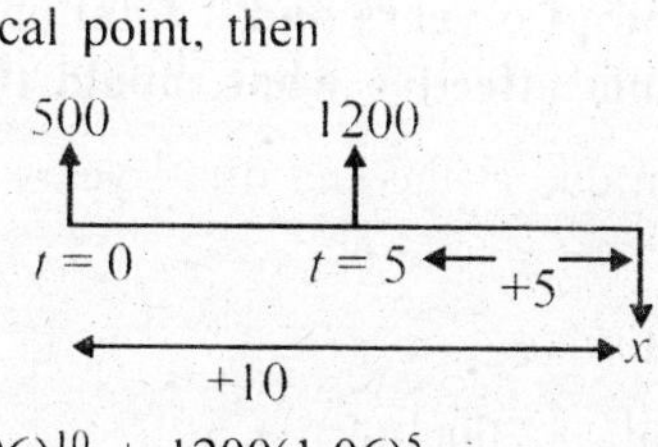

$$x = 500(1.06)^{10} + 1200(1.06)^5$$
$$= 500(1.7908) + 1200(1.3382)$$
$$= 895.4 + 1605.84$$
$$x = 2501.24$$

From the above numericals, it can be concluded if the debt is getting discharged after a payment has been made, payment shall be compounded and if it is getting discharged before a payment is made, it shall be discounted.

Following problems are based on the situation when a debt or series of debt is to be discharged by more than one payment.

Example 25 : **Mr. *X* would receive two payments – one payment of Rs. 200 today and another payment of Rs. 700 would be received five year hence. Mr. *X* wants to discharge the debt in form of two equal instalments. First payment three year hence and second payment six year hence. Find the size of each payment, if the rate of interest is 5%.**

Solution : Let x be the size of each payment. Now measuring the payment and receipt on time scale, we have

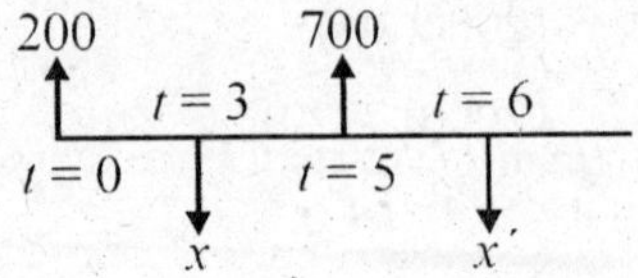

$x' = x, (1 + 5\%)^3$

If we take $t = 3$ as focal point, we have

$$x + x\,(1 + 5\%)^3 = 200(1 + 5\%)^{+3} + 700(1 + 5\%)^{-2}$$

$$x + x\,(1.05)^3 = 200(1.05)^3 + 700(1.05)^{-2}$$

$$x + x\,(1.1576) = 200(1.1576) + 700(0.9070)$$

$$x\,(2.1576) = 231.52 + 634.90$$

$$x\,(2.1576) = 866.42$$

$$x = \frac{866.42}{2.1576} = 401.56$$

$\therefore$ First instalment $= 401.56$

Second instalment $= 401.56\,(1 + 5\%)^3$

$= 401.56\,(1.05)^3$

$= 464.84.$

Example 26 : **In return of a promise to pay Rs. 500 at the end of 10 years, a person agreed to pay Rs. 100 now, Rs. 200 at the end of 6 years and a final payment at the end of 12 years. If the rate of interest is 2% per annum effective what should the final payment be?**

Solution : Let x be the final payment due at the end of 12 years and let the focal date be 12 years hence.

Then, we have equation of the form.

$$500(1.02)^2 = 100(1.02)^{12} + 200(1.02)^6 + x$$

$$\therefore \quad x = 500(1.02)^2 - 100(1.02)^{12} - 200(1.02)^6$$

$$x = 500(1.0404) - 100(1.268242) - 200(1.126162)$$

$$x = 520.20 - 126.8242 - 225.2324$$

$$= \text{Rs. } 168.1434.$$

Example 27 : **In a return promise to pay Rs. 800 at the end of 8 years, Mr. *X* agree to pay Rs. 200 now, Rs. 200 at the end of fourth year and final payment at the end of tenth year. If the rate of interest is 6% per annum effective, what should be the final payment be?**

Solution : Let 'x' be the final payment. Measuring on time scale we have

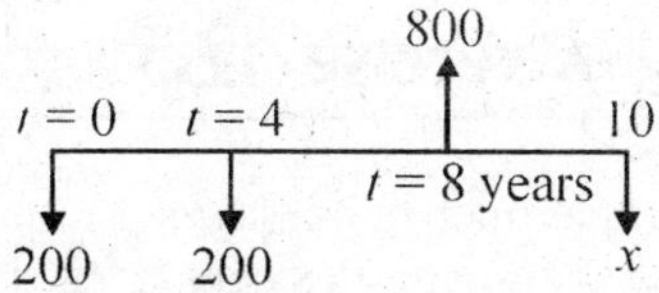

If we take 10th year as a focal date, we have

$$800(1 + 6\%)^2 = 200(1 + 6\%)^{10} + 200(1 + 6\%)^6 + x$$

$$800(1.1236) = 200(1.7908) + 283.7 + x$$

$$\therefore \quad x = 257.02$$

$\therefore$ Final payment shall be = Rs. 257.02

Example 28 : **A man owes Rs. 8000 due in 2 years without interest and Rs. 3000 due in 9 years with 6% annual effective rate of interest. He wishes to pay these debts in two equal instalments due 4 and 5 years hence, respectively. If the money is worth 4% converted semiannually how much should each instalment be?**

Solution : Let the focal date be 5 years hence and the amount of each instalment be x.

The equation of value will be

$$x\,(1.02)^2 + x = 8000\,(1.02)^6 + 3000\,(1.06)^9\,(1.02)^8$$

$$2.0404x = 9009.3 + 4325.9$$

$$x = \frac{13,335.2}{2.0404} = 6535.58$$

Example 29 : **The sums of Rs. 2000, Rs. 3000 and Rs. 4000 are due at the end of 2, 4 and 8 years respectively. It is proposed to replace this series of payments by a single sum of Rs. 9000 payable at the end of n years. If the rate of interest is 10% per annum effective, find the value of n.**

Solution : Let the focal date be 0 year. The equation of value would be

$$9000(1 + 0.10)^{-n} = 2000(1 + 0.10)^{-2} + 3000(1 + 0.10)^{-4} + 4000(1 + 0.10)^{-8}$$

$$\Rightarrow \quad 9(1.10)^{-n} = 2(1.10)^{-2} + 3(1.10)^{-4} + 4(1.10)^{-8}$$

$$= 2(0.8264) + 3(0.6830) + 4(0.4665)$$

$$= 5.5678$$

$$\therefore \quad (1.10)^{-n} = \frac{5.5678}{9} = 0.6186$$

Taking logarithm of both sides, we obtain

$$-n \log(1.10) = \log(0.6186) = -0.2086$$

$$n(0.0414) = 0.2086$$

$$n = \frac{0.2086}{0.0414} = 5 \text{ years (approx)}.$$

Exercise 12.5

1. X borrowed Rs. 30000 at 8% simple interest and agreed to pay Rs. 15000 on loan in 6 months. What payment 1 year from now will settle the debt. **[Ans.** 16800]

2. Mr. X would get Rs. 500 at the end of seven years from now for which he is required to pay Rs. 100 today, Rs. 200 three years from now and an amount ten years from now. If the rate of interest is 5%, find the amount to be paid to balance the debt. **[Ans.** 134.50]

3. Mr. X would be getting Rs. 700 and Rs. 900 after 3 and 9 years respectively against which he is required to make payment after 5 years to discharge both the debt. Find the size of the payment which will discharge both the debts, if the rate of interest is 6%. Compounded quarterly. **[Ans.** Rs. 1497.68]

4. A debt of Rs. 15000 due in 5 years is to be repaid by a payment of Rs. 7500 now and a second payment at the end of 7 years. What should be the second payment if the interest rate is 8% compounded quarterly. **[Ans.** 4516.50]

5. Mr. X owes Rs. 15000 due in 1 year and Rs. 25000 due in 4 years. He agrees to pay Rs. 10000 today and the remainder in 2 years. How much must he pay at the end of 2 years if money is with 5% compounded semiannually. **[Ans.** 27369.50]

6. A debt of Rs. 5000 which is due 4 years from now is to be paid off by three payments; 1200 now, Rs. 1300 after three years and Rs. 4000 after n years. Find the value of n; if rate of interest is 5% p.a. **[Ans.** $n = 16.54$ years.

7. A debt of Rs. 7000 due in 3 years and Rs. 8000 in 7 years is to be repaid by a single payment of Rs. 5000 now and two equal payments which are due 1 year from now and 4 years from now. If the interest rate is 6% compounded annually, how much are each of the equal payment. **[Ans.** Rs. 3571.25]

8. The sum of Rs. 3000 due 2 years hence and another of Rs. 7000 due 5 years hence are to be repaid by a single sum of 7500 at the end of n years. If the rate of interest is 4% (*i*) compounded annually (*ii*) compounded semiannually, find the value of n.
[Ans. (*i*) 6.4 years. (*ii*) 3.2 years]

9. A owes B two sums of money Rs. 2000 due in 2 years and Rs. 1500 due in 5 years. If A wishes to pay off the total debt now by a single payment. find how much should the payment be if money is worth 8% compounded quarterly. **[Ans.** 2716.15]

10. Mr. X secured two loan firm the bank. One for Rs. 700 due in 3 years and one for Rs. 13000 due in 6 years, both at an interest of 10% per annum compounded semiannually. The bank has agreed to allow the two loans to be repaid though a single payment in 5 years at the same interest rate. What amount will Mr. X be required to pay the bank at the end of 5 years.
[Ans. Rs. 32577.8]

11. A owes B two sum of money. Rs. 1200 plus interest at 7% compounded annually, which is due in 5 years, and Rs. 2500 plus interest at 8% compounded semiannually, which is due in 7 years. If both debts are to be paid off by a single payment at the end of 6 years, find the amount of the payment if money is worth 6% compounded quarterly. **[Ans.** 5864.50]

DISCOUNT

Discount may be defined as the deduction allowed on a financial obligation. For example, a person is required to make payment of Rs. 500 and if he is given discount of 15% then he would be required to make payment of Rs. $\left(500 - \frac{15}{100} \text{ of } 500\right)$ = Rs. 425. There is another term called discounting which means determining the present value of a sum due to be received in figure. For example, if a person is likely to get Rs. 500 after two years and he is interest is knowing what is its value today, he may use the following present value formula.

$$\text{Present value} = 500/(1 + r)^2$$

where r is the rate of interest.

Discounting can also be used in another way. For example. a bank has to make loan of Rs. 500 for a year to a borrower. The bank while making payment may deduct a part of money from Rs. 500 and pays balance to the borrower. Let us say bank deducts Rs. 75 from Rs. 500 and pays Rs. 425. Then, we have

$$500 = 75 + 425$$

or $$500 - 75 = 425$$

i.e., Amount – Interest = Principal

The borrower would be required to pay back Rs. 500 to the bank at the end of a year. Thus, it can be concluded that discount is based on amount where as interest is based on principal.

NOMINAL RATE OF DISCOUNT, EFFECTIVE RATE OF DISCOUNT AND FORCE OF DISCOUNT

Nominal rate of discount is the stipulated or specified rate of discount. For example, a person purchased a National Saving Certificate worth Rs. 100 for Rs. 92 carrying a term of one year. It implies a person is required to pay Rs. 92 for the certificate against which he get Rs. 100 from the Government after one year. Thus, it is said that the certificate is being issued at a discount of 8%. In other words,

$$A(1 - d) = P$$

i.e., $$100(1 - 8\%) = 92.$$

Now, recall the case of compounding, where when compounding is done more than once in a year, we have to multiply time with number of times compounding is done and divide the rate with number of times to incorportate the effect. Likewise, in case of discounting, if discounting is done two or four times depending upon the fact that it is being done semiannually or quarterly, the effect is incorporated by dividing the discount rate by number of times and multiplying the time with the same figure. Thus, in the above example, if discounting is done on semi-annual basis, we have

$$100\left(1 - \frac{8}{2}\%\right)^{1\times 2} = 100\,(1 - 4\%)^2 = 92.16$$

$\therefore$ discount rate = 100 – 92.16 = 7.84%

Hence, the nominal rate of discount is 8% but effective rate of discount is 7.84% *i.e.,* less than the nominal rate of discount.

The difference has arisen due to number of times discounting is effected in a year.

Thus, if *de* denotes the effective rate of discount, *d* denotes nominal rate of discount and *m* denotes frequency of discounting.

$$\therefore \quad (1 - de) = \left(1 - \frac{d}{m}\right)^m$$

If *m* becomes very large *i.e.*, m → ∞, we have

$$(1 - de) = \underset{m \to \infty}{Lt} \left(1 - \frac{d}{m}\right)^m$$

$$= \underset{m \to \infty}{Lt} \left[\left(1 - \frac{d}{m}\right)^{m/d}\right]^d$$

$$(1 - de) = e^{-d}$$

$$\therefore \quad de = 1 - e^{-d}$$

The nominal rate of discount *d* converted continually and equivalent to a given effective rate *de* is called force of discount.

Example 30 : **What is the present value of a continuous income stream of Rs. 5000 per year for three years if it is discounted continuously at the rate of 6% per year.**

Solution : The present value of a continuous income stream of Rs. 5000 per year for 3 years discounted continuously at the rate of 6% per annum is given by

$$P = \int_0^3 5000e^{-0.06t} . dt = 5000\int_0^3 e^{-0.06t} . dt$$

$$= 5000\left|\frac{e^{-0.06t}}{-0.06}\right|_0^3$$

$$= 5000\left[-\frac{1}{0.06}\left(e^{-0.18} - e^0\right)\right]$$

$$= \frac{5000}{0.06}(1 - 0.83527)$$

$$= \frac{5000 \times 0.16473 \times 100}{6} = 13725.50$$

Example 31 : **The amount of Re 1 in 2 years at a certain nominal rate of interest plus the present value of Re 1, due in 2 years, at the same nominal rate of discount, both rates convertible half yearly, is 2.00480032. Find the rate.**

Solution : Let *r* be the nominal rate of interest convertible half yearly. Then the interest rate per period is $i = r/2$. Further, we are given that

$$(1 + i)^4 + (1 + i)^4 = 2.00480032$$

$$2i^4 + 12i^2 + 2 = 2.00480032$$

$$i^4 + 6i^2 - 0.00240016 = 0$$

$$i^2 = \frac{-6 \pm \sqrt{36.00960064}}{2} = 0.0004$$

$$i^2 = 0.002 \quad \text{or} \quad r = 4\%$$

Exercise 12.6

1. Find the present value and discount on Rs. 4000 due in 3 years at 5% effective rate of discount. [**Ans.** PV = 3429.50, Discount = 570.50]
2. Find the present value and discount on Rs. 3000 due in 2 years and 6% discount rate, convertible half yearly. [**Ans.** PV = 2655.87, Discount = 344.13]
3. The present value of Rs. 100 due in 2 years at a certain nominal rate of discount convertible semiannually, is Rs. 90. Find the rate of discount. [**Ans.** 5.24%]
4. The amount of Re 1 in one year at a certain nominal rate of interest plus the present value of Re 1 due in one year, at the same nominal rate of discount both rates convertible quarterly, is 2.00480032. Find the rate of discount. [**Ans.** 8%]
5. What is meant by rate of discount? How does it differ from the rate of interest? Bring out the relationship among effective rate of discount, nominal rate of discount and force of discount?
6. The amount of Re. 1 in 2 years at a certain nominal rate of interest plus the present value of Re 1 due in 2 years, at the same nominal rate of discount both rates convertible half yearly, is 2.00480032. Find the rate of discount. [**Ans.** 4%]

DEPRECIATION

Depreciation means allowance provided in the value of assets due to 'wear and tear'. As we know that when assets like plant and machinery are used for business purpose, there value keeps on decreasing over a period of time. Thus, the asset worth Rs. 1000 would not have same value throughout its life rather it will keep on declining with time. The value of the asset at the end of year 1 would be less than its value in the beginning of the year. The rate at which the decline takes place is known as **rate of depreciation.** The amount with which the value of the asset decrease is known as **depreciation.** The value of the depreciable asset at the end of its useful life is called the **scrap value.**

Methods of computing the Annual Depreciation

(1) ***Straight line method :*** Under this method, the depreciation is calculated by dividing the total cost of the asset by the life of the asset. In case, the asset has any salvage value then the same be deducted from the original cost of the asset. The formula for calculating depreciation under this method is given as.

$$\text{Depreciation} = \frac{(\text{Original cost} - \text{salvage value})}{\text{life of an asset}}$$

(2) ***Reducing balance depreciation :*** Under this method, the depreciation is calculated at a constant rate of the book value of the asset. For example, if 'A' is a value of the asset at the beginning and 'd' is the rate of depreciation then the depreciated value of the asset, D, could be given as

$$D = A(1 - d)$$

After two years, 'D' would be given as

$$D = A(1 - d)^2$$

Likewise, after 'n' years, D would be given as

$$D = A(1 - d)^n.$$

***Example 32 :* A machine costing Rs. 70000 depreciates at a constant rate of 6% what is the depreciation for 9th year. If the estimated useful life of the machine is 10 years, determine the scrap value of the machine.**

Solution : Given

$$C = \text{Rs. } 70000$$

$$r = 6\%$$

Depreciation of 9th year would.

= value of machine at the end of year 8 – value of machine at end of year 9

$= 70000(1 - 6\%)^8 - 70000\ (1 - 6\%)^9$

$= 70000\ (0.6095) - 70000\ (0.5729)$

$= 42665 - 40103$

$\therefore$ Depreciation for 9th year = 2562

Scrap value of the machine $= C(1 - 6\%)^{10}$

$= 7000\ (0.5386)$

$= 37702$

Depreciation for 10 years $= 70000 - 37702$

$= 32298$

***Example 33 :* A machine is purchased for Rs. 20000. It is subject to depreciation at the rate of 10% for first three years and thereafter at the rate of 15% for two years. Find value of machine at the end of five years.**

Solution : Given $C = 2000$

rate of dep = 10% for three years

rate of dep = 15% for two years

$\therefore$ Cost of machine after five years $= 20000\ (1 - 10\%)^3\ (1 - 15\%)^2$

$= 20000(0.729)\ (0.7225)$

$= 20000(0.5267025)$

$= 10534.5$

***Example 34 :* An asset costing Rs. 1500 will depreciate to a scrap value of Rs. 120 in 10 years. Find the rate of depreciation.**

Solution : Let the rate of depreciation be r, then we have

$$120 = 1500(1 - r)^{10}$$

Taking log of both the sides

$$\log 120 = \log 1500 + 10 \log (1 - r)$$

$$2.0792 = 3.1761 + 10 \log (1 - r)$$

$$\therefore \quad 10 \log (1 \quad r) = -3.1761 + 2.1761 = -1.0969$$

$$10 \log (1 - r) = -1.0969$$

$$\log (1 - a) = -0.10969 = \bar{1}.89032$$

$$(1 - r) = \text{Antilog } (\bar{1}.89031) = 0.7767$$

$$r = 1 - 0.7767 = 0.2233 = 2233\%$$

Example 35 : **A machine depreciates at the rate of 10% per annum for the first two years and then 7% per annum for the next 3 years, depreciation being calculated on the diminishing value. If the value of the machine be Rs. 10000 initially, find the average rate of depreciation and the depreciated value of the machine at the end of the fifth year.**

Solution : Depreciated value at the end of 5th year would be

$$= 10000\,(1 - 10/100)^2 \left(1 - \frac{7}{100}\right)^3 = \text{Rs. } 6516$$

Let 'r' be the average rate of depreciation. Then 'r' is given by

$$(1 - r)^5 = \left(1 - \frac{10}{100}\right)^2 \left(1 - \frac{7}{100}\right)^3 = \left(\frac{9}{10}\right)^3 \left(\frac{93}{100}\right)^3$$

$$5 \log (1 - r) = 2 (\log 9 - \log 10) + 3 (\log 93 - \log 100)$$

$$= 2(0.9542 - 1) + 3 (1.9685 - 2)$$

$$= -0.0916 - 0.0945 = -0.1861$$

$$\log (1 - r) = -0.0372 = \bar{1}.9628$$

$$(1 - r) = AL\ (\bar{1}.9628) = 0.9179$$

$$r = 1 - 0.9179 = 0.0821$$

$$= 8.21\%$$

$\therefore$ The average rate of depreciation is 8.21%.

Exercise 12.7

1. The initial cost of a machine and the scrap value are Rs. 40000 and Rs. 4000 respectively. If the life is 9 years, find the annual depreciation using straight line method. **[Ans.** 4000]
2. The initial cost of machine is Rs. 15000 and it has life of 5 years. Find annual depreciation using sum of the year digit method. **[Ans.** 1000, 2000, 3000, 4000, 5000]
3. An asset is purchased for Rs. 1, 10,000. It will depreciate to a scrap value of 6000 in 5 years. (*i*) If the reducing balance method of depreciation is used, find the rate of depreciation. Find the book value of the asset at the end of third year. What would have been the book value at

the end of third year if the straight line method of depreciation had been used.

[**Ans.** rate = 44.11% BV = 19204.14, BV with SLM = 41600]

4. A machine costing Rs. 80000 would reduce to Rs. 20000 in 8 years. Find the rate of yearly depreciation, given that depreciation is calculated using diminishing balances method.

[**Ans.** 15.91%]

5. A machine was purchased for Rs. 100000. It is subject to depreciation at the rate of 8% p.a. Find the value of the machine after four years. [**Ans.** Rs. 71639.3]

6. A machine was purchased for Rs. 150000. The value of the machine after twelve years was found to be Rs. 55150. Find the rate of depreciation. [**Ans.** 8%]

7. A machine was purchased for Rs. 200000. The machine was subject to 12% rate of depreciation Find the time after which the value of the machine would reduce to Rs. 55700.

[**Ans.** 10 years approx]

8. A machine was purchased for Rs. 300000. It is subject to depreciation at the rate of 10%. Find the depreciation for the eleventh year. Also find the value of the machine after 15 years.

[**Ans.** Rs. 10460.35, 61767.34]

9. A machine was purchased for Rs. 500000. It is subject to depreciation at the rate of 8% for first three years and thereafter at the rate of 10%. Find the value of the machine after 8 years.

[**Ans.** Rs. 229903.7]

10. A machine was purchased for Rs. 350000. It is subject to depreciation at the rate of 6% for first three years and thereafter at the rate of 8%. Find the value of the machine after 5 years.

[**Ans.** Rs. 240817.1]

AMORTIZATION OF LOAN

When we take loan from a bank or any financial institution, it is to be repaid in the form of series of equal payment for a given period of time. Each payment can be considered to be comprising of two parts.

1. Interest on the outstanding loan, and
2. Repayment of part of Loan.

For example, X takes a loan of Rs. 1000 form a bank to be repaid is 10 equal annual instalments. Thus, the size of each instalment would be Rs. 100 if we presume the case where rate of interest in nil. But, in actual, interest is also charged on the loan. In such a case when size of instalments are determined, it includes interest payment besides the part of principal repayment. The bank on receiving the instalment breaks it into two parts. First part is treated as Interest on the outstanding loan and the remaining part is adjusted against principal repayment. This process of repaying the loan is known as amortization of loan.

The size of instalment for any principal 'R' carrying interest rate of 'i' to be paid over 'n' period can be determined using the formula given below.

$$R = \frac{P}{a_{\overline{n}|i}}$$

Principal outstanding at beginning of rth period

$$R a_{\overline{n-r+1}|i} = R \cdot \frac{1-(1+i)^{-n+r-1}}{i}$$

Interest in r^{th} period : $R a_{\overline{n-r+1}|i}$

Principal contained in r^{th} payment : $R\left[1 - i a_{\overline{n-k+1}|i}\right]$

Total interest paid $= nR - P$

Example 36 : **Find the present value of an annuity of Rs. 300 payable at the end of each month for 4 years, if money is 6% converted monthly.**

Solution : Present value of the annuity is given as

$$P = R a_{\overline{n}|i}$$

$$P = ?$$

$$R = 300$$

$$n = 4 \times 12 = 48$$

$$i = \frac{6}{12} = 0.5\%$$

$\therefore \quad a_{\overline{n}|i} = 42.58031778$ (Using table IV)

$$\therefore \quad P = (300)\ (42.5803)$$

$$P = 12774.9$$

Example 37 : **Mr. X purchase a house for Rs. 200000. He agrees to pay for the house in 5 equal instalments at the end of each year. If the money is worth 5% effective, what would be the size of each instalment.**

In case X makes down payment of Rs. 50000, then what would be size of each instalment.

Solution : Present value of annuity

$$P = R a_{\overline{n}|i}$$

$$P = 200{,}000$$

$$R = ?$$

$$n = 5$$

$$i = 5\%$$

$$\therefore \quad a_{\overline{5}|5} = 4.3294$$

$$\therefore \quad R = \frac{P}{a_{\overline{n}|i}} = \frac{200000}{4.3294} = 46195.77$$

If X makes cash down payment of 50,000 then X is required to pay only (200000 − 50000) = 150000.

$\therefore$ Size of Instalment $= \dfrac{150000}{4.3294} = 34646.83$

Example 38 : **In the above question, if *X* has made annual instalment of Rs. 35000 at the end of each year then what would have been the cash down payment by *X*.**

Solution : We have

$$P = 200{,}000$$
$$R = 35000$$
$$n = 5$$
$$i = 5\%$$

$\therefore$ P = Cash down payment + $R\,a_{\overline{n}|i}$

$\therefore$ 200000 = Cash down payment + 35000(4.3294)

$\therefore$ 200000 = Cash down payment + 151529

$\therefore$ Cash down payment = 200000 – 151529

= 48471

Example 39 : **Mr. *X* purchased an asset by paying cash down payment of Rs. 200,000 and promising to pay Rs. 25000 at the end of year for next 10 years. If the seller charges interest at the rate of 5% per annum, find**

(*i*) Cash price of the asset

(*ii*) If *X* miss the first two instalment, what should be the size of the third instalment to make him uptodate?

(*iii*) After making seven instalment, he want to discharge the remaining instalment through a single payment at the time of 8th instalment. What should added to the 8th instalment to discharge the entire payment.

Solution : Given

Cash down payment = 200000

Size of instalment = Rs. 25000 per annum

Time of payment = 10 years

Interest = 5%

Cash price = Cash down payment + present value of ordinary annuity of Rs. 25000 for ten years.

$= 200000 + 25000\ a_{\overline{10}|5}$

$= 200000 + 25000(7.7217)$

$= 200000 + 193042.5$

$= 393042.5$

(*ii*) If *X* misses the first two instalment and want to pay the same while making third payment, then the size of third instalment would be

= Third instalment + second instalment (5%, 1) + First instalment (5%, 2).

$= 25000 + 25000\ (1 + 5\%) + 25000(1 + 5\%)^2$

$= 25000 + 26250 + 27562.50$

$= 78812.50$

Alternatively

Size of third instalment $= 25000\ S_{\overline{3}|0.05}$

$= 25000 \times 3.1525$

$= 78812.5$

(*iii*) Since seven instalments have already been made and 8th instalment is due, which is required to include all future payments as well so as to discharge the entire debt. Thus the size of 8th instalment.

= 8th instalment + Present value of 9th and 10th payment

$= 25000 + 25000/(1 + 0.05) + 25000/(1 + 0.05)^2$

$= 25000 + 23809.52 + 22675.73$

$= 71485.25$

Alternatively

$= 25000 + 25000\ a_{\overline{2}|0.05}$

$= 25000 + 25000\ (1.8594)$

$= 25000 + 46485$

$= 71485$

Example 40 : **'A' purchased a television paying Rs. 5000 down and promising to pay Rs. 200 every three months for next 4 years. The seller charges interest at 8% per annum compounded quarterly.**

(*i*) What is the cash price of television.

(*ii*) If 'A' missed the first three payments, what must he pay at the time the fourth is due to bring him upto date?

Solution :

(*i*) The cash price of television = 5000 + Present value of ordinary annuity of 16 payment of Rs. 200 each at the rate of 0.02 per period.

$= 5000 + 200\ a_{\overline{16}|0.02}$

$= 5000 + 200\ (13.5777)$

$= 5000 + 2715.54$

= Rs. 7715.54

(*ii*) In case, A missed the first three payments, then he is required to pay at the time the fourth is due the amount of an ordinary annuity consisting of 4 quarterly payments of Rs. 200 each at the rate 0.02 per quarter. The amount is calculated as under :

$$200\, s_{\overline{4}|0.02} = 200\ (4.1216)$$

$$= \text{Rs. } 824.32$$

Example 41 : **What should be the monthly sales value of a company if it desires to earn a 12% annual return convertible monthly on its investment of Rs. 2,00,000? Monthly costs are Rs. 3,000. The investment will have eight year life with no scrap value.**

Solution : Let monthly sales volume be Rs. x. Therefore, 'x' will be given by the relation.

$$2{,}00{,}000 = (x - 3000)\ a_{\overline{96}|0.01}$$

$$= (x - 3000)\ (61.52770299)$$

$$\Rightarrow \quad x - 3000 = \frac{2,00,000}{61.52770299} = 3250.57$$

$$\Rightarrow \quad x = 3000 + 3250.57 = \text{Rs. } 6250.57.$$

Example 42 : **A loan of Rs. 50000, at the interest rate of 5% compounded annually, is to be amortized by equal payments at the end of each year for 10 years. Find :**

(*i*) **the annual payment**

(*ii*) **the principal outstanding at beginning of 8th period.**

(*iii*) **interest in 8th payment**

(*iv*) **principal contained in 8th payment**

(*v*) **total interest paid.**

Solution : (*i*) The annual payment, R, would be

$$R = \frac{50000}{a_{\overline{n}|i}} = \frac{50000}{a_{\overline{10}|0.05}} = \frac{50000}{7.7217}$$

$$= 6475.25$$

(*ii*) Principal outstanding at the beginning of 8th period

$$= R\, a_{\overline{n-k+1}|i} = 6475.25 \times a_{\overline{10-8+1}|0.05}$$

$$= 6475.25 \times a_{\overline{3}|0.05}$$

$$= 6475.25 \times 2.7232$$

$$= 17633.40$$

(*iii*) Interest in 8th payment

$$= R\, i\, a_{\overline{n-k+1}|i}$$

$$17633.40 \times 0.50$$

$$= 881.67$$

(*iv*) Principal contained in 8th payment

$$= R\left[1 - i\, a_{\overline{n-k+1}|i}\right]$$

$$= 6475.25 - 881.67 = 5593.58$$

Total Interest paid $= nR - P$

$$= 64752.5 - 50000$$

$$= 14752.50$$

Example 43 : **Find amortized monthly payment necessary to pay off a house building loan of Rs. 250000 at 12% per annum in 8 years. Further, find the amount of loan paid after the payment of 56 instalments.**

Solution : We have

$$r = \frac{12\%}{12} = 0.01$$

$$n = 8 \times 12 = 84$$

$$\therefore \quad R = \frac{250000}{130.6722} = 1913.18$$

Amount of loan paid after 56th instalment

$$= 250000 - R\, s_{\overline{n}|i}$$

$$= 250000 \quad 1913.18\, S_{\overline{56}|0.05}$$

$$= 250000 \quad 1913.18(74.5809)$$

$$= 250000 \quad 142686.68$$

$$= 107313.32.$$

Example 44 : **A loan of Rs. 10,000 is to be repaid by equal annual instalments of principal and interest over a period of 20 years. The rate of interest is 3% per annum effective. Find;**

(*i*) **The annual instalment;**

(*ii*) **The capital contained in 8th instalment; and**

(*iii*) **The principal repaid after 12 instalments have been paid.**

Solution : Let the size of each annual instalment be Rs. R. Therefore, R is given by

$$R = \frac{P}{a_{\overline{n}|i}},$$

where $P = 10{,}000$, n 20 and i - 0.03

$$\therefore \quad R = \frac{10,000}{a_{\overline{20}|0.03}} = \frac{10,000}{14.87747486} = \text{Rs. } 672.16$$

(*ii*) The capital contained in 8th instalment will be

$$= R\left[1 - i\, a_{\overline{20-8+1}|i}\right]$$

$$= 672.16\left[1 - 0.03 \times a_{\overline{13}|0.03}\right]$$

$$= 672.16\ [1 \quad 0.03 \times 10.63495533]$$

$$= 672.16 \times 0.680951341$$

$$= \text{Rs. } 457.71.$$

(*ii*) The principal repaid after 12 instalments have been paid

= loan amount – principal outstanding at beginning of 13th payment interval

$$= 10{,}000 - R\ a_{\overline{20-13+1}|i}$$

$$= 10000 - 672.16 \times a_{\overline{8}|0.03}$$

$$= 10000 - 672.16 \times 7.01969219$$

$$= 10000 - 4718.36 = \text{Rs. } 5281.64$$

Exercise 12.8

1. Find the present value of Rs. 5000 due in 10 years at 6% compounded annually. [**Ans.** 2791.97]
2. Find the present value of Rs. 3000 due after 5 years if the interest rate is 5% compounded semiannually. [**Ans.** 2343.59]
3. Find the present value of Rs. 2000 due after 4 years of the interest rate is 9% compounded monthly. [**Ans.** 1397.22]
4. A person wish to have Rs. 25000 at the end of 10 years. If the interest is compounded continuously at the rate of 10%, how much money should be paid into the fund initially? [**Ans.** 9197]
5. M purchased a television paying Rs. 5000 down and promising to pay Rs. 200 every quarter for next 10 years. The seller charges interest at the rate of 12% per annum Compounded quarterly. If *M* missed the first 10 payments, what must he pay when the 11th payment is due to discharge his entire loan? [**Ans.** Rs. 6339.26]
6. Find the present value of an annuity of Rs. 2000 payable at the end of each year for 8 years, if money is worth 5% effective. [**Ans.** Rs. 12926.42]
7. Find the present value of an annuity of Rs. 900 payable at the end of each month for 7 years, if money is worth 6% converted monthly. [**Ans.** Rs. 61607.74]
8. Find the present value of an annuity of Rs. 1300 payable at the end of every six month for 5 years, if money is worth 6% converted semiannually. [**Ans.** Rs. 11089.26]
9. A person purchases an asset for which he agreed to pay Rs. 500 at the end of every six month for 5 years. If money is worth 6% converted semiannually, find the cash price of the asset. [**Ans.** Rs. 4265.10]
10. A loan of Rs. 50000, at the interest rate of 6% compounded annually, is to be amortized by equal payments at the end of each years for 5 years. Find the annual payment. [**Ans.** Rs. 11869.82]

11. A loan of Rs. 15000 is to be repaid by equal annual instalments of principal and interest over a period of 20 years. Find the annual instalment when the rate of interest is 3% per annum effective.

[**Ans.** Rs. 1008.26]

12. What is the present value of a continuous income stream of Rs. 1500 per year for two years if it is discounted continuously a the rate of 0.06 per year? [**Ans.** Rs. 2827.50]

13. A loan of Rs. 70000, at the interest rate of 6% compounded annually, is to be amortized by equal payments at the end of each year for 5 years. Find :

(*a*) the annual payment

(*b*) the principal outstanding at beginning of 4th period.

(*c*) Interest in the 4th payment

(*d*) Principal contained in 4th payment, and

(*e*) Total interest paid.

[**Ans.** (*a*) 16617.75, (*b*) 30466.86, (*c*) 1828.011, (*d*) 14789.74, (*e*) 13088.74]

14. A loan of Rs. 110000, at the interest rate of 6% compounded annually, is to be amortized by equal payments at the end of each year for 5 years. Find :

(*f*) the annual payment.

(*g*) the principal outstanding at beginning of 4th period.

(*h*) Interest in the 4th payment.

(*i*) Principal contained in 4th payment, and

(*j*) Total interest paid.

[**Ans.** (*f*) 24926.62, (*g*) 45700.29, (*h*) 2740.017, (*i*) 22174.6, (*j*) 19533.11]

15. Mr. *X* sold the old machine for Rs. 200000 to buy a new machine for Rs. 6,00,000. What cash payment will be necessary so that the balance can be liquidated by payments of Rs. 20,000 at the end of cash of each month for 20 months when interest is charged at the rate of 9% compounded monthly.

[**Ans.** Rs. 29839.62]

16. Mr. and Mrs. *X* wishes to purchase a house for Rs. 1500000 with the down payment of Rs. 300000. If they can amortize the balance at 9% for 20 years, what is their monthly payment? What is the total interest paid? What is their equity after 10 years.

[**Ans.** 10769.72, 1391212, 647689.907]

17. Mohan has first purchased a house for Rs. 700000 and has made a down payment of Rs. 1,50,000. He proposes to repay the balance in 25 years by monthly instalments at 9%.

(*i*) What are the monthly payments?

(*ii*) What is the total interest payment? [**Ans.** (*i*) 4719, 865700]

18. Calculate the present value of an annuity of Rs. 30,000 per annum, assumed to be payable continuously for 10 years, at the rate of interest of 8 percent per annum compounded continuously.

[**Ans.** Rs. 206501.54]

19. A two-wheeler is purchased on instalment basis such that Rs. 1800 is to be paid each year for 5 years. If interest is charged @ 11% per annum compounded continuously, what would be the cash price or present value of the two-wheeler? [**Ans.** Rs. 6922.64]

20. Derive, by using calculus, the present value of an annuity of Re. 1 per annum assumed to be payable continuously for n years at the rate of interest i per rupee per annum convertible continuously.

LEASING, CAPITAL EXPENDITURE AND BONDS

Leasing

Leasing is a financial arrangement under which a person can use an asset on payment of rent. known as lease rental, for certain specified period. Thus, is case of lease rental, out flow takes place in the form of equal rentals, say R. If 'r' is the rate of interest, we may be interest in finding present value of these lease rentals which is compared with the purchase price and accordingly a final decision is taken – whether to buy a machine or to avail its utility through leasing.

Capital Expenditure

When a firm plans any capital expenditure towards acquisition of assets, it assess the benefits offered by the assets against the cost of the assets. The asset which offers highest net benefit is preferred. The benefits which are normally offered are in the form of saving in labour cost, operational cost, etc.

BOND

A bond is a like debenture in which a person is required to make a payment to the firm issuing bond, which is basically purchase price of the bond. Against this one time payment, the person gets series of interest payment at specified intervals of time at a specified rate. After the expiry of the specified period. the person return back the bond to the firm and get back his original payment. This process is known as **redemption** of bond. When a person gets same amount which he had invested, a bond is said to be redeemed at per. When he gets more than what he paid, it is known as redemption at premium. When he gets less than what he paid, it is known as redemption at discount.

Thus, we may summaries that an investor in bond gets two benefits against payment of purchase price of bond.

1. Interest payments.
2. Principal repayment at the time of redemption.

Therefore, the purchase price of bond should be equal to the present value of the annuity formed by its interest payment and the present value of principal repayment at the time of redemption.

Bonds are sold and purchased in the open market where their price may not be equal to the purchase price. Therefore when purchase price is compared with the benefits accuring from the bond, the rate of return may be different from their regular interest payment from the firm. This is **known as effective rate or yield rate.**

Example 45 : **A company may obtain a particular machine either by leasing it for 5 years at an annual rent of Rs. 800 or by purchasing the machine for Rs. 3200.**

(*i*) Which alternative is preferable if the company can invest money at 6% per annum?

(*ii*) What would be your decision, if it can invest at 8% per annum.

Solution : (*i*) Let us calculate present value of annual payment made by the company over next five years.

$$P = 800\ a_{\overline{n}|i} = 800\ a_{\overline{5}|0.06}$$

$$= 800 \times 4.2123 = 3369.84$$

Since the present value of series of payments to be made by the company aggregate to Rs. 3369.84 which is higher than the purchase price of Rs. 3200, hence purchasing is preferable.

(*ii*) At 8%, the present value is

$$= 800\ a_{\overline{5}|0.08} = 800 \times 3.9927 = 3194.16$$

which is less than purchase price, therefore, leasing is preferable.

Example 46 : **A bond has a face amount of Rs. 1000 and maturity period of 10 years. The nominal interest rate is 6%. What should be the price of the bond to yield an effective interest rate of 8%.**

Solution : Amount of each annual interest payment

$$= \frac{6}{100} \times 100 = 60$$

Present value of annuity of Rs. 60

$$= 60\ a_{\overline{n}|i} = 60\ a_{\overline{10}|0.08}$$

$$= 60 \times 6.7100 = 402.6$$

Present value of Maturity payment

$$= 1000\ (1 + 0.08)^{-10}$$

$$= 1000 \times 0.4631 = 463.10$$

$\therefore$ Price of the Bond = Present value of Interest + Present value of principal

$$= 402.60 + 463.10$$

$$= 865.70$$

Example 47 : **An investor want to purchase a 3 year Rs. 100 face value bond having nominal interest rate of 6%. What should be the purchase price if the investors required rate of return is 8% and the bond is the mature at par.**

Solution : Given Maturity value = Rs. 100

$$\text{Interest} = \frac{6}{100} \times 100 = 60$$

$$\text{Time} = 3 \text{ years}$$

$$\therefore \quad \text{Purchase price} = 6\ a_{\overline{n}|i} + 100\ (1 + 0.08)^{-3}$$

$$= 6\ a_{\overline{3}|0.08} + 100\ (1 + 0.08)^{-3}$$

$$= 6(2.5770) + 100(0.7938)$$

$$= 15.342 + 79.38 = 94.7$$

Example 48 : **Machine *A* costs Rs. 10000 and has useful life of 8 years. Machine *B* costs Rs. 8000 and has useful life of 6 years. Suppose machine *A* generates an annual labour savings of Rs. 2000 while machine *B* generates an annual labour savings of Rs. 1800. Assuming the time value of money is 10% per annum, find which machine is preferable?**

Solution : In order to find better machine out of the given two machines, we shall calculate equivalent cost of each machine, as under.

	Machine A	*Machine B*
Cost	10000	8000
Life	8 years	6 years
PV Annuity factor	$a_{\overline{8}\|0.10} = 5.335$	$a_{\overline{6}\|0.10} = 4.356$
Equivalent Annual Cost (∴ Cost/PVAF)	1874.41	1836.55

∴ Net Annual saving in the case of two machines will be.

	Machine A	*Machine B*
Labour Savings per annum	2000	1800
Equivalent Annual cost	1874.41	1836.55
Net Savings	Rs. 125 59	R< 36.55

∴ Machine *A* is preferable.

Exercise 12.9

1. Find the purchase price of Rs. 1000 bond, redeemable at the end of 10 years at par, and paying annual dividends at 4%, if the yield rat is to be 5% effective. [**Ans.** 922.77]
2. Find the purchase price of Rs. 500, 5% bond, dividends payable semiannually, redeemable at Rs. 550 in 5 years, it the yield rate is to be 6% compounded semiannually. [**Ans.** 515.83]
3. Find the purchase price of a bond paying annual dividend at 8.5% and having maturity period 10 years. The bond would be redeemed at Rs. 1100 and the expected investor yield is 8%. [**Ans.** 1079.76]
4. Machine *A* costs Rs. 20000 and has useful life of 10 years. Machine *B* costs Rs. 12000 and has useful life of 8 years. Machine *A* generates an annual labour savings of Rs. 3000 and machine *B* generates an annual labour savings of Rs. 2000. Assuming the time value of money is 8% per annum, find which machine in preferable. [**Ans.** Machine *A* is preferable]
5. A company may obtain a particular machine either by leasing it for 5 years (the useful life) at an annual rent of Rs. 2000 or by purchasing the machine for Rs. 1800. If the company can borrow money at 10% per annum, which alternative is preferable. [**Ans.** Leasing is preferable]
6. Mr. Ram, businessman, plans to shift his business from Delhi to Faridabad because of closure of certain type of industries in Delhi. He has to make a decision between two machines, both of which are designed to improve operation by saving a labour cost. Machine *A* costs Rs. 9750

and will generate the annual labour savings of Rs. 2400. Machine B costs Rs. 7750 and will save Rs. 2300 annually. Machine A has a useful life of 8 years while Machine B has a useful life of 6 years only. If time value of money is 10% per annum, which machine is preferable?

(Assume annual compounding and that the savings is realised at the end of each year).

[**Ans.** Machine A is preferable].

7. A company may obtain a particular machine either by leasing it for 5 year at an annual rent of Rs. 1500 or by purchasing the machine for Rs. 5500.

   (*a*) Which alternative is preferable if the company can borrow money at 10% per annum?

   (*b*) What if the cost of borrowing is 14% per annum?

   [**Ans.** (*a*) Purchase is preferable as Rs. 5686.2 is more than Rs. 5500,
   (*b*) Leasing is preferable as Rs. 5149.65 is less than Rs. 5500.]

8. The management of a company has an option either to construct a new godown for Rs. 500000 or rent an equivalent one with a 25 year lease for an annual rental of Rs. 40000 payable at the beginning of each year and an option to purchase a readymade room for Rs. 25000 at the expiration of the contract. If the company expects to earn 8% per annum after taxes from other investment opportunities, should management construct or rent an equivalent factory building?

   [**Ans.** Cost of option II = 464800.30, therefore management should take it on rent]

9. The debenture holders of a company receive interest at 10% per annum half yearly on 30th June and 31th December and an additional interest at 2% per annum payable annually on 31 December each year. If an investor purchases one debenture of Rs. 100 for Rs. 90 on 1st January, find his yield expressed as an effective rate of interest per half year. What would be the yield per annum? [**Ans.** 6.63%, 13.7%]

PERPETUITY

Perpetuity is an annuity for infinite number of period. The sum of perpetuity would be different in the cases, when annuity starts from the beginning of a period and in the case when it starts from the end of the given period. For example, a payment required to be made in the financial year 2004–05 can either be made on 1 April, 2004 or on 31 March, 05. But, the dates will have different implications. When the payment starts from **the first day of a financial year,** we have case of annuity due. In such case, the sum of payment for using period *i.e.*, perpetuity would be given as

$$S = R + \frac{R}{i} \quad \text{(where 'R' is the annual payment and 'i' is the rate of interest)}$$

When payment is **made at the end of year,** it is a case of annuity and sum would be given as

$$S = \frac{R}{i}$$

Example 49 : **Find the present value of a sequence of payment of Rs. 125 made at the end of each quarter and continuing for ever, if effective rate of interest is 8%.**

Solution : This is a case of perpetuity

The present value of perpetuity is given as

$$P \propto = \frac{R}{i}$$

Here $R = 125$

$$i = \frac{8}{4} = 2\% = 0.02$$

$$P\infty = \frac{125}{0.02} = \text{Rs. } 6250.$$

Example 50 : **Find the rate at which present value of a perpetuity of Rs. 500 payable at the end of each quarter be Rs. 10000?**

Solution : We have

$$P\infty = \frac{R}{i}$$

$$P\mu = 10000$$

$$R = \text{Rs. } 500$$

$$i = ?$$

$\therefore$ Effective rate $(r) = 5 \times 4 = 20\% \left(\text{Since } i = \frac{r}{4}\right)$

Example 51 : **How much money is needed to conduct a series of lectures costing Rs. 2500 at the beginning of each year indefinitely, if money is worth 3% compounded annually?**

Solution : In this case payment starts from the beginning of the year

$\therefore$ We have $P\infty = R + \frac{R}{i}$

Here $R = 2500$

$$i = 0.03$$

$$P\infty = 2500 + \frac{2500}{0.03}$$

$$= 85633.33$$

Exercise 12.10

1. How much money is needed to endure a series of lectures costing Rs. 5000 at the beginning of each year indefinitely, if money is worth 3% compounded annually? [**Ans.** Rs. 171666.66]
2. What amount shall be deposited today so as to provide an yearly allowance of Rs. 15000 at the beginning of arch year indefinitely, if money is worth 6% compounded annually? [**Ans.** Rs. 265000]
3. Find the rate of which present value of the perpetuity of Rs. 800 payable at the end of each quarter will accumulate to Rs. 50000 [**Ans.** Rate = 6.4% p.a.]
4. Find the rate at which present value of the perpetuity of Rs. 800 payable at the end of each half year will accumulate to Rs. 50000. [**Ans.** Rate = 3.2% p.a.]

5. A man want to deposit a certain amount with a college so that the college can give scholar-ship of Rs. 500 every year, indefinitely, to the best student of the year. Find the amount to be deposited by the man, if money is worth 6% compounded annually [**Ans.** Amount = 8833.33]

ANNUITY DUE

As already mentioned, in case of annuity due, it will be made in the battening of the year and therefore it will remain invested for n periods.

If R is the payment to be made in the first year, it will be made in the beginning of the year and therefore it will remain invested for n periods.

$\therefore$ Amount of Ist payment $= R(1 + i)^n$

Similarly Amount of IInd payment $= R(1 + i)^{n-1}$

Amount of IIIrd payment $= R(1 + i)^{n-2}$

$\vdots$

Amount of later n^{th} payment $= R(1 + i)^{n-(n-1)}$

$= R(1 + i)$

Thus, the sum of these payment would be given as

$$S = R(1 + i) + R(1 + i)^2 \ldots + R(1 + i)^n$$

This is a geometric series where

$$\text{first term} = R(1 + i)$$

$$\text{Common Ratio} = \frac{R(1+i)^2}{R(1+i)} = (1+i)$$

$$\therefore \text{ Sum of the series} = S = \frac{R(1+i)\left[(1+i)^n - 1\right]}{(1+i-1)} = \frac{R(1+i)\left[(1+i)^n - 1\right]}{i}$$

$$= R\left(S_{\overline{n+1}|i} - 1\right)$$

Example 52 : **Find the amount at the end of 10 years of an annuity of Rs. 500 payable at the beginning of each year until 10 payments have been made if rate of interest is 6% effective.**

Solution : Since payments are being made in the beginning of each year, it is a case of annuity due.

$$\therefore \quad S = R\left(S_{\overline{n+1}|i} - 1\right)$$

where $R = 500$, $n = 10$, $i = 0.06$

$$\therefore \quad S = 500\left(S_{\overline{10+1}|0.06} - 1\right)$$

$$= 500(14.97164 - 1)$$

$$= 500(13.97164)$$

$$= 6985.82$$

Example 53 : **Mr. *X* deposits Rs. 500 at be beginning of each quarter in bank account carrying interest rate of 6% compounded quarterly. Find the balance at the end of 4 years.**

Solution : Here

$$R = 500$$

$$i = \frac{6}{4} = 1.5\%$$

$$n = 4 \times 4 = 16$$

$$\text{Sum of annuity} = R\left(S_{\overline{n+1}|i} - 1\right)$$

$$= 500\left(S_{\overline{16+1}|0.015} - 1\right)$$

$$= 500\left(S_{\overline{17+1}|0.015} - 1\right)$$

$$= 500(19.2013 - 1) = 500\ (18.2013)$$

$$= 9100.65.$$

Example 54 : **Mr. *X* wants Rs. 500,000 at end of 7 years. If the rate of interest is 8%, what amount shall be deposited in the beginning of each quarter so as to get the above amount.**

Solution : Let 'R' be the amount deposited in the beginning of each quarter.

We have $S = R\left(S_{\overline{n+1}|i} - 1\right)$

Here $S = 500000$

$$n = 7 \times 4 = 28 \qquad \therefore \quad n + 1 = 29$$

$$i = \frac{8\%}{4} = 2\%$$

$$\therefore \quad S_{\overline{29}|0.02} = 38.7922$$

$$\therefore \quad 500000 = R(38.7922 - 1)$$

$$500000 = R(37.7922)$$

$$R = \frac{500000}{37.7922} = 13230.24$$

$\therefore$ Amount to be deposited in the beginning of each quarter = Rs. 13230.24

PRESENT VALUE OF ANNUITY DUE

As the name itself reflects, present value of Annuity Due refers to determination of present value of each payment in form of annuity due and aggregating them, as shown below.

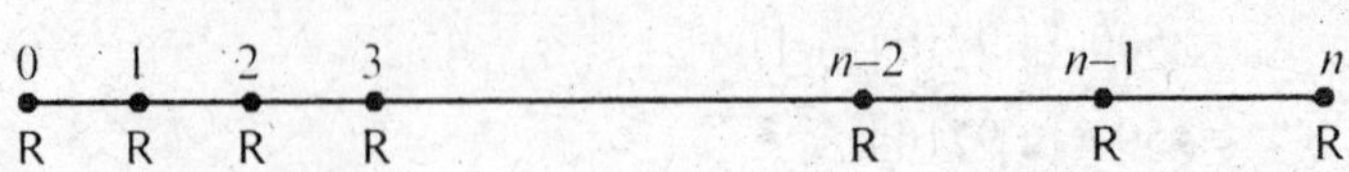

Present value of Ist payment $R = R(1 + i)^0 = R$

Present value of IInd payment $R = R(1+i)^{-1}$

Present value of IIIrd payment $R = R(1+i)^{-2}$

Therefore the sum of present value of annuity due can be written as

$$S = R + \text{Sum of ordinary annuity having } (n-1) \text{ terms.}$$

[$\therefore$ Since first term is R]

$$= R + R\, a_{\overline{n-1}|\,i}$$

$$S = R\left(a_{\overline{n-1}|\,i} + 1\right)$$

***Example 55* : Find the present value of an annuity due of Rs. 500 payable annually for 10 years at the rate of 7%.**

Solution : Present value of Annuity due

$$P = R\left(a_{\overline{n-1}|\,i} + 1\right)$$

$$= 500\left(a_{\overline{10-1}|\,0.07} + 1\right)$$

$$= 6.5152$$

$$\therefore \quad a_{\overline{9}|\,0.07} = 6.5152$$

$$\therefore \quad P = R(6.5152 + 1)$$

$$= 500(6.5152 + 1)$$

$$= 500(7.5152)$$

$$P = 3757.6$$

***Example 56* : Mr. *X* purchased an asset for which he agreed to pay Rs. 1000 at the beginning of each quarter for 5 years. If the rate of interest is 6%, find the case price of the asset.**

Solution : Let the cash price of the asset $= P$

$$\therefore \quad P = R\left(a_{\overline{n-1}|\,i} + 1\right)$$

Here

$$R = 1000$$

$$n = 5 \times 4 = 20$$

$$i = \frac{6}{4} = 1.5\% = 0.015$$

$$\therefore \quad P = 1000\left(a_{\overline{20-1}|\,0.015} + 1\right)$$

$$= 1000\left(a_{\overline{19}|\,0.015} + 1\right)$$

$$= 1000(16.4261 + 1)$$

$$= 1000\,(17.4261) = 17426.1$$

Example 57 : **Mr. *X* purchased an asset for Rs. 100,000 on instalment basis. Each instalment is to be paid at the beginning of each quarter. Find the size of each instalment if the money is to be repaid in three years and effective rate of interest is 6%.**

Solution : We have

$$P = R\left(a_{\overline{n-1}|i} + 1\right)$$

$$P = 100000$$

$$R = ?$$

$$n = 3 \times 4$$

$$i = \frac{6}{4} = 1.5\% = 0.015$$

$$1000 = R\left(a_{\overline{12-1}|0.015} + 1\right)$$

$$1000 = R\left(a_{\overline{11}|0.015} + 1\right)$$

$$1000 = R(10.0711 + 1)$$

$$R = \frac{100000}{11.0711} = 9032.52$$

$\therefore$ size of each instalment = Rs. 9032.52.

Exercise 12.11

1. Find the amount at the end of 10 years of an annuity of Rs. 500 payable at the beginning of each year if money is worth 6% effective. **[Ans.** 6985.82]
2. Find the amount at the end of 3 year if Rs. 300 is deposited in an account paying 8% compounded quarterly. **[Ans.** 4104.09]
3. At the beginning of each quarter, Rs. 900 is deposited into a saving account that pays 6% compounded quarterly. Find the balance is the account at the end of 5 years. **[Ans.** 21123.45]
4. A man purchase a house from *B* and agrees to pay *B* twenty instalments of Rs. 15000 each. The instalments would be paid at the begin of each period. If the money's work 8% effective, find the equivalent cash price of the house. **[Ans.** Rs. 159053.85]
5. A man purchases a house for which he agrees to pay Rs. 3000 at the beginning of each 3 months until the has made 10 payments. If money is worth 6% compounded quarterly, what is the equivalent cash price of the house. **[Ans.** 28081.50]
6. What equal payments made at the beginning of each month for 4 years will pay for a house priced at Rs. 500000, if money is worth 15% compounded annually? **[Ans.** 13743.58]
7. A debt of Rs. 25000 with interest rate of 8% compounded quarterly is to be discharged by 10 equal quarterly payment. The payment would be made at the beginning of each period. Find the size of each payment. **[Ans.** 2728.60]

DEFERRED ANNUITY

As already mentioned, in case of deferred annuity the series of payment is made after interval of time. For example, if a person borrows loan of Rs. 100,000 to be repaid in ten equal annual instalments and the repayment is to start after certain period of time say 'm' periods. Thus, the payment of annual instalment commences after the gap of certain number of years. Therefore, we may say that it is an annuity starting after certain period of time.

The present value of deferred annuity for n periods, deferred for certain number of period say 'm' year will be given as

$$P = R\left(a_{\overline{m+n}|i} - a_{\overline{m}|i}\right)$$

Also $$P = \frac{R}{i}\left[\frac{1}{(1+i)^m} - \frac{1}{(1+i)^{m+n}}\right]$$

Example 58 (a) : **Find the present value of series of annual payments of Rs. 700 each, the first payment being made at the end of 6 year and the last at the end of 15 years, if the effective rate of interest 8%.**

Solution : Present value of deferred annuity is given by the formula

$$P = R\left(a_{\overline{m+n}|i} - a_{\overline{m}|i}\right)$$

Here $R = 700$

$m = 5$

$n = 10\ (\because\ 15 - 5)$

$i = 8\%$

$\therefore\quad a_{\overline{m+n}|i} = a_{\overline{15}|0.05} = 8.5594$

$\therefore\quad a_{\overline{m}|i} = a_{\overline{5}|0.05} = 3.9927$

$\therefore\quad P = 700\ (8.5594 - 3.9927)$

$P = 700\ (4.5667)$

$= 3196.69$

Example 58 (b) : **Find the present value of an annuity of Rs. 200 per quarter for 8 years, deferred $3\frac{1}{2}$ years, if money is worth 8% converted quarterly.**

Solution : Present value of deferred annuity is given by the formula

$$P = \frac{R}{i}\left(\frac{1}{(1+i)^m} - \frac{1}{(1+i)^{m+n}}\right)$$

Here $R = 200$

$$m = \frac{7}{2} \times 4$$

$= 14$

$n = 18$

$i = 2\%$

$$P = \frac{200}{.02}\left[\frac{1}{(1+.02)^{14}} - \frac{1}{(1+.02)^{32}}\right]$$

$P = 10000\ [.7578 - .5306]$

$P = 1000\ [.2272]$

$P = \text{Rs. } 2272.$

Example 59 : **A bungalow sells for Rs. 50000 downpayment and 10 semiannual payments of Rs. 5000 each, the first due 3 years hence. Find the cash price of the bungalow if money is worth 6% compounded semiannually.**

Solution : Present value of deferred annuity is given by the formula

$$P = \frac{R}{i}\left(\frac{1}{(1+i)^m} - \frac{1}{(1+i)^{m+n}}\right)$$

Here $R = 5000$

$m = 5$

$n = 10$

$i = 3\%$

$$P = \frac{5000}{.03}\left[\frac{1}{(1+.03)^5} - \frac{1}{(1+.03)^{15}}\right]$$

$$P = \frac{5000}{.03}\left[\frac{1}{(1.03)^5} - \frac{1}{(1.03)^{15}}\right]$$

$$P = \frac{5000}{.03}[.8626 - .6418]$$

$P = 166667\ [.2208]$

$P = 36800.$

$\therefore$ Cash price of the bungalow = Downpayment + present value of deferred annuity

= 50000 + 36800

= Rs. 86800

Example 60 : **Mr. *X* purchased an asset for which he agrees to make payment in 5 equal annual instalments of Rs. 15000 each. The payment would commence from the end of 3rd years. If the effective rate of interest is 7%, find the cash price of the asset.**

Solution : This is case of deferred annuity

$$\therefore \quad P = R\left(a_{\overline{m+n}|i} - a_{\overline{m}|i}\right)$$

Here $R = \text{Rs. } 15000$

$$m = 2$$

$$n = 5$$

$$i = 0.07$$

$$\therefore \quad P = 15000\left(a_{\overline{2+5}|0.07} - a_{\overline{2}|0.07}\right)$$

$$= 15000\left(a_{\overline{7}|0.07} - a_{\overline{2}|0.07}\right) = 15000\,(5.3892 - 1.8080)$$

$$P = 15000(3.5812) = 53718$$

Exercise 12.12

1. Find the present value of a sequence of annual payments of Rs. 800 each, the first being made at the end of 5 year and the last at the end of 12 years, if money is worth 6% effective.
   [**Ans.** 3934]

2. An annuity consist of 6 annual payments of Rs. 3500 each, the first being made at the end of 5 years. Find the amount of this annuity, if money is worth 8% compounded annually.
   [**Ans.** 25675.75]

3. Find the present value of series of annual payments of Rs. 5000 each, the first being made at the end of 5 years and the last at the end of 10 years, if money is worth 5% effective.
   [**Ans.** 20878.792]

4. A man borrowed Rs. 75000 at compound interest of 7% per annum and has to repay the money in 20 equal yearly instalments. If the first payment is to be made 3 years hence, find the size of each instalment. [**Ans.** 8105.31]

5. A house is sold for Rs. 70000 down and 10 semiannual payments of Rs. 5000 each, the first due 3 years hence. Find the cash price of the house if money is worth 6% compounded semiannually. [**Ans.** 106789.89]

6. Mr. *X* took a loan which was to be repaid by monthly instalment of Rs. 3000 p.m. for 5 years. He paid the instalment upto the end of two years. He could not pay any instalment in the third year. He want to restart the payment from the beginning of fourth year. Find how much he should pay each month so that his loan is cleared by the end of five years.

13

Logarithms

Highlights of the Chapter

- **Introduction**
- **Procedure for Finding Log**
- **Finding Characteristic and Mantissa**
- **Antilogarithm**
- **Basic Changing Formula**
- **Practical Problems**

INTRODUCTION

Logarithms facilitate process of complex calculation. Before understanding process of computing logarithm, one must get familiar with the basic concepts of logarithm.

The most important issue is the base with reference to which logarithm is being computed. For example,

$$Y = \log_a X$$

The above representation shows 'Log of X' to the base 'a'.

Normally, we calculate log to the base 10 which is called as common logarithm. When 'base' is not specifically mentioned, it is presumed that computation is being done with reference to base 10.

PROCEDURE FOR FINDING LOGARITHM

When we compute log of any number, two parts are to be calculated. The first part is called characteristic and the second part is Mantissa.

Characteristic is an integer (positive, negative or zero) whereas mantissa is a positive proper fraction.

For example, if the log of a number is 3.524 then characteristic is 3 and mantissa is 524. Similarly, if log of any number is –2.334, its characteristic is 2 and mantissa is 334. In this case, characteristic can also be written as $\bar{2}$.

PROCEDURE FOR FINDING CHARACTERISTIC

Case I : If the given number is greater than or equal to one, the characteristic is one less than the number of digits contained in its integral part. For example, if the given number is 642.8, the number of digits before decimal are three , therefore characteristic is (3 – 1) = 2.

Similarly, if the given number is 64.28, the integral part comprises of two digits therefore characteristic is (2 – 1) = 1.

Case II : If the given number is less than one, the characteristic of such number will be negative and one more than the number of ciphers immediately after the decimal point before any non zero number. For example, if the given number is 0.0058. The given number is less than one and has two ciphers after decimal point and before any non zero number. The characteristic of this number will be –(1 + 2) *i.e.* –3. Similarly, if the given number is 0.1238. This is also less than one and there are no Ciphers after decimal point therefore its characteristic is – (1 + 0) = – 1. The negative characteristic can also be written $\bar{1}$ (*i.e.* with bar sign on the number instead of '–ve' sign).

***Example 1 :* Find the characteristic of the logarithm of following numbers.**

(*i*) 2498.56	**(*ii*) 2.4985**
(*iii*) 0.0248	**(*iv*) 0.00024**
(*v*) 0.2458	

Solution

(*i*) Given number 2498.56 is greater than one. Therefore, characteristic is (4 – 1) = 3 *i.e.* one less than the number of digits before decimal (or the number of digits contained in its integral part).

(*ii*) Given number 2.4985 is greater than one. Therefore characteristic is (1 – 1) = 0.

(*iii*) Given number 0.0248 is less than one. Therefore, characteristic is – (1 + 1) = – 2 or 2 *i.e* characteristic is negative and one more than the number of ciphers immediately after the decimal point before any non zero figure.

(*iv*) Given number is 0.000224 is less than one. Therefore, characteristic is – (1 + 3) = – 4 or $\bar{4}$.

(*v*) Given number is 0.2458 is less than one therefore, characteristic is – (1 + 0) = – 1 or $\bar{1}$.

CALCULATION OF MANTISSA

Mantissa as already mentioned is a positive fraction part of a log. In order to calculate mantissa of any number, log table are used. While calculating mantissa, first four digits of a number are considered ignoring the decimal sign. For example, given number is 23.825 then for calculating mantissa, we will consider 2382. If number of digits are not four after ignoring decimal point then it shall be made four digit number by inserting Ciphers at the end of the number. For example, the given number is 2.3 then we shall make it to four digit by adding two ciphers at the end *i.e.*, 2300 and we shall look for mantissa of 2300 in the log table. In order to find mantissa of a given number from the log table, we take first two digit and locate them in the extreme left hand column. We move row-wise to find intersecting number between first two digits and the third digit. Note down this number and further move row-wise to find intersecting number between first two digits and fourth digit appearing is mean difference column. Add the number obtained earlier and the number obtained in mean difference column. Prefix the decimal to the number so obtained.

For Example : Mantissa of 5.379 is to be calculated. We take first two digit 53 in the extreme left and move row-wise to find intersecting number between 53 and 7 (third digit). The number is 7300. Now we move further row-wise to find intersecting number between 53 and 9 (fourth digit) under mean difference column. The number is 7. The resulting mantissa is 7300 + 7 = 7307.

After prefixing decimal, we have mantissa as 0.7307.

Once characteristic and mantissa has been calculated, the value of logarithm of a number is Characteristic + Mantissa.

ANTILOGARITHM

If $\log_a Y = x$, then Y is referred as antilogarithm of x to the base 'a' and it is written as antilog $_a x$.

The procedure of finding antilogarithm is similar to that of finding mantissa from log tables with slight modification. In order to find antilogarithm, separate tables with heading antilogarithm are used.

The following two examples of finding antilogarithm would help in understanding the procedure.

(*a*) To find Antilog of 2.5378.

Refer decimal part of the number and find value corresponding to it from Antilog table in the manner exactly similar to finding mantissa. The number intersecting at 53 and 7 is 3443 and number corresponding to fourth digit *i.e.* 8 is 6 (in the mean difference column).

Adding the two number we have, 3443 + 6 = 3449.

Now we consider the integral part of the number. If it is greater than or equal to zero, add '1' one to it. For example, in this case the number is '2'. Adding '1' to it, we have '3'. Prefix decimal after three digits in value obtained above. Therefore, we have Antilog of 2.5378 as 344.9.

(*b*) Finding Antilog of –2.5378 or $\bar{2}$.5378.

In this case, so far the use of antilog table is concerned, it will be similar as is previous case since decimal part is same. The main issue is prefixing the decimal for which integral part is used.

In this case integral part is negative, therefore, subtract 1 from the integral part *i.e.* 2. The resulting value is 2 – 1 = 1. Insert one cipher to the left hand side of 3449 and then prefix the decimal point. Therefore, the required number is 0.03449.

Example 2 : **Find the log of following numbers.**

(*i*) 5892 **(*ii*) 589.2**

(*iii*) 5.892 **(*iv*) 0.5892**

(*v*) 0.05892

Solution

(*i*) Characteristic = 4 – 1 = 3.

Mantissa = 7701 + 1 = 7702

∴ Log = 3 + 0.7702 = 3.7702

(*ii*) Characteristic = 3 – 1 = 2

Mantissa = 7701 + 1 = 7702

Log = 2 + 0.7702 = 2.7702

(*iii*) Characteristic = 1 – 1 = 0

Mantissa = 7701 + 1 = 7702

Log = 0 + 0.7702 = 0.7702

(*iv*) Characteristic = – (0 + 1) = $\bar{1}$

Mantissa = 7701 + 1 = 7702

Log = $\bar{1}.7702$

(*v*) Characteristic = – (1 + 1) = – 2 = $\bar{2}$

Mantissa = 7701 + 1 = 7702

Log = $\bar{2}.7702$

Properties of Logarithm

(*a*) The logarithm of a product of any two or more numbers is equal to sum of their respective logarithm.

$$\log_a(mn) = \log_a m + \log_a n$$

(*b*) The logarithm of a fraction is equal to the logarithm of numerator subtracted by logarithm of the denominator.

$$\log_a\left(\frac{m}{n}\right) = \log_a m - \log_a n$$

(*c*) The logarithm of the pth power of a number is '*p*' times the logarithm of that number.

$$\log_a m^p = p \log_a m$$

The example given below highlights the use log properties in solving complex mathematical expressions.

Example 2 : **Find the value of $\frac{(4872)^{1/2} \times (368)^{1/5}}{(1928)^{1/7}}$ using log and antilog tables.**

Solution : Let

$$y = \frac{(4872)^{1/2} \times (368)^{1/5}}{(1928)^{1/7}}$$

Taking log both the sides, we have

$$\log y = \frac{1}{2}\log(4872) + \frac{1}{5}\log(368) - \frac{1}{7}\log(1928)$$

$$= \frac{1}{2} \times (3.6877) + \frac{1}{5} \times (2.565) - \frac{1}{7} \times (3.285)$$

$$= 1.8438 + 0.5130 - 0.4692$$

$$\log y = 1.8876$$

$$y = \text{Antilog } (1.8876)$$

$$y = 77.20$$

Hence the required solution is 77.20.

BASE CHANGING FORMULA

Normally, we use log to the base 10 for calculation purpose because these log tables are available with us. However, we may calculate log of any given number with respect to any given base. Though, computer facilitates us in computing log to the base 'e' directly (known as natural logarithm) but in actual practice, we shall convert the given base to base 10 so that we can make use of log table for calculation. The formula of base conversion is given below :

Suppose we have

$$\log_{(\text{old base})} X$$

$$\log_{(\text{New base})} X = \frac{\log_{(\text{old base})} X}{\log_{(\text{new base})}(\text{Old base})}$$

This has been proved below :

Suppose we have

$$\log_m X \quad a \qquad (1)$$

We are required to calculate $\log_n X$ *i.e.*, we have to change base from 'm' to 'n'.

Let $\quad Y = \log_n X \qquad (2)$

$\therefore \quad n^Y = X$

Taking $\log_m$ both the sides, we have

$$Y \log_m n = \log_m X$$

$$\therefore \quad Y = \frac{\log_m X}{\log_m n} \qquad (3)$$

Using (2) and (3), we have

$$\log_n X = \frac{\log_m X}{\log_m n}$$

The following examples would explain the procedure of base conversion.

(Change of base method)

Example 3 : **Calculate the value of following (in terms of log to the base 10).**

(*i*) $\log_7 23$ **(*ii*) $\log_4 20 \times \log_3 48$**

Solution : (*i*) First we have to change base from 7 to 10, as shown below :

$$\log_7 23 = \frac{\log_{10} 23}{\log_{10} 7} = \frac{1.3617}{0.8451} = 1.611$$

(*ii*) First we have to change base from 4 and 3 to 10, as shown below :

$$\log_4 20 \times \log_3 48$$

$$= \frac{\log_{10} 20}{\log_{10} 4} \times \frac{\log_{10} 48}{\log_{10} 3}$$

$$= \frac{1.3010}{0.6021} \times \frac{1.6812}{0.4771}$$

$$= 2.1607 \times 3.5237$$

$$= 7.613$$

***Example 4 :* Given log 2 = 0.30103, find the number of digits in 2^{32}**

Solution : Let $x = 2^{32}$

$$\therefore \quad \log x = 32 \log 2$$

$$= 32 \times 0.30103 = 9.6329$$

As characteristic of log x is 9 therefore number of digits is the number 2^{32} is $(9 + 1) = 10$.

***Example 5 :* Given log 3 = 0.4771, find the position of first non zero figure in 3^{-40}.**

Solution Let $x = 3^{-40}$

$$\therefore \quad \log x = -40 \log 3$$

$$= -40 \times 0.4771$$

$$= -19.084$$

$$= -19 - 1 + (1 - 0.084)$$

$$= -20 + 0.916$$

$$= \overline{20}.916$$

This implies x has 19 Ciphers immediately after decimal point so that first significant or non zero is 20th digit.

***Example 6 :* Find the cube root of 6.284 using log and antilog table.**

Solution : Let $x = (6.284)^{1/3}$

Taking log both the sides, we have

$$\log x = \frac{1}{3} \log (6.284)$$

$$\log x = \frac{1}{3} \times (0.7983)$$

$$\log x = 0.2661$$

$$\therefore \quad x = \text{Antilog } (0.2661)$$

$$= 1845 + 0$$

$$x = 1.845 \text{ (approx)}$$

***Example 7 :* Evaluate $\dfrac{24.395 \times (3.16)^3}{8.79}$.**

Solution : Let $x = \dfrac{24.395 \times (3.16)^3}{8.79}$

Then $\log x = \log 24.395 + 3 \log 3.16 - \log 8.79$

$$= 1.3874 + 1.4991 - .9440$$

$$= 1.9425$$

So, $x = 87.60$

***Example 8* : Use log tables to find the value of x if x satisfies the equation.**

$$\frac{20}{14.7} = \left(\frac{.0613}{x}\right)^{1.32}$$

Solution : $\dfrac{20}{14.7} = \left(\dfrac{.0613}{x}\right)^{1.32}$

$\Rightarrow$ $\log 20 - \log 14.7 = 1.32\ [\log .0613 - \log x]$

$\Rightarrow$ $1.32 \log x = 1.32 \log .0613 - \log 20 + \log 14.7$

$\Rightarrow$ $$\log x = \frac{(1.32) \times (\bar{2}.7874) - 1.3010 + 1.1673}{1.32}$$

$\Rightarrow$ $$= \frac{(1.32) \times (-2) + (1.32 \times 7874) + 1.1673 - 1.3010}{1.32}$$

$\Rightarrow$ $x = .049$ (using antilog).

***Example 9* : Evaluate** $\sqrt[7]{\dfrac{1}{.8176 \times 36.21}}$

***Solution* :** Let $x = \sqrt[7]{\dfrac{1}{.8176 \times 36.21}}$

Then $$\log x = \frac{1}{7}[\log 1 - \log .8176 - \log 36.21]$$

$$= \frac{1}{7}[0 - (\bar{1}.9125) - (1.5588)]$$

$$= \frac{1}{7}[-1.4713]$$

$$= \frac{-7 + 7 - 1.4713}{7}$$

$$= \frac{-7 + 5.5287}{7}$$

$$= -1 + .7898$$

$$= \bar{1}.7898$$

$x = .616.$

***Example 10* : Solve $5^x + 5^{(x+2)} = 250$**

***Solution* :** We have

$$5^x + 5^{(x+2)} = 260$$

$$5^x (1 + 5^2) = 260$$

$$5^x\,(2.6) = 260$$

$$5^x = \frac{260}{26} = 10$$

$$x \log 5 = \log^{10}$$

$$x = \frac{1}{\log 5} = \frac{1}{0.6990} = 1.4306$$

Example 11 : **Solve for x, $\log_x (8x - 3) - \log_x 4 = 2$.**

Solution : $\log_x (8x - 3) - \log_x 4 = 2$

$$\Rightarrow \quad \log_x \left(\frac{8x - 3}{4}\right) = 2$$

$$\Rightarrow \quad x^2 = \frac{8x - 3}{4}$$

$$\Rightarrow \quad 4x^2 - 8x + 3 = 0$$

$$\Rightarrow \quad x = \frac{8 \pm 4\overline{\,64 - 48\,}}{8}$$

$$= \frac{8 \pm 4}{8} = \frac{1}{2}, \frac{3}{2}.$$

Example 12 (i) : **Prove that $\log 2 + 16 \log \frac{16}{15} + 12 \log \frac{25}{24} + 7 \log \frac{81}{80} = 1$ (assuming that base is 10 in each logarithm).**

Solution : LHS $= \log 2 + 16 \log \frac{16}{15} + 12 \log \frac{25}{24} + 7 \log \frac{81}{80}$

$= \log 2 + 16 \log 16 - 16 \log 15 + 12 \log 25$

$= \log 2 + 16 \log 2^4 - 16 \log 3 \times 5 + 12 \log 5^2$

$- 12 \log 2^3 \times 3 + 7 \log 3^4 - 7 \log 2^4 \times 5$

$= \log 2 + 64 \log 2 - 16 \log 3 - 16 \log 5 + 24 \log 5$

$- 12 \log 3 - 36 \log 2 + 28 \log 3 - 28 \log 2 - 7 \log 5$

$= (1 + 64 - 36 - 28) \log 2 + (28 - 12 - 16) \log 3 + (24 - 16 - 7) \log 5$

$= \log 2 + \log 5$

$= \log 2 \times 5$

$= \log 10$

$= 1.$

Example 12 (ii) : **If $a^x = b^y = c^z$ and $b^2 = ac$ prove that**

$$y = \frac{2 \times z}{x + z}.$$

Solution : Let $a^x = b^y = c^z = u$ (say)

$$\Rightarrow \qquad x = \frac{\log u}{\log a} \quad y = \frac{\log u}{\log b} \quad z = \frac{\log u}{\log c}$$

Example 13 : **If *a, b, c,* are any three consecutive integers, prove that log (1 + *ac*) = 2 log *b*.**

Solution : RHS $= 2 \log b$

$= 2 \log (a + 1)$ (Since $b = a + 1$)

$= \log (a + 1)^2$

$= \log (a^2 + 1 + 2a)$

$= \log [1 + a (a + 2)]$ (Since $c = a + 2$)

$\log [1 + ac] =$ LHS.

Example 14 : **Simplify $\log_a b \log_b c \log_c d \log_d a$**

Solution : $\log_a b \log_b c \log_c d \log_d a$

$$= \frac{\log_k b}{\log_k a} \frac{\log_k c}{\log_k b} \frac{\log_k d}{\log_k c} \frac{\log_k a}{\log_k d}$$

$= 1.$

Example 15 : **Prove that $\log x = \log [1 - \{1 - x^2)^{-1}\}^{-1}]_{-1/2}$**

Solution : RHS $= -\frac{1}{2} \log\left[1 - \left\{1 - \left(1 - x^2\right)^{-1}\right\}^{-1}\right]$

$$= -\frac{1}{2} \log\left[1 - \left\{1 - \frac{1}{1 - x}\right\}^{-1}\right]$$

$$= -\frac{1}{2} \log\left[1 - \left\{\frac{1 - x^2 - 1}{1 - x^2}\right\}^{-1}\right]$$

$$= -\frac{1}{2} \log\left[1 - \left\{\frac{1 - x^2}{1 - x^2}\right\}^{-1}\right]$$

$$= -\frac{1}{2} \log\left[1 + \frac{1 - x^2}{x^2}\right]$$

$$= -\frac{1}{2} \log\left[\frac{x^2 + 1 - x^2}{x^2}\right]$$

$$= -\frac{1}{2} \log \frac{1}{x^2}$$

$$= -\frac{1}{2} \log \left(x^2\right)^{-1}$$

$$= \frac{1}{2} \log x^2$$

$$= \log x = \text{LHS}.$$

Example 16 : **If $\log_2 x + \log_4 x + \log_{16} x = \frac{21}{4}$ find x.**

Solution :

$$\text{LHS} = \log_2 x + \frac{\log_2 x}{\log_2 4} + \frac{\log_2 x}{\log_2 16}$$

$$= \log_2 x + \frac{\log_2 x}{2} + \frac{\log_2 x}{4}$$

$$= \frac{7}{4} \log_2 x$$

Therefore, $\frac{7}{4} \log_2 x = \frac{21}{4}$

$\Rightarrow \qquad \log_2 x = 3$

$\Rightarrow \qquad x = 2^3 \Rightarrow x = 8.$

Example 17 : **Find the simplest value of $\log_3 \sqrt[4]{729 \sqrt[3]{9^{-1}.27^{-4/3}}}$**

Solution :

$$\log_3 \sqrt[4]{729 \sqrt[3]{9^{-1}.27^{-4/3}}}$$

$$= \log_3 \sqrt[4]{3^6 \sqrt[3]{9^{-1}.27^{-4/3}}}$$

$$= \log_3 \sqrt[4]{3^6 \sqrt[3]{3^{-2} 3^{-4}}}$$

$$= \log_3 \sqrt[4]{3^6 . 3^{-2}}$$

$$= \log_3 \sqrt[4]{3^4}$$

$$= \log_3 3 = 1.$$

Example 18 : **The first and fifth term of a G.P. are respectively 7 and 112 respectively. Find the common ratio.**

Solution : L a, ar, ar^2, ar^3 and ar^4 be first five terms of G.P.

Then $\qquad a = 7$ and $ar^4 = 112$

$$\therefore \qquad \frac{ar^4}{a} = r^4 = \frac{112}{7} = 16$$

Taking lob both the sides, we have

$$4 \log r = \log 16$$

$$= 1.2041$$

$$\log r = \frac{1.2041}{4} = 0.30102$$

$\therefore$ $r = \text{Antilog } (0.3010)$

$r = 2$

Example 19 : **Prove that $X^{\log y/z}. Y^{\log z/x}. Z^{\log x/y} = 1$**

Solution : Let $p = X^{\log y/z}. Y^{\log z/x}. Z^{\log x/y}$

Using properties of log, we have

$$\log p = (\log y - \log z). \log x + (\log Z - \log X) \log Y$$
$$+ (\log x - \log y) . \log z$$

Solving the above expression, we have

$\log p = 0$

$p = a^0$ (where 'a' is any base)

$\therefore$ $p = 1$ (anything raise to power 0 is 1).

Example 20 : **Solve the equation**

$$3^x + 4^y = 18$$

$$3^{x+2} + 4^{y+2} = 227$$

Solution : Let $p = 3^x$ and $q = 4^y$

We have $p + q = 18$

$9p = 16q = 227$

Solving above equations, we have

$p = 7$ and $q = 11$

$\therefore$ $3^x = 7.$

Taking log both the sides, we have

$x \log 3 = \log 7$

$x (0.4771) = (0.8451)$

$\therefore$ $x = 1.771$

Similarly $4^y = 11$

Taking log both sides, we have

$y \log 4 = \log 11$

$y (0.6021) = 1.0414$

$$y = \frac{1.0414}{0.6021} = 1.729$$

Example 21 **: Find the value of $\log_x 6561$ when $x^3 = 9$.**

Solution : Let $y = \log_x 6561$

$\therefore$ $x^y = 6561$

$x^y = 9^3 \times 9$ ...(*i*)

Substituting $x^3 = 9$ is equation (*i*)

We have $x^y = (x^3)^3 \times x^3$

$\therefore$ $x^y = x^{12}$

$\therefore$ $y = 12$

Hence $\log_x 6561 = 12$

Example 22 **: If $\log_a m = n$ show that $\log_{1/a} m = n$.**

Solution : Given

$$\log_a m = n$$

$\therefore$ $a^n = m$

$\therefore$ $\left(\frac{1}{a}\right)^n = \frac{1}{m}$

$$\left(\frac{1}{a}\right)^{-n} = \left(\frac{1}{m}\right)^{-1} = m$$

Taking $\log_{1/a}$ both the sides, we have

$$-n \log_{(1/a)} (1/a) = \log_{(1/a)} m$$

$\Rightarrow$ $-n = \log_{(1/a)} m$

Example 23 **: If x, y, z are in G.P., show that $\log_x a$, $\log_y a$ and $\log_z a$ are in H.P.**

Solution : Given

$\log_x a$, $\log_y a$ and $\log_z a$ are in H.P.

$\therefore$ $\frac{1}{\log_x a}$, $\frac{1}{\log_y a}$ and $\frac{1}{\log_z a}$ are in A.P.

or $\log_a x$, $\log_a y$ and $\log_a z$ are in A.P.

$\therefore$ $\log_a y - \log_a x = \log_a z - \log_a y$

$2 \log_a y = \log_a z + \log_a + x$

$\log_a y \log_a(z x)$

$y^2 = zx$

$\therefore$ x, y, z are in G.P.

Exercise 13.1

1. The characteristic of the number 0.0283 is

   (*i*) 2 (*ii*) –1 (*iii*) –2 (*iv*) 3

2. For computing mantissa we need first _______ digits of the given number

   (*i*) Five (*ii*) four (*iii*) four digits after decimal

   (*iv*) three digits.

3. The value of $\log_x 32$ is

   (*i*) 5 (*ii*) 7 (*iii*) 3 (*iv*) Indeterminate.

4. The value of $\log_{100} 1000$ is

   (*i*) 10 (*ii*) 1.5 (*iii*) 2 (*iv*) Indeterminate

5. If $\log_x (5x - 6) = 2$, the value of x will be

   (*i*) 3 and 2 (*ii*) 3 and 5 (*iii*) 5 and 2 (*iv*) 6 and 2

6. If log 2 = 0.30103, the number of digits in 2^{16}

   (*i*) five (*ii*) sixteen (*iii*) four (*iv*) eight

7. The value of log 2 + log 5 is

   (*i*) Ten (*ii*) One (*iii*) Twenty five (*iv*) Indeterminate

8. The value of log 5 × log 5 × log 4 is

   (*i*) Two (*ii*) Five (*iii*) Four (*iv*) None of the above.

9. The value of log 20 – log 2 is

   (*i*) Ten (*ii*) one (*iii*) log 18 (*iv*) none of the above.

10. The value of log 25 + log 4 is

    (*i*) Two (*ii*) Ten (*iii*) log 29 (*iv*) none of the above.

Answers

1. (*iii*)	2. (*ii*)	3. (*i*)	4. (*ii*)	5. (*i*)
6. (*i*)	7. (*ii*)	8. (*i*)	9. (*ii*)	10. (*i*)

Exercise 13.2

1. Find the value of $\dfrac{\log\sqrt{27} + \log 8 - \log\sqrt{1000}}{\log 1.2}$ [**Ans.** 3/2]

2. Find $\log_8 25$ given that $\log_{10} 2 = 0.3010$. **[Ans.** 1.5482]

3. If $a_{24}12$, $b = \log_{36}{}^{24}$, $c = \log_{48}{}^{36}$

Prove that $1 + abc = 2bc$

4. Find the value of

$$\log 2_{43}(3^3) + \log 2_{43}\left(9^{\frac{5}{2}+\frac{7}{2}}\right) + \log 2_{43}\left(27^{\frac{9}{3}+\frac{11}{3}+\frac{13}{3}}\right) + \log 2_{43}\left(81^{\frac{15}{4}+\frac{17}{4}+\frac{19}{4}+\frac{21}{4}}\right)$$

[Ans. 24]

5. Prove that

$$\log 2\left(\frac{75}{16}\right) - \log 2\left\{\frac{\sqrt[4]{\left(\frac{25}{81}\right)^3}\,\sqrt[3]{\left(\frac{25}{81}\right)}}{\sqrt[12]{\left(\frac{25}{81}\right)^7}}\right\} + \frac{1}{3}\log 2\left(2^{15}\cdot 3^{-15}\right) = 1.$$

6. Prove that $\log_b a \times \log_c b \times \log_a c = 1$.

7. Find the value of x and y, using log, from the given equations

$$2^x + 3^y = 44$$

$$2^{x+2} + 3^{y+2} = 221$$

[Ans. $x = 5.1299$ $y = 2$]

8. Find the value of $\dfrac{2\log 6 + 6\log 2}{4\log 2 + \log 27 - \log 9}$. **[Ans.** 2]

9. Find the value of the following :

(*i*) $\log_9 27\sqrt{3}$

(*ii*) $\dfrac{(16)^{1/5}\,(5)^2}{(108)^3}$ (Given $\log 2 = 0.3010$ and $\log 3 = 0.4771$)

[Ans. (*i*) 7/4 (*ii*) –4.4611]

10. Using log properties, prove

$$\log_{mn} x = \frac{\log_n x}{(1 + \log_n m)}$$

If m, n and x are positive numbers.

14

Theory of Sets

HIGHLIGHTS OF THE CHAPTER

- **Description of a Set**
- **Types of Sets**
- **Venn Diagram**
- **Operation on Sets**
- **Algebra of Sets**
- **Application of Set Theory**

INTRODUCTION

A set is a collection of well defined objects. The objects are well distinguished also. For example, a set of all natural numbers from 1 to 50. The numbers are :

(*i*) Well defined

(*ii*) Well distinguished.

The objects that constitutes set are called its members or elements. For example, in the above case, all numbers from 1 to 50 are elements of the above set. If x is any natural number defined as $1 \leq x \leq 50$, x belongs to the set. Symbolically, it will be indicated as $x \in A$, where x is a member of the set A.

If $1 > x > 50$, x does not belong to the above set and it will be indicated as $x \notin A$.

DESCRIPTION OF A SET

A set is described in the following two ways :

I. Roster Method : Under this method a set is described by listing elements, separated by commas, within braces {}. For example : *The set of vowels of English Alphabet may be described as {a, e, i, o, u}.*

The order in which the elements are written in a set does not make any difference.

Therefore, $\{a, e, i, o, u\}$ and $\{e, a, i, o, u\}$ denote the same set.

II. Set-Builder Method : Under this method, a set is described by a characterizing property $P(x)$ of its elements x. In such a case the set is described by $\{x : P(x) \text{ holds}\}$ or, $\{x \mid P(x) \text{ holds}\}$, which is read as 'the set of all x such that $P(x)$ holds'. The symbol '|' or ':' is read as 'such that'. For example: *The set* $A = \{1, 2, 3, 4, 5, 6, 7\}$ *can be written as* $A = \{x \in N : x \leq 7\}$.

Example 1 : **Write the set of all vowels in English alphabet which precede *j*.**

Solution : The vowels in English alphabet which precede *j* are *a, e, i.* Therefore, the set $A = \{a, e, i\}$ is the set of all vowels in English alphabet which preceded.

Example 2 : **Write the set** $\left\{\frac{1}{2}, \frac{2}{3}, \frac{3}{4}, \frac{4}{5}, \frac{5}{6}, \frac{6}{7}, \frac{7}{8}, \frac{8}{9}\right\}$ **in the set builder form.**

Solution : It can be observed that each element in the given set has the denominator one more than the numerator. Also, the numerator begins from 1 and do not exceed 8. Hence, in the set builder form the given set can be written as

$$\left\{x : x = \frac{n}{n+1}, n \in N, n \leq 8\right\}$$

TYPES OF SETS

Empty Set : *A set is said to be empty or null or void set if it has no element and it is denoted by* ϕ.

In Roster method, ϕ is denoted by $\{\}$.

It follows from this definition that a set A is an empty set if the statement $x \in A$ is not true for any x. For example, $[x \in N : 6 < x < 7] = \phi$.

A set consisting of at least one element is called a non empty or non-void set.

Singleton Set : *A set consisting of a single element is called a singleton set.* For example, the set $\{6\}$ is a singleton set.

Finite Set : *A set is called a finite set if it is either void set or its elements can be listed (counted, labelled) by natural numbers 1, 2, 3,... and the process of listing terminates at a certain natural number n (say).*

Cardinal Number of a Finite Set : *The number n in the above definition is called the cardinal number or order of a finite set A and is denoted by n(A).*

Infinite Set : *A set whose elements cannot be listed by the natural numbers 1, 2, 3,..., n, for any natural number n is called an infinite set.*

For example, (*1*) *Each one of the following sets is a finite set :*

(*i*) Set of odd natural numbers less than 100.

(*ii*) Set of boys in a given class.

(2) *Each one of the following sets is an infinite set :*

(*i*) Set of all points in a plane

(*ii*) Set of all lines in a plane.

Equivalent Sets : *Two finite sets A and B are equivalent if their cardinal numbers are same i.e.,* $n(A) = n(B)$.

Equal Sets : *Two sets A and B are said to be equal if every element of A is a member of B, and every element of B is a member of A.*

If sets A and B are equal, we write $A = B$ and $A \neq B$, when A and B are not equal.

If $A = \{1, 2, 5, 6\}$ and $B = \{5, 6, 2, 1\}$. Then $A = B$, because each element of A is an element of B and vice-versa. The elements of a set may be listed in any order.

It implies equal sets are equivalent but equivalent sets need not be equal.

For example, $A = \{1, 2, 3\}$ and $B = \{a, b, c\}$ are equivalent sets but not equal sets.

***Example 3 :* Which of the following sets are empty sets?**

(*i*) $A = \{x : x^2 - 5 = 0$ and x is rational$\}$

(*ii*) $B = \{x : x$ is an even prime number$\}$

(*iii*) $C = \{x : 8 < x < 9, x \in N\}$

Solution :

(*i*) Since there is no rational number whose square is 5. Therefore $x^2 - 5 = 0$ is not satisfied by any rational number. Hence, A is an empty set.

(*ii*) Since 2 is the only even prime number. Therefore, $B = \{2\}$. Therefore, B is not an empty set.

(*iii*) Since there is no natural number between 8 and 9. Therefore, C is an empty set.

***Example 4 :* Which of the following pairs of sets are equal? Justify your answer.**

(*i*) $A = \{x : x$ is a letter in the word "REAP"$\}$

$B = \{x : x$ is a letter in the word "PAPER"$\}$

(*ii*) $A = \{x : x \in Z$ and $x^2 \leq 8\}$, $B = \{x : x \in R$ and $x^2 - 5x + 6 = 0\}$

Solution :

(*i*) $A = \{R, E, A, P\}$

and, $B = \{P, A, P, E, R\} = \{R, E, A, P\}$

Clearly, $A = B$.

(*ii*) $A = \{x : x \in Z$ and $x^2 \leq 8\} = \{-2, -1, 0, 1, 2\}$

and, $B = \{x : x \in R$ and $x^2 - 5x + 6 = 0\} = \{3, 2\}$

Since $3 \in B$ but $3 \notin A$

Therefore, $A \neq B$.

***Example 5 :* State which of the following sets are finite and which are infinite:**

(*i*) $A = \{x : x \in Z$ and $x^2 - 4x + 3 = 0\}$

(*ii*) $B = \{x : x \in Z$ and x^2 is even$\}$

(*iii*) $C = \{x : x \in Z$ and $x^2 = 49\}$

(*iv*) $D = \{x : x \in Z$ and $x > -9\}$

Solution :

(*i*) $A = \{x : x \in Z$ and $x^2 - 4x + 3 = 0\} = \{1, 3\}$

So, A is a finite set

(*ii*) $B = \{x : x \in Z \text{ and } x^2 \text{ is even}\}$

$= \{..., -6, -4, -2, 0, 2, 4, 6, ...\}$

Clearly, B is an infinite set.

(*iii*) $C = \{x : x \in Z \text{ and } x^2 = 49\}$

$= \{7, -7\}$

Clearly, A is a finite set.

(*iv*) $D = \{x : x \in Z \text{ and } x > -9\}$

$= \{-8, -7, ...\}$

Clearly, D is an infinite set.

Subsets

Let A and B be two sets. If every element of A is an element of B, then A is called a subset of B.

If A is a subset of B, we write $A \subseteq B$, which is read as "A is a subset of B" or "A is contained in B".

Thus, $A \subseteq B$ if $a \in A \Rightarrow a \in B$.

If A is a subset of B, we say that B contains A or B is a super set of A and we write $B \supset A$.

If A is not a subset of B, we write $A \not\subset B$.

Obviously, every set is a subset of itself and the empty set is subset of every set. These two subsets are called **improper subsets.** A subset A of a set B is called a **proper subset** of B if $A \neq B$ and we write $A \subset B$. In such a case, we also say that B is a super set of A.

Universal Set

In set theory, there is a set that contains all sets under consideration *i.e.*, it is a super set of each of the given sets. Such a set is called the universal set and is denoted by U. In other words, a set that contains all sets in a given context is called the universal set. For example,

If $A = \{1, 2, 3, 4\}$, $B = \{2, 3, 4, 5, 6\}$ and $C = \{1, 3, 5, 7\}$, then $U = \{1, 2, 3, 4, 5, 6, 7\}$ can be taken as the universal set.

Power Set

Let A be a set. Then the collection or family of all subsets of A is called the power set of A and is denoted by $P(A)$.

Let $A = \{1, 2, 3\}$. Then the subsets of A are :

$$\phi, \{1\}, \{2\}, \{3\}, \{1, 2\}, \{1, 3\}, \{2, 3\} \text{ and } \{1, 2, 3\}.$$

Hence $P(A) = [\phi, \{1\}, \{2\}, \{3\}, \{1, 2\}, \{1, 3\}, \{2, 3\}\{1, 2, 3\}\}$.

***Example 6 :* Let $A = \{a, b, c, d\}$, $B = \{a, b, c\}$ and $C = \{b, d\}$. Find all sets X such that :**

(*i*) $X \subset B$ and $X \subset C$ (*ii*) $X \subset A$ and $X \not\subset B$.

Solution : We have,

(*i*) $P(A) = \{\phi, \{a\}, \{b\}, \{c\}, ...\}$

$P(B) = \{\phi, \{a\}, \{b\}, \{c\}, \{a, b\}, \{a, c\}, \{b, c\}, \{a, b, c\}\}$

and, $P(C) = \{\phi, \{b\}, \{d\}, \{b, d\}\}$

Given, $X \subset B$ and $X \subset C$

$\Rightarrow$ $X \in P(B)$ and $X \in P(C)$.

$\Rightarrow$ $X = \phi, \{b\}$

(*ii*) We have,

$X \subset A$ and $X \not\subset B$

$\Rightarrow$ X is a subset of A but X is not a subset of B

$\Rightarrow$ $X \in P(A)$ but $X \notin P(B)$

$\Rightarrow$ $X = \{d\}, \{a, b, d\}, \{b, c, d\}, \{a, c, d\}, \{a, d\}, \{b, d\}, \{c, d\}, \{a, b, c, d\}$.

***Example 7 :* Let $A = \{1, 2, 3, 4\}$, $B = \{1, 2, 3\}$ and $C = \{2, 4\}$. Find all sets X satisfying each pair of conditions.**

(*i*) $X \subset B$ and $X \not\subset C$ **(*ii*) $X \subset A$, $X \subset B$ and $X \subset C$.**

Solution : We have,

(*i*) $X \subset B$ and $X \not\subset C$

$\Rightarrow$ X is a subset of B but X is not a subset of C

$\Rightarrow$ $X \in P(B)$ but $x \notin P(C)$

$\Rightarrow$ $X = \{1\}, \{3\}, \{1, 2\}, \{1, 3\}, \{2, 3\}, \{1, 2, 3\}$

(*ii*) We have,

$X \subset A$, $X \subset B$ and $X \subset C$

$\Rightarrow$ $X \in P(A)$, $X \in P(B)$ and $X \in P(C)$

$\Rightarrow$ X is a subset of A, B and C.

$\Rightarrow$ $X = \phi, \{2\}$.

VENN DIAGRAMS

Swiss mathematician Euler and British mathematician John-Venn gave idea of representing set through pictures. The diagrams drawn to represent sets are called **Venn-Euler diagrams** or simply Venn-diagrams. In Venn-diagrams the universal set U is represented by points within a rectangle and its subsets are represented by points in closed curves (usually circles) within the rectangle. If a set A is a subset of a set B, then the circle representing A is drawn inside the circle representing B. If A and B are not equal but they have some common elements, then to represent A and B we draw two intersecting circles. Two disjoint sets are represented by two non-intersecting circles.

OPERATIONS ON SETS

In this section, we shall introduce some operations on sets to construct new sets from given ones.

Union of Sets : *Let A and B be two sets. The union of A and B is the set of all those elements which belong to A or to B or to both A and B.*

We shall use the notation $A \cup B$ (read as "A union B") to denote the union of A and B.

Thus, $A \cup B = \{x : x \in A \text{ or } x \in B\}$.

Clearly, $x \in A \cup B \Leftrightarrow x \in A$ or $x \in B$.

And, $x \notin A \cup B \Leftrightarrow x \notin A$ and $x \notin B$.

In Fig. 1 the shaded part represents $A \cup B$.

For example, If $A = \{2, 3\}$ and $B = \{1, 3, 5, 7\}$, then $A \cup B = \{1, 2, 3, 5, 7\}$.

Intersection of Sets : Let A and B be two sets. The intersection of A and B is the set of all those elements that belong to both A and B.

The intersection of A and B is denoted by $A \cap B$ (read as "A intersection B")

Thus, $A \cap B = \{x : x \in A \text{ and } x \in B\}$

Clearly, $x \in A \cap B \Leftrightarrow x \in A$ and $x \in B$

In Fig. 2 the shaded region represents $A \cap B$.

For example, If $A = \{1, 2, 3, 4, 5\}$ and $B = \{1, 3, 9, 12\}$, then $A \cap B = \{1, 3\}$.

Disjoint Sets : Two sets A and B are said to be disjoint, if $A \cap B = \phi$.

If $A \cap B \neq \phi$, then A and B are said to be intersecting or overlapping sets.

***For example,* If $A = \{1, 2, 3, 4, 5, 6\}$, $B = \{7, 8, 9, 10, 11\}$ and $C = \{6, 8, 10, 12, 14\}$, then A and B are disjoint sets, while A and C are intersecting sets.**

Difference of Sets : Let A and B be two sets. The difference of A and B, written as $A - B$, is the set of all those elements of A which do not belong to B.

Thus, $A - B = \{x : x \in A \text{ and } x \notin B\}$

or, $A - B = \{x \in A : x \notin B\}$.

Clearly, $x \in A - B \Leftrightarrow x \in A$ and $x \notin B$.

In Fig. 3, the shaded part represents $A - B$.

Similarly, the difference $B - A$ is the set of all those elements of B that do not belong to A *i.e.*,

$$B - A = \{x \in B : x \notin A\}.$$

In Fig. 4, the shaded part represents $B - A$.

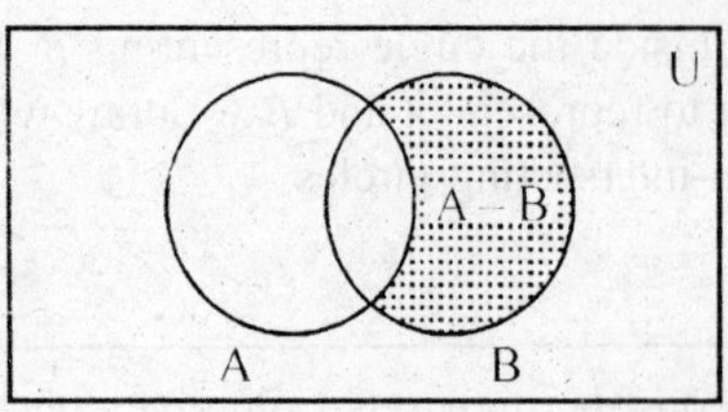

Fig. 4

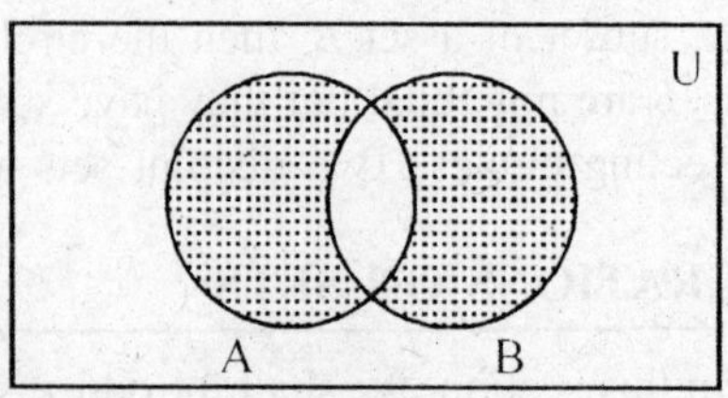

Fig. 5

***For example,* If $A = \{2, 3, 4, 5, 6, 7\}$ and $B = \{3, 5, 7, 9, 11, 13\}$, then $A - B = \{2, 4, 6\}$ and $B - A = \{9, 11, 13\}$.**

Symmetric Difference of Two Sets : Let A and B be two sets. The symmetric difference of sets A and B is the set $(A - B) \cup (B - A)$ and is denoted by $A \Delta B$.

Thus, $A \Delta B = (A - B) \cup (B - A) = \{x : x \notin A \cap B\}$

The shaded part in Fig. 5 represents $A \Delta B$.

***For example,* If $A = \{1, 2, 3, 4, 5, 6, 7, 8\}$ and $B = \{1, 3, 5, 6, 7, 8, 9\}$, then $A - B = \{2, 4\}$, $B - A = \{9\}$.**

$\therefore$ $A \Delta B = \{2, 4, 9\}$.

Complement of a Set : Let U be the universal set and let A be a set such that $A \subset U$. Then, the complement of A with respect to U is denoted by A' or A^c or $U - A$ and is defined the set of all those elements of U which are not in A.

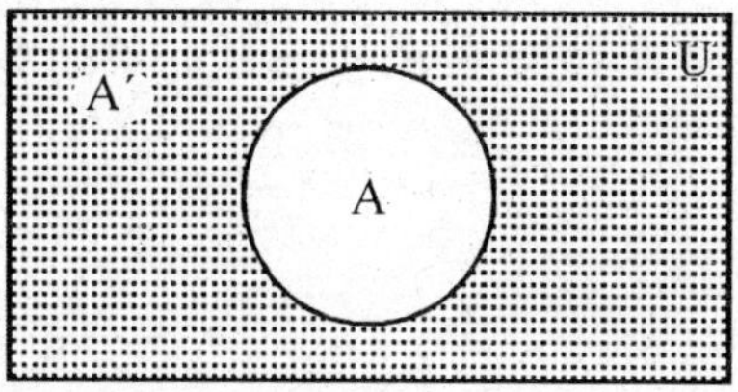

Fig. 6

Thus $A' = \{x \in U : x \notin A\}$.

Clearly, $x \in A' \Leftrightarrow x \notin A$.

For example, If $U = \{1, 2, 3, 4, 5, 6, 7, 8, 9\}$ and $A = \{1, 3, 5, 7, 9\}$, then $A' = \{2, 4, 6, 8\}$.

LAWS OF ALGEBRA OF SETS

In this section, we shall state and prove some fundamental laws of algebra of sets.

I. Idempotent Laws : For any set A, we have

(*i*) $A \cup A = A$

(*ii*) $A \cap A = A$

Proof

(*i*) $A \cup A = \{x : x \in A \text{ or } x \in A\} = [x : x \in A] = A$

(*ii*) $A \cap A = \{x : x \in A \text{ and } x \in A\} = [x : x \in A] = A$.

II. Identity Laws : For any set A, we have

(*i*) $A \cup \phi = A$

(*ii*) $A \cap U = A$.

i.e., ϕ and U are identify elements for union and intersection respectively

Proof

(*i*) $A \cup \phi = \{x : x \in A \text{ or } x \in \phi\} = [x : x \in A] = A$

(*ii*) $A \cap U = \{x : x \in A \text{ and } x \in U\} = [x : x \in A] = A.$

III. Commutative Laws : For any two sets A and B, we have

(*i*) $A \cup B = B \cup A$

(*ii*) $A \cap B = B \cap A$

i.e., union and intersection are commutative.

Proof

Recall that two sets X and Y are equal if $X \subseteq Y$ and $Y \subseteq X$. Also, $X \subseteq Y$ if every element of X belongs to Y.

(*i*) Let x be an arbitrary element of $A \cup B$. Then

$$x \in A \cup B \Rightarrow x \in A \text{ or } x \in B \Rightarrow x \in B \text{ or } x \in A \Rightarrow x \in B \cup A$$

$\therefore \quad A \cup B \subseteq B \cup A.$

Similarly, $B \cup A \subseteq A \cup B.$

Hence, $A \cup B = B \cup A.$

IV. Associative Laws : If A, B and C are any three sets, then

(*i*) $(A \cup B) \cup C = A \cup (B \cup C)$

(*ii*) $A \cap (B \cap C) = (A \cap B) \cap C$

i.e., union and intersection are associative.

Proof

(*i*) Let x be an arbitrary element of $(A \cup B) \cup C$. Then,

$$x \in (A \cup B) \cup C$$

$$\Rightarrow \quad x \in (A \cup B) \text{ or } x \in C$$

$$\Rightarrow \quad (x \in A \text{ or } x \in B) \text{ or } x \in C$$

$$\Rightarrow \quad x \in A \text{ or } (x \in B \text{ or } x \in C)$$

$$\Rightarrow \quad x \in A \text{ or } x \in (B \cup C)$$

$$\Rightarrow \quad x \in A \cup (B \cup C)$$

$$\therefore \quad (A \cup B) \cup C \subseteq A \cup (B \cup C).$$

Similarly, $A \cup (B \cup C) \subseteq (A \cup B) \cup C.$

Hence, $(A \cup B) \cup C = A \cup (B \cup C).$

(*ii*) Let x be an arbitrary element of $A \cap (B \cap C)$. Then,

$$x \in A \cap (B \cap C)$$

$\Rightarrow \quad x \in A$ and $x \in (B \cap C)$

$\Rightarrow \quad x \in A$ and $(x \in B$ and $x \in C)$

$\Rightarrow \quad (x \in A$ and $x \in B)$ and $x \in C$

$\Rightarrow \quad x \in (A \cap B)$ and $x \in C$

$\Rightarrow \quad x \in (A \cap B) \cap C$

$\therefore \quad A \cap (B \cap C) \subseteq (A \cap B) \cap C.$

Similarly, $(A \cap B) \cap C \subseteq A \cap (B \cap C)$.

Hence. $A \cap (B \cap C) = (A \cap B) \cap C.$

V. Distributive Laws : If A, B and C are any three sets, then

(*i*) $A \cup (B \cap C) = (A \cup B) \cap (A \cup C)$

(*ii*) $A \cap (B \cup C) = (A \cap B) \cup (A \cap C)$.

i.e., union and intersection are distributive over intersection and union respectively.

Proof

(*i*) Let x be an arbitrary element of $A \cup (B \cap C)$. Then.

$x \in A \cup (B \cap C)$

$\Rightarrow \quad x \in A$ or $x \in (B \cap C)$

$\Rightarrow \quad x \in A$ or $(x \in B$ and $x \in C)$

$\Rightarrow \quad (x \in A$ or $x \in B)$ and $(x \in A$ or $x \in C)$ [$\because$ 'or' is distributive over 'and']

$\Rightarrow \quad x \in (A \cup B)$ and $x \in (A \cup C)$

$\Rightarrow \quad x \in ((A \cup B) \cap (A \cup C))$

$\therefore \quad A \cup (B \cap C) \subseteq (A \cup B) \cap (A \cup C)$

Similarly, $(A \cup B) \cap (A \cup C) \subseteq A \cup (B \cap C)$.

Hence. $A \cup (B \cap C) = (A \cup B) \cap (A \cup C)$.

(*ii*) Let x be an arbitrary element of $A \cap (B \cup C)$. Then,

$x \in A \cap (B \cup C)$

$\Rightarrow \quad x \in A$ and $x \in (B \cup C)$

$\Rightarrow \quad x \in A$ and $(x \in B$ or $x \in C)$

$\Rightarrow \quad (x \in A$ and $x \in B)$ or $(x \in A$ and $x \in C)$

$\Rightarrow \quad x \in (A \cap B)$ or $x \in (A \cap C)$

$\Rightarrow \quad x \in (A \cap B) \cup (A \cap C)$

$\therefore \quad A \cap (B \cup C) \subseteq (A \cap B) \cup (A \cap C)$

Similarly, $(A \cap B) \cup (A \cap C) \subseteq A \cap (B \cup C)$.

Hence, $A \cap (B \cup C) = (A \cap B) \cup (A \cap C)$.

VI. De-Morgan's Laws : If A, B and C are any two sets, then

(*i*) $(A \cup B)' = A' \cap B'$

(*ii*) $(A \cap B)' = A' \cup B'$

Proof

(*i*) Let x be an arbitrary element of $(A \cup B)'$. Then,

$x \in (A \cup B)'$

$\Rightarrow \quad x \notin (A \cup B)$

$\Rightarrow \quad x \notin A$ and $x \notin B$

$\Rightarrow \quad x \in A'$ and $x \in B'$

$\Rightarrow \quad x \in A' \cap B'$.

$\therefore \quad (A \cup B)' \subseteq A' \cap B'$.

Again, let y be an arbitrary element of $A' \cap B'$. Then,

$y \in A' \cap B'$

$\Rightarrow \quad y \in A'$ and $y \in B'$

$\Rightarrow \quad y \notin A$ and $y \notin B$

$\Rightarrow \quad y \notin A \cup B$.

$\Rightarrow \quad y \in (A \cup B)'$

$\therefore \quad A' \cap B' \subseteq (A \cup B)'$.

Hence, $(A \cup B)' = A' \cap B'$

(*ii*) Let x be an arbitrary element of $(A \cap B)'$. Then,

$x \in (A \cap B)'$

$\Rightarrow \quad x \notin (A \cap B)$

$\Rightarrow \quad x \notin A$ or $x \notin B$

$\Rightarrow \quad x \in A'$ or $x \in B'$

$\Rightarrow \quad x \in A' \cup B'$

$\Rightarrow \quad (A \cap B)' \subseteq A' \cup B'$.

Again, let y be an arbitrary element of $A' \cup B'$. Then,

$$y \in (A' \cup B')$$

$\Rightarrow$ $y \in A'$ or $y \in B'$

$\Rightarrow$ $y \notin A$ or $y \notin B$

$\Rightarrow$ $y \notin (A \cap B)$

$\Rightarrow$ $y \in (A \cap B)'$

$\therefore$ $A' \cup B' \subseteq (A \cap B)'$.

Hence, $(A \cap B)' = A' \cup B'$.

Some Important Results on Number of Elements in Sets

If A, B and C are finite sets, and U be the finite universal set, then

(*i*) $n(A \cup B) = n(A) + n(B) - n(A \cap B)$

(*ii*) $n(A \cup B) = n(A) + n(B) \Leftrightarrow A, B$ are disjoint non-void sets.

(*iii*) $n(A - B) = n(A) - n(A \cap B)$ *i.e.*, $n(A - B) + n(A \cap B) = n(A)$

(*iv*) $n(A \Delta B) =$ No. of elements which belong to exactly one of A or B

$= n((A - B) \cup (B - A))$

$= n(A - B) + n(B - A)$ [$\because$ $(A - B)$ and $(B - A)$ are disjoint]

$= n(A) - n(A \cap B) + n(B) - n(A \cap B)$

$= n(A) + n(B) - 2n(A \cap B)$

(*v*) $n(A \cup B \cup C) = n(A) + n(B) + n(C) - n(A \cap B) - n(B \cap C)$
$- n(A \cap C) + n(A \cap B \cap C)$

(*vi*) No. of elements in exactly two of the sets A, B, C

$= n(A \cap B) + n(B \cap C) + n(C \cap A) - 3n(A \cap B \cap C)$.

(*vii*) No. of elements in exactly one of the sets A, B, C

$= n(A) + n(B) + n(C) - 2n(A \cap B) - 2n(B \cap C)$
$- 2n(A \cap C) + 3n(A \cap B \cap C)$

(*viii*) $n(A' \cup B') = n((A \cap B)') = n(U) - n(A \cap B)$

(*ix*) $n(A' \cap B') = n((A \cup B)') = n(U) - n(A \cup B)$.

APPLICATIONS OF SET THEORY

Example 6 : **In a group of 800 people, 500 can speak Hindi and 400 can speak English. How many can speak both Hindi and English?**

Solution : Let H denote the set of people speaking Hindi and E denote the set of people speaking English. We are given that

$$n(H) = 500, n(E) = 400 \text{ and } n(H \cup E) = 800.$$

We are required to find $n(H \cap E)$.

We know that

$$n(H \cup E) = n(H) + n(E) - n(H \cap E)$$

$$\Rightarrow \quad n(H \cap E) = n(H) + n(E) - n(H \cup E)$$

$$\Rightarrow \quad n(H \cap E) = 500 + 400 - 800 = 100$$

Hence, 100 persons can speak both Hindi and English.

Example 7 : **In a class of 50 students, 40 speak Hindi, 20 speak both English and Hindi and all the students speak at least one of the two languages. How many students speak only English and not Hindi? How many students speak English?**

Solution : Let H denote the set of students speaking Hindi and E the set of students speaking English. Then, it is given that

$$n(H \cup E) = 50, n(H) = 40, n(H \cap E) = 20.$$

Now, $\quad n(E - H) = n(H \cup E) - n(H) = 50 - 40 = 10$

Thus, the number of students speaking English but no Hindi is 10.

We have, $\quad n(H \cup E) = n(H) + n(E) - n(H \cap E)$

$$\Rightarrow \quad 50 = 40 + n(E) - 20 \Rightarrow n(E) = 30.$$

Hence, the number of students who speaks English is 30.

Example 8 : **A survey company investigated 800 car owners and found, 650 owned Maruti car and 300 owned Hyundai car; 100 owned both cars. Is this data correct?**

Solution : Let U be the set of all car owners investigated, M be the set of persons who owned Maruti cars and H be the set of persons who owned Hyundai cars.

It is given that

$$n(U) = 800, n(M) = 650, n(H) = 300 \text{ and } n(M \cap H) = 100.$$

$$\therefore \quad n(M \cup H) = n(M) + n(H) - n(M \cap H)$$

$$= 650 + 300 - 100 = 850$$

But, $M \cup H \subseteq U$. Therefore,

$$n(M \cup H) \leq n(U)$$

$$n(M \cup H) \leq 800$$

This is a contradiction. This implies the given data is incorrect.

***Example 9 :* In a survey of 2000 mobile it was found that 1700 users liked Nokia and 1500 users liked Motorola. What is the least number that must have liked both the products?**

Solution : Let U be the set of all users, A be the set of users who liked Nokia and B be the set of users who liked Motorola.

It is given that

$$n(U) = 2000,\ n(A) = 1700,\ n(B) = 1500$$

$$n(A \cup B) = n(A) + n(B) \cap -n(A \cap B)$$

$$n(A \cup B) = 1700 + 1500 - n(A \cap B) = 3200 - n(A \cap B)$$

Since, $\quad A \cup B \subset U$

$\therefore \quad n(A \cup B) \leq n(U)$

$\Rightarrow \quad 3200 - n(A \cap B) \leq 2000$

$\Rightarrow \quad 3200 - 2000 \leq n(A \cap B)$

$\Rightarrow \quad n(A \cap B) \geq 1200$

Thus, the least value of $n(A \cap B)$ is 1200.

Hence the least number of users who liked both the mobile phone is 1200.

***Example 10 :* If A, B and C are three sets and U is the universal set such that $n(U) = 1000$, $n(A) = 400$, $n(B) = 500$ and $n(A \cap B) = 100$. Find $n(A' \cap B')$.**

Solution : We have $A' \cap B' = (A \cup B)'$

$$\therefore \quad n(A' \cup B') = n((A \cup B)') = n(U) - (A \cup B)$$

$$= n(U) - [n(A) + n(B) - n(A \cap B)]$$

$$= 1000 - (400 + 500 - 100) = 200.$$

***Example 11 :* In a survey of 500 students in a college 180 were listed as drinking Tea, 275 as drinking coffee and 95 were listed as both drinking Tea as well as Coffee. Find how many students were drinking neither Tea nor Coffee.**

Solution : Let U be the set of all surveyed students, A denote the set of students drinking Tea and B be the set students drinking Coffee.

It is given that

$$n(U) \quad 500,\ n(A) = 180,\ n(B) = 275 \text{ and } n(A \cap B) = 95$$

We are required to find,

$$n(A' \cap B')$$

Now, $n(A' \cap B') = n(A \cup B)'$

$= n(U) - n(A \cup B)$

$= n(U) - \{n(A) + n(B) \cap -n(A \cap B)\}$

$= 500 - \{180 + 275 - 95\}$

$= 500 - 360 = 140.$

Example 12 : **In a survey of 35 students, 17 have opted Management, 10 have opted Management, but not Engineering. Find the number of Students who have opted both Management and Engineering and the number of students who have opted Engineering but not Management, if it is given that each student has opted either Management or Engineering or both.**

Solution : Let A denote the set of students who have opted Management and B be the set of students who have opted Engineering

It is given that

$$n(A \cup B) = 35, n(A) = 17 \text{ and } n(A - B) = 10.$$

Now, $n(A) = n(A - B) + n(A \cap B)$

$\Rightarrow$ $17 = 10 + n(A \cap B)$

$\Rightarrow$ $n(A \cap B) = 7.$

Thus, 7 students have opted both Management and Engineering.

Now, $n(A \cup B) = n(A) + n(B) - n(A \cap B)$

$\Rightarrow$ $35 = 17 + n(B) - 7$

$\Rightarrow$ $n(B) = 25.$

Now, $n(B) = n(B - A) + n(A \cap B)$

$\Rightarrow$ $25 = n\ (B - A) + 7$

$\Rightarrow$ $n(B - A) = 18.$

Thus, 18 students have opted Engineering but not Managements.

Example 13 : **In a survey of Magazine 10,000 families it was found that 4000 families buy Magazine *A*, 2000 families buy Magazine *B* and 1000 families buy Magazine *C*. 5% families buy *A* and *B*, 3% buy *B* and *C*, 4% buy *A* and *C*. If 2% families buy all the three news papers, find the number of families which buy (*i*) A only (*ii*) *B* only (*iii*) none of *A*, *B* and *C*.**

Solution : Let P, Q and R be the sets of families buying Magazine A, B and C respectively. Let U be the universal set. Then,

$n(P) = 4000,$ $\quad n(Q) = 2000,$

$n(R) = 1000,$ $\quad n(P \cap Q) = 5\% \text{ of } 10,000 = 500,$

$n(Q \cap R) = 300,$ $\quad n(R \cap Q) = 4\% \text{ of } 10,000 = 400$

(*i*) Required number $= n(P \cap Q' \cap R') = n(P \cap (Q \cup R)')$

$= n(P) - n[P \cap (Q \cup R)]$ $\quad [\because n(A \cap B') = n(A) \cap -n(A \cap B)]$

$= n(P) - n[(P \cap Q) \cup (P \cap R)]$

$= n(P) - [n(P \cap Q) \cup (P \cap R) - n\{(P \cap Q) \cap (P \cap R)\}]$

$= n(P) - [n(P \cap Q) + n(P \cap Q) - n(P \cap Q \cap R)]$

$= 4000 - [500 + 400 - 200] = 3300$

(*ii*) Required number $= n(P' \cap Q \cap R') = n(Q \cap P' \cap R')$

$= n(Q \cap (P \cup R)')$

$= n(Q) - n(Q \cap (P \cup R))$

$[\because n(A \cap B') = n(A) - n(A \cap B)]$

$= n(Q) - n[(Q \cap P) \cup (Q \cap R)]$

$= n(Q) - [n(Q \cap P) + n(Q \cap R) - n\{(Q \cap P) \cap (Q \cap R)\}]$

$= 2000 - [500 + 300 - 200] = 1400$

(*iii*) Required number $= n(P' \cap Q' \cap' R) = n[(P \cup Q \cup R)']$

$= n(U) - n(P \cup Q \cup R)$

$= n(U) - n(P) + n(Q) + n(R) - n(P \cap Q) - n(Q \cap R)$

$- n(R \cap P) + n(P \cap Q \cap R)$

$= 10000 - [4000 + 2000 + 1000 - 500 - 300 - 400 + 200] = 4000$

***Example 14 :* A Business News channel issued awards to various companies. 38 awards were given on financial performance, 15 on the basis of Business Growth and 20 on the basis of company profile. In all 58 awards were given and three companies got award for all three parameters. How many companies received award for exactly two parameters.**

Solution : Let F denote the set of companies who received award for financial performance, B the set, who received award for Business Growth and C the set who received award for Company profile. Then, we have

$n(F) = 38, n(B) = 15, n(C) = 20, n(F \cup B \cup C)$

$= 58$ and $n(F \cap B \cap C) = 3$

$\Rightarrow \quad 59 = 38 + 15 + 20 - n(F \cap B) - n(B \cap C) - n(F \cap C) + 3$

$\Rightarrow \quad n(F \cap B) + n(B \cap C) + n(F \cap C) = 76 \cap -58 = 18$

Number of men who received medals in exactly two of the three sports

$= n(F \cap B) + n(B \cap C) + n(F \cap C) - 3n(F \cap B \cap C)$

$= 18 - 3 \times 3$

$= 9$

Thus, 9 men received medals in exactly two of the three sports.

Example 15 : **In an apartment of 25 houses, it was observed**

15 houses posses Matiz car,

12 houses posses Palio car,

and 11 houses posses Chevrelot,

5 had Matiz and Chevrelot, 9 had Matiz and Palio,

4 had Palio and Chevrelot and 3 had taken all the three cars. Find the number of that had

(*i*) **Only chevrelot**

(*ii*) **Only Matiz**

(*iii*) **Only Palio**

(*iv*) **Palio and Chevlot but not Matiz**

(*v*) **Matiz and Palio and not chevlot**

(*vi*) **Only one of the car**

(*vii*) **at least one of the car**

(*viii*) **none of the car.**

Solution : Let M denote the set house who had taken Matiz, P the set of house who had taken Palio and C the set of house who had taken

Then we have

$$n(U) = 25, n(M) = 15, n(P) = 12, n(C) = 11, n(M \cap C) = 5,$$

$$n(M \cap P) = 9, n(P \cap C) = 4, n(M \cap P \cap C) = 3$$

(*i*) Required number of houses

$$= n(M' \cap P' \cap C)$$

$$= n((M \cup P)' \cap C)$$

$$= n(C) - n((M \cup P) \cap C) \qquad [\because n(A \cap B') = n(A) - n(A \cap B)]$$

$$= n(C) - n(M \cap C) \cup (P \cap C)$$

$$= n(C) - \{n(M \cap C) \cup (P \cap C) - n(M \cap P \cap C)\}$$

$$= 11 - \{5 + 4 - 3\}$$

$$= 5.$$

(*ii*) Required number of house

$$= n(M \cap P' \cap C')$$

$$= n(M \cap (P \cap C)')$$

$$= n(M) - n(M \cap (P \cap C))$$

$$= n(M) - n((M \cap P) \cup (M \cap C))$$

$$= n(M) - \{n(M \cap P) + n(M \cap C) \cap -(M \cap P \cap C)\}$$

$$= 15 - \{9 + 5 - 3\}$$

$$= 4.$$

(*iii*) Required number of house

$= n(P \cap M' \cap C')$

$= n(P \cap (M \cap C)')$

$= n(P) - n(P \cap (M \cap C))$

$= n(P) - n((P \cap M) \cup (M \cap C))$

$= n(P) - \{n(P \cap M) + n(P \cap C) \cup (P \cap M \cap C)\}$

$= 12 - \{9 + 4 - 3\}$

$= 2.$

(*iv*) Required number of house

$= n(P \cap C \cap M')$

$= n(P \cap C) - n(P \cap C \cap M)$ $\quad [\because n(A \cap B') = n(A) \cap -n(A \cap B)]$

$= 4 - 3 = 1.$

(*v*) Required number of house

$= n(M \cap P \cap C')$

$= n(M \cap P) - n(M \cap P \cap C)$

$= 9 - 3 = 6.$

(*vi*) Required number of house

$$= n(M) + n(P) + n(C) - 2\{n(M \cap P) + n(P \cap C) + n(M \cap C) + 3n(M \cap P \cap C)\}$$

$= 15 + 12 + 11 - 2\ \{9 + 4 + 5\} + 3 \times 3$

$= 38 - 36 + 9$

$= 11$

(*vii*) Required number of house

$= n(M \cup P \cup C)$

$$= n(M) + n(P) + n(C) - n(M \cap P) \cap -n(P \cap C) - n(M \cap C) + n(M \cap P \cap C)$$

$= 15 + 12 + 11 - 9 - 4 - 5 + 3$

$= 23$

(*viii*) Required number of house

$= n(M' \cap P' \cap C')$

$= n(M \cup P \cup C)'$

$= n(U) - n(M \cup P \cup C)$

$= 25 - 23 = 2.$

Objective Type Questions

1. A set having no element is called

   (*i*) void set (*ii*) sub set (*iii*) Universal Set (*iv*) Proper set

2. The sets whose cardinal numbers are same are set to be

   (*i*) Singleton set (*ii*) Equivalent set (*iii*) Universal Set (*iv*) Proper set

3. When a set is describe with the help of character of elements, it is

   (*i*) Roaster method (*ii*) Set builder method

   (*iii*) Universal method (*iv*) none of the above.

4. The set which contains all sets under consideration is called

   (*i*) Singleton set (*ii*) Equivalent set

   (*iii*) Universal Set (*iv*) Proper set

5 Empty set is also called

   (*i*) Singleton set (*ii*) Equivalent set

   (*iii*) Universal Set (*iv*) Improper subset

Answers

1. (*i*) 2. (*ii*) 3. (*ii*) 4. (*iii*) 5. (*iv*)

Exercise 14.1

1. Write the following sets by listing elements enclosed in brackets { }.

   (*i*) A is the set whose elements are first ten letters of the alphabet.

   (*ii*) X is the set of all two digit positive numbers which are divisible by 10.

   [(*i*) $A = \{a, b, c, d, e, f, g, h, i,\}$ (*ii*) $A = \{10, 20, 30, 40, 50, 60, 70, 80, 90\}$]

2. Write the following sets using a statement to designate each :

   (*i*) $A = \{3, 6, 9, 12, 15, 18, 21\}$

   (*ii*) $B = \{s, t, u, v, w, x, y, z\}$.

   [(*i*) $A = \{x/x$ is a positive integer less than 21 and multiple of 3$\}$

   (*ii*) $B = \{x|x$ is one of the last letter of alphabet$\}$]

3. Determine which of the following sets are equal?

$A = \{1, 2, 4\}$, $B = \{2, 4, 1\}$, $C = \{1, 2, 3\}$

$D = \{x \mid x$ is a positive integer less than 6.

$E = \{1, 2, 3, 4, 5\}$.

[$A = B \neq C$, $D = E$]

4. Indicate which of the following sets are finite?

(*i*) $A = \{x|x$ is a positive integer$\}$

(*ii*) $B = \{x|x$ is an even integer lying between 2 and 100$\}$.

(*iii*) $C = \{x|x$ is a letter of the alphabet.

(*iv*) $D =$ the set of all employees of ABC Ltd.

(*v*) $E = \{x|x$ is an integer less than 20$\}$

[B, C, D are finite sets]

5. Perform the indicated operations on

$A = \{a, b, c, d, e, f\}$

$B = \{a, e, i, o, u\}$

$C = \{m, n, o, p, q, r, s, t, u,\}$

(*i*) $A \cup B$; (*ii*) $A \cap B$; (*iii*) $A \cup B \cup C$; (*iv*) $A \cap B \cap C$.

[(*i*) $\{a, b, c, d, e, f, i, o, u\}$ (*ii*) $\{a, e\}$
(*iii*) $\{a, b, c, d, e, f, i, o, u, m, n, p, q, r, s, t\}$ (*iv*) ϕ]

6. If $A = \{1, 2, 3, 4, 5\}$, $B = \{2, 4, 6, 8, 10\}$, $C = \{3, 6, 9, 12, 15\}$

Find

(*i*) $(A \cup B) \cap C$; (*ii*) $A \cup (B \cap C)$;

(*iii*) $(A \cap C) \cup B$.

[(*i*) $\{6\}$, (*ii*) $\{1, 2, 3, 4, 5, 6\}$ (*iii*) $\{2, 3, 4, 6, ,8, 10\}$]

7. If $A = \{1, 2, 3, 4\}$, $B = \{3, 4, 5, 6\}$, $C = \{4, 5, 6, 7\}$

Find (*i*) $A - B$;

(*ii*) $(A \cup B) - C$;

(*iii*) $A - (B \cap C)$;

(*iv*) $(A \cap B) - (B \cap C)$.

[(*i*) $\{1, 2\}$; (*ii*) $\{1, 2, 3\}$; (*iii*) $\{1, 2, 3\}$]

8. If $U = \{1, 2, 3, 4, 5, 6, 7, 8, 9, 10\}$

$A = \{1, 4, 7, 10\}$

$B = \{2, 5, 8\}$

Find (*i*) A' (*ii*) B' (*iii*) $A \cap B'$ (*iv*) $A' \cap B$ (*iv*) $A' \cap B'$.

[(*i*) $\{2, 3, 5, 6, 8, 9\}$, (*ii*) $\{1, 3, 4, 6, 7, 9, 10\}$ (*iii*) $\{1, 4, 7, 10\}$]

9. In a survey of 500 consumers, it was found that 425 liked product *I* and 375 liked product *II*. What is the least number of consumers that must have liked both products assuming that there may be consumers of products different from *I* and *II*. [300]

10 Suppose that in a survey concerning the reading habits of students it is found that :

60 per cent read magazine *A*,

50 per cent read magazine *B*,

50 per cent read magazine *C*.

30 per cent read magazine *A* and *B*.

20 per cent read magazine *B* and *C*.

300 per cent read magazine *A* and *C*.

10 per cent read all three magazines.

(*i*) What percent read exactly two magazines?

(*ii*) What percent do not read any of the magazines? [(*i*) 50; (*ii*) 10]

11. In a Chemistry class there are 20 students, and in a Physics class there are 30 students. Find the number either in Physics class or Chemistry class if,

(*i*) the two classes meet at the same hour.

(*ii*) the two classes meet at different and 10 students are enrolled in both courses.

[(*i*) 50; (*ii*) 40]

12. A college awarded 38 medals in Football, 15 in Basket ball and 20 in Cricket. If these medals went to a total of 58 men and only three of these men got medals in all the three sports, how many men received medals in exactly two of the three sports? [9]

13. In a recent survey of 5000 people, it was found that 2800 read Economic Times and 2300 read Business Standard while 400 read both the papers. How many read neither Economic Times nor Business standard. [300]

14. In an Institute of the 100 students, the numbers studying the various languages were found to be :

German only 18; German but not Spanish 23; German and French 8; German 26; French 48; French and Spanish 8: no language 24.

(*i*) How many students took Spanish?

(*ii*) How many took German and Spanish but not French?

(*iii*) How many took French if and only if they did not take Spanish?

[(*i*) 18; (*ii*) None; (*iii*) 50]

15. In a survey of 30 students, it was found that 19 take Mathematics, 17 take Music, 11 take History, 7 take Mathematics and History, 12 take Mathematics and Music, 5 take Music and History and 2 take all three courses. Find (*i*) the number of students that take Mathematics but do not take History (*ii*) the number that take exactly two of the three courses. [12]

15

Permutations and Combinations

Highlights of the Chapter

- Introduction
- Factorial Notation
- Different Types of Permutation
- Derivation of Permutation Formula
- Combinations
- Types of Combinations

INTRODUCTION

The word 'Permutations' refers to the different arrangement of objects in a set where all elements are different. For example, if there are 3 alphabets A, B, C, then number of permutations or arrangements possible are ABC, CAB, BCA, BAC, CBA, ACB. Thus, there are six ways in which these alphabets can be arranged.

Important Concepts

(*i*) **Addition Principle :** If an operation can be performed in m ways and if another operation can be performed in n ways and only one operation can be done at a time then *either* of the two operations can be performed in $(m + n)$ ways.

(*ii*) **Multiplication Principle :** If an operation can be performed in m ways and if another operation in n ways independent of the first, then the number of ways of performing both the operations simultaneously is $m \times n$.

FACTORIAL NOTATION

Before we proceed further, we must understand factorial notation. It is a continued product of the first n natural numbers beginning with 1 and ending with n. It is denoted by the symbol $n!$ and read as **factorial** n.

Thus $\quad n! = 1 \times 2 \times 3 \times \ldots \times n$

$$9! = 1 \times 2 \times 3 \times 4 \times 5 \times 6 \times 7 \times 8 \times 9$$

The process of arrangement is affected in case of following situations :

(*i*) When out of '*n*' objects, '*r*' have been taken out at a time

Let us consider 'n' objects and 'r' places to be fixed. For first place, 'n' object are available. For second place, $(n - 1)$ objects are available. Likewise, for 'r' places, $n - (r - 1)$ places *i.e.*, $(n - r + 1)$ places are available.

Applying multiplication rule, we have

$$^nP_r = n\,(n-1)\,(n-2)\,.......\,(n-r+1)$$

This can be written as

$$^nP_r = \frac{n!}{(n-r)!}$$

For example, if there are n different objects and 'r' are taken at a time then it is usually denoted by the symbol ^nP_r.

(*i*) the permutations of the three numbers 1, 2, 3 taken only one of them at a time are (1, 2, 3)

(*ii*) the permutations of three numbers 1, 2, 3 taken two of them at a time are (12, 13, 23)

(*iii*) the permutations of the three letters, *a, b, c* taken all at a time are (*abc; acb; bac; bca; cab; cba*).

Practical Question based on above concepts.

Example 1 : **There are six doors in an auditorium. In how many can a person enter from one door and leave the auditorium from a different door?**

Solution. A person can enter the auditorium from any one of the six doors and can leave it by any of the remaining five doors.

∴ Total number of ways = 6 × 5 = 30 ways.

Example 2 : **How many different words can be formed using the letters M, O, B, I, L, E, taken**

(*a*) all at a time, and

(*b*) four letters at a time

(*c*) every word begins with M

(*d*) None of the words begins with M.

Solution : (*a*) All the six letters are different

$$\therefore \quad 6p_6 = 6! = 720 \text{ words}$$

(*b*) If we take four letters at a time, $n = 6$ and $r = 4$

$$\therefore \quad 6p_4 = \frac{6!}{(6-4)!} = 6 \times 5 \times 4 \times 3 = 360 \text{ words}$$

(*c*) If first letter is M, then remaining five letters can be arranged in $5p_5$ ways = 120 ways.

(*d*) None of the words begins with M = Total number of words which can be formed using these six letters – Number of words starting with M = 720 – 120 = 500 ways.

(*ii*) Permutation of 'r' objects out of 'n' different objects when particular object is always taken.

When out of 'n' different objects, one has to make permutation of 'r' different objects while particular objects 'x' is always taken, the particular objects can be placed at anywhere is different positions in rp_x ways and the remaining in $^{(n-x)}p_{(r-x)}$ ways.

$\therefore$ Total number of permutations $= rp_x \times {}^{(n-x)}p_{(r-x)}$

For example '5' objects are to be taken out of '10' objects such that '3' objects are always present.

Since '3' objects are always to be taken, this can be done in $5p_3$ ways. Now there '2' positions left to be acquired by $(10 - 3) = 7$ objects which can be permutated in $7p_2$ ways. Therefore, total number of permutations available are

$$5p_3 \times 7p_2 = \frac{5!}{2!} \times \frac{7!}{5!}$$

$$= \frac{7 \times 6 \times 5 \times 4 \times 3 \times 2 \times 1}{2 \times 1}$$

$$= 2520 \text{ ways.}$$

(*iii*) Permutations excluding '*p*' particular items

If there are '*n*' objects and '*p*' item are to be specifically excluded then '*r*' objects can be taken in following manner :

$${}^{(n-p)}p_r.$$

For example, if out of '10' objects, '5' are to be chosen such that '3' objects are always excluded then we have number of permutations as

$$(10 - 3)\, p_5 = 7p_5 = \frac{7!}{2!} = 7 \times 6 \times 5 \times 4 \times 3$$

$$= 2520 \text{ ways.}$$

(*iv*) Circular Permutation

In case of circular permutation, different items are to be placed on perimeter of the circle. After fixing position of one object, the remaining $(n - 1)$ items can be placed in $(n - 1)!$ ways.

Example 3 : **In how many ways 5 ladies and 5 gents be seated at a round table, so that no two ladies sit together?**

Solution : If we allow gents to sit first, then the gents can sit in $(5 - 1)! = 4!$ ways.

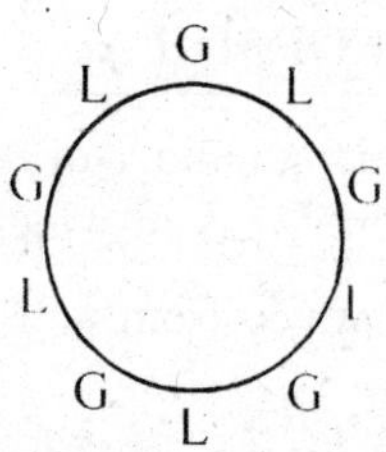

There will be five positions vacant between two successive gents, which can be acquired by ladies in 5! ways.

$\therefore$ Total number of ways $= 4! \times 5! = 24 \times 120 = 2880$ ways.

Example 4 : **Find the number of arrangements of 12 students taken 5 at a time in which 3 particular students are always included.**

Solution : Among five students, there particular student are always included which means among remaining 9 students, only '2' students are to be considered.

∴ Total number of permutation

$$= 5p_3 \times 9p_2 = 4320 \text{ ways.}$$

***Example 5 :* How many permutations can be made out of letters of the word "MUMBAI'?**

Solution : In the given word (MUMBAI), there are six letters, one alphabet has been repeated twice, therefore

$$\text{Number of permutations} = \frac{6!}{2!} = 6 \times 5 \times 4 \times 3 = 360 \text{ ways.}$$

***Example 6 :* In how many ways can the letter of following be arranged?**

(*i*) ECONOMICS

(*ii*) DAUGHTER

Solution : (i) The word ECONOMICS has a letters in it. The letter 'C' and 'D' have been repeated twice.

$$\therefore \text{Number of permutations} = \frac{9!}{2!2!} = 90720 \text{ ways.}$$

(*ii*) The word DAUGHTER has 8 different letters.

∴ Number of permutations = 8! = 40320.

***Example 7 :* Taking all the letters used in SHARP, find the number of different words if**

(*i*) Every word begin with S.

(*ii*) None of the word begins with S.

Solution : (*i*) There are five alphabets in the word SHARP and first word should always be 'S'. Remaining four words can be changed in

$$4p_4 \text{ ways} = 4! \text{ ways} = 2 \text{ ways.}$$

(*ii*) None of the word begins with S.

Five words can be formed using 5 alphabets in $5p_5$ ways = 120 ways.

∴ Words not starting with 'S' = 120 − 24 = 96 ways.

DERIVATION OF PERMUTATION FORMULA

When we want to calculate number of permutations of *n* different things taken *r* at a time, basically we are required to find number of different ways in which *r* places can be filled up by *n* things.

The first place can be occupied in *n* ways, from any one of the *n* things can be put in it.

$$\therefore \qquad {}^np_1 = n$$

When the first place has been occupied in any one of the *n* ways, the second place can be filed up in $(n - 1)$ different ways, from any one of the remaining $n - 1$ things.

$$\therefore \qquad {}^np_2 = n(n - 1)$$

When the first two places have been filled up in any one of the $n(n - 1)$ ways, third place can be filled up in $(n - 2)$ ways.

∴ the first three places can be filled up in $n(n - 1)(n - 2)$ ways, *i.e.*,

$$^{n}p_3 = n(n-1)(n-2)$$

If we generalizes the above procedure for 'r' ways will be given as

$$^{n}p_r = (n-1)(n-2)....(n-\overline{r-1})$$

$$= n(n-1)(n-2)....(n-r+1)$$

$$= \frac{n(n-1)(n-2)....(n-r+1)\{(n-r)!\}}{(n-r)!} = \frac{n!}{(n-r)!}$$

Permutations in which objects are repeated. The number of permutations of n different objects taken r at a time in which each objects is repeated r times in any arrangements in n^r.

Permutations of objects not all different. The number of permutations of n objects of which p objects are alike of one kind, q objects are alike of a second kind and all the rest are different is $\frac{n!}{p!\,q!}$.

Example 8 : **There are four bus lines between town A and town B and three bus lines between town B and town C.**

(*i*) In how many ways can a man travel by bus from *A* to *C* by way of *B*?

(*ii*) In how many ways can a man travel round trip by bus from *A* to *C* by way of *B*, if he does not want to use a bus line more than once?

Solution : (*i*) There are 4 bus lines from *A* to *B* and 3 bus lines from *B* to *C* therefore a man can travel by bus from *A* to *C* by way of *B* in $4 \times 3 = 12$ ways.

(*ii*) There are four bus lines from *A* to *B* and three bus lines from *B* to *C*. However the man does not want to use the bus line more than once, the number of bus lines from *C* to *B* are 2 and from *B* to *A* are 3.

∴ the number of ways in which he can travel from *A* to *C* by ways of $B = 4 \times 3 = 12$ ways.

Also the number of ways in which he can travel from *C* to *A* by way of *B* not using the bus line more than once $= 2 \times 3 = 6$ ways.

Therefore the total number of ways in which a man can travel round trip by bus from *A* to *C* by way of *B* not using the bus line more than once $= 12 \times 6 = 72$ ways.

Example 9 : **Find the number of words that can be formed by considering all possible permutations of the letters of the word 'MOTHER'. How many of these words begin with M and end with R?**

Solution : The number of words that can be formed by considering all possible permutations of the letters of the word "MOTHER" is

$$^{6}p_6 = 6! = 720$$

If, *M* occupies the first place and *R* the last place, there remain 4 letters. If these 4 letters are permuted in the remaining 4 places in all possible ways, the required number of permutations will be $^{4}p_4$, *i.e.*, 24 ways.

Example 10 : **Six book are to be kept on a shelf, of which two are science. In how many different ways can the books be arranged so that :**

(i) the two science books are together, and

(ii) the two science books are not together.

Solution : (i) If the two science books are always kept together and consider as one unit, the total number of permutations is 5!. But the science books can be arranged between themselves in 2! ways. Hence the number of permutations in which these two books are always together is

$$5! \times 2! = 120 \times 2 = 240.$$

(ii) The total number of permutations of the books without any restriction is 6! = 720. So the number of permutations in which the two science books are not together is 720 – 240 = 480.

Example 11 : **(a) In how many ways can the letters of the word "LAUGHTER" be arranged so that the vowels may never be separated?**

(b) How many arrangement in (a) is possible if vowels are never together?

Solution : (a) Considering the 3 vowels as one, we have only 6 letters *l, g, h, t, r, (a, u, e)* to arrange. Therefore, the number of arrangements of the letters in which the vowels are together

= 6! = 720 ways.

Vowels, being 3 in number can be arranged among themselves in 3! or 6 ways.

∴ the total no. of required arrangements = 720 × 6 = 4,320.

(b) Total number of permutations without any restriction is 8! = 40320 ways.

Total no. of permutations when vowels are not together = 40320 – 4320

= 36,000 ways.

Example 12 : **How many arrangements of the letters of the word "SOCIETY" can be made: (i) if the vowels are to occupy only odd places, (ii) the relative positions of vowels and consonants are not changed.**

Solution : There are 7 different letters in the word 'SOCIETY' of which 3 are vowels and 4 consonants.

(i) There are 4 odd and 3 even places. Since the vowels are to occupy odd places, and the four consonants the remaining 4 places, the vowels can be arranged in ${}^4p_3$ ways and the consonants can be arranged in ${}^4p_4 = 4!$ ways.

Therefore, the total number of required ways

$$= {}^4p_3 \times 4! = 576.$$

(ii) It is given that vowels and constants have to retain the places they occupy in the word. Therefore 3 vowels can be arranged in their places in 3! ways, and depending on these arrangements, the 4 consonants can be arranged in their places in 4! ways.

Therefore the total number of required ways

$$= 3! \times 4! = 144.$$

Example 13 : **How many numbers greater than a million can be formed with the digits 8, 7, 7, 0, 8,7, 4.**

Solution : There are 7 digits in all, of which there are 2 eight 3 seven, and rest numbers are different.

$\therefore$ the total numbers $= \dfrac{7!}{2!\,3!} = 420.$

Since some number would begin with 0 and are less than one million. These numbers shall be rejected.

The number of numbers beginning with $0 = \dfrac{6!}{2!\,3!} = 60.$

The required numbers $= 420 - 60 = 360.$

Example 14 : **(*a*) In how many ways can the letters of the word "MOBILE" be arranged so that the consonants always occupy the odd places.**

(*b*) How many words can be formed out of the letters "ARTICLE", so that the vowels occupy the even places?

Solution : (*a*) In the given word, MOBILE, there are 6 letters of which 3 (MBL) are consonants and (OIE) are vowels.

The 3 positions to be filled up with consonants is shown below :

1	2	3	5	5	6
(*M*)		(*B*)		(*L*)	

The 3 consonants can be placed in the 3 positions marked 1, 3, 5. The total number of ways in which this can be done is $^3P_3 = 3! = 6$, one such arrangement is shown above. For this arrangement the 3 vowels can occupy the three remaining positions in 3! or 6 ways.

$\therefore$ total number of arrangements are $6 \times 6 = 36.$

(*b*) In the given word, ARTICLE, the position to be occupied by vowels is shown below :

1	2	3	4	5	67
	(*A*)		(*I*)		(*E*)

These three vowels can be arranged in the three even places (2, 4, 6) in $^3P_3$ ways. After this, the remaining four letters can be arranged in the remaining four places in $^4P_4$ ways.

$\therefore$ by the fundamental theorem, the total number of arrangements

$$= {}^3P_3 \times {}^4P_4 = 3! \times 4! = 144.$$

COMBINATIONS

The different groups that can be formed out of a given set of objects by taking some or all of them at a time without giving any consideration to the arrangements are called their combinations. It is to be noted that placement of various items in a group is immaterial in case of combination whereas it is material in case of permutations.

For example :

(*i*) the combination of the three numbers 1, 2, 3 taken one at time are (1, 2, 3).

(*ii*) the combination of the three numbers 1, 2, 3 taken two at a time are (12, 13, 23).

The number of combinations of n different objects taken r at a time is denoted by the symbol ^nC_r and is given by

$$^nC_r = \frac{n!}{(n-r)!\,r!}$$

Types of Combinations

(*i*) The number of combinations of *n* different objects taken *r* at a time is equal to the number of combinations of *n* different objects taken $(n - r)$ at a time, *i.e.*, $^nC_r = {}^nC_{n-r}$.

(*ii*) The number of combinations of *n* objects taken *r* at time plus the number of combinations of *n* objects taken $(r - 1)$ at a time is equal to the number of combinations of $(n + 1)$ objects taken *r* at a time and is given by $^nC_r + {}^nC_{r-1} = {}^{n+1}C_r$.

To calculate number of combination taking '*r*' objects out of '*n*' objects when '*p*' are (*i*) always included (*ii*) never included.

(*i*) If '*p*' things always included then we are left with $(n - p)$ objects and we have to choose $(r - p)$ objects, number of combinations will be

$$^{(n-p)}C_{(r-p)}$$

(*ii*) If '*p*' things are never taken then we are left with $(n - p)$ objects and we have to choose '*r*' objects, number of combinations will be

$$^{(n-p)}C_r$$

Example 15 : **In how many ways a team of 6 players can be formed out of 9 players.**

Solution : We have to choose any 6 players out of 9 players, therefore number of combinations

$$9C_6 = \frac{9!}{(9-6)!\,6!} = \frac{9 \times 8 \times 7}{3 \times 2 \times 1} = 84 \text{ ways.}$$

Example 16 : **How many teams of 6 players can be formed out of 15 players if 2 particular players.**

(*i*) are always taken

(*ii*) are never taken

Solution : (*i*) If '2' players are always taken, then we have to choose $(6 - 2)$ players out of $(15 - 2)$ players. Therefore

$$\text{number of combinations} = {}^{13}C_4 = \frac{13!}{9! \times 4!}$$

$$= \frac{13 \times 12 \times 11 \times 10}{4 \times 3 \times 2 \times 1} = 715 \text{ ways.}$$

(*ii*) If '2' players are never taken then we have to choose '6' players out of $(15 - 2)$ players. Therefore number of combinations $= {}^{13}C_6$

$$= \frac{13!}{7! \times 6!} = \frac{13 \times 12 \times 11 \times 10 \times 9 \times 8}{6 \times 5 \times 4 \times 3 \times 2 \times 1}$$

$$= 1716 \text{ ways.}$$

(*iv*) Division into Groups

If we have $(m + n)$ items which are to be divided into groups of '*m*' and '*n*' items of unequal groups, then following formulae is used.

$$^{(m+n)}C_m = \frac{(m+n)!}{(m+n-m)\,m!} = \frac{(m+n)!}{n!\,m!}$$

If $m = n$, this implies both the groups are equal then the number will be

$$^{2m}C_m = \frac{(2m)!}{(2m-m)!\,m!} = \frac{2m}{(m!)^2}$$

The above formula is used when groups cannot be inter changed. However, if the groups can be interchanged then we have above formula as

$$= \frac{(2m)}{(m!)^2\,2!}$$

(*v*) Method of getting number of combinations from '*n*' different objects taken some or all at a time.

If there are '*n*' objects and one has to take some or all at a time then for any object, there are two choices, either to be included or not to be included *i.e.,* 2 ways.

Thus, if there are '*n*' objects, there will be 2^n ways. However, in one case, all the objects will be taken, therefore, total number of combinations in this case will be $(2^n - 1)$ ways.

***Example 17* : How many ways can a person invite his five friends by sending invitation to one or more at a time?**

Solution. In this case, a person can invite 1, 2, 3, 4 or 5 friends at a time

$= 2^5 - 1 = 32 - 1 = 31$ ways.

***Example 18* : Three persons enter in a room where 5 seats are vacant. In how many ways can they seat themselves?**

***Solution* :** First person can occupy any of the 5 seats. So there are 5 ways.

Second person can occupy any of the remaining 4 seats. So there are 4 ways.

Similarly, third can occupy a seat in 3 ways.

Hence, by fundamental principle of counting, required number of ways $= 5 \times 4 \times 3 = 60$

***Example 19* : How many 3–digit odd numbers can be formed using the digits 1, 2, 3, 4, 5 when**

(*i*) repetition of digit is not allowed.

(*ii*) repetition of digit is allowed.

***Solution* :** (*i*) In order to form odd number, we shall have 1, 3 or 5 at unit place in 3 ways.

Since repetition of digit is not allowed, at ten's place we can have any of the remaining 4 numbers and at hundred's place any of the remaining 3 numbers

$\therefore$ Number of ways $= 3 \times 4 \times 3 = 36$ ways.

(*ii*) Again, unit place can be filled in 3 ways.

Since repetition of digit is allowed therefore ten and hundred place can be filled in 5 ways.

$\therefore$ Number of ways $= 5 \times 5 \times 3$

$= 75$

Example 20 : **How many different signals can be given with 5 different flags by hoisting.**

(*i*) two flags at a time

(*ii*) all at a time

Solution : (*i*) Number of ways of hoisting two flags at a time = $5p_2 = 5 \times 4 = 20$

(*ii*) Number of ways of hoisting all flags at a time = $5p_5 = 5! = 120$.

Example 21 : **Find the number of ways in which 5 students and 3 teachers can be seated in a row so that no two teachers are together.**

Solution : 5 students can occupy 5 places in $5p_5 = 5! = 120$ ways.

Since no two teachers have to sit together, their positions are shown below.

T S T S T S T S T S T

Therefore, three teachers can occupy 6 places in

$$6p_3 \text{ ways} = 6 \times 5 \times 4 = 120 \text{ ways.}$$

∴ Required number of ways = 120 × 120 = 14400.

Example 22 : **In how many ways, five student can be arranged in**

(*i*) a line **(*ii*) a circle**

Solution : (*i*) Number of ways in which five students can be arranged in a line = 5! = 120 ways

(*ii*) Number of ways in which five students can be arranged in a circle = (5 – 1)! = 4! = 24 ways.

Example 23 : **In how many ways ten employees including chairman and vice chairman be seated on a round table if chairman and vice chairman have to sit together.**

Solution : If we treat chairman and vice chairman as one then 9 person can be arranged in (9 – 1)! = 8! ways.

The chairman and vice-chairman can be arranged among themselves in 2!.

∴ Required number of ways = 2 × 8!.

Example 24 : **How many different groups of 3 students can be formed out of 12 students?**

Solution : Total number of combinations = $^{12}C_3$

$$= \frac{12!}{9!\,3!} = \frac{12 \times 11 \times 10}{3 \times 2 \times 1} = 220 \text{ ways.}$$

Example 25 : **How many different groups of 3 males and 3 females can be formed out of 12 males and 16 females?**

Solution : Number of ways for taking 3 males out of 12 = $^{12}C_3$

Number of ways for taking 3 females out of 16 = $^{16}C_3$

Total number of combinations = $^{12}C_3 \times {}^{16}C_3$

= 123200 ways.

Example 26 : **A committee of 5 employees is to formed taking 2 from Accounts, 2 from Marketing and 1 from HRD division. If there are total 12 employees in account, 7 in marketing and 5 in HRD division, in how many ways, the committee can be formed.**

Solution : Number of ways of choosing 2 employees.

from Account division = ${}^{12}C_2$ ways. Likewise,

for Marketing and HRD, we have ${}^7C_2$ and ${}^5C_1$ ways.

$\therefore$ Total number of ways = ${}^{12}C_2 \times {}^7C_2 \times {}^5C_1$

$= 66 \times 21 \times 5 = 6930$ ways.

Example 27 : **In a BPO company, three branches in a particular country are managed by 4, 5 and 8 persons. In how many ways can 20 persons be allotted to the different branches.**

Solution : Let the three branches be designated as *A, B* and *C* respectively. Now 4 persons for branch *A* can be selected out of 20 in ${}^{20}C_4$ ways.

Having selected 4 persons for branch *A* in one of the ${}^{20}C_4$ ways : 5 persons can be selected out of the remaining 16 for branch *B* in ${}^{16}C_5$ ways and thereafter 8 persons can be selected for branch *C* out of the remaining 11 in ${}^{11}C_8$ ways.

Using Fundamental theorem, the selection of persons can be made in ${}^2C_1 \times {}^{16}C_5 \times {}^{11}C_8$ ways.

$= 4845 \times 4368 \times 165 = 3491888400$

Since $${}^{20}C_4 = \frac{20 \times 19 \times 18 \times 17}{4 \times 3 \times 2 \times 1} = 4845$$

$${}^{16}C_5 = \frac{16 \times 15 \times 14 \times 13 \times 12}{5 \times 4 \times 3 \times 2 \times 1} = 4368$$

$${}^{11}C_8 = {}^{11}C_8 = \frac{11 \times 10 \times 9}{3 \times 2 \times 1} = 165.$$

Example 28 : **Out of 4 officers and 10 clerks in an office, a committee consisting of 2 officers and 3 clerks is to be formed. In how many ways can this be done if : (*i*) any officer and any clerk can be included, (*ii*) one particular clerk must be on the committee, (*iii*) one particular officer cannot be on the committee?**

Solution : (*i*) Number of ways in which a committee of 2 officers and 3 clerks can be formed.

$$= {}^4C_2 \times {}^{10}C_3 = \frac{4 \times 3}{1 \times 2} \times \frac{10 \times 9 \times 8}{1 \times 2 \times 3} = 720 \text{ ways.}$$

(*ii*) Since, the specified clerk must be in each committee, the remaining 2 clerks out of the 9 can be selected in ${}^9C_2$ ways.

$\therefore$ number of ways in which a required committee can be formed in this case

$$= {}^4C_2 \times {}^9C_2 = \frac{4 \times 3}{1 \times 2} \times \frac{9 \times 8}{1 \times 2} = 216 \text{ ways.}$$

(*iii*) Since one specified officer cannot be on any committee, 2 officers out of remaining three can be selected in ${}^3C_2$ ways.

$\therefore$ number of ways of forming committee in this case.

$= {}^3C_2 \times {}^{10}C_3 = 360$ ways.

Example 28 : **For sales promotion in 3 zones *A*, *B* and *C* a company requires 10, 15 and 20 men respectively. If 45 men are available in how many particular ways can they be allotted to the**

different zones? If out of in how many man must be posted to *A*, 5 to *B* and 2 to *C*, 45, 3 ways the remaining persons can be distributed?

Solution : Selection of men from zone *A* out can be made out of 45 men in $^{45}C_{10}$. Out of the remaining 35 men, 15 men for zone *B* can be selected in $^{35}C_{15}$ ways, leaving 20 men for zone *C*. Hence 45 men can be distributed to 3 different zones in

$$^{45}C_{10} \cdot {}^{35}C_{15} = \frac{45!}{10!\,35!} \times \frac{35!}{15!\,20!} = \frac{45!}{10!\,15!\,20!} \text{ ways.}$$

Now, if 3 particular men must be allotted to zone *A*, 5 to *B* and 2 to *C*, the remaining 35 men can be distributed to *A*, *B* in

$$^{35}C_7 \cdot {}^{28}C_{10} = \frac{35!}{7!\,28!} \times \frac{28!}{10!\,18!} = \frac{35!}{7!\,10!\,18!} \text{ ways.}$$

Example 29 : **In a company there are 20 full time employees including the chairman and the vice chairman from whom a committee of 5 is to be appointed. In how many ways committee can be formed so that it shall include**

(*i*) the chairman and the vice-chairman;

(*ii*) the chairman but not the vice-chairman;

(*iii*) neither the chairman nor the vice chairman.

Solution : (*i*) As the chairman and the vice chairman are to be included, we can choose any 3 from 18 employees to form a committee of 5. This can be done in $^{18}C_3$ ways. Hence the number of committees is 816.

(*ii*) Since only the chairman is to be included, therefore the selection of 4 employees from 18 can be made in $^{18}C_4$ ways. Hence the number of committees containing the chairman, and 4 employees is 3060.

(*iii*) When neither the chairman nor the vice chairman is to be included, the selection will have to be done from the remaining employees only. This can be done in $^{18}C_5$ ways. Hence the number of committees with neither the chairman nor the vice chairman included is 8568.

Example 30 : **A Board of Directors of a company shall consists of 10 members. 6 belonging to the independent and 4 to the whole time employee. In how many ways can a committee of 5 be selected so that the members of the independent directors are in majority?**

Solution : The following table shows the possible of selections under given conditions:

Type	*Independent*	*Whole time Employee*
I	5	0
II	4	1
III	3	2

Let us first find the number of ways of making a selection of type I. 5 members can be selected from Independent in $^6C_5$ ways; 0 member can be selected from whole time employee in $^4C_0$ ways.

Applying Fundamental theorem, the number of ways of making a choice of type I = $^6C_5 \times {}^4C_0$.

Similarly, the number of ways in which each type of selection which can be made is shown below :

Type	*No. of ways of making the choice*
I	${}^6C_5 \times {}^4C_0$
II	${}^6C_4 \times {}^4C_1$
III	${}^6C_3 \times {}^4C_2$

Hence, the total number of ways in which a committee of 5 be selected so that the members of the independent directors are in majority.

$$= {}^6C_5 \times {}^4C_0 + {}^6C_4 \times {}^4C_1 + {}^6C_3 \times {}^4C_2$$

$$= 6 \times 1 + \frac{6 \times 5}{1 \times 2} \times 4 + \frac{6 \times 5 \times 4}{1 \times 2 \times 3} \times \frac{4 \times 3}{1 \times 2} = 186.$$

Example 31 : **In how many ways 10 cabins can be allotted to a group of 5,3 and 2 employees?**

Solution : If there are 'm' and 'n' number of persons in two groups of total 'p' objects then number of ways, combinations can take place

$$= \frac{P\,!}{m\,!\;n\,!}$$

Applying same rule, we have

$$= \frac{10\,!}{5\,!\;3\,!\;2\,!} = 2520 \text{ ways.}$$

Example 32 : **In how many ways 15 files be put in three trays in equal number?**

Solution : There are 15 files and each tray is to contain five files, therefore formula will be

$$= \frac{3m\,!}{(m\,!)^3\;3\,!}$$

$$= \frac{3 \times 5\,!}{(15)\,!\;3\,!} = 126126 \text{ ways.}$$

Objective Type Questions

1. If $\frac{1}{9!} + \frac{1}{10!} = \frac{x}{11!}$ the value of x is

(*i*) 100 (*ii*) 110 (*iii*) 120 (*iv*) 121

2. The number of words of three distinct letters of English alphabets are

(*i*) 15600 (*ii*) 14500 (*iii*) 13200 (*iv*) 17200

3. The number which lie between 100 and 1000 in which all digits are distinct

(*i*) 570 (*ii*) 648 (*iii*) 742 (*iv*) 692

4. The number of ways in which 5 letters be posted in 4 letters boxes

(*i*) 5^4 (*ii*) 4^5 (*iii*) 20^5 (*iv*) 5^{20}

5. A coin is tossed 5 times. the possible outcomes are

(*i*) 16 (*ii*) 24 (*iii*) 30 (*iv*) 32

6. If $P(n, 4) = 20 \times P(n, 2)$, the value of n is

(*i*) 7 (*ii*) 8 (*iii*) 9 (*iv*) 10

7. The number of ways in which 6 person can stand in a queue is

(*i*) 12 (*ii*) 230 (*iii*) 720 (*iv*) 688

8. The number of ways by which 7 pictures can be hung from 5 picture nails on a wall is

(*i*) 2500 (*ii*) 2502 (*iii*) 2510 (*iv*) 2520

9. The number of ways 5 boys and 3 girls can be seated in a row so that no two girls are together

(*i*) 14440 (*ii*) 13478 (*iii*) 14448 (*iv*) 14000

10. The number of ways in which the letters of the word FAILURE be arranged so that consonants may only occupy odd positions

(*i*) 550 (*ii*) 576 (*iii*) 540 (*iv*) 567

11. If ${}^nC_7 = {}^nC_7$, the value of n would be

(*i*) 7 (*ii*) 9 (*iii*) 11 (*iv*) 13

12. The number of ways in which 4 students are chosen out of 32 students

(*i*) 35960 (*ii*) 34781 (*iii*) 30451 (*iv*) 39842

13. A polygon has 44 diagonal. The number of sides would be

(*i*) 9 (*ii*) 10 (*iii*) 11 (*iv*) 12

14. The number of triangles that can be made by joining 12 points, 5 of which are collinear

(*i*) 188 (*ii*) 198 (*iii*) 200 (*iv*) 210

15. Out of 7 component and 4 vowels the words of 3 component and 2 vowels can be

(*i*) 20,200 (*ii*) 22200 (*iii*) 24,200 (*iv*) 25,200

16. The number of words that can be formed by taking letters at a time out of the word 'MATHEMATICS' so two letters are distinct and two are alike

(*i*) 458 (*ii*) 756 (*iii*) 348 (*iv*) 689

17. The number of ways in which 7 plus (+1) sign and 5 minus (–1) signs be arranged in a row so that no two minus sign are together.

(*i*) 48 (*ii*) 56 (*iii*) 63 (*iv*) 42

18. The number of triangle that can be formed by joining the vertices of a hexagon

(*i*) 6 (*ii*) 18 (*iii*) 20 (*iv*) 24

19. The number of 5 cards combination out of a deck of 52 cards if at least one of the 5 cards has to be king

(*i*) 886656 (*ii*) 883496 (*iii*) 8846 (*iv*) 479827

20. A student has to answer 4 question out of 5 question however question 1 and 2 are compulsory. The number of ways in which the student can make the choice is

(*i*) 3 (*ii*) 5 (*iii*) 7 (*iv*) 4

Answers

1. (*iv*)	2. (*i*)	3. (*ii*)	4. (*ii*)	5. (*iv*)
6. (*i*)	7. (*iii*)	8. (*iv*)	9. (*i*)	10. (*ii*)
11. (*iii*)	12. (*i*)	13. (*iii*)	14. (*iv*)	15. (*iv*)
16. (*ii*)	17. (*ii*)	18. (*iii*)	19. (*i*)	20. (*i*)

Exercise 15.1

1. Compute

(*i*) $\frac{9!}{(5!) \times (3!)}$ (*ii*) $\frac{32!}{29!}$

(*iii*) $\frac{(12!) - (10!)}{9!}$ [**Ans.** (*i*) 504; (*ii*) 29760; (*iii*) 1310]

2. Find n if

(*i*) $(n + 2)! = 60 \times (n - 1)!$

(*ii*) $(n + 2)! = 2550 \times (n!)$ [**Ans.** (*i*) 3; (*ii*) 49]

3. Prove that

(*i*) $\frac{n!}{r!} = n(n-1)(n-2).....(r+1)$

(*ii*) $\frac{n!}{r!(n-1)!} + \frac{n!}{(r-1)!(n-r+1)} = \frac{(n+1)!}{r!(n-r+1)!}$

4. There are 10 buses running between Mumbai and Pune. In how many ways a man can go from Mumbai to Pune and return by a different bus? [**Ans.** 90]

5. In how many ways can a vowel a consonant and a digit can be chosen out of the 26 letters of the English alphabet and the 10 digits? [**Ans.** 1050]

6. There are 6 books on Physics and 5 books on chemistry in a bookshop. In how many ways can a student purchase either a book on Physics or a book on chemistry? [**Ans.** 11]

7. Evaluate :

(*i*) ${}^{10}P_4$;

(*ii*) ${}^{62}P_3$

(*iii*) ${}^{9}P_9$ [**Ans.** (*i*) 5040; (*ii*) 226920; (*iii*) 362880]

8. Prove that ${}^{9}P_3 + 3\,{}^{9}P_3 = {}^{10}P_3$

9. If ${}^{11}P_r = {}^{12}P_{r-1}$, find r. [**Ans.** 9]

10. Prove that ${}^nP_n = 2\,{}^nP_{n-2}$

11. In how many ways can 5 person occupy 3 vacant seat? **[Ans.** 60]

12. How many 4 letter words, with or without meaning, can be formed out of the letter of the word 'LOGARITHMS', if repetition of letters is not allowed. **[Ans.** 5040]

13. How many permutation can be formed by the letter of the words 'VOWEL' when

(*i*) there is no restriction on letters? **[Ans.** 720]

(*ii*) each word begin with *E*? **[Ans.** 120]

(*iii*) all vowels come together? **[Ans.** 240]

(*iv*) all consonants come together? **[Ans.** 144]

(*v*) Each word begin with 0 and ends with L? **[Ans.** 24]

14. How many different number greater than 50,000 can be formed with the digits 0, 1, 1, 5, 9. **[Ans.** 24]

15. In how many ways 3 yellow and 2 green discs be arranged in a row if the discs of the same colour are indistinguishable? **[Ans.** 1260]

16. If ${}^nC_7 = {}^nC_4$, find the value of *n*. **[Ans.** 11]

17. If ${}^8C_r - {}^7C_3 = {}^7C_2$, find *r*. **[Ans.** 3.5]

18. Evaluate ${}^{20}C_5 + \sum_{r=2}^{5} {}^{25-r}C_4$. **[Ans.** 42504]

19. How many triangles can be formed joining the vertics of a hexagon? **[Ans.** 20]

20. In how many ways a team of 11 players be selected from 16 players? How many of these will

(*i*) include 2 particular players?

(*ii*) exclude 2 particular players? **[Ans.** 4368 (*i*) 2002; (*ii*) 364]

21. A student has to answer 10 question, choosing at least 4 from each part of A and part B. If there are 6 question in part A and 7 in part B. In how many ways can the student choose 10 questions? **[Ans.** 226]

22. Determine the number of 5 cards combination out of a deck of 52 cards if at least one of the 5 card has to be king?

23. How many four letters words can be formed using the letter of the word "INEFFECTIVE"? **[Ans.** 1422]

24. How many triangles can be obtained by joining 12 points, five of which are collinear? **[Ans.** 210]

25. A tea party is arranged for 16 persons along two side of a long table with 8 chair on each side four person wish to sit on a particular side and two on the other side. In how ways can they be seated? **[Ans.** ${}^{10}C_4 \times (8!)^2$]

16

Mathematical Induction

Highlights of the Chapter

- **Introduction**
- **Principles of Mathematical Induction**
- **Solved Practical Problems**

INTRODUCTION

In order to understand mathematical induction, one needs to be familiar with mathematical statements. Mathematical statements are normal sentences or descriptions which involve mathematical relations.

For example, let $P(n)$ be the statement "$n^2 + n$" is visible by 2. This is a mathematical statement. Now, if we put $n = 1$, 2, and 3 and find the results, we will observe that the statement is true.

However, if we apply same technique for the statement "$P(n) = n^2$ is divisible by 2", the result will hold good for $n = 1$ and 2 but not for $n = 3$.

PRINCIPLES OF MATHEMATICAL INDUCTION

Let $P(n)$ be a statement involving the natural number n such that

(*i*) $P(1)$ is true, and

(*ii*) $P(m + 1)$ is true, whenever $P(m)$ is true.

Then, $P(n)$ is true for all $n \in N$.

Let $P(n)$ be a statement involving the natural number n such that

(*i*) $P(1)$ is true, and

(*ii*) $P(m + 1)$ is true, whenever $P(n)$ is true for all $n \leq m$.

Then, $P(n)$ is true for all $n \in N$.

The principles of Mathematical induction helps in ascertaining the validity of any given mathematical statement for all natural number. The procedure of testing validity of mathematical statement using mathematical induction is given below :

(*i*) Find if the statement is true for $n = 1$.

(*ii*) Assume that the statement is true for $n = k$.

(*iii*) On the basis of relation derived under step (*ii*), prove that statement is true for $n = k + 1$. The procedure would become clear from the following examples :

***Example 1* : Prove that $n^2 + n$ is even natural number for all $n \in N$.**

***Solution* :** Let $P(n) = n^2 + n$

When $n = 1$

$$P(1) = 1^2 + 1 = 2$$

The statement holds good for $n = 1$.

Now, let the statement be true for $n = k$ *i.e.*

$$P(k) = k^2 + k = 2\lambda \text{ for some } \lambda \in N$$

Based on above statements, we need to show.

$$P(k + 1) = (k + 1)^2 + (k + 1) \text{ is an even natural number}$$

$$\begin{aligned} P(k + 1) &= k^2 + 1 + 2k + k + 1 \\ &= (k^2 + k) + (2k + 2) \\ &= 2\lambda + 2(k + 1) \\ &= 2(\lambda + k + 1) = 2\alpha \end{aligned}$$

where $\alpha = \lambda + k + 1 \in N$

For any value of α belonging to natural number, 2α is an even natural number. Hence it is proved that

$$P(k + 1) = (k + 1)^2 + (k + 1) \text{ is an even natural number.}$$

***Example 2* : Prove using mathematical induction**

$$1 + 4 + 7 + ... + (3n - 2) = \frac{1}{2} n(3n - 1) \text{ for } n \in N.$$

***Solution* :**

Let $P(n) = 1 + 4 + 7 + ... + (3n - 2) = \frac{1}{2} n(3n - 1)$

when $n = 1$, we have

$$= P(1) = [3(1) - 2] = \frac{1}{2} \cdot 1 \cdot (3(1) - 1)$$

$$= 1 = 1$$

Let the statement be true for $n = k$, we have

$$P(k) = 1 + 4 + 7 + ... + (3k - 2) = \frac{1}{2} k(3k - 1) \qquad ...(1)$$

Now we are required to prove that the statement holds good for $P(k + 1)$

$$P(k + 1) = 1 + 4 + 7 + ... + (3k - 2) + (3(k + 1) - 2) = \frac{1}{2}(k + 1)(3(k + 1) - 1) \qquad ...(2)$$

To prove statement (2) using statement (1), we add $[3(k + 1) - 2]$ on both sides of statement (1) we have

$$1 + 4 + 7 + \ldots + (3k - 2) + [3(k + 1) - 2] = \frac{1}{2}k(3k - 1) + [3(k + 1) - 2]$$

Now using R.H.S.,

$$\frac{1}{2}k(3k - 1) + [3(k + 1) - 2] = \frac{1}{2}k(3k - 1) + (3k + 1)$$

$$= \frac{1}{2}[3k^2 - k + 6k + 2]$$

$$= \frac{1}{2}[3k^2 + 5k + 2]$$

$$= \frac{1}{2}(k + 1)(3k + 2)$$

$$= \frac{1}{2}(k + 1)[3(k + 1) - 1] = P(k + 1)$$

Hence proved the given result holds good for all $n \in N$.

Example 3 : **Prove using mathematical that the sum $S_n = n^3 + 3n^2 + 5n + 3$ is divisible by 3 for all $n \in N$.**

Solution : Let $P(n)$ be the statement given by

$P(n) : S_n = n^3 + 3n^2 + 5n + 3$ is divisible by 3

Let $n = 1$, we have

$P(1) : S_1 = 1^3 + 3(1)^2 + 5(1) + 3$ is divisible by 3.

Since, $1^3 + 3(1)^2 + 5(1) + 3 = 12$, which is divisible by 3

$\therefore$ $P(1)$ is true

Let the statement be true for $n = k$, then we have

$S_k = k^3 + 3k^2 + 5k + 3$ is divisible by 3

$\Rightarrow$ $S_k = k^3 + 3k^2 + 5k + 3 = 3\lambda$, for some $\lambda \in N$ ...(i)

Now we need to show that $P(k + 1)$ is true. For this we have to show that $(k + 1)^3 + 3(k + 1)^2 + 5(k + 1) + 3$ is divisible by 3.

Now, $(k + 1)^3 + 3(k + 1)^2 + 5(k + 1) + 3$

$= (k^3 + 3k^2 + 5k + 3) + 3k^2 + 9k + 9$

$= 3\lambda + 3(k^2 + 3k + 3)$

$= 3[\lambda + k^2 + 3k + 3]$ [Using (i)]

$= 3\mu$, where $\mu = \lambda + k^2 + 3k + 3 \in N$

$\therefore$ $P(k + 1)$ is true

Hence, by the principle of mathematical induction the statement is true for all $n \in N$.

Example 4 : **Using the principle of mathematical induction, prove that $(2^{3n} - 1)$ is divisible by 7 for all $n \in N$.**

Solution : Let $P(n)$ be the statement given by

$P(n) : 2^{3n} - 1$ is divisible by 7

Let $n = 1$, we have

$P(1) = 2^{3\times1} - 1 = 8 - 1 = 7$, which is divisible by 7.

So, $P(1)$ is true

Let $P(k)$ be true. Then

$2^{3k} - 1$ is divisible by 7.

$\Rightarrow$ $2^{3k} - 1 = 7l$, for some $\lambda \in N$ ...(*i*)

We are now required to prove that $P(k + 1)$ is true. For this we have to show that $2^{3(k+1)} - 1$ is divisible by 7.

Now, $2^{3(k+1)} - 1 = 2^{2k}.2^3 - 1 = (7\lambda + 1)\, 2^3 - 1$ [Using (i)]

$= 56\lambda + 8 - 1 = 7(8\lambda + 1)$, which is divisible by 7

$\therefore$ $P(k + 1)$ is true.

Hence, by the principle of mathematical inducation, $P(n)$ is true for all $n \in N$ *i.e.* $2^{3n} - 1$ is divisible by 7 for all $n \in N$.

***Example 5 :* Prove by the principle of induction that for all $n \in N$, $(10^{2n-1} + 1)$ is divisible by 11.**

Solution : Let $P(n)$ be the statement given by

$P(n) : 10^{2n-1} + 1$ is divisible by 11

Let $n = 1$, we have

$P(1) : 10^{2\cdot1-1} + 1$ is divisible by 11.

Since $10^{2\cdot1-1} + 1 = 11$, which is divisible by 11.

So, $P(k)$ be true. Then,

$10^{2k-1} + 1$ is divisible by 11

$\Rightarrow$ $10^{k-1} + 1 = 11\lambda$, for some $\lambda \in N$ ...(i)

We are required to show that $P(k + 1)$ is true. For this we have to show that $10^{2(k+1)} + 1$ is divisible by 11.

Now,

$10^{2(k+1)-1} + 1 = 10^{2k+1} = 10^{2k-1}\, 10^2 + 1$

$\Rightarrow$ $10^{2(k+1)-1} + 1 = (11\lambda - 1)\, 100 + 1$ [Using (i)]

$\Rightarrow$ $10^{2(k+1)-1} + 1 = 1100\lambda - 99 = 11(100\lambda - 9) = 11\mu$, where $\mu = 100\lambda - 9 \in N$

$\Rightarrow$ $10^{2(k+1)} - 1$ is divisible by 11

$\Rightarrow$ $P(k + 1)$ is true

Hence, by the principle of mathematical induction $P(k)$ is true for all $n \in N$ *i.e* $10^{2n-1} + 1$ is divisible by 11 for all $n \in N$.

***Example 6 :* Prove by the principle of mathematical induction that for all $n \in N$, 3^{2n} when divided by 8, the remainder is always 1.**

Solution : Let $P(n)$ be the statement given by

$P(n)$: 3^{2n} when divided by 8, the remainder is 1

or, $P(n) : 3^{2n} = 8\lambda + 1$ for some $\lambda \in N$

Let $n = 1$, we have

$P(1) : 3^2 = 8\lambda + 1$ for some $\lambda \in N$.

$\therefore$ $3^2 = 8 \times 1 + 1 = 8\lambda + 1$, where $\lambda = 1$

$\therefore$ $P(1)$ is true

Let $P(k)$ be true. Then

$$3^{2k} = 8\lambda + 1 \text{ for some } \lambda \in N \qquad ...(i)$$

We are required to show that $P(k + 1)$ is true for which we have to show that $3^{2(k+1)}$ when divided by 8, the remainder is 1 *i.e.* $3^{2(k+1)} = 8\mu + 1$ for some $\mu \in N$.

Now, $3^{2(k+1)} = 3^{2k} . 3^2 = (8\lambda + 1) \times 9$ [Using (i)]

$= 72\lambda + 9 = 72\lambda + 8 + 1 = 8(9\lambda + 1) + 1 = 8\mu + 1$, where $\mu = 9\lambda + 1 \in N$

$\Rightarrow$ $P(k + 1)$ is true

Hence, by the principle of mathematical induction $P(n)$ is true for all $n \in N$ *i.e.* 3^{2n} when divided by 8 the remainder is always 1.

Example 7 : **Prove that for $n \in N$, $10^n + 3.4^{n+2} + 5$ is divisible by 9.**

Solution : Let $P(n)$ be the statement given by

$P(n) : 10^n + 3.4^{n+2} + 5$ is divisible by 9

Let $n = 1$, we have

$P(1) : 10^1 + 3.(4^{1+2}) + 5$ is divisible by 9.

$\therefore$ $10^1 + 3(4^{1+2}) + 5 = 10 + 192 + 5 = 207$, which is divisible by 9

$\therefore$ $P(1)$ is true.

Let $P(k)$ be true. Then.

$10^k + 3.(4^{k+2}) + 5$ is divisible by 9

$$\Rightarrow \quad 10^k + 3.(4^{k+2}) + 5 = 9\lambda, \lambda \in N \qquad ...(i)$$

We are now required to prove that $P(k + 1)$ is true for which we have to show that $10^{(k+1)} + 3(4^{k+3}) + 5$ is divisible by 9.

Now,

$10^{k+1} + 3.4^{k+3} + 5$

$= 10^k.10 + 3.4^{k+3} + 5$

$= [9\lambda - 3(4^{k+2}) - 5] \times 10 + 3.4^{k+3} + 5$ [Using (i)]

$= 90\lambda - 30 \times 4^{k+2} - 50 + 3 \times 4 \times 4^{k+2} + 5$

$= 90\lambda - 30 \times 4^{k+2} + 12 \times 4^{k+2} - 45$

$= 90\lambda - 18 \times 4^{k+2} - 45$

$= 9\,(10\lambda - 2 \times 4^{k+2} - 5) = 9\mu$, where $\mu = 10\lambda - 2 \times 4^{k+2} - 5$

$\Rightarrow$ $10^{k+1} + 3.4^{k+3} + 5$ is divisible by 9

$\Rightarrow$ $P\,(k + 1)$ is true

Hence, by the principle of mathematical induction $P(n)$ is true for all $n \in N$.

Example 8 : **Using principle of mathematical induction prove that $4^n + 15n - 1$ is divisible by 9 for all natural numbers n.**

Solution : Let $P(n)$ be the statement given by

$P(n) : 4^n + 15n - 1$ is divisible by 9

Let $n = 1$, we have

$P(1) : 4^1 + 15 \times 1 - 1$ is divisible by 9.

$\therefore$ $4^1 + 15 \times 1 - 1 = 18$, which is divisible by 9

$\therefore$ $P(1)$ is true

Let $P(k)$ be true. Then,

$4^k + 15k - 1$ is divisible by 9

$\Rightarrow$ $4^k + 15k - 1 = 9\lambda$, for some $\lambda \in N$

We are required to prove that $P(k + 1)$ is true, for which we have to show that $4^{k+1} + 15(k + 1) - 1$ is divisible by 9.

Now, $4^{k+1} + 15\,(k + 1) - 1$

$= 4^k.4 + 15\,(k + 1) - 1$

$= (9\lambda - 15\,k + 1) \times 4 + 15\,(k + 1) - 1$

$= 36\,\lambda - 45\,k + 18$

$= 9\,(4\,\lambda - 5\,k + 2)$, which is divisible by 9.

$\therefore$ $P(k + 1)$ is true.

Hence, by the principle of mathematical induction $P(n)$ is true for all $n \in N$ *i.e.* $4^n + 15n - 1$ is divisible by 9.

Example 9 : **Prove that $1^2 + 2^2 + 3^2 + ... + n^2 = \dfrac{n(n+1)(2n+1)}{6}$ for all natural numbers using mathematical induction.**

Solution : Let $P(n)$ be the statement given by

$$P_{(n)} = 1^2 + 2^2 + 3^2 + ... + n^2 = \frac{n(n+1)(2n+1)}{6}$$

Let $n = 1$, we have

$$P(1) = 1^2 = \frac{1(1+1)(2+1)}{6} = 1$$

Let the statement be true for $n = k$.

$$P(k) = 1^2 + 2^2 + 3^2 + ... + k^2 = \frac{k(k+1)(2k+1)}{6}.$$

Now, we have to prove that statement is true for $P(k + 1)$

$$P(k+1) = 1^2 + 2^2 + 3^2 + ... + k^2 + (k+1)^2$$

$$= \frac{1}{6}(k+1)((k+1)+1)(2(k+1)+1)$$

Now, $\quad 1^2 + 2^2 + 3^2 + ... + k^2 + (k+1)^2$

$$= [1^2 + 2^2 + 3^2 + ... + k^2] + (k+1)^2$$

$$= \frac{1}{6}k(k+1)(2k+1) + (k+1)^2$$

$$= \frac{1}{6}(k+1)\{k(2k+1) + 6(k+1)\} = \frac{1}{6}(k+1)\{2k^2 + 7k + 6\}$$

$$= \frac{1}{6}(k+1)(k+2)(2k+3) = \frac{1}{6}(k+1)((k+1)+1)(2(k+1)+1)$$

$\therefore \quad P(k + 1)$ is true

Hence, by the principle of mathematical induction, the given result is true for all $n \in N$.

Example 10 : **Prove by the principle of mathematical induction that**

$n < 2^n$ for all $n \in N$

Solution : Let $P(n)$ be the statement given by $P(n) : n < 2^n$

Let $n = 1$, we have

$P(1) : 1 < 2^1$.

$\therefore \quad 1 < 2^1$

$\therefore \quad P(1)$ is true

Let $P(k)$ be true. Then, $k < 2^k$

We are required to prove that $P(k + 1)$ is true for which we will have to prove that $(k + 1) < 2^{k+1}$.

Since, $\quad P(k)$ is true

Therefore $\quad k < 2^k$

$\Rightarrow \quad 2k < 2.2^k \Rightarrow 2k < 2^{k+1} \Rightarrow (k + k) < 2^{k+1}$

$\Rightarrow \quad k + 1 \leq k + k < 2^{k+1} \qquad [\because 1 \leq k \therefore k + 1 \leq k + k]$

$\Rightarrow \quad (k + 1) < 2^{k+1}$

$\Rightarrow \quad P(k + 1)$ is true

So, by the principle of mathematical induction $P(n)$ is true for all $n \in N$ *i.e.* $n < 2^n$ for all $n \in N$.

Exercise 16.1

Prove the following by the principle of mathematical induction :

1. $\frac{1}{1.2}+\frac{1}{2.3}+\frac{1}{3.4}+\ldots+\frac{1}{n(n+1)}=\frac{n}{n+1}$.

2. $1^2+2^2+3^2+\ldots+n^2=\frac{n(n+1)(2n+1)}{6}$.

3. $1+2+3+\ldots+n=\frac{n(n+1)}{2}$.

4. $1+3+5+\ldots+(2n-1)=n^2$ *i.e.* the sum of first n odd natural numbers is n^2.

5. $1^3+2^3+3^3+\ldots+n^3=\left(\frac{n(n+1)}{2}\right)^2$.

6. $\frac{1}{3.7}+\frac{1}{7.11}+\frac{1}{11.15}+\ldots+\frac{1}{(4n-1)(4n+3)}=\frac{n}{3(4n+3)}$.

7. $1^2+3^2+5^2+\ldots+(2n-1)^2=\frac{1}{3}n\left(4n^2-1\right)$.

8. $5^{2n}-1$ is divisible by 24 for all $n \in N$.

9. $3^{2n}+7$ is divisible by 8 for all $n \in N$.

10. $7^{2n}+2^{3n-3}.3^{n-1}$ is divisible by 25 for all $n \in N$.

17

Sequence and Series

HIGHLIGHTS OF THE CHAPTER

- **Arithmetical Progression**
- **Properties of Arithmetical Progression**
- **Insertion of Arithmetic Mean**
- **Geometric Progression**
- **Properties of Geometric Progression**
- **Harmonic Progression**
- **Finding nth term**
- **Insertion of HP between two terms**

ARITHMETICAL PROGRESSION

The numbers, a, a_2, a_3 ...a_n are said to be in Arithmetical Progression if $a_n - a_{n-1}$ is constant for all integers $n > 1$. For example, following series are in *A.P.*

(*i*) 1, 3, 5, 7...

(*ii*) –1, – 5, – 9, – 13......

The number $a_n - a_{n-1}$ is referred as common difference. In the above case, the common difference for series (*i*) and series (*ii*) is 2 and –4 respectively. The common difference is denoted as '*d*'.

Properties of Arithmetic Progression

(*i*) The nth term of arithmetic progression is given by :

$$a_n = a_1 + (n - 1)d$$

where a_n = n^{th} term of A.P.

a_1 = first term of A.P.

n = required number of terms.

d = common difference.

Example 1 : **Find the 8th term of the series 4, 7, 10, ...**

Solution : In this case

$$a_1 = 4, \quad d = 7 - 4 = 3, \quad n = 8$$

∴ 8th term will be given as

$$a_8 = 4 + (8 - 1) \,.\, 3$$
$$= 4 + 7 \times 3$$
$$= 25$$

Example 2 : **Which term of the A.P. 28, 24, 20, 16.... is 8.**

Solution : Let n^{th} term be 8.

Given $d = 24 - 28 = -4$, $a = 28$ using the formula $a_n = a_1 + (n - 1)d$

∴ $8 = 28 + (n - 1)(-4)$

$8 = 28 - 4n + 4$

∴ $4n = 24$

$n = 6$

∴ 8 is the 6th term of the given series.

(*ii*) Finding sum of Finite Numbers of terms in A.P.

The sum of finite term of A.P. is given by :

$$S_n = \frac{n}{2}\left[2a_1 + (n-1)d\right]$$

If first and last terms are given, $S_n = \dfrac{n}{2}[a + l]$

(*iii*) n^{th} term of *A.P.* from the end.

Left there be an *A.P.* with first term '*a*' and common difference '*d*'. If there are '*m*' terms in the A.P., then n^{th} term from the end = $(m - n + 1)^{th}$ term from the beginning.

n^{th} term from the end = a_{m-n+1}

n^{th} term from the end = $a + (m - n + 1 - 1)d$

n^{th} term from the end = $a + (m - n)d$.

If '*l*' is the last term of the *A.P.* then we can find n^{th} term from the end using common difference as '$-d$' instead of '*d*'.

n^{th} term from the end = $l + (n - 1)(-d) = l - (n - 1)d$

Example 3 : **Find the 6th term from the end of the *A.P.* 17, 14, 11, ...1, –40.**

Solution : We have

l = Last term = –40, Common difference = –3

6th term from the end = $l - (6 - 1)d = -40 - 5 \times (-3)$

$= -25$.

Example 4 : **The 10th term of an *A.P.* is 30 and 16th term is 60. Find the**

(*i*) 18th term.

(*ii*) General term.

Solution : (*i*) Let 'a' be the first term and 'd' be the common difference

$$a_{10} = 30 \text{ and } a_{16} = 60$$

$$\therefore \quad a_{10} = a + (10 - 1)d = 30 \quad ...(1)$$

$$a_{16} = a + (16 - 1)d = 60 \quad ...(2)$$

Subtracting (1) from (2), we have

$$6d = 30$$

$$d = 5$$

$$\therefore \quad a + (10 - 1)(5) = 30$$

$$a = 30 - 45 = -15$$

$\therefore$ 18th term will be given as

$$a_{18} = a + (18 - 1)d$$

$$= -15 + (17).5$$

$$= 70$$

(*ii*) General term $\quad a_n = a + (n - 1)d$

$$= a_n = -15 + (n - 1)(5) = 5n - 20$$

Example 5 : **The sum of three numbers of A.P. is –6 and the product is 24. Find the numbers.**

Solution : Let the three numbers be $a - d, a, a + d$

$$\therefore \quad a - d + a + a + d = -6$$

$$3a = -2$$

Further $(a - d) . a(a + d) = 24$

$$a . (a^2 - d^2) = 24$$

Substituting $a = -2$, we have

$$(-2)(4 - d^2) = 24$$

$$4 - d^2 = -12$$

$$-d^2 = -12 - 4$$

$$d^2 = 16$$

$$d = \pm 4$$

$\therefore$ Numbers are $(-2 + 4), -2, (-2 - 4)$

$$-2 -4, -2, -2 + 4$$

i.e., $\quad 2, -2, -6 \quad$ or $\quad -6, -2, 2$

Example 6 : **Find the Sum of 3, 7, 11 .... upto 16 terms.**

Solution : Given $a_1 = 3, d = 7 - 3 = 4, n = 16$

Substituting these values in the formula

$$S_n = \frac{n}{2}\left[2a_1 + (n-1)d\right]$$

$$S_n = \frac{16}{2}\left[2(3) + (16-1)(4)\right]$$

$$= 8\ [6 + 60]$$

$$= 8 \times 66 = 528$$

Example 7 : **How many terms of the series 1, 6, 11, ... be taken so that their sum is 148.**

Solution : Given a = first term = 1

d = common difference = 5

Using the formula

$$S_n = \frac{n}{2}\left[2a + (n-1)d\right]$$

We have $148 = \frac{n}{2}\left[2(1) + (n-1)5\right]$

$$5n^2 - 3n - 296 = 0$$

$$(n - 8)(5n + 37) = 0$$

$$n = 8,\ n = -37/5$$

Since 'n' cannot be negative therefore, total number of terms is 8.

Example 8 : **The sum of the first p, q, r terms of an A.P. are a, b, c respectively. Show that**

$$\frac{a}{p}(q-r) + \frac{b}{q}(r-p) + \frac{c}{r}(p-q) = 0.$$

Solution : Let 'a', be first term and 'd' be common difference

$\therefore$ We have

$$a = \text{sum of } p \text{ terms} = \frac{p}{2}\left[2a_1 + (p-1)d\right]$$

Similarly $b = \frac{q}{2}\left[2a_1 + (q-1)d\right]$

$$c = \frac{r}{2}\left[2a_1 + (r-1)d\right]$$

The above equations can be written as

$$\frac{2a}{p} = \left[2a_1 + (p-1)d\right] \quad ...(i)$$

$$\frac{2b}{q} = \left[2a_1 + (q-1)d\right] \quad ...(ii)$$

$$\frac{2c}{r} = \left[2a_1 + (r-1)d\right] \qquad ...(iii)$$

Multiplying (*i*), (*ii*) and (*iii*) by $(q - r)$, $(r - p)$ and $(p - q)$ respectively and adding, we get

$$\frac{2a}{p}(q-r) + \frac{2b}{q}(r-p) + \frac{2c}{r}(p-q)$$

$$= 2a\,(q - r + r - p + p - q) + d\,[(p - 1)(q - r)(r - p) + (r - 1)(p - q)]$$

$$= 2a_1 \times 0 + d \times 0 = 0$$

Example 9 **: If the sum of *m* terms of an A.P. is the same as the sum of its *n* terms. Show that the sum of its (*m* + *n*) terms is zero.**

Solution : Let a be the first term and d be the common difference.

Given $S_m = S_n$

$$\therefore \quad \frac{m}{2}\left[2a + (m-1)d\right] = \frac{n}{2}\left[2a + (n-1)d\right]$$

$$2a\,(m - n) + [m\,(m - 1) - n\,(n - 1)]\,d = 0$$

$$2a\,(m - n) + [(m^2 - n^2) - (m - n)]\,d = 0$$

$$(m - n)\,[2a + (m + n - 1)\,d] = 0$$

Since $m - n \neq 0$

$$\therefore \quad 2a + (m + n - 1)\,d = 0$$

By definition $S_{m+n} = \dfrac{(m+n)}{2}\left[2a + (m+n-1)d\right]$

$$\therefore \quad S_{m+n} = \frac{(m+n)}{2}[0] = 0$$

Hence proved.

Example 10 **: The ratio of the sum of *n* terms of two A.P.'s is (7*n* + 1) : (4*n* + 27). Find the ratio of their m^{th} terms.**

Solution : Let a_1, a_2 be the first terms and d_1, d_2 be common difference of two given A.P.'s.

$$S_n = \frac{n}{2}\left[2a_1 + (n-1)d_1\right]$$

$$S_n^{1} = \frac{n}{2}\left[2a_2 + (n-1)d_2\right]$$

Given $\dfrac{S_n}{S_n^{1}} = \dfrac{2a_1 + (n-1)d_1}{2a_2 + (n-1)d_2} = \dfrac{(7n+1)}{(4n+27)}$

In order to find ratio of the mth term, replace n with $(2m - 1)$ is the above equation.

$$\therefore \quad \frac{2a_1 + (2m-2)d_1}{2a_2 + (2m-2)d_2} = \frac{(7(2m-1)+1)}{(4(2m-1)+27)}$$

$$\therefore \quad \frac{a_1 + (m-1)d_1}{a_2 + (m-1)d_2} = \frac{14m-6}{8m+23}$$

∴ Ratio of mth terms of two A.P.'s is $(14m - 6) : (8m + 23)$

INSERTION OF ARITHMETIC MEANS

(*i*) Insertion of n Arithmetic Means between a and b.

Let $A_1, A_2, ..., A_n$ be n arithmetic means between a and b

∴ $a, A_1, A_2, ... A_n\ b$ is an $A.P.$

Let d be common difference.

The series contains $(n + 2)$ terms

∴ $b = (n+2)^{th}$ term $= a + (n+1)d$

$$\therefore \quad d = \frac{b-a}{(n+1)}$$

$$\therefore \quad A_1 = a + d = a + \frac{(b-a)}{(n+1)}$$

Likewise $A_n = a + \dfrac{n(b-a)}{(n+1)}$

(*ii*) Insertion of Single Arithmetic Mean between a and b.

Let A be arithmetic mean of a an b. Then

a, A, b are in A.P.

$A - a = b - A$

$$\therefore \quad 2A = a + b \quad \Rightarrow \quad A = \frac{(a+b)}{2}$$

***Example 11 :* Insert 4 A.M.s between 4 and 19.**

Solution : Let A_1, A_2, A_3, A_4 be four $A.M.s$

∴ $4, A_1, A_2, A_3, A_4, 18$

Let d be common difference between each term.

$$d = \frac{b-a}{(n+1)} = \frac{19-4}{(4+1)} = \frac{15}{5} = 3$$

$A_1 = a + d = 4 + 3 = 7$

$A_2 = a + 2d = 4 + 2(3) = 10$

$$A_3 = a + 3d = 4 + 3(3) = 13$$

$$A_4 = a + 4d = 4 + 4(3) = 16.$$

Example 12 : **For what value of n, $\frac{a^{n+1} + b^{n+1}}{a^n + b^n}$ is the arithmetic mean of a and b?**

Solution : A.M. of a and b $= \frac{a + b}{2}$

Given $$\frac{a^{n+1} + b^{n+1}}{a^n + b^n} = \frac{a + b}{2}$$

$$2(a^{n+1} + b^{n+1}) = (a + b)(a^n + b^n)$$

$$2a^{n+1} + 2b^{n+1} = a^{n+1} + ab^n + ba^n + b^{n+1}$$

$$a^{n+1} + b^{n+1} = ab^n + ba^n$$

$$a^n (a - b) = b^n (a - b)$$

$\therefore$ $$a^n = b^n$$

$\therefore$ $$\left(\frac{a}{b}\right)^n = 1$$

This implies $$n = 0$$

Example 13 : **There are n A.M.s between 3 and 17. The ratio of last mean to the first mean is 3 : 1. Find the value of n.**

Solution : Let $A_1, A_2, ..., A_n$ be n A.M's between 3 and 17.

Common difference $$d = \frac{b - a}{n + 1} = \frac{17 - 3}{n + 1} = \frac{14}{n + 1}$$

$\therefore$ $$A_1 = 3 + d = 3 + \frac{14}{(n + 1)}$$

$$A_n = 3 + nd = 3 + \frac{14n}{(n + 1)}$$

$\therefore$ $$A_1 = \frac{3n + 17}{(n + 1)}, \quad A_n = \frac{3 + 17n}{(n + 1)}$$

Given $$\frac{A_n}{A_1} = \frac{3}{1}.$$

$$\frac{(3 + 17n)/(n + 1)}{(3n + 17)/(n + 1)} = \frac{3}{1}$$

$\therefore$ $$(3 + 17n) = 3(3n + 17)$$

$$3 + 17n = 9n + 51$$

$$8n = 48$$

$$n = 6$$

Example 14 : **Insert A.M.s between 7 and 71 in such a way that the 5th A.M. is 27. Find the number of A.M.s.**

Solution : Common difference

$$d = \frac{b-a}{(n+1)} = \frac{(71-7)}{(n+1)} = \frac{64}{(n+1)}$$

Given $A_5 = 27$

$$\therefore \quad A_5 = a + 5d = \frac{7 + 5(64)}{(n+1)}$$

$$27 = 7 + \frac{320}{(n+1)}$$

$$20(n+1) = 320$$

$$20n = 300$$

$$n = 15.$$

Example 15 : **In *a*, *b*, *c* are in A.P., prove that the following are also in A.P.**

(*i*) $b + c, c + a, a + b$;

(*ii*) $\frac{1}{bc}, \frac{1}{ca}, \frac{1}{ab}$;

(*iii*) $\frac{1}{\sqrt{b}+\sqrt{c}}, \frac{1}{\sqrt{c}+\sqrt{a}}, \frac{1}{\sqrt{a}+\sqrt{b}}$.

Solution : (*i*) If $b + c, c + a, a + b$ are in A.P.

therefore $(c + a) - (b + c) = (a + b) - (c + a)$

$$\Rightarrow \quad a - b = b - c$$

$$\Rightarrow \quad a + c = 2b$$

Since, it is given *a*, *b*, *c* are in A.P., the relation is proved.

(*ii*) Given *a*, *b*, *c* are in A.P.

Divide each term by *abc*, we have

$$\frac{a}{abc}; \frac{b}{abc}, \frac{c}{abc}$$

$$\therefore \quad \frac{1}{bc}, \frac{1}{ac}, \frac{1}{ab} \text{ are in A.P.}$$

(*iii*) $\frac{1}{\sqrt{b}+\sqrt{c}}, \frac{1}{\sqrt{a}+\sqrt{c}}, \frac{1}{\sqrt{a}+\sqrt{b}}$ will be in A.P.

if $$\frac{1}{\sqrt{c}+\sqrt{a}} - \frac{1}{\sqrt{b}+\sqrt{c}} = \frac{1}{\sqrt{a}+\sqrt{b}} - \frac{1}{\sqrt{c}+\sqrt{a}}$$

$$\frac{\sqrt{b}-\sqrt{a}}{\left(\sqrt{c}+\sqrt{a}\right)\left(\sqrt{b}+\sqrt{c}\right)}=\frac{\sqrt{c}-\sqrt{b}}{\left(\sqrt{a}+\sqrt{b}\right)\left(\sqrt{c}+\sqrt{a}\right)}$$

$$\Rightarrow \quad \frac{\sqrt{b}-\sqrt{a}}{\sqrt{b}+\sqrt{c}}=\frac{\sqrt{c}-\sqrt{b}}{\sqrt{a}+\sqrt{b}}$$

$$\Rightarrow \quad b-a=c-b$$

$$\Rightarrow \quad 2b=a+c.$$

Since a, b, c are in A.P., hence relation is proved.

***Example 16 :* If $\frac{1}{b+c}, \frac{1}{c+a}, \frac{1}{a+b}$ are in A.P. Prove that a^2, b^2, c^2 are also in A.P.**

Solution : Given $\frac{1}{b+c}, \frac{1}{c+a}, \frac{1}{a+b}$ are in A.P.

$$\therefore \quad \frac{1}{c+a}-\frac{1}{b+c}=\frac{1}{a+b}-\frac{1}{c+a}$$

$$\frac{b+c-c-a}{(c+a)(b+c)}=\frac{c+a-a-b}{(a+b)(c+a)}$$

$$\frac{(b-a)}{(c+a)(b+c)}=\frac{(c-b)}{(a+b)(c+a)}$$

$$\frac{(b-a)}{(b+c)}=\frac{(c-b)}{(a+b)}$$

$$b^2-a^2=c^2-b^2$$

This implies a^2, b^2, c^2 are in A.P.

***Example 17 :* *XYZ* Ltd. produced 600 units during 3rd year of its operation. The company maintained its constant growth of production and produced 700 units in the 7th year. Find the initial production in the first year.**

Solution : Let 'a_1' be the initial production and 'd' be the constant growth of production.

Given $a_3 = 600$, $a_7 = 700$

Using Arithmetic Progression, we have

$$a_3 = 600 = a_1 + (3-1)d$$

$$a_7 = 700 = a_1 + (7-1)d$$

$$\therefore \quad 600 = a_1 + 2d \qquad ...(1)$$

$$700 = a_2 + 6d \qquad ...(2)$$

Subtracting (1) from (2), we have

$$100 = 4d$$

$$\therefore \quad d = 25$$

Substituting this value of 'd' in equation (1), we have

$$a_1 = 550$$

$\therefore$ Initial Production = 550 units.

Example 18 : **Mr X was drawing Rs. 400 a month during 11th year of his service, and Rs. 760 during the 29th year. The past record shows that his salary has increased annually in Arithmatical Progression. Find**

(*i*) Starting Salary of *X*;

(*ii*) Annual Increment;

(*iii*) Salary at the time of retirement, if *X* will retire on completion of 40 years of service.

Solution : Given $a_{11} = 400$, $a_{29} = 760$

Let a, be starting Salary and 'd' be annual increment.

Using A.P., we have

$$a_{11} = 400 = a_1 + 10\,d \quad \text{...(1)}$$

$$a_{29} = 760 = a_1 + 28d \quad \text{...(2)}$$

Subtracting (1) from (2), we have

$$360 = 18d$$

$$\therefore \quad d = 20$$

Substituting $d = 20$ in (1), we have

$$a_1 = 200$$

Salary at the time of retirement will be

$$a_{40} = 200 + (40 - 1)(20)$$

$$a_{40} = 980.$$

Example 19 : **Mr *X* saved Rs. 18500 in 10 years. In each year after the first he saved Rs. 200 more than he did in the preceding year. How much did he save in the first year.**

Solution : Let 'a', be the amount saved in the first year.

Using Arithmetic progression, we have

$$S_n = \frac{n}{2}\left[2a_1 + (n-1)d\right]$$

$$\therefore \quad 18500 = \frac{10}{2}\left[2a_1 + (10-1)200\right]$$

$$\therefore \quad 2a_1 = 1900$$

$$a_1 = 950.$$

Example 20 : **A money lender lends Rs. 1500 and charges Rs. 240 as overall interest. The amount was recovered in 12 equal instalment each less by Rs. 10 than the preceding one. Find the amount of first instalment.**

Solution : Let 'a' be the amount of first instalment.

Using A.P., we have

$$S_n = \frac{n}{2}[2a_1 + (n-1)d]$$

$$1740 = \frac{12}{2}[2a_1 + (12-1)(-10)]$$

$$1740 = 12a_1 - 660$$

$$\therefore \quad 12a_1 = 2400$$

$$a_1 = 200.$$

Example 21 : **Mr *X* borrowed interest free loan of Rs. 12000 from *Y*. The loan is to be repaid in ten installments. Mr *X* paid Rs. 800 as first instalment and then increases each instalment by equal amount over the preceding instalment. What will be the last instalment?**

Solution : Let '*l*' be the last instalment.

Using A.P., we have

$$S_n = \frac{n}{2}[a + l]$$

$$12000 = \frac{10}{2}[800 + l]$$

$$2400 = 800 + l$$

$$\therefore \quad l = 1600$$

Last Instalment = Rs. 1600.

Example 22 : **A lamp lighter has to light 100 gas lamps. He takes 1½ minutes to go from one lamp post to the next. Each lamp post burns 10 c.c. of gas per hour. How many c.c. of gas has been burnt by 8:30 P.M. if he lights the first lamp at 6 P.M.**

Solution : Total time period = 6 P.M. to 8:30 P.M. = 150 minutes.

$$S_n = \frac{25}{3}(300 - 1.5 \times 33) = 1262.25 \text{ c.c.}$$

Example 23 : **The monthly salary of a person was Rs. 320 for each of the first three years. He next got annual increments of Rs. 40 per month for each of the following successive 12 years. His Salary remained stationary till retirement when he found that his average monthly salary during the service period was Rs. 698. Find the period of his service.**

Solution : Let *n* be the total number of year of the person's service.

$\therefore$ Total Salary = 12 . n . 698 ...(1)

Total Salary in first three years = $320 \times 3 \times 12 = 960 \times 12$

Monthly Salary for 4th year = 360

Likewise Salary for 5th year = 400

We may conclude there would be A.P.,

$a = 360,\ d = 40,\ n = 12$

$\therefore$ Total Salary for next 12 years $= 12 \times \left[\frac{12}{2}\left[720 + 11(40)\right]\right]$

$= 12 \times 6\ (720 + 440)$

$= 12 \times 6960$

At the end of 12 years, his monthly Salary was

$\Rightarrow \quad 360 + (12 - 1)\ 40 = \text{Rs. } 800.$

He got Rs. 800 p.m. for the remaining period $(n - 15)$.

$\therefore$ Total Salary throughout his Service period

$= 12\ [960 + 6960 + 800\ (n - 15)]$

$= 12\ [800n - 4080]$ ...(2)

Comparing (1) and (11)

$12n \times 698 = 12\ (800n - 4080)$

$102\ n = 4080$

$n = 40$ years.

Example 24 : **B arranges to pay a debt of Rs. 9600 in 48 annual instalments which form an arithmetic series. When 40 of these instalments are paid, B becomes insolvent and his creditor, finds that Rs. 2400 still remains unpaid. Find the value of each of first three instalments of B ignore interest.**

Solution : Given $S_n = 9600\ n = 48$

$\therefore \quad 9600 = \frac{48}{2}\left[2a + (48 - 1)\,d\right] \Rightarrow 2a + 47d = 400$ ...(1)

Amount already paid through 40 instalments $= 9600 - 2400 = 7200$

$\therefore \quad 7200 = \frac{48}{2}\left[2a + (40 - 1)\,d\right] \Rightarrow 2a + 39d = 360$ ...(2)

Solving (1) & (2), we have $a = 82.50,\ d = 5$.

$\therefore$ First three instalment are Rs. 82.50, Rs. 87.50 and Rs. 92.50.

Example 25 : **A piece of equipment cost a certain factory Rs. 6,00,000. If it depreciates in value, 15% the first year, 13½% the next year 12% the third year, and so on, what will be its value at the end of 10 years, all percentages applying to original cost.**

Solution : The rates of depreciation are in A.P. with common difference $-$ 1.5 and $a = 15$.

$\therefore$ 10th year depreciation $= 15 + (10 - 1)\ (-1.5)$

$= 15 - 13.5 = 1.5$

Assume original cost of equipment $= 100$

$\therefore$ Depreciation for first year $= 15$

and Depreciation for 10th year $= 1.5 = \dfrac{3}{2}$

$\therefore$ Total Depreciation during 10 years $= \dfrac{10}{2}(15 + 1.5)$

$$= \frac{165}{2}$$

$\therefore$ Value of equipment at the end of 10 years $= 100 - \dfrac{165}{2} = \dfrac{35}{2}$

$\therefore$ Value of equipment costing 600000 at the end of 10 year

$$= \frac{600000}{100} \times \frac{35}{2} = 105000.$$

Example 26 : **80 coins are placed in a straight line on the ground. The distance between any two consecutive coins is 10 metres. How far must a person travel to bring then one by one to a basket placed 10 metres behind the first coin.**

Solution : Time taken to bring back Ist coin $= 10 + 10 = 20$

Time taken to bring back IInd coin $= 20 + 20 = 40$

Time taken to bring back IIIrd coin $= 30 + 30 = 60$

$\therefore$ there is A.P. with $a = 20$ and $d = 20$.

Total distance covered $S_n = \dfrac{n}{2}[2a + (n-1)d]$

$$= \frac{80}{2}[2(20) + (80-1)(20)]$$

$$= 40(40 + 1580) = 64800.$$

GEOMETRIC PROGRESSION

It is a series of numbers where each number is related to its preceding or succeeding number with a common ratio. For example 2, 4, 8, 16, ... In this case, the common ratio is 2. Each number can be derived by multiplying its preceding number with 2.

(*i*) Finding n^{th} term of a G.P.

The nth term of G.P. is given as

$$t_n = ar^{n-1}$$

where a = first term

r = common ratio

(*ii*) Finding the sum of first n terms of a G.P.

$$S_n = \frac{a(1-r^n)}{(1-r)} \quad [r \neq 1]$$

For $r = 1$, $S_n = na$

The sum of an infinite G.P. is given by

$$S_n = \frac{a}{1-r}$$

Example 27 : **Find the 9th term of G.P.**

$$\frac{1}{4}, -\frac{1}{2}, 1, -2$$

Solution : $T_n = ar^{n-1}$

$$a = \frac{1}{4} \qquad r = \frac{\text{Second term}}{\text{First term}} = \frac{-1/2}{1/4} = -2$$

$$T_9 = \frac{1}{4}(-2)^{9-1} = 64$$

Example 28 : **Which term of the G.P.**

5, 10, 20, ... is 5120

Solution : Given $a = 5$, $r = \frac{10}{5} = 2$

Let 5120 be n^{th} term

$$t_n = ar^{n-1}$$

$\therefore$ $5120 = 5(2)^{n-1}$

$\therefore$ $2^{n-1} = 1024 = 2^{10}$

$\therefore$ $n - 1 = 10 \Rightarrow n = 11$

Example 29 : **The 4th and 9th terms of a G.P. are 54 and 13122 respectively. Find the G.P.**

Solution : Given $t_4 = 54 = ar^3$ ...(1)

$t_9 = 13122 = ar^8$ ...(2)

Dividing (2) by (1), we have

$$r^5 = 243$$

$\therefore$ $r = 3$

$\therefore$ $54 = a(3)^3$

$\Rightarrow$ $a = 2$

$\therefore$ G.P. is 2, 6, 18, ...

Example 30 : **Find the sum of 10 terms of the G.P.**

1, 1/2, 1/4, 1/8, ...

Solution : Given a = 1, r = 1/2

$$\therefore \quad S_n = a.\left[\frac{r^n - 1}{r - 1}\right]$$

$$S_{10} = 1.\left[\frac{(1/2)^{10} - 1}{1/2 - 1}\right] = \frac{1023}{512}$$

Example 31 : **How many terms of G.P. 1 + 4 + 16 + 64 + ... will make the sum 5461?**

Solution : Given $a = 1$, $r = 4$, $S_n = 5461$

$$S_n = \frac{a\left[r^n - 1\right]}{\left[r - 1\right]}$$

$$5461 = \frac{1.\left[4^n - 1\right]}{\left[4 - 1\right]}$$

$$\therefore \quad 4^n - 1 = 16383$$

$$4^n = 16384$$

$$4^n = 47$$

$$\therefore \quad n = 7.$$

Example 32 : **(*i*) Find the sum of series**

7 + 77 + 777 + ... + *n* terms

Solution : Given

$$7 + 77 + 777 + ... + n \text{ terms}$$

$$7\left[1 + 11 + 111 + ... + n\right]$$

$$\frac{7}{9}\left[9 + 99 + 999 + ... + n\right]$$

$$\frac{7}{9}\left[(10 - 1) + (100 - 1) + (1000 - 1) + ... + 10^n - 1\right]$$

$$\therefore \quad \frac{7}{9}\left[\left(10 + 10^2 + 10^3 + ... + 10^n\right) - (1 + 1 + 1 + ... + n \text{ times})\right]$$

$$= \frac{7}{9}\left[10 \times \frac{\left(10^n - 1\right)}{(10 - 1)} - n\right]$$

$$= \frac{7}{81}\left[10^{n+1} - 10 - 9n\right]$$

Example 33 : **Find the sum of 0.7 + 0.77 + 0.777 ... + n terms.**

Solution :

$$S_n = 0.7 + 0.77 + 0.777 + ... + n \text{ terms}$$

$$= 7[0.1 + 0.11 + 0.111 + ... + n \text{ terms}]$$

$$= \frac{7}{9}[0.9 + 0.99 + 0.999 + ... + n \text{ terms}]$$

$$= \frac{7}{9}[(1 - 0.1) + (1 - 0.01) + (1 - 0.001) + ... + n \text{ terms}]$$

$$= \frac{7}{9}\left[\left(1 - \frac{1}{10}\right) + \left(1 - \frac{1}{10^2}\right) + \left(1 - \frac{1}{10^3}\right) + ... n \text{ terms}\right]$$

$$= \frac{7}{9}\left[n - \frac{1}{10} \cdot \frac{1 - \left(\frac{1}{10}\right)^n}{1 - \left(\frac{1}{10}\right)}\right]$$

$$= \frac{7}{9}\left[n - \frac{1}{9}\left(1 - \frac{1}{10^n}\right)\right]$$

Example 34 : **Find the sum to infinity of the G.P.**

$$\frac{-5}{4}, \frac{5}{16}, \frac{-5}{64}, ...$$

Solution : Given

$$a = \frac{-5}{4}$$

$$r = -\frac{1}{4}$$

$$S_\alpha = \frac{a}{1 - r} = \frac{-5/4}{1 - (-1/4)} = -1$$

Example 35 : **Prove that $6^{1/2} . 6^{1/4} . 6^{1/8}$ ..... $\alpha = 6$**

Solution : We have

$$6^{1/2} . 6^{1/4} . 6^{1/8} .... \alpha$$

$$= 6^{\left[\frac{1}{2} + \frac{1}{4} + \frac{1}{8} + ... + \alpha\right]}$$

$$= 6^{[1/2/(1-1/2)]} = 6^{[1/2/1/2]} = 6^1$$

Example 36 : **The sum of an infinite G.P. is 8, its second term is 2, find the first term.**

Solution : Let 'a' be the first term and r is the common ratio. Then

$$S_\alpha = 8 \quad \text{and} \quad ar = 2$$

$$\frac{a}{1-r} = 8$$

$$r = \frac{2}{a}$$

$$\frac{a}{1-\left(\frac{2}{a}\right)} = 8$$

$$a^2 - 8a + 16 = 0$$

$$(a-4)^2 = 0$$

$$a = 4$$

INSERTION OF GEOMETRIC MEANS BETWEEN TWO GIVEN NUMBERS

(*i*) Insertion of N Geometric means between two given numbers a and b.

Let $G_1, G_2, \ldots G_n$ be n geometric means between two given numbers a and b.

$\therefore$ $a, G_1, G_2, \ldots, G_n, b$ consist of $(n + z)$ terms.

$$b = (n+2)^{\text{th}} \text{ term} = ar^{n+1}$$

$$\therefore \quad r = \left(\frac{b}{a}\right)^{1/n+1}$$

$$G_1 = ar = a\left(\frac{b}{a}\right)^{1/n+1}$$

$$G_2 = ar^2 = a\left(\frac{b}{a}\right)^{2/n+1}$$

Likewise $G_n = a\left(\frac{b}{a}\right)^{n/n+1}$

***Example 37 :* Insert 5 GMs between 576 and 9.**

Solution : Let G_1, G_2, G_3, G_4, G_5 be GMs between 576 and 9.

$$\therefore \quad r = \left(\frac{b}{a}\right)^{1/n+1} = \left(\frac{9}{576}\right)^{1/5+1} = \left(\frac{1}{64}\right)^{1/6} = \frac{1}{2}$$

$$\therefore \quad G_1 = ar = 576 \times \frac{1}{2} = 288$$

$$G_2 = ar^2 = 576 \times \frac{1}{2} \times \frac{1}{2} = 144$$

$$G_3 = 72, \; G_4 = 36, \; G_5 = 18$$

Example 38 : **The sum of three numbers in G.P. is 35 and their product is 1000. Find the numbers.**

Solution : Let the numbers be $\frac{a}{2}$, a, ar

$\therefore$ Their product $a^3 = 1000$

$\therefore$ $a = 10$

$\therefore$ Numbers are $\frac{10}{r}$, 10, $10r$.

Given Sum of numbers = 35

$$\therefore \quad \frac{10}{r} + 10 + 10r = 35$$

$$2r^2 - 5r + 2 = 0$$

$$r = 2, \frac{1}{2}$$

$\therefore$ Numbers are 5, 10, 20 or 20, 10, 5.

Example 39 : **If *S* is the sum, *P* the product and *R* the sum of reciprocals of *n* terms in G.P., prove that**

$$P^2R^n = S^n$$

Solution : Let $a, ar, ar^2, \ldots$ be the given G.P.

$$\therefore \quad S = a + ar + ar^2 + \ldots + ar^n$$

$$= a\frac{\left(1 - r^n\right)}{(1 - r)} \qquad \ldots(1)$$

$$P = a \,.\, ar \,.\, ar^2 \ldots ar^{n-1}$$

$$= a^n\, r^{0 + 1 + 2 + \ldots + n - 1}$$

$$= a^n r^{\frac{(n-1)(n)}{2}} \qquad \ldots(2)$$

$$R = \frac{1}{a} + \frac{1}{ar} + \frac{1}{ar^2} + \ldots + n \text{ terms}$$

$$= \frac{\frac{1}{a}\left(1 - \frac{1}{r^n}\right)}{(1 - 1/r)} \Rightarrow \frac{\left(1 - r^n\right)}{a(1 - r)r^{n-1}} \qquad \ldots(3)$$

Using (2) and (3), we have $P^2R^n = \dfrac{a^{2n} r^{n(n-1)} \left(1 - r^n\right)^n}{a^n (1 - r)^n r^{n(n-1)}}$

$$= \frac{a^n\left(1-r^n\right)^n}{(1-r)^n} = S^n$$

Hence proved.

Example 40 : **For three consecutive months, a person deposits some amount of money on the first day of each month in small savings fund. These three successive amounts in the deposit, the total value of which is Rs. 65, form a G.P. If the two extreme amounts be multiplied each by 3 and the mean by 5, the products form an A.P. Find the amount in the first and second deposits.**

Solution : Let the three successive deposits be Rs. a, Rs. ar and Rs. ar^2.

$\therefore \quad a + ar + ar^2 = 65$

Also give $3a$, $5ar$ and $3ar^2$ form an A.P.

$\therefore \quad 3a - 5ar = 5ar - 3ar^2$

$\Rightarrow \quad 3ar^2 - 10ar + 3a = 0$

$(r - 3)(3r - 1) = 0$

$\Rightarrow \quad r = 3,\ r = 1/3$

When $r = 3$, $a = 5$ and the amounts are Rs. 5, Rs. 15, Rs. 45.

When $r = 1/3$, $a = 45$ and the amounts are Rs. 45, Rs. 15 and Rs. 5.

HARMONIC PROGRESSION

Harmonic progression is a sequence or series of terms whose reciprocals form arithmetic progression. For example, if $a, b, c....$ are in harmonic progression then $\frac{1}{a}, \frac{1}{b}, \frac{1}{c}$......... are in arithmetic progression.

For example, the number $\frac{1}{3}, \frac{1}{5}, \frac{1}{7}, \frac{1}{9}$......... are in H.P, since 3, 5, 7, 9.....are is A.P.

Example 41 : If a, b, c are in H.P., show that

$$\frac{a}{b+c}, \frac{b}{c+a}, \frac{c}{a+b} \text{ are also is H.P.}$$

Solution : Given a, b, c are in H.P.

$\therefore \quad \frac{1}{a}, \frac{1}{b}, \frac{1}{c}$ are in H.P.

$\therefore$ Multiplying all terms with $a + b + c$, we have

$$\frac{a+b+c}{a}, \frac{a+b+c}{b}, \frac{a+b+c}{c} \text{ are in A.P.}$$

$$1 + \frac{b+c}{a}, 1 + \frac{a+c}{b}, 1 + \frac{a+b}{c} \text{ are in A.P.}$$

$\therefore \quad \frac{b+c}{a}, \frac{a+c}{b}, \frac{a+b}{c}$ are in A.P.

This implies

$$\frac{a}{(b+c)}, \frac{b}{(a+c)}, \frac{c}{(a+b)} \text{ are in H.P.}$$

The general form of Harmonic progression is given as

$$\frac{1}{a}, \frac{1}{a+d}, \frac{1}{a+2d}, \ldots\ldots\ldots\ldots$$

The nth *term of a* Harmonic Progression is given as

$$t_n = \frac{1}{(n\text{th term of the corresponding A.P.})}$$

$$t_n = \frac{1}{a+(n-1)d}$$

where a is first term and d is the common difference.

Based on above facts, following problems can be solved.

Example 41(a) : **Find the 7th term of H.P.** $\frac{1}{3}, \frac{1}{5}, \frac{1}{7} \ldots\ldots$

Solution : Here $a = 3$, $d = 5 - 3 = 2$ $n = 7$

$$t_7 = \frac{1}{3+(7-1).2} = \frac{1}{15}$$

$\therefore \quad$ 7th term is $\frac{1}{15}$.

Example 42 : Find the 9th term of harmonic progression

$$\frac{1}{4}, \frac{1}{9}, \frac{1}{14} \ldots\ldots\ldots\ldots$$

Solution : The nth term of H.P. is given as

$$t_n = \frac{1}{a+(n-1)d}$$

The reciprocal terms of the seris will be 4, 9, 14....*i.e.* in form of Arthmetic progression (A.P.), where first term $a = 4$ and common difference $d = 9 - 4 = 5$.

$\therefore \quad$ n^{th} term will be $t_n = 4 + (n - 1) .5$

Subsituting $n = 9$,

We have $\quad t_9 = 4 + (9 - 1) 5$

$= 4 + 40 = 44$

The reciprocal term will be $\frac{1}{44}$

$\therefore$ 9th term of H.P. $= \frac{1}{44}$.

Insertion of harmonic progression terms between two terms.

Let x and y be two given numbers. Let h_1; h_2....., h_n be the 'n' terms to be inserted between x and y. Then, the reciprocal terms

$$\frac{1}{x}, \frac{1}{h_1}, \frac{1}{h_2}, \ldots\ldots, \frac{1}{h_n}, \frac{1}{y}$$

are in A.P. with first term 'a' as $\frac{1}{x}$; commons difference 'd' and last term is $(n + 2)^{th}$ *i.e.* $\frac{1}{y}$.

The $(n + 2)^{th}$ term will be given as

$$\frac{1}{y} = \frac{1}{a} + (n + 2 - 1)\,d = \frac{1}{x} + (n + 1)\,d$$

$$\therefore \quad d = \frac{(x - y)}{xy\,(n + 1)}$$

$$\therefore \quad \frac{1}{h_1} = \frac{1}{x} + \frac{(x - y)}{xy\,(n + 1)},\ \frac{1}{h_2} = \frac{1}{h_1} + d = \frac{y\,(n - 1) + 2x}{xy\,(n + 1)}$$

Similarly $\quad \frac{1}{h_n} = \frac{y + x.n}{xy\,(n + 1)}$.

Example 43 : Insert 3 terms between $\frac{1}{2}$ and $\frac{1}{14}$ if the given series is in harmonic progression.

Solution : Given harmonic progression series.

$\therefore$ Arithmetic progression will be 2,....., 14. where first term = 2 and the value of common difference can be calulated usign n^{th} term formula.

Since '14' in this case is 5th term,

$$\therefore \quad 14 = a + (5–1)\,d = 2 + 4d$$

$$d = 3$$

$$\therefore \quad t_2 = a + d = 2 + 3 = 5$$

$$t_3 = t_2 + d = 5 + 3 = 8$$

$$t_4 = t_3 + d = 8 + 3 = 11$$

$\therefore$ The three terms between $\frac{1}{2}$ to $\frac{1}{14}$ are $\frac{1}{5}, \frac{1}{8}, \frac{1}{11}$.

Objective Type Questions

Q 1. The 16th term of an A.P. defined by 9, 12, 15, 18........... is

(*i*) 50 (*ii*) 52 (*iii*) 54 (*iv*) 56

Q 2. Which term of the sequence 72, 70, 68, 66........ is 40

(*i*) 16 (*ii*) 17 (*iii*) 15 (*iv*) 20

Q 3. The number of terms in A.P. 3, 6, 9, 12, ... 111 is

(*i*) 30 (*ii*) 32 (*iii*) 35 (*iv*) 37

Q 4. The first negative term of the A.P. 20, $19\frac{1}{4}$, $18\frac{1}{2}$, $17\frac{3}{4}$, ... is

(*i*) 27 (*ii*) 30 (*iii*) 31 (*iv*) 28

Q 5. The term of the A.P. $8 - 6i$, $7 - 4i$, $6 - 2i$, ... which is purely real

(*i*) 4 (*ii*) 6 (*iii*) 7 (*iv*) 8

Q 6. The two digit numbers that are divisible by 7 are

(*i*) 10 (*ii*) 11 (*iii*) 12 (*iv*) 13

Q 7. In A.P. 3, 7, 11, ... 407, the 20th term from the end will be

(*i*) 330 (*ii*) 331 (*iii*) 332 (*iv*) 340

Q 8. The 6th and 7th term of an A.P. are 19 and 41 respectively, the 40th term would be

(*i*) 80 (*ii*) 82 (*iii*) 84 (*iv*) 86

Q 9. The sum of all odd, intigers between 2 and 100 divisible by 3 is

(*i*) 800 (*ii*) 860 (*iii*) 867 (*iv*) 870

Q 10. The value of x in A.P. 1 + 6 11 + 16 + ... + x = 148 would be

(*i*) 30 (*ii*) 32 (*iii*) 34 (*iv*) 36

Q 11. The 9th term of the progression is

(*i*) 60 (*ii*) 62 (*iii*) 64 (*iv*) 70

Q 12. The 4th term from the end of the G.P. 3, 6, 12, 24............ 3072 is

(*i*) 370 (*ii*) 350 (*iii*) 382 (*iv*) 384

Q 13. In G.P. 2, 1, $\frac{1}{2}$, $\frac{1}{4}$, ... which term is $\frac{1}{128}$?

(*i*) 10 (*ii*) 9 (*iii*) 8 (*iv*) 12

Q 14. The first term of a G.P. is 1. The sum of 3rd and 5th term is 90. The common ratio would be

(*i*) $r = \pm 2$ (*ii*) $r = \pm 3$ (*iii*) $r = 3$, (*iv*) $r = 2$

Q 15. The 3rd term of a G.P. is 4. The product of first five terms would be

(*i*) 2^5 (*ii*) 3^5 (*iii*) 4^5 (*iv*) 5^5

Q 16. The three number in G.P. whose sum is 38 and product is 1728

(*i*) $3, \frac{9}{4}, \frac{27}{8}$ (*ii*) 6, 14, 36 (*iii*) 12, 24, 36 (*iv*) 8, 12, 18

Q 17. The sum of 7 terms of G.P. 3, 6, 12, ... is

(*i*) 300 (*ii*) 350 (*iii*) 378 (*iv*) 381

Q 18. The number of terms in G.P. 1 + 4 + 16 + 64 .... will mate the sum 5461

(*i*) 7 (*ii*) 8 (*iii*) 10 (*iv*) 12

Q 19. The rational number whose decimal expansion is 0.423

(*i*) $\frac{419}{990}$ (*ii*) $\frac{420}{999}$ (*iii*) $\frac{400}{990}$ (*iv*) $\frac{920}{900}$

Q 20. The value of $9^{1/3}, 9^{1/9}, 9^{1/27}$ .... ¥ is

(*i*) 27 (*ii*) 9 (*iii*) 36 (*iv*) 3

Answers

1. (*iii*)	2. (*ii*)	3. (*iv*)	4. (*i*)	5. (*i*)
6. (*iv*)	7. (*ii*)	8. (*iii*)	9. (*iii*)	10. (*iv*)
11. (*iii*)	12. (*iv*)	13. (*ii*)	14. (*ii*)	15. (*iii*)
16. (*iv*)	17. (*iv*)	18. (*i*)	19. (*i*)	20. (*iv*)

Exercise 17.1

1. Find

(*i*) 10th term of the A.P. 1, 4, 7, ...

(*ii*) 16th term of the A.P. 9, 12, 15, ... [(*i*) 28, (*ii*) 54]

2.

(*i*) The 6th and 7th terms of an A.P. are 19 and 41 respectively, find the 40th term.

(*ii*) The 10th and 18th terms of an A.P. are 41 and 73 respectively, find 26th term.

[(*i*) 87, (*ii*) 105]

3. How many terms are there in the sequence

(*i*) 3, 6, 9, ..., 111

(*ii*) $-1, -\frac{5}{6}, \frac{-2}{3}, ..., \frac{10}{3}.$ **[(*i*) 37, (*ii*) 27]**

4. Find the sum of the following arithmatical progressian.

(*i*) 49, 44, 39, ... upto to 17 terms.

(*ii*) 50, 46, 42, ... upto to 10 terms.

(*iii*) 41, 36, 31, ... upto to 12 terms. [(*i*) 153, (*ii*) 320, (*iii*) 162]

5. If a, b, c are in A.P. then show that

(*i*) $b + c - a, c + a - b, a + b - c$ are in A.P.

(*ii*) $a^2 (b + c), b^2 (c + a), c^2 (a + b)$ are in A.P.

6. Insert three arithmetic means between 3 and 19. [7, 11, 15]

7. Insert six A.M.s between 15 and – 13. [11, 7, 3, – 1, – 5, – 9]

8. Mr X repays a loan of Rs. 3250 by paying Rs. 20 in the first month and then increases the payment by Rs. 15 every month. How long will it take him to clear the loan. [$n = 20$]

9. A man saved Rs. 16500 in ten years. In each year after the first he saved Rs. 100 more than he did in the preceding year. How much did he save in the first year? [Rs. 1200]

10. A man secure an interest free loan of Rs. 14500 from a friend and agrees to repay it in ten instalments. He pays Rs. 1000 as first instalment and then increases each instalment by equal amount over the preceding instalment. What will be his last instalment? [Rs. 1900]

11. A manufacturer of T.V. sets produced 600 units in the third year and 700 units in the seventh year. Assuming the product units in the seventh year. Assuming the product increases uniformly by a fixed number every year, find

(*i*) Total product in 7 years.

(*ii*) the product in the 10th year. [(*i*) 4375; (*ii*) 775]

12. Mr. X saves Rs. 32 during the first year and Rs. 36 in the second year. Find the time in which he will be saving Rs. 200, if he increases his savings by Rs. 4 every year. [5 yrs]

13. Mr. X takes a loan of Rs. 2000 from Mr. Y and agrees to repay in number of instalments, each instalment exceeding the previous one by Rs. 10. If the first instalment be Rs. 5, fixed how many instalment will be necessary to wipe out the loan completely. [20]

14. To verify cash balances, the auditor of certain bank, employs his assistant to count cash in hand of Rs. 4500. After he counts quickly at the rate of Rs. 150 per minute for 10 minutes only, at the end of that time he begins to count at the rate of Rs. 2 less every minute than he could count in the previous minute. Ascertain how much time he will take to count this sum of Rs. 4500? [34 minutes]

15. A person pays Rs. 975 by monthly instalments each less than the former by Rs. 5. The first instalment is Rs. 100. In what time the entire amount be paid. [15 months]

16. Find

(*a*) the ninth term of the G.P. 1, 4, 16, 64....

(*b*) the tenth term of the G.P. $\sqrt{2}, \frac{1}{\sqrt{2}}, \frac{1}{2\sqrt{2}}$ $\left[(a)\ 4^8, (b)\ \frac{1}{\sqrt{2}} \times \frac{1}{2^8}\right]$

17. Which term of the G.P. 18, –12, 8, ... is $\frac{512}{729}$ [9]

18. The fourth term of a G.P. is 27 and the 7th term is 729, find the G.P. [1, 3, 9,...]

19. Find the sum of following series

(*i*) 5 + 55 + 555 + ... to *n* terms.

(*ii*) 0.5 + 0.55 + 0.555 + ... + to *n* terms.

20. The fifth term of a G.P. is 81 whereas its second term is 24. Find the series and sum of its first eight terms.

$$\left[a = 16,\ r = 3/2,\ S_8 = \frac{65 \times 97}{8}\right]$$

21. Find the sum of the following series to infinity.

(*i*) $8 + 4\sqrt{2} + 4 + \ldots + \alpha$

(*ii*) $9^{1/3} \cdot 9^{1/9} \cdot 9^{1/27} \ldots \alpha$ $\left[8\left(2 + \sqrt{2}\right), 3\right]$

22. Insert 6 GMs between 27 and $\frac{1}{81}$. $\left[9, 3, 1, \frac{1}{3}, \frac{1}{9}, \frac{1}{27}\right]$

23. If a is the GM of 2 and $\frac{1}{4}$, find a. $\left[1/\sqrt{2}\right]$

24. If a, b, c, d are in G.P., prove that $a + b, b + c, c + d$ are also in G.P.

25. If a, b, c are in G.P., prove that the following are also in G.P.

(*i*) a^2, b^2, c^2

(*ii*) $a^2 + b^2, ab + bc, b^2 + c^2$

26. Find the 8th term of the harmonic progression in fue following cases.

(*a*) $\frac{1}{3}, \frac{1}{8}, \frac{1}{13}, \ldots$

(*b*) $\frac{1}{2}, \frac{1}{6}, \frac{1}{10}, \frac{1}{14}, \ldots$ $\left[\textbf{Ans. } (a)\frac{1}{38}, (b)\frac{7}{30}\right]$

12. Insert four terms between $\frac{1}{5}$ and $\frac{1}{15}$ of harmonic progression. $\left[\textbf{Ans. } \frac{1}{7}, \frac{1}{9}, \frac{1}{11}, \frac{1}{13}\right]$

18

Binomial Theorem

Highlights of the Chapter

- **Introduction**
- **Binomial Theorem for Positive Integral Index**
- **Finding General Term and Middle Term**
- **Finding Greatest Term**
- **Solve Practical Problems**

INTRODUCTION

An algebraic expression which contains two terms is called a binomial expression.

For example, $(a + b)$, $(5x - 3y)$ etc., are binomial expressions.

Likewise, an algebraic expression containing three terms is called a *trinomial.* In general, expressions containing more than two terms are known as multinomial expression.

The general form of the binomial expression is $(x + a)$ and the expansion of $(x + a)^n$, $n \in N$ is called the *binomial theorem.* It gives us formula for the expansion of the powers of a binomial expression. For example,

$$(x + a)^0 = 1$$

$$(x + a)^1 = x + a$$

$$(x + a)^2 = x^2 + 2ax + a^2$$

$$(x + a)^3 = x^3 + 3x^2a + 3xa^2 + a^3$$

It shall be observed that the coefficients in the above expansions follow a particular pattern as shown below :

Index of the binomial	*Coefficients of various terms*
0	1
1	1 1
2	1 2 1
3	1 3 3 1

The pattern has a unique structure because each row is bounded by 1 on both sides and any entry, except the first and last, in a row is the sum of two entries in the preceding row, one on the immediate left and the other on the immediate right. The pattern is known as ***Pascal's triangle***.

BINOMIAL THEOREM FOR POSITIVE INTEGRAL INDEX

If x and a are real numbers, then for all $n \in N$,

$$(x + a)^n = {}^nC_0x^n a^0 + {}^nC_1x^{n-1} a^1 + {}^nC_2x^{n-2} a^2 + \ldots. + {}^nC_rx^{n-r} a^r + \ldots. + {}^nC_{n-1} x^1 a^{n-1} + {}^nC_nx^0 a^n$$

i.e. $$(x + a)^n = \sum_{r=0}^{n} {}^nC_rx^{n-r}a^r$$

Using the above expansion, some important properties relating to binomial expression have been discussed below :

(1) Finding number of terms in the expansion of Binomial expression.

We have

$$(x + a)^n = \sum_{r=0}^{n} {}^nC_rx^{n-r}a^r.$$

$r = 0$

$$= {}^nC_0\, x^n a^0 + {}^nC_1\, x^{n-1} a^1 + {}^nC_2\, x^{n-2} a^2 + \ldots. + {}^nC_r\, x^{n-r} a^r + \ldots + {}^nC_n\, x^0 a^n$$

As r can have values from 0 to n, the total number of terms in the expansion is $(n + 1)$.

If we replace a by $-a$, we will have above expression as

$$(x - a)^n = {}^nC_0\, x^n a^0 - {}^nC_1\, x^{n-1} a^1 + {}^nC_2\, x^{n-2} a^2 - {}^nC_3\, x^{n-3} a^3 + \ldots$$
$$+ (-1)^r\, {}^nC_r\, x^{n-r} a^r + \ldots + (-1)^n\, {}^nC_n\, x^0 a^n.$$

i.e. $$(x + a)^n = \sum_{r=0}^{n} (-1)^r\, {}^nC_rx^{n-r}a^r.$$

Thus, the terms in the expansion of $(x - a)^n$ are alternatively positive and negative, the last term is positive or negative according as n is even or odd.

Substitute $x = 1$ and $a = x$ in the expansion of $(x + a)^n$ we have

$$(1 + x)^n = {}^nC_0 + {}^nC_1x + {}^nC_2x^2 + \ldots + {}^nC_rx^r + \ldots + {}^nC_nx^n$$

i.e. $$(1 + x)^n = \sum_{r=0}^{n} {}^nC_rx^r.$$

This is the expansion of $(1 + x)^n$, we have

$$(1 + x)^n = {}^nC_0x^n + {}^nC_1x^{n-1} + {}^nC_2x^{n-2} + \ldots + {}^nC_rx^{n-r} + \ldots + {}^nC_{n-1}x + {}^nC_n$$

$$(1 + x)^n = \sum_{r=0}^{n} {}^nC_rx^{n-r}$$

This is the expansion of $(1 + x)^n$ in descending powers of x.

Substituting $x = 1$ and $a = -x$ in the expansion of $(x + a)^n$, we get

$$(1 - x)^n = {}^nC_0 - {}^nC_1x + {}^nC_2x^2 - {}^nC_3x^3 + ... + (-1)^r\,{}^nC_rx^r + ... + (-1)^n\,{}^nC_n\,x^n.$$

i.e. $$(1 + x)^n = \sum_{r=0}^{n} (-1)^r\,{}^nC_rx^r.$$

Combining expansion of $(x + a)^n$ and $(x - a)^n$, we have following relationship

$$(x + a)^n + (x - a)^n = 2[{}^nC_0x^n\,a^0 + {}^nC_2x^{n-2}\,a^2 + {}^nC_4\,x^{n-4} + ...]$$

and,

$$(x + a)^n - (x - a)^n = 2[{}^nC_1x^{n-1}\,a^1 + {}^nC_3x^{n-3}\,a^3 + ...]$$

If n is odd than $\{(x + a)^n + (x - a)^n\}$ and $\{(x + a)^n - (x - a)^n\}$ both have the same number of terms equal to $\left(\frac{n+1}{2}\right)$ whereas if n is even, then $\{(x + a)^n + (x - a)^n\}$ has $\left(\frac{n}{2}+1\right)$ terms and $\{(x + a)^n - (x - a)^n\}$ has $\left(\frac{n}{2}\right)$ terms.

Example 1 : **Find the number of terms in the expansions of the following :**

(*i*) $(5x - 3y)^9$ (*ii*) $\left(1 + 3\sqrt{2}x\right)^9 + \left(1 - 3\sqrt{2}x\right)^9$

(*iii*) $\left(\sqrt{x} + \sqrt{y}\right)^{10} + \left(\sqrt{x} - \sqrt{y}\right)^{10}$ (*iv*) $[8x + y)^8 - (8x - y)^8]$

Solution :

(*i*) The expansion of $(x + a)^n$ has $(n + 1)$ terms.

Therefore, the expansion of $(2x - 3y)^9$ has 10 terms.

(*ii*) If n is odd, then the expansion of $(x + a)^n + (x - a)^n$ contains $\left(\frac{n+1}{2}\right)$ terms.

Therefore, the expansion of $(1 + 3\sqrt{2}x)^9 + (1 - 3\sqrt{2}x)^9$ has $\left(\frac{9+1}{2}\right) = 5$ terms.

(*iii*) If n is even, then the expansion of $\{(x + a)^n + (x - a)^n\}$ has $\left(\frac{n}{2} + 1\right)$ terms.

Therefore, $\left(\sqrt{x} + \sqrt{y}\right)^{10} + \left(\sqrt{x} - \sqrt{y}\right)^{10}$ has 6 terms.

(*iv*) If n is even, then $\{(x + a)^n - (x - a)^n\}$ has $\frac{n}{2}$ terms.

Therefore $(8x + y)^8 - (8x - y)^8$ has 4 terms.

FINDING GENERAL TERM AND MIDDLE TERMS IN A BINOMIAL EXPANSION

Again, refer to expansion of $(x + a)^n$, as shown below :

$$(x + a)^n = {}^nC_0x^n\,a^0 + {}^nC_1x^{n-1}\,a^1 + {}^nC_2x^{n-2}\,a^2 + ... + {}^nC_rx^{n-r}\,a^r + ... + {}^nC_nx^0\,a^n$$

In this care

The first term $= {}^nC_0x^na^0$

The second term $= {}^nC_1 x^{n-1} a^1$

The third term $= {}^nC_2 x^{n-2} a^2$, and so on

It shall be observed that the suffix of C in any term is one less than the number of terms, the index of x is n minus the suffix of C and the index of a is the same as the suffix of C.

Using the above basis, we can generalize that the $(r + 1)$th term is given by ${}^nC_r x^{n-r} a^r$

Thus, $(r + 1)$th term will be given as $T_{r+1} = {}^nC_2 x^{n-r} a^r$

This is called the *general term,* because by giving different values to r we can determine all terms of the expansion.

Similarly, in the binomial expansion of $(x - a)^n$, the general term is given by

$$T_{r+1} = (-1)^r \, {}^nC_r \, x^{n-r} \, a^r$$

In the binomial expansion of $(1 + x)^n$, we have

$$T_{r+1} = {}^nC_r x^r$$

In the binomial expansion of $(1 - x)^n$, we have

$$T_{r+1} = (-1)^r \, {}^nC_r \, x^r$$

Middle Terms in a Binomial Expansion

Since the binomial expansion of $(x + a)^n$ contains $(n + 1)$ terms. Therefore,

(*i*) If n is even, then $\left(\frac{n}{2} + 1\right)$th term is the middle term.

(*ii*) If n is odd, then $\left(\frac{n+1}{2}\right)$th and $\left(\frac{n+3}{2}\right)$th terms are the two middle terms.

***Example 2 :* Write the general term in the expansion of $(x^2 - y)^8$.**

Solution : We have $(x^2 - y)^8 = \{x^2 + (-y)\}^8$.

The general term in the expansion of the above binomial is given by

$$T_{r+1} = {}^8C_r (x^2)^{8-r} (-y)^r \qquad [\because T_{r+1} = {}^nC_r \, x^{n-r} \, a^r]$$

$$\Rightarrow \quad T_{r-1} = (-1)^r \, {}^8C_r \, x^{16-2r} \, y^r$$

***Example 3 :* Find the 9th term in the expansion of $\left(x - \frac{3a}{x^2}\right)^{12}$.**

Solution : We know that the $(r + 1)$th term in the expansion of $(x + a)^n$ is given by

$$T_{r+1} = {}^nC_r \, x^{n-r} \, a^r$$

In the expansion of $\left(x - \frac{3a}{x^2}\right)^{12}$, we have

$$\Rightarrow \quad T_9 = T_{8+1} = {}^{12}C_8 \, (x)^{12-8} \left(\frac{-3a}{x^2}\right)^8 = {}^{12}C_8 \, (x)^4 \left(\frac{-3a}{x^2}\right)^8$$

$$\Rightarrow \quad T_9 = {}^{12}C_4 . 3^8 \frac{a^8}{x^{12}} = \left({}^{12}C_4 x^{-12} a^8\right) 3^8$$

Example 4 : **Find the 6th term in the expansion of** $\left(\frac{4x}{3} - \frac{3}{2x}\right)^9$.

Solution : We have, $\left(\frac{4x}{3} - \frac{3}{2x}\right)^9 = \left\{\frac{4x}{3} + \left(-\frac{3}{2x}\right)\right\}^9$

$$\therefore \quad T_6 = T_{5+1} = {}^9C_5 \left(\frac{4x}{3}\right)^{9-5} \left(-\frac{3}{2x}\right)^5 \qquad [\because T_{r+1} = {}^nC_r x^{n-r} a^r]$$

$$\Rightarrow \quad T_6 = {}^9C_5 \left(\frac{4x}{3}\right)^4 (-1)^5 \left(\frac{3}{2x}\right)^5 = -{}^9C_4 \left(\frac{4x}{3}\right)^4 \left(\frac{3}{2x}\right)^5 \qquad [\because {}^9C_5 = {}^9C_4]$$

$$\Rightarrow \quad T_6 = -\frac{9 \times 8 \times 7 \times 6}{4 \times 3 \times 2 \times 1}\left(\frac{2^8}{3^4} . x^4\right)\left(\frac{3^5}{2^5 \cdot x^5}\right) = -\frac{3024}{x}$$

Example 5 : **Find the 4th term from the end in the expansion of** $\left(\frac{5}{x^2} - \frac{x^3}{10}\right)^7$.

Solution : Clearly, the given expansion contains 8 terms.

So, 4th term from the end = (8 – 4 + 1)th = 5th term from the beginning

$$\therefore \quad \text{Required term} = T_5 = T_{4+1} = {}^7C_4 \left(\frac{5}{x^2}\right)^{7-4} \left(-\frac{x^3}{10}\right)^4$$

$$= {}^7C_3 \left(\frac{5}{x^2}\right)^3 \left(\frac{x^3}{10}\right)^4 \qquad [\because {}^7C_3 = {}^7C_4]$$

$$= \frac{7 \times 6 \times 5}{3 \times 2 \times 1}\left(\frac{5^3}{x^6}\right)\left(\frac{x^{12}}{10^4}\right) = \frac{35}{80} x^6$$

Example 6 : **Find the middle term in the expansion of** $\left(\frac{5}{3}x^2 - \frac{3}{5x}\right)^{10}$.

Solution : Here $n = 10$, which is an even number.

So, $\left(\frac{10}{2} + 1\right)$th term *i.e.* 6th term is the middle term.

Hence, the middle term $= T_6 = T_{5+1} = {}^{10}C_5 \left(\frac{5}{3}x^2\right)^{10-5} \left(-\frac{3}{5x}\right)^5$

$$= -{}^{10}C_5 x^5$$

Example 7 : **Find the middle terms in the expansion of** $\left(5x - \frac{x^3}{3}\right)^7$.

Solution : The given expression $= \left(5x - \frac{x^3}{3}\right)^7$. Here $n = 7$, which is an odd number.

So, $\left(\frac{7+1}{2}\right)$th and $\left(\frac{7+1}{2}+1\right)$th i.e. 4th and 5th terms are two middle terms.

Now, $T_4 = T_{3+1} = {}^7C_3 (5x)^{7-3}\left(-\frac{x^3}{3}\right)^3 = (-1)^3 \cdot {}^7C_3 (5x)^4 \left(\frac{x^3}{3}\right)^3$

$\Rightarrow \quad T_4 = -35 \times 625 \times x^4 \times \frac{x^9}{27} = -\frac{21875\, x^{13}}{27}$

and, $T_5 = T_{4+1} = {}^7C_4 (5x)^{7-4}\left(-\frac{x^3}{3}\right)^4 = {}^7C_4 (5x)^3\left(-\frac{x^3}{3}\right)^4$

$\Rightarrow \quad T_5 = 35 \times 125x^3 \times \frac{x^{12}}{81} = \frac{4375}{81}x^{15}$

Hence, the middle terms are $-\frac{21875}{27}x^{13}$ and $\frac{4375}{81}x^{15}$

Example 8 : **Prove that the middle term in the expansion of $(1 + x)^{2n}$ is**

$$\frac{1.3.5\ldots(2n-1)}{n!}2^n \cdot x^n$$

Solution : The given expression $= (1 + x)^{2n}$. In this case the index $2n$ is even, therefore $(n + 1)$th term is the middle term.

Hence, the middle term

$$= T_{n+1} = {}^{2n}C_n (1)^{2n-n} x^n = {}^{2n}C_n x^n$$

$$= \frac{(2n)!}{(2n-n)!\,n!}x^n$$

$$= \frac{1\cdot 2\cdot 3\cdot 4\cdot 5\cdot 6\ldots(2n-3)(2n-2)(2n-1)(2n)}{n!\,n!}x^n$$

$$= \frac{\{1\cdot 3\cdot 5\ldots(2n-3)(2n-1)\}\{2\cdot 4\cdot 6\ldots(2n-2)(2n)\}}{n!\,n!}x^n$$

$$= \frac{\{1\cdot 3\cdot 5\ldots(2n-3)(2n-1)\}\{1\cdot 2\cdot 3\ldots(n-1)(n)\}2^n}{n!\,n!}x^n$$

$$= \frac{\{1\cdot 3\cdot 5\ldots(2n-3)(2n-1)\}\,n!\cdot 2^n\cdot x^n}{n!\,n!}$$

$$= \frac{1\cdot 3\cdot 5\ldots(2n-1)}{n!}2^n x^n$$

***Example 9* : Find the coefficient of x^{13} in the binomial expansion of $\left(2x^2 - \frac{3}{x}\right)^{11}$, where $x \neq 0$.**

***Solution* :** Suppose $(r + 1)$th term contains x^{13} in the binomial expansion of $\left(2x^2 - \frac{3}{x}\right)^{11}$.

Now, $$T_{r+1} = {}^{11}C_r \left(2x^2\right)^{11-r} \left(-\frac{3}{x}\right)^r = (-1)^r \, {}^{11}C_r 2^{(11-r)} \cdot 3^r \cdot x^{22-3r} \quad \text{...(i)}$$

This term will contain x^{13}, if

$$22 - 3r = 13 \Rightarrow r = 3.$$

So, $(3 + 1)$th *i.e.* 4th term contains x^{13}.

Putting $r = 3$ in (*i*), we get

$$T_4 = (-1)^4 \, {}^{11}C_3 \, 2^8.3^3.x^{13}$$

$\therefore$ Coefficient of $x^{13} = {}^{11}C_3 \, 2^8 3^3$.

***Example 10* : Prove that there is no term involving x^8 in the expansion of $\left(5x^2 - \frac{8}{x}\right)^{11}$, where $r \neq 0$.**

***Solution* :** Suppose x^6 occurs in $(r + 1)$th term in the expansion of $\left(5x^2 - \frac{8}{x}\right)^{11}$.

Now, $$T_{r+1} = {}^{11}C_r \left(5x^2\right)^{11-r} \left(-\frac{8}{x}\right)^r = {}^{11}C_r (-1)^r \, 5^{11-r} 8^r x^{22-3r}$$

For this term to contain x^8, we must have

$$22 - 3r = 8 \Rightarrow r = \frac{14}{3}, \text{ which is a fraction.}$$

Since r is a fraction, therefore, we conclude that there is no term having coefficient of x^8.

***Example 11* : Find the coefficients of x^{12} and x^{-3} in the expansion of $\left(x^2 - \frac{1}{x}\right)^{12}$.**

***Solution* :** Let $(r + 1)$th term involves x^{12} in the expansion of $\left(x^2 - \frac{1}{x}\right)^{12}$.

$$\therefore \quad T_{r+1} = {}^{12}C_r \left(x^2\right)^{12-r} \left(-\frac{1}{x}\right)^r$$

$$= (-1)^r \, {}^{12}C_r \, x^{24-3r} \quad \text{....(1)}$$

For this term to contain x^{12}, we shall have

$$24 - 3r = 12$$

$\therefore \quad r = 4$

Subsituting $r = 4$, in above equation (1), we have

$$T_5 = (-1)^4\ {}^{12}C_5\ x^{12}$$
$$= 495\ x^{12}$$

$\therefore$ Coefficient of x^{12} is 495.

Finding coefficient of x^{-3}, we shall have

$$24 - 3r = -3$$
$$-3r = -27$$
$$r = 9$$

$$\therefore \quad T_{9+1} = (-1)^9\ {}^{12}C_9\ x^{24-27}$$
$$= -220\ x^{-3}$$

$\therefore$ Coefficient of x^{-3} is -220.

Example 12 : **Find the term independent of x in the expansion of $\left(x - \frac{1}{x}\right)^8$.**

Solution : We have $(r + 1)$th term as

$$T_{r+1} = {}^8C_r x^{8-r}\left(-\frac{1}{x}\right)^r$$
$$= (-1)^r\ {}^8C_r\ x^{8-2r}$$

Since the required term is independent of x,

$$\therefore \quad 8 - 2r = 0$$
$$r = 4$$

$\therefore$ T_5 is the required term, which will be given as

$$\therefore \quad T_5 = {}^8C_4 x^{8-4}\left(-\frac{1}{x}\right)^4 = 70$$

Finding the greatest term (Numerically) in the expansion of $(x + a)^n$

Let $\quad$ rth term of $(x + a)^n$ be T_r

and $\quad$ $(r + 1)$th term of $(x + a)^n$ be T_{r+1}

$$\therefore \quad T_{r+1} = {}^nC_r\ x^{n-r} a^r$$
$$T_r = {}^nC_{r-1}\ x^{n-r+1}\ a^{r-1}$$

$$\therefore \quad \frac{T_{r+1}}{T_r} = \frac{n!}{(n-r)!\,r!}\ \frac{(n-r+1)!\,(r-1)!}{n!}\ \frac{x^{n-r} \cdot a^r}{x^{n-r+1}\, a^{r-1}}$$

$$= \frac{(n-r+1)}{r} \cdot \frac{a}{x}$$

Since our requirement is to find greatest term, therefore, for any given value of 'r', $T_{r+1} \geq T_r$

$$\therefore \quad \frac{T_{r+1}}{T_r} \geq 1$$

$$\therefore \quad \frac{n-r+1}{r} \cdot \frac{a}{x} \geq 1$$

$$= \left(\frac{(n+1)}{r} - \frac{r}{r}\right)\frac{a}{x} \geq 1$$

$$\frac{(n+1)}{r} - 1 \geq \frac{x}{a}$$

$$\frac{n+1}{r} \geq \frac{x+a}{a}$$

$$\therefore \quad r \leq \frac{a(n+1)}{(x+a)}$$

Set $\dfrac{a(n+1)}{(x+a)} = m$

If m is integer, t_m and t_{m+1} are equal and are greatest term.

If m is not integer, then t_{m+1} is the greatest term.

Example 13 : **Find numerically the greatest term in the expansion of $(3 + 5x)^9$ when $x = \dfrac{3}{5}$.**

Solution : We have $(3+5x)^9 = 3^9\left(1 + \dfrac{5}{3}x\right)^9$

Here $m = \dfrac{x(n+1)}{(x+1)}$ and $n = 9$

Given $x = 3/5$

$$\therefore \quad m = \frac{3}{5} \times \frac{(9+1)}{8} \times 5$$

$$m = \frac{150}{40} = 3.5$$

Since m is not integer, then t_{m+1} *i.e.* t_{3+1} is the greatest term

$$T_4 = 3^9 \cdot {}^9C_3\left(\frac{5}{3}x\right)^3$$

$$= 7654500\, x^3$$

Objective Type Questions

Q. 1 The number of terms in the expansion of $[(3x + y)^8 - (3x - y)^8]$ are

(*i*) 4 (*ii*) 6 (*iii*) 8 (*iv*) 10

Q. 2 Using the Binomial theorem, the value of $\{(\sqrt{2}+1)^5 + (\sqrt{2}-1)^5\}$ is

(*i*) $48\sqrt{2}$ (*ii*) 50 (*iii*) $50\sqrt{2}$ (*iv*) $58\sqrt{2}$

Q. 3 The number of terms in the expansion of $(2x - 3y)^9$ are

(*i*) 8 (*ii*) 9 (*iii*) 10 (*iv*) 12

Q. 4 The 10th term in the expansion of $\left(2x^2 + \frac{1}{x}\right)^{12}$ is

(*i*) $\frac{1520}{x^2}$ (*ii*) $\frac{1520}{x^3}$ (*iii*) $\frac{1760}{x^2}$ (*iv*) $\frac{1760}{x^3}$

Q. 5 The middle term in the expansion of $\left(\frac{2}{3}x^2 - \frac{3}{2}x\right)^{20}$ is

(*i*) ${}^{20}C_{10}\, x^{10}$ (*ii*) ${}^{20}C_9\, x^9$ (*iii*) ${}^{20}C_{11}\, x^{11}$ (*iv*) ${}^{20}C_{12}\, x^{12}$

Q. 6 The term independent of x in the expansion of $\left(x - \frac{1}{x}\right)^{12}$ is

(*i*) ${}^{12}C_5$ (*ii*) ${}^{12}C_6$ (*iii*) ${}^{12}C_7$ (*iv*) ${}^{12}C_8$

Q. 7 The coefficient of three consecutive terms in the expansion of $(1 + x)^n$ are in the ratio 1 : 7 : 42. The value of n is

(*i*) 30 (*ii*) 40 (*iii*) 45 (*iv*) 55

Q. 8 The number of terms free from radical sign in the expansion of $(x^{1/5} + y^{1/10})^{55}$ are

(*i*) 10 (*ii*) 7 (*iii*) 6 (*iv*) 5

Q. 9 The relation between a and b so that the coefficient of x^7 in $\left(ax^2 + \frac{1}{bx}\right)^{11}$ and of x^{-7} in $\left(ax - \frac{1}{bx^2}\right)^{11}$ are equal is

(*i*) $ab = 1$ (*ii*) $a^2b^2 = 1$ (*iii*) $a^3b^3 = 5$ (*iv*) $ab = 6$

Q. 10 The coefficient of $(2r + 4)^{th}$ and $(r - 2)^{th}$ term in the expansion of $(1 + x)^{18}$ are equal, the value of r is

(*i*) 4 (*ii*) 5 (*iii*) 6 (*iv*) 7

Answers

1. (*i*)	2. (*iv*)	3. (*iii*)	4. (*iv*)	5. (*i*)
6. (*ii*)	7. (*iv*)	8. (*iii*)	9. (*i*)	10. (*iii*)

Exercise 18.1

1. Using Binomial theorem, expand each of the following :

   (i) $(3x + 2y)^4$ (ii) $(x^2 - 2/x)^7$

   (iii) $[\sqrt{x} - \sqrt{6}]^6$ (iv) $(1 + 2x - 3x^2)^5$

2. Evaluate –

   (i) $(\sqrt{2}+1)^6 + (\sqrt{2}-1)^6$ (ii) $(999)^4$ (iii) $(1.01)^5$

   [**Ans.** (i) 198; (ii) 996005996001; (iii) 1.0510100501]

3. Find the 5th term from the end in the expansion of $\left(x - \frac{1}{x}\right)^{12}$. [**Ans.** $495x^4$]

4. Find the coefficient of

   (i) x^7 in the expansion of $\left(x^2 + \frac{1}{x}\right)^{11}$ [**Ans.** 462]

   (ii) x^{10} in the expansion of $(x^2 - 2)^{11}$ [**Ans.** 29568]

5. Find the middle term in the expansion of

   (i) $\left(1 - \frac{x^2}{2}\right)^{14}$ $\left[\textbf{Ans. } \frac{-429}{16}x^{14}\right]$

   (ii) $\left(\frac{a}{3} + 9b\right)^8$ [**Ans.** $5670\, a^4b^4$

6. Find two middle term in the expansion of

   (i) $(x^2 + a^2)^5$ [**Ans.** $10x^6a^4$]

   (ii) $\left(x^4 - \frac{1}{x^3}\right)^{11}$ [**Ans.** $-462x^9$, $462x^2$]

7. Find the term independent of x in the expansion of

   (i) $\left(x + \frac{1}{x}\right)^{10}$ (ii) $\left(\sqrt{x} + \frac{1}{3x^2}\right)^{10}$ (iii) $\left(\frac{3x^2}{2} - \frac{1}{3x^2}\right)^9$ (iv) $\left(x - \frac{1}{x^2}\right)^{3n}$

   [**Ans.** (i) 252; (ii) 5; (iii) 7.18; (iv) $(-1)^n\, {}^{3n}C_n$]

8. Prove that the coefficient of $(r + 1)^{th}$ term in the expansion of $(1 + x)^{n+1}$ is equal to the sum of coefficient of rth and $(r + 1)^{th}$ terms in the expansion of $(1 + x)^n$.

9. The coefficient of 5th, 6th and 7th term in the expansion of $(1 + x)^n$ are in A.P, find n?

10. If in the expansion of $(1 + x)^n$, the coefficient of pth and q^{th} terms are equal. Prove that $p + q = n + 2$ where $p \neq q$.

19

Algebra of Vectors

HIGHLIGHTS OF THE CHAPTER

- Introduction
- Important Characteristics of Vector
- Types of Vector
- Section Formula
- Linear Combination of Vectors
- Collinear and Non-Collinear Vectors
- Linear Independence and Dependence of Vectors
- The Scalar or Dot Product
- Angle Between Two Vectors
- Applications of Scalar Product in Mechanics
- vector or cross product
- Scalar Triple Product
- Scalar Triple Product in Terms of Components
- Vector Triple Product

INTRODUCTION

Vectors are represented by line segments. The length of the line segment represent the magnitude of the vector and the direction of arrow marked at one end represent the direction of the vector. A vector, denoted by $\overrightarrow{PQ}$, is determined by two points P, Q such that the magnitude of the vector is the length of the straight line PQ and its direction is that from P to Q. The point P is called the *initial point of vector* $\overrightarrow{PQ}$ and Q is called the *terminal point* or tip. In practice, vectors are denoted by $\vec{a}, \vec{b}, \vec{c}$ etc.

Fig. 1.1.

The modulus, or module, or magnitude of a vector $\vec{a}$ is the positive number which is the measure of its length and is denoted by $|\vec{a}|$. The modulus $|\vec{a}|$ of a vector $\vec{a}$ is sometimes written as **a**.

IMPORTANT CHARACTERISTICS OF VECTOR

Length : *The length of* $\overrightarrow{PQ}$ *will be denoted by* $|\overrightarrow{PQ}|$ *or PQ.*

Support : *The line of unlimited length of which PQ is segment is called the support of the vector* $\overrightarrow{PQ}$.

Sense : *The sense of* $\overrightarrow{PQ}$ *is from P to Q and that of* $\overrightarrow{QP}$ *is from Q to P. Thus, the sense of a directed line segment is from its initial point to the terminal point.*

Equal Vectors : *Two vectors* $\vec{a}$ *and* $\vec{b}$ *are said to be equal, written as* $\vec{a} = \vec{b}$, *if they have*

(i) *the same length*

(ii) *the same or parallel support, and*

(iii) *the same sense.*

TYPES OF VECTOR

Zero or Null Vectors : *A vector whose initial and terminal points are coincident is called the zero or the null vector.*

The modulus of the null vector is zero but it can be thought of as having any line as its line of support. The null vector is denoted by $\vec{0}$.

Vectors other than the null vector are called *proper vectors.*

Unit Vector : *A vector whose modulus is unity, is called a unit vector. The unit vector in the direction of a vector* $\vec{a}$ *is denoted by* $\hat{a}$, *read 'a cap'. Thus,* $|\hat{a}| = 1$.

Like and Unlike Vectors : *Vectors are said to be like when they have the same sense of direction and unlike when they have opposite directions.*

Collinear or Parallel Vectors : *Vectors having the same or parallel supports are called collinear vectors.*

Co-Initial Vectors : *Vector having the same initial point are called co-initial vectors.*

Co-Planar Vectors : *A vectors is said to be coplanar, if their supports are parallel to the same plane.*

Note that two vectors are always coplanar.

Coterminous Vectors : *Vectors having the same terminal point are called coterminous vectors.*

Negative of a Vectors : *The vector which has the same magnitude as the vector* $\vec{a}$ *but opposite direction, is called the negative of* $\vec{a}$ *and is denoted by* $-\vec{a}$.

Thus, if $\overrightarrow{PQ} = \vec{a}$, *then* $\overrightarrow{QP} = -\vec{a}$.

Reciprocal of a Vector : *A vector having the same direction as that of a given vector* $\vec{a}$ *but magnitude equal to the reciprocal of the given vector is known as the reciprocal of* $\vec{a}$ *and is denoted by* $\vec{a}^{-1}$.

Localized and Free Vectors : *A vector which is drawn parallel to a given vector through a specified point in space is called a localized vector. For example, a force acting on a rigid body is a localized vector as its effect depends on the line of action of the force. If the value of a vector depends only on its length and direction and is independent of its position in the space, it is called a free vector.*

PROPERTIES OF ADDITION AND SUBTRACTION OF VECTORS

(i) *Vector addition is commutative i.e.,* $\vec{a} + \vec{b} = \vec{b} + \vec{a}$ *for any two vectors* $\vec{a}$ and $\vec{b}$.

(ii) *Vector addition is associative i.e.,* $(\vec{a} + \vec{b}) + \vec{c} = \vec{a} + (\vec{b} + \vec{c})$ *for any three vectors* $\vec{a}, \vec{b}, \vec{c}$.

(iii) *(Existence of additive identity) For every vector* $\vec{a}$, *we have* $\vec{a} + \vec{0} = \vec{a} = \vec{0} + \vec{a}$, *where* $\vec{0}$ *is the null vectors.*

Subtraction of Vectors

If $\vec{a}$ and $\vec{b}$ are two vectors, then the subtraction of $\vec{b}$ from $\vec{a}$ is defined as the vector sum of $\vec{a}$ and $-\vec{b}$ is denoted by $\vec{a} - \vec{b}$ *i.e.,* $\vec{a} - \vec{b} = \vec{a} + (-\vec{b})$.

From the above definition it is evident that two vectors $\vec{a}$ and $\vec{b}$ are collinear or parallel if $\vec{a} = m\vec{b}$ for some non-zero scalar m.

For any vector $\vec{a}$, we also define

$$1\vec{a} = \vec{a}, (-1)\vec{a} = -\vec{a} \text{ and } 0\vec{a} = \vec{0}.$$

If we have vectors $\vec{a}, \vec{b}$ and scalars m, n we have

(i) $m(-\vec{a}) = (-m)\vec{a} = -(m\vec{a})$

(ii) $(-m)(-\vec{a}) = m\vec{a}$

(iii) $m(m\vec{a}) = (mn)\vec{a} = n\vec{a}$

(iv) $(m + n)\vec{a} = m\vec{a} + n\vec{a}$

(v) $m(\vec{a} + \vec{b}) = m\vec{a} + m\vec{b}$.

SECTION FORMULA

Theorem 1 : (Internal division) Let A and B be two points with position vectors $\vec{a}$ and $\vec{b}$ respectively, and let C be a point dividing AB internally in the ration $m : n$. Then the position vector of C is given by

$$\overrightarrow{OC} = \frac{m\vec{b} + n\vec{a}}{m+n}.$$

Remarks 1 : If c is the mid point of AB, then it divides AB in the ratio 1 : 1. Therefore, position vector of C is

$$\frac{1.\vec{a} + 1.\vec{b}}{1+1} = \frac{\vec{a}+\vec{b}}{2}.$$

Thus, the position vector of the mid point of AB is $\frac{1}{2}\left(\vec{a}+\vec{b}\right)$.

Theorem 2 : (*External division*) Let A and B be two points with position vectors $\vec{a}$ and $\vec{b}$ respectively and let C be a point dividing AB externally in the ratio $m : n$. Then the position vector of C is given by

$$\overrightarrow{OC} = \frac{m\vec{b} - n\vec{b}}{m-n}.$$

***Example 1 :* Find the position vector of the points which divide the join of the points $2\vec{a} - 3\vec{b}$ and $3\vec{a} - 2\vec{b}$ internally and externally in the ratio 2 : 3.**

Solution : Let P and Q be the given points with position vectors $2\vec{a} - 3\vec{b}$ and $3\vec{a} - 2\vec{b}$ respectively. Let P and Q be the points dividing AB in the ratio 2 : 3 internally and externally respectively. Then,

$$\text{Position vector of } P = \frac{3\left(2\vec{a} - 3\vec{b}\right) + 2\left(3\vec{a} - 2\vec{b}\right)}{3+2} = \frac{12\vec{a}}{5} - \frac{13\vec{b}}{5}$$

$$\text{Position vector of } Q = \frac{3\left(2\vec{a} - 3\vec{b}\right) - 2\left(3\vec{a} - 2\vec{b}\right)}{3-2} = -5\vec{b}.$$

LINEAR COMBINATION OF VECTORS

Definition : A vector $\vec{r}$ is said to be a linear combination of vectors $\vec{a}, \vec{b}, \vec{c}$ ... etc. if there exist scalars, x, y, z etc., such that $\vec{r} = x\vec{a} + y\vec{b} + z\vec{c} + \ldots$

For examples, vectors $\vec{r_1} = 3\vec{a} + \vec{b} + 8\vec{c}$, $\vec{r_2} = 2\vec{a} + 3\vec{b} + \sqrt{7}\vec{c}$ are linear combinations of the vectors, $\vec{a}, \vec{b}, \vec{c}$.

COLLINEAR AND NON-COLLINEAR VECTORS

Let $\vec{a}$ and $\vec{b}$ be two collinear vectors and let $\hat{x}$ be the unit vector in the direction of $\vec{a}$.

Then the unit vector in the direction of $\vec{b}$ is $\hat{x}$ or $-\hat{x}$ according as $\vec{a}$ and $\vec{b}$ are like or unlike parallel vectors.

Now $\vec{a} = \left|\vec{a}\right|\hat{x}$ and $\vec{b} = \pm\left|\vec{b}\right|\hat{x}$

$$\therefore \vec{a} = \left(\frac{|\vec{a}|}{|\vec{b}|}\right)|\vec{b}|\,\hat{x} \Rightarrow \vec{a} = \left(+\frac{|\vec{a}|}{|\vec{b}|}\right)\vec{b} \Rightarrow \vec{a} = \lambda\vec{b}, \text{ where } \lambda = \pm\frac{|\vec{a}|}{|\vec{b}|}.$$

Thus, if $\vec{a}, \vec{b}$ are collinear vectors, then $\vec{a} = \lambda\vec{b}$ or $\vec{b} = \lambda\vec{a}$ for some scalar λ.

Theorem : If $\vec{a}, \vec{b}$ are any two non-zero non-collinear vectors and x, y are scalars such that $x\vec{a} = y\vec{b}$, then $x = y = 0$.

Collinear Points

Let A, B, C be three Points. Then,

A, B, C are collinear

$$\Leftrightarrow \overrightarrow{AB} \text{ and } \overrightarrow{BC} \text{ are colinear}$$

$$\Leftrightarrow \overrightarrow{AB} \text{ and } \lambda\overrightarrow{BC} \text{ for some scalar } \lambda.$$

Thus, if A, B, C are three points in a plain such that $\overrightarrow{AB} = \lambda\overrightarrow{BC}$ or, $\overrightarrow{AB} = \lambda\overrightarrow{AC}$ or $\overrightarrow{BC} = \lambda\overrightarrow{AC}$ for some scalar l, then A, B, C are collinear.

***Example 2* : Show that the points with position vectors $\vec{a} - 2\vec{b} + 3\vec{c}, -2\vec{a} + 3\vec{b} - \vec{c}$ and $4\vec{a} - 7\vec{b} + 7\vec{c}$ are collinear.**

***Solution* :** Let P, Q, R be the points with position vectors $\vec{a} - 2\vec{b} + 3\vec{c}, -2\vec{a} + 3\vec{b} - \vec{c}$ and $\vec{a} - 2\vec{b} + 3\vec{c}, -4\vec{a} - 7\vec{b} + 7\vec{c}$ respectively. Then, we have

$$\overrightarrow{PQ} = \left(-2\vec{a} + 3\vec{b} - \vec{c},\right) - \left(\vec{a} - 2\vec{b} + 3\vec{c}\right) = -3\vec{a} + 5\vec{b} - 4\vec{c}$$

and
$$\overrightarrow{QR} = \left(4\vec{a} - 7\vec{b} + 7\vec{c},\right) - \left(-2\vec{a} + 3\vec{b} - \vec{c}\right) = 6\vec{a} - 10\vec{b} + 8\vec{c}.$$

It can be observed, $\overrightarrow{QR} = -2\overrightarrow{PQ}$, which shows that $\overrightarrow{PQ}$ and $\overrightarrow{QR}$ are parallel vectors. However Q is a points common to them. Therefore, $\overrightarrow{PQ}$ and $\overrightarrow{QR}$ are collinear. Hence, points P, Q and R are collinear.

Addition, Substraction and Multiplication of a Vector by a Scalar and Equality in Terms of Components

For any two vectors $\vec{a} = a_1\hat{i} + a_2\hat{k} + a_3\hat{k}$ and $\vec{a} = b_1\hat{i} + b_2\hat{k} + b_3\hat{k}$, we define

(*i*) $\vec{a} + \vec{b} = (a_1 + b_1)\hat{i} + (a_2 + b_2)\hat{j} + (a_3 + b_3)\hat{k}$

(*ii*) $\vec{a} - \vec{b} = (a_1 - b_1)\hat{i} + (a_2 - b_2)\hat{j} + (a_3 - b_3)\hat{k}$

(*iii*) $m\vec{a} = (ma_1)\hat{i} + (ma_2)\hat{j} + (ma_3)\hat{k}$, where m is a scalar

(*iv*) $\vec{a} = \vec{b} \Leftrightarrow a_1 = b_1, a_2 = b_2$ and $a_3 = b_3$.

Distance Between Two Points : Let $P(x_1, y_1, z_1)$ and $Q(x_2, y_2, z_2)$ be two points. Then, $\overrightarrow{PQ}$ = Position vector of Q – Position vector of P.

$$\Rightarrow \quad \overrightarrow{PQ} = \left(x_2\hat{i} + y_2\hat{j} + z_2\hat{k}\right) - \left(x_1\hat{i} + y_1\hat{j} + z_1\hat{k}\right)$$

$$\Rightarrow \quad \overrightarrow{PQ} = (x_1 - x_1)\hat{i} + (y_2 - y_1)\hat{j} + (z_2 - z_1)\hat{k}$$

$$\therefore \quad PQ = \left|\overrightarrow{PQ}\right| = \sqrt{(x_2 - x_1)^2 + (y_2 - y_1)^2 + (z_2 - z_1)^2}.$$

Thus the distance between the points $P(x_1, y_1, z_1)$ and $Q(x_1, y_2, z_2)$ is given by :

Example 3 : **Find the unit vector in the direction of $3\hat{i} - 6\hat{j} + 2\hat{k}$.**

Solution : Let $\vec{a} = 3\hat{i} - 6\hat{j} + 2\hat{k}$. Then,

$$\left|\vec{a}\right| = \sqrt{3^2 + (-6)^2 + 2^2} = 7.$$

So, unit vector in the direction of $\vec{a}$ is given by

$$\hat{a} = \frac{1}{\left|\vec{a}\right|}\vec{a} = \frac{1}{7}\left(3\hat{i} - 6\hat{j} + 2\hat{k}\right) = \frac{3}{7}\hat{i} - \frac{6}{7}\hat{j} + \frac{2}{7}\hat{k}.$$

Example 4 : **Show that the three points $A(-2, 3, 5)$, $B(1, 2, 3)$ and $C(7, 0, -1)$ are collinear.**

Solution : We have

$$\overrightarrow{AB} = \left(\hat{i} + 2\hat{j} + 3\hat{k}\right) - \left(-2\hat{i} + 3\hat{j} + 5\hat{k}\right) = 3\hat{i} - \hat{j} - 2\hat{k}$$

$$\overrightarrow{BC} = \left(7\hat{i} + 0\hat{j} - 3\hat{k}\right) - \left(\hat{i} + 2\hat{j} + 3\hat{k}\right) = 6\hat{i} - 2\hat{j} - 4\hat{k}$$

$$= 2\left(3\hat{i} - \hat{j} - 2\hat{k}\right)$$

Clearly, $\overrightarrow{BC} = 2\,\overrightarrow{AB}$.

This shows that the vectors $\overrightarrow{AB}$ and $\overrightarrow{BC}$ are parallel. But, B is a common point. So, the given points A, B and C are collinear.

Example 5 : **Find the distance between the points $A(2, 3, 1)$, $B(-1, 2, -3)$, using vector method.**

Solution : We have

$$\overrightarrow{AB} = \left(\hat{i} + 2\hat{j} - 3\hat{k}\right) - \left(2\hat{i} + 3\hat{j} + \hat{k}\right) = -3\hat{i} - \hat{j} - 4\hat{k}$$

$$\therefore \quad AB = \left|\overrightarrow{AB}\right| = \sqrt{(-3)^2 + (-1)^2 + (-4)^2} = \sqrt{26}.$$

Example 6 : **If $\vec{a} = 3\hat{i} - 2\hat{j} + \hat{k}$ and $\vec{b} = 2\hat{i} - 4\hat{j} - 3\hat{k}$, find $\left|\vec{a} - 2\vec{b}\right|$.**

Solution : We have,

$$\vec{a}-2\vec{b} = \left(3\hat{i}-2\hat{j}+\hat{k}\right)-2\left(2\hat{i}-4\hat{j}-3\hat{k}\right) = -\hat{i}+6\hat{j}+7\hat{k}$$

$$\therefore \quad \left|\vec{a}-2\vec{b}\right| = \left|-\hat{i}+6\hat{j}+7\hat{k}\right| = \sqrt{(-1)^2+6^2+7^2} = \sqrt{86}.$$

Example 7 : **The position vectors of the points *P, Q, R* are**

$$\left|\vec{a}-2\vec{b}\right| = \hat{i}+2\hat{j}+3\hat{k},\ -2\hat{i}+3\hat{j}+5\hat{k} \text{ and } 7\hat{i}-\hat{k} \text{ respectively.}$$

Prove that *P, Q* and *R* are collinear.

Solution : We have,

$$\overrightarrow{PQ} = \left(-2\hat{i}+3\hat{j}+5\hat{k}\right), \left(\hat{i}+2\hat{j}+3\hat{k}\right) = -3\hat{i}+\hat{j}+2\hat{k}$$

and

$$\overrightarrow{QR} = \left(-7\hat{i}-\hat{k}\right)-\left(-2\hat{i}+3\hat{j}+5\hat{k}\right) = 9\hat{i}-3\hat{j}-6\hat{k}.$$

Clearly, $\overrightarrow{QR} = -3\,\overrightarrow{PQ}.$

This shows that the vectors $\overrightarrow{PQ}$ and $\overrightarrow{QR}$ are collinear. But Q is common point between $\overrightarrow{PQ}$ and $\overrightarrow{QR}$. Therefore, given points P, Q and R are collinear.

Theorem 1 : (Test of collinearity of three points) Three points with position vectors $\vec{a}, \vec{b}, \vec{c}$ are collinear iff there exist scalars x, y, z not all zero such that $x\vec{a}, + y\vec{b}, + z\vec{c} = \vec{0}$, where $x+y+z=0$.

LINEAR INDEPENDENCE AND DEPENDENCE OF VECTORS

Linearly Independent Vectors : A set of non-zero vectors $\vec{a_1}, \vec{a_2}, \ldots \vec{a_n}$ is said to be linearly independent, if

$$x\vec{a_1}, x_2\vec{a_2}, \ldots x_n\vec{a_n} = 0 \Rightarrow x_1 = x_2 = \ldots = x_n = 0$$

Linearly Dependent Vectors : A set of vectors $\vec{a_1}, \vec{a_2}, \ldots \vec{a_n}$ is said to be linearly dependent if there exist scalars $x_1, x_2, \ldots, x_n$ not all zero such that

$$x_1\vec{a_1}, x_2\vec{a_2}, \ldots x_n\vec{a_n} = \vec{0}.$$

It follows from this definition that a set of vectors is linearly dependent if one of them is expressible as a linear combination of others.

Example 8 : **Prove that two non-zero, non-collinear vectors are linearly independent.**

Solution : Let $\vec{a}$ and $\vec{b}$ be two non-zero non-collinear vectors such that $x\vec{a} + y\vec{b} = \vec{0}$.

In order to prove that $\vec{a}, \vec{b}$ are linearly independent, we just show that $x = y = 0$.

If possible, let $x \neq 0$. Then,

$$x\vec{a} + y\vec{b} = \vec{0} \Rightarrow \vec{a} = -\frac{y}{x}\vec{b} \qquad [\because x \neq 0]$$

This shows that $\vec{a}$ and $\vec{b}$ are collinear vectors. This is a contradiction.

So, $x = 0$.

Similarly, we have $y = 0$.

Thus, $x\vec{a} + y\vec{b} = \vec{0} \Rightarrow x = y = 0$.

Hence $\vec{a}$ and $\vec{b}$ are linearly independent vectors.

Example 9 : **Prove that any two collinear vectors are linearly dependent.**

Solution : Let $\vec{a}$, $\vec{b}$ be two collinear vectors. Then,

$\vec{b} = x\vec{a}$ for some scalar x.

$\Rightarrow \quad x\vec{a} + (-1)\vec{b} = \vec{0}$

$\Rightarrow \quad x\vec{a} + y\vec{b} = \vec{0}$, where $y = -1 \neq 0$.

This shows that the vectors $\vec{a}, \vec{b}$ are linearly dependent.

SCALAR OR DOT PRODUCT

THE SCALAR OR DOT PRODUCT

Scalar or Dot Product : Let $\vec{a}$ and $\vec{b}$ be two non-zero vectors inclined at an angle θ. Then the scalar product of $\vec{a}$ with $\vec{b}$ is denoted by $\vec{a}.\vec{b}$ and is defined as the scalar $|\vec{a}||\vec{b}|\cos\theta$.

Thus, $\vec{a}.\vec{b} = |\vec{a}||\vec{b}|\cos\theta$.

Clearly, the scalar product of two vectors is a scalar quantity, due to which this product is called scalar product. Since we are putting a dot between $\vec{a}$ and $\vec{b}$. Therefore, it is also called dot product.

Property I : (*Commutatively*) The scalar product of two vectors is commutative *i.e.,*

$$\vec{a}.\vec{b} = \vec{b}.\vec{a}.$$

Property II : (*Distributivity of scalar product over vector addition*). The scalar product of vectors is distributive over vector addition *i.e.,*

(*i*) $\vec{a}.\left(\vec{b} + \vec{c}\right) = \vec{a}.\vec{b} + \vec{a}.\vec{c}$ (*Left distributivity*)

(ii) $\left(\vec{b} + \vec{c}\right).\vec{a} = \vec{b}.\vec{a} + \vec{c}.\vec{a}$ *(Right distributivity)*

Property III : Let $\vec{a}$ and $\vec{b}$ be two non-zero vectors. Then,

$$\vec{a}.\vec{b} = 0 \quad \Leftrightarrow \quad \vec{a} \text{ is perpendicular to } \vec{b}.$$

Property IV : For any vector $\vec{a}$, we have

$$\vec{a}.\vec{a} = \left|\vec{a}\right|^2.$$

Property V : If m is a scalar and $\vec{a}, \vec{b}$ be any two vectors, then

$$\left(m\vec{a}\right).\vec{b} = m\left(\vec{a}.\vec{b}\right) = \vec{a}.\left(m\vec{b}\right).$$

Property VI : If m, n are scalars and $\vec{a}, \vec{b}$ be two vectors. Then,

$$m\vec{a}.n\vec{b} = mn\left(\vec{a}.\vec{b}\right) = \left(mn\vec{a}\right).\vec{b} = \vec{a}.\left(mn\vec{b}\right)$$

Property VII : For any two vectors $\vec{a}$ and $\vec{b}$, we have

(i) $\vec{a}.\left(-\vec{b}\right) = -\left(\vec{a}.\vec{b}\right) = \left(-\vec{a}\right).\vec{b}$

(ii) $\left(-\vec{a}\right).\left(-\vec{b}\right) = \vec{a}.\vec{b}$.

Property VIII : For any two vectors $\vec{a}$ and $\vec{b}$, we have

(i) $\left|\vec{a} + \vec{b}\right|^2 = \left|\vec{a}\right|^2 + \left|\vec{b}\right|^2 + 2\vec{a}.\vec{b}$

(ii) $\left|\vec{a} - \vec{b}\right|^2 = \left|\vec{a}\right|^2 + \left|\vec{b}\right|^2 - 2\vec{a}.\vec{b}$

(iii) $\left(\vec{a} + \vec{b}\right).\left(\vec{a} - \vec{b}\right) = \left|\vec{a}\right|^2 + \left|\vec{b}\right|^2$.

Example 10 : **If $\vec{a} = 2\hat{i} - \hat{j} + 2\hat{k}$, $\vec{b} = 3\hat{i} + 2\hat{j} + 3\hat{k}$ find $\vec{a}.\vec{b}$.**

Solution : We have,

$$\vec{a}.\vec{b} = \left(2\hat{i} - \hat{j} + 3\hat{k}\right).\left(3\hat{i} + 2\hat{j} + 3\hat{k}\right)$$

$$= (2)(3) + (-1)(2) + (2)(3) = 10.$$

ANGLE BETWEEN TWO VECTORS

Let $\vec{a}, \vec{b}$ be two vectors inclined at an angle θ. Then,

$$\vec{a}.\vec{b} = \left|\vec{a}\right|\left|\vec{b}\right|\cos\theta$$

$$\Rightarrow \quad \cos\theta = \frac{\vec{a}\cdot\vec{b}}{|\vec{a}|\,|\vec{b}|}$$

$$\Rightarrow \quad \theta = \cos^{-1}\left\{\frac{\vec{a}\cdot\vec{b}}{|\vec{a}|\,|\vec{b}|}\right\}. \qquad ...(ii)$$

Example 11 : **Find the angle between two vectors**

$$\hat{i} - 2\hat{j} + 3\hat{k} \text{ and } 3\hat{i} - 2\hat{j} + \hat{k}.$$

Solution : Let $\vec{a} = \hat{i} - 2\hat{j} + 3\hat{k}\,c$ and $\vec{b} = 3\hat{i} - 2\hat{j} + \hat{k}$

Let θ be the angle between vectors $\vec{a}$ and $\vec{b}$. Then,

$$\cos\theta = \frac{\vec{a}\cdot\vec{b}}{|\vec{a}|\,|\vec{b}|}$$

We have,

$$\vec{a} = \hat{i} - 2\hat{j} + 3\hat{k} \text{ and } \vec{b} = 3\hat{i} - 2\hat{j} + \hat{k}.$$

Then,

$$\vec{a}\cdot\vec{b} = 1\times 3 + (-2)\times(-2) + 3\times 1 = 3 + 4 + 3 = 10$$

$$|\vec{a}| = \sqrt{1+4+9} = \sqrt{14} \text{ and } |\vec{b}| = \sqrt{9+4+1} = \sqrt{14}$$

$$\therefore \quad \cos\theta = \frac{\vec{a}\cdot\vec{b}}{|\vec{a}|\,|\vec{b}|}$$

$$\Rightarrow \quad \cos\theta = \frac{10}{14}$$

$$\Rightarrow \quad \cos\theta = \frac{5}{7}$$

$$\Rightarrow \quad \theta = \cos^{-1}\left(\frac{5}{7}\right).$$

Hence, the angle between the given vectors is $\cos^{-1}\left(\frac{5}{7}\right)$.

Example 12 : **Find** $\left(\vec{a} + 3\vec{b}\right).\left(2\vec{a} - \vec{b}\right)$, ***if*** $= \vec{a} = \hat{i} + \hat{j} + 2\hat{k}$ **and** $\vec{b} = 3\hat{i} + 2\hat{j} - \hat{k}$.

Solution : We have

$$\vec{a} + 3\vec{b} = \left(\hat{i} + \hat{j} + 2\hat{k}\right) + 3\left(3\hat{i} + 2\hat{j} - \hat{k}\right) = 10\hat{i} + 7\hat{j} - \hat{k}$$

and $$2\vec{a} - \vec{b} = 2\left(\hat{i} + \hat{j} + 2\hat{k}\right) - 3\left(3\hat{i} + 2\hat{j} - \hat{k}\right) = -\hat{i} + 0\hat{j} - 6\hat{k}$$

$$\therefore \quad (\vec{a} + 3\vec{b}).(2\vec{a} - \vec{b}) = (10\hat{i} + 7\hat{j} - \hat{k}).(-\hat{i} + 0\hat{j} - 5\hat{k})$$

$$= (10)(-1) + (7) + (-1)(5) = -10 + 0 - 5 = -15.$$

Example 13 : **Dot products of a vector with vectors $3\hat{i} - 5\hat{k}$, $2\hat{i} + 7\hat{j}$ and $\hat{i} + \hat{j} + \hat{k}$ are respectively –1, 6 and 5. Find the vector.**

Solution : Let $\vec{a} = 3\hat{i} + 0\hat{j} - 5\hat{k}$, $\vec{b} = 2\hat{i} + 7\hat{j} + 0\hat{k}$ and $\vec{c} = \hat{i} + \hat{j} + \hat{k}$ be three given vectors. Let $\vec{r} = x\hat{i} + y\hat{j} + z\hat{k}$ ne a vector such that its dot products with $\vec{a}$, $\vec{b}$ and $\vec{c}$ are –1, 6 and 5 respectively. Then,

$$\vec{r}.\vec{a} = 1 \Rightarrow (x\hat{i} + y\hat{j} + z\hat{k}).(3\hat{i} + 0\hat{j} + 5\hat{k}) = -1 \Rightarrow 3x + 0y - 5z = -1 \quad ....(i)$$

$$\vec{r}.\vec{b} = 6 \Rightarrow (x\hat{i} + y\hat{j} + z\hat{k}).(2\hat{i} + 7\hat{j} + 0\hat{k}) = 6 \Rightarrow 2x + 7y + 0z = 6 \quad ...(ii)$$

and $\vec{r}.\vec{c} = 5 \Rightarrow (x\hat{i} + y\hat{j} + z\hat{k}).(\hat{i} + \hat{j} + \hat{k}) = 5 \Rightarrow x + y + z = 5 \quad ...(iii)$

Solving (*i*), (*ii*) and (*iii*), we get $x = 3$, $y = 0$, $z = 2$.

Hence, the required vector $\vec{r}$ is given by

$$\vec{r} = 3\hat{i} + 0\hat{j} + 2\hat{k}.$$

Example 14 : **Find the value of λ so that the vectors $\vec{a} = 2\hat{i} + \lambda\hat{j} + \hat{k}$ and $\vec{b} = \hat{i} - 2\hat{j} + 3\hat{k}$ are perpendicular to each other.**

Solution : The vector $\vec{a}$ and $\vec{b}$ are perpendicular to each other.

$$\therefore \quad \vec{a}.\vec{b} = 0$$

$$\Rightarrow \quad (2\hat{i} + \lambda\hat{j} + \hat{k}).(\hat{i} - 2\hat{j} + 3\hat{k}) = 0$$

$$\Rightarrow \quad (2)(1) + \lambda(-2) + (1)(3) = 0$$

$$\Rightarrow \quad -2\lambda + 5 = 0 \Rightarrow \lambda = 5/2.$$

Example 15 : **Find the value of p for which the vectors $\vec{a} = 3\hat{i} + 2\hat{j} + 9\hat{k}$ and $\vec{b} = \hat{i} + p\hat{j} + 3\hat{k}$ are (*i*) perpendicular (*ii*) parallel.**

Solution : (*i*) If vector $\vec{a}$ and $\vec{b}$ are perpendicular, then

$$\vec{a}.\vec{b} = 0$$

$$\Rightarrow \quad (3\hat{i} + 2\hat{j} + 9\hat{k}).(\hat{i} + p\hat{j} + 3\hat{k}) = 0$$

$$\Rightarrow \quad 3 + 2p + 27 = 0 \Rightarrow p = -15.$$

(*ii*) We know that the vectors $\vec{a} = a_1\hat{i} + a_2\hat{j} + a_3\hat{k}$ and $\vec{b} = b_1\hat{i} + b_2\hat{j} + b_3\hat{k}$ are parallel iff $\vec{a} = \lambda\vec{b}$.

$$\Leftrightarrow \quad \left(a_1\hat{i} + a_2\hat{j} + a_3\hat{k}\right) = \lambda\left(b_1\hat{i} + b_2\hat{j} + b_3\hat{k}\right)$$

$$\Leftrightarrow \quad a_1 = \lambda b_1,\ a_2 = \lambda b_2,\ a_3 = \lambda b_3$$

$$\Leftrightarrow \quad \frac{a_1}{b_1} = \frac{a_2}{b_2} = \frac{a_3}{b_3} (= \lambda)$$

So given vectors $\vec{a} = 3\hat{i} + 2\hat{j} + 9\hat{k}$ and $\vec{b} = \hat{i} + p\hat{j} + 3\hat{k}$ will be parallel iff

$$\frac{3}{1} = \frac{2}{p} = \frac{9}{3} \Rightarrow 3 = \frac{2}{p} \Rightarrow p = \frac{2}{3}.$$

Example 16 : **Find the projection of the vector $7\hat{i} + \hat{j} - 4\hat{k}$ on $2\hat{i} + 6\hat{j} + 3\hat{k}$.**

Solution : Let $\vec{a} = 7\hat{i} + \hat{j} - 4\hat{k}$ and $\vec{b} = 2\hat{i} + 6\hat{j} + 3\hat{k}$

We have,

$$\text{Projection of } \vec{a} \text{ on } \vec{b} = \frac{\vec{a}.\vec{b}}{|\vec{b}|}$$

Now,

$$\vec{a}\cdot\vec{b} = \left(7\hat{i} + \hat{j} - 4\hat{k}\right)\cdot\left(2\hat{i} + 6\hat{j} + 3\hat{k}\right) = 14 + 6 - 12 = 8$$

and

$$\vec{b} = \sqrt{2^2 + 6^2 + 3^2} = 7$$

$$\therefore \quad \text{Projection of } \vec{a} \text{ on } \vec{b} = \frac{\vec{a}.\vec{b}}{|\vec{b}|} = \frac{8}{7}.$$

APPLICATIONS OF SCALAR PRODUCT IN MECHANICS

If force is acted on a particle, then work is said to be done if the particle is displaced in a direction which is not perpendicular to the force.

The work done by a force is a scalar quantity. The measure of force is equal to the product of the magnitude of the force and the amount of the displacement in the direction of the force.

Let a particle be placed at O and a force $\vec{F}$ represented by $\vec{OB}$ be a acting on the particle at O. Due to the application of force $\vec{F}$ the particle is displaced in the direction of $\vec{OA}$. Let $\vec{OA}$ be the displacement. Then the component of $\vec{OA}$ in the direction of the force $\vec{F}$ is $|\vec{OA}| \cos\theta$.

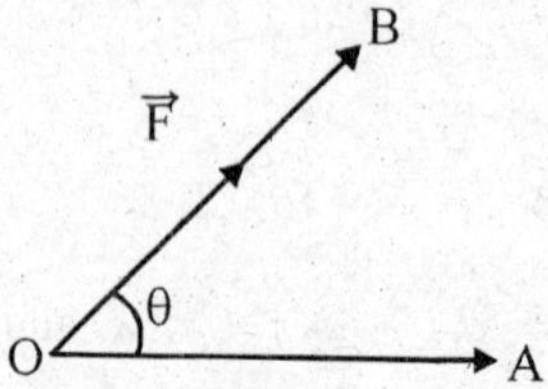

Fig. 1

$\therefore$ Work done $= |\vec{F}|\,|\vec{OA}| \cos\theta.$

$$= \vec{F} . \vec{OA} = \vec{F} . \vec{d}, \text{ where } \vec{d} = \vec{OA}$$

or, Work done = (Force) . (Displacement)

If a number of force are acting on a particle, then the sum of the works done by the separate forces is equal to the work done by the resultant force.

VECTOR OR CROSS PRODUCT

Definition

Vector (or Cross) Product : Let $\vec{a}, \vec{b}$ be two non-zero non-parallel vectors. Then the vector product $\vec{a} \times \vec{b}$, in that order, is defined as a vector whose magnitude is $|\vec{a}|\,|\vec{b}| \sin\theta$, where θ is the angle between $\vec{a}$ and $\vec{b}$ and whose direction is perpendicular to the plane of $\vec{a}$ and $\vec{b}$ in such a way that $\vec{a}, \vec{b}$ and this direction constitute a right handed system.

Property 1 : Vector product is not commutative *i.e.,* $\vec{a}$ and $\vec{b}$ are any two vector, then, $\vec{a} \times \vec{b} = -\left(\vec{b} \times \vec{a}\right)$.

Property 2 : If $\vec{a}, \vec{b}$ are two vectors and m is a scalar, then

$$m\,\vec{a}, \vec{b} = m\left(\vec{b} \times \vec{a}\right) = \vec{a} \times m\,\vec{b}$$

Property 3 : If $\vec{a}, \vec{b}$ are two vectors and m, n are scalars, then

$$m\,\vec{a} \times n\,\vec{b} = m\,n\left(\vec{a} \times \vec{b}\right) = n\left(\vec{a} \times n\,\vec{b}\right) = n\left(\vec{a} \times \vec{b}\right).$$

Property 4 : The vector product of two non-zero vectors is zero vector iff they are parallel (collinear).

i.e., $\vec{a} \times \vec{b} = \vec{0} \Leftrightarrow \vec{a} \parallel \vec{b}, \vec{a}, \vec{b}$ are non-zero vectors.

Example 17 : **Find $\vec{a} \times \vec{b}$, if $\vec{a} = 2\hat{i} + \hat{k}$ and $\vec{b} = \hat{i} + \hat{j} + \hat{k}$.**

Solution : We have,

$$\vec{a} \times \vec{b} = \begin{vmatrix} \hat{i} & \hat{j} & \hat{k} \\ 2 & 0 & 1 \\ 1 & 1 & 1 \end{vmatrix}$$

$$= (0-1)\hat{i} - (2-1)\hat{j} + (2-0)\hat{k} = -\hat{i} - \hat{j} + 2\hat{k}.$$

Example 18 : **Find the magnitude of $\vec{a}$ given by $\vec{a} = (\hat{i} + 3\hat{j} - 2\hat{k}) \times (-\hat{i} + 3\hat{k})$.**

Solution : We have

$$\vec{a} = (\hat{i} + 3\hat{j} - 2\hat{k}) \times (-\hat{i} + 0\hat{j} + 3\hat{k})$$

$$\Rightarrow \quad \vec{a} = \begin{vmatrix} \hat{i} & \hat{j} & \hat{k} \\ 1 & 3 & -2 \\ -1 & 0 & 3 \end{vmatrix} = (9 - 0)\hat{k} - (3 - 2)\hat{j} + (0 + 3)\hat{k} = 9\hat{i} - \hat{j} + 3\hat{k}$$

$$|\vec{a}| = \sqrt{9^2 + (-1)^2 + 3^2} = \sqrt{91}.$$

Example 19 : **Find a unit vector perpendicular to both the vectors $\hat{i} - 2\hat{j} + 3\hat{k}$ and $\hat{i} + 2\hat{j} - \hat{k}$.**

Solution : Let $\vec{a} = \hat{i} - 2\hat{j} + 3\hat{k}$ and $\vec{b} = -2\hat{i} + \hat{j} - 2\hat{k}$. Then

$$\vec{a} \times \vec{b} = \begin{vmatrix} \hat{i} & \hat{j} & \hat{k} \\ 1 & -2 & 3 \\ 1 & 2 & -1 \end{vmatrix} = (2 - 6)\hat{i} - (-1 - 3)\hat{j} + (2 + 2)\hat{k} = -4\hat{i} - 4\hat{j} + 4\hat{k}.$$

$$\Rightarrow \quad |\vec{a} \times \vec{b}| = \sqrt{(-4)^2 + 4^2 + 4^2} = 4\sqrt{3}.$$

So, a unit vector perpendicular to both the vectors $\vec{a}$ and $\vec{b}$ is given by

$$\hat{n} = \frac{\vec{a} \times \vec{b}}{|\vec{a} \times \vec{b}|} = \frac{(-4\hat{i} + 4\hat{j} + 4\hat{k})}{4\sqrt{3}} = \frac{1}{\sqrt{3}}(-\hat{i} + \hat{j} + \hat{k}).$$

Example 20 : **Find a unit vector perpendicular to the plane ABC where *A, B, C* are the points (3, – 1, 2), (1, – 1, – 3), (4, – 3, 1) respectively.**

Solution : The vector $\vec{AB} \times \vec{AC}$ is perpendicular to the vectors $\vec{AB}$ and $\vec{AC}$.

$$\therefore \quad \text{Required vector} = \frac{\vec{AB} \times \vec{AC}}{|\vec{AB} \times \vec{AC}|}$$

Now, $\vec{AB}$ of position vector of B – Position vector of A

$$= \hat{i} - 3\hat{j} - 3\hat{k} - (3\hat{i} - \hat{j} + 2\hat{k}) = -2\hat{i} + 0\hat{j} - 5\hat{k}$$

and $\quad \vec{AC}$ = P.V. of C – $P.V.$ of

$$A = (4\hat{i} - 3\hat{j} + \hat{k}) - (3\hat{i} - \hat{j} + 2\hat{k}) = \hat{i} - 2\hat{j} - \hat{k}$$

$$\therefore \quad \vec{AB} \times \vec{AC} = \begin{vmatrix} \hat{i} & \hat{j} & \hat{k} \\ -2 & 0 & -5 \\ 1 & -2 & -1 \end{vmatrix}$$

$$= (0 - 10)\hat{i} - (2 + 5)\hat{j} + (4 - 0)\hat{k} = -10\hat{i} - 7\hat{j} + 4\hat{k}$$

$$\Rightarrow \quad \left|\vec{AB} \times \vec{AC}\right| = \sqrt{(10)^2 + (-7)^2 + 4^2} = \sqrt{165}.$$

Hence, required vector $= \dfrac{\vec{AB} \times \vec{AC}}{\left|\vec{AB} \times \vec{AC}\right|} = \dfrac{1}{\sqrt{165}} = \left(-10\hat{i} - 7\hat{j} + 4\hat{k}\right).$

PRODUCT OF THREE VECTORS

SCALAR TRIPLE PRODUCT

Definition : Let $\vec{a}, \vec{b}, \vec{c}$ be three vectors. Then the scalar $\left(\vec{a} \times \vec{b}\right).\vec{c}$ is called the scalar triple product of $\vec{a}, \vec{b}$ and $\vec{c}$ and is denoted by $\left[\vec{a}\,\vec{b}\,\vec{c}\right]$.

Thus, $\quad \left[\vec{a}\,\vec{b}\,\vec{c}\right] = \left(\vec{a} \times \vec{b}\right).\vec{c}.$

SCALAR TRIPLE PRODUCT IN TERMS OF COMPONENTS

Theorem : Let $\vec{a} = a_1\hat{i} + a_2\hat{j} + a_3\hat{k},\ \vec{b} = b_1\hat{i} + b_2\hat{j} + b_3\hat{k},\ \vec{c} = c_1\hat{i} + c_2\hat{j} + c_3\hat{k}$ be three vectors. Then,

$$\left[\vec{a}\,\vec{b}\,\vec{c}\right] = \begin{vmatrix} a_1 & a_2 & a_3 \\ b_1 & b_2 & b_3 \\ c_1 & c_2 & c_3 \end{vmatrix}.$$

Example 21 : **Show that the vector $\vec{a} = -2\hat{i} - 2\hat{j} + 4\hat{k},\ \vec{b} = -2\hat{i} + 4\hat{j} - 2\hat{k}$ and $\vec{c} = 4\hat{i} - 2\hat{j} - 2\hat{k}$ are coplanar.**

Solution : We know that three vectors, $\vec{a}, \vec{b}, \vec{c}$ are coplanar iff their scalar triple product is zero *i.e.*, $\left[\vec{a}\,\vec{b}\,\vec{c}\right] = 0.$

Here, $\quad \left[\vec{a}\,\vec{b}\,\vec{c}\right] = \begin{vmatrix} -2 & -2 & 4 \\ -2 & 4 & -2 \\ 4 & -2 & -2 \end{vmatrix} = -2(-8 - 4) + 2(4 + 8) + 4(4 - 16)$

$$= 24 + 24 - 48 = 0.$$

Hence, the given vectors are coplanar.

VECTOR TRIPLE PRODUCT

Definition : Let $\vec{a}, \vec{b}, \vec{c}$ be any three vectors, then the vectors $\vec{a} \times \left(\vec{b} \times \vec{c}\right)$ and $\left(\vec{a} \times \vec{b}\right) \times \vec{c}$ are called vector triple products of $\vec{a}, \vec{b}, \vec{c}$.

Theorem : For any three vectors, $\vec{a}, \vec{b}, \vec{c}$ we have, $\vec{a} \times \left(\vec{b} \times \vec{c}\right) = \left(\vec{a} \,.\, \vec{b}\right)\vec{b} - \left(\vec{a} \,.\, \vec{b}\right)\vec{c}.$

Example 22 : **Prove that $\vec{a} \times \left(\vec{b} \times \vec{c}\right) + \vec{b} \times \left(\vec{c} \times \vec{a}\right) + \vec{c} \times \left(\vec{a} \times \vec{b}\right) = \vec{0}.$**

Solution : We have,

$$\vec{a} \times \left(\vec{b} \times \vec{c}\right) + \vec{b} \times \left(\vec{c} \times \vec{a}\right) + \vec{c} \times \left(\vec{a} \times \vec{b}\right)$$

$$= \left[\left(\vec{a} \,.\, \vec{c}\right)\vec{b} - \left(\vec{a} \,.\, \vec{b}\right)\right] + \left[\left(\vec{b} \,.\, \vec{a}\right)\vec{c} - \left(\vec{b} \,.\, \vec{c}\right)\vec{a}\right] + \left[\left(\vec{c} \,.\, \vec{b}\right)\vec{a} - \left(\vec{c} \,.\, \vec{a}\right)\vec{b}\right]$$

$$= \left[\left(\vec{a} \,.\, \vec{c}\right)\vec{b} - \left(\vec{a} \,.\, \vec{b}\right)\vec{c}\right] + \left[\left(\vec{a} \,.\, \vec{b}\right)\vec{c} - \left(\vec{b} \,.\, \vec{c}\right)\vec{a}\right] + \left[\left(\vec{b} \,.\, \vec{c}\right)\vec{a} - \left(\vec{a} \,.\, \vec{c}\right)\vec{b}\right]$$

$$= \vec{0}.$$

Example 23 : **For any vector $\vec{a}$, prove that $\vec{a} = \hat{i}\times\left(\vec{a} \times \hat{i}\right) + \hat{j}\left(\vec{a} \times \hat{j}\right)\hat{k} \times \left(\vec{a} \times \hat{k}\right) = 2\vec{a}.$**

Solution : Let $\vec{a} = a_1\hat{i} + a_2\hat{j} + a_3\hat{k}.$ Then,

$$\hat{i}\times\left(\vec{a} \times \hat{i}\right) + \hat{j} \times \left(\vec{a} \times \hat{j}\right) + \hat{k} \times \left(\vec{a} \times \hat{k}\right)$$

$$= \left[\left(\hat{i} \,.\, \hat{i}\right)\vec{a} - \left(\hat{i} \,.\, \vec{a}\right)\hat{i}\right] + \left[\left(\hat{j} \,.\, \hat{j}\right)\vec{a} - \left(\hat{j} \,.\, \vec{a}\right)\hat{j}\right]\left[\left(\hat{k} \,.\, \hat{k}\right)\vec{a} - \left(\hat{k} \,.\, \vec{a}\right)\hat{k}\right]$$

$$= \left[\vec{a} - \left(\hat{i} \,.\, \vec{a}\right)\right] + \left[\vec{a} - \left(\hat{j} \,.\, \vec{a}\right)\hat{j}\right]\left[\vec{a} - \left(\hat{k} \,.\, \vec{a}\right)\hat{k}\right] \qquad \left[\because \hat{i} \,,\hat{i} = \hat{j} \,.\hat{j} = \hat{k} \,.\hat{k} = 1\right]$$

$$= 3\vec{a} - \left[\left(\hat{i} \,.\, \vec{a}\right)\hat{i} + \left(\hat{j} \,.\, \vec{a}\right)\hat{j} + \left(\hat{k} \,.\, \vec{a}\right)\hat{k}\right]$$

$$= 3\vec{a} - \left(a_1\hat{i} + a_2\hat{j} + a_3\hat{k}\right) \qquad \left[\because \hat{i} \,.\, \vec{a} = a_1,\ \hat{j} \,.\, \vec{a} = a_2 \text{ and } \hat{k} \,.\, \vec{a} - a_3\right]$$

$$= 3\vec{a} - \vec{a} = 2\vec{a}.$$

Example 24 : **Prove that $= \left[\vec{a} \times \vec{b} \;\; \vec{b} \times \vec{c} \;\; \vec{c} \times \vec{a}\right] = \left[\vec{a}\,\vec{b}\,\vec{c}\right]^2.$**

Solution : We have,

$$\left[\vec{a} \times \vec{b} \;\; \vec{b} \times \vec{c} \;\; \vec{c} \times \vec{a}\right]$$

$$= \left[\left(\vec{a} \times \vec{b}\right) \times \left(\vec{b} \times \vec{c}\right)\right] . \left(\vec{c} \times \vec{a}\right)$$

$$= \left[\vec{d} \times \left(\vec{b} \times \vec{c}\right)\right] . \left(\vec{c} \times \vec{a}\right), \text{ where } \vec{d} = \vec{a} \times \vec{b}$$

$$= \left[\left(\vec{d} \,.\, \vec{c}\right)\vec{b} \times \left(\vec{d} \,.\, \vec{b}\right)\vec{c}\right] . \left(\vec{c} \times \vec{a}\right)$$

$$= \left[\left(\left(\vec{a} \times \vec{b}\right).\vec{b}\right)\vec{b} \times \left(\left(\vec{a} \times \vec{b}\right)\vec{c}\right)\vec{c}\right].\left(\vec{c} \times \vec{a}\right)$$

$$= \left\{\left[\vec{a}\ \vec{b}\ \vec{c}\right].\vec{b} - \left[\vec{a}\ \vec{b}\ \vec{b}\right]\vec{c}\right\}.\left(\vec{c} \times \vec{a}\right)$$

$$= \left[\vec{a}\ \vec{b}\ \vec{c}\right]\left\{\vec{b}.\left(\vec{c} \times \vec{a}\right)\right\}$$

$$= \left[\vec{a}\ \vec{b}\ \vec{c}\right]\left[\vec{b}\ \vec{c}\ \vec{a}\right] = \left[\vec{a}\ \vec{b}\ \vec{c}\right]^2.$$

Example 25 : **Prove that**

(*i*) $\left(\vec{a} \times \vec{b}\right) \times \left(\vec{c} \times \vec{d}\right) = \left[\vec{a}\ \vec{b}\ \vec{d}\right] c - \left[\vec{a}\ \vec{b}\ \vec{c}\right]\vec{d}$.

(*ii*) $\left(\vec{a} \times \vec{b}\right) \times \left(\vec{c} \times \vec{d}\right) = \left[\vec{a}\ \vec{c}\ \vec{d}\right] - \left[\vec{b}\ \vec{c}\ \vec{d}\right]\vec{a}$.

Solution : (*i*) We have,

$$\left(\vec{a} \times \vec{b}\right) \times \left(\vec{c} \times \vec{d}\right)$$

$$= \vec{r} \times \left(\vec{c} \times \vec{d}\right), \quad \text{where } \vec{r} = \vec{a} \times \vec{b}$$

$$= \left(\vec{r}\ .\ \vec{d}\right)\vec{c} - \left(\vec{r}\ .\ \vec{a}\right)\vec{d}$$

$$= \left\{\left(\vec{a} \times \vec{b}\right).\vec{d}\right\} - \left\{\left(\vec{a} \times \vec{b}\right).\vec{c}\right\}\vec{d}$$

$$= \left[\vec{a}\ \vec{b}\ \vec{d}\right]\vec{c} - \left[\vec{a}\ \vec{b}\ \vec{c}\right]\vec{d}.$$

(*ii*) $\left(\vec{a} \times \vec{b}\right) \times \left(\vec{c} \times \vec{d}\right)$

$$= \left(\vec{a} \times \vec{b}\right) \times \vec{r}$$

$$= -\vec{r} \times \left(\vec{a} \times \vec{b}\right)$$

$$= \left\{\left(\vec{r}\ .\ \vec{b}\right)\vec{a} - \left(\vec{r}\ .\ \vec{a}\right)\vec{b}\right\}$$

$$= \left(\vec{r}\ .\ \vec{a}\right)\vec{b} - \left(\vec{r}\ .\ \vec{b}\right)\vec{a}$$

$$= \left\{\left(\vec{c} \times \vec{d}\right).\vec{a}\right\}\left\{\vec{b} - \left(\vec{c} \times \vec{d}\right)\right\}\vec{a}$$

$$= \left\{\vec{a}.\left(\vec{c} \times \vec{d}\right)\right\}\vec{b} - \left\{\vec{b}\ .\left(\vec{b}\ .\left\{\vec{c} \times \vec{d}\right)\right\}\vec{a}$$

$$= \left[\vec{a}\ \vec{c}\ \vec{d}\right]\vec{b} - \left[\vec{b}\ \vec{c}\ \vec{d}\right]\vec{a}.$$

Example 26 : **Prove that** $\vec{a}\left\{\vec{b}\left(\vec{c} \times \vec{d}\right)\right\} = \left(\vec{b}\ .\ \vec{d}\right)\left(\vec{a} \times \vec{c}\right) - \left(\vec{b}\ .\ \vec{c}\right)\left(\vec{a} \times \vec{d}\right).$

Solution : We have,

$\vec{a} \times \left\{\vec{b}\left(\vec{c} \times \vec{d}\right)\right\}$

$= \vec{a} \times \left\{\left(\vec{b} . \vec{d}\right)\vec{c} - \left(\vec{b} . \vec{c}\right)\vec{d}\right\}$

$= \vec{a} \times \left\{\left(\vec{b} . \vec{d}\right)\vec{c}\right\} - \vec{a} \times \left\{\left(\vec{b} . \vec{c}\right)\vec{d}\right\}$ [By distributive law]

$= \left(\vec{b} . \vec{d}\right)\left(\vec{a} \times \vec{c}\right) - \left(\vec{b} . \vec{c}\right)\left(\vec{a} \times \vec{d}\right).$

APPLICATION OF VECTORS

Example 27 **: Find the area of the parallelogram determined by the vectors**

$$\hat{i} + 2\hat{j} + 3\hat{k} \text{ and } 3\hat{i} - 2\hat{j} + \hat{k}.$$

Solution : Let $\vec{a} = \hat{i} + 2\hat{j} + 3\hat{k}$ and $\vec{b} = 3\hat{i} - 2\hat{j} + \hat{k}$. The vector area of the parallelogram whose adjacent sides area represented by the vectors $\vec{a}$ and $\vec{b}$ is $\vec{a} \times \vec{b}$.

$$\vec{a} \times \vec{b} = \begin{vmatrix} \hat{i} & \hat{j} & \hat{k} \\ 1 & 2 & 3 \\ 3 & -2 & 1 \end{vmatrix} = (2 + 6)\hat{i} - (1 - 9)\hat{j} + (-2 - 6)\hat{k} = 8\hat{i} + 8\hat{j} - 8\hat{k}$$

Hence, area of the parallelogram $= \vec{a} \times \vec{b} = \sqrt{8^2 + 8^2 + (-8)^2} = 8\sqrt{3}$ square unit.

Example 28 **: Show that the area of the parallelogram having diagonals**

$$3\hat{i} + \hat{j} - 2\hat{k} \text{ and } \hat{i} - 3\hat{j} + 4\hat{k} \text{ is } 5\sqrt{3}.$$

Solution : Let $\vec{a} = 3\hat{i} + \hat{j} - 2\hat{k}$ and $\vec{b} = \hat{i} - 3\hat{j} + 4\hat{k}$. Then,

$$\vec{a} \times \vec{b} = \begin{vmatrix} \hat{i} & \hat{j} & \hat{k} \\ 3 & 1 & -2 \\ 1 & -3 & 4 \end{vmatrix} = (4 - 6)\hat{i} - (12 + 2)\hat{j} + (-9 - 1)\hat{k}$$

$$= -2\hat{i} - 14\hat{j} - 10\hat{k}$$

$\therefore \quad \vec{a} \times \vec{b} = \sqrt{(-2)^2 + (-14)^2 + (-10)^2} = \sqrt{300}$

$\therefore$ Area of parallelogram $= \frac{1}{2}\left|\vec{a} \times \vec{b}\right| = \frac{1}{2}\sqrt{300}$ sq. units.

Example 29 **: Given $\left|\vec{a}\right| = 10, \left|\vec{b}\right| = 2$ and $\vec{a} . \vec{b} = 12$, find $\left|\vec{a} \times \vec{b}\right|$.**

Solution : As already explained,

$$\left(\vec{a} . \vec{b}\right)^2 + \left|\vec{a} \times \vec{b}\right|^2 = \left|\vec{a}\right|^2 \left|\vec{b}\right|^2$$

$\therefore \quad 12^2 + \left|\vec{a} \times \vec{b}\right|^2 = (10)^2 \times (2)^2$

$\therefore \quad \left|\vec{a} \times \vec{b}\right|^2 = 400 - 144$

$\therefore \quad \left|\vec{a} \times \vec{b}\right|^2 = 256$

$\therefore \quad \left|\vec{a} \times \vec{b}\right|^2 = 16.$

Example 30 : **Find the area of the triangle whose vertices are $A(3, -1, 2)$, $B(1, -1, -3)$ and $C(4, -3, 1)$.**

Solution : Let $\vec{a}, \vec{b}$ and $\vec{c}$ be the position vectors of points A, B and C respectively. Therefore,

$$\vec{a} = 3\hat{i} - \hat{j} + 2\hat{k}, \ \vec{b} = \hat{i} - \hat{j} - 3\hat{k} \text{ and } \vec{c} = 4\hat{i} - 3\hat{j} + \hat{k}$$

We have,

$$\text{Area of } \Delta ABC = \frac{1}{2}\left|\vec{AB} \times \vec{AC}\right|$$

Now $\quad \vec{AB}$ = Position vector of B – Position vector of A

$\Rightarrow \quad \vec{AB} = \vec{b} - \vec{a}$

$\Rightarrow \quad \vec{AB} = \left(\hat{i} - \hat{j} - 3\hat{k}\right) - \left(3\hat{i} - \hat{j} + 2\hat{k}\right) = 2\hat{i} + 0\hat{j} - 5\hat{k},$

Similarly, $\quad \vec{AC}$ = Position vector of C – Position vector of A

$\Rightarrow \quad \vec{AC} = \vec{c} - \vec{a}$

$\Rightarrow \quad \vec{AC} = \left(4\hat{i} - 3\hat{j} + \hat{k}\right) - \left(3\hat{i} - \hat{j} + 2\hat{k}\right) = \hat{i} - 2\hat{j} - \hat{k},$

$$\Rightarrow \quad \vec{AB} \times \vec{AC} = \begin{vmatrix} \hat{i} & \hat{j} & \hat{k} \\ -2 & 0 & -5 \\ 1 & -2 & -1 \end{vmatrix} = (0 - 10)\hat{i} - (2 + 5)\hat{j} + (4 - 0)\hat{k}$$

$\Rightarrow \quad \vec{AB} \times \vec{AC} = -10\hat{i} - 7\hat{j} + 4\hat{k}$

$\Rightarrow \quad \left|\vec{AB} \times \vec{AC}\right| = \sqrt{(-10)^2 + (-7)^2 + 4^2} = \sqrt{165}$

Hence, area of $\Delta ABC = \frac{1}{2}\left|\vec{AB} \times \vec{AC}\right| = \frac{1}{2}\sqrt{165}.$

Example 31 : **For any three vector $\vec{a}, \vec{b}, \vec{c}$ show that**

$$\vec{a} \times \left(\vec{b} + \vec{c}\right) + \vec{b} \times \left(\vec{c} + \vec{a}\right) + \vec{c} \times \left(\vec{a} + \vec{b}\right) = \vec{0}.$$

Solution : We have,

$$\vec{a} \times \left(\vec{b} + \vec{c}\right) + \vec{b} \times \left(\vec{c} + \vec{a}\right) + \vec{c} \times \left(\vec{a} + \vec{b}\right)$$

$$= \vec{a} \times \vec{b} + \vec{a} \times \vec{c} + \vec{b} \times \vec{c} + \vec{b} \times \vec{a} + \vec{c} \times \vec{a} + \vec{c} \times \vec{b} \quad \text{[Using distributive law]}$$

$$= \vec{a} \times \vec{b} + \vec{a} \times \vec{c} + \vec{b} \times \vec{c} - \vec{a} \times \vec{b} - \vec{a} \times \vec{c} - \vec{b} \times \vec{c}$$

$$= \vec{0}. \quad \left[\because \vec{a} \times \vec{b} = -\vec{b} \times \vec{a} \text{ etc.}\right]$$

Example 32 : **If $\vec{a} \times \vec{b} = \vec{c} \times \vec{d}$ and $\vec{a} \times \vec{c} = \vec{b} \times \vec{d}$, show that $\vec{a} - \vec{d}$ is parallel to $\vec{b} - \vec{c}$, where $= \vec{a} \neq \vec{d}$ and $\vec{b} \neq \vec{c}$.**

Solution : Two non-zero vectors are parallel where their cross-product is zero vector.

Therefore, we have

$$\left(\vec{a} - \vec{d}\right) \times \left(\vec{b} - \vec{c}\right) = \vec{a} \times \vec{b} - \vec{a} \times \vec{c} - \vec{d} \times \vec{b} + \vec{d} \times \vec{c}$$

[Using distributive law]

$$\left(\vec{a} - \vec{d}\right) \times \left(\vec{b} - \vec{c}\right) = \vec{c} \times \vec{d} - \vec{b} \times \vec{d} + \vec{b} \times \vec{d} - \vec{c} \times \vec{d}$$

$$\left[\begin{array}{r} \because \vec{a} \times \vec{b} = \vec{c} \times \vec{d},\ \vec{a} \times \vec{c} = \vec{b} \times \vec{d} - \vec{d} \times \vec{b} = \vec{b} \times \vec{d} \\ \text{and } \vec{d} \times \vec{c} = -\vec{b} \times \vec{d} \end{array}\right]$$

$$\left(\vec{a} - \vec{d}\right) \times \left(\vec{b} - \vec{c}\right) = \vec{0}$$

So, $\left(\vec{a} - \vec{d}\right)$ is parallel to $\left(\vec{b} - \vec{c}\right)$.

Example 33 : If $\vec{a}\ \vec{b}, \vec{c}$ are three vectors such that $\vec{a} + \vec{b} + \vec{c} = \vec{0}$, **then prove that** $\vec{a} \times \vec{b} = \vec{b} \times \vec{c} = \vec{c} \times \vec{a}$

Solution : We have,

$$\vec{a} + \vec{b} + \vec{c} = \vec{0}$$

$$\Rightarrow \quad \vec{a} \times (\vec{a} + \vec{b} + \vec{c}) = \vec{a} \times \vec{0} \quad \text{[Taking cross-product with } \vec{a}\text{]}$$

$$\Rightarrow \quad \vec{a} \times \vec{a} + \vec{a} \times \vec{b} + \vec{a} \times \vec{c} = \vec{0} \quad \text{[Using distributive law]}$$

$$\Rightarrow \quad \vec{a} \times \vec{b} - \vec{c} \times \vec{a} = \vec{0} \quad \left[\because \vec{a} \times \vec{a} = \vec{0} \text{ and } \vec{a} \times \vec{c} = -\vec{c} \times \vec{a}\right]$$

$$\Rightarrow \quad \vec{a} \times \vec{b} = \vec{c} \times \vec{a} \quad (1)$$

Again, $\vec{a} + \vec{b} + \vec{c} = \vec{0}$

$$\Rightarrow \quad \vec{b} \times (\vec{a} + \vec{b} + \vec{c}) = \vec{b} \times \vec{0} \qquad \text{[Taking cross-product with } \vec{b}\text{]}$$

$$\Rightarrow \quad \vec{b} \times \vec{a} + \vec{b} \times \vec{b} + \vec{b} \times \vec{c} = \vec{0}$$

$$\Rightarrow \quad -\vec{a} \times \vec{b} + \vec{0} + \vec{b} \times \vec{c} = \vec{0} \qquad \left[\because \vec{b} \times \vec{b} = \vec{0} \text{ and } \vec{b} \times \vec{a} = -\vec{a} \times \vec{b}\right]$$

$$\Rightarrow \quad \vec{a} \times \vec{b} = \vec{b} \times \vec{c} \qquad (2)$$

From (1) and (2), we obtain

$$\vec{a} \times \vec{b} = \vec{b} \times \vec{c} = \vec{c} \times \vec{a}.$$

Example 34 : If $\vec{a} = \hat{i} + \hat{j} + \hat{k}$, $\vec{c} = \hat{j} - \hat{k}$ **are given vectors, then find a vector** $\vec{b}$ **satisfying the equation** $\vec{a} \times \vec{b} = \vec{c}$ ***and*** $\vec{a} \cdot \vec{b} = 3$.

Solution : Let $\vec{b} = x\hat{i} + y\hat{j} + 3\hat{k}$. Then,

$$\vec{a} \times \vec{b} = \vec{c}$$

$$\therefore \quad \begin{vmatrix} \hat{i} & \hat{j} & \hat{k} \\ 1 & 1 & 1 \\ x & y & z \end{vmatrix} = (\hat{j} - \hat{k})$$

$$(z - y)\hat{i} - (z - x)\hat{j} + (y - x)\hat{k} = \hat{j} - \hat{k}$$

$$z - y = 0, \; -(z - x) = 1, \; y - x = -1$$

$$y = z, \; x - z = 1, \; x - y = 1$$

$$x - z = 1, \; x - y = 1 \qquad [\because \text{These two equations are equivalent to } y = z]$$

$$z = x - 1 \text{ and } y = x - 1.$$

Given, $\quad \vec{a} \cdot \vec{b} = 3$

$$\therefore \quad (\hat{i} + \hat{j} + \hat{k}).(x\hat{i} + y\hat{j} + z\hat{k}) = 3$$

$$x + y + z = 3$$

$$x + x - 1 - x - 1 = 3 \qquad \text{(Using } (i)\text{)]}$$

$$3x = 5 \Rightarrow x = \frac{5}{3}$$

$$\therefore \quad y = x - 1 \Rightarrow y = \frac{5}{3} - 1 = \frac{2}{3}.$$

Also, $\quad y = z \Rightarrow z = \frac{2}{3}.$

Hence, $\quad \vec{b} = \frac{5}{3}\hat{i} + \frac{2}{3}\hat{j} + \frac{2}{3}\hat{k}.$

Example 35 : *Find* $\vec{a} \times \vec{b}$, *if* $\vec{a} = 2\hat{i} + \hat{k}$ *and* $\vec{b} = \hat{i} + \hat{j} + \hat{k}$.

Solution : We have,

$$\vec{a} \times \vec{b} = \begin{vmatrix} \hat{i} & \hat{j} & \hat{k} \\ 2 & 0 & 1 \\ 1 & 1 & 1 \end{vmatrix}$$

$$\Rightarrow \quad \vec{a} \times \vec{b} = (0-1)\hat{i} - (2-1)\hat{j} + (2-0)\hat{k} = -\hat{i} - \hat{j} + 2\hat{k}$$

Example 36 : *Find the magnitude of* $\vec{a}$ *given by* $\vec{a}\ (\hat{i} + 3\hat{j} - 2\hat{k}) \times (-\hat{i} + 3\hat{k})$

Solution : We have,

$$\vec{a} = (\hat{i} + 3\hat{j} - 2\hat{k}) \times (-\hat{i} + 0\hat{j} + 3\hat{k})$$

$$\Rightarrow \quad \vec{a} = \begin{vmatrix} \hat{i} & \hat{j} & \hat{k} \\ 1 & 3 & -2 \\ -1 & 0 & 3 \end{vmatrix} = (9-0)\hat{i} - (3-2)\hat{j} + (0+3)\hat{k} = 9\hat{i} - \hat{j} + 3\hat{k}$$

$$\therefore \quad |\vec{a}| = \sqrt{9^2 + (-1)^2 + 3^2} = \sqrt{91}.$$

Example 37 : *Find a unit vector perpendicular to both the vectors* $\hat{i} - 2\hat{j} + 3\hat{k}$ and $\hat{i} + 2\hat{j} - \hat{k}$.

Solution : Let $\vec{a} = \hat{i} - 2\hat{j} + 3\hat{k}$ and $\vec{b} = -2\hat{i} + \hat{j} - 2\hat{k}$. Then,

$$\vec{a} \times \vec{b} = \begin{vmatrix} \hat{i} & \hat{j} & \hat{k} \\ 1 & -2 & 3 \\ 1 & 2 & -1 \end{vmatrix} = (2-6)\hat{i} - (-1-3)\hat{j} + (2+2)\hat{k}$$

$$= -4\hat{i} + 4\hat{j} + 4\hat{k}.$$

$$\Rightarrow \quad \left|\vec{a} \times \vec{b}\right| = \sqrt{(-4)^2 + 4^2 + 4^2} = 4\sqrt{3}.$$

So, a unit vector perpendicular to both the vectors $\vec{a}$ and $\vec{b}$ is given by

$$\hat{n} = \frac{\vec{a} \times \vec{b}}{\left|\vec{a} \times \vec{b}\right|} = \frac{(-4\hat{i} + 4\hat{j} + 4\hat{k})}{4\sqrt{3}} = \frac{1}{\sqrt{3}}(-\hat{i} + \hat{j} + \hat{k})$$

Example 38 : *Find a vector of magnitude 9, which is perpendicular to both the vectors* $4\hat{i} - \hat{j} + 3\hat{k}$ and $-2\hat{i} + \hat{j} - 2\hat{k}$.

Solution : Let $\vec{a} = 4\hat{i} - \hat{j} + 3\hat{k}$ and $\vec{b} = -2\hat{i} + \hat{j} - 2\hat{k}$. Then,

$$\vec{a} \times \vec{b} = \begin{vmatrix} \hat{i} & \hat{j} & \hat{k} \\ 4 & -1 & 3 \\ -2 & 1 & -2 \end{vmatrix} = (2-3)\hat{i} - (-8+6)\hat{j} + (4-2)\hat{k}$$

$$= -\hat{i} + 2\hat{j} + 2\hat{k}$$

$$\Rightarrow \quad \left|\vec{a} \times \vec{b}\right| = \sqrt{(-1)^2 + 2^2 + 2^2} = 3$$

$$\therefore \quad \text{Required vector} = 9\left\{\frac{\vec{a} \times \vec{b}}{\left|\vec{a} \times \vec{b}\right|}\right\} = \frac{9}{3}(-\hat{i} + 2\hat{j} + 2\hat{k}) = -3\hat{i} + 6\hat{j} + 6\hat{k}.$$

Exercise 19.1

1. Write a unit vector in the direction $\vec{a} = 3\hat{i} - 2\hat{j} + 6\hat{k}$.

Ans. $\hat{a} = \frac{3}{7}\hat{i} \frac{-2}{7}\hat{j} + \frac{6}{7}\hat{k}$

2. If $\vec{a} = \hat{i} + 2\hat{j} + -3\hat{k}$ and $\vec{b} = 2\hat{i} + 4\hat{j} + 9\hat{k}$, find a unit vector parallel to $\vec{a} + \vec{b}$.

Ans. $\frac{3}{7}\hat{i} + \frac{6}{7}\hat{j} + \frac{6}{7}\hat{k}$

3. If $\vec{a} + \vec{b} + \vec{c} = 0$, $|\vec{a}| = 3$, $|\vec{b}| = 5$ and $|\vec{c}| = 7$, find the angle between $\vec{a}$ and $\vec{b}$.

Ans. Cos $\theta = \frac{1}{2}$.

4. For what value of λ are the vector $\vec{a}$ and $\vec{b}$ perpendicular to each other?

(*i*) $\vec{a} = \lambda\hat{i} + 2\hat{j} + \hat{k}$ and $\vec{b} = 4\hat{i} - a\hat{j} + 2\hat{k}$

(*ii*) $\vec{a} = \lambda\hat{i} + 2\hat{j} + \hat{k}$ and $\vec{b} = 5\hat{i} - a\hat{j} + 2\hat{k}$

(*iii*) $\vec{a} = \lambda\hat{i} + 3\hat{j} + 2\hat{k}$ and $\vec{b} = \hat{i} - \hat{j} + 3\hat{k}$

Ans. (*i*) $\lambda = 4$, (*ii*) $\lambda = \frac{16}{5}$, (*iii*) -3

5. Dot product of a rector with $\hat{i} + \hat{j} - 3\hat{k}$, $\hat{i} + 3\hat{j} - 2\hat{k}$ and $2\hat{i} + \hat{j} + 4\hat{k}$ are 0, 5 and 8 respectively. Find the vector.

Ans. $\hat{i} + 2\hat{j} + \hat{k}$.

6. If $\vec{a}, \vec{b}, \vec{c}$ are three mutually perpendicular vectors of equal magnitude, prove that $\vec{a} + \vec{b} + \vec{c}$ is equally inclined with vectors $\vec{a}, \vec{b}$ and $\vec{c}$.

7. Find the angle between the vector $\vec{a} = \hat{i} - \hat{j} + \hat{k}$ and $\vec{b} = \hat{i} + \hat{j} - \hat{k}$.

Ans. $\text{Cos}^{-1}\left(-\frac{1}{3}\right)$.

8. For what value of λ are the vectors $\vec{a} = 2\hat{i} + \lambda\hat{j} + \hat{k}$ and $\vec{b} = \hat{i} - 2\hat{j} + 3\hat{k}$ perpendicular to each other.

Ans. $\frac{5}{2}$

9. Find the magnitude of $\vec{a} \times \vec{b}$ in the following cases :

(i) $\vec{a} \times \hat{i} + 3\hat{j} - 2\hat{k}$ and $\vec{b} = -\hat{i} + 3\hat{k}$

(ii) $\vec{a} = 3\hat{i} + 4\hat{j}$ and $\vec{b} = \hat{i} + \hat{j} + \hat{k}$

(iii) $\vec{a} = 2\hat{i} + \hat{k}$ and $\vec{b} = \hat{i} + \hat{j} + \hat{k}$

Ans. (i) $\sqrt{91}$, (ii) $\sqrt{26}$, (iii) $\sqrt{6}$

10. If $|\vec{a}| = 13$, $|\vec{b}| = 5$ and $\vec{a} \cdot \vec{b} = 60$, then find $\left|\vec{a} \times \vec{b}\right|$.

Ans. 13

11. If $|\vec{a}| = 2$, $|\vec{b}| = 5$ and $\vec{a} \times \vec{b} = 8$, find $\vec{a} \cdot \vec{b}$.

Ans. 6

12. Find a unit vector perpendicular to both the vectors $4\hat{i} - \hat{j} + 3\hat{k}$ and $-2\hat{i} + \hat{j} - 2\hat{k}$.

Ans. $\frac{1}{3}(-\hat{i} + 2\hat{j} + 2\hat{k})$

13. Find the area of the parallelogram determined by the vectors

(i) $2\hat{i}$ and $3\hat{j}$ (ii) $2\hat{i} - 3\hat{j} + 3\hat{k}$ and $\hat{i} - \hat{j}$ (iii) $\hat{i} - 3\hat{j} + \hat{k}$ and $\hat{i} + \hat{j} + \hat{k}$

Ans. (i) 6 squints, (ii) $3\sqrt{3}$ sq units, (iii) $4\sqrt{2}$ sq. units.

14. If $\vec{a} = \hat{i} - \hat{j} + \hat{k}$, $\vec{c} = \hat{j} - \hat{k}$ are given vectors, find a vector $\vec{b}$ satisfying the equations $\vec{a} \times \vec{b} = \vec{c}$ and $\vec{a} \cdot \vec{b} = 3$.

Ans. $\vec{b} = \frac{5}{3}\hat{i} + \frac{2}{3}\hat{j} + \frac{2}{3}\hat{k}$

15. Find a vector whose length is 3 and which is perpendicular to the vector.

$\vec{a} = 3\hat{i} + \hat{j} - 4\hat{k}$ and $\vec{b} = 6\hat{i} + 5\hat{j} - 2\hat{k}$.

Ans. $42\hat{i} + 14\hat{j} - 21\hat{k}$.

TABLE 1
AMOUNT AT COMPOUND INTEREST
$$s = (1 + i)^n$$

Periods	Rate i				
n	.0025 ($\frac{1}{4}$%)	.004167 ($\frac{5}{12}$%)	.005 ($\frac{1}{2}$%)	.005833 ($\frac{7}{12}$%)	.0075 ($\frac{3}{4}$%)
1	1.0025 0000	1.0041 6667	1.0050 0000	1.0058 3333	1.0075 0000
2	1.0050 0625	1.0083 5069	1.0100 2500	1.0117 0069	1.0150 5625
3	1.0075 1877	1.0125 5216	1.0150 7513	1.0176 0228	1.0226 6917
4	1.0100 3756	1.0167 7112	1.0201 5050	1.0235 3830	1.0303 3919
5	1.0125 6266	1.0210 0767	1.0252 5125	1.0295 0894	1.0380 6673
6	1.0150 9406	1.0252 6187	1.0303 7751	1.0355 1440	1.0458 5224
7	1.0176 3180	1.0295 3379	1.0355 2940	1.0415 5490	1.0536 9613
8	1.0201 7588	1.0338 2352	1.0407 0704	1.0476 3064	1.0615 9885
9	1.0227 2632	1.0381 3111	1.0459 1058	1.0537 4182	1.0695 6084
10	1.0252 8313	1.0424 5666	1.0511 4013	1.0598 8865	1.0775 8255
11	1.0278 4634	1.0468 0023	1.0563 9583	1.0660 7133	1.0856 6441
12	1.0304 1596	1.0511 6190	1.0616 7781	1.0722 9008	1.0938 0690
13	1.0329 9200	1.0555 4174	1.0669 8620	1.0785 4511	1.1020 1045
14	1.0355 7448	1.0599 3983	1.0723 2113	1.0848 3662	1.1102 7553
15	1.0381 6341	1.0643 5625	1.0776 8274	1.0911 6483	1.1186 0259
16	1.0407 5882	1.0687 9106	1.0830 7115	1.0975 2996	1.1269 9211
17	1.0433 6072	1.0732 4436	1.0884 8651	1.1039 3222	1.1354 4455
18	1.0459 6912	1.0777 1621	1.0939 2894	1.1103 7182	1.1439 6039
19	1.0485 8404	1.0822 0670	1.0993 9858	1.1168 4899	1.1525 4009
20	1.0512 0550	1.0867 1589	1.1048 9558	1.1233 6395	1.1611 8414
21	1.0538 3352	1.0912 4387	1.1104 2006	1.1299 1690	1.1698 9302
22	1.0564 6810	1.0957 9072	1.1159 7216	1.1365 0808	1.1786 6722
23	1.0591 0927	1.1003 5652	1.1215 5202	1.1431 3771	1.1875 0723
24	1.0617 5704	1.1049 4134	1.1271 5978	1.1498 0602	1.1964 1353
25	1.0644 1144	1.1095 4526	1.1327 9558	1.1565 1322	1.2053 8663
26	1.0670 7247	1.1141 6836	1.1384 5955	1.1632 5955	1.2144 2703
27	1.0697 4015	1.1188 1073	1.1441 5185	1.1700 4523	1.2235 3523
28	1.0724 1450	1.1234 7244	1.1498 7261	1.1768 7049	1.2327 1175
29	1.0750 9553	1.1281 5358	1.1556 2197	1.1837 3557	1.2419 5709
30	1.0777 8327	1.1328 5422	1.1614 0008	1.1906 4069	1.2512 7176
31	1.0804 7773	1.1375 7444	1.1672 0708	1.1975 8610	1.2606 5630
32	1.0831 7892	1.1423 1434	1.1730 4312	1.2045 7202	1.2701 1122
33	1.0858 8687	1.1470 7398	1.1789 0833	1.2115 9869	1.2796 3706
34	1.0886 0159	1.1518 5346	1.1848 0288	1.2186 6634	1.2892 3434
35	1.0913 2309	1.1566 5284	1.1907 2689	1.2257 7523	1.2989 0359
36	1.0940 5140	1.1614 7223	1.1966 8052	1.2329 2559	1.3086 4537
37	1.0967 8653	1.1663 1170	1.2026 6393	1.2401 1765	1.3184 6021
38	1.0995 2850	1.1711 7133	1.2085 7725	1.2473 5167	1.3283 4866
39	1.1022 7732	1.1760 5121	1.2147 2063	1.2546 2789	1.3383 1128
40	1.1050 3301	1.1809 5142	1.2207 9424	1.2619 4655	1.3483 4861
41	1.1077 9559	1.1858 7206	1.2268 9821	1.2693 0791	1.3584 6133
42	1.1105 6508	1.1908 1319	1.2330 3270	1.2767 1220	1.3686 4969
43	1.1133 4149	1.1957 7491	1.2391 9786	1.2841 5969	1.3789 1456
44	1.1161 2485	1.2007 5731	1.2453 9385	1.2916 5062	1.3892 5642
45	1.1189 1516	1.2057 6046	1.2516 2082	1.2991 8525	1.3996 7584
46	1.1217 1245	1.2107 8446	1.2578 7892	1.3067 6383	1.4101 7341
47	1.1245 1673	1.2158 2940	1.2641 6832	1.3143 8662	1.4207 4971
48	1.1273 2802	1.2208 9536	1.2704 8916	1.3220 5388	1.4314 0533
49	1.1301 4634	1.2259 8242	1.2768 4161	1.3297 6586	1.4421 4087
50	1.1329 7171	1.2310 9068	1.2832 2581	1.3375 2283	1.4529 5693

TABLE 1
AMOUNT AT COMPOUND INTEREST

$$s = (1 + i)^n$$

Periods	Rate i				
n	.0025 ($\frac{1}{4}$%)	.004167 ($\frac{5}{12}$%)	.005 ($\frac{1}{2}$%)	.005833 ($\frac{7}{12}$%)	.0075 ($\frac{3}{4}$%)
50	1.1329 7171	1.2310 9068	1.2832 2581	1.3375 2283	1.4529 5693
51	1.1358 0414	1.2362 2022	1.2896 4194	1.3453 2504	1.4638 5411
52	1.1386 4365	1.2413 7114	1.2960 9015	1.3531 7277	1.4748 3301
53	1.1414 9026	1.2465 4352	1.3025 7060	1.3610 6628	1.4858 9426
54	1.1443 4398	1.2517 3745	1.3090 8346	1.3690 0583	1.4970 3847
55	1.1472 0484	1.2569 5302	1.3156 2887	1.3769 9170	1.5082 6626
56	1.1500 7285	1.2621 9033	1.3222 0702	1.3850 2415	1.5195 7825
57	1.1529 4804	1.2674 4946	1.3288 1805	1.3931 0346	1.5309 7509
58	1.1558 3041	1.2727 3050	1.3354 6214	1.4012 2990	1.5424 5740
59	1.1587 1998	1.2780 3354	1.3421 3946	1.4094 0374	1.5540 2583
60	1.1616 1678	1.2833 5868	1.3488 5015	1.4176 2526	1.5656 8103
61	1.1645 2082	1.2887 0601	1.3555 9440	1.4258 9474	1.5774 2363
62	1.1674 3213	1.2940 7561	1.3623 7238	1.4342 1246	1.5892 5431
63	1.1703 5071	1.2994 6760	1.3691 8424	1.4425 7870	1.6011 7372
64	1.1732 7658	1.3048 8204	1.3760 3016	1.4509 9374	1.6131 8252
65	1.1762 0977	1.3103 1905	1.3829 1031	1.4594 5787	1.6252 8139
66	1.1791 5030	1.3157 7872	1.3898 2486	1.4679 7138	1.6374 7100
67	1.1820 9817	1.3212 6113	1.3967 7399	1.4765 3454	1.6497 5203
68	1.1850 5342	1.3267 6638	1.4037 5785	1.4851 4766	1.6621 2517
69	1.1880 1605	1.3322 9458	1.4107 7664	1.4938 1102	1.6745 9111
70	1.1909 8609	1.3378 4580	1.4178 3053	1.5025 2492	1.6871 5055
71	1.1939 6356	1.3434 2016	1.4249 1968	1.5112 8965	1.6998 0418
72	1.1969 4847	1.3490 1774	1.4320 4428	1.5201 0550	1.7125 5271
73	1.1999 4084	1.3546 3865	1.4392 0450	1.5289 7279	1.7253 9685
74	1.2029 4069	1.3602 8298	1.4464 0052	1.5378 9179	1.7383 3733
75	1.2059 4804	1.3659 5082	1.4536 3252	1.5468 6283	1.7513 7486
76	1.2089 6291	1.3716 4229	1.4609 0069	1.5558 8620	1.7645 1017
77	1.2119 8532	1.3773 5746	1.4682 0519	1.5649 6220	1.7777 4400
78	1.2150 1528	1.3830 9645	1.4755 4622	1.5740 9115	1.7910 7708
79	1.2180 5282	1.3888 5935	1.4829 2395	1.5832 7334	1.8045 1015
80	1.2210 9795	1.3946 4627	1.4903 3857	1.5925 0910	1.8180 4398
81	1.2241 5070	1.4004 5729	1.4977 9026	1.6017 9874	1.8316 7931
82	1.2272 1108	1.4062 9253	1.5052 7921	1.6111 4257	1.8454 1691
83	1.2302 7910	1.4121 5209	1.5128 0561	1.6205 4090	1.8592 5753
84	1.2333 5480	1.4180 3605	1.5203 6964	1.6299 9405	1.8732 0196
85	1.2364 3819	1.4239 4454	1.5279 7148	1.6395 0235	1.8872 5098
86	1.2395 2928	1.4298 7764	1.5356 1134	1.6490 6612	1.9014 0536
87	1.2426 2811	1.4358 3546	1.5432 8940	1.6586 8567	1.9150 6590
88	1.2457 3468	1.4418 1811	1.5510 0585	1.6683 6134	1.9300 3339
89	1.2488 4901	1.4478 2568	1.5587 6087	1.6780 9344	1.9445 0865
90	1.2519 7114	1.4538 5829	1.5665 5468	1.6878 8232	1.9590 9246
91	1.2551 0106	1.4599 1603	1.5743 8745	1.6977 2830	1.9737 8565
92	1.2582 3882	1.4659 9902	1.5822 5939	1.7076 3172	1.9885 8905
93	1.2613 8441	1.4721 0735	1.5901 7069	1.7175 9290	2.0035 0346
94	1.2645 3787	1.4782 4113	1.5981 2154	1.7276 1219	2.0185 2974
95	1.2676 9922	1.4844 0047	1.6061 1215	1.7376 8993	2.0336 6871
96	1.2708 6847	1.4905 8547	1.6141 4271	1.7478 2646	2.0489 2123
97	1.2740 4564	1.4967 9624	1.6222 1342	1.7580 2211	2.0642 8814
98	1.2772 3075	1.5030 3289	1.6303 2449	1.7682 7724	2.0797 7030
99	1.2804 2383	1.5092 9553	1.6384 7611	1.7785 9219	2.0953 6858
100	1.2836 2489	1.5155 8426	1.6466 6849	1.7889 6731	2.1110 8384

TABLE 1
AMOUNT AT COMPOUND INTEREST
$$s = (1 + i)^n$$

Periods	Rate i				
n	.01 (1%)	.01125($1\frac{1}{8}$%)	.0125 ($1\frac{1}{4}$%)	.015 ($1\frac{1}{2}$%)	.0175 ($1\frac{3}{4}$%)
1	1.0100 0000	1.0112 5000	1.0125 0000	1.0150 0000	1.0175 0000
2	1.0201 0000	1.0226 2656	1.0251 5625	1.0302 2500	1.0353 0625
3	1.0303 0100	1.0341 3111	1.0379 7070	1.0456 7838	1.0534 2411
4	1.0406 0401	1.0457 6509	1.0509 4534	1.0613 6355	1.0718 5903
5	1.0510 1005	1.0575 2994	1.0640 8215	1.0772 8400	1.0906 1656
6	1.0615 2015	1.0694 2716	1.0773 8318	1.0934 4326	1.1097 0235
7	1.0721 3535	1.0814 5821	1.0908 5047	1.1098 4491	1.1291 2215
8	1.0828 5671	1.0936 2462	1.1044 8610	1.1264 9259	1.1488 8178
9	1.0936 8527	1.1059 2789	1.1182 9218	1.1433 8998	1.1689 8721
10	1.1046 2213	1.1183 6958	1.1322 7083	1.1605 4083	1.1894 4449
11	1.1156 6835	1.1309 5124	1.1464 2422	1.1779 4894	1.2102 5977
12	1.1268 2503	1.1436 7444	1.1607 5452	1.1956 1817	1.2314 3931
13	1.1380 9328	1.1565 4078	1.1752 6395	1.2135 5244	1.2529 8950
14	1.1494 7421	1.1695 5186	1.1899 5475	1.2317 5573	1.2749 1682
15	1.1609 6896	1.1827 0932	1.2048 2918	1.2502 3207	1.2972 2786
16	1.1725 7864	1.1960 1480	1.2198 8955	1.2689 8555	1.3199 2935
17	1.1843 0443	1.2094 6997	1.2351 3817	1.2880 2033	1.3430 2811
18	1.1961 4748	1.2230 7650	1.2505 7739	1.3073 4064	1.3665 3111
19	1.2081 0895	1.2368 3611	1.2662 0961	1.3269 5075	1.3904 4540
20	1.2201 9004	1.2507 5052	1.2820 3723	1.3468 5501	1.4147 7820
21	1.2323 9194	1.2648 2146	1.2980 6270	1.3670 5783	1.4395 3681
22	1.2447 1586	1.2790 5071	1.3142 8848	1.3875 6370	1.4647 2871
23	1.2571 6302	1.2934 4003	1.3307 1709	1.4083 7715	1.4903 6146
24	1.2697 3465	1.3079 9123	1.3473 5105	1.4295 0281	1.5164 4279
25	1.2824 3200	1.3227 0613	1.3641 9294	1.4509 4535	1.5429 8054
26	1.2952 5631	1.3375 8657	1.3812 4535	1.4727 0953	1.5699 8269
27	1.3082 0888	1.3526 3442	1.3985 1092	1.4948 0018	1.5974 5739
28	1.3212 9097	1.3678 5156	1.4159 9230	1.5172 2218	1.6254 1290
29	1.3345 0388	1.3832 3989	1.4336 9221	1.5399 8051	1.6538 5762
30	1.3478 4892	1.3988 0134	1.4516 1336	1.5630 8022	1.6828 0013
31	1.3613 2740	1.4145 3785	1.4697 5853	1.5865 2642	1.7122 4913
32	1.3749 4068	1.4304 5140	1.4881 3051	1.6103 2432	1.7422 1349
33	1.3886 9009	1.4465 4398	1.5067 3214	1.6344 7918	1.7727 0223
34	1.4025 7699	1.4628 1760	1.6255 6629	1.6589 9637	1.8037 2452
35	1.4166 0276	1.4792 7430	1.5446 3587	1.6838 8132	1.8352 8970
36	1.4307 6878	1.4959 1613	1.5639 4382	1.7091 3954	1.8674 0727
37	1.4450 7647	1.5127 4519	1.5834 9312	1.7347 7663	1.9000 8689
38	1.4595 2724	1.5297 6357	1.6032 8678	1.7607 9828	1.9333 3841
39	1.4741 2251	1.5469 7341	1.6233 2787	1.7872 1025	1.9671 7184
40	1.4888 6373	1.5643 7687	1.6436 1946	1.8140 1841	2.0015 9734
41	1.5037 5237	1.5819 7611	1.6641 6471	1.8412 2868	2.0366 2530
42	1.5187 8989	1.5997 7334	1.6849 6677	1.8688 4712	2.0722 6624
43	1.5339 7779	1.6177 7079	1.7060 2865	1.8968 7982	2.1085 3090
44	1.5493 1757	1.6359 7071	1.7273 5421	1.9253 3302	2.1454 3019
45	1.5648 1075	1.6543 7538	1.7489 4614	1.9542 1301	2.1829 7522
46	1.5804 5885	1.6729 8710	1.7708 0797	1.9835 2621	2.2211 7728
47	1.5962 6344	1.6918 0821	1.7929 4305	2.0132 7910	2.2600 4789
48	1.6122 2608	1.7108 4105	1.8153 5485	2.0434 7829	2.2995 9872
49	1.6283 4834	1.7300 8801	1.8380 4679	2.0741 3046	2.3398 4170
50	1.6446 3182	1.7495 5150	1.8610 2237	2.1052 4242	2.3807 8893

TABLE 1
AMOUNT AT COMPOUND INTEREST
$$s = (1 + i)^n$$

Periods *n*	Rate *i*: .01 (1%)	.01125 ($1\frac{1}{8}$%)	.0125 ($1\frac{1}{4}$%)	.015 ($1\frac{1}{2}$%)	.0175 ($1\frac{3}{4}$%)
50	1.6446 3182	1.7495 5150	1.8610 2237	2.1052 4242	2.3807 8893
51	1.6610 7814	1.7692 2395	1.8842 8515	2.1368 2106	2.4224 5274
52	1.6776 8892	1.7891 3784	1.9078 3872	2.1688 7337	2.4648 4566
53	1.6944 6581	1.8092 6564	1.9316 8670	2.2014 0647	2.5079 8046
54	1.7114 1047	1.8296 1988	1.9558 3279	2.2344 2757	2.5518 7012
55	1.7285 2457	1.8502 0310	1.9802 8070	2.2679 4398	2.5965 2785
56	1.7458 0982	1.8710 1788	2.0050 3420	2.3019 6314	2.6419 6708
57	1.7632 6792	1.8920 6684	2.0300 9713	2.3364 9259	2.6882 0151
58	1.7809 0060	1.9133 5259	2.0554 7335	2.3715 3998	2.7352 4503
59	1.7987 0960	1.9348 7780	2.0811 6676	2.4071 1308	2.7831 1182
60	1.8166 9670	1.9566 4518	2.1071 8135	2.4432 1978	2.8318 1628
61	1.8348 6367	1.9786 5744	2.1335 2111	2.4798 6807	2.8813 7306
62	1.8532 1230	2.0009 1733	2.1601 9013	2.5170 6609	2.9317 9709
63	1.8717 4443	2.0234 2765	2.1871 9250	2.5548 2208	2.9831 0354
64	1.8904 6187	2.0461 9121	2.2145 3241	2.5931 4442	3.0353 0785
65	1.9093 6649	2.0692 1087	2.2422 1407	2.6320 4158	3.0884 2574
66	1.9284 6015	2.0924 8949	2.2702 4174	2.6715 2221	3.1424 7319
67	1.9477 4475	2.1160 2999	2.2986 1976	2.7115 9504	3.1974 6647
68	1.9672 2220	2.1398 3533	2.3273 5251	2.7522 6896	3.2534 2213
69	1.9868 9442	2.1639 0848	2.3564 4442	2.7935 5300	3.3103 5702
70	2.0067 6337	2.1882 5245	2.3858 9997	2.8354 5629	3.3682 8827
71	2.0268 3100	2.2128 7029	2.4157 2372	2.8779 8814	3.4272 3331
72	2.0470 9931	2.2377 6508	2.4459 2027	2.9211 5796	3.4872 0990
73	2.0675 7031	2.2629 3994	2.4764 9427	2.9649 7533	3.5482 3607
74	2.0882 4601	2.2883 9801	2.5074 5045	3.0094 4996	3.6103 3020
75	2.1091 2847	2.3141 4249	2.5387 9358	3.0545 9171	3.6735 1098
76	2.1302 1975	2.3401 7659	2.5705 2850	3.1004 1059	3.7377 9742
77	2.1515 2195	2.3665 0358	2.6026 6011	3.1469 1674	3.8032 0888
78	2.1730 3717	2.3931 2675	2.6351 9336	3.1941 2050	3.8697 6503
79	2.1947 6754	2.4200 4942	2.6681 3327	3.2420 3230	3.9374 8592
80	2.2167 1522	2.4472 7498	2.7014 8494	3.2906 6279	4.0063 9192
81	2.2388 8237	2.4748 0682	2.7352 5350	3.3400 2273	4.0765 0378
82	2.2612 7119	2.5026 4840	2.7694 4417	3.3901 2307	4.1478 4260
83	2.2838 8390	2.5308 0319	2.8040 6222	3.4409 7492	4.2204 2984
84	2.3067 2274	2.5592 7473	2.8391 1300	3.4925 8954	4.2942 8737
85	2.3297 8997	2.5880 6657	2.8746 0191	3.5449 7838	4.3694 3740
86	2.3530 8787	2.6171 8232	2.9015 3444	3.5981 5306	4.4459 0255
87	2.3766 1875	2.6466 2562	2.9469 1612	3.6521 2535	4.5237 0584
88	2.4003 8494	2.6764 0016	2.9837 5257	3.7069 0723	4.6028 7070
89	2.4243 8879	2.7065 0966	3.0210 4948	3.7625 1084	4.6834 2093
90	2.4486 3267	2.7369 5789	3.0588 1260	3.8199 4851	4.7653 8080
91	2.4731 1900	2.7677 4867	3.0970 4775	3.8762 3273	4.8487 7496
92	2.4978 5019	2.7988 8584	3.1357 6085	3.9343 7622	4.9336 2853
93	2.5228 2869	2.8303 7331	3.1749 5786	3.9933 9187	5.0199 6703
94	2.5480 5698	2.8622 1501	3.2146 4483	4.0532 9275	5.1078 1645
95	2.5735 3755	2.8944 1492	3.2548 2789	4.1140 9214	5.1972 0324
96	2.5992 7293	2.9269 7709	3.2955 1324	4.1758 0352	5.2881 5429
97	2.6252 6565	2.9599 0559	3.3367 0716	4.2384 4057	5.3806 9699
98	2.6515 1831	2.9932 0452	3.3784 1600	4.3020 1718	5.4748 5919
99	2.6780 3349	3.0268 7807	3.4206 4620	4.3665 4744	5.5706 6923
100	2.7048 1383	3.0609 3045	3.4634 0427	4.4320 4565	5.6681 5594

TABLE 1
AMOUNT AT COMPOUND INTEREST
$$s = (1 + i)^n$$

Periods	Rate i				
n	.02 (2%)	.0225 ($2\frac{1}{4}$%)	.025 ($2\frac{1}{2}$%)	.0275 ($2\frac{3}{4}$%)	.03 (3%)
1	1.0200 0000	1.0225 0000	1.0250 0000	1.0275 0000	1.0300 0000
2	1.0404 0000	1.0455 0625	1.0506 2500	1.0557 5625	1.0609 0000
3	1.0612 0800	1.0690 3014	1.0768 9063	1.0847 8955	1.0927 2700
4	1.0824 3216	1.0930 8332	1.1038 1289	1.1146 2126	1.1255 0881
5	1.1040 8080	1.1176 7769	1.1314 0821	1.1452 7334	1.1592 7407
6	1.1261 6242	1.1428 2544	1.1596 9342	1.1767 6836	1.1940 5230
7	1.1486 8567	1.1685 3901	1.1886 8575	1.2091 2949	1.2298 7387
8	1.1716 5938	1.1948 3114	1.2184 0290	1.2423 8055	1.2667 7008
9	1.1950 9257	1.2217 1484	1.2488 6297	1.2765 4602	1.3047 7318
10	1.2189 9442	1.2492 0343	1.2800 8454	1.3116 5103	1.3439 1638
11	1.2433 7431	1.1273 1050	1.3120 8666	1.3477 2144	1.3842 3387
12	1.2682 4179	1.3060 4999	1.3448 8882	1.3847 8378	1.4257 6089
13	1.2936 0663	1.3354 3611	1.3785 1104	1.4228 6533	1.4685 3371
14	1.3194 7876	1.3654 8343	1.4129 7382	1.4619 9413	1.5125 8972
15	1.3458 6834	1.3962 0680	1.4482 9817	1.5021 9896	1.5579 6742
16	1.3727 8571	1.4276 2146	1.4845 0562	1.5435 0944	1.6047 0644
17	1.4002 4142	1.4597 4294	1.5216 1826	1.5859 5595	1.6528 4763
18	1.4282 4625	1.4925 8716	1.5596 5872	1.6295 7313	1.7024 3506
19	1.4568 1117	1.5261 7037	1.5986 5019	1.6743 8290	1.7535 0605
20	1.4859 4740	1.5605 0920	1.6386 1644	1.7204 2843	1.8061 1123
21	1.5156 6634	1.5956 2066	1.6795 8185	1.7677 4021	1.8602 9457
22	1.5459 7967	1.6315 2212	1.7215 7140	1.8163 5307	1.9161 0341
23	1.5768 9926	1.6682 3137	1.7646 1068	1.8663 0278	1.9735 8651
24	1.6084 3725	1.7057 6658	1.8087 2595	1.9176 2610	2.0327 9411
25	1.6406 0599	1.7441 4632	1.8539 4410	1.9703 6082	2.0937 7793
26	1.6734 1811	1.7833 8962	1.9002 9270	2.0245 4575	2.1565 9127
27	1.7068 8648	1.8235 1588	1.9478 0002	2.0802 2075	2.2212 8901
28	1.7410 2421	1.8645 4499	1.9964 9502	2.1374 2682	2.2879 2768
29	1.7758 4469	1.9064 9725	2.0464 0739	2.1962 0606	2.3565 6551
30	1.8113 6158	1.9493 9344	2.0975 6758	2.2566 0173	2.4272 6247
31	1.8475 8882	1.9932 5479	2.1500 0677	2.3186 5828	2.5000 8035
32	1.8845 4059	2.0381 0303	2.2037 5694	2.3824 2138	2.5750 8276
33	1.9222 3140	2.0839 6034	2.2588 5086	2.4479 3797	2.6523 3524
34	1.9606 7603	2.1308 4945	2.3153 2213	2.5152 5626	2.7319 0530
35	1.9998 8955	2.1787 9356	2.3732 0519	2.5844 2581	2.8138 6245
36	2.0398 8734	2.2278 1642	2.4325 3532	2.6554 9752	2.8982 7833
37	2.0806 8509	2.2779 4229	2.4933 4870	2.7285 2370	2.9852 2667
38	2.1222 9879	2.3291 9799	2.5656 8242	2.8035 5810	3.0747 8348
39	2.1647 4477	2.3816 0290	2.6195 7448	2.8806 5595	3.1670 2698
40	2.2080 3966	2.4351 8897	2.6850 6384	2.9598 7399	3.2620 3779
41	2.2522 0046	2.4899 8072	2.7521 9043	3.0412 7052	3.3598 9893
42	2.2972 4447	2.5460 0528	2.8209 9520	3.1249 0546	3.4606 9589
43	2.3431 8936	2.6032 9040	2.8915 2008	3.2108 4036	3.5645 1677
44	2.3900 5314	2.6618 6444	2.9638 0808	3.2991 3847	3.6714 5227
45	2.4378 5421	2.7217 5639	3.0379 0328	3.3898 6478	3.7815 9584
46	2.4866 1129	2.7829 9590	3.1138 5086	3.4830 8606	3.8950 4372
47	2.5363 4352	2.8456 1331	3.1916 9713	3.5788 7093	4.0118 9503
48	2.5870 7039	2.9096 3961	3.2714 8956	3.6772 8988	4.1322 5188
49	2.6388 1179	2.9751 0650	3.3532 7680	3.7784 1535	4.2562 1944
50	2.6915 8803	3.0420 4640	3.4371 0872	3.8823 2177	4.3839 0602

TABLE 1
AMOUNT AT COMPOUND INTEREST
$$s = (1 + i)^n$$

Periods	Rate i				
n	.02 (2%)	.0225 ($2\frac{1}{4}$%)	.025 ($2\frac{1}{2}$%)	.0275 ($2\frac{3}{4}$%)	.03 (3%)
50	2.6915 8803	3.0420 4640	3.4371 0872	3.8823 2177	4.3839 0602
51	2.7454 1979	3.1104 9244	3.5230 3644	3.9890 8562	4.5154 2320
52	2.8003 2819	3.1804 7852	3.6111 1235	4.0987 8547	4.6508 8590
53	2.8563 3475	3.2520 3929	3.7013 9016	4.2115 0208	4.7904 1247
54	2.9134 6144	3.3252 1017	3.7939 2491	4.3273 1838	4.9341 2485
55	2.9717 3067	3.4000 2740	3.8887 7303	4.4463 1964	5.0821 4859
56	3.0311 6529	3.4765 2802	3.9859 9236	4.5685 9343	5.2346 1305
57	3.0917 8859	3.5547 4990	4.0856 4217	4.6942 2975	5.3916 5144
58	3.1536 2436	3.6347 3177	4.1877 8322	4.8233 2107	5.5534 0098
59	3.2166 9685	3.7165 1324	4.2924 7780	4.9559 6239	5.7200 0301
60	3.2810 3079	3.8001 3479	4.3997 8975	5.0922 5136	5.8916 0310
61	3.3466 5140	3.8856 3782	4.5097 8449	5.2322 8827	6.0683 5120
62	3.4135 8443	3.9730 6467	4.6225 2910	5.3761 7620	6.2504 0173
63	3.4818 5612	4.0624 5862	4.7380 9233	5.5240 2105	6.4379 1379
64	3.5514 9324	4.1538 6394	4.8565 4464	5.6759 3162	6.6310 5120
65	3.6225 2311	4.2473 2588	4.9779 5826	5.8320 1974	6.8299 8273
66	3.6949 7357	4.3428 9071	5.1024 0721	5.9924 0029	7.0348 8222
67	3.7688 7304	4.4406 0576	5.2299 6739	6.1571 9130	7.2459 2868
68	3.8442 5050	4.5405 1939	5.3607 1658	6.3265 1406	7.4633 0654
69	3.9211 3551	4.6426 8107	5.4947 3449	6.5004 9319	7.6872 0574
70	3.9995 5822	4.7471 4140	5.6321 0286	6.6792 5676	7.9178 2191
71	4.0795 4939	4.8539 5208	5.7729 0543	6.8629 3632	8.1553 5657
72	4.1611 4038	4.9631 6600	5.9172 2806	7.0516 6706	8.4000 1727
73	4.2443 6318	5.0748 3723	6.0651 5876	7.2455 8791	8.6520 1778
74	4.3292 5045	5.1890 2107	6.2167 8773	7.4448 4158	8.9115 7832
75	4.4158 3546	5.3057 7405	6.3722 0743	7.6495 7472	9.1789 2567
76	4.5041 5216	5.4251 5396	6.5315 1261	7.8599 3802	9.4542 9344
77	4.5942 3521	5.5472 1993	6.6948 0043	8.0760 8632	9.7379 2224
78	4.6861 1991	5.6720 3237	6.8721 7044	8.2981 7869	10.0300 5991
79	4.7798 4231	5.7996 5310	7.0337 2470	8.5263 7861	10.3309 6171
80	4.8754 3916	5.9301 4530	7.2095 6782	8.7608 5402	10.6408 9056
81	4.9729 4794	6.0635 7357	7.3898 0701	9.0017 7751	10.9601 1727
82	5.0724 0690	6.2000 0397	7.5745 5219	9.2493 2639	11.2889 2079
83	5.1738 5504	6.3395 0406	7.7639 1599	9.5036 8286	11.6275 8842
84	5.2773 3214	6.4821 4290	7.9580 1389	9.7650 3414	11.9764 1607
85	5.3828 7878	6.6279 9112	8.1569 6424	10.0335 7258	12.3357 0855
86	5.4905 3336	6.7771 2092	8.3608 8834	10.3094 9583	12.7057 7981
87	5.6003 4708	6.9296 0614	8.5699 1055	10.5930 0696	13.0869 5320
88	5.7123 5402	7.0855 2228	8.7841 5832	10.8843 1465	13.4795 6180
89	5.8266 0110	7.2449 4653	9.0037 6228	11.1836 3331	13.8839 4865
90	5.9431 3313	7.4079 5782	9.2288 5633	11.4911 8322	14.3004 6711
91	6.0619 9579	7.5746 3688	9.4595 7774	11.8071 9076	14.7294 8112
92	6.1832 3770	7.7450 6621	9.6960 6718	12.1318 8851	15.1713 6556
93	6.3069 0042	7.9193 2030	9.9384 6886	12.4655 1544	15.6265 0652
94	6.4330 3843	8.0975 1512	10.1869 3058	12.8083 1711	16.0953 0172
95	6.5616 9920	8.2797 0921	10.4416 0352	13.1605 4584	16.5781 6070
96	6.6929 3318	8.4660 0267	10.7026 4395	13.5224 6085	17.0755 0559
97	6.8267 9184	8.6564 8773	10.9702 1004	13.8943 2852	17.5877 7076
98	6.9633 2768	8.8512 5871	11.2444 6530	14.2764 2255	18.1154 0388
99	7.1025 9423	9.0504 1203	11.5255 7693	14.6690 2417	18.6588 6600
100	7.2446 4612	9.2540 4630	11.8137 1635	15.0724 2234	19.2186 3198

TABLE 1
AMOUNT AT COMPOUND INTEREST
$$s = (1 + i)^n$$

Periods	Rate i				
n	.035 $(3\frac{1}{2}\%)$	.04 (4%)	.045 $(4\frac{1}{2}\%)$	.05 (5%)	.055 $(5\frac{1}{2}\%)$
1	1.0350 0000	1.0400 0000	1.0450 0000	1.0500 0000	1.0550 0000
2	1.0712 2500	1.0816 0000	1.0920 2500	1.1025 0000	1.1130 2500
3	1.1087 1788	1.1248 6400	1.1411 6613	1.1576 2500	1.1742 4138
4	1.1475 2300	1.1698 5856	1.1925 1860	1.2155 0625	1.2388 2465
5	1.1876 8631	1.2166 5290	1.2461 8194	1.2762 8156	1.3069 6001
6	1.2292 5533	1.2653 1902	1.3022 6012	1.3400 9564	1.3788 4281
7	1.2722 7926	1.3159 3178	1.3608 6183	1.4071 0042	1.4546 7916
8	1.3168 0904	1.3685 6905	1.4221 0061	1.4774 5544	1.5346 8651
9	1.3628 9735	1.4233 1181	1.4860 9514	1.5513 2822	1.6190 9427
10	1.4105 9876	1.4802 4428	1.5529 6942	1.6288 9463	1.7081 4446
11	1.4599 6972	1.5394 5406	1.6228 5305	1.7103 3936	1.8020 9240
12	1.5110 6866	1.6010 3222	1.6958 8143	1.7958 5633	1.9012 0749
13	1.5639 5606	1.6650 7351	1.7021 9610	1.8856 4914	2.0057 7390
14	1.6186 9452	1.7316 7645	1.8519 4492	1.9799 3160	2.1160 9146
15	1.6753 4843	1.8009 4351	1.9352 8244	2.0789 2818	2.2324 7649
16	1.7339 8604	1.8729 8125	2.0223 7015	2.1828 7459	2.3552 6270
17	1.7946 7555	1.9479 0050	2.1133 7681	2.2920 1832	2.4848 0215
18	1.8574 8920	2.0258 1652	2.2084 7877	2.4066 1923	2.6214 6627
19	1.9225 0132	2.1068 4918	2.3078 6031	2.5269 5020	2.7656 4691
20	1.9897 8886	2.1911 2314	2.4117 1402	2.6532 9771	2.9177 5749
21	2.0594 3147	2.2787 6807	2.5202 4116	2.7859 6259	3.0782 3415
22	2.1315 1158	2.3699 1879	2.6336 5201	2.9252 6072	3.2475 3703
23	2.2061 1448	2.4647 1554	2.7521 6635	3.0715 2376	3.4261 5157
24	2.2833 2849	2.5633 0416	2.8760 1383	3.2250 9994	3.6145 8990
25	2.3632 4498	2.6658 3633	3.0054 3446	3.3863 5494	3.8133 9235
26	2.4459 5856	2.7724 6978	3.1406 7901	3.5556 7269	4.0231 2893
27	2.5315 6711	2.8833 6858	3.2820 0956	3.7334 5632	4.2444 0102
28	2.6201 7196	2.9987 0332	3.4296 9999	3.9201 2914	4.4778 4307
29	2.7118 7798	3.1186 5145	3.5840 3649	4.1161 3560	4.7241 2444
30	2.8067 9370	3.2433 9751	3.7453 1813	4.3219 4238	4.9839 5129
31	2.9050 3148	3.3731 3341	3.9138 5745	4.5380 3949	5.2580 6861
32	3.0067 0759	3.5080 5875	4.0899 8104	4.7649 4147	5.5472 6238
33	3.1119 4235	3.6483 8110	4.2740 3018	5.0031 8854	5.8523 6181
34	3.2208 6033	3.7943 1634	4.4663 6154	5.2533 4797	6.1742 4171
35	3.3335 9045	3.9460 8899	4.6673 4781	5.5160 1537	6.5138 2501
36	3.4502 6611	4.1039 3255	4.8773 7846	5.7918 1614	6.8720 8538
37	3.5710 2543	4.2680 8986	5.0968 6049	6.0814 0694	7.2500 5008
38	3.6960 1132	4.4388 1345	5.3262 1921	6.3854 7729	7.6488 0283
39	3.8253 7171	4.6163 6599	5.5658 9908	6.7047 5115	8.0694 8699
40	3.9592 5972	4.8010 2063	5.8163 6454	7.0399 8871	8.5133 0877
41	4.0978 3381	4.9930 6145	6.0781 0094	7.3919 8815	8.9815 4076
42	4.2412 5799	5.1927 8391	6.3516 1548	7.7615 8756	9.4755 2550
43	4.3897 0202	5.4004 9527	6.6374 3818	8.1496 6693	9.9966 7940
44	4.5433 4160	5.6165 1508	6.9361 2290	8.5571 5028	10.5464 9677
45	4.7023 5855	5.8411 7568	7.2482 4843	8.9850 0779	11.1265 5409
46	4.8669 4110	6.0748 2271	7.5744 1961	9.4342 5818	11.7385 1456
47	5.0372 8404	6.3178 1562	7.9152 6849	9.9059 7109	12.3841 3287
48	5.2135 8898	6.5705 2824	8.2714 5557	10.1412 6965	13.0652 6017
49	5.4960 6459	6.8333 4937	8.6436 7107	10.9213 3313	13.7838 4948
50	5.5849 2686	7.1066 8335	9.0326 3627	11.4673 9979	14.5419 6120

TABLE 1
AMOUNT AT COMPOUND INTEREST
$$s = (1 + i)^n$$

Periods	Rate i				
n	.06 (6%)	.065 ($6\frac{1}{2}$%)	.07 (7%)	.075 ($7\frac{1}{2}$%)	.08 (8%)
1	1.0600 0000	1.0650 0000	1.0700 0000	1.0750 0000	1.0800 0000
2	1.1236 0000	1.1342 2500	1.1449 0000	1.1556 2500	1.1664 0000
3	1.1910 1600	1.2079 4963	1.2250 4300	1.2422 9688	1.2597 1200
4	1.2624 7696	1.2864 6635	1.3107 9601	1.3354 6914	1.3604 8896
5	1.3382 2558	1.3700 8666	1.4025 5173	1.4356 2933	1.4693 2808
6	1.4185 1911	1.4519 4230	1.5007 3035	1.5433 0153	1.5868 7432
7	1.5036 3026	1.5539 8655	1.6057 8148	1.6590 4914	1.7138 2427
8	1.5938 4807	1.6549 9567	1.7181 8618	1.7834 7783	1.8509 3021
9	1.6894 7896	1.7625 7039	1.8384 5921	1.9172 3866	1.9990 0463
10	1.7908 4770	1.8771 3747	1.9671 5136	2.0610 3156	2.1589 2500
11	1.8982 9856	1.9991 5140	2.1048 5195	2.2156 0893	2.3316 3900
12	2.0121 9647	2.1290 9624	2.2521 9159	2.3817 7960	2.5181 7012
13	2.1329 2826	2.2674 8750	2.4098 4500	2.5604 1307	2.7196 2373
14	2.2609 0396	2.4148 7418	2.5785 3415	2.7524 4405	2.9371 9362
15	2.3965 5819	2.5718 4101	2.7590 3154	2.9588 7735	3.1721 6911
16	2.5403 5168	2.7390 1067	2.9521 6375	3.1807 9315	3.4259 4264
17	2.6927 7279	2.9170 4637	3.1588 1521	3.4193 5264	3.7000 1805
18	2.8543 3915	3.1066 5438	3.3799 3228	3.6758 0409	3.9960 1950
19	3.0255 9950	3.3085 8691	3.6165 2754	3.9514 8940	4.3157 0106
20	3.2071 3547	3.5236 4506	3.8696 8446	4.2478 5110	4.6609 5714
21	3.3995 6360	3.7526 8199	4.1405 6237	4.5664 3993	5.0338 3372
22	3.6035 3742	3.9966 0632	4.4304 0174	4.9089 2293	5.4365 4041
23	3.8197 4966	4.2563 8573	4.7405 2986	5.2770 9215	5.8714 6365
24	4.0489 3464	4.5330 5081	5.0723 6695	5.6728 7406	6.3411 8074
25	4.2918 7072	4.8276 9911	5.4274 3264	6.0983 3961	6.8484 7520
26	4.5493 8296	5.1414 9955	5.8073 5292	6.5557 1508	7.3963 5321
27	4.8223 4594	5.4756 9702	6.2138 6763	7.0473 9371	7.9880 6147
28	5.1116 8670	5.8316 1733	6.6488 3836	7.5759 4824	8.6271 0639
29	5.4183 8790	6.2106 7245	7.1142 5705	8.1441 4436	9.3172 7490
30	5.7434 9117	6.6143 6616	7.6122 5504	8.7549 5519	10.0626 5689
31	6.0881 0064	7.0442 9996	8.1451 1290	9.4115 7683	10.8676 6944
32	6.4533 8668	7.5021 7946	8.7152 7080	10.1174 4509	11.7370 8300
33	6.8405 8988	7.9898 2113	9.3253 3975	10.8762 5347	12.6760 4964
34	7.2510 2528	8.5091 5950	9.9781 1354	11.6919 7248	13.6901 3361
35	7.6860 8679	9.0622 5487	10.6765 8148	12.5688 7042	14.7853 4429
36	8.1472 5200	9.6513 0143	11.4239 4219	13.5115 3570	15.9681 7184
37	8.6360 8712	10.2786 3603	12.2236 1814	14.5249 0088	17.2456 2558
38	9.1542 5235	10.9467 4737	13.0792 7141	15.6142 6844	18.6252 7563
39	9.7035 0749	11.6582 8595	13.9948 2041	16.7853 3858	20.1152 9768
40	10.2857 1794	12.4160 7453	14.9744 5784	18.0442 3897	21.7245 2150
41	10.9028 6101	13.2231 1938	16.0226 6989	19.3975 5689	23.4624 8322
42	11.5570 3267	14.0826 2214	17.1442 5678	20.8523 7366	25.3394 8187
43	12.2504 5463	14.9979 9258	18.3443 5475	22.4163 0168	27.3666 4042
44	12.9854 8191	15.9728 6209	19.6284 5959	24.0975 2431	29.5559 7166
45	13.7646 1083	17.0110 9813	21.0024 5176	25.9048 3863	31.9204 4939
46	14.5904 8748	18.1168 1951	22.4726 2338	27.8477 0153	34.4740 8534
47	15.4659 1673	19.2944 1278	24.0457 0702	29.9362 7915	37.2320 1217
48	16.3938 7173	20.5485 4961	25.7289 0651	32.1815 0008	40.2105 7314
49	17.3775 0403	21.8842 0533	27.5299 2997	34.5951 1259	43.4274 1899
50	18.4201 5427	23.3066 7868	29.4570 2506	37.1897 4603	46.9016 1251

TABLE II
PRESENT VALUE AT COMPOUND INTEREST
$= v^n \; 1/(1+i)^n = (1+i)^{-n}$

Periods	Rate i				
n	.0025 ($\frac{1}{4}$%)	.004167 ($\frac{5}{12}$%)	.005 ($\frac{1}{2}$%)	.005833 ($\frac{7}{12}$%)	.0075 ($\frac{3}{4}$%)
1	0.9975 0623	0.9958 5062	0.9950 2488	0.9942 0050	0.9925 5583
2	0.9950 1869	0.9917 1846	0.9900 7450	0.9884 3463	0.9851 6708
3	0.9925 3734	0.9876 0345	0.9851 4876	0.9827 0220	0.9778 3333
4	0.9900 6219	0.9835 0551	0.9802 4752	0.9770 0301	0.9705 5417
5	0.9875 9321	0.9794 2457	0.9753 7067	0.9713 3688	0.9633 2920
6	0.9851 3038	0.9753 6057	0.9705 1808	0.9657 0361	0.9561 5802
7	0.9826 7370	0.9713 1343	0.9656 8963	0.9601 0301	0.9490 4022
8	0.9802 2314	0.9672 8308	0.9608 8520	0.9545 3489	0.9419 7540
9	0.9777 7869	0.9632 6946	0.9561 0468	0.9489 9906	0.9349 6318
10	0.9753 4034	0.9592 7249	0.9513 4794	0.9434 9534	0.9280 0315
11	0.9729 0807	0.9552 9211	0.9466 1487	0.9380 2354	0.9210 9494
12	0.9704 8187	0.9513 2824	0.9419 0534	0.9325 8347	0.9142 3815
13	0.9680 6171	0.9473 8082	0.9372 1924	0.9271 7495	0.9074 3241
14	0.9656 4759	0.9434 4978	0.9325 5646	0.9217 9779	0.9006 7733
15	0.9632 3949	0.9395 3505	0.9279 1688	0.9164 5182	0.8939 7254
16	0.9608 3740	0.9356 3657	0.9233 0037	0.9111 3696	0.8873 1766
17	0.9584 4130	0.9317 5426	0.9187 0684	0.9058 5272	0.8807 1231
18	0.9560 5117	0.9278 8806	0.9141 3616	0.9005 9922	0.8741 5614
19	0.9536 6700	0.9240 3790	0.9095 8822	0.8953 7619	0.8676 4878
20	0.9512 8878	0.9202 0372	0.9050 6290	0.8901 8346	0.8611 8985
21	0.9489 1649	0.9163 8544	0.9005 6010	0.8850 2084	0.8547 7901
22	0.9465 5011	0.9125 8301	0.8960 7971	0.8798 8815	0.8484 1589
23	0.9441 8964	0.9087 9636	0.9816 2160	0.8747 8524	0.8421 0014
24	0.9418 3505	0.9050 2542	0.8771 8567	0.8697 1192	0.8358 3140
25	0.9394 8634	0.9012 7013	0.8827 7181	0.8646 6802	0.8296 0935
26	0.9371 4348	0.8975 3042	0.8783 7991	0.8596 5338	0.8234 3358
27	0.9348 0646	0.8938 0623	0.8740 0986	0.8546 6782	0.8173 0380
28	0.9324 7527	0.8900 9749	0.8696 6155	0.8497 1117	0.8112 1966
29	0.9301 4990	0.8864 0414	0.8653 3488	0.8447 8327	0.8251 8080
30	0.9278 3032	0.8827 2611	0.8610 2973	0.8398 8394	0.7991 8690
31	0.9255 1653	0.8790 6335	0.8567 4600	0.8350 1303	0.7932 3762
32	0.9232 0851	0.8754 1578	0.8524 8358	0.8301 7037	0.7873 3262
33	0.9209 0624	0.8717 8335	0.8482 4237	0.8253 5580	0.7814 7158
34	0.9186 0972	0.8681 6599	0.8440 2226	0.8205 6914	0.7756 5418
35	0.9163 1892	0.8645 6365	0.8398 2314	0.8158 1025	0.7698 8008
36	0.9140 3384	0.8609 7624	0.8356 4492	0.8110 7896	0.7641 4896
37	0.9117 5445	0.8574 0373	0.8314 8748	0.8063 7510	0.7584 6051
38	0.9094 8075	0.8538 4604	0.8273 5073	0.8016 9853	0.7528 1440
39	0.9072 1272	0.8503 0311	0.8232 3455	0.7970 4907	0.7472 1032
40	0.9049 5034	0.8467 7488	0.8191 3886	0.7924 2659	0.7416 4796
41	0.9026 9361	0.8432 6129	0.8150 6354	0.7878 3091	0.7361 2701
42	0.9004 4250	0.8397 6228	0.8110 0850	0.7832 6188	0.7306 4716
43	0.8981 9701	0.8362 7779	0.8069 7363	0.7787 1935	0.7252 0809
44	0.8959 5712	0.8328 0776	0.8029 5884	0.7742 0316	0.7198 0952
45	0.8937 2281	0.8293 5212	0.7989 6402	0.7697 1317	0.7144 5114
46	0.8914 9407	0.8259 1083	0.7949 8907	0.7652 4922	0.7091 3264
47	0.8892 7090	0.8224 8381	0.7910 3390	0.7608 1115	0.7038 5374
48	0.8870 5326	0.8190 7102	0.7870 9841	0.7563 9883	0.6986 1414
49	0.8848 4116	0.8156 7238	0.7831 8250	0.7520 1209	0.6934 1353
50	0.8826 3457	0.8122 8785	0.7792 8607	0.7476 5079	0.6882 5165

TABLE II
PRESENT VALUE AT COMPOUND INTEREST

$$= v^n \; 1/(1 + i)^n = (1 + i)^{-n}$$

Periods	Rate i				
n	.0025 ($\frac{1}{4}$%)	.004167 ($\frac{5}{12}$%)	.005 ($\frac{1}{2}$%)	.005833 ($\frac{7}{12}$%)	.0075 ($\frac{3}{4}$%)
50	0.8826 3457	0.8122 8785	0.7792 8607	0.7476 5079	0.6882 5165
51	0.8804 3349	0.8089 1736	0.7754 0902	0.7433 1479	0.6831 2819
52	0.8782 3790	0.8055 6086	0.7715 5127	0.7390 0393	0.6780 4286
53	0.8760 4778	0.8022 1828	0.7677 1270	0.7347 1808	0.6729 9540
54	0.8716 6312	0.7955 8957	0.7638 9324	0.7304 5708	0.6679 8551
55	0.8716 8391	0.7955 7468	0.7600 9277	0.7262 2079	0.6630 1291
56	0.8695 1013	0.7922 7354	0.7563 1122	0.7220 0907	0.6580 7733
57	0.8673 4178	0.7889 8610	0.7525 4847	0.7178 2178	0.6531 7849
58	0.8651 7883	0.7857 1230	0.7488 0445	0.7136 5877	0.6483 1612
59	0.8630 2128	0.7824 5208	0.7450 7906	0.7095 1990	0.6434 8995
60	0.8608 6911	0.7792 0539	0.7413 7220	0.7054 0504	0.6386 9970
61	0.8587 2230	0.7759 7217	0.7376 8378	0.7013 1404	0.6339 4511
62	0.8565 8085	0.7727 5237	0.7340 1371	0.6972 4677	0.6292 2592
63	0.8544 4474	0.7695 4593	0.7303 6190	0.6932 0308	0.6245 4185
64	0.8523 1395	0.7663 5279	0.7267 2826	0.6891 8285	0.6198 9266
65	0.8501 8848	0.7631 7291	0.7231 1269	0.6851 8593	0.6152 7807
66	0.8480 6831	0.7600 0621	0.7195 1512	0.6812 1219	0.6106 9784
67	0.8459 5343	0.7568 5266	0.7159 3544	0.6772 6150	0.6061 5170
68	0.8438 4382	0.7537 1219	0.7123 7357	0.6733 3372	0.6061 3940
69	0.8417 3947	0.7505 8476	0.7088 2943	0.5694 2872	0.5971 6070
70	0.8396 4037	0.7474 7030	0.7053 0291	0.6655 4637	0.5927 1533
71	0.8375 4650	0.7443 6876	0.7017 9394	0.6616 8653	0.5883 0306
72	0.8354 5786	0.7412 8009	0.6983 0243	0.6578 4908	0.5829 2363
73	0.8333 7442	0.7382 0424	0.6948 2829	0.6540 3388	0.5795 7681
74	0.8312 9618	0.7351 4115	0.6913 7143	0.6502 4081	0.5752 6234
75	0.8292 2312	0.7320 9078	0.6879 3177	0.6464 6973	0.5709 7999
76	0.8271 5523	0.7290 5306	0.6845 0923	0.6427 2053	0.5657 2952
77	0.8250 9250	0.7260 2794	0.6811 0371	0.6389 9306	0.5625 1069
78	0.8230 3491	0.7230 1537	0.6777 1513	0.6352 8723	0.5583 2326
79	0.8209 8246	0.7200 1531	0.6743 4342	0.6316 0288	0.5541 6701
80	0.8189 3512	0.7170 2770	0.6709 8847	0.6279 3980	0.5500 4170
81	0.8168 9289	0.7140 5248	0.6676 5022	0.6242 9816	0.5459 4710
82	0.8148 5575	0.7110 8960	0.6643 2858	0.6206 7754	0.5418 8297
83	0.8128 2369	0.7081 3902	0.6610 2346	0.6170 7792	0.5378 4911
84	0.8107 9670	0.7052 0069	0.6577 3479	0.6134 9917	0.5388 4527
85	0.8087 7476	0.7022 7454	0.6544 6248	0.6099 4118	0.5298 7123
86	0.8067 5787	0.6993 6054	0.6512 0644	0.6064 0382	0.5259 2678
87	0.8047 4600	0.6964 5863	0.6479 6661	0.6028 8698	0.5220 1169
88	0.8027 3915	0.6935 6876	0.6447 4290	0.5993 9054	0.5181 2575
89	0.8007 3731	0.6906 9088	0.6415 3522	0.5959 1437	0.5142 6873
90	0.7987 4046	0.6878 2495	0.6383 4350	0.5924 5836	0.5104 4043
91	0.7967 4859	0.6849 7090	0.6351 6766	0.5890 2240	0.5066 4063
92	0.7947 6168	0.6821 2870	0.6320 0763	0.5856 0636	0.5028 6911
93	0.7927 7973	0.6792 9829	0.6288 6331	0.5822 1014	0.4991 2567
94	0.7908 0273	0.6764 7962	0.6257 3464	0.5788 3361	0.4954 1009
95	0.7888 3065	0.6736 7265	0.6226 2153	0.5754 7666	0.4917 2217
96	0.7868 6349	0.6708 7733	0.6195 2391	0.5721 3918	0.4880 6171
97	0.7849 0124	0.6680 9361	0.6164 4170	0.5688 2106	0.4844 2850
98	0.7829 4388	0.6653 2143	0.6133 7483	0.5655 2218	0.4808 2233
99	0.7809 9140	0.6625 6076	0.6103 2321	0.5622 4243	0.4772 4301
100	0.7790 4379	0.6598 1155	0.6072 8678	0.5579 5171	0.4736 9033

TABLE II
PRESENT VALUE AT COMPOUND INTEREST
$$v^n = (1 + i)^{-n}$$

Periods	Rate i				
n	.01 (1%)	.01125 $(1\frac{1}{8}\%)$	.0125 $(1\frac{1}{4}\%)$	.015 $(1\frac{1}{2}\%)$	.0175 $(1\frac{3}{4}\%)$
1	0.9900 9901	0.9888 7515	0.9876 5432	0.9852 2167	0.9828 0098
2	0.9802 9605	0.9778 7407	0.9754 6106	0.9706 6175	0.9658 9777
3	0.9705 9015	0.9669 9537	0.9634 1833	0.9563 1699	0.9492 8528
4	0.9609 8034	0.9562 3770	0.9515 2428	0.9421 8423	0.9329 5851
5	0.9514 6569	0.9455 9970	0.9397 7706	0.9282 6033	0.9169 1254
6	0.9420 4524	0.9350 8005	0.9281 7488	0.9145 4219	0.9011 4254
7	0.9327 1805	0.9246 7743	0.9167 1593	0.9010 2679	0.8856 4378
8	0.9234 8322	0.9143 9054	0.9053 9845	0.8877 1112	0.8704 1157
9	0.9143 3982	0.9042 1808	0.8942 2069	0.8745 9224	0.8554 4135
10	0.9052 8695	0.8941 5880	0.8831 8093	0.8616 6723	0.8407 2860
11	0.8963 2372	0.8842 1142	0.8722 7746	0.8489 3323	0.8262 6889
12	0.8874 4923	0.8743 7470	0.8615 0860	0.8353 8742	0.8120 5788
13	0.8746 6260	0.8646 4742	0.8508 7269	0.8240 2702	0.7980 9128
14	0.8699 6297	0.8550 2835	0.8403 8809	0.8118 4928	0.7843 6490
15	0.8613 4947	0.8455 1629	0.8299 9318	0.7998 5150	0.7708 7459
16	0.8528 2126	0.8361 1005	0.8197 4635	0.7880 3104	0.7576 1631
17	0.8443 7749	0.8268 0846	0.8096 2602	0.7763 8526	0.7445 8605
18	0.8360 1731	0.8176 1034	0.7996 3064	0.7649 1159	0.7317 7990
19	0.8277 3992	0.8085 1455	0.7897 5866	0.7536 0747	0.7191 9401
20	0.8195 4447	0.7995 1995	0.7800 0855	0.7424 7042	0.7068 2458
21	0.8114 3017	0.7906 2542	0.7703 7881	0.7314 9795	0.6946 6789
22	0.8035 9621	0.7818 2983	0.7608 6796	0.7206 8763	0.6827 2028
23	0.7954 4179	0.7731 3210	0.7514 7453	0.7100 3708	0.6709 7817
24	0.7871 6613	0.7645 3112	0.7421 9707	0.6995 4392	0.6594 3800
25	0.7797 6844	0.7560 2583	0.7330 3414	0.6892 0583	0.6480 9632
26	0.7720 4796	0.7476 1516	0.7239 8434	0.6790 2052	0.6369 4970
27	0.7644 0392	0.7392 9806	0.7150 4626	0.6689 8574	0.6259 9479
28	0.7568 3557	0.7310 7348	0.7062 1853	0.6590 9925	0.6152 2829
29	0.7493 4215	0.7229 4040	0.6974 9978	0.6493 5887	0.6046 4697
30	0.7419 2292	0.7148 9780	0.6888 8867	0.6397 6243	0.5942 4764
31	0.7345 7715	0.7069 4467	0.6803 8387	0.6303 0781	0.5840 2716
32	0.7273 0411	0.6990 8002	0.6719 8407	0.6209 9292	0.5739 8247
33	0.7201 0307	0.6913 0287	0.6636 8797	0.6118 1568	0.5641 1053
34	0.7129 7334	0.6836 1223	0.6554 9429	0.6027 7407	0.5544 0839
35	0.7059 1420	0.6760 0715	0.6474 0177	0.5938 6608	0.5448 7311
36	0.6989 2495	0.6684 8667	0.6394 0916	0.5850 8974	0.5355 0183
37	0.6920 0490	0.6610 4986	0.6315 1522	0.5764 4309	0.5262 9172
38	0.6851 5337	0.6536 9578	0.6237 1873	0.5679 2423	0.5172 4002
39	0.6783 6967	0.6464 2352	0.6160 1850	0.5595 3126	0.5083 4400
40	0.6716 5314	0.6392 3216	0.6084 1334	0.5512 6232	0.4996 0098
41	0.6650 0311	0.6321 2080	0.6009 0206	0.5431 1559	0.4910 0834
42	0.6584 1892	0.6250 8855	0.5934 8352	0.5350 8925	0.4825 6348
43	0.6518 9992	0.6181 3454	0.5861 5656	0.5271 8153	0.4742 6386
44	0.6454 4546	0.6112 5789	0.5789 2006	0.5153 9067	0.4661 0699
45	0.6390 5492	0.6044 5774	0.5717 7290	0.5117 1494	0.4580 9040
46	0.6327 2764	0.5977 3324	0.5647 1397	0.5041 5265	0.4502 1170
47	0.6264 6301	0.5910 8355	0.5577 4219	0.4967 0212	0.4424 6850
48	0.6202 6041	0.5845 0784	0.5508 5649	0.4893 6170	0.4348 5848
49	0.6141 1921	0.5780 0528	0.5440 5579	0.4821 2975	0.4273 7934
50	0.6080 3842	0.5715 7506	0.5373 3905	0.4750 0468	0.4200 2883

TABLE II
PRESENT VALUE AT COMPOUND INTEREST
$$v^n = (1 + i)^{-n}$$

Periods	Rate i				
n	.01 (1%)	.01125 ($1\frac{1}{8}$%)	.0125 ($1\frac{1}{4}$%)	.015 ($1\frac{1}{2}$%)	.0175 ($1\frac{3}{4}$%)
50	0.6080 3882	0.5715 7506	0.5373 3905	0.4750 0468	0.4200 2883
51	0.6020 1864	0.5652 1637	0.5307 0524	0.4679 8491	0.4128 0475
52	0.5960 5806	0.5589 2843	0.5241 5332	0.4610 6887	0.4057 0492
53	0.5901 5649	0.5527 1044	0.5176 8229	0.4542 5505	0.3987 4719
54	0.5843 1336	0.5465 6162	0.5112 9115	0.4475 4192	0.3918 6947
55	0.5785 2808	0.5404 8120	0.5049 7892	0.4409 2800	0.3851 2970
56	0.5728 0008	0.5344 6843	0.4987 4461	0.4344 1182	0.3785 0585
57	0.5671 2879	0.5285 2256	0.4925 8727	0.4279 9194	0.3719 9592
58	0.5615 1365	0.5226 4282	0.4865 0594	0.4216 6694	0.3655 9796
59	0.5559 5411	0.5168 2850	0.4804 9970	0.4154 3541	0.3593 1003
60	0.5504 4962	0.5110 7887	0.4745 6760	0.4092 9597	0.3531 3025
61	0.5449 9962	0.5053 9319	0.4687 0874	0.4025 4726	0.3470 5676
62	0.5396 0358	0.4997 7077	0.4629 2222	0.3972 8794	0.3410 8772
63	0.5342 6097	0.4942 1090	0.4572 0713	0.3914 1669	0.3352 2135
64	0.5289 7126	0.4887 1288	0.4515 6259	0.3856 3221	0.3294 5587
65	0.5237 3592	0.4832 7602	0.4459 8775	0.3799 3321	0.3237 8956
66	0.5185 4844	0.4778 9965	0.4404 8175	0.3743 1843	0.3182 2069
67	0.5134 1429	0.4725 8309	0.4350 4368	0.3687 8663	0.3127 4761
68	0.5083 3099	0.4673 2568	0.4296 7277	0.3633 3658	0.3073 6866
69	0.5032 9801	0.4621 2675	0.4243 6817	0.3579 6708	0.3020 8222
70	0.4983 1486	0.4569 8566	0.4191 2905	0.3526 7692	0.2968 8670
71	0.4933 8105	0.4519 0177	0.4139 5462	0.3474 6495	0.2917 8054
72	0.4884 9609	0.4468 7443	0.4088 4407	0.3423 3000	0.2867 6221
73	0.4836 5949	0.4419 0302	0.4037 9661	0.3572 7093	0.2818 3018
74	0.4788 7078	0.4369 8692	0.3988 1147	0.3322 8663	0.2769 8298
75	0.4741 2949	0.4321 2551	0.3938 8787	0.3273 7599	0.2722 1914
76	0.4694 3514	0.4273 1818	0.3890 2506	0.3225 3793	0.2675 3724
77	0.4647 8726	0.4225 6433	0.3842 2228	0.3177 7136	0.2629 3586
78	0.4601 8541	0.4178 6337	0.3794 7879	0.3130 7523	0.2584 1362
79	0.4556 2912	0.4132 1470	0.3747 9387	0.3084 4850	0.2539 6916
80	0.4511 1794	0.4086 1775	0.3701 6679	0.3038 9015	0.2496 0114
81	0.4466 5142	0.4040 7194	0.3655 9643	0.2993 9916	0.2453 0825
82	0.4422 2913	0.3995 7670	0.3610 8329	0.2949 7454	0.2410 8919
83	0.4378 5063	0.3951 3148	0.3566 2547	0.2906 1531	0.2369 4269
84	0.4335 1547	0.3907 3570	0.3522 2268	0.2863 2050	0.2328 6751
85	0.4292 2324	0.3863 8882	0.3478 7426	0.2820 8917	0.2288 6242
86	0.4249 7350	0.3820 9031	0.3435 7951	0.2779 2036	0.2249 2621
87	0.4207 6585	0.3778 3961	0.3393 3779	0.2738 1316	0.2210 5770
88	0.4165 9985	0.3736 3621	0.3351 4843	0.2697 6666	0.2172 5572
89	0.4124 7510	0.3694 7956	0.3310 1080	0.2657 7996	0.2135 1914
90	0.4083 9119	0.2653 6913	0.3269 2425	0.2618 5218	0.2098 4682
91	0.4043 4771	0.3613 0448	0.3228 8814	0.2579 8245	0.2062 3766
92	0.4003 4427	0.3572 8503	0.3189 0187	0.2541 6990	0.2026 9057
93	0.3963 8046	0.3533 1029	0.3149 6481	0.2504 1369	0.1992 0450
94	0.3924 5590	0.3493 7976	0.3110 7636	0.2467 1300	0.1957 7837
95	0.3885 7020	0.3454 9297	0.3072 3591	0.2430 6699	0.1924 1118
96	0.3847 2297	0.3416 4941	0.3034 4287	0.2394 7487	0.1891 0190
97	0.3809 1383	0.3378 4861	0.2996 9666	0.2359 3583	0.1858 4953
98	0.3771 4241	0.3340 9010	0.2959 9670	0.2324 4909	0.1826 5310
99	0.3734 0832	0.3503 7340	0.2923 4242	0.2290 1389	0.1795 1165
100	0.3697 1121	0.3266 9805	0.2887 3326	0.2556 2944	0.1764 2422

TABLE II
PRESENT VALUE AT COMPOUND INTEREST
$$v^n = (1 + i)^{-n}$$

Periods	Rate i				
n	.02 (2%)	.0225 ($2\frac{1}{4}$%)	.025 ($2\frac{1}{2}$%)	.0275 ($2\frac{3}{4}$%)	.03 (3%)
1	0.9803 9216	0.9779 9511	0.9756 0976	0.9732 3601	0.9708 7379
2	0.9611 6878	0.9564 7444	0.9518 1440	0.9471 8833	0.9425 9591
3	0.9423 2233	0.9354 2732	0.9285 9941	0.9218 3779	0.9151 4166
4	0.9238 4543	0.9148 4335	0.9059 5064	0.8971 6573	0.8884 8705
5	0.9057 3081	0.8947 1232	0.8838 5429	0.8731 5400	0.8626 0878
6	0.8879 7138	0.8750 2427	0.8622 9687	0.8497 8491	0.8374 8426
7	0.8705 6018	0.8557 6946	0.8412 6524	0.8270 4128	0.8130 9151
8	0.8534 9037	0.8369 3835	0.8207 4657	0.8049 0635	0.7894 0923
9	0.8367 5527	0.8185 2161	0.8007 2836	0.7833 6385	0.7664 1673
10	0.8203 4830	0.8005 1013	0.7811 9840	0.7623 9791	0.7440 9391
11	0.8042 6304	0.7828 9499	0.7621 4478	0.7419 9410	0.7224 2128
12	0.7884 9318	0.7656 6748	0.7435 5589	0.7221 3440	0.7013 7988
13	0.7730 3253	0.7488 1905	0.7254 2038	0.7028 0720	0.6809 5134
14	0.7578 0502	0.7323 4137	0.7077 2720	0.6839 9728	0.6611 1781
15	0.7430 1473	0.7162 2628	0.6904 6556	0.6656 9078	0.6418 6195
16	0.7284 4581	0.7004 6580	0.6736 2493	0.6478 7424	0.6231 6694
17	0.7141 6256	0.6850 5212	0.6571 9506	0.6305 3454	0.5060 1645
18	0.7001 5937	0.6699 7763	0.6411 6591	0.6136 5892	0.5873 9461
19	0.6864 3076	0.6552 3484	0.6255 2772	0.5972 3496	0.5207 8603
20	0.6729 7133	0.6408 1647	0.6102 7094	0.5812 5057	0.5536 7575
21	0.6597 7582	0.6267 1538	0.5953 8629	0.5656 9398	0.5375 4928
22	0.6468 3904	0.6129 2457	0.5808 6467	0.5505 5375	0.5218 9250
23	0.6341 5592	0.5994 3724	0.5666 9724	0.5358 1874	0.5066 9175
24	0.6217 2149	0.5862 4668	0.5528 7535	0.5214 7809	0.4919 3374
25	0.6095 3087	0.5733 4639	0.5393 9059	0.5075 2126	0.4776 0557
26	0.5975 7928	0.5607 2997	0.5262 3472	0.4939 3796	0.4636 9473
27	0.5858 6204	0.5483 9117	0.5133 9973	0.4807 1821	0.4501 8906
28	0.5743 7455	0.5363 2388	0.5008 7778	0.4678 5227	0.4370 7675
29	0.5631 1231	0.5245 2213	0.4886 6125	0.4553 3068	0.4243 4636
30	0.5520 7089	0.5129 8008	0.4767 4269	0.4431 4421	0.4119 8676
31	0.5412 4597	0.5016 9201	0.4551 1481	0.4312 8391	0.3999 8715
32	0.5306 3330	0.4906 5233	0.4537 7055	0.4197 4103	0.3883 3703
33	0.5202 2873	0.4798 5558	0.4427 0298	0.4085 0708	0.3770 2625
34	0.5100 2817	0.4692 9641	0.4319 0534	0.3975 7380	0.3660 4490
35	0.5000 2761	0.4589 6960	0.4213 7107	0.3669 3314	0.3553 8340
36	0.4902 2315	0.4488 7002	0.4110 9372	0.3765 7727	0.3450 3243
37	0.4806 1093	0.4389 9268	0.4010 6705	0.3664 9856	0.3349 8294
38	0.4711 8719	0.4293 3270	0.3912 8492	0.3566 8959	0.3252 2615
39	0.4619 4822	0.4198 8528	0.3817 4139	0.3471 4316	0.3157 5355
40	0.4528 9042	0.4106 4575	0.3724 3062	0.3378 5222	0.3065 5684
41	0.4440 1021	0.4016 0954	0.3633 4695	0.3288 0995	0.2976 2800
42	0.4353 0413	0.3927 7213	0.3544 8483	0.3200 0968	0.2889 5922
43	0.4267 6875	0.3841 2925	0.3458 3886	0.3114 4495	0.2805 4294
44	0.4184 0074	0.3756 7653	0.3374 0376	0.3031 0944	0.2723 7178
45	0.4101 9680	0.3674 0981	0.3291 7440	0.2940 9702	0.2644 3862
46	0.4021 5373	0.3593 2500	0.3211 4576	0.2871 0172	0.2567 3653
47	0.3942 6836	0.3514 1809	0.3133 1294	0.2794 1773	0.2492 5876
48	0.3865 3761	0.3465 8518	0.3056 7116	0.2719 3940	0.2419 9880
49	0.3789 5844	0.3661 2242	0.2982 1576	0.2646 6122	0.2349 5029
50	0.3715 2788	0.3287 2608	0.2909 4221	0.2575 7783	0.2281 0708

TABLE II
PRESENT VALUE AT COMPOUND INTEREST
$$v^n = (1 + i)^{-n}$$

Periods	Rate *i*				
n	.02 (2%)	.0225 ($2\frac{1}{4}$%)	.025 ($2\frac{1}{2}$%)	.0275 ($2\frac{3}{4}$%)	.03 (3%)
50	0.3715 2788	0.3287 2608	0.2909 4221	0.2575 7783	0.2281 0708
51	0.3642 4302	0.3214 9250	0.2838 4606	0.2506 8402	0.2214 6318
52	0.3571 0100	0.3144 1810	0.2769 2298	0.2439 7471	0.2150 1280
53	0.3500 9902	0.3074 9936	0.2701 6876	0.2374 4497	0.2287 5029
54	0.3432 3433	0.3007 3287	0.2635 7928	0.2310 9000	0.2026 1719
55	0.3565 0425	0.2941 1528	0.2571 5052	0.2249 0511	0.1967 6717
56	0.2909 0613	0.2876 4330	0.2508 7855	0.2188 8575	0.1910 3609
57	0.3234 3738	0.2813 1374	0.2447 5956	0.2130 2749	0.1854 7193
58	0.3170 9547	0.2751 2347	0.2387 8982	0.2073 2603	0.1800 6984
59	0.3108 7791	0.2690 6940	0.2329 6568	0.2017 7716	0.1748 2508
60	0.3047 8227	0.2631 4856	0.2272 8359	0.1963 7679	0.1697 3309
61	0.2988 0614	0.2573 5801	0.2217 4009	.1911 2097	0.1647 8941
62	0.2929 4720	0.2516 9487	0.2163 3179	0.1860 0581	0.1599 8972
63	0.2872 0314	0.2461 5635	0.2110 5541	0.1810 2755	0.1553 2982
64	0.2815 7170	0.2407 3971	0.2059 0771	0.1761 8253	0.1508 0565
65	0.2760 5069	0.2354 4226	0.2008 8557	0.1714 6718	0.1464 1335
66	0.2706 3793	0.2302 6138	0.1959 8593	0.1668 7804	0.1421 4879
67	0.2653 3130	0.2251 9450	0.1912 0578	0.1624 1172	0.1380 0853
68	0.2601 2873	0.2202 3912	0.1865 4223	0.1580 6493	0.1339 8887
69	0.2550 2817	0.2153 9278	0.1819 9241	0.1538 3448	0.1346 8628
70	0.2500 2761	0.2106 5309	0.1775 5358	0.1497 1726	0.1262 9736
71	0.2451 2511	0.2060 1769	0.1732 2300	0.1457 1023	0.1226 1880
72	0.2403 1874	0.2014 8429	0.1689 9805	0.1418 1044	0.1190 4737
73	0.2356 0661	0.1970 5065	0.1648 7615	0.1380 1503	0.1155 7998
74	0.2309 8687	0.1927 1458	0.1608 5478	0.1343 2119	0.1122 1357
75	0.2264 5771	0.1884 7391	0.1569 3149	0.1307 2622	0.1089 4521
76	0.2220 1737	0.1843 2657	0.1531 0389	0.1272 2747	0.1057 7205
77	0.2176 6408	0.1802 7048	0.1493 6965	0.1238 2235	0.1026 9131
78	0.2133 9616	0.1763 0365	0.1457 2649	0.1205 0837	0.0997 0030
79	0.2092 1192	0.1724 2411	0.1421 7218	0.1172 8309	0.0967 9641
80	0.2051 0973	0.1686 2993	0.1387 0457	0.1141 4412	0.0939 7710
81	0.2010 8797	0.1649 1925	0.1353 2153	0.1110 8917	0.0912. 3990
82	0.1971 4507	0.1612 9022	0.1320 2101	0.1081 1598	0.0885 8243
83	0.1932 7948	0.1577 4105	0.1288 0098	0.1052 2237	0.0860 0236
84	0.1804 8968	0.1542 6997	0.1256 5949	0.1024 0620	0.0834 9743
85	0.1857 7420	0.1508 7528	0.1255 9463	0.0996 6540	0.0810 6547
86	0.1821 3157	0.1475 5528	0.1196 0452	0.0969 9795	0.0787 0434
87	0.1785 6036	0.1443 0835	0.1166 8733	0.0944 0190	0.0764 1198
88	0.1750 5918	0.1411 3236	0.1138 4130	0.0918 7533	0.0741 8639
89	0.1716 2665	0.1380 2724	0.1110 6468	0.0894 1638	0.0720 2562
90	0.1682 6142	0.1349 8997	0.1083 5579	0.0870 2324	0.0699 2779
91	0.1649 6217	0.1320 1953	0.1057 1296	0.0846 9415	0.0678 9105
92	0.1617 2762	0.1291 1445	0.1031 3460	0.0824 2740	0.0659 1364
93	0.1585 5649	0.1262 7331	0.1006 1912	0.8002 2131	0.0639 9383
94	0.1554 4754	0.1234 9468	0.0981 6500	0.0780 7487	0.0621 2993
95	0.1523 9955	0.1207 7719	0.0957 7073	0.0759 8469	0.0603 2032
96	0.1494 1132	0.1181 1950	0.0934 3486	0.0739 5104	0.0585 6342
97	0.1464 8169	0.1155 2029	0.0911 5596	0.0719 7181	0.0568 5769
98	0.1436 0950	0.1129 7828	0.0880 3264	0.0700 4556	0.0552 0164
99	0.1407 9363	0.1104 9221	0.0867 6355	0.0681 7086	0.0535 9383
100	0.1380 3297	0.1080 6084	0.0846 4737	0.0663 4634	0.0520 3284

TABLE II
PRESENT VALUE AT COMPOUND INTEREST
$$v^n = (1 + i)^{-n}$$

Periods	Rate i				
n	.035 $(3\frac{1}{2}\%)$	.04 (4%)	.045 $(4\frac{1}{2}\%)$	.05 (5%)	.055 $(5\frac{1}{2}\%)$
1	0.9661 8357	0.9615 3846	0.9569 3780	0.9523 8095	0.9478 6730
2	0.9335 1070	0.9245 5621	0.9157 2995	0.9070 2948	0.8984 5242
3	0.9019 4271	0.8889 9636	0.8762 9660	0.8638 3760	0.8516 1366
4	0.8714 4223	0.8548 0419	0.8385 6134	0.8227 0247	0.8072 1674
5	0.8419 7317	0.8219 2711	0.8024 5105	0.7835 2617	0.7651 3435
6	0.8135 0064	0.7903 1453	0.7678 9574	0.7462 1540	0.7252 4583
7	0.7859 9096	0.7599 1781	0.7348 2846	0.7106 8133	0.6874 3681
8	0.7594 1156	0.7306 9021	0.7031 8513	0.6768 3936	0.6515 9887
9	0.7337 3097	0.7025 8674	0.6729 0443	0.6446 0892	0.6176 2926
10	0.7089 1881	0.6755 6417	0.6439 2768	0.6139 1325	0.5854 3058
11	0.6849 4571	0.6495 8093	0.6161 9874	0.5846 7929	0.5549 1050
12	0.6617 8330	0.6245 9705	0.5896 6386	0.5568 3742	0.5259 8152
13	0.6394 0415	0.6005 7409	0.5642 7164	0.5303 2135	0.4985 6068
14	0.6177 8179	0.5774 7508	0.5399 7286	0.5050 6795	0.4725 6937
15	0.5968 9062	0.5552 6450	0.5167 2044	0.4810 1710	0.4479 3305
16	0.5767 0591	0.5339 0818	0.4944 6932	0.4581 1152	0.4245 8109
17	0.5572 3378	0.5133 7325	0.4731 7639	0.4362 9669	0.4024 4653
18	0.5383 6114	0.4936 2812	0.4528 0037	0.4155 2065	0.3814 6590
19	0.5201 5569	0.4746 4242	0.4333 0179	0.3937 3396	0.3615 7906
20	0.5025 6588	0.4563 8695	0.4146 4286	0.3768 8948	0.3427 2896
21	0.4855 7090	0.4388 3360	0.3967 8743	0.3589 4236	0.3248 6158
22	0.4691 5063	0.4219 5539	0.3797 0089	0.3418 4987	0.3079 2567
23	0.4532 8563	0.4057 2633	0.3633 5013	0.3255 7131	0.2918 7267
24	0.4379 5713	0.3901 2147	0.3477 0347	0.3100 6791	0.2766 5656
25	0.4231 4699	0.3751 1680	0.3327 3060	0.2953 0277	0.2622 3370
26	0.4088 3767	0.3606 8923	0.3184 0248	0.2812 4073	0.2485 6275
27	0.3950 1224	0.3468 1657	0.3046 9137	0.2678 4832	0.2356 0450
28	0.3816 5434	0.3334 7747	0.2915 7069	0.2550 9364	0.2233 2181
29	0.3687 4815	0.3206 5141	0.2790 1502	0.2429 4632	0.2116 7944
30	0.3562 7841	0.3083 1867	0.2670 0002	0.2313 7745	0.2006 4402
31	0.3442 3035	0.2964 6026	0.2555 0241	0.2203 5947	0.1901 8390
32	0.3325 8971	0.2850 5794	0.2444 9991	0.2098 6617	0.1802 6910
33	0.3213 4271	0.2740 9417	0.2339 7121	0.1998 7254	0.1708 7119
34	0.3104 7605	0.2635 5209	0.2238 9589	0.1903 5480	0.1619 6321
35	0.2999 7686	0.2534 1547	0.2142 5444	0.1812 9029	0.1535 1963
36	0.2898 3272	0.2436 6872	0.2050 2817	0.1726 5741	0.1455 1624
37	0.2800 3161	0.2342 9685	0.1961 9921	0.1644 3563	0.1379 3008
38	0.2705 6194	0.2252 8543	0.1877 5044	0.1566 0536	0.1307 3941
39	0.2614 1250	0.2166 2061	0.1796 6549	0.1491 4797	0.1239 2362
40	0.2525 7247	0.2082 8904	0.1719 2870	0.1420 4568	0.1174 6314
41	0.2440 3137	0.2002 7793	0.1645 2507	0.1352 8160	0.1113 3947
42	0.2357 7910	0.1925 7493	0.1574 4026	0.1288 3962	0.1055 3504
43	0.2278 0590	0.1851 6820	0.1506 6054	0.1227 0440	0.1000 3322
44	0.2201 0231	0.1780 4635	0.1441 7276	0.1168 6133	0.0948 1822
45	0.2126 5924	0.1711 9841	0.1379 6437	0.1112 9651	0.0898 7509
46	0.2054 6787	0.1646 1386	0.1320 2332	0.1059 9668	0.0851 8965
47	0.1985 1968	0.1582 8256	0.1263 3810	0.1009 4921	0.0807 4849
48	0.1918 0645	0.1521 9476	0.1208 9771	0.0961 4211	0.0765 3885
49	0.1853 2024	0.1463 4112	0.1156 9158	0.0915 6391	0.0725 4867
50	0.1790 5337	0.1407 1262	0.1107 0965	0.0872 0373	0.0687 6652

TABLE II
PRESENT VALUE AT COMPOUND INTEREST
$$v^n = (1 + i)^{-n}$$

Periods	Rate i				
n	.06 (6%)	.065 ($6\frac{1}{2}$%)	.07 (7%)	.075 ($7\frac{1}{2}$%)	.08 (8%)
1	0.9433 9623	0.9389 6714	0.9345 7944	0.9302 3256	0.9259 2593
2	0.8899 9644	0.8816 5928	0.8734 3873	0.8653 3261	0.8573 3882
3	0.8396 1928	0.8278 4909	0.8162 9788	0.8049 6057	0.7938 3224
4	0.7920 9366	0.7773 2309	0.7628 9521	0.7488 0053	0.7350 1950
5	0.7472 5817	0.7298 8084	0.7129 8618	0.6965 5863	0.6805 8320
6	0.7049 6054	0.6853 3412	0.6663 4222	0.6479 6152	0.6301 6963
7	0.6650 5711	0.6435 0621	0.6227 4974	0.6027 5490	0.5834 9040
8	0.6274 1237	0.6042 3119	0.5820 0910	0.5607 0223	0.5402 6888
9	0.5918 9846	0.5673 5323	0.5439 3374	0.5215 8347	0.5002 4897
10	0.5583 9478	0.5327 2604	0.5083 4929	0.4851 9393	0.4631 9349
11	0.5267 8753	0.5002 1224	0.4750 9280	0.4713 4319	0.4288 8286
12	0.4969 6936	0.4696 8285	0.4440 1196	0.4198 5413	0.3971 1376
13	0.4688 3902	0.4410 1676	0.4149 6445	0.3905 6198	0.3676 9792
14	0.4423 0096	0.4141 0025	0.3878 1724	0.3633 1347	0.3404 6104
15	0.4172 6506	0.3886 2652	0.3624 4602	0.3579 6602	0.3152 4170
16	0.3936 4628	0.3650 9533	0.3387 3460	0.3143 8699	0.2918 9047
17	0.3713 6442	0.3428 1251	0.3165 7439	0.2924 5302	0.2702 6895
18	0.3503 4379	0.3218 8969	0.2958 6392	0.2720 4932	0.2502 4903
19	0.3305 1301	0.3022 4384	0.2765 0833	0.2530 6913	0.2317 1206
20	0.3118 0473	0.2837 9703	0.2584 1900	0.2354 1315	0.2145 4821
21	0.2941 5540	0.2664 7608	0.2415 1309	0.2189 8897	0.1986 5575
22	0.2775 0510	0.2502 1228	0.2257 1317	0.2037 1067	0.1839 4051
23	0.2617 9726	0.2349 4111	0.2109 4688	0.1894 9830	0.1703 1528
24	0.2469 7855	0.2206 0198	0.1971 4662	0.1762 7749	0.1576 9934
25	0.2329 9863	0.2071 3801	0.1842 4918	0.1639 7906	0.1460 1790
26	0.2198 1003	0.1944 9579	0.1721 9549	0.1525 3866	0.1352 0176
27	0.2076 6795	0.1826 2515	0.1609 3037	0.1418 9643	0.1251 8682
28	0.1956 3014	0.1714 7902	0.1504 0021	0.1319 9668	0.1159 1372
29	0.1845 5674	0.1110 1316	0.1405 6282	0.1227 8761	0.1073 2752
30	0.1741 1013	0.1511 8607	0.1313 6712	0.1142 2103	0.0993 7733
31	0.1642 5484	0.1419 5875	0.1227 7301	0.1062 5212	0.0920 1605
32	0.1549 5740	0.1332 9460	0.1147 4113	0.0988 3918	0.0852 0005
33	0.1461 8622	0.1251 5925	0.1072 3470	0.0919 4343	0.0788 8893
34	0.1379 1153	0.1175 2042	0.1002 1934	0.0855 2877	0.0730 4531
35	0.1301 0522	0.1103 4781	0.0936 6294	0.0795 6164	0.0676 3454
36	0.1227 4077	0.1036 1297	0.0875 3546	0.0740 1083	0.0626 2458
37	0.1157 9318	0.0972 8917	0.0818 0884	0.0688 4729	0.0579 8572
38	0.1092 3885	0.0913 5134	0.0764 5686	0.0640 4399	0.0536 9048
39	0.1030 5552	0.0857 7590	0.0714 5501	0.0595 7580	0.0497 1341
40	0.0972 2219	0.0805 4075	0.0667 8038	0.0554 1935	0.0460 3093
41	0.0917 1905	0.0756 2512	0.0624 1157	0.0515 5288	0.0426 2123
42	0.0865 2740	0.0710 0950	0.0583 2857	0.0479 5617	0.0394 6411
43	0.0816 2962	0.0666 7559	0.0545 1268	0.0446 1039	0.0365 4084
44	0.0770 0908	0.0626 0619	0.0509 4643	0.0414 9804	0.0338 3411
45	0.0726 5007	0.0587 8515	0.0476 1349	0.0386 0283	0.0313 2788
46	0.0685 3781	0.0551 9733	0.[illegible]44 9859	0.0359 0961	0.0290 0730
47	0.0646 5831	0.0518 2848	0.0415 8747	0.0334 0428	0.0268 5861
48	0.0609 9840	0.0486 6524	0.0388 6679	0.0310 7375	0.0248 6908
49	0.0575 4566	0.0456 9506	0.0363 2410	0.0289 0582	0.0230 2693
50	0.0542 8836	0.0429 0616	0.0339 4776	0.0268 8913	0.0213 2123

TABLE III
AMOUNT OF AN ANNUITY

$$s_{\overline{n}|}\, i = \frac{(1+i)^n - 1}{i}$$

Periods	Rate i				
n	.0025 ($\frac{1}{3}$%)	.004167 ($\frac{5}{12}$%)	.005 ($\frac{1}{2}$%)	.005833 ($\frac{7}{12}$%)	.0075 ($\frac{3}{4}$%)
1	1.0000 0000	1.0000 0000	1.0000 0000	1.0000 0000	1.0000 0000
2	2.0025 0000	2.0041 6667	2.0050 0000	2.0058 3333	2.0075 0000
3	3.0075 0625	3.0125 1736	3.0150 2500	3.0175 3403	3.0225 5625
4	4.0150 2502	4.0250 6952	4.0301 0013	4.0351 3631	4.0452 2542
5	5.0250 6258	5.0418 4064	5.0502 5063	5.0586 7460	5.0755 6461
6	6.0376 2523	6.0628 4831	6.0755 0188	6.0881 8354	6.1136 3135
7	7.0527 1930	7.0881 1018	7.1058 7939	7.1236 9794	7.1594 8358
8	8.0703 5110	8.1176 4397	8.1414 0879	8.1652 5285	8.2131 7971
9	9.0905 2697	9.1514 6749	9.1121 1583	9.2128 8349	9.2747 7856
10	10.1132 5329	10.1895 9860	10.2280 2641	10.2666 2531	10.3443 3940
11	11.1385 3642	11.2320 5526	11.2791 6654	11.3265 1396	11.4219 2194
12	12.1663 8277	12.2788 5549	12.3355 6237	12.3925 8529	12.5075 8636
13	13.1967 9872	13.3300 1739	13.3972 4018	13.4648 7537	13.6013 9325
14	14.2297 9072	14.3855 5913	14.4642 2639	14.5434 2048	14.7034 0370
15	15.2653 6520	15.4454 9896	15.5365 4752	15.6282 5710	15.8136 7923
16	16.3035 2861	16.5098 5520	16.6142 3026	16.7194 2193	16.9322 8183
17	17.3442 8743	17.5786 4627	17.6973 0141	17.8169 5189	17.0592 7394
18	18.3876 4815	18.6518 9063	18.7857 8791	18.9208 8411	19.1947 1849
19	19.4336 1727	19.7296 0684	19.8797 1685	20.0312 5593	19.3386 7888
20	20.4822 0131	20.8118 1353	20.9791 1544	21.1481 0493	20.4912 1897
21	21.5334 0682	21.8985 2942	22.0840 1101	22.2714 6887	21.6524 0312
22	22.5872 4035	22.9897 7320	23.1944 3107	23.4013 8577	22.8222 9614
23	23.6437 0843	24.0855 8402	24.3104 0323	24.5378 9386	25.0009 6336
24	24.1728 1770	25.1859 2053	25.4319 5524	25.6810 3157	26.1884 7059
25	25.7645 7475	26.2908 6187	26.5591 1502	26.8308 3759	27.3848 8411
26	26.8289 8619	27.4004 0713	27.6919 1059	27.9873 5081	28.5902 7075
27	27.8960 5865	28.5145 7549	28.8303 7015	29.1506 1036	29.8046 9778
28	28.9657 9880	29.6333 8622	29.9745 2200	30.3206 5558	31.0282 3301
29	30.0382 1330	30.7568 5866	31.1243 9461	31.4975 2607	32.2609 4476
30	31.1133 0883	31.8850 1224	32.2800 1658	32.6812 6164	33.5029 0184
31	32.1910 9210	33.0178 6646	33.4414 1666	33.8719 0233	34.7541 7361
32	33.2715 6983	34.1554 4090	34.6086 2375	35.0694 8843	36.0148 2991
33	34.3547 4876	35.2977 5524	35.7816 6686	36.2740 6045	37.2849 4113
34	35.4406 3563	36.4448 2922	36.9605 7520	37.4856 5913	38.5645 7819
35	36.5292 3722	37.5966 8268	38.1453 7807	38.7043 2548	39.8538 1253
36	36.6205 6031	38.7533 3552	39.3361 0497	39.9301 0071	41.1537 1612
37	38.7146 1171	39.9148 0775	40.5327 8549	41.1630 2630	42.4613 6149
38	39.8113 9824	41.0811 1945	41.7354 4942	42.4031 4395	43.7798 2170
39	40.9109 2674	42.2522 9078	42.9441 2666	43.6504 9562	45.1081 7037
40	42.0132 0405	43.4283 4199	44.1588 4730	44.9051 2352	46.4464 8164
41	43.1182 3706	44.6092 9343	45.3796 4153	46.1670 7007	47.7948 3026
42	44.2260 3265	45.7951 6547	46.6065 3974	47.4363 7798	49.1532 9148
43	45.3365 9774	46.9859 7866	47.8395 7244	48.7130 9018	50.5219 4117
44	46.4499 3923	48.1817 5357	49.0787 7030	49.9972 4988	51.9008 5573
45	47.5660 6408	49.3825 1088	50.3241 6415	51.2889 0050	53.2901 1215
46	48.6849 7924	50.5882 7134	51.5757 8498	52.5880 8575	54.6897 8799
47	49.8066 9169	51.7990 5581	52.8336 6390	53.8948 4959	56.0999 6140
48	50.9312 0842	53.0148 8521	54.0978 3222	55.2092 3621	57.5207 1111
49	52.0585 3644	54.2357 8056	55.3683 2138	56.5312 9009	58.9521 1644
50	53.1886 8278	55.4617 6298	56.6451 6299	57.8610 5595	60.3942 5732

TABLE III
AMOUNT OF AN ANNUITY

$$s_{\overline{n|}\,i} = \frac{(1+i)^n - 1}{i}$$

Periods	Rate i				
n	.0025 ($\frac{1}{4}$%)	.004167 ($\frac{5}{12}$%)	.005 ($\frac{1}{2}$%)	.005833 ($\frac{7}{12}$%)	.0075 ($\frac{3}{4}$%)
50	53.1886 828	55.4617 630	56.6451 630	57.8610 559	60.3942 573
51	54.2316 545	56.6928 537	57.9283 888	59.1985 788	61.8472 142
52	55.4574 586	57.9290 739	59.2180 307	60.5439 038	63.3110 684
53	56.5961 023	59.1704 450	60.5141 209	61.8970 766	64.7859 014
54	57.7375 925	60.4169 885	61.8166 915	63.2581 429	66.2717 956
55	58.8819 365	61.6687 260	63.1257 750	64.6271 487	67.7688 341
56	60.0291 413	62.9256 790	64.4414 038	66.0041 404	69.2771 003
57	61.1792 142	64.1878 694	63.7636 109	67.3891 646	70.7966 786
58	62.3321 622	65.4553 188	67.0924 289	68.7822 680	72.3276 537
59	63.4879 926	66.7280 493	68.4278 911	70.1834 979	73.8701 111
60	64.6467 126	68.0060 828	69.7700 305	71.5929 016	75.4241 369
61	65.8083 294	69.2894 415	71.1188 807	73.0105 269	76.9898 180
62	66.9728 502	70.5781 475	72.4744 751	74.4364 216	78.5672 416
63	68.1402 824	71.8722 231	73.8368 474	75.8706 341	80.1564 959
64	69.3106 331	73.1716 907	75.2060 317	77.3132 128	81.7576 696
65	70.4839 096	74.4765 728	76.5820 618	78.7642 065	83.3708 521
66	71.6601 194	75.7868 918	77.9649 721	80.2236 644	84.9901 335
67	72.8392 697	77.1026 706	79.3547 970	81.6916 358	86.6336 045
68	74.0213 679	78.4239 317	80.7515 710	83.1681 703	88.2833 566
69	75.2064 213	79.7506 981	82.1553 288	84.6533 180	89.9454 817
70	76.3944 374	81.0829 926	83.5661 055	86.1471 290	91.6200 729
71	77.5854 235	82.4208 384	84.9839 360	87.6496 539	93.3072 234
72	78.7793 870	83.7642 586	86.4088 557	89.1609 436	95.0070 276
73	79.9763 355	85.1132 763	87.8409 000	90.6810 491	96.7195 803
74	81.1762 763	86.4679 150	89.2801 045	92.2100 219	98.4449 771
75	82.3792 170	87.8281 980	90.7265 050	93.7479 137	100.1933 145
76	83.5851 651	89.1941 488	92.1801 375	95.2947 765	101.9346 893
77	84.7941 280	90.5657 911	93.6410 382	96.8506 627	103.6991 995
78	86.0061 133	91.9431 485	95.1090 434	98.4156 249	105.4769 435
79	87.2211 286	93.3262 485	96.5847 896	99.9897 160	107.2680 206
80	88.4391 814	94.7151 044	98.0677 136	101.5729 894	109.0725 307
81	89.6602 793	96.1097 506	99.5580 521	103.1654 985	110.8905 747
82	90.8844 300	97.5102 079	101.0558 424	104.7672 972	112.7222 540
83	92.1116 411	98.9165 004	102.5611 216	106.3784 398	114.5676 709
84	93.3419 202	100.3286 525	104.0739 272	107.9080 807	116.4269 284
85	94.5752 750	101.7466 886	105.5942 969	109.6289 748	118.3001 304
86	95.8117 132	103.1706 331	107.1222 683	111.2684 771	120.1873 814
87	97.0512 425	104.6005 108	108.6578 707	112.9175 432	122.0887 867
88	98.2938 706	106.0363 462	110.2011 691	114.5762 289	124.0044 526
89	99.5396 053	107.4781 643	111.7521 749	116.2445 902	125.9344 860
90	100.7884 543	108.9259 900	113.3109 358	117.9226 837	127.8789 947
91	102.0404 254	110.3798 483	114.8774 905	119.6105 660	129.8380 871
92	103.2955 265	111.8397 643	116.4518 779	121.3082 943	131.8118 728
93	104.5537 653	113.3057 634	118.0341 373	123.0159 260	133.8004 618
94	105.8151 497	114.7778 707	119.6243 080	124.7335 189	135.8039 653
95	107.0796 876	116.2561 118	121.2224 295	126.4611 311	137.8224 951
96	108.3473 868	117.7405 123	122.8285 417	128.1988 210	139.8561 638
97	109.6182 553	119.2310 978	124.4426 844	129.9466 475	141.9050 850
98	110.8923 009	120.7278 940	126.0648 978	131.7046 696	143.9693 731
99	112.1665 317	122.2309 269	127.6952 223	134.4729 468	146.0491 434
100	113.4499 555	123.7204 224	129.3336 984	135.2515 390	148.1445 120

TABLE III
AMOUNT OF AN ANNUITY

$$s_{\overline{n}|}\, i = \frac{(1+i)^n - 1}{i}$$

Periods	Rate i				
n	.01 (1%)	.01125 ($1\frac{1}{2}$%)	.0125 ($1\frac{1}{4}$%)	.015 ($1\frac{1}{2}$%)	.0175 ($1\frac{3}{4}$%)
1	1.0000 0000	1.0000 0000	1.0000 0000	1.0000 0000	1.0000 0000
2	2.0100 0000	2.0112 5000	2.0125 0000	2.0150 0000	2.0175 0000
3	3.0301 0000	3.0338 7656	3.0376 5625	3.0452 2500	3.0528 0625
4	4.0604 0100	4.0680 0767	4.0756 2695	4.0909 0338	4.1062 3036
5	5.1010 0501	5.1137 7276	5.1265 7229	5.1522 6693	5.1780 8939
6	6.1520 1506	6.1713 0270	6.1906 5444	6.2295 5053	6.2687 0596
7	7.2135 3521	7.2407 2986	7.2680 3762	7.3229 9419	7.3784 0831
8	8.2856 7056	8.3221 8807	8.3588 8809	8.4328 3911	8.5075 3045
9	9.3685 2727	9.4158 1269	9.4633 7420	9.5593 3169	9.6564 1224
10	10.4622 1254	10.5217 4058	10.5816 6637	10.7027 2167	10.8253 9945
11	11.5668 3467	11.6401 1016	11.7139 3720	11.8632 6249	12.0148 4394
12	12.6825 0301	12.7710 6140	12.8603 6142	13.0412 1143	13.2251 0371
13	13.8093 2804	13.9147 3584	13.0211 1594	14.2368 2960	14.4565 4303
14	14.9474 2132	15.0712 7662	15.1963 7988	15.4503 8205	15.7095 3253
15	16.0968 9554	16.2408 2848	16.3863 3463	16.6821 3778	16.9844 4935
16	17.2578 6449	17.4235 3780	17.5911 6382	17.9323 6984	18.2816 7721
17	18.4304 4314	18.6195 5260	18.8110 5336	19.2013 5539	19.6016 0656
18	19.6147 4757	19.8290 2257	20.0461 9153	20.4893 7572	20.9446 3468
19	20.8108 9504	21.0520 9907	21.2967 6893	21.7967 1636	22.3111 6578
20	22.0190 0399	22.2889 3519	22.5629 7854	23.1236 6710	23.7016 1119
21	23.2391 9403	23.5396 8571	23.8450 1577	24.4705 2211	25.1163 8938
22	24.4715 8598	24.8045 0717	25.1430 7847	25.8375 7994	26.5559 2620
23	25.7163 0183	26.0835 5788	26.4573 6695	27.2251 4364	28.0206 5490
24	26.9734 6485	27.3769 9790	27.7880 8403	28.6335 2080	29.5110 1637
25	28.2431 9950	28.6849 8913	29.1354 3508	30.0630 2361	31.0274 5915
26	29.5256 3150	30.0076 9526	30.4996 2802	31.5139 6896	32.5704 3969
27	30.8208 8781	31.3452 8183	31.8808 7337	32.9866 7850	34.1404 2238
28	32.1290 9669	32.6979 1625	33.2793 8429	34.4814 7867	35.7378 7977
29	33.4503 8766	34.0657 6781	34.6953 7659	35.9985 0087	37.3632 9267
30	34.7848 9153	35.4490 0769	36.1290 6880	37.5386 8137	39.0171 5029
31	36.1327 4045	36.8478 0903	37.5806 8216	39.1017 6159	40.6999 5042
32	37.4940 6785	38.2623 4688	39.0504 4069	40.6882 8801	42.4121 9955
33	38.8690 0853	39.6927 9829	40.5385 7120	42.2986 1233	44.1544 1305
34	40.2576 9862	41.1393 4227	42.0453 0334	43.9330 9152	45.9271 1527
35	41.6602 7560	42.6021 5987	43.5708 6963	45.5920 8789	47.7308 3979
36	43.0768 7836	44.0814 3417	45.1155 0550	47.2759 6921	49.5661 2949
37	44.5076 4714	45.5773 5030	46.6794 4932	48.9851 0874	51.4335 3675
38	45.9527 2361	47.0900 9549	48.2629 4243	50.7198 8538	53.3326 2365
39	47.4122 5085	48.6198 5906	49.8662 2921	52.4806 8366	55.2669 6206
40	48.8863 7336	50.1688 3248	51.4895 5708	54.2678 9391	57.2341 3390
41	50.3752 3709	51.7312 0934	53.1331 7654	56.0819 1232	59.2357 3124
42	51.8789 8946	53.3131 8545	54.7973 4125	57.9231 4100	61.2723 5654
43	53.3977 7936	54.9129 5879	56.4823 0801	59.7919 8812	63.3446 2278
44	54.9317 5715	56.5307 2957	58.1883 3686	61.6888 6794	65.4531 5367
45	56.4810 7472	58.1667 0028	59.9156 9108	63.6142 0096	67.5985 8386
46	58.0458 8547	59.8210 7566	61.6646 3721	65.5684 1398	69.7815 5908
47	59.6263 4432	61.4940 6276	63.4354 4518	67.5519 4018	72.0027 3637
48	61.2226 0777	63.1858 7097	65.2283 8824	69.5652 1929	74.2627 8425
49	62.8348 3385	64.8087 1201	67.0437 4310	71.6086 9758	76.5623 8298
50	64.4631 8218	66.6268 0002	68.8817 8989	73.6828 2804	78.9022 2468

TABLE III
AMOUNT OF AN ANNUITY

$$s_{\overline{n}|}\, i = \frac{(1+i)^n - 1}{i}$$

Periods	Rate i				
n	.01 (1%)	.01125 ($1\frac{1}{8}$%)	.0125 ($1\frac{1}{4}$%)	.015 ($1\frac{1}{2}$%)	.0175 ($1\frac{3}{4}$%)
50	64.4631 822	66.6268 000	68.8817 899	73.6828 280	78.9022 247
51	66.1078 140	68.3763 515	70.7428 123	75.7880 705	81.2830 136
52	67.7688 921	70.1455 855	72.6270 974	77.9248 915	83.7054 663
53	69.4465 811	71.9347 233	74.5349 361	80.0937 649	86.1703 120
54	71.1410 469	73.7439 890	76.4666 228	82.2951 714	88.6782 925
55	72.8524 573	75.5736 088	78.4224 556	84.5295 989	91.2301 626
56	74.5809 819	77.4238 119	80.4027 363	86.7975 429	93.8266 904
57	76.3267 917	79.2948 298	82.4077 705	89.0995 061	96.4686 575
58	78.0900 597	81.1868 966	84.4378 676	91.4359 987	99.1568 590
59	79.8709 603	83.1002 492	86.4933 410	93.8075 386	101.8921 041
60	81.6696 699	85.0351 270	88.5745 078	96.2146 517	104.6752 159
61	83.4863 666	86.9917 722	90.6816 891	98.6578 715	107.5070 322
62	85.3212 302	88.9704 297	92.8152 102	101.1377 396	110.3884 052
63	87.1744 425	90.9713 470	94.9754 003	103.6548 057	113.3202 023
64	89.0461 869	92.9947 446	97.1625 928	106.2096 277	116.3033 058
65	90.9366 488	95.0409 659	99.3771 253	108.8087 722	119.3386 137
66	92.8460 153	97.1101 767	101.6193 393	111.4348 137	122.4270 394
67	94.7744 755	99.2026 662	103.8895 811	114.1063 359	125.5695 126
68	96.7222 202	101.3186 962	106.1882 008	116.8179 310	128.7669 791
69	98.6894 424	103.4585 315	108.5155 553	119.5701 999	132.0204 012
70	100.6763 368	105.6224 400	110.8719 978	122.3637 529	135.3307 583
71	102.6831 002	107.8106 925	113.2578 977	125.1992 092	138.6990 465
72	104.7099 312	110.0235 628	115.6736 215	128.0771 974	142.1263 798
73	106.7570 305	112.2613 278	118.1195 417	130.9983 553	145.6134 897
74	108.8246 008	114.5242 678	120.5960 360	133.9633 307	149.1617 258
75	110.9128 468	116.8126 658	123.1034 864	136.9727 806	152.7720 560
76	113.0219 753	119.1268 083	125.6422 800	140.0273 723	156.4455 670
77	115.1521 951	121.4669 849	128.2128 085	143.1277 829	160.1833 644
78	117.3037 170	123.8334 865	130.8154 686	146.2746 997	163.9865 733
79	119.4767 542	126.2266 152	133.4506 620	149.4688 202	167.8563 383
80	121.6715 217	128.6466 646	136.1187 953	152.7108 525	171.7938 242
81	123.8882 369	131.0939 306	138.8202 802	156.0015 153	175.8002 162
82	126.1271 193	133.5687 464	141.5555 337	159.3415 380	179.8767 200
83	128.3883 905	136.0713 948	144.3249 779	162.7316 611	184.0245 625
84	130.6722 744	138.6021 980	147.1290 401	166.1726 360	188.2449 924
85	132.9789 971	141.1614 727	149.9681 531	169.6652 255	192.5392 798
86	135.3087 871	143.7495 393	152.8427 550	173.2102 039	196.9087 172
87	137.6618 750	146.3667 216	155.7532 895	176.8083 569	201.3546 197
88	140.0384 937	149.0133 472	158.7002 056	180.4604 823	205.8783 256
89	142.4388 787	151.6897 474	161.6839 581	184.1673 895	210.4811 962
90	144.8632 675	154.3962 572	164.7050 076	187.9299 004	215.1646 172
91	147.3119 001	157.1332 169	167.7638 202	191.7488 489	219.9299 980
92	149.7850 191	159.9009 636	170.8608 680	195.6250 816	224.7787 729
93	152.2828 693	162.6998 495	173.9966 288	199.5594 578	229.7124 015
94	154.8056 980	165.5302 228	177.1715 867	203.5528 497	234.7323 685
95	157.3537 550	168.3924 378	180.3862 315	207.6061 425	239.8401 850
96	159.9272 926	171.2628 527	183.6410 594	211.7202 346	245.0373 882
97	162.5265 655	174.2138 298	186.9365 726	215.8960 381	250.3255 425
98	165.1518 311	177.1737 354	190.2732 798	220.1344 787	255.7062 395
99	167.8033 494	180.1669 399	193.6516 958	224.4364 959	261.1810 987
100	170.4813 829	183.1938 180	197.0723 420	228.8030 433	266.7517 679

TABLE III
AMOUNT OF AN ANNUITY

$$s_{\overline{n}|}\, i = \frac{(1+i)^n - 1}{i}$$

Periods	Rate i				
n	.02 (2%)	.0225 ($2\frac{1}{4}$%)	.025 ($2\frac{1}{2}$%)	.0275 ($2\frac{3}{4}$%)	.03 (3%)
1	1.0000 0000	1.0000 0000	1.0000 0000	1.0000 0000	1.0000 0000
2	2.0200 0000	2.0225 0000	2.0250 0000	2.0275 0000	2.0300 0000
3	3.0604 0000	3.0680 0625	3.0756 2500	3.0832 5625	3.0909 0000
4	4.1216 0800	4.1370 3639	4.1525 1563	4.1680 4580	4.1836 2700
5	5.2040 4016	5.2301 1971	5.2563 2852	5.2826 6706	5.3091 3581
6	6.3081 2096	6.3477 9740	6.3877 3673	6.4279 4040	6.4684 0988
7	7.4342 8338	7.4906 2284	7.5474 3015	7.6047 0876	7.6624 6218
8	8.5829 6905	8.6591 6186	8.7361 1590	8.8138 3825	8.8923 3605
9	9.7546 2843	9.8539 9300	9.9545 1880	9.0562 1880	9.1591 0613
10	10.9497 2100	11.0757 0784	11.2033 8177	11.3327 6482	11.4638 7931
11	12.1687 1542	12.3249 1127	12.4834 6631	12.6444 1585	12.8077 9569
12	13.4120 8973	13.6022 2177	13.7955 5297	13.9921 3729	14.1920 2956
13	14.6803 3152	14.9082 7176	15.1404 4179	15.3769 2107	15.6177 9045
14	15.9739 3815	16.2437 0788	16.5189 5284	16.7997 8639	17.0863 2416
15	17.2934 1692	17.6091 9130	17.9319 2666	18.2617 8052	18.5989 1389
16	18.6392 8525	19.0053 9811	19.3802 2483	19.7639 7948	20.1568 8130
17	20.0120 7096	20.4330 1957	20.8647 3045	21.3074 8892	21.7615 8774
18	21.4123 1238	21.8927 6251	22.3863 4871	22.8934 4487	23.4140 3537
19	22.8405 5863	23.3853 4966	23.9460 0743	24.5230 1460	25.1168 6844
20	24.2973 6980	24.9115 2003	25.5446 5761	26.1973 9750	26.8703 7449
21	25.7833 1719	26.4720 2923	27.1832 7405	27.9178 2593	28.6764 8572
22	27.2989 8354	28.0676 4989	28.8628 5590	29.6855 6615	30.5367 8030
23	28.8449 6321	29.6991 7201	30.5844 2730	31.5019 1921	32.4528 8370
24	30.4218 6247	31.3674 0338	32.3490 3798	33.3682 2199	34.4264 7022
25	32.0302 9972	33.0731 6996	34.1577 6393	35.2858 4810	36.4592 6432
26	33.6709 0572	34.8173 1628	36.0117 0803	37.2562 0892	38.5530 4225
27	35.3443 2383	36.6007 0590	37.9120 0073	39.2807 5467	40.7096 3352
28	37.0512 1031	38.4242 2178	39.8598 0075	41.3609 7542	42.9309 2252
29	38.7922 3451	40.2887 6677	41.8562 9577	43.4984 0224	45.2188 5020
30	40.5680 7921	42.1952 6402	43.9027 0316	45.6946 0831	47.5724 1571
31	42.3794 4079	44.1446 5746	46.0002 7074	47.9512 1003	50.0026 7818
32	44.2270 2961	46.1379 1226	48.1502 7751	50.2698 6831	52.5027 5852
33	46.1115 7020	48.1760 1528	50.3540 3445	52.6522 8969	55.0778 4128
34	48.0338 0160	50.2599 7563	52.6128 8531	55.1002 2765	57.7301 7652
35	49.9944 7763	52.3908 2508	54.9282 0744	57.6154 8391	60.4620 8181
36	51.9943 6719	54.5696 1864	57.3014 1263	60.1999 0972	63.2759 4427
37	54.0342 5453	56.7974 3506	59.7339 4794	62.8554 0724	66.1742 2259
38	56.1149 3962	59.0753 7735	62.2272 9664	65.5839 3094	69.1594 4927
39	58.2372 3841	61.4045 7334	64.7829 7906	68.3874 8904	72.2342 3275
40	60.4019 8318	63.7861 7624	67.4025 5354	71.2681 4499	75.4012 5973
41	62.6100 2284	66.2213 6521	70.0876 1737	74.2228 1898	78.6632 9753
42	64.8622 2330	68.7113 4592	72.8398 0781	77.2692 8950	82.0231 9645
43	67.1594 6777	71.2573 5121	75.6608 0300	80.3941 9496	85.4838 9234
44	69.5026 5712	73.8606 4161	78.5523 2308	83.6050 3532	89.0484 0911
45	71.8927 1027	76.5225 0605	81.5161 3116	86.9041 7379	92.7198 6139
46	74.3305 6447	79.2442 6243	84.5540 3443	90.2940 3857	96.5014 5723
47	76.8171 7576	82.0272 5834	87.6678 8530	93.7771 2463	100.3965 0095
48	79.3535 1928	84.8728 7165	90.8595 8243	97.3559 9556	104.4083 9598
49	81.9405 8966	87.7825 1126	94.1310 7199	101.0332 8544	108.5406 4785
50	84.5794 0145	90.7576 1776	97.4843 4879	104.8117 0079	112.7968 6729

TABLE III
AMOUNT OF AN ANNUITY

$$s_{\overline{n}|}\, i = \frac{(1+i)^n - 1}{i}$$

Periods n	Rate i: .02 (2%)	.0225 ($2\frac{1}{4}$%)	.025 ($2\frac{1}{2}$%)	.0275 ($2\frac{3}{4}$%)	.03 (3%)
50	84.5794 015	90.7576 178	97.4843 488	104.8117 008	112.7968 673
51	87.2709 895	93.7996 642	100.9214 575	108.6940 226	117.1807 733
52	90.0164 093	96.9101 566	104.4444 939	112.6831 082	121.6961 965
53	92.8167 375	100.0906 351	108.0556 063	116.7818 937	126.3470 824
54	95.6730 722	103.3426 744	111.7569 965	120.9933 957	131.1374 949
55	98.5865 337	106.6678 846	115.5509 214	125.3207 141	136.0716 197
56	101.5582 643	110.0679 120	119.4396 944	129.7670 337	141.1537 683
57	104.5894 296	113.5444 400	123.4256 868	134.3356 272	146.3883 814
58	107.6812 182	117.0991 899	127.5113 289	139.0298 569	151.7800 328
59	110.8348 426	120.7339 217	131.6991 121	143.8531 780	157.3334 338
60	114.0515 394	124.4504 349	135.9915 900	148.8091 404	163.0534 168
61	117.3325 702	128.2505 697	140.3913 797	153.9013 917	168.9450 399
62	120.6792 216	132.1362 075	144.9011 642	159.1336 800	175.0133 911
63	124.0928 060	136.1092 722	149.5236 933	164.5098 562	181.2637 928
64	127.5746 622	140.1717 308	154.2617 856	170.0338 773	187.7017 066
65	131.1261 554	144.3255 948	159.1183 303	175.7098 089	194.3327 578
66	134.7486 785	148.5729 207	164.0962 885	181.5418 286	201.1627 406
67	138.4436 521	152.9158 114	169.1986 957	187.5342 289	208.1976 228
68	142.2125 251	157.3564 171	174.4286 631	193.6914 202	215.4435 515
69	146.0567 756	161.8969 365	179.7893 797	200.0179 343	222.9068 580
70	149.9779 111	166.5396 176	185.2841 142	206.5184 275	230.5940 637
71	153.9774 694	171.2867 590	190.9162 171	213.1976 842	238.5118 856
72	158.0570 188	176.1407 111	196.6891 225	220.0606 205	246.6672 422
73	162.2181 591	181.1038 771	202.6063 506	227.1122 876	255.0672 595
74	166.4625 223	186.1787 143	208.6715 093	234.3578 755	263.7192 773
75	170.7917 728	191.3677 354	214.8882 270	241.8027 171	272.6308 556
76	175.2076 082	196.6735 094	221.2605 045	249.4522 918	281.8097 813
77	179.7117 604	202.0986 634	227.7920 171	257.3122 298	291.2640 747
78	184.3059 956	207.6458 833	234.4868 175	265.3883 162	302.0019 969
79	188.9921 155	213.3179 157	241.3489 880	273.6864 948	311.0320 568
80	193.7719 578	219.1175 688	248.3827 126	282.2128 735	321.3630 185
81	198.6473 970	225.0477 141	255.5922 805	290.9737 275	322.0039 091
82	203.6203 449	231.1112 876	262.9820 875	299.9755 050	342.9640 264
83	208.6927 518	237.3112 916	270.5566 397	309.2248 314	354.2529 472
84	213.8666 068	243.6507 957	278.3205 557	318.7285 142	365.8805 356
85	219.1439 390	250.1329 386	286.2785 695	328.4935 484	377.8369 517
86	224.5268 178	256.7609 297	294.4355 338	338.5271 209	390.1926 602
87	230.0173 541	263.5380 506	302.7964 221	348.8366 168	402.8984 400
88	235.6177 012	270.4676 567	311.3663 327	359.4296 237	415.9853 932
89	241.3300 552	277.5531 790	320.1504 310	370.3139 384	429.4649 550
90	247.1566 563	284.7981 255	329.1542 533	481.4975 717	443.3489 037
91	253.0997 894	292.2060 834	338.3831 096	392.9887 549	457.6493 708
92	259.1617 852	299.7807 202	347.8426 873	404.7959 457	472.3788 519
93	265.3450 209	307.5257 865	357.5387 545	416.9278 342	487.5502 174
94	271.6519 214	315.4451 166	367.4772 234	490.3933 496	503.1767 240
95	278.0849 598	323.5426 318	377.6641 540	442.2016 667	519.2720 257
96	284.6466 590	331.8223 410	388.1057 578	455.3622 126	535.8501 865
97	291.3395 922	340.2883 437	398.8084 018	468.8846 734	552.9256 920
98	298.1663 840	348.9448 314	409.7786 118	482.7790 019	570.5134 628
99	305.1297 117	357.7960 901	421.0230 271	497.0554 245	588.6288 667
100	312.2323 059	366.8465 021	432.5486 540	511.7244 487	604.2877 327

TABLE III
AMOUNT OF AN ANNUITY

$$s_{\overline{n}|}\, i = \frac{(1+i)^n - 1}{i}$$

Periods	Rate i				
n	.035 ($3\frac{1}{2}$%)	.04 (4%)	.045 ($4\frac{1}{2}$%)	.05 (5%)	.055 ($5\frac{1}{2}$%)
1	1.0000 000	1.0000 000	1.0000 000	1.0000 000	1.0000 000
2	2.0350 000	2.0400 000	2.0450 000	2.0500 000	2.0550 000
3	3.1062 250	3.1216 000	3.1370 250	3.1525 000	3.1680 250
4	4.2149 429	4.2464 640	4.2781 911	4.3101 250	4.3422 664
5	5.3624 659	5.4163 226	5.4707 097	5.5256 313	5.5810 910
6	6.5501 522	6.6329 755	6.7168 217	6.8019 128	6.8880 510
7	7.7794 075	7.8982 945	8.0191 518	8.1420 085	8.2668 938
8	9.0516 868	9.2142 263	9.3800 136	9.5491 089	9.7215 730
9	10.3684 958	10.5827 953	10.8021 142	11.0265 643	11.2562 598
10	11.7313 932	12.0061 071	12.2882 094	12.5778 925	12.8753 538
11	13.1419 919	13.4863 514	13.8411 788	14.2067 872	14.5834 982
12	14.6019 916	15.0258 055	15.4640 318	15.9171 265	16.3855 907
13	16.1130 303	16.6268 377	17.1599 133	17.7129 828	18.2867 981
14	17.6769 864	18.2919 112	18.9321 094	19.5986 320	20.2925 720
15	19.2956 809	20.0235 876	20.7840 543	21.5785 636	22.4086 635
16	20.9710 297	21.8245 311	22.7193 367	23.6574 918	24.6411 400
17	22.7050 157	23.6975 124	24.7417 069	25.8403 664	26.9964 027
18	24.4996 913	25.6454 129	26.8550 837	28.1323 847	29.4812 048
19	26.3571 805	27.6712 294	29.0635 625	30.5390 039	32.1026 711
20	28.2796 818	29.7780 786	31.3714 228	35.0659 541	34.8683 180
21	30.2694 707	31.9692 017	35.7831 368	35.7192 518	37.7860 755
22	32.3289 022	34.2479 698	36.3033 780	38.5052 144	40.8643 097
23	34.4604 137	36.6178 886	38.9370 300	41.4304 751	44.1118 467
24	36.6665 282	39.0826 041	41.6891 963	44.5019 989	47.5379 983
25	38.9498 567	41.6459 083	44.5652 101	47.7270 988	51.1525 882
26	41.3131 017	44.3117 446	47.5706 446	51.1134 538	54.9659 805
27	43.7590 602	47.0842 144	50.7113 236	54.6691 264	58 9891 094
28	46.2906 273	49.9675 830	53.9933 332	58.4025 828	63.2335 105
29	48.9107 993	52.9662 863	57.4230 332	62.3227 119	67.7113 535
30	51.6226 773	56.0849 378	61.0070 697	66.4388 475	72.4354 780
31	54.4294 710	59.3283 353	54.7523 878	70.7607 899	77.4194 293
32	57.3345 025	62.7014 687	68.6662 452	75.2988 294	82.6774 979
33	60.3412 101	66.2095 274	72.7562 263	80.0637 708	88.2247 603
34	63.4531 524	69.8579 085	77.0302 565	85.0679 594	94.0771 221
35	66.6740 127	73.6522 249	81.4966 180	90.3203 074	100.2513 638
36	70.0076 032	77.5983 138	86.1639 658	95.8363 227	106.7651 888
37	73.4578 693	81.7022 464	91.0413 443	101.6281 389	113.6372 742
38	77.0288 947	85.9703 363	96.1382 048	107.7095 458	120.8873 242
39	80.7249 060	90.4091 497	101.4644 240	114.0950 231	128.5361 271
40	84.5502 777	95.0255 157	107.0303 231	120.7997 742	136.6056 141
41	88.5095 375	99.8265 363	112.8466 876	127.8397 630	145.1189 228
42	92.6073 713	104.8195 978	118.9247 885	135.2317 511	154.1004 636
43	96.8486 293	110.0123 817	125.2764 040	142.9933 387	163.5759 891
44	101.2383 313	115.4128 770	131.9138 422	151.1430 056	173.5726 685
45	105.7816 729	121.0293 920	138.8499 651	159.7001 569	184.1191 653
46	110.4840 314	126.8705 677	146.0982 135	168.6851 637	195.2457 194
47	115.3509 725	132.9453 904	153.6726 331	178.1194 218	206.9842 339
48	120.3882 566	139.2632 060	161.5879 016	188.0253 929	219.3683 668
49	125.6018 456	145.8337 343	169.8593 572	198.4266 626	232.4336 270
50	130.9979 102	152.6670 837	178.5030 283	209.3479 957	246.2174 764

TABLE III
AMOUNT OF AN ANNUITY

$$s_{\overline{n|}\,i} = \frac{(1+i)^n - 1}{i}$$

Periods	Rate *i*				
n	.06 (6%)	.065 $(6\frac{1}{2}\%)$	.07 (7%)	.075 $(7\frac{1}{2}\%)$	.08 (8%)
1	1.0000 000	1.0000 000	1.0000 000	1.0000 000	1.0000 000
2	2.0600 000	2.0650 000	2.0700 000	2.0750 000	2.0600 000
3	3.1836 000	3.1992 250	3.2149 000	3.2306 250	3.2464 000
4	4.3746 160	4.4071 746	4.4399 430	4.4729 219	4.5061 120
5	5.6370 930	5.6936 410	5.7507 390	5.8083 910	5.8666 010
6	6.9753 185	7.0637 276	7.1532 907	7.2440 930	7.3359 290
7	8.3938 376	8.5228 699	8.6540 211	8.7873 219	8.9228 034
8	9.8974 679	10.0758 565	10.2598 026	10.4463 710	10.6366 276
9	11.4913 160	11.7318 522	11.9779 887	12.2298 488	12.4875 578
10	13.1807 949	13.4944 225	13.8164 480	14.1470 875	14.4865 625
11	14.9716 426	15.3715 600	15.7835 993	16.2081 191	16.6454 875
12	16.8699 412	17.3707 114	17.8884 513	18.4237 280	18.9771 265
13	18.8821 377	19.4998 076	20.1406 429	20.8055 076	21.4952 966
14	21.0150 659	21.7672 951	22.5504 879	23.3659 207	24.2149 203
15	23.2759 699	24.1821 693	25.1290 220	26.1183 647	27.1521 139
16	25.6725 281	26.7540 103	27.8880 536	29.0772 421	30.3242 830
17	28.2128 798	29.4930 210	30.8402 173	32.2580 352	35.7502 257
18	30.0056 525	32.4100 674	33.9990 325	35.6773 879	37.4502 437
19	33.7599 917	35.5167 218	37.3789 648	39.3531 919	41.4462 632
20	36.7855 912	38.8253 087	40.9954 923	43.3046 813	45.7619 643
21	39.9927 267	42.3489 537	44.8651 768	47.5525 324	50.4229 214
22	43.3922 903	46.1016 357	49.0057 392	52.1189 724	55.4567 552
23	46.9958 277	50.0982 420	53.4861 409	57.0278 953	60.8932 956
24	50.8155 774	54.3546 278	58.1766 708	62.3049 874	66.7647 592
25	54.8645 120	58.8876 786	63.2490 377	67.9778 615	73.1059 400
26	59.1563 827	63.7153 777	68.6764 704	74.0762 011	79.9544 151
27	63.7057 657	68.8568 772	74.4838 233	80.6319 162	87.3507 684
28	68.5281 116	74.3325 743	80.6976 909	87.6793 099	95.3588 298
29	73.6397 983	80.1641 916	87.3465 293	95.2552 582	103.9659 362
30	79.0581 862	86.3748 640	94.4607 863	103.3994 025	113.2832 111
31	84.8016 774	92.9892 302	102.0730 414	112.1543 577	123.3458 680
32	90.8897 780	100.0335 302	110.2181 543	121.5659 345	134.2135 374
33	97.3431 647	107.5357 096	118.9334 251	131.6833 796	145.9506 204
34	104.1837 546	115.5255 308	128.2587 648	142.5596 331	158.6266 701
35	111.4347 799	124.0346 903	138.2368 784	154.2516 056	172.3168 037
36	119.1208 667	133.0969 451	148.9134 598	166.8204 760	187.1021 480
37	127.2681 187	142.7482 466	160.3374 020	180.3320 117	203.0703 198
38	135.9042 058	153.0268 826	172.5610 202	194.8569 126	220.3159 454
39	145.0584 581	163.9736 300	185.6402 916	210.4711 810	238.9412 210
40	154.7619 656	175.6319 159	199.6351 120	227.2565 196	259.0565 187
41	165.0476 836	188.0479 904	214.6095 698	245.3007 586	280.7810 402
42	175.9505 446	201.2711 098	230.6322 397	264.6983 155	304.2435 234
43	187.5075 772	215.3537 320	247.7764 965	285.5506 891	329.5830 053
44	199.7580 319	230.3517 245	266.1208 513	307.9669 908	356.9496 457
45	212.7435 138	246.3245 866	285.7493 108	332.0645 151	386.5056 174
46	226.5081 246	263.3356 848	306.7517 626	357.9693 537	418.4260 668
47	241.0986 121	281.4525 043	329.2243 860	385.8170 553	452.9001 521
48	256.5645 288	300.7469 170	353.2700 930	415.7533 344	490.1321 643
49	272.9584 006	321.2954 666	378.9989 995	447.9348 345	530.3427 374
50	290.3359 046	343.1796 720	406.5289 295	482.5299 471	573.7701 564

TABLE IV
PRESENT VALUE OF AN ANNUITY

$$a_{\overline{n}|}\, i = \frac{1-(1+i)^{-n}}{i}$$

Periods	Rate i				
n	.0025 ($\frac{1}{4}$%)	.004167 ($\frac{5}{12}$%)	.005 ($\frac{1}{2}$%)	.005833 ($\frac{7}{12}$%)	.0075 ($\frac{3}{4}$%)
1	0.9975 0623	0.9958 5062	0.9950 2488	0.9942 0050	0.9925 5383
2	1.9925 2492	1.9875 6908	1.9850 9938	1.9826 3513	1.9777 2291
3	2.9850 6227	2.9751 7253	2.9702 4814	2.9653 3732	2.9555 5624
4	3.9751 2446	3.9586 7804	3.9504 9566	3.9423 4034	3.9261 1041
5	4.9627 1766	4.9381 0261	4.9258 6633	4.9136 7722	4.8894 3961
6	5.9478 4804	5.9134 6318	5.8963 8441	5.8793 8083	5.8455 9763
7	6.9305 2174	6.8847 7661	6.8620 7404	6.8394 8384	6.7946 3785
8	7.9107 4487	7.8520 5970	7.8229 5924	7.7940 1874	7.7366 1325
9	8.8825 2357	8.8153 2916	8.7790 6392	8.7430 1780	8.6715 7642
10	9.8638 6391	9.7746 0165	9.7304 1186	9.6865 1314	9.5995 7958
11	10.8367 7196	10.7298 9376	10.6770 2673	10.6245 3667	10.5206 7452
12	11.8072 5384	11.6812 2200	11.6189 3207	11.5571 2014	11.4349 1267
13	12.7753 1555	12.6286 0283	12.5561 5131	12.4842 9509	12.3423 4508
14	13.7409 6314	13.5720 5261	13.4887 0777	13.4060 9288	13.2430 2242
15	14.7042 0264	14.5115 8766	14.4166 2465	14.3225 4470	14.1369 9495
16	15.6650 4004	15.4472 2422	15.3399 2502	15.2336 8156	15.0243 1261
17	16.6234 8133	16.3789 7848	16.2586 3186	16.1365 3427	15.9050 2492
18	17.5795 3250	17.3068 6654	17.1727 6802	17.0401 3350	16.7791 8107
19	18.5331 9950	18.2309 0443	18.0823 5624	17.9355 0969	17.6468 2984
20	19.4844 8828	19.1511 0815	18.9874 1915	18.8256 9315	18.5080 1969
21	20.4334 0477	20.0674 9359	19.8879 7925	19.7107 1398	19.3627 9870
22	21.3799 5488	20.9800 7661	20.7840 5896	20.5906 0213	20.2122 1459
23	22.3241 4452	21.8888 7297	21.6756 8055	21.4653 8738	21.0533 1473
24	23.2659 7957	22.7938 9839	22.5628 6622	22.3350 9930	21.8891 4614
25	24.2054 6591	23.6951 6853	23.4456 3803	23.1997 6732	22.7187 5547
26	25.1426 0939	24.5926 9895	24.3240 1794	24.0594 2070	23.5421 8905
27	26.0774 1585	25.4865 0517	25.1980 2780	24.9140 8852	24.3594 9286
28	27.0098 9112	26.3766 0266	26.0676 8936	25.7937 9968	25.1707 1251
29	27.9400 4102	27.2630 0680	26.9330 2424	26.6085 8295	25.9758 9331
30	28.8678 7134	28.1457 3291	27.7940 5397	27.4484 6689	26.7750 8021
31	29.7933 8787	29.0247 9626	28.6507 9997	28.2834 7993	27.5683 1783
32	30.7165 9638	29.9002 1205	29.5032 8355	29.1136 5030	20.3556 5045
33	31.6375 0262	30.7719 9540	30.3515 2592	29.9390 0610	29.1371 2203
34	32.5561 1234	31.6401 6139	31.1955 4818	30.7595 7524	29.9127 7621
35	33.4724 3126	32.5047 2504	32.0353 7132	31.5753 8549	30.6826 5629
36	34.3864 6510	35.3657 0128	32.8710 1624	32.3864 6445	31.4468 0525
37	35.2982 1955	34.2231 0501	33.7025 0372	33.1928 3955	32.2052 6576
38	36.2077 0030	35.0769 5105	34.5298 5445	33.9945 3808	32.9580 8016
39	37.1149 1302	35.9272 5416	35.3530 8900	34.7915 8716	33.7052 9048
40	38.0198 6336	36.7740 2904	36.1722 2786	35.5840 1374	34.4469 3844
41	38.9225 5697	37.6172 9033	36.9872 9141	36.3718 4465	35.1830 6545
42	39.8229 9947	38.4570 5261	37.7982 9991	37.1551 0653	35.9137 1260
43	40.7211 9648	39.2933 3040	38.6052 7354	37.9338 2588	36.6389 2070
44	41.6171 5359	40.1261 3816	39.4082 3238	38.7080 2904	37.3587 3022
45	42.5108 7640	40.9554 9028	40.2071 9640	39.4777 4221	38.0731 8136
46	43.4023 7048	41.7814 0111	41.0021 8547	40.2429 9143	38.7823 1401
47	44.2916 4137	42.6038 8492	41.7932 1937	41.0038 0258	39.4861 6775
48	45.1786 9464	43.4229 5594	42.5803 1778	41.7602 0141	40.1847 8189
49	46.0635 3580	44.2386 2832	43.3635 0028	42.5122 1349	40.8781 9542
50	46.9461 7037	45.0509 1617	44.1427 8635	43.2598 6428	41.5664 4707

TABLE IV
PRESENT VALUE OF AN ANNUITY

$$a_{\overline{n}|}\, i = \frac{1-(1+i)^{-n}}{i}$$

Periods	Rate i				
n	.0025 ($\frac{1}{4}$%)	.004167 ($\frac{5}{12}$%)	.005 ($\frac{1}{2}$%)	.005833 ($\frac{7}{12}$%)	.0075 ($\frac{3}{4}$%)
50	46.9461 7037	45.0509 1617	44.1427 8635	43.2598 6428	41.5664 4707
51	47.8266 0386	45.8598 3353	44.9181 9537	44.0031 7907	42.2495 7525
52	48.7048 4176	46.6653 9439	45.6897 4664	44.7421 8301	42.9276 1812
53	49.5808 8953	47.4676 1267	46.4574 5934	45.4769 0108	43.6006 1351
54	50.4547 5265	48.2665 0224	47.2213 5258	46.2073 5816	44.2685 9902
55	51.3264 3656	49.0620 7692	47.9814 4535	46.9335 7895	44.9316 1193
56	52.1959 4669	49.8543 5046	48.7377 5657	47.6555 8802	45.5896 8926
57	53.0632 8847	50.6433 3656	49.4903 0505	48.3734 0980	46.2428 6776
58	53.9284 6730	51.4290 4885	50.2391 0950	49.0870 6856	46.8911 8388
59	54.7914 8858	52.2115 0093	50.9841 8856	49.7965 8846	47.5346 7382
60	55.6523 5769	52.9907 0632	51.7255 6075	50.5019 9350	48.1733 7352
61	56.5110 7999	53.7666 7850	52.4632 4453	51.2033 0754	48.8073 1863
62	57.3676 6083	54.5394 3087	53.1972 5824	51.9005 5431	49.4365 4455
63	58.2221 0557	55.3089 7680	53.9276 2014	52.5937 5739	50.0610 8640
64	59.0744 1952	56.0753 2959	54.6543 4840	53.2829 4024	50.6809 7906
65	59.9246 0800	56.8385 0250	55.3774 6109	53.9681 2617	51.2962 5713
66	60.7726 7631	57.5985 0871	56.0969 7621	54.6493 3836	51.9069 5497
67	61.6186 2974	58.3553 6137	56.8129 1165	55.3265 9986	52.5131 0667
68	62.4624 7355	59.1090 7357	57.5252 8522	55.9999 3358	53.1147 4607
69	63.3042 1302	59.8596 5832	58.2341 1465	56.6693 6230	53.7119 0677
70	64.1438 5339	60.6071 2862	58.9394 1756	57.3349 0867	54.3046 2210
71	64.9813 9989	61.3514 9738	59.6412 1151	57.9965 9520	54.8929 2516
72	65.8168 5774	62.0927 7748	60.3395 1394	58.6544 4427	55.4768 4880
73	66.6502 3216	62.8309 8172	61.0343 4222	59.3084 7815	56.0564 2561
74	67.4815 2834	63.5661 2287	61.7257 1366	59.9587 1896	56.6316 8795
75	68.3107 5146	64.2982 1365	62.4136 4543	60.6051 8869	57.2026 6794
76	69.1379 0670	65.0272 6670	63.0981 5466	61.2479 0922	57.7693 9746
77	69.9629 9920	65.7532 9464	63.7792 5836	61.8869 0229	58.3319 0815
78	70.7860 3411	66.4763 1002	64.4569 7350	62.5221 8952	58.8902 3141
79	71.6070 1657	67.1963 2533	65.1313 1691	63.1537 9239	59.4443 9842
80	72.4259 5169	67.9133 5303	65.8023 0539	63.7817 3229	59.9944 4012
81	73.2428 4458	68.6274 0550	66.4699 5561	64.4060 3044	60.5403 8722
82	74.0577 0033	69.3384 9511	67.1342 8419	65.0267 0798	61.0822 7019
83	74.8705 2402	70.0466 3413	67.7953 0765	65.6437 8590	61.6201 1930
84	75.6813 2072	70.7518 3482	68.4530 4244	66.2572 8507	62.1539 6456
85	76.4900 9548	71.4541 0936	69.1075 0491	66.8672 2625	62.6838 3579
86	77.2968 5335	72.1534 6991	69.7587 1135	67.4736 3007	63.2097 6257
87	78.1015 9935	72.8499 2854	70.4066 7796	68.0765 1706	63.7317 7427
88	78.9043 3850	73.5434 9730	71.0514 2086	68.6759 0759	64.2499 0002
89	79.7050 7581	74.2341 8618	71.6929 5608	69.2718 2197	65.7641 6872
90	80.5038 1627	74.9220 1313	72.3312 9958	69.8642 8033	65.2746 0918
91	81.3005 6486	75.6069 8403	72.9664 6725	70.4533 0273	65.7812 4981
92	82.0953 2654	76.2891 1272	73.5984 7487	71.0389 0910	66.2841 1892
93	82.8881 0628	76.9684 1101	74.2273 3818	71.6211 1923	66.7832 4458
94	83.6789 0901	77.6448 9063	74.8530 7282	72.1999 5284	67.2786 5467
95	84.4677 3966	78.3185 6329	75.4756 9434	72.7754 2950	67.7703 7685
96	85.2546 0315	78.9894 4062	76.0952 1825	73.3475 6869	68.2584 3856
97	86.0395 0439	79.6575 3422	76.7116 5995	73.9163 8975	68.7428 6705
98	86.8224 4827	80.3228 5566	77.3250 3478	74.4819 1193	69.2236 8938
99	87.6034 3967	80.9854 1642	77.9353 5799	75.0441 5436	69.7009 3239
100	88.3824 8346	81.6452 2797	78.5426 4477	75.6031 3607	70.1746 2272

TABLE IV
PRESENT VALUE OF AN ANNUITY

$$a_{\overline{n}|}\, i = \frac{1-(1+i)^{-n}}{i}$$

Periods	Rate i				
n	.01 (1%)	.01125 $\left(1\frac{1}{8}\%\right)$	.0125 $\left(1\frac{1}{4}\%\right)$	.015 $\left(1\frac{1}{2}\%\right)$	.0075 $\left(1\frac{3}{4}\%\right)$
1	0.9900 9901	0.9888 7515	0.9876 5432	0.9852 2167	0.9828 0098
2	1.9703 9506	1.9667 4923	1.9631 1538	1.9558 8342	1.9486 9875
3	2.9409 8521	2.9337 4460	2.9265 3371	2.9122 0042	2.8979 8403
4	3.9019 6555	3.8899 8230	3.8780 5798	3.8543 8465	3.8309 4254
5	4.8534 3124	4.8355 8200	4.8178 3504	4.7826 4497	4.7478 5508
6	5.7954 7647	5.7706 6205	5.7460 0992	5.6971 8717	5.6489 9762
7	6.7281 9453	6.6953 3948	6.6627 2585	6.5982 1396	6.5346 4139
8	7.6516 7775	7.6097 3002	7.5681 2429	7.4859 2508	7.4050 5297
9	8.5660 1758	8.5139 4810	8.4623 4498	8.3605 1732	8.2604 9432
10	9.4713 0453	9.4081 0690	9.3455 2591	9.2221 8455	9.1012 2291
11	10.3676 2825	10.2923 1832	10.2178 0337	10.0711 1779	10.9274 9181
12	11.2550 7747	11.1666 9302	11.0793 1197	10.9075 0521	10.7395 4969
13	12.1337 4007	12.0313 4044	11.9301 8466	11.7315 3222	11.5376 4097
14	13.0037 0304	12.8863 6880	12.7705 5275	12.5433 8150	12.3220 0587
15	13.8650 5252	13.7318 8509	13.6005 4592	13.3432 3301	13.0928 8046
16	14.7178 7378	14.5679 9514	14.4202 9227	14.1312 6405	13.8504 9677
17	15.5622 5127	15.3948 0360	15.2299 1829	14.9076 4931	14.5950 8282
18	16.3982 6858	16.2124 1395	16.0295 4893	15.6725 6089	15.3268 6272
19	17.2260 0850	17.0209 2850	16.8193 0759	16.4261 6837	16.0460 5673
20	18.0455 5297	17.8204 4845	17.5993 1613	17.1686 3879	16.7528 8130
21	18.8569 8313	18.6110 7387	18.3696 9495	17.9001 3673	17.4475 4919
22	19.6603 7934	19.3929 0371	19.1305 6291	18.6208 2437	18.1302 6948
23	20.4558 2113	20.1660 3580	19.8820 3744	19.3308 6145	18.8012 4764
24	21.2433 8726	20.9305 6693	20.6242 3451	20.0304 0537	19.4606 8565
25	22.0231 5570	21.6865 9276	21.3572 6865	20.7196 1120	20.1087 8196
26	22.7952 0366	22.4342 0792	22.0812 5299	21.3986 3172	20.7457 3166
27	23.5596 0759	23.1735 0598	22.7962 9925	22.0676 1746	21.3717 2644
28	24.3164 4316	23.9045 7946	23.5025 1778	22.7267 1671	21.9869 5474
29	25.0657 8530	24.6275 1986	24.2000 1756	23.3760 7558	22.5916 0171
30	25.8077 0822	25.3434 1766	24.8889 0623	24.0158 3801	23.1858 4934
31	26.5422 8537	26.0493 6233	25.5692 9010	24.6461 4582	23.7698 7650
32	27.2695 8947	26.7484 4236	26.2412 7418	25.2671 3874	24.3438 5897
33	27.9896 9255	27.4397 4522	26.9049 6215	25.8789 5442	24.9079 6951
34	28.7026 6589	28.1233 5745	27.5604 5644	26.4817 2849	25.4623 7789
35	29.4085 8009	28.7993 6460	28.2078 5822	27.0755 9458	26.0072 5100
36	30.1075 0504	29.4678 5127	28.8472 6737	27.6606 8431	26.5427 5283
37	30.7995 0994	30.1289 0114	29.4787 8259	28.2371 2740	27.0690 4455
38	31.4846 6330	30.7825 9692	30.1025 0133	28.8050 5163	27.5862 8457
39	32.1630 3298	31.4290 2044	30.7185 1983	29.3645 8288	28.0946 2857
40	32.8346 8611	32.0682 5260	31.3269 3316	29.9158 4520	28.5942 2955
41	33.4996 8922	32.7003 7340	31.9278 3522	30.4589 6079	29.0852 3789
42	34.1581 0814	33.3254 6195	32.5213 1874	30.9940 5004	29.5678 0136
43	34.8100 0806	33.9435 9649	33.1074 7530	31.5212 3157	30.0420 6522
44	35.4554 5352	34.5548 5438	33.6863 9536	32.0406 2223	30.5081 7221
45	36.0945 0844	35.1593 1212	34.2581 6825	32.5523 3718	30.9662 6261
46	36.7272 3608	35.7570 4536	34.8228 8222	33.0564 8983	31.4164 7431
47	37.3536 9909	36.3481 2891	35.3806 2442	33.5531 9195	31.8589 4281
48	37.9739 5949	36.9326 3674	35.9314 8091	34.0425 5365	32.2938 0129
49	38.5880 7871	37.5106 4202	36.4755 3670	34.5246 8339	32.7211 8063
50	39.1961 1753	38.0822 1708	37.0128 7575	34.9996 8807	33.1412 0946

TABLE IV
PRESENT VALUE OF AN ANNUITY

$$a_{\overline{n}|}\, i = \frac{1 - (1 + i)^{-n}}{i}$$

Periods	Rate i				
n	.01 (1%)	.01125 $\left(1\frac{1}{8}\%\right)$	.0125 $\left(1\frac{1}{4}\%\right)$	.015 $\left(1\frac{1}{2}\%\right)$	.0175 $\left(1\frac{3}{4}\%\right)$
50	39.1961 1753	38.0822 1708	37.0128 7575	34.9996 8807	33.1412 0946
51	39.7981 3617	38.6474 3345	37.5435 8099	35.4676 7298	33.5540 1421
52	40.3941 9423	39.2063 6188	38.0677 3431	35.9287 4185	33.9597 1913
53	40.9843 5072	39.7590 7232	38.5854 1660	36.3829 9690	34.3584 4632
54	41.5686 6408	40.3056 3394	39.0967 0776	36.8305 3882	34.7503 1579
55	42.1471 9216	40.8461 1514	39.6016 8667	37.2714 6681	35.1354 4550
56	42.7199 9224	41.3805 8358	40.1004 3128	37.7058 7863	35.5139 5135
57	43.2871 2102	41.9091 0613	40.5930 1855	38.1338 7058	35.8859 4727
58	43.8486 3468	42.4317 4896	41.0795 2449	38.5555 3751	36.2515 4523
59	44.4045 8879	42.9485 7746	41.5600 2419	38.9709 7292	36.6108 5526
60	44.9550 3841	43.4596 5633	42.0345 9179	39.3802 6889	36.9639 8552
61	45.5000 3803	43.9650 4952	42.5033 0054	39.7835 1614	37.3110 4228
62	46.0396 4161	44.4648 2029	42.9662 2275	40.1808 0408	37.6521 3000
63	46.5739 0258	44.9590 3119	43.4234 2988	40.5722 2077	37.9873 5135
64	47.1028 7385	45.4477 4407	43.8749 9247	40.9578 5298	38.3168 0723
65	47.6266 0777	45.9310 2009	44.3209 8022	41.3377 8618	38.6405 9678
66	48.1451 5621	46.4089 1975	44.7614 6195	41.7121 0461	38.9588 1748
67	48.6585 7050	46.8815 0284	45.1965 0563	42.0808 9125	39.2715 6509
68	49.1669 0149	47.3488 2852	45.6261 7840	42.4442 2783	39.5789 3375
69	49.6701 9949	47.8109 5527	46.0505 4656	42.8021 9490	39.8810 1597
70	50.1685 1435	48.2679 4094	46.4696 7562	43.1548 7183	40.1779 0267
71	50.6618 9539	48.7198 4270	46.8836 3024	43.5023 3678	40.4696 8321
72	51.1503 9148	49.1667 1714	47.2924 7431	43.8446 6677	40.7564 4542
73	51.6340 5097	49.6086 2016	47.6962 7093	44.1819 3771	41.0382 7560
74	52.1129 2175	50.0456 0708	48.0950 8240	44.5142 2434	41.3152 5857
75	52.5870 5124	50.4777 3259	48.4889 7027	44.8416 0034	41.5874 7771
76	53.0564 8638	50.9050 5077	48.8779 9533	45.1641 3826	41.8550 1495
77	53.5212 7364	51.3276 1510	49.2622 1761	45.4819 0962	42.1179 5081
78	53.9814 5905	51.7454 7847	49.6416 9640	45.7949 8485	42.3763 6443
79	54.4370 8817	52.1586 9317	50.0164 9027	46.1034 3335	42.6303 3359
80	54.8882 0611	52.5673 1092	50.3866 5706	46.4073 2349	42.8799 3474
81	55.3348 5753	52.9713 8286	50.7522 5389	46.7067 2265	43.1252 4298
82	55.7770 8666	53.3709 5957	51.1133 3717	47.0016 9720	43.3663 3217
83	56.2149 3729	53.7660 9104	51.4699 6264	47.2923 1251	43.6032 7486
84	56.6484 5276	54.1568 2674	51.8221 8532	47.5786 3301	43.8361 4237
85	57.0776 7600	54.5432 1557	52.1700 5958	47.8607 2218	44.0650 0479
86	57.5026 4951	54.9253 0588	52.5136 3909	48.1386 4254	44.2899 3099
87	57.9234 1535	55.3031 4549	52.8529 7688	48.4124 5571	44.5109 8869
88	58.3400 1520	55.6767 8169	53.1881 2531	48.6822 2237	44.7282 4441
89	58.7524 9030	56.0462 6126	53.5191 3611	48.9480 0234	44.9417 6355
90	59.1608 8148	56.4116 3041	53.8460 6035	49.2098 5452	45.1516 1037
91	59.5652 2919	56.7729 3490	54.1689 4850	49.4678 3696	45.3578 4803
92	59.9655 7346	57.1302 1992	54.4878 5037	49.7220 0686	45.5605 3860
93	60.3619 5392	57.4835 3021	54.8028 1518	49.9724 2055	45.7597 4310
94	60.7544 0982	57.8329 0997	55.1138 9154	50.2191 3355	45.9555 2147
95	61.1829 8002	58.1784 0294	55.4211 2744	50.4622 0054	46.1479 3265
96	61.5277 0299	58.5200 5235	55.7245 7031	50.7016 7541	46.3370 3455
97	61.9086 1682	58.8579 0096	56.0242 6698	50.9376 1124	46.5228 8408
98	62.2857 5923	59.1919 9106	56.3202 6368	51.1700 6034	46.7055 3718
99	62.6591 6755	59.5223 6446	56.6126 0610	51.3990 7422	46.8850 4882
100	63.0288 7877	59.8490 6251	56.9013 3936	51.6247 0367	47.0614 7304

TABLE IV
PRESENT VALUE OF AN ANNUITY

$$a_{\overline{n}|}\, i = \frac{1-(1+i)^{-n}}{i}$$

Periods	Rate i				
n	.02 (2%)	.0225 $(2\frac{1}{4}\%)$	.025 $(2\frac{1}{2}\%)$	.0275 $(2\frac{3}{4}\%)$	.03 (3%)
1	0.9803 9216	0.9779 9511	0.9756 0976	0.9732 3601	0.9708 7379
2	1.9415 6094	1.9344 6955	1.9274 2415	1.9204 2434	1.9134 6970
3	2.8838 8327	2.8698 9687	2.8560 2356	2.8422 6213	2.8286 1135
4	3.8077 2870	3.7847 4021	3.7619 7421	3.7394 2787	3.7170 9810
5	4.7134 5951	4.6794 5253	4.6458 2850	4.6125 8186	4.5797 0719
6	5.6014 3089	5.5544 7680	5.5081 2536	5.4623 6678	5.4171 9144
7	6.4719 9107	6.4102 4626	6.3493 9060	6.2894 0806	6.2302 8296
8	7.3254 8144	7.2471 8461	7.1701 3717	7.0943 1441	7.0196 9119
9	8.1622 3671	8.0657 0622	7.9708 6553	7.8776 7826	7.7861 0892
10	8.9825 8501	8.8662 1635	8.7520 6393	8.6400 7616	8.5302 0284
11	9.7868 4805	9.6491 1134	9.5142 0871	9.3820 6926	9.2526 2411
12	10.5753 4122	10.4147 7882	10.2577 6460	10.1042 0366	9.9540 0399
13	11.3483 7375	11.1635 9787	10.9831 8497	10.8070 1086	10.6349 5533
14	12.1062 4877	11.8959 3924	11.6909 1217	11.4910 0814	11.2960 7314
15	12.8492 6350	12.6121 6551	12.3813 7773	12.1566 9892	11.9379 3509
16	13.5777 0931	13.3126 3131	13.0550 0266	12.8045 73:5	12.5611 0203
17	14.2918 7188	13.9976 8343	13.7121 9772	13.4351 0769	13.1661 1847
18	14.9920 3125	14.6676 6106	14.3533 6363	14.0487 6661	13.7535 1308
19	15.6784 6201	15.3228 9590	14.9788 9134	14.6430 0157	14.3237 9911
20	16.3514 3334	15.9637 1237	15.5891 6229	15.2772 5213	14.8774 7486
21	17.0112 0916	16.5904 2775	16.1845 4857	15.7929 4612	15.4150 2414
22	17.6580 4820	17.2033 5232	16.7654 1324	16.3434 9987	15.9369 1664
23	18.2922 0412	17.8027 8955	17.3321 1048	16.8793 1861	16.4436 0839
24	18.9139 2560	18.3890 3624	17.8849 8583	17.4007 9670	16.9355 4212
25	19.5234 5647	19.9623 8263	18.4243 7642	17.9083 1795	17.4131 4769
26	20.1210 3576	19.5231 1260	18.9506 1114	18.4022 5592	17.8768 4242
27	20.7068 9780	20.0715 0376	19.4640 1087	18.8829 7413	18.3270 3147
28	21.2812 7236	20.6078 2764	19.9648 8866	19.3508 2640	18.7641 0823
29	21.8443 8466	21.1323 4977	20.4535 4991	19.8061 5708	19.1884 5459
30	22.3964 5555	21.6453 2985	20.9302 9259	20.2493 0130	19.6004 4135
31	22.9377 0152	22.1470 2186	21.3954 0741	20.6805 8520	20.0004 2849
32	23.4683 3482	22.6376 7419	21.8491 7796	21.1003 2623	20.3887 6553
33	23.9885 6355	23.1175 2977	22.2918 8094	21.5088 3332	20.7657 9178
34	24.4985 9172	23.5868 2618	22.7237 8628	21.9064 0712	21.1318 3668
35	24.9986 1933	24.0457 9577	23.1451 5734	22.2933 4026	21.4872 2007
36	25.4888 4248	24.4946 6579	23.5562 5107	22.6699 1753	21.8322 5250
37	25.9694 5341	24.9336 5848	23.9573 1812	23.0364 1609	22.1672 3544
38	26.4406 4060	25.3629 9118	24.3486 0304	23.3931 0568	22.4924 6159
39	26.9025 8883	25.7828 7646	24.7303 4443	23.7402 4884	22.8082 1513
40	27.3554 7924	26.1935 2221	25.1027 7505	24.0781 0106	23.1147 7197
41	27.7994 8945	26.5951 3174	25.4661 2200	24.4069 1101	23.4123 9997
42	28.2347 9358	26.9879 0390	25.8206 0683	24.7269 2069	23.7013 5920
43	28.6615 6233	27.3720 3316	26.1664 4569	25.0383 6563	23.9319 0213
44	29.0799 6307	27.7477 0969	25.5038 4945	25.3414 7507	24.2542 7392
45	29.4901 5987	28.1151 1950	26.8330 2386	25.6364 7209	24.5187 1254
86	29.8923 1360	28.4744 4450	27.1541 6962	25.9235 7381	24.7754 4907
47	30.2865 8196	28.8258 6259	27.4674 8255	26.2029 9154	25.0247 0783
48	30.6731 1957	29.1695 4777	27.7731 5371	26.4749 3094	25.2667 0664
49	31.0520 7801	29.5056 7019	28.0713 6947	26.7395 9215	25.5016 5693
50	31.4236 0589	29.8343 9627	28.3623 1168	26.9971 6998	25.7297 6401

TABLE IV
PRESENT VALUE OF AN ANNUITY

$$a_{\overline{n}|}\, i = \frac{1-(1+i)^{-n}}{i}$$

Periods	Rate i				
n	.02 (2%)	.0225 ($2\frac{1}{4}$%)	.025 ($2\frac{1}{2}$%)	.0275 ($2\frac{3}{4}$%)	.03 (3%)
50	31.4236 0589	29.8343 9627	28.3623 1168	26.9971 6998	25.7297 6401
51	31.7878 4892	30.1558 8877	28.6461 5774	27.2478 5400	25.9512 2719
52	32.1449 4992	30.4703 0687	28.9230 8072	27.4918 2871	26.1662 3999
53	32.4950 4894	30.7778 0623	29.1932 4948	27.7292 7368	26.3749 9028
54	32.8382 8327	31.0785 3910	29.4568 2876	27.9603 6368	26.5776 6047
55	33.1747 8752	31.3726 5438	29.7139 7928	28.1852 6879	26.7744 2764
56	33.5046 9365	31.6602 9768	29.9648 5784	28.4041 5454	26.9654 6373
57	33.8281 3103	31.9416 1142	30.2096 1740	28.6171 8203	27.1509 3566
58	34.1452 2650	32.2167 3489	30.4484 0722	28.8245 0806	27.3310 0549
59	34.4561 0441	32.4858 0429	30.6813 7290	29.0262 8522	27.5058 3058
60	34.7608 8668	32.7489 5285	30.9086 5649	29.2226 6201	27.6755 6367
61	35.0596 9282	33.0063 1086	31.1303 9657	29.4137 8293	27.8403 5307
62	35.3526 4002	33.2580 0573	31.3467 2836	29.5997 8879	28.0003 4279
63	35.6398 4316	33.5041 6208	31.5577 8377	29.7808 1634	28.1556 7261
64	35.9214 1486	33.7449 0179	31.7636 9148	29.9569 9887	28.3064 7826
65	36.1974 6555	33.9803 4405	31.9645 7705	30.1284 6605	28.4528 9152
66	36.4681 0348	34.2106 0543	32.1605 6298	30.2953 4409	28.5950 4031
67	36.7334 3478	34.4357 9993	32.3517 6876	30.4577 5581	28.7330 4884
68	36.9935 6351	34.6560 3905	32.5383 1099	30.6158 2974	28.8670 3771
69	37.2485 9168	34.8714 3183	32.7203 0340	30.7696 5522	28.9971 2399
70	37.4986 1929	35.0820 8492	32.8978 5698	30.9193 7247	29.1234 2135
71	37.7437 4441	35.2881 0261	33.0710 7998	31.0650 8270	29.2460 4015
72	37.9840 6314	35.4895 8691	33.2400 7803	31.2068 9314	29.3650 8752
73	38.2196 6975	35.6866 3756	33.4049 5417	31.3440 0816	29.4806 6750
74	38.4506 5662	35.8793 5214	33.5658 0895	31.4792 2936	29.5928 8107
75	38.6771 1433	36.0678 2605	33.7227 4044	31.6099 5558	29.7018 2628
76	38.8991 3170	36.2521 5262	33.8758 4433	31.7371 8304	29.8075 9833
77	39.1167 9578	36.4324 2310	34.0252 1398	31.8610 0540	29.9102 8964
78	39.3301 9194	36.6087 2675	34.1709 4047	31.9815 1377	30.0099 8994
79	39.5394 0386	36.7811 5085	34.3131 1265	32.0987 9685	30.1067 8635
80	39.7445 1359	36.9497 8079	34.4518 1722	32.2129 4098	30.2007 6345
81	39.9456 0156	37.1147 0004	34.5871 3875	32.3240 3015	30.2920 0335
82	40.1427 4663	37.2759 9026	34.7191 5976	32.4321 4613	30.3805 8577
83	40.3360 2611	37.4337 3130	34.8479 6074	32.5373 6850	30.4665 8813
84	40.5255 1579	37.5880 0127	34.9736 2023	32.6397 7469	30.5500 8556
85	40.7112 8999	37.7388 7655	35.0962 1486	32.7394 4009	30.6311 5103
86	40.8934 2156	37.8864 3183	35.2158 1938	32.8364 3804	30.7098 5537
87	41.0719 8192	38.0307 4018	35.3325 0671	32.9308 3994	30.7862 6735
88	41.2470 4110	38.1718 7304	35.4463 4801	33.0227 1527	30.8604 5374
89	41.4186 6774	38.3099 0028	35.5574 1269	33.1121 3165	30.9324 7936
90	41.5869 2916	38.4448 9025	35.6657 6848	33.1991 5489	31.0024 0714
91	41.7518 9133	38.5769 0978	35.7714 8144	33.2838 4905	31.0702 9820
92	41.9136 1895	38.7060 2423	35.8746 1604	33.3662 7644	31.1362 1184
93	42.0721 7545	38.8322 9754	35.9752 3516	33.4464 9776	31.2002 0567
94	42.2276 2299	38.9557 9221	36.0734 0016	33.5245 7202	31.2623 3560
95	42.3800 2254	39.0765 6940	36.1691 7089	33.6005 5671	31.3226 5592
96	42.5294 3386	39.1946 8890	36.2626 0574	33.6745 0775	31.3812 1934
97	42.6759 1555	39.3102 0920	36.3537 6170	33.7464 7956	31.4380 7703
98	42.8195 2505	39.4231 8748	36.4426 9434	33.8165 2512	31.4932 7867
99	42.9603 1867	39.5336 7968	36.5294 5790	33.8846 9598	31.5468 7250
100	43.0983 5164	39.6417 4052	36.6141 0526	33.9510 4232	31.5989 0534

TABLE IV
PRESENT VALUE OF AN ANNUITY

$$a_{\overline{n}|}\, i = \frac{1-(1+i)^{-n}}{i}$$

Periods	Rate i				
n	.035 ($3\frac{1}{2}$%)	.04 (4%)	.045 ($4\frac{1}{2}$%)	.05 (5%)	.055 ($5\frac{1}{2}$%)
1	0.9661 8357	0.9615 3846	0.9569 3780	0.9523 8095	0.9478 6730
2	1.8996 9428	1.8860 9467	1.8726 6775	1.8594 1043	1.8463 1971
3	2.8016 3698	2.7750 9103	2.7489 6435	2.7232 4803	2.6979 3338
4	3.6730 7921	3.6298 9522	3.5875 2570	3.5459 5050	3.5051 5012
5	4.5150 5238	4.4518 2233	4.3899 7674	4.3294 7667	4.2702 8448
6	5.3285 5302	5.2421 3686	5.1578 7248	5.0756 9207	4.9955 3031
7	6.1145 4398	6.0020 5467	5.8927 0094	5.7863 7340	5.6829 6712
8	6.8739 5554	6.7327 4487	6.5958 8607	6.4632 1276	6.3345 6599
9	7.6076 8651	7.4353 3161	7.2687 9050	7.1078 2168	6.9521 9525
10	8.3166 0532	8.1108 9578	7.9127 1818	7.7217 3493	7.5376 2583
11	9.0015 5104	8.7604 7671	8.5289 1692	8.3064 1422	8.0925 3633
12	9.6633 3433	9.3850 7376	9.1185 8078	8.8632 5164	8.6185 1785
13	10.3027 3849	9.9856 4785	9.6828 5242	9.3935 7299	9.1170 7853
14	10.9205 2028	10.5631 2293	10.2228 2528	9.8986 4094	9.5896 4790
15	11.5174 1090	11.1183 8743	10.7395 4573	10.3796 5804	10.0375 8094
16	12.0941 1681	11.6522 9561	11.2340 1505	10.8377 6956	10.4621 6203
17	12.6513 2059	12.1656 6885	11.7071 9143	11.2740 6625	10.8646 0856
18	13.1896 8173	12.6592 9697	12.1599 9180	11.6895 8690	11.2460 7447
19	13.7098 3742	13.1339 3940	12.5932 9359	12.0853 2086	11.6076 5352
20	14.2124 0330	13.5903 2634	13.0079 3645	12.4622 1034	11.9503 8248
21	14.6979 7420	14.0291 5995	13.4047 2388	12.8211 5271	12.2752 4406
22	15.1671 2484	14.4511 1533	13.7844 2476	13.1630 0258	12.5831 6973
23	15.6204 1047	14.8568 4167	14.1477 7489	13.4885 7388	12.8750 4239
24	16.0583 6760	15.2469 6314	14.4954 7837	13.7986 4179	13.1516 9895
25	16.4815 1459	15.6220 7994	14.8282 0896	14.0939 4457	13.4139 3266
26	16.8903 5226	15.9827 6918	15.1466 1145	14.3751 8530	13.6624 9541
27	17.2853 6451	16.3295 8575	15.4512 0282	14.6430 3362	13.8980 9991
28	17.6670 1885	16.6630 6322	15.7428 7351	14.8981 2726	14.1214 2172
29	18.0357 6700	16.9837 1463	16.0218 8853	15.1410 7358	14.3331 0116
30	18.3920 4541	17.2920 3330	16.2888 8854	15.3724 5103	14.5337 4517
31	18.7362 7576	17.5884 9356	16.5443 9095	15.5928 1050	14.7239 2907
32	19.0688 6547	17.8735 5150	16.7888 9086	15.8026 7667	14.9041 9817
33	19.3902 0818	18.1476 4567	17.0228 6207	16.0025 4921	15.0750 6936
34	19.7006 8423	18.4111 9776	17.2467 5796	16.1929 0401	15.2370 3257
35	20.0006 6110	18.6646 1323	17.4610 1240	16.3741 9429	15.3905 5220
36	20.2904 9381	18.9082 8195	17.6660 4058	16.5468 5171	15.5360 6843
37	20.5705 2542	19.1425 7880	17.8622 3979	16.7112 8734	15.6739 9851
38	20.8410 8736	19.3678 6423	18.0490 9023	16.8678 9271	15.8047 3793
39	21.1024 9987	19.5844 8484	18.2296 5572	17.0170 4067	15.9286 6154
40	21.3550 7234	19.7927 7388	18.4015 8442	17.1590 8635	16.0461 2469
41	21.5991 0371	19.9930 5181	18.5661 0949	17.2943 6796	16.1574 6416
42	21.8348 8281	20.1856 2674	18.7235 4975	17.4232 0758	16.2629 9920
43	22.0626 8870	20.3707 9494	18.8742 1029	17.5459 1198	16.3630 3242
44	22.2827 9102	20.5488 4129	19.0183 8305	17.6627 7331	16.4578 5063
45	22.4954 5026	20.7200 3970	19.1563 4742	17.7740 6982	16.5477 2572
46	22.7009 1813	20.8846 5356	19.2883 7074	17.8800 6650	16.6329 1537
47	22.8994 3780	21.0429 3612	19.4147 0884	17.9810 1571	16.7136 6386
48	23.0912 4425	21.1951 3088	19.5356 0654	18.0771 5782	16.7902 0271
49	23.2765 6450	21.3414 7200	19.6512 9813	18.1687 2173	16.8627 5139
50	23.4556 1787	21.4821 8462	19.7620 0778	18.2559 2546	16.9315 1790

TABLE IV
PRESENT VALUE OF AN ANNUITY

$$a_{\overline{n}|}\, i = \frac{1-(1+i)^{-n}}{i}$$

Periods	Rate i				
n	.06 (6%)	.065 ($6\frac{1}{2}$%)	.07 (7%)	.075 ($7\frac{1}{2}$%)	.08 (8%)
1	0.9433 9623	0.9389 6714	0.9345 7944	0.9302 3256	0.9259 2593
2	1.8333 9267	1.8206 2642	1.8080 1817	1.7955 6517	1.7832 6475
3	2.6730 1195	2.6484 7551	2.6243 1604	2.6005 2574	2.5770 9699
4	3.4651 0561	3.4257 9860	3.3872 1126	3.3493 2627	3.3121 2684
5	4.2123 6379	4.1556 7944	4.1001 9744	4.0458 8490	3.9927 1004
6	4.9173 2433	4.8410 1356	4.7665 3966	4.6938 4642	4.6228 7966
7	5.5823 8144	5.4845 1977	5.3892 8940	5.2966 0132	5.2063 7006
8	6.2097 9381	6.0887 5096	5.9712 9851	5.8573 0355	5.7466 3894
9	6.8016 9227	6.6561 0419	6.5152 3225	6.3788 8703	6.2468 8791
10	7.3600 8705	7.1888 3022	7.0235 8154	6.8640 8096	6.7100 8140
11	7.8868 7458	7.6890 4246	7.4986 7434	7.3154 2415	7.1389 6426
12	8.3838 4394	8.1587 2532	7.9426 8630	7.7352 7827	7.5360 7802
13	8.8526 8296	8.5997 4208	8.3576 5074	8.1258 4026	7.9037 7594
14	9.2949 8393	9.0138 4233	8.7454 6799	8.4891 5373	8.2442 3698
15	9.7122 4899	9.4026 6885	9.1079 1401	8.8271 1975	8.5594 7869
16	10.1058 9527	9.7677 6418	9.4466 4860	9.1415 0674	8.8513 6916
17	10.4772 5969	10.1105 7670	9.7632 2299	9.4339 5976	9.1216 3811
18	10.8276 0348	10.4324 6638	10.0590 8691	9.7060 0908	9.3718 8714
19	11.1581 1649	10.7347 1022	10.3355 9524	9.9590 7821	9.6035 9920
20	11.4699 2122	11.0185 0725	10.5940 1425	10.1944 9136	9.8181 4741
21	11.7640 7662	11.2449 8333	10.8355 2733	10.4134 8033	10.0168 0316
22	12.0415 8172	11.5351 9562	11.0612 4050	10.6171 9101	10.2007 4366
23	12.3033 7898	11.7701 3673	11.2721 8738	10.8066 8931	10.3710 5895
24	12.5503 5753	11.9907 3871	11.4693 3400	10.9828 6680	10.5287 5828
25	12.7833 5616	12.1978 7673	11.6535 8318	11.1469 4586	10.6747 7619
26	13.0031 6619	12.3923 7251	11.8257 7867	11.2994 8452	10.8099 7795
27	13.2105 3414	12.5749 9766	11.9867 0904	11.4413 8095	10.9351 6477
28	13.4061 6428	12.7464 7668	12.1371 1125	11.5733 7763	11.0510 7849
29	13.5907 2102	12.9074 8984	12.2776 7407	11.6961 6524	11.1584 0601
30	13.7648 3115	13.0586 7591	12.4090 4118	11.8103 8627	11.2577 8334
31	13.9290 8599	13.2006 3465	12.5318 1419	11.9166 3839	11.3497 9939
32	14.0840 4339	13.3339 2925	12.6465 5532	12.0154 7757	11.4349 9944
33	14.2302 2961	13.4590 8850	12.7537 9002	12.1074 2099	11.5138 8837
34	14.3681 4114	13.5766 0892	12.8540 0936	12.1929 4976	11.5869 3367
35	14.4982 4636	13.6869 5673	12.9476 7230	12.2725 1141	11.6545 6822
36	14.6209 8713	13.7905 6970	13.0352 0776	12.3465 2224	11.7171 9279
37	14.7367 8031	13.8878 5887	13.1170 1660	12.4153 6952	11.7751 7851
38	14.8460 1916	13.9792 1021	13.1934 7345	12.4794 1351	11.8288 6899
39	14.9490 7468	14.0649 8611	13.2649 2846	12.5389 8931	11.8785 8240
40	15.0462 9687	14.1455 2687	13.3317 0884	12.5944 0866	11.9246 1333
41	15.1380 1592	14.2211 5199	13.3941 2041	12.6459 6155	11.9672 3457
42	15.2245 4332	14.2921 6149	13.4524 4898	12.6939 1772	12.0066 9867
43	15.3061 7294	14.3588 3708	13.5069 6167	12.7385 2811	12.0432 3951
44	15.3831 8202	14.4214 4327	13.5570 0810	12.7800 2615	12.0770 7362
45	15.4558 3209	14.4802 2842	13.6055 2159	12.8186 2898	12.1084 0150
46	15.5243 6990	14.5354 2575	13.6500 2018	12.8545 3858	12.1374 0880
47	15.5890 2821	14.5872 5422	13.6913 0764	12.8879 4247	12.1642 6741
48	15.6500 2661	14.6359 1946	13.7304 7443	12.9190 1662	12.1891 3649
49	15.7075 7227	14.6816 1451	13.7667 9853	12.9479 2244	12.2121 6341
50	15.7618 6064	14.7245 2067	13.8007 4629	12.9748 1157	12.2334 8464

TABLE V
TABLE OF e^x AND e^{-x}

x	e^x	e^{-x}
0.00	1.0000	1.00000
0.01	1.0101	0.99005
0.02	1.0202	.98020
0.03	1.0305	.97045
0.04	1.0408	.96079
0.05	1.0513	.95123
0.06	1.0618	.94176
0.07	1.0725	.93239
0.08	1.0833	.92312
0.09	1.0942	.91393
0.10	1.1052	.90484
0.11	1.1163	.89583
0.12	1.1275	.88692
0.13	1.1388	.87809
0.14	1.1503	.86936
0.15	1.1618	.86071
0.16	1.1735	.85214
0.17	1.1853	.84366
0.18	1.1972	.83527
0.19	1.2092	.82696
0.20	1.2214	.81873
0.21	1.2337	.81058
0.22	1.2461	.80252
0.23	1.2586	.79453
0.24	1.2712	.78663
0.25	1.2840	.77880
0.26	1.2969	.77105
0.27	1.3100	.76338
0.28	1.3234	.75578
0.29	1.3364	.74826
0.30	1.3499	.74082
0.31	1.3634	.73345
0.32	1.3771	.72615
0.33	1.3910	.71892
0.34	1.4049	.71177
0.35	1.4191	.70469
0.36	1.4333	.69768
0.37	1.4477	.69073
0.38	1.4623	.68386
0.39	1.4770	.67706
0.40	1.4918	.67032
0.41	1.5068	.66365
0.42	1.5220	.65705
0.43	1.5373	.65051
0.44	1.5527	.64404
0.45	1.5683	.63763
0.46	1.5841	.63128
0.47	1.6000	.62500
0.48	1.6161	.61878
0.49	1.6323	.61263
0.50	1.6487	.60653
0.51	1.6653	.60050

x	e^x	e^{-x}
0.52	1.6820	.59452
0.53	1.6989	.58860
0.54	1.7160	.58275
0.55	1.7333	.57695
0.56	1.7507	.57121
0.57	1.7683	.56553
0.58	1.7860	.55990
0.59	1.8040	.55433
0.60	1.8221	.54881
0.61	1.8404	.54335
0.62	1.8589	.53794
0.63	1.8776	.53259
0.64	1.8965	.52729
0.65	1.9166	.52205
0.66	1.9384	.51685
0.67	1.9542	.51171
0.68	1.9739	.50662
0.69	1.9937	.50158
0.70	2.0138	.49659
0.71	2.0340	.49164
0.72	2.0544	.48675
0.73	2.0751	.48191
0.74	2.0959	.47711
0.75	2.1170	.47237
0.76	2.1383	.46767
0.77	2.1598	.46301
0.78	2.1815	.45841
0.79	2.2034	.45384
0.80	2.2255	.44933
0.81	2.2479	.44486
0.82	2.2705	.44043
0.83	2.2933	.43605
0.84	2.3164	.43171
0.85	2.3396	.42741
0.86	2.3632	.42316
0.87	2.3869	.41895
0.88	2.4109	.41478
0.89	2.4351	.41066
0.90	2.4596	.40657
0.91	2.4843	.40252
0.92	2.5093	.39852
0.93	2.5345	.39455
0.94	2.5600	.39063
0.95	2.5857	.38674
0.96	2.6117	.38289
0.97	2.6379	.37908
0.98	2.6645	.37531
0.99	2.6912	.37158
1.00	2.7183	.36788
1.10	3.0042	.33287
1.20	3.3201	.30119
1.30	3.6693	.27253
1.40	4.0552	.24660
1.50	4.4817	.22313

x	e^x	e^{-x}
1.60	4.9530	.20190
1.70	5.4739	.18268
1.80	6.0496	.16530
1.90	6.6859	.14957
2.00	7.3891	.13534
2.10	8.1662	.12246
2.20	9.2050	.11080
2.30	9.9742	.10026
2.40	11.023	.09072
2.50	12.182	.08208
2.60	13.464	.07427
2.70	14.880	.06721
2.80	16.445	.06081
2.90	18.174	.05502
3.00	20.086	.04979
3.10	22.198	.04505
3.20	24.533	.04076
3.30	27.113	.03688
3.40	29.964	.03337
3.50	33.115	.03020
3.60	36.598	.02732
3.70	40.447	.02472
3.80	44.701	.02237
3.90	49.402	.02024
4.00	54.598	.01832
4.10	60.340	.01657
4.20	66.686	.01500
4.30	73.700	.01357
4.40	81.451	.01227
4.50	90.107	.01111
4.60	99.484	.01005
4.70	109.95	.00910
4.80	121.51	.00823
4.90	134.29	.00745
5.00	148.41	.00674
5.10	164.02	.00610
5.20	181.27	.00552
5.30	200.34	.00499
5.40	221.41	.00452
5.50	244.69	.00409
5.60	270.43	.00370
5.70	298.87	.00335
5.80	330.30	.00303
5.90	365.04	.00274
6.00	403.43	.00248
6.25	518.01	.00193
6.50	665.14	.00150
6.75	854.06	.00117
7.00	1096.6	.00091
7.50	1808.0	.00055
8.00	2981.0	.00034
8.50	4914.8	.00020
9.00	8103.1	.00012
9.50	13360	.00007
10.00	22026	.00005

LOGARITHMS

	0	1	2	3	4	5	6	7	8	9	Mean Differences 1	2	3	4	5	6	7	8	9
10	0000	0043	0086	0128	0170						5	9	13	17	21	26	30	34	38
						0212	0253	0294	0334	0374	4	8	12	16	20	24	28	32	36
11	0414	0453	0492	0531	0509						4	8	12	16	20	23	27	31	35
						0607	0645	0682	0719	0755	4	7	11	15	18	22	26	29	33
12	0792	0828	0864	0899	0934						3	7	11	14	18	21	25	28	32
						0969	1004	1038	1072	1106	3	7	10	14	17	20	24	27	31
13	1139	1173	1206	1239	1271						3	6	10	13	16	19	23	26	29
						1303	1335	1367	1399	1430	3	7	10	13	16	19	22	25	29
14	1461	1492	1523	1553	1584						3	6	9	12	15	19	22	25	28
						1614	1644	1673	1703	1732	3	6	9	12	14	17	20	23	26
15	1761	1790	1818	1847	1875						3	6	9	11	14	17	20	23	26
						1903	1931	1959	1987	2014	3	6	8	11	14	17	19	22	25
16	2041	2068	2095	2122	2148						3	6	8	11	14	16	19	22	24
						2175	2201	2227	2253	2279	3	5	8	10	13	16	18	21	23
17	2304	2330	2355	2380	2405						3	5	8	10	13	15	18	20	23
						2430	2455	2480	2504	2529	3	5	8	10	12	15	17	20	22
18	2553	2577	2601	2625	2648						2	5	7	9	12	14	17	19	21
						2672	2695	2718	2742	2765	2	4	7	9	11	14	16	18	21
19	2788	2810	2833	2856	2878						2	4	7	9	11	13	16	18	20
						2900	2923	2945	2967	2989	2	4	6	8	11	13	15	17	19
20	3010	3032	3054	3075	3096	3118	3139	3160	3181	3201	2	4	6	8	11	13	15	17	19
21	3222	3243	3263	3284	3304	3324	3345	3365	3385	3404	2	4	6	8	10	12	14	16	18
22	3424	3444	3464	3483	3502	3522	3541	3560	3579	3598	2	4	6	8	10	12	14	15	17
23	3617	3636	3655	3674	3692	3711	3729	3747	3766	3784	2	4	6	7	9	11	13	15	17
24	3802	3820	3838	3856	3874	3892	3909	3927	3945	3962	2	4	5	7	9	11	12	14	16
25	3979	3997	4014	4031	4048	4065	4082	4099	4116	4133	2	3	5	7	9	10	12	14	15
26	4150	4166	4183	4200	4216	4232	4249	4265	4281	4298	2	3	5	7	8	10	11	13	15
27	4314	4330	4346	4362	4378	4393	4409	4425	4440	4456	2	3	5	6	8	9	11	13	14
28	4472	4487	4502	4518	4533	4548	4564	4579	4594	4609	2	3	5	6	8	9	11	12	14
29	4624	4639	4654	4669	4683	4698	4713	4728	4742	4757	1	3	4	6	7	9	10	12	13
30	4771	4786	4800	4814	4829	4843	4857	4871	4886	4900	1	3	4	6	7	9	10	11	13
31	4914	4928	4942	4955	4969	4983	4997	5011	5024	5038	1	3	4	6	7	8	10	11	12
32	5051	5065	5079	5092	5105	5119	5132	5145	5159	5172	1	3	4	5	7	8	9	11	12
33	5185	5198	5211	5224	5237	5250	5263	5276	5289	5302	1	3	4	5	6	8	9	10	12
34	5315	5328	5340	5353	5366	5378	5391	5403	5416	5428	1	3	4	5	6	8	9	10	11
35	5441	5453	5465	5478	5490	5502	5514	5527	5539	5551	1	2	4	5	6	7	9	10	11
36	5563	5575	5587	5599	5611	5623	5635	5647	5658	5670	1	2	4	5	6	7	8	10	11
37	5682	5694	5705	5717	5729	5740	5752	5763	5775	5786	1	2	3	5	6	7	8	9	10
38	5798	5809	5821	5832	5843	5855	5866	5877	5888	5899	1	2	3	5	6	7	8	9	10
39	5911	5922	5933	5944	5955	5966	5977	5988	5999	6010	1	2	3	4	5	7	8	9	10
40	6021	6031	6042	6053	6064	6075	6085	6096	6107	6117	1	2	3	4	5	6	8	9	10
41	6128	6138	6149	6160	6170	6180	6191	6201	6212	6222	1	2	3	4	5	6	7	8	9
42	6232	6243	6253	6263	6274	6284	6294	6304	6314	6325	1	2	3	4	5	6	7	8	9
43	6335	6345	6355	6365	6375	6385	6395	6405	6415	6425	1	2	3	4	5	6	7	8	9
44	6435	6444	6454	6464	6474	6484	6493	6503	6513	6522	1	2	3	4	5	6	7	8	9
45	6532	6542	6551	6561	6571	6580	6590	6599	6609	6618	1	2	3	4	5	6	7	8	9
46	6628	6637	6646	6656	6665	6675	6684	6693	6702	6712	1	2	3	4	5	6	7	7	8
47	6721	6730	6739	6749	6758	6767	6776	6785	6794	6803	1	2	3	4	5	5	6	7	8
48	6812	6821	6830	6839	6848	6857	6866	6875	6884	6893	1	2	3	4	4	5	6	7	8
49	6902	6911	6920	6928	6937	6946	6955	6964	6972	6981	1	2	3	4	4	5	6	7	8

LOGARITHMS

	0	1	2	3	4	5	6	7	8	9	Mean Differences								
											1	2	3	4	5	6	7	8	9
50	6990	6998	7007	7016	7024	7033	7042	7050	7059	7067	1	2	3	3	4	5	6	7	8
51	7076	7084	7093	7101	7110	7118	7126	7135	7143	7152	1	2	3	3	4	5	6	7	8
52	7160	7168	7177	7185	7193	7202	7210	7218	7226	7235	1	2	2	3	4	5	6	7	7
53	7243	7251	7259	7267	7275	7284	7292	7300	7308	7316	1	2	2	3	4	5	6	6	7
54	7324	7332	7340	7348	7356	7364	7372	7380	7388	7396	1	2	2	3	4	5	6	6	7
55	7404	7412	7419	7427	7435	7443	7451	7459	7466	7474	1	2	2	3	4	5	5	6	7
56	7482	7490	7497	7505	7513	7520	7528	7536	7543	7551	1	2	2	3	4	5	5	6	7
57	7559	7566	7574	7582	7589	7597	7604	7612	7619	7627	1	2	2	3	4	5	5	6	7
58	7634	7642	7649	7657	7664	7672	7679	7686	7694	7701	1	1	2	3	4	4	5	6	7
59	7709	7716	7723	7731	7738	7745	7752	7760	7767	7774	1	1	2	3	4	4	5	6	7
60	7782	7789	7796	7803	7810	7818	7825	7832	7839	7846	1	1	2	3	4	4	5	6	6
61	7853	7860	7868	7875	7882	7889	7896	7903	7910	7917	1	1	2	3	4	4	5	6	6
62	7924	7931	7938	7945	7952	7959	7966	7973	7980	7987	1	1	2	3	3	4	5	6	6
63	7993	8000	8007	8014	8021	8028	8035	8041	8048	8055	1	1	2	3	3	4	5	5	6
64	8062	8069	8075	8082	8089	8096	8102	8109	8116	8122	1	1	2	3	3	4	5	5	6
65	8129	8136	8142	8149	8156	8162	8169	8176	8182	8189	1	1	2	3	3	4	5	5	6
66	8195	8202	8209	8215	8222	8228	8235	8241	8248	8254	1	1	2	3	3	4	5	5	6
67	8261	8267	8274	8280	8287	8293	8299	8306	8312	8319	1	1	2	3	3	4	5	5	6
68	8325	8331	8338	8344	8351	8357	8363	8370	8376	8382	1	1	2	3	3	4	4	5	6
69	8388	8395	8401	8407	8414	8420	8426	8432	8439	8445	1	1	2	2	3	4	4	5	6
70	8451	8457	8463	8470	8476	8482	8488	8494	8500	8506	1	1	2	2	3	4	4	5	6
71	8513	8519	8525	8531	8537	8543	8549	8555	8561	8567	1	1	2	2	3	4	4	5	5
72	8573	8579	8585	8591	8597	8603	8609	8615	8621	8627	1	1	2	2	3	4	4	5	5
73	8633	8639	8645	8651	8657	8663	8669	8675	8681	8686	1	1	2	2	3	4	4	5	5
74	8692	8698	8704	8710	8716	8722	8727	8733	8739	8745	1	1	2	2	3	4	4	5	5
75	8751	8756	8762	8768	8774	8779	8785	8791	8797	8802	1	1	2	2	3	3	4	5	5
76	8808	8814	8820	8825	8831	8837	8842	8848	8854	8859	1	1	2	2	3	3	4	5	5
77	8865	8871	8876	8882	8887	8893	8899	8904	8910	8915	1	1	2	2	3	3	4	5	5
78	8921	8927	8932	8938	8943	8949	8954	8960	8965	8971	1	1	2	2	3	3	4	4	5
79	8976	8982	8987	8993	8998	9004	9009	9015	9020	9025	1	1	2	2	3	3	4	4	5
80	9031	9036	9042	9047	9053	9058	9063	9069	9074	9079	1	1	2	2	3	3	4	4	5
81	9085	9090	9096	9101	9106	9112	9117	9122	9128	9133	1	1	2	2	3	3	4	4	5
82	9138	9143	9149	9154	9159	9165	9170	9175	9180	9186	1	1	2	2	3	3	4	4	5
83	9191	9196	9201	9206	9212	9217	9222	9227	9232	9238	1	1	2	2	3	3	4	4	5
84	9243	9248	9253	9258	9263	9269	9274	9279	9264	9489	1	1	2	2	3	3	4	4	5
85	9294	9299	9304	9309	9315	9320	9325	9330	9335	9340	1	1	2	2	3	3	4	4	5
86	9345	9350	9355	9360	9365	9370	9375	9380	9385	9390	1	1	2	2	3	3	4	4	5
87	[illegible]	9400	9405	9410	9415	9420	9425	9430	9435	9440	0	1	1	2	2	3	3	4	4
88	9445	9450	9455	9460	9465	9469	9474	9479	9484	9489	0	1	1	2	2	3	3	4	4
89	9494	9499	9504	9509	9513	9518	9523	9528	9533	9538	0	1	1	2	2	3	3	4	4
90	9542	9547	9552	9557	9562	9566	9571	9576	9581	9586	0	1	1	2	2	3	3	4	4
91	9590	9595	9600	9605	9609	9614	9619	9624	9628	9633	0	1	1	2	2	3	3	4	4
92	9638	9643	9647	9652	9657	9661	9666	9671	9675	9680	0	1	1	2	2	3	3	4	4
93	9685	9689	9694	9699	9703	9708	9713	9717	9722	9727	0	1	1	2	2	3	3	4	4
94	9731	9736	9741	9745	9750	9754	9759	9763	9768	9773	0	1	1	2	2	3	3	4	4
95	9777	9782	9786	9791	9795	9800	9805	9809	9814	9818	0	1	1	2	2	3	3	4	4
96	9823	9827	9832	9836	9841	9845	9850	9854	9859	9863	0	1	1	2	2	3	3	4	4
97	9868	9872	9877	9881	9886	9890	9894	9899	9903	9908	0	1	1	2	2	3	3	4	4
98	9912	9917	9921	9926	9930	9934	9939	9943	9948	9952	0	1	1	2	2	3	3	4	4
99	9956	9961	9965	9969	9974	9978	9983	9987	9991	9996	0	1	1	2	2	3	3	3	4

ANTILOGARITHMS

	0	1	2	3	4	5	6	7	8	9	Mean Differences								
											1	2	3	4	5	6	7	8	9
.00	1000	1002	1005	1007	1009	1012	1014	1016	1019	1021	0	0	1	1	1	1	2	2	2
.01	1023	1026	1028	1030	1033	1035	1038	1040	1042	1045	0	0	1	1	1	1	2	2	2
.02	1047	1050	1052	1054	1057	1059	1062	1064	1067	1069	0	0	1	1	1	1	2	2	2
.03	1072	1074	1076	1079	1081	1084	1086	1089	1091	1094	0	0	1	1	1	1	2	2	2
.04	1096	1099	1102	1104	1107	1109	1112	1114	1117	1119	0	1	1	1	1	2	2	2	2
.05	1122	1125	1127	1130	1132	1135	1138	1140	1143	1146	0	1	1	1	1	2	2	2	2
.06	1148	1151	1153	1156	1159	1161	1164	1167	1169	1172	0	1	1	1	1	2	2	2	2
.07	1175	1178	1180	1183	1186	1189	1191	1194	1197	1199	0	1	1	1	1	2	2	2	2
.08	1202	1205	1208	1211	1213	1216	1219	1222	1225	1227	0	1	1	1	1	2	2	2	3
.09	1230	1233	1236	1239	1242	1245	1247	1250	1253	1256	0	1	1	1	1	2	2	2	3
.10	1259	1262	1265	1268	1271	1274	1276	1279	1282	1285	0	1	1	1	1	2	2	2	3
.11	1288	1291	1294	1297	1300	1303	1306	1309	1312	1315	0	1	1	1	2	2	2	2	3
.12	1318	1321	1324	1327	1330	1334	1337	1340	1343	1346	0	1	1	1	2	2	2	2	3
.13	1349	1352	1355	1358	1361	1365	1368	1371	1374	1377	0	1	1	1	2	2	2	3	3
.14	1380	1384	1387	1390	1393	1396	1400	1403	1406	1409	0	1	1	1	2	2	2	3	3
.15	1413	1416	1419	1422	1426	1429	1432	1435	1439	1442	0	1	1	1	2	2	2	3	3
.16	1445	1449	1452	1455	1459	1462	1466	1469	1472	1476	0	1	1	1	2	2	2	3	3
.17	1479	1483	1486	1489	1493	1496	1500	1503	1507	1510	0	1	1	1	2	2	2	3	3
.18	1514	1517	1521	1524	1528	1531	1535	1538	1542	1545	0	1	1	1	2	2	2	3	3
.19	1549	1552	1556	1560	1563	1567	1570	1574	1578	1581	0	1	1	1	2	2	3	3	3
.20	1585	1589	1592	1596	1600	1603	1607	1611	1614	1618	0	1	1	1	2	2	3	3	3
.21	1622	1626	1629	1633	1637	1641	1644	1648	1652	1656	0	1	1	2	2	2	3	3	3
.22	1660	1663	1667	1671	1675	1679	1683	1687	1690	1694	0	1	1	2	2	2	3	3	3
.23	1698	1702	1706	1710	1714	1718	1722	1726	1730	1734	0	1	1	2	2	2	3	3	4
.24	1738	1742	1746	1750	1754	1758	1762	1766	1770	1774	0	1	1	2	2	2	3	3	4
.25	1778	1782	1786	1791	1795	1799	1803	1807	1811	1816	0	1	1	2	2	2	3	3	4
.26	1820	1824	1828	1832	1837	1841	1845	1849	1854	1858	0	1	1	2	2	3	3	3	4
.27	1862	1866	1871	1875	1879	1884	1888	1892	1897	1901	0	1	1	2	2	3	3	3	4
.28	1905	1910	1914	1919	1923	1928	1932	1936	1941	1945	0	1	1	2	2	3	3	4	4
.29	1950	1954	1959	1963	1968	1972	1977	1982	1986	1991	0	1	1	2	2	3	3	4	4
.30	1995	2000	2004	2009	2014	2018	2023	2028	2032	2037	0	1	1	2	2	3	3	4	4
.31	2042	2046	2051	2056	2061	2065	2070	2075	2080	2084	0	1	1	2	2	3	3	4	4
.32	2089	2094	2099	2104	2109	2113	2118	2123	2128	2133	0	1	1	2	2	3	3	4	4
.33	2138	2143	2148	2153	2158	2163	2168	2173	2178	2183	0	1	1	2	2	3	3	4	4
.34	2188	2193	2198	2203	2208	2213	2218	2223	2228	2234	1	1	2	2	3	3	4	4	5
.35	2239	2244	2249	2254	2259	2265	2270	2275	2280	2286	1	1	2	2	3	3	4	4	5
.36	2291	2296	2301	2307	2312	2317	2323	2328	2333	2339	1	1	2	2	3	3	4	4	5
.37	2344	2350	2355	2360	2366	2371	2377	2382	2388	2393	1	1	2	2	3	3	4	4	5
.38	2399	2404	2410	2415	2421	2427	2432	2438	2443	2449	1	1	2	2	3	3	4	4	5
.39	2455	2460	2466	2472	2477	2483	2489	2495	2500	2506	1	1	2	2	3	3	4	5	5
.40	2512	2518	2523	2529	2535	2541	2547	2553	2559	2564	1	1	2	2	3	4	4	5	5
.41	2570	2576	2582	2588	2594	2600	2606	2612	2618	2624	1	1	2	2	3	4	4	5	5
.42	2630	2636	2642	2649	2655	2661	2667	2673	2679	2685	1	1	2	2	3	4	4	5	6
.43	2692	2698	2704	2710	2716	2723	2729	2735	2742	2748	1	1	2	3	3	4	4	5	6
.44	2754	2761	2767	2773	2780	2786	2793	2799	2805	2812	1	1	2	3	3	4	4	5	6
.45	2818	2825	2831	2838	2844	2851	2858	2864	2871	2877	1	1	2	3	3	4	5	5	6
.46	2884	2891	2897	2904	2911	2917	2924	2931	2938	2944	1	1	2	3	3	4	5	5	6
.47	2951	2958	2965	2972	2979	2985	2992	2999	3006	3013	1	1	2	3	3	4	5	5	6
.48	3020	3027	3034	3041	3048	3055	3062	3069	3076	3083	1	1	2	3	4	4	5	6	6
.49	3090	3097	3105	3112	3119	3126	3133	3141	3148	3155	1	1	2	3	4	4	5	6	6

ANTILOGARITHMS

	0	1	2	3	4	5	6	7	8	9	Mean Differences 1	2	3	4	5	6	7	8	9
.50	3162	3170	3177	3184	3192	3199	3206	3214	3221	3228	1	1	2	3	4	4	5	6	7
.51	3236	3243	3251	3258	3266	3273	3281	3289	3296	3304	1	2	2	3	4	5	5	6	7
.52	3311	3319	3327	3334	3342	3350	3357	3365	3373	3381	1	2	2	3	4	5	5	6	7
.53	3388	3396	3404	3412	3420	3428	3436	3443	3451	3459	1	2	2	3	4	5	6	6	7
.54	3467	3475	3483	3491	3499	3508	3516	3524	3532	3540	1	2	2	3	4	5	6	6	7
.55	3548	3556	3565	3573	3581	3589	3597	3606	3614	3622	1	2	2	3	4	5	6	7	7
.56	3631	3639	3648	3656	3664	3673	3681	3690	3698	3707	1	2	3	3	4	5	6	7	8
.57	3715	3724	3733	3741	3750	3758	3767	3776	3784	3793	1	2	3	3	4	5	6	7	8
.58	3802	3811	3819	3828	3837	3846	3855	3864	3873	3882	1	2	3	4	4	5	6	7	8
.59	3890	3899	3908	3917	3926	3936	3945	3954	3963	3972	1	2	3	4	5	5	6	7	8
.60	3981	3990	3999	4009	4018	4027	4036	4046	4055	4064	1	2	3	4	5	6	6	7	8
.61	4074	4083	4093	4102	4111	4121	4130	4140	4150	4159	1	2	3	4	5	6	7	8	9
.62	4169	4178	4188	4198	4207	4217	4227	4236	4246	4256	1	2	3	4	5	6	7	8	9
.63	4266	4276	4285	4295	4305	4315	4325	4335	4345	4355	1	2	3	4	5	6	7	8	9
.64	4365	4375	4385	4395	4406	4416	4426	4436	4446	4457	1	2	3	4	5	6	7	8	9
.65	4467	4477	4487	4498	4508	4519	4529	4539	4550	4560	1	2	3	4	5	6	7	8	9
.66	4571	4581	4592	4603	4613	4624	4634	4645	4656	4667	1	2	3	4	5	6	7	9	10
.67	4677	4688	4699	4710	4721	4732	4742	4753	4764	4775	1	2	3	4	5	7	8	9	10
.68	4786	4797	4808	4819	4831	4842	4853	4864	4875	4887	1	2	3	4	6	7	8	9	10
.69	4898	4909	4920	4932	4943	4955	4966	4977	4989	5000	1	2	3	5	6	7	8	9	10
.70	5012	5023	5035	5047	5058	5070	5082	5093	5105	5117	1	2	4	5	6	7	8	9	11
.71	5129	5140	5152	5164	5176	5188	5200	5212	5224	5236	1	2	4	5	6	7	8	10	11
.72	5248	5260	5272	5284	5297	5309	5321	5333	5346	5358	1	2	4	5	6	7	9	10	11
.73	5370	5383	5395	5408	5420	5433	5445	5458	5470	5483	1	3	4	5	6	8	9	10	11
.74	5495	5508	5521	5534	5546	5559	5572	5585	5598	5610	1	3	4	5	6	8	9	10	12
.75	5623	5636	5649	5662	5675	5689	5702	5715	5728	5741	1	3	4	5	7	8	9	10	12
.76	5754	5768	5781	5794	5808	5821	5834	5848	5861	5875	1	3	4	5	7	8	9	11	12
.77	5888	5902	5916	5929	5943	5957	5970	5984	5998	6012	1	3	4	5	7	8	10	11	12
.78	6026	6039	6053	6067	6081	6095	6109	6124	[illegible]	6152	1	3	4	6	7	8	10	11	13
.79	6166	6180	6194	6209	6223	6237	6252	6266	6281	6295	1	3	4	6	7	9	10	11	13
.80	6310	6324	6339	6353	6368	6383	6397	6412	6427	6442	1	3	4	6	7	9	10	12	13
.81	6457	6471	6486	6501	6516	6531	6546	6561	6577	6592	2	3	5	6	8	9	11	12	14
.82	6607	6622	6637	6653	6668	6683	6699	6714	6730	6745	2	3	5	6	8	9	11	12	14
.83	6761	6776	6792	6808	6823	6839	6855	6871	6887	6902	2	3	5	6	8	9	11	13	14
.84	6918	6934	6950	6966	6982	6998	7015	7031	7047	7063	2	3	5	6	8	10	11	13	15
.85	7079	7096	7112	7129	7145	7161	7178	7194	7211	7228	2	3	5	7	8	10	12	13	15
.86	7244	7261	7278	7295	7311	7328	7345	7362	7379	7396	2	3	5	7	8	10	12	13	15
.87	7413	7430	7447	7464	7482	7499	7516	7534	7551	7568	2	3	5	7	9	10	12	14	16
.88	7586	7603	7621	7638	7656	7674	7691	7709	7727	7745	2	4	5	7	9	11	12	14	16
.89	7762	7780	7798	7816	7834	7852	7870	7889	7907	7925	2	4	5	7	9	11	13	14	16
.90	7943	7962	7980	7998	8017	8035	8054	8072	8091	8110	2	4	6	7	9	11	13	15	17
.91	8128	8147	8166	8185	8204	8222	8241	8260	8279	8299	2	4	6	8	9	11	13	15	17
.92	8318	8337	8356	8375	8395	8414	8433	8453	8472	8492	2	4	6	8	10	12	14	15	17
.93	8511	8531	8551	8570	8590	8610	8630	8650	8670	8690	2	4	6	8	10	12	14	16	18
.94	8710	8730	8750	8770	8790	8810	8831	8851	8872	8892	2	4	6	8	10	12	14	16	18
.95	8913	8933	8954	8974	8995	9016	9036	9057	9078	9099	2	4	6	8	10	12	15	17	19
.96	9120	9141	9162	9183	9204	9226	9247	9268	9290	9311	2	4	6	8	11	13	15	17	19
.97	9333	9354	9376	9397	9419	9441	9462	9484	9506	9528	2	4	7	9	11	13	15	17	20
.98	9550	9572	9594	9616	9638	9661	9683	9705	9727	9750	2	4	7	9	11	13	16	18	20
.99	9772	9795	9817	9840	9863	9886	9908	9931	9954	9977	2	5	7	9	11	14	16	18	20